PUBLISHED BY

Practical PowerShell Press
Naperville, IL 60565

This book contains material contributions from Dave Stork.

Library of Congress Control Number: 2018939057
ISBN: 978-0-9987498-8-4

Paperback Edition - Printed and bound in the United States of America

First Printing

Technical Reviewer: Dave Stork
Indexing: Indexmatic2 by Indiscripts
CopyEditor: Deb Scoles

Cover: Damian Scoles * Yoho National Park

FOREWORD

My first introduction to PowerShell was at Microsoft TechEd 2005 in Orlando, Florida. A guy named Jeffrey Snover with a funky bow tie talked about this new thing he created called Monad. It was going to revolutionize IT administration forever. His excitement and enthusiasm was the same as a new father talking about his baby. The talk was, "Next-Generation Command Line Scripting: Monad" and the standing room crowd was mesmerized.

This object-oriented programming language was built on, and fully leveraged, the .NET framework, which at the time was still relatively new itself. Jeffrey described how to use its simple verb-noun syntax to get, set, and manage objects and collections in an entirely new way.

I had quite a bit of experience writing scripts in VB, Visual Basic Scripting (VBS) and Windows Management Instrumentation (WMI), but none of those languages provided the power, flexibility, and ease of use that Monad provided. It opened a whole new world, as I realized how much time it would save me.

We had little idea that it would become the framework for Exchange Server 2007 and later Exchange Online. Who would have thought that it could be extended in such a way? When Microsoft marketing got wind of it they just had to change the name to Windows PowerShell (they get paid by the syllable).

Microsoft's first foray into cloud computing came in the form of BPOS, the Business Productivity Online Suite, which was based on Exchange 2007. At that time, remote PowerShell was still a new thing and BPOS couldn't take advantage of it. Admins would have to forward their task requests to Microsoft, and an engineer would (maybe) run a PowerShell script to implement them. Obviously, this was not scalable, so Microsoft worked on the next generation of cloud computing, Office 365, running on Exchange 2010 with much improved remote PowerShell support.

Being able to remotely manage cloud services using PowerShell is fantastic but knowing how to use it properly can be a daunting challenge. That's where this book comes in. Whether you're new to PowerShell or you're a seasoned administrator, "Practical PowerShell – Office 365: Exchange Online" will guide you through the basics and beyond. You'll develop good scripting techniques using real-world examples that you can refer to over and over again.

As you may have already learned, everything that can be done in the Exchange Online Admin Center can be done with PowerShell, but not everything you can do with PowerShell is in the GUI. A lot of learning PowerShell content out there forces you to test the weight of your eyelids. Damian does an excellent job showing you the tips and techniques for managing Exchange Online without diving too much into the weeds. His examples are on point and give you the information you need to start using it right away.

I'm sure you will get a lot of useful information from this book and will continue to use it as a resource for those not-so-common tasks.

Jeff Guillet
Microsoft MVP | MCM and Founder EXPTA Consulting

DAMIAN SCOLES

Damian Scoles is an Exchange/Office Servers and Services MVP since 2013. He is currently based out of the Chicago area and started out managing Exchange 5.5 and Windows NT. He has worked with Exchange Server since 1997 and has remained active in the Exchange community by contributing to TechNet forums, creating scripts for Exchange Admins on the TechNet wiki, writing detailed Exchange blog articles (https://justauc-guy.wordpress.com/) and running an Exchange/Office 365 User Group in Chicago. As a second time author, Damian has poured his knowledge of Exchange Online and PowerShell into this book. He hopes you will enjoy reading it as much as he did writing it.

DAVE STORK

Dave Stork started his Exchange career with Exchange 2003 and that version got him hooked. He blogs (https://dirteam.com/dave) and tweets (https://twitter.com/dmstork) about Exchange and other relevant topics for several years now and in time has expanded this community work with contributing to podcasts, speaking at several events and user group meetings in and outside his native Netherlands. He poured most of his knowledge and experience into the Practical PowerShell Exchange Server 2016 book last year. Now he is expanding his skills with reviewing this Exchange Online book. He is also an Exchange/Office Servers and Services MVP since 2014.

Acknowledgments

About this book

As PowerShell is a crucial tool in administrating cloud services, it's an important and valuable skill to possess. Unfortunately learning it by yourself can be a daunting task. That is why this book was written, to help the average IT Pro/Administrator learn the fundamentals (and perhaps a little beyond that) of PowerShell. Believing that a practical approach will help the reader understand and learn these useful skills and help him or her to become proficient in Exchange PowerShell for all of their work and become more productive and a valuable employee almost immediately after reading this book.

Damian Scoles

I would like to thank my kids for their support and understanding while I worked on my second book. The writing of this book was a bit easier and harder at the same time. However, now that it is completed, I can spend more time with them. I especially want to thank my wife who put in a lot of time correcting my mistakes and lack of consistency. Without her help I would not have been able to produce such a high quality book.

I would also like to acknowledge and thank other IT professionals/MVPs who have helped me in various ways with advice, feedback, etc. to achieve this end product. Those include: Tony Redmond, Paul Cunningham, Bhargav Shukla and many others.

Errata

In writing this book, a lot of effort was put into making the information as accurate as possible. Any errors that are reported will be recorded here:

http://www.practicalpowershell.com/errata

Expect this document to be updated if any issues are found. If, for some reason, you want to report something that is not there go ahead and report it on that page.

Additional support can be found by emailing *input@practicalpowershell.com*.

Table of Contents

Introduction

Exchange and PowerShell...1

Why PowerShell and Not the Exchange Admin Center [a.k.a. the GUI] 1

Exchange Management Shell 2

Command Structure 2

   Cmdlet Examples...3

Piping 3

Protecting Yourself and What If 5

Command Discovery Techniques..5

PowerShell Modules 6

Getting Help!?!...7

Idiosyncrasies..9

Cloud-Only vs Synced Environments and PowerShell Cmdlets...............9

   Non-Synced Accounts (Cloud Only) 10

   Synced Accounts 11

   Book Methodology 11

1. PowerShell Basics

Exchange Online PowerShell: Where to Begin 12

Variables 12

Arrays 13

Hash Tables 14

CSV Files...14

Operators 15

Loops...16

   Foreach 16

   Do { } While () 17

   Export-CSV 18

   How to Use these Cmdlets 19

Functions 19

PowerShell Tools 20

   PowerShell ISE 20

   Alternatives to ISE..23

   ISE Plug-ins and Additional Tools 23

2. Beyond the Basics

Formatting 26
  Capitalization 26
  Commenting 27
  Mind Your Brackets! 30
Command Output 31
  Cmdlet Output Formatting 31
  Filtering 33
  Splitting 34
Scripting in Color 37
  Color Coding Examples 37
Miscellaneous Topics 40
  Quotes 40
  Obfuscated Information 42
  Code Signing 43

3. Building Scripts

How to Begin 47
Scenario One - Inactive Groups in Office 365 48
  Completing the Code Section 59
  Conclusion 59
Scenario Two - PowerShell and Change 60
  Coding the Script 61
  Script Summary 65
Script Building Conclusion 65

4. What's New

Introduction 66
Office 365 Roadmap 67
Launched Features 68
Rolling Out Now 70
Canceled Features 71
In Development 71
Desktop Clients 73

5. Connecting to ExO

Connecting to Office 365 75
  PowerShell Cmdlets 76
  Office 365 Cmdlets 77
  Connect to Azure Active Directory 77
  Managing Office 365 Mailboxes from On-Premises PowerShell 77
UPN and Primary SMTP Address Updates 85

6. Identity Management

Introduction 86
Directory Synchronization 87
    History 87
    Two Phrases and Their Distinctions 88
Preparing Your AD - IDFIX 88
Install of Azure AD Connect 93
    Option 1 – Express Installation 93
    Option 2 – Customize 94
PowerShell and Directory Synchronization 98
What Needs to be Performed Where? 99
    Active Directory 99
    Azure Active Directory Connect 103
    Azure AD Connect – Connectors 105
Licensing 108
Azure AD Recycle Bin 116

7. ExO Configuration

Client Access 120
    *-CASMailboxPlan Cmdlets 123
    Outlook Web Access (OWA) 124
GAL Segmentation 129
    Enable Address Book Policy Routing 130
    Create Recipient Filter 130
    Create Address Lists 131
    Create Global Address List (GAL) and Offline Address Book (OAB) 133
    Create a New Address Book Policy 135
Accepted Domains 136
POP3 and IMAP4 138
    Where To Start 138
    PowerShell Cmdlet Determination 138
Client Access Rules 142
    Cmdlet Review 142
    Creating a Rule 143
    Testing Rules 145
    Final Thoughts on Client Access Rules 146

8. Users

Types of Objects 147
Creating Users 148
    Mailbox or Mail Enabled User 148
Enabling Mailbox 150

Enabling Archive Mailbox 151
New Mail Contacts 151
Deleting Users 152
Modifying Users 152
User 152
Mailbox 153
OWA 155
Calendar 155
Policies 156
Permissions 157
Often Requested Changes 159
Converting Mailbox Types 160
Reporting 161
General Remarks 161
Cmdlets 161

9. Non-User Objects

Shared Mailboxes 175
PowerShell 175
Resource Mailboxes 178
Equipment Mailboxes 178
Equipment Mailbox Management 180
Room Mailboxes 181
Room Lists 183
Public Folder Mailboxes 185
Distribution Groups 187
PowerShell 187
Management 188
Get-MessageTrace 191
Group Moderation 193
PowerShell 193
Controlling Group Mail Flow 194
Office 365 Groups 196
Putting It All Together 199

10. Mail Flow

Mail Flow Connectors 201
Removing Connectors 204
Connector Reporting 204
Centralized Mail Transport 206
Message Tracing 207
Transport Rules 207

Accepted Domains 209
    Postmaster Check 210
    Removing An Accepted Domain 211

11. Mail Flow - Compliance

Message Hygiene 213
    External Controls 213
    Exchange Online Protection 214
Data Loss Prevention 222
    Features of DLP 223
    DLP PowerShell 223
    DLP Templates 223
    DLP Policies 225
    Policy Tips 226
    Document Fingerprinting 228
Journaling 232
    PowerShell 232
    Journaling Verification 235
    Reporting on Journaling Rules 236
    Disabling Rules 236
    Removing Rules 236
Azure Information Protection 237
    Outlook Protection Rules 241
    Mobile Protection 242
Office 365 Message Encryption (OME) 243

12. Security and Compliance Center

Security and Compliance Center 249
Connecting with PowerShell 250
Permissions 251
Classifications - Labels and DLP 254
    Labels 254
    Sensitive Information Types 256
Search and Investigation 259
    Compliance Searches 259
    Compliance Cases 259

13. Permissions and Compliance

Layered Security 262
    Management Roles 263
    Management Role Entries - Granular Permissions 268
    Management Role Groups 271

Special Management Role Groups. 272
Default User Role. 275
Impersonation 279
Management Scopes 280
Auditing 281
Admin Audit Logs. 281
Mailbox Audit Logs 286

14. Migrations

Introduction. 291
Basics (Migrations from On-Premises) 292
Migration Batch. 292
Move Requests 296
Checking Migration Status and Reports 300
Status 300
Reporting 302
Public Folder Migrations 303

15. Mobile Devices

Mobile Device Policies 305
Managing Mobile Device Mailbox Policies 305
Creating and Assigning. 306
Encrypted Device and Memory Card. 308
Managing Devices 310
Device Access ABQ. 310
Default Access Level 312
Allowing a Blocked/Quarantined Device. 313
Getting Devices for a Mailbox 313
Device Wipe 314
Removing a Device 315
ActiveSync Device Limit. 315
Reporting 315
Blocked/Quarantined Devices. 316
Wiped Devices 316
ActiveSync Enabled/Disabled Accounts. 317

16. Public Folders

Introduction 318
Background - Legacy Public Folders 318
Modern Public Folders 318
The Basics 319
New Public Folder Replication Model 319

Creating Public Folder Mailboxes 320
Creating Public Folders 321
Removing Public Folders 324
Get-PublicFolder* 325
Mail Enabled Public Folders 327
Public Folder Permissions 328
Troubleshooting 333

17. Unified Messaging

Overview 335
UM Basics 336
Basic Configuration 336
Skype for Business Integration 343
User Management 344
Modifying UM Mailbox 344
Removing UM Mailbox 345
Reporting 345

18. Reporting

Screenshots 349
TXT Files 349
CSV Files 353
HTML Files 356
Quick HTML Reports 356
Adding Polish – Refining HTML Reports 358
Detailed, Complex HTML Reporting 360
Delivery Methodologies 363
SMTP Delivery 364
File Copy 365

19. Troubleshooting

An Intro to Troubleshooting 368
Breaking up the Script 369
Pause and Sleep 369
Write-Host 371
Comments 372
PowerShell ISE 374
Debugging 375
Try and Catch 376
ErrorAction 378
Transcript 378
Deciphering Error Messages 380

    Basic Steps...380
    Sample Error Troubleshooting...............................380
Access Denied..381
Variables..382
Arrays..385
Conclusion...386

A. Best Practices

What is a Best Practice?...387
Summary of Best Practices.......................................387
PowerShell Best Practices..388
    Commenting..388
    Useful Comments..388
    Variable Naming..389
    Variable Block...389
    Matching Variables to Parameters.....................390
    Preference Variables...390
    Naming Conventions, this time for Functions and Scripts...........391
    Singular Task Functions....................................391
    Signing Your Code...392
    Filter vs. Where..392
    Error Handling..392
    Write-Output / Write-Verbose............................393
    '# Requires'...394
    Set-StrictMode -Version Latest...........................396
    Capitalization..398
    Using full command names................................398
    Cmdlet Binding...399
    Script Structure..400
    Quotes...400
    Running Applications.......................................401
    Conclusion and Further Help.............................401

B. Miscellaneous

Menus..404
Aliases..409
    New-Alias..410
    Set-Alias...410
    Removing an Alias...411
Foreach-Object (%)..412
PowerShell Interface Customization........................416
Command Logging..419

Introduction

Exchange and PowerShell

Beginning with Exchange Server 2007, Microsoft introduced PowerShell to enhance the Exchange Server product. PowerShell was a radical change at the time when Microsoft was known for its GUI interfaces. Yes, Microsoft had some command line access to its OS's (think DOS). By adding a command line interface, Microsoft had suddenly put the gauntlet down and announced to the world that it was serious about it products and providing an enhancement that would appeal to those who would look down on Microsoft because of the GUI based approach.

While Exchange Server 2007 ran what was then known as PowerShell 1.0, and while it was a good addition to existing Exchange Server management it was not perfect. It was not as flexible as it is today and was sorely in need of enhancement. With the introduction of Exchange Server 2010 and Exchange Server 2013, PowerShell advanced from 2.0 to 4.0. Currently Exchange Online supports PowerShell version 4.0 and 5.0. We won't cover the enhancements between versions, however suffice it to say that the product has changed drastically over the years since it was first introduced in 2007.

As PowerShell has advanced feature-wise, the commands that are exposed to Exchange Server have changed from 2007 to 2010 to 2013 to 2016 and now Exchange Online. This book is focused on Exchange Online, however a lot of the cmdlets, one-liners and scripts will work on Exchange 2016, 2013 and even Exchange 2010. We will make references to changes that have occurred in case you have written scripts in previous versions and are unaware of changes that need to be made in those scripts.

Why PowerShell and Not the Exchange Admin Center [a.k.a. the GUI]

There are many reasons to use PowerShell to manage and manipulate your Exchange Online Tenant. Some of the reasons are obvious while others may require some explanation. Let's lay out why you should use and become familiar with when it comes to PowerShell for Exchange Online:

- PowerShell allows the use of standard Windows commands that you would run in the Command Prompt.
- PowerShell brings powerful commands to the table to enable you to work with a complex environment. These commands use a verb-noun based syntax.
- PowerShell is integrated with almost all of Microsoft's on-premises and cloud applications.
- PowerShell allows for heavy automation. While this would seem to be geared to larger environments, smaller shops can utilize scheduling for common tasks – reporting, maintenance, bulk maintenance, etc. – to reduce the time needed and human errors in managing their Exchange server(s).
- Some things just cannot be done in the GUI. This is important. This is not advertised or spelled out by Microsoft. There are many options or configurations that can ONLY be performed with PowerShell. To make this clear, PowerShell is not limited in its management of Exchange as the GUI is. So it is important to learn it when learning about Exchange Servers in general.
- PowerShell works with objects. These objects can enable you to do powerful tasks in Exchange.
- PowerShell can get a task done in fewer lines than say VBScript. Some will find this to be an advantage as it can take less time to accomplish a task by writing it in PowerShell.
- PowerShell works with many technologies – XML, WMI, CIM, .NET, COM and Active Directory. The last one is important as you will see later, we can tie scripts together between Active Directory queries and Exchange commands.

- PowerShell provides a powerful help and search function. When working with PowerShell and a command is new to you, Get-Help is extremely useful as it can provide working examples of code. Searching for commands is easy as well and if you know what you want to manipulate (e.g. mailboxes), just searching for commands with a keyword of 'mailbox' can help direct your Get-Help query to find the relevant command.

As we get further into the book, we will cover these important features and more. One thing to remember about Exchange Server PowerShell is that it can be run local on an Exchange Server or remote (if PowerShell remoting is enabled). This can ease manageability of your messaging environment.

** **Note** ** For this book, we'll access Exchange Online with PowerShell 5.0.

Exchange Management Shell

Simply put, the Exchange Management Shell is the original Windows PowerShell with a module loaded specifically with Exchange Server oriented cmdlets.

Cmdlet (definition) – is a single PowerShell command like Get-Mailbox. Pronunciation: 'commandlet'.

Module (definition) – is a collection of additional PowerShell commands that are grouped together for one purpose or function. Example modules are Exchange Server, Active Directory and Windows Azure. There are many, many more, but these examples are relevant to this book.

Command Structure

PowerShell cmdlets come in two basic groupings - safe exploratory cmdlets (ones starting with 'GET' for example) and others that can configure or modify the Exchange configuration (SET, REMOVE, etc. - not as safe and can be dangerous to a production Exchange messaging environment).

Anatomy of a PowerShell Cmdlet:

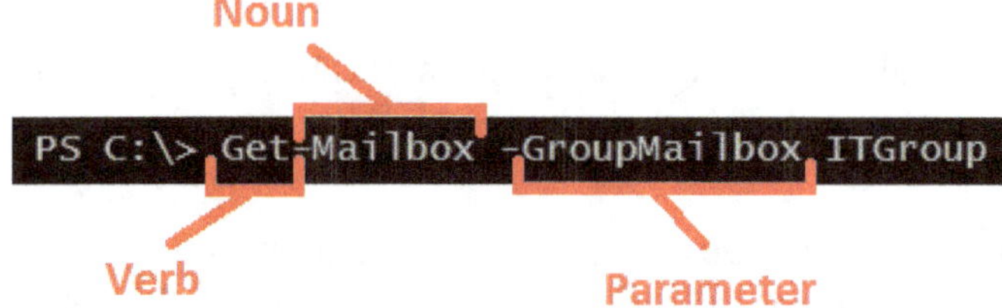

Verb - The action part of the cmdlet. Whether this is Get, Remove, List, Set or Add and more that are less common. These words are the first word of the Cmdlet and to the left of the dash of the cmdlet name.
Noun - The word or words to the right of the dash of the PowerShell cmdlet name. These words help describe what is being affected in Exchange Server 2016. Examples include - FederationTrust, FocusedMailbox, AddressList and more.
Parameter(s) - These are the options which are selected and upon which the PowerShell cmdlet will act. To get an idea of what parameters are present for each cmdlet you will need to do run a Get-Help <cmdlet> -full. We will review that later in this chapter.
Switch - Options that can be toggled for a cmdlet that don't need additional information (-WhatIf for example).

Cmdlet Examples

Get-UnifiedGroup
Provides a list of Unified Groups in the Exchange Online

Set-UnifiedGroup
Allows for the configuration of your Unified Groups in Exchange Online

When exploring PowerShell for Exchange for the first time, it is advisable to start with the Get cmdlets as these cmdlets will provide the beginner to PowerShell the following items:

- A view into Exchange and its configuration
- Practice with parameters, output, piping and more
- Non-destructive PowerShell practice
- A means to generating reports on Exchange

Get-cmdlets are benign in the sense that the current environment is not being changed or re-configured. This provides for safe learning or exploration not only for PowerShell but Exchange as well. It is highly recommended that you review some basic cmdlets like the following as a good starting point for your venture into Exchange PowerShell:

Get-AcceptedDomain	Get-AddressBookPolicy	Get-CASMailbox
Get-Clutter	Get-DlpPolicy	Get-MobileDevice
Get-QuarantineMessage	Get-SyncRequest	Get-UMMailbox

Piping

Single cmdlets are the meat and potatoes of PowerShell. However you can combine the results gathered by one cmdlet and feed this to another cmdlet in PowerShell which then processes results from the previous cmdlet. This process is known as piping. By combing two cmdlets together like this we now have a very powerful tool to use to construct one-liners. Caution should be used as not all cmdlets can be piped into another or vice versa.

One-liner (definition) – In PowerShell a one-liner literally is either a single command that performs a function or it is comprised of a set of cmdlets that are paired together with a pipe symbol '|'.

For an example of piping we are passing information from Get-Mailbox to Get-MailboxStatistics to produce results in a single table. If we did not use the pipelining feature, you would have to perform the Get-MailboxStatistics for each mailbox instead of using the pipeline method, which will run this for all mailboxes in one cmdlet. The pipe allows us to do that in bulk, which saves time and produces a single table of results.

Get-Mailbox | Get-MailboxStatistics

** **Note** ** Some cmdlets may return too many results and are often restricted to a set limit. In the above 'Get-Mailbox' example, the results are often limited to the first 1000. A way around this limit is to use '-ResultSize' and specifying a larger number, like 2,000, or using 'Unlimited' which will provide as many results it can find without restrictions.

Sample output:

```
DisplayName                    ItemCount StorageLimitStatus        LastLogonTime
-----------                    --------- ------------------        -------------
Administrator                  15                                  12/19/2014 3:39:49 PM
Backup                         6
Corporate User                 7
Corporate User2                12
Damian Scoles                  246359                              1/28/2016 3:40:06 PM
Discovery Search Mailbox       1
John Smith                     10
Postmaster                     7                                   7/7/2013 8:18:25 PM
SCOM Agent                     3
SearchResults                  1
```

To see the advantage of this, if we needed to gather the same information using just Get-MailboxStatistics, we would need to run the command for each mailbox:

```
[PS] C:\>get-mailboxstatistics damian
Creating a new session for implicit remoting of "Get-MailboxStatistics" command...
DisplayName                    ItemCount     StorageLimitStatus
-----------                    ---------     ------------------
Damian Scoles                  252601

[PS] C:\>get-mailboxstatistics administrator
DisplayName                    ItemCount     StorageLimitStatus
-----------                    ---------     ------------------
Administrator                  15
```

As you can see, the pipeline method enables us to move past a simple single line. What this also allows us to do is save time and allow us to work more efficiently in our scripting.

An alternative to piping would require quite a bit more effort, and some techniques we have not covered yet. The code would involve basically gathering all the mailboxes and storing their identities in a variable and the reading through the variable and running Get-MailboxStatistics for each mailbox stored in that variable:

```
$Mailboxes = Get-Mailbox
Foreach ($Mailbox in $Mailboxes) {
    Get-MailboxStatistics $Mailbox.Alias
}
```

The results are the same, while the complexity has gone up substantially some combined cmdlets can save server resources in terms of CPU and memory usage.

For another example of pipeline, let's take a more advanced topic like Mailbox Database health in a mailbox cluster. In order to get a complete picture of database health in a cluster we need to find all the databases and then get a status of each copy on each node that has that copy. How do we do this? We pipe Get-PublicFolder to the Get-PublicFolderStatistics cmdlet. These commands work in tandem to produce this:

```
PS C:\> Get-PublicFolder "\" -Recurse | Get-PublicFolderStatistics

Name              ItemCount     LastModificationTime
----              ---------     --------------------
IPM_SUBTREE       0             9/8/2015 1:11:11 AM
Company1          209           9/8/2015 1:11:24 AM
andD              41            9/8/2015 1:13:01 AM
HR                0             9/8/2015 1:12:57 AM
IT                915           9/8/2015 1:12:54 AM
Company2          534           9/8/2015 1:12:34 AM
```

Notice that we can see the status, as well as the ContentIndexStatus. Both of these are important in knowing the health of your mailbox databases.

Protecting Yourself and What If

PowerShell is powerful. PowerShell can thus do some serious damage to Exchange Online and Azure Active Directory. How can you protect your infrastructure from your missteps?

- Run Get cmdlets first to get a general familiarity of PowerShell in Exchange.
- Use the WhatIf switch when running cmdlets, this will show what would have occurred if a cmdlet was run.

An example of the WhatIf switch would be what would happen if you were to get all mailboxes in Exchange and remove the mailboxes:

> Get-Mailbox testclouduser | Remove-Mailbox -WhatIf
>
> **What if**: Removing the mailbox "testclouduser" will mark the mailbox and the archive, if present, for deletion. The associated Windows Live ID "testclouduser@tenant.onmicrosoft.com" will also be deleted and will not be available for any other Windows Live service.

The one caveat to this is if the mailbox is synchronized from Active Directory, you will see this error message instead:

> Get-Mailbox User | Remove-Mailbox -WhatIf

```
PS C:\> Get-Mailbox User01 | Remove-Mailbox -WhatIf
The following error occurred during validation in agent 'Windows LiveId Agent': 'Unable to perform
the save operation. 'user01' is not within a valid server write scope. '
    + CategoryInfo          : NotSpecified: (:) [Remove-Mailbox], ProvisioningValidationException
    + FullyQualifiedErrorId : [Server=BN3PRO8MB1985,RequestId=4edce40c-1abd-43d4-acde-1ff096ba1ab0
    ,TimeStamp=8/28/2017 4:36:32 AM] [FailureCategory=Cmdlet-ProvisioningValidationException] B9D5
    5EA1,Microsoft.Exchange.Management.RecipientTasks.RemoveMailbox
    + PSComputerName        : ps.outlook.com
```

Notice the WhatIf statement in front of each result. If this command was run in production, all mailboxes would be deleted. However, because we ran the same command with the WhatIf switch only a simulation was run, no mailboxes were removed.

Command Discovery Techniques

A certain amount of discovery involves knowing Exchange. With this knowledge, finding commands that are necessary to perform actions becomes easier. For example users in your environment that receive email have mailboxes. This may seem like a simple example, but it will help illustrate the idea of knowing Exchange will help with PowerShell cmdlets.

So, going back to mailboxes. We need to manipulate some information or create a report on mailboxes in your Exchange Online tenant. If you don't know what commands that can be run, we rely on a specific cmdlet called 'Get-Command'. With this we can find cmdlets we need:

> Get-Command *mailbox*

Running this will look for any PowerShell cmdlet that has the work mailbox in it. The wildcard '*' that is located in front and behind the word 'mailbox' just means that we are searching for any command that may or may not have additional letters before or after the word 'mailbox'. A small portion of the results are listed below:

```
PS C:\> Get-Command *mailbox*

CommandType     Name                                     Version    Source
-----------     ----                                     -------    ------
Function        Add-MailboxFolderPermission              1.0        tmp_fqap2abx.svy
Function        Add-MailboxLocation                      1.0        tmp_fqap2abx.svy
Function        Add-MailboxPermission                    1.0        tmp_fqap2abx.svy
Function        Disable-Mailbox                          1.0        tmp_fqap2abx.svy
Function        Disable-UMMailbox                         1.0        tmp_fqap2abx.svy
Function        Enable-Mailbox                           1.0        tmp_fqap2abx.svy
Function        Enable-UMMailbox                          1.0        tmp_fqap2abx.svy
Function        Export-MailboxDiagnosticLogs             1.0        tmp_fqap2abx.svy
Function        Get-ActiveSyncMailboxPolicy              1.0        tmp_fqap2abx.svy
Function        Get-CASMailbox                           1.0        tmp_fqap2abx.svy
Function        Get-CASMailboxPlan                       1.0        tmp_fqap2abx.svy
Function        Get-GroupMailbox                         1.0        tmp_fqap2abx.svy
Function        Get-Mailbox                              1.0        tmp_fqap2abx.svy
```

Now, let's say we actually need to look at Public Folders in the environment:

```
Get-Command *PublicFolder*
```

```
CommandType     Name                                              Version    Source
-----------     ----                                              -------    ------
Function        Add-PublicFolderClientPermission                  1.0        tmp_fqap2abx.svy
Function        Disable-MailPublicFolder                          1.0        tmp_fqap2abx.svy
Function        Enable-MailPublicFolder                           1.0        tmp_fqap2abx.svy
Function        Get-MailPublicFolder                              1.0        tmp_fqap2abx.svy
Function        Get-PublicFolder                                  1.0        tmp_fqap2abx.svy
Function        Get-PublicFolderClientPermission                  1.0        tmp_fqap2abx.svy
Function        Get-PublicFolderItemStatistics                    1.0        tmp_fqap2abx.svy
Function        Get-PublicFolderMailboxDiagnostics                1.0        tmp_fqap2abx.svy
Function        Get-PublicFolderMailboxMigrationRequest           1.0        tmp_fqap2abx.svy
Function        Get-PublicFolderMailboxMigrationRequestStatistics 1.0        tmp_fqap2abx.svy
Function        Get-PublicFolderMigrationRequest                  1.0        tmp_fqap2abx.svy
Function        Get-PublicFolderMigrationRequestStatistics        1.0        tmp_fqap2abx.svy
Function        Get-PublicFolderStatistics                        1.0        tmp_fqap2abx.svy
Function        New-PublicFolder                                  1.0        tmp_fqap2abx.svy
```

As you can see, the Get-Command is useful for finding cmdlets in PowerShell that you can use in Exchange Online.

PowerShell Modules

When working with Exchange and because of its dependency on Azure Active Directory we may need other cmdlets in order to perform certain actions. When working in the default Exchange Management Shell, PowerShell cmdlets for Azure Active Directory are not preloaded. In order to load these cmdlets, we may need to install the module. With PowerShell 5.0 we can download modules of all sorts using the 'Install-Module' cmdlet like so:

```
Install-Module -Name AzureAD
```

** **Note** ** If this is the first time the Install-Module cmdlet has been run, you may receive a message about a 'NuGet Provider'. This provider is what allows the interaction between PowerShell and the NuGet repository where the modules are stored. Make sure to answer yes as to whether to install it.

```
PS C:\> Install-Module -Name AzureAD

NuGet provider is required to continue
PowerShellGet requires NuGet provider version '2.8.5.201' or newer to interact with NuGet-based
repositories. The NuGet provider must be available in 'C:\Program
Files\PackageManagement\ProviderAssemblies' or
'C:\Users\Administrator\AppData\Local\PackageManagement\ProviderAssemblies'. You can also install
the NuGet provider by running 'Install-PackageProvider -Name NuGet -MinimumVersion 2.8.5.201
-Force'. Do you want PowerShellGet to install and import the NuGet provider now?
[Y] Yes  [N] No  [S] Suspend  [?] Help (default is "Y"): y
```

Once the NuGet module has installed, we can now install the AzureAD module via the NuGet provider:

```
Untrusted repository
You are installing the modules from an untrusted repository. If you trust this repository, change
its InstallationPolicy value by running the Set-PSRepository cmdlet. Are you sure you want to
install the modules from 'PSGallery'?
[Y] Yes  [A] Yes to All  [N] No  [L] No to All  [S] Suspend  [?] Help (default is "N"): y
```

Once the module is installed we can now to connect to AzureAD to work with this part of an Office 365 tenant:

    Connect-AzureAD

After the PowerShell module has loaded, additional cmdlets are available.

Getting Help!?!

Along with Get-Command, Get-Help will assist you in exploring PowerShell for Exchange Online.

When faced with running a new cmdlet in PowerShell or just figuring out what other options are available for a PowerShell cmdlet, the Get-Help and Get-Command are extremely helpful. If you've used Linux or Unix they are like the man pages of old where a description of what the command can do, where it can be run, various examples of how the command can be used and more. When using the Get-Help and Get-Command, just like other PowerShell commands, there are switches that you can use to help enhance the basic cmdlet. For example, take this cmdlet:

    Get-Help Get-RetentionPolicy

The above command returns some information on the Get-Mailbox cmdlet:

```
NAME
    Get-RetentionPolicy

SYNOPSIS
    This cmdlet is available in on-premises Exchange Server 2016 and in the cloud-based service.
    Some parameters and settings may be exclusive to one environment or the other.

    Use the Get-RetentionPolicy cmdlet to retrieve the settings for retention policies.

    For information about the parameter sets in the Syntax section below, see Exchange cmdlet
    syntax.

SYNTAX
    Get-RetentionPolicy [-Identity <MailboxPolicyIdParameter>] [-DomainController <Fqdn>]
    [<CommonParameters>]

DESCRIPTION
    A retention policy is associated with a group of retention policy tags that specify retention
    settings for items in a mailbox. A policy may contain one default policy tag to move items to
    an archive mailbox, one default policy tag to delete all items, one default policy tag to
    delete voicemail items, and multiple personal tags to move or delete items. A mailbox can have
    only one retention policy applied to it. The Get-RetentionPolicy cmdlet displays all policy
    settings associated with the specified policy.

    You need to be assigned permissions before you can run this cmdlet. Although all parameters
    for this cmdlet are listed in this topic, you may not have access to some parameters if
    they're not included in the permissions assigned to you. To see what permissions you need, see
    the "Messaging records management" entry in the Messaging policy and compliance permissions in
    Exchange 2016 topic.

RELATED LINKS
    Online Version
    http://technet.microsoft.com/EN-US/library/7a05203e-894b-4109-9647-ca7afc44a08f(EXCHG.160).aspx
REMARKS
```

Notice the main sections: Name, Synopsis, Syntax, Description, Related Links and Remarks. The command we ran provided us with a nice summary of what this command can do and the Related Link section points you to the online documentation for this cmdlet. However, what is missing is the switches or options that are available for the cmdlet as well as some examples on how to use the cmdlet as well. To get these, run the following:

```
Get-Help Get-RetentionPolicy -Full
```

The same first section appear: Name, Synopsis, Syntax and Description. However, a few addition sections appear now: Parameters, Inputs, Outputs and Examples:

```
PARAMETERS
    -DomainController <Fqdn>
        This parameter is available only in on-premises Exchange 2016.

        The DomainController parameter specifies the domain controller that's used by this cmdlet
        to read data from or write data to Active Directory. You identify the domain controller by
        its fully qualified domain name (FQDN). For example, dc01.contoso.com.

        Required?                    false
        Position?                    Named
        Default value
        Accept pipeline input?       False
        Accept wildcard characters?  false

    -Identity <MailboxPolicyIdParameter>
        The Identity parameter specifies the policy name.

        Required?                    false
        Position?                    1
        Default value
        Accept pipeline input?       True
        Accept wildcard characters?  false

    <CommonParameters>
        This cmdlet supports the common parameters: Verbose, Debug,
        ErrorAction, ErrorVariable, WarningAction, WarningVariable,
        OutBuffer, PipelineVariable, and OutVariable. For more information, see
        about_CommonParameters (http://go.microsoft.com/fwlink/?LinkID=113216).

INPUTS

        To see the input types that this cmdlet accepts, see Cmdlet Input and Output Types
        (http://go.microsoft.com/fwlink/p/?linkId=616387). If the Input Type field for a cmdlet is
        blank, the cmdlet doesn't accept input data.


OUTPUTS

        To see the return types, which are also known as output types, that this cmdlet accepts,
        see Cmdlet Input and Output Types (http://go.microsoft.com/fwlink/p/?linkId=616387). If
        the Output Type field is blank, the cmdlet doesn't return data.

    -------------------------- Example1 --------------------------
```

When you work with a command that you are unfamiliar with, it would be advisable to start with the -Full switch to get all information on the cmdlet as well as some examples on how to use the command. The major weakness of the help command as well as the Online help is that some commands are very complex and have so many options that they don't feel as complete as they might. This means that even after finding the right parameters, it may take some time to get the right results. If you find yourself in this situation, you can turn to your favorite Internet search engine to find the right syntax OR possibly get a close enough example that a bit of tweaking will make the cmdlet run the way you expect.

Idiosyncrasies

Let's end this chapter on a cautionary note. We covered commands like Get-Help and Get-Command. These will come in handy as you build your own scripts. After writing scripts for a while you may notice that not everything in Exchange PowerShell is perfect or logical. This is especially true when it comes to PowerShell cmdlet naming conventions. Let's take for example any cmdlet with the word 'Mobile' in it. Here is the list of all the cmdlets:

    Get-Command *Mobile*

Which will give us this for results:

However, there is another set of cmdlets that appear for mobile devices, under their original name of Active Sync.

```
Name
----
Clear-MobileDevice
Get-MobileDevice
Get-MobileDeviceDashboardSummaryReport
Get-MobileDeviceMailboxPolicy
Get-MobileDeviceStatistics
New-MobileDeviceMailboxPolicy
Remove-MobileDevice
Remove-MobileDeviceMailboxPolicy
Set-MobileDeviceMailboxPolicy
```

These cmdlets were once the only available ones because the Active Sync protocol used to be THE way to connect to Exchange. With the advent of modern protocols, apps and the cloud, the cmdlet base is slowly changing. Here are all the cmdlets with 'ActiveSync' in their name:

    Get-Command *ActiveSync*

```
Name
----
Clear-ActiveSyncDevice
Get-ActiveSyncDevice
Get-ActiveSyncDeviceAccessRule
Get-ActiveSyncDeviceClass
Get-ActiveSyncDeviceStatistics
Get-ActiveSyncMailboxPolicy
Get-ActiveSyncOrganizationSettings
New-ActiveSyncDeviceAccessRule
New-ActiveSyncMailboxPolicy
Remove-ActiveSyncDevice
Remove-ActiveSyncDeviceAccessRule
Remove-ActiveSyncMailboxPolicy
Set-ActiveSyncDeviceAccessRule
Set-ActiveSyncMailboxPolicy
Set-ActiveSyncOrganizationSettings
```

As you can see this leaves a bit to be desired for consistency sake. The best way to handle these situations is to do what we did above to get all cmdlets that have a similar word or function to them.

Cloud-Only vs Synced Environments and PowerShell Cmdlets

For anyone who manages Exchange Online, knowing what PowerShell cmdlets will with their environment is a crucial piece of information. In that spirit we want to make sure that these differences are clearly delineated in the rest of the book and when we are working with PowerShell. The important thing to remember is that if your accounts, mailboxes and other objects are not synced to the cloud you will need to make your changes in Office 365 directly and not to anything on-premises like Active Directory. This is simply because Office 365 is in this scenario your source of truth and it is the master copy of these objects. If, however, you have Active Directory and you are syncing these objects to the cloud your on-premises Active Directory is the source of truth or Start of Authority. Those synced objects need to be changed in your on-premises Active Directory, to be more precise those synced attributes are actual only read-only in the cloud. This currently also means that if you have Exchange attributes that need to be changed in those synced objects, you require an Exchange server on-premises. This is currently the only supported way to achieve those changes (like adding an additional SMTP address to a synced object). You might find blog posts and well-intentioned advices to use third party tool or perhaps even ADSIedit, but those aren't officially supported. This does not preclude you from running PowerShell cmdlets against your Exchange Online tenant. Or on fully cloud objects.

** **Note** ** Please note that the defining feature here is the synchronization of objects, NOT the fact that an Exchange environment is hybrid or not. AD synchronization is a prerequisite for an Exchange hybrid environment.

Hybrid environment (things to consider):

- **Creation of Shared Mailbox** - the process includes creating a remote mailbox and then converting this mailbox into a Shared Mailbox
- **Creation of Archive Mailbox** - PowerShell cmdlet run on-premises Exchange and attribute synced to Exchange Online
- **Handling of self-management distribution lists** - On by default in User Roles of Exchange Online
- We use a sync script to create copy lists in Exchange Online (ExO) so that both sides can be self-managed independent of the mailbox location.

Non-Synced Accounts (Cloud Only)

For those who do not want any infrastructure for their email services, this is a common setup. In this configuration, all your objects exist in Exchange Online only. All management tools and scripts will run against these cloud-only objects. The Admin Console for your tenant should show all of these objects as 'Cloud-Only' and this only manageable from Office 365's connections.

Sample Management Scenarios

Creating a new mailbox
    (1) Log into Exchange Online PowerShell with an account with the correct login privileges
    (2) Create an account using the New-Mailbox cmdlet.
    (3) Add license in Office 365
    (4) Configure mailbox attributes - Retention policy, ActiveSync policy, OWA policy and more

** **Note** ** There is no need to wait for synchronization or for an object to be updated in two places. All changes are made in Exchange Online.

Create Mail Transport Rule
    (1) Log into Exchange Online PowerShell
    (2) Run New-TransportRule to create the new rule - refer to page 205 for more information.

Synced Accounts

It is common, but not entirely true of all of these environments, that a synced environment will have Exchange on-premises for management. This is simply because Microsoft does not support managing synced objects to the cloud with ADSIEdit. The supported method is to have an Exchange Server on-premises to serve as a management console. Due to this requirement and the nature of this server, Microsoft will also provide what is known as a Hybrid license key for you to license an Exchange 2010, 2013 or 2016 server to use it for Exchange Online management.

Sample Management Scenarios

Creating a new mailbox

    (1) Log into an Exchange Server with an account with the correct login privileges
    (2) Create an account using the New-RemoteMailbox cmdlet.
    (3) Wait for Azure AD Connect to sync this newly created object to Exchange Online
    (4) Log into Exchange Online PowerShell
    (5) Add license in Office 365
    (6) Configure mailbox attributes - retention policy, ActiveSync policy, OWA policy and more

** **Note** ** Notice that we are logging into both Exchange On-Premises and Exchange Online depending on what the task is to be performed.

Create Mail Transport Rule

For a synced environment this situation is one of 'It Depends'. The reasoning behind that is, depending on your configuration, email may still be flowing through Exchange on-premises/ In this scenario, let assume that we need the rules in ExO because mail flow from internal and external recipients all flows through Exchange Online Protection (EOP).

    (1) Log into Exchange Online PowerShell
    (2) Run New-TransportRule to create the new rule - refer to page 205 for more information.

Book Methodology

For most of the scenarios and cmdlets laid out, we are assuming that there is an Active Directory on-premises that has synced to Exchange Online. As such, we will assume that there will be some split management. Some will require modification from an on-premises Exchange server as well as connecting to ExO to make some changes. As such, we'll try to point out when there is a deviation from this scenario.

What's Next?

In this introduction we have just scratched the surface of what is available in PowerShell for Exchange Online. Let's go ahead and get in deep with PowerShell in Chapter 1.

In This Chapter

- Variables
- Arrays
- Hash Tables
- CSV Files
- Operators
- Loops
- Functions
- PowerShell Tools
  - ISE
  - ISE Plug-Ins

Exchange Online PowerShell: Where to Begin

This book is not a beginner's guide to PowerShell and while we assume that you, the reader, know at least something about PowerShell, we will quickly cover some basic PowerShell topics. What is covered in this chapter is necessary in order to form our building blocks for the more advanced chapters later in this book. Those building blocks will provide practical knowledge for using PowerShell with Exchange Online. Theory can be useful, but for production messaging environments, practical tips and tricks (and scripts!) are far more useful for working in your environment.

In the Introduction, we covered one-liners, cmdlets and getting help in the PowerShell interface. We are now going to turn our attention to building PowerShell parts that make up these elements in PowerShell. Remember that a PowerShell cmdlet consists of a verb and a noun. Remember that PowerShell cmdlets provide various parameters as we saw with the Get-Help in the Introduction to this book.

In the next few pages we will introduce you to some important concepts that are key to building your scripts for Exchange Online. These concepts include variables, arrays, loops and more. Learning these will provide you with the building blocks for your scripts. There will be some basic topics which will introduce you to these elements. These topics will give you the tools to begin building scripts in future chapters of this book.

Variables

When scripting, a variable is a place for storing data. A variable can store data for different lengths of time, but most importantly, the data stored in the variable can be retrieved or referenced by cmdlets later in a script for performing a task. The data stored in variables is of a certain type, such as strings, numerals, arrays and more. Variables are essential in PowerShell scripting, and it should become apparent how useful they are when working with Exchange Online.

Example - Variables

Variable	Variable Type
$Value = 1	Numeric
$FirstName = "Damian"	String

Variables are not restricted to static content or a single object or value, and they can store complex, nested structures as well. For example, if we use a variable to store information on all mailboxes:

$AllMailboxes = Get-Mailbox

The $AllMailboxes variable stores information on each mailbox as a single object and can contain as many objects as there are mailboxes in the Exchange environment. This content is unlikely to change as the script using that information will likely be stored for repeated use in a script. However, a variable containing the current value of a property of a mailbox or server might change repeatedly in a script loop, replacing the variable content on each pass. For example, while looping through an array (example on page 4), the mailbox name could be stored in a temporary variable (e.g. $name) and with each pass of in the loop, the contents of $name would change to the mailbox name in the current line of an array. Thus, the contents of a variable is not necessarily static and can be changed during the processing of a script.

Arrays

Arrays are used to store a collection of objects. This collection of data is more complex than what would be stored in a normal variable (above).

Example

$Values = 1,2,3,4,5
$Names = "Dave","Matt","John","Michael"

As you can see from the above example, the array contains a row of values which can be used by a script for queries or manipulation.

Even more complex than arrays are multi-dimensional arrays. The $AllMailboxes variable example above is an example of this type of variable. This type is used to store more complex, structured information.

Example of Arrays (Multi-dimensional)

If we were to store all the information about all the Exchange Servers in an array of arrays, there would be a 'list' of arrays. Each line is essentially its own array of values. Visually, this is how the data is stored in the array [the top line contains the column descriptions for the underlying values]:

"Alias","ArchiveQuota","RetentionHoldEnabled","RecipientType"
"Damian","100 GB (107,374,182,400 bytes)","False","MailUser"
"Dave","100 GB (107,374,182,400 bytes)","False","MailUser"
"Brian","100 GB (107,374,182,400 bytes)","False","MailUser"
"RoomTest","100 GB (107,374,182,400 bytes)","False","MailUser"

Hash Tables

Hash tables are similar in form and function to arrays, but with a twist. To initialize a hash table, the command is similar to an array:

    $Hash = @ { }

Notice the use of the '{' brackets and not '('. Once initialized we can populate the data like so:

Example

In the below data sample, the name of each mailbox matched up with the Quota size for their mailbox. As can be seen by the data set, the data is stored in pairs:

    $Mailboxes = @{Damian = '100 GB '; Dave= '100 GB ' ; Brian= '100 GB'}

To display the contents of the hash table, simply run '$Mailboxes':

```
PS C:\> $Mailboxes

Name            Value
----            -----
Brian           100 GB
Damian          100 GB
Dave            100 GB
```

In most scenarios, an array is the way to go for data storage and manipulation. However, hash tables provide for more complex data storage and indexing with its data pairs.

CSV Files

CSV files are files used to store static data, outside of using variables. This data can be pre-created and then used by a script post creation or a CSV file can be generated by a script either as an end result or an intermediary step for a script to be used at a later point. CSV files can be considered an alternative option to using arrays. They can be used to contain data in a way similar to how an array would store data. One of the differences is that CSVs are files and arrays are stored in memory (RAM), which means that arrays only exist while a script is running and CSV files can be used to store information which should be kept, like for input or output purposes. They can also be looped through, like an array. CSV files can be manually created in a program like Excel for total control or created by a running script with an Export-CSV cmdlet to export the data.

Arrays are preferable for storing data within a script because no file is created and left behind to cleanup at a later date. The exception would be if I have an external program or process that generates a CSV file which contains lists of values that need to be imported or used for a process involving a PowerShell script.

The format of the CSV file looks something like this:

```
DisplayName,Alias,PrimarySMTPAddress,SendQuota,ReceiveQuota,RetentionPolicy
Damian Scoles,DamianScoles,Damian@PracticalPowerShell.Com,20GB,30GB,BigCorpDefault
Dave Stork,DaveStork,DaveStork@PracticalPowerShell.Com,25GB,35GB,BigCorpDefault
John Doe,JohnDoe,JohnDoe@PracticalPowerShell.Com,10GB,20GB,BigCorpRestricted
```

Column Headers

Static data to be used by the script

```
DisplayName,Alias,PrimarySMTPAddress,SendQuota,ReceiveQuota,RetentionPolicy
Damian Scoles,DamianScoles,Damian@PracticalPowerShell.Com,20GB,30GB,BigCorpDefault
Dave Stork,DaveStork,DaveStork@PracticalPowerShell.Com,25GB,35GB,BigCorpDefault
John Doe,JohnDoe,JohnDoe@PracticalPowerShell.Com,10GB,20GB,BigCorpRestricted
```

PowerShell scripts that use CSV files commonly read CSV files and store the contents in a variable to be used by the script. Import-CSV is the command to perform this task.

Example

$CSVFileData = Import-CSV "C:\Temp\MailboxData.csv"

In the section on Loops, we will review what can be done with data stored in the variable, after it has been imported from a CSV file.

Operators

Operators are used in PowerShell to compare two objects or values. This can be particularly useful for when "If.. Then" or "Where-Object" is used.

Operators can include the following:

-eq	Equal	-and	TRUE when both are TRUE
-lt	Less than		e.g. (3 -eq 3) -and (1 -lt 3)
-gt	Greater than		TRUE
-ne	Not equal	-or	TRUE when either is TRUE
-ge	Greater than or equal		e.g. (3 -lt 3) -or (2 -eq 2)
-le	Less than or equal		TRUE
-like	Like Good for single wildcards e.g. "*mailbox"	-xor	TRUE when only one is TRUE e.g. (1 -eq 1) -xor (2 -eq 2) FALSE
-match	Matches criteria (non-case sensitive) Also can use double wildcards e.g. "*mailbox*"	-not / !	When a condition is not TRUE e.g. -not (1 -eq 1) FALSE
-cmatch	Match criteria (case-sensitive) e.g. "*Mailbox*"		
-contains	Exact match		

Example

```
 $Mailbox = Get-Mailbox
If ($Mailbox -eq "Damian") {
    Set-Mailbox $Mailbox -ForwardingSMTPAddress DaveStork@PracticalPowershell.Com
}
```
The above example configures email forwarding for a mailbox that matches the name Damian and

forwards all messages to the email address of ***DaveStork@PracticalPowershell.Com.***

Another example would be if there are mailboxes with small quotas (2GB) that need to be increased to 5GB:

```
If ($Quota -lt 2000000) {
    Set-Mailbox $Mailbox -IssueWarningQuota 5gb
}
```

Operators will work with strings and numbers types. Less than and greater than operators will work against text:

```
If ("Mouse" -lt "Wolf) {
    Write-Host "The Wolf eats the Mouse!"
}
```

The output from this comparison would result in:

```
The Wolf eats the Mouse!
```

The operators, with strings, work off the numerical values of each letter in the words added together and compared.

Loops

Loops can be used to process or generate a series of data, perhaps an array (or an array of arrays) of data stored in variables (like our $CSVFileData variable in the previous section). A loop can also use a counter for a series of values as well. Here are a few different ways to create loops in PowerShell:

Types

```
Foreach { }
Do { } While ()
```


Foreach

Foreach loops can be used to process each element of an array either stored in a variable or a CSV file. The array can have a single or multiple elements. The Foreach loop will stop when there are no more lines to read or process, although the more lines there are, the longer it will take to complete.

Example

Let's take our $CSVFileData variable that has stored the data we pre-created in a CSV file. The variable now contains three 'rows' of usable data. We can use the data to manipulate mailboxes by changing parameters, creating a report to send to IT Admins or maybe to move mailboxes to different mailbox databases.

** **Note** ** In the below code, with each loop, the variable $line, will be filled with a row from the CSV variable. You can then do something with that data in $line. After the loop is finished, Foreach will read the next line in $CSVFIleData and enter it in $line. And so forth until all rows have been read.

A simple example of a Foreach loop would look like this: (Complete code):

```
$CSVFileData = Import-CSV "C:\Data.csv"
Foreach ($Line in $CSVFileData) {
    $DisplayName = $Line.DisplayName
    $Size = $Line.ReceiveQuota
    Write-Host "The user $DisplayName has a mailbox Receive Quota of $Size."
}
```

The output would look like this:

```
The user Damian Scoles has a Receive Quota of 30GB.
The user Dave Stork has a Receive Quota of 35GB.
The user John Doe has a Receive Quota of 20GB.
```

In this example, the loop created a simple visual representation of the data, but the representation was repeated in a standard manner using a loop and a write-host cmdlet.

Do { } While ()

Do While and While loops allow a loop to continuously run until a condition has been met. The key difference between the two is that a While loop will evaluate a condition prior to any code executing (the code between the brackets of a While loop may not even run once) whereas a Do While loop will execute code first (guaranteeing at least one time execution of code) and then checking for a particular condition. Whether this conditional exit is an incremental counter, waiting for a query result or a certain key to be pressed, the Do While loop provides some interesting functionality that can be used in PowerShell and with your Exchange Online.

When looping code with a While loop, an example of conditional exit is the counter variable. Simply put, the counter variable keeps track of the number of times a loop has run. Each time the below loop runs, the counter value increases by 1 ($Counter++). When the $counter variable reaches 1,000, the script block will stop processing and PowerShell will move on to the next section of code.

Example – While Loop

```
$Counter = 1
While ($Counter -lt 1000) {
    Write-Host "This is pass # $Counter for this loop."
    $Counter++
}
```

** **Note** ** The $Counter++ near the end of the loop, which is shorthand for $Counter = $Counter +1.

Also notice that the 'While' statement is at the top of the loop unlike the Do...While loop that follows.

Example – Do While Loop

```
$Counter = 1
Do {
```

```
    Write-Host "This is pass # $Counter for this loop."
    $Counter++
} While ($Counter -ne 1000)
```

In the above sample, we use a counter variable ($counter) which is incremented by 1's using $Counter++. On each pass the script writes a line to the screen (write-host "This is pass # $Counter for this loop."). The resulting output from the code loops something like this:

```
This is pass # 4 for this loop.
This is pass # 5 for this loop.
This is pass # 6 for this loop.
This is pass # 7 for this loop.
This is pass # 8 for this loop.
This is pass # 994 for this loop.
This is pass # 995 for this loop.
This is pass # 996 for this loop.
```

Once the variable ($Counter) gets to 1,000, the script will exit.

```
This is pass # 994 for this loop.
This is pass # 995 for this loop.
This is pass # 996 for this loop.
This is pass # 997 for this loop.
This is pass # 998 for this loop.
This is pass # 999 for this loop.
```

Notice that a result with 1,000 is not shown above and this is because the counter is increased after the write-host statement and the $Counter variable is increased from 999 to 1,000 and exits. In order to show a result with 1,000 the $counter variable needs to be moved:

Example

```
$Counter = 0
Do {
    $Counter++
    Write-Host "This is pass # $Counter for this loop."
} While ($Counter -ne 1000)
```

Export-CSV

Export-CSV – This cmdlet can create a CSV file to be used by another script or another section of code in the same script.

When exporting to a CSV file, make sure to use the –NoType option in order to remove the extraneous line that gets inserted into the exported CSV. This extra line can affect the use of the CSV file later. See below for an example of what happens when exporting a complete list of mailboxes to a CSV file:

Export-CSV -NoType

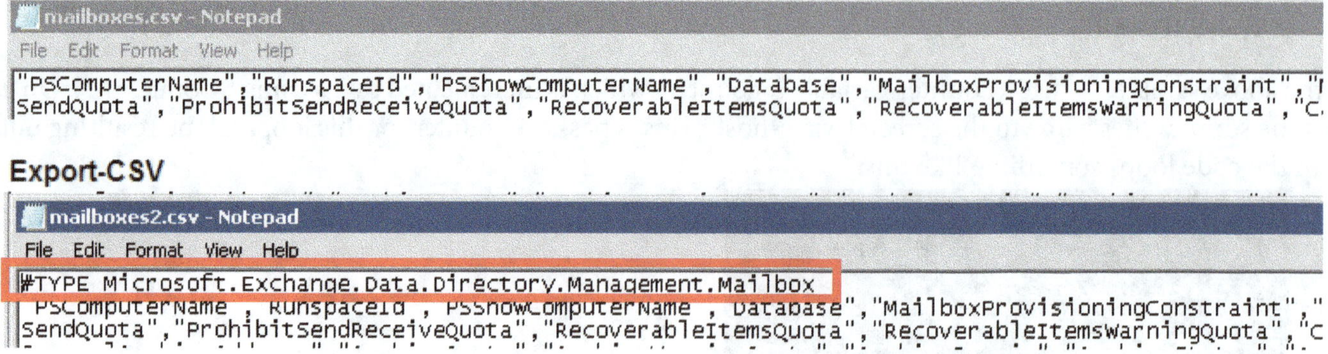

Export-CSV

** **Note** ** In order to use the CSV later in the script, the –NoType option should be used.

How to Use these Cmdlets

These cmdlets are most useful for pulling in information from an external source or exporting the information for a later script or for reporting purposes. When importing the contents of a CSV file, we can use a variable to store the contents to be pulled out later by a loop or some other method.

Functions

Functions are blocks of code that can be called upon within the same script. This block of code becomes a reusable operation that can be called on multiple times in a script. The function, since it is comprised of reusable code, helps to save time in coding by removing duplicate coding efforts as well as reducing the size of the script removing duplicate code. Which, depending on how much code is involved and how often it is called, can improve the performance and efficiency of a PowerShell script, as well as make it more maintainable.

Example

```
# Check for Old Disclaimers
Function Check-OldDisclaimers {
    $RuleCheck = (Get-TransportRule).ApplyHtmlDisclaimerText
    $RuleCheck2 = Get-TransportRule | Where {$_.ApplyHtmlDisclaimerText -ne $Null}
    If ($RuleCheck -eq $Null) {
        Write-Host "There are no disclaimers in place now." -ForegroundColor Green
    } Else {
        Foreach ($Line in $RuleCheck2) {
            Write-Host "There is a transport rule in place called $Line that is a disclaimer rule."
        }
    }
} #End of the Check-OldDisclaimers function

Check-OldDisclaimers
```

In the above example, the function is begun with the word 'Function' and enclosed in { } brackets. The function is then called by the very last line where the 'Check-OldDisclaimers' matches the name of the function, which executes the code contained within the brackets.

The previous code sample checks for disclaimers configured in Exchange Online. The last line of the script above calls the function (with the code contained within the '{' and '}' brackets) and the code in the brackets executes. The PowerShell function by itself will not do anything unless it is called upon.

PowerShell Tools

PowerShell ISE

PowerShell ISE [*Integrated Scripting Environment*] is one of **THE** tools you should get familiar with when working with PowerShell. The tool comes installed by default with Windows 2012, 2012 R2 and 2016. If you are using an older version of Windows (2008R2 and before) ISE is not pre-installed and it will be necessary to download the installation and install it on the server.

The ISE has many useful features such as color coding of PowerShell cmdlet types as well as the indicators that are provided for loops (Foreach, If Else, etc.), to aid in checking matching brackets for example. ISE's built-in spell checker make this tool very useful. ISE is also PowerShell-aware which means you can quickly find the relevant cmdlet or recently defined variable after only typing a few characters. If working with Exchange, the Exchange PowerShell Module needs to be available for ISE to use otherwise it won't be able to look up those cmdlets needed or used with Exchange Servers.

PowerShell ISE Graphical Interface

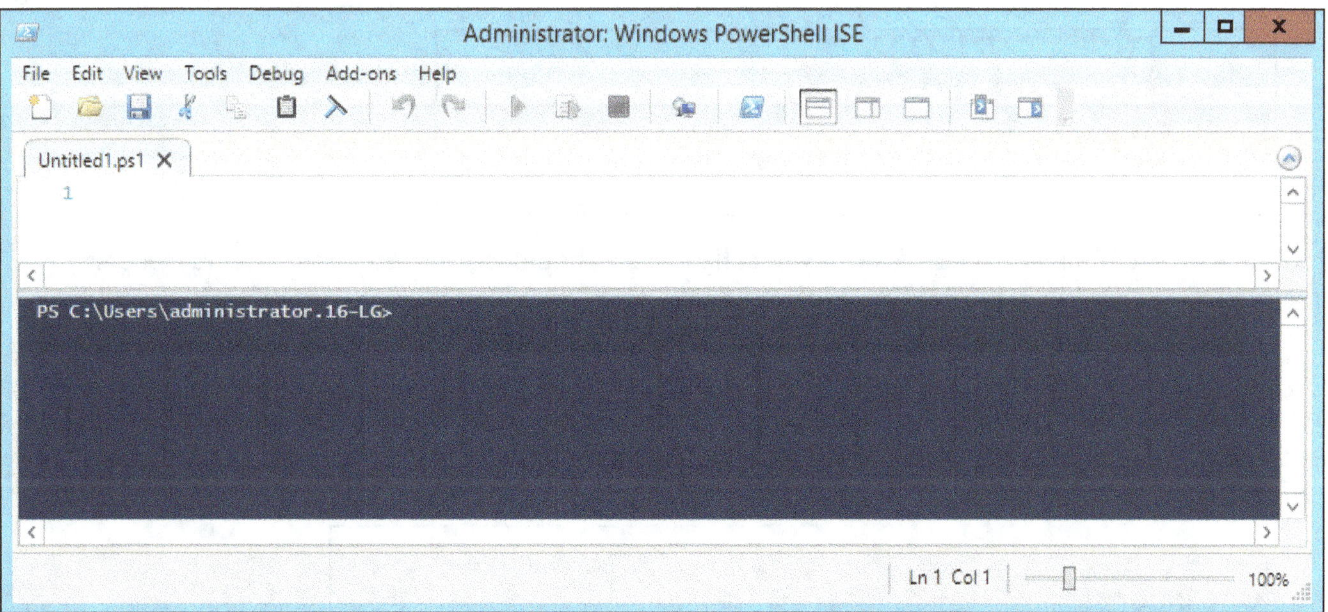

The ISE tool is a great way to help visualize a script (indentation, color, etc), while not necessary or required to assist the coder visually in writing PowerShell scripts. ISE can also be used to interactively debug scripts, stepping through the code as it is executed, allowing you to inspect variables for example.

Logical groupings are denoted by the '-' symbol on the left of the screen:

```
Licensing.ps1 ×
 1 ⊟Foreach ($Line in $Users) {
 2      # Configure variables
 3      $Upn = $Line.upn
 4      $Location = (Get-MsolUser -UserPrincipalName $Upn).UsageLocation
 5      $Licensed = (Get-MsolUser -UserPrincipalName $Upn).IsLicensed
 6      If ($Locaton -eq $Null) {
 7          Set-msoluser -UserPrincipalName $Upn -UsageLocation "US"
 8      }
 9      If ($Licensesd -eq $False) {
10          Set-MsolUserLicense -UserPrincipalName $Upn -AddLicenses "<tenant>:ENTERPRISEPACK"
11      }
12      $LicenseOptions = New-MsolLicenseOptions -AccountSkuId "<tenant>:ENTERPRISEPACK" -DisabledPlans $Disabledoptions
13      Set-MsolUserLicense -User $upn -LicenseOptions $LicenseOptions
14      $Status = (Get-MsolUser -User $Upn).Licenses[0].ServiceStatus
15 }
16
```

Different components of the PowerShell scripts are shown in different colors. Comments are green, variables are red and cmdlets are color coded blue:

```
Licensing.ps1 ×                    Variable       Comment
 1 ⊟Foreach ($Line in $Users) {           Cmdlet
 2      # Configure variables
 3      $Upn = $Line.upn
 4      $Location = (Get-MsolUser -UserPrincipalName $Upn).UsageLocation
 5      $Licensed = (Get-MsolUser -UserPrincipalName $Upn).IsLicensed
 6      If ($Locaton -eq $Null) {
 7          Set-msoluser -UserPrincipalName $Upn -UsageLocation "US"
 8      }
 9      If ($Licensesd -eq $False) {
10          Set-MsolUserLicense -UserPrincipalName $Upn -AddLicenses "<tenant>:ENTERPRISEPACK"
11      }
12      $LicenseOptions = New-MsolLicenseOptions -AccountSkuId "<tenant>:ENTERPRISEPACK" -DisabledPlans $Disabledoptions
13      Set-MsolUserLicense -User $upn -LicenseOptions $LicenseOptions
14      $Status = (Get-MsolUser -User $Upn).Licenses[0].ServiceStatus
15 }
16
```

Loops can be verified by click at or near a bracket to see where the closing bracket is [paired brackets highlighted]:

```
66  if ($success -ne $false) {
67      write-verbose "Test passed for server $name."
68  } else {
69      write-verbose "Test failed for server $name."
70  }
```

If we click on the '-' sign on the left side, it will collapse A section of code is enclosed by a bracket pair:

```
66  if ($success -ne $false) {...} else {
69      write-verbose "Test failed for server $name."
70  }
```

Some of the formatting is NOT done by the ISE tool. Indentation is up to you to do. I recommend the use of indenting each loop. Following is an example of this. This technique is used for readability and is not required for the code to run properly:

```
              $n = 0
            ⊟foreach ($line in $csv) {
                if ($line -eq $true) {
                    if ($n -lt 10) {
                        write-host "We are at number $n"
                    }
                }
                $n++
            }
```

One indent for each loop that is present.

** **Note** ** Each indent is created by using the TAB key.

In the next example of indentation, without indentation, the script would be hard to read and understand where the different loops or groupings start / end:

```
2      if( $tryWMI ) {
3          ## WMI depends on RPC. CIM depends on WinRM, but C
4          try {$Page_Managed = Get-WMIObject -computer $name
5          } catch {Write-Verbose "$($TestID): Was not able t
6          $nulldata = $true
7          }
8      }
```

Now notice the red brackets highlight the bracketing to show the way cmdlets are grouped.

```
if( $tryWMI ) {
    ## WMI depends on RPC. CIM depends on WinRM
    try {
        $Page_Managed = Get-WMIObject -computer
    } catch {
        Write-Verbose "$($TestID): Was not able
        $nulldata = $true
    }
}
```

Indentation falls into the same category as comments. While not required to be used, they make the script much easier to use, understand and troubleshoot in case of problems or errors. Creating a script is one of many uses for the tool, as the ISE tool also allows for running the script. In the lower portion of the tool is a PowerShell interface used for script execution.

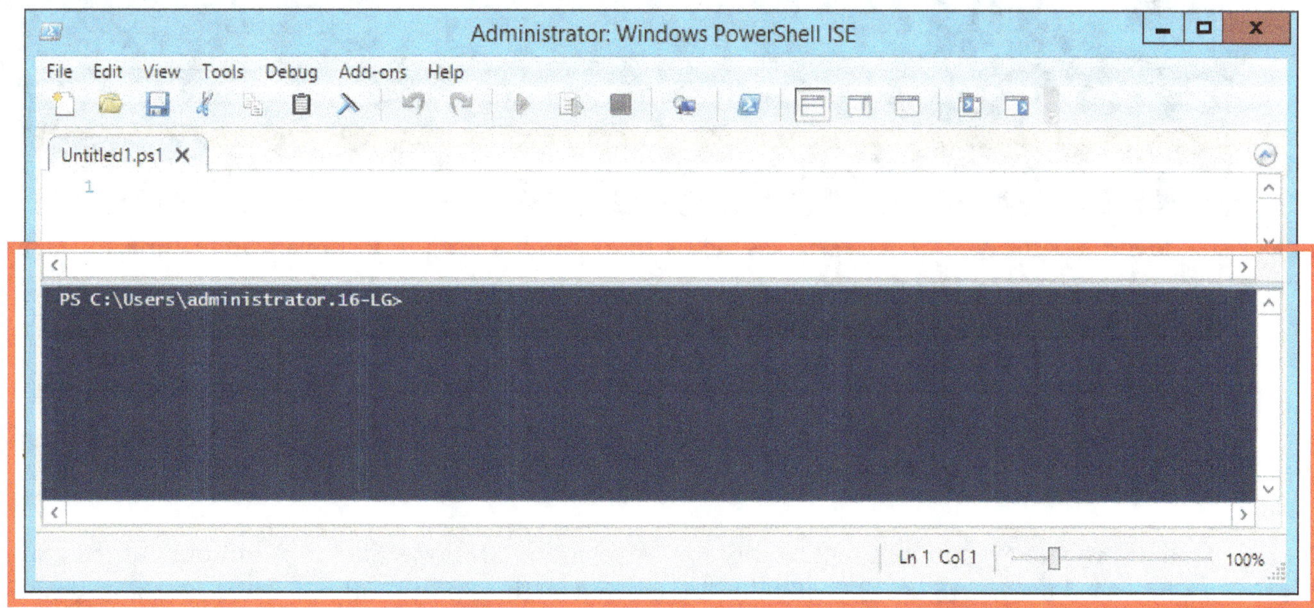

PowerShell modules can be imported in order to expand its capabilities. For Active Directory this module can be loaded with this one-liner.

Active Directory

```
import-module activedirectory
```

After the module is loaded, AD cmdlets such as Get-AdUser and Get-ADDomain Controller can now be run.

Modules can also be pre-loaded into a PowerShell profile to make this even easier. Read up more on this here:

https://blogs.technet.microsoft.com/heyscriptingguy/2012/05/24/use-a-module-to-simplify-your-power-shell-profile/

Alternatives to ISE

Notepad and Notepad++. Notepad is a very basic way to edit a PowerShell script. It is best used for quickly copying and pasting scripts or scripts that require very little work. Notepad++ is program similar to the PowerShell ISE in that it can handle multiple languages, however the ISE is much more versatile. Auto-Completion of PowerShell cmdlets and variable names are incredibly useful while coding longer scripts.

Visual Studio Code is also a viable alternative to PowerShell ISE. The product is a noteworthy take on PowerShell script editing and is worth a look at here - https://4sysops.com/archives/visual-studio-code-vscode-as-power-shell-script-editor/. Visually it has a more modern take on script editing:

```
Licensing.ps1 - Visual Studio Code

File  Edit  View  Go  Help

Licensing.ps1  ✕

 1    Foreach ($Line in $Users) {
 2
 3        $Upn = $Line.upn
 4        $Location = (Get-MsolUser -UserPrincipalName $Upn).UsageLocation
 5        $Licensed = (Get-MsolUser -UserPrincipalName $Upn).IsLicensed
 6        If ($Locaton -eq $Null) {
 7            Set-msoluser -UserPrincipalName $Upn -UsageLocation "US"
 8        }
 9        If ($Licensesd -eq $False) {
10        Set-MsolUserLicense -UserPrincipalName $Upn -AddLicenses "<tenant>:ENTERPRISEPACK"
11        }
```

It has visual identifiers for comments, variables, text strings and has even more advanced features for identifying correct brackets keywords and more.

ISE Plug-ins and Additional Tools

Plug-ins for ISE provide even more functionality for those coding in PowerShell.   Additional functionality and features can be added to PowerShell ISE with plug-ins created by third party authors. Here are some sample plug-ins for the PowerShell ISE program:

ISE Steroids - http://www.powertheshell.com/isesteroids/

ISE Steroids makes coding within the ISE more interactive. The plug-in provides assistance with your coding, making sure that the correct syntax is used.

For example, the right use of quotes ' or " is shown below:

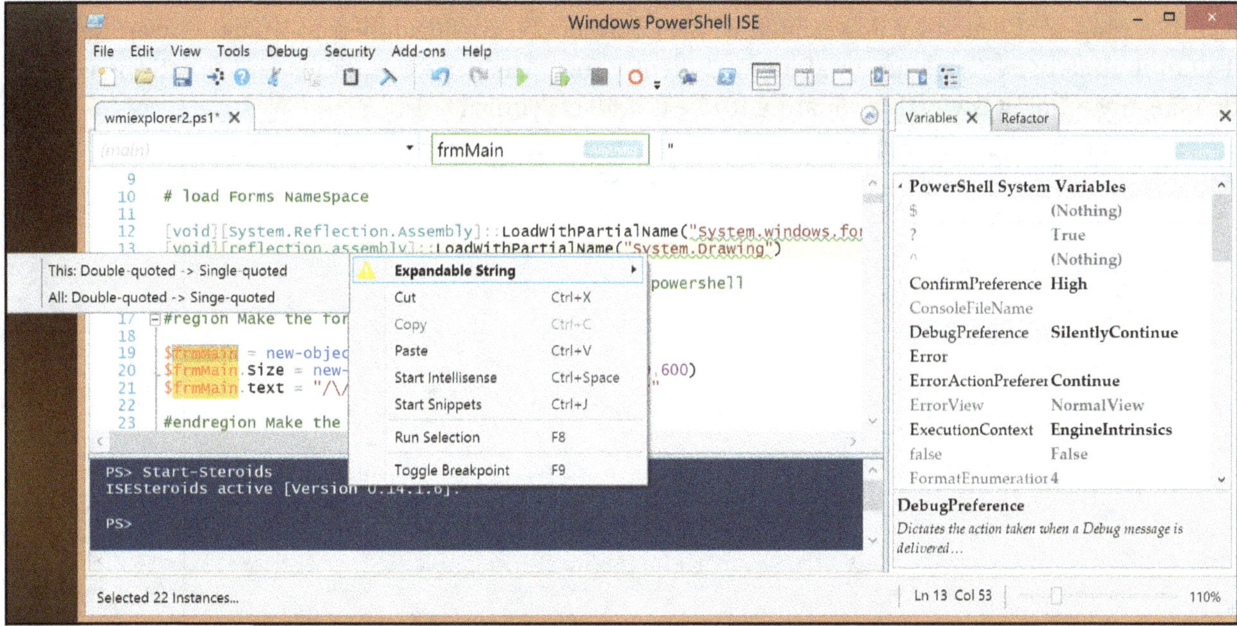

The plug-in also provides help on PowerShell cmdlets:

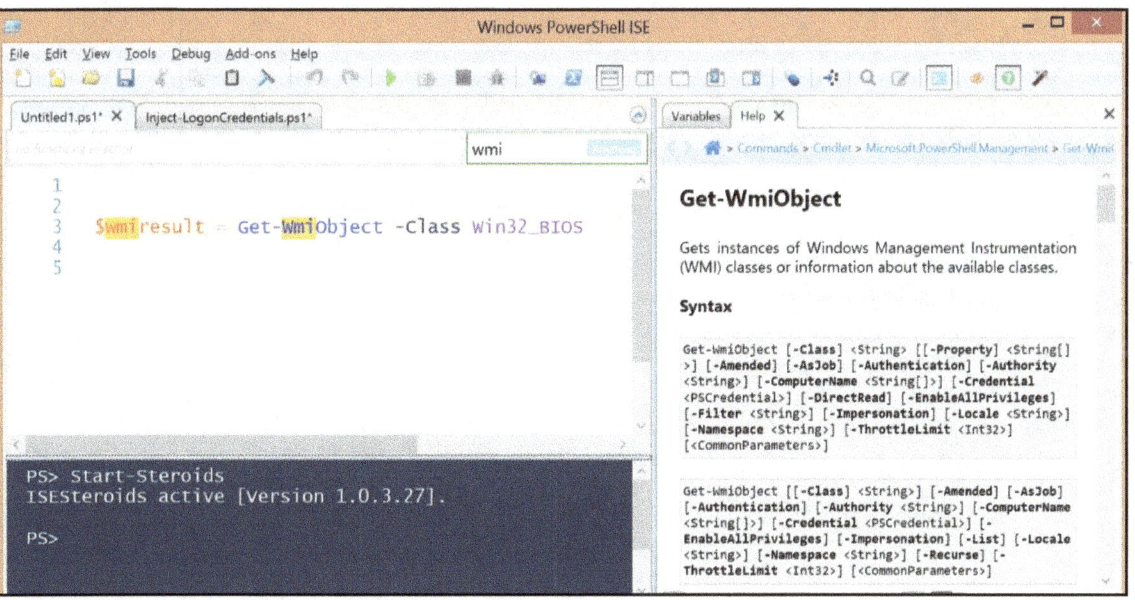

PSharp Plug-in for PowerShell

The PSharp ISE plug-in, created by PowerShell MVP Doug Finke, was designed to make PowerShell ISE more powerful than it already is. The plug-in allows for identifying variables, commands and functions with a single keystroke. Like any other, it is worth evaluating to see if it meets your needs.

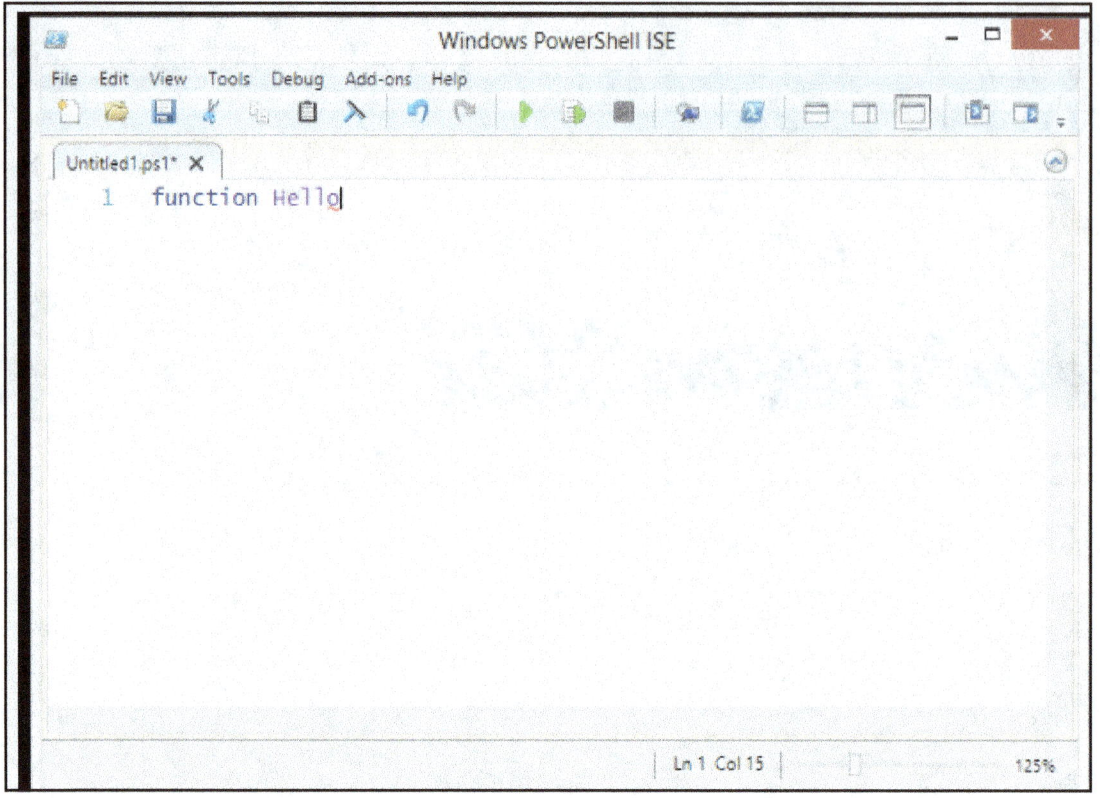

http://www.powershellmagazine.com/2013/08/18/psharp-makes-powershell-ise-better/

In This Chapter

Formatting
- Capitalization
- Commenting
- Mind Your Brackets

Command Output
- Cmdlet Output Formatting
- Filtering
- Splitting
- Scripting in Color

Miscellaneous
- Quotes
- CIM / WMI
- Obfuscated Information
- Code Signing

Formatting

A good working PowerShell script can be written quickly and without any formal formatting or standards. The script will probably function and perform the tasks it was coded for. However, a useful well-coded script should have more. A script should be easily read by another person, there should be a description of the script at the top and plenty of commenting in the script to provide information about its workings.

In this section, we will cover topics like capitalization, comments and bracketing. The use of these techniques will make your PowerShell scripts more usable and readily accessible to those who may use your scripts.

Capitalization

We must note that even though capitalization can be used throughout our scripts, PowerShell is NOT case sensitive. One use case scenario for Capitalization is to help make PowerShell cmdlets and their arguments more readable:

PowerShell Cmdlet Example:

No capitalization
```
get-mobiledevicedashboardsummaryreport
```

Each word is capitalized
Get-MobileDeviceDashboardSummaryReport

Visually the second cmdlet example would make the scripts more readable. We can see the individual words in the cmdlet and possibly allow us to decipher what the cmdlet is used for. While the non-capitalized one seems flat, with the words seemingly running together.

Capitalization can vastly improve the readability of the script by providing visual clues for each new word in a variable where words are mashed together:

Variable Example:

No capitalization
$mailboxnames

Each word is capitalized
$MailboxNames

This capitalization is analogous to syllable emphasis in pronouncing words. The capital letters emphasize the important parts and give the read a visual cue as to what is being run. While this convention is not required by PowerShell as it is case-insensitive. Another example would be function names:

Function Example:

No capitalization
function unifiedgroupcreation {
}

Each word is capitalized
Function UnifiedGroupCreation {
}

In summary, while these changes will not increase the speed of your script, nor make the script run cleaner, it will make it easier for troubleshooting and understanding how a script is structured.

Commenting

Comments. Do we really need these? Comments in PowerShell are not required, however they are extremely useful. If you have a team that shares scripts, then comments can be quiet beneficial to all. Not only can scripting logic be explained, or versioning be tracked, but each section of the script can be described and documented for yourself or others who will run the script.

PowerShell 1.0

If you write a script that needs to run on all versions of Exchange and Exchange Online, even legacy versions, be aware that Exchange 2007, which uses PowerShell 1.0, does not like certain commenting syntax. The '#' is the only accepted way of making a block of comments. The '#' needs to be in front of each line that needs to be treated as a comment versus executable content.

```
# ********************************************************
# *      This section is for the Windows 2008 R2 SP1 OS  *
# ********************************************************
```

PowerShell 2.0+

The more 'modern' versions of Exchange PowerShell have more options in formatting comments that are put into scripts. The below example shows the starting of a comment block with a '<#' and ending the same comment block with '>#'.

```
<#
.SYNOPSIS
        Distribution Group Cleanup Script - Office 365 Hybrid with Exchange 2013 or 201

.DESCRIPTION
        This script will cleanup all distribution groups that have not been used within
    that are running in a Hyrid mode with groups synched from an on-premises Active Di
    message logs in Office 365 to see what activity there is on certain groups.  This
    hide on-premises groups.


.NOTES
    Version             : 1.0
    Date Created        : 05/01/2016
    Change Log          : 1.0 - Script first set up, modified version of Exchange 2010,

.EXAMPLE
                .\Office365-DistributionGroupCleanup.ps1

        To be run once per month as a recurring task

.INPUTS
                None. You cannot pipe objects to this script, at this time.
#>
```

Comments can also use the format of '#' in front of each line just like we had from PowerShell 1.0. The example under PowerShell 1.0 can also be used in Exchange 2016. Comments can be single lines as well:

```
# Get-ADUser -Filter {SamAccountName -eq $UserID} | Set-ADUser .....
```

The example above is an instance where I wanted to comment out a line for troubleshooting other code around this one line. Another example is inline commenting, however that is not recommended as is makes reading more challenging:

```
Set-Mailbox –Identity UserA –PrimarySMTPAddress usera@contoso.com # Set Primary SMTP address
```

Uses

What are the main drivers for comment utilization in scripts?

- Providing a detailed description of the purpose of the script as well as how to use the script
- Breaking the script into sections
- Providing a quick description of a section
- To block out a line of code for future use
- To block out a line of code that did not work

Take time to provide at least a very basic framework for other script users to get the gist of your script. Adding comments will provide an additional benefit to your scripts. It allows you, the coder, to go back to an old script and quickly figure out what the script was for and allow for possible modification of one or more sections, as needed. Reusable code will also save time down the line when coding new scripts for new purposes.

With script writing, you might find it easier to comment as the script is built, if nothing else it provides a helpful reminder to yourself of which parts are performing certain functions in the script. For example, while building a script for checking Pagefile settings, making sure to comment on what step you're on in the process: (the code below is a sample and not a complete script):

```
# Set the ideal PageFile size
$Page_Ideal = $RAMinMB + 10

# Retrieve the Minimum PageFile size
try {$Page_min = (Get-CIMInstance -ComputerName $name -ClassName win32_pagefilesetting -Property * -ErrorAction Stop).initialsize
}catch {$WMI=$true;write-host "The server $name is inaccessible by CIM, trying WMI." -foregroundcolor yellow}
if( $WMI ) {
    ## WMI depends on RPC. CIM depends on WinRM, but CIM failed, so we try WMI before we give up.
    try {$Page_min = (Get-WMIObject -Computer $name -Class win32_pagefilesetting -Property * -ErrorAction Stop).initialsize
    } catch {$up=$false;write-host " The server $name is inaccessible by WMI, this is not good." -foregroundcolor red}
}

# Retrieve the Maximum PageFile size
try {$Page_max = (Get-CIMInstance -ComputerName $name -ClassName win32_pagefilesetting -Property * -ErrorAction Stop).maximumsize
}catch {$WMI=$true;write-host "The server $name is inaccessible by CIM, trying WMI." -foregroundcolor yellow}
if( $WMI ) {
    ## WMI depends on RPC. CIM depends on WinRM, but CIM failed, so we try WMI before we give up.
    try {$Page_max = (Get-WMIObject -Computer $name -Class win32_pagefilesetting -Property * -ErrorAction Stop).maximumsize
    } catch {$up=$false;write-host " The server $name is inaccessible by WMI, this is not good." -foregroundcolor red}
}
```

Note the comments lines that are enclosed in red rectangles. Each comment block describes a logical section of the script, almost like a script block. I did this so I could describe each section of my script with a single concise line of text.

The symbol for commenting (#) can also be used to remove a line in the script from executing. Using the '#' in front of a one-liner in a script would essentially turn the cmdlet into a comment and no longer be executable in PowerShell. This technique is commonly used in order to duplicate a line of code, allowing for the original line to be saved while new versions of the line are concocted:

Example – Troubleshooting Code

Original line (which fails and needs more options for output)
Get-Mailbox DamianScoles | ft DisplayName, Server, Database

Comment the line, duplicate and modify
Get-Mailbox DamianScoles | ft DisplayName, Server, Database
Get-Mailbox DamianScoles | ft DisplayName, ServerName, Database

Notice the original line above and the new corrected line below. I did this because the first command failed to actually display the 'Server' where the mailbox was, because the parameter was incorrect and should have been 'Server Name'.

Another reason to comment out a line is PowerShell is to either remove old code or remove troubleshooting code.

Example – Removing Old Code
$Mailbox = Get-Mailbox $Name

```
Write-Host "The current mailbox is $Mailbox."

Becomes....
$Mailbox = Get-Mailbox $Name
# Write-Host "The current mailbox is $Mailbox."
```

Note on this, that after a script has tested out and verified as performing its function, these sorts of lines should be cleaned up to get rid of code no longer needed.

Mind Your Brackets!

One of the more important aspects of writing loops and code sections in PowerShell is making sure your brackets are all correct and in the right place. Take a look at the code section below. Red arrows are drawn below to show which bracket goes with which set of code:

```
5  $files = get-childitem $location
7
8  # Loop for each file to get IP Addresses
9  foreach ($file in $files) {
10     $name = $file.name
11     $csv = import-csv $location"\"$name
12     foreach ($line in $csv) {
13        if ($line -like "#") { }
14        else {
15
16 # Get the Client IP
17           $info = $line.cip
18           if ($info -ne "cip") {
19              foreach ($value in $info) {
20                 if ($value -ne $null) {
21
22 # Client IP also contains the port number which we will remove here
23                    $ID = $value.Split([char]0x003A)
24                    $CIP = $ID[0]
25                    $cipresults += $cip
26                 }
27              }
28           }
29        }
30     }
31 }
32
32 # Optional - Remove Duplicates
33 $location = (Get-POPSettings -server $server).logfilelocation
```

Why are brackets important? If each section of code is not closed properly, it could execute incorrectly or not execute at all. If you are using Windows PowerShell ISE, any issues with brackets should be obvious:

```
        Missing Bracket                    All Brackets Present
  foreach ($line in $var) {          foreach ($line in $var) {
     if ($line -eq "20") {              if ($line -eq "20") {
                                           }
  }                                    }
```

As PowerShell ISE will show related brackets with gray marking the other bracket in a pair.

Notice the underlined bracket in the red rectangle in the left code sample as well as the missing '-' in the blue rectangle as well. These are two visual clues that the PowerShell ISE can provide for us while coding in PowerShell. These clues let us know that are brackets are not correct and that something is amiss. The only weakness with this visual clue is that sometimes the red squiggly does not mean that the exact same kind of bracket is missing:

Example – Different Bracket Missing

```
foreach ($line in $csv) {
    if ($that -eq $that {
    }
}
```

The correct code block looks like this:

```
foreach ($line in $csv) {
    if ($that -eq $that) {
    }
}
```

Notice that the if () block on the top code block was missing the right bracket. Notice that the '{' bracket actually had the red squiggly under it, even though a ')' was missing. In the same vein, a missing quote can also cause a bracket to get a red squiggly placed under it:

```
write-host "B... Bl... Bla... Blah!"
foreach ($line in $csv) {
    write-host "
}
```

One missing quote causes all of this. Corrected:

```
write-host "B... Bl... Bla... Blah!"
foreach ($line in $csv) {
    write-host "That was the quote we needed."
}
```

No more issues.

Command Output

The default results that are provided by PowerShell cmdlets are lackluster and in some cases not useful at all. The output needs to be tweaked. This section will cover ways to improve PowerShell cmdlet output, from filtering out unwanted results, to tweaking values stored in variables, to formatting tables and even adding a bit of color to PowerShell output.

Cmdlet Output Formatting

Formatting. Boring. Do we really need to format our output? Who's going to care?

Any PowerShell script author should. By default the formatting for PowerShell leaves much to be desired. Property values on objects could be truncated, values you need may not be the defaults and more. Formatting will help you create better output, more usable output and allow you to get more out of Exchange 2016 via PowerShell.

How do we do this? Let's cover some of the basics. At the end of a PowerShell cmdlet we can add some more characters to change to format of the output. The characters are:

Switch	Name	Purpose
| FL	Format List	All object properties are displayed in a list format
| FT	Format Table	Object properties displayed in a table format
| FT -auto	Format Table + Auto	Object properties displayed in a table format extra spaces removed
| FT -wrap	Format Table + Wrap	Object properties displayed in multi-line fashion

Get-UnifiedGroup cmdlet using FL which will display 'all' an objects properties in list format:

```
PS C:\> Get-UnifiedGroup | FL

RunspaceId                                   : cce32c88-30fd-4817-bf64-d96ce210c0e0
AccessType                                   : Public
AutoSubscribeNewMembers                      : True
AlwaysSubscribeMembersToCalendarEvents       : False
CalendarMemberReadOnly                       :
CalendarUrl                                  :
Database                                     : NAMPR08DG185-db124
ExchangeGuid                                 : 0cbf11af-2040-4288-b927-6a09963a3dda
FileNotificationsSettings                    :
GroupSKU                                     : Default
HiddenGroupMembershipEnabled                 : False
InboxUrl                                     :
IsExternalResourcesPublished                 : True
IsMailboxConfigured                          : True
Language                                     : en-US
MailboxProvisioningConstraint                :
ManagedByDetails                             : {Damian Scoles}
```

Get-UnifiedGroup cmdlet using FT which will display a select number of attributes in a table format:

```
PS C:\> Get-UnifiedGroup | FT

Name                       Alias                  ServerName        AccessType
----                       -----                  ----------        ----------
TestDL-Regular_5bd1b2e44a  TestDL-Regular         b12pr08mb705      Public
MicrosoftAzurePowerShe...  MicrosoftAzurePow...   co2pr0801mb2277   Private
```

Why would we want to use FT or FL? FT allows us to create a usable table, mostly for reporting purposes. It also allows us to copy and paste the information and share it outside of PowerShell. FL will allow you to see all the properties on an object. The list of attributes could then be used to create a better or more concise list of properties in table format:

```
PS C:\> Get-UnifiedGroup | Fl *share*


SharePointSiteUrl     :
SharePointDocumentsUrl :
SharePointNotebookUrl  :

SharePointSiteUrl      : https://scoles.sharepoint.com/sites/MicrosoftAzurePowerShellBook
SharePointDocumentsUrl : https://scoles.sharepoint.com/sites/MicrosoftAzurePowerShellBook/Shared
                         Documents
SharePointNotebookUrl  :
```

Using the property list from the above FL we can now select relevant properties to put in a table format. Also notice the use of an asterisk ('*') which is used as a wildcard character representing any number of characters on its side of the string. Let's pick Prohibit Send Quotas and the Issue Warning Quota. We can now run this in a table format:

```
PS C:\> Get-UnifiedGroup | Ft Alias,SubscriptionEnabled,WelcomeMessageEnabled,ConnectorsEnabled,IsMembershipDynamic

Alias                    SubscriptionEnabled WelcomeMessageEnabled ConnectorsEnabled IsMembershipDynamic
-----                    ------------------- --------------------- ----------------- -------------------
TestDL-Regular           True                True                  True              False
MicrosoftPowerShellBook  True                False                 True              False
```

What if we pick too many attributes and the values could become truncated as is evidenced above with the '...' displayed.

```
PS C:\> Get-UnifiedGroup | Ft Alias,*URL*

Alias                           CalendarUrl InboxUrl PeopleUrl PhotoUrl SharePointSiteUrl
-----                           ----------- -------- --------- -------- -----------------
TestDL-Regular
MicrosoftPowerShellBook                                                 https://scoles.sharepoint.com/sites/MicrosoftA...
```

To fix this, first we need to widen the PowerShell Windows to a number greater that the normal 80. You may need some trial and error on exact size numbers. After that, we can run the same cmdlet with the | FT, but now followed by an '-auto' switch. The '-auto' switch will take all of the results and create a 'neat table' that makes all property values fit on the screen. The downside to the switch is that it will hold the results from being displayed as Power-Shell is calculating how the properties will all fit on the screen properly.

```
PS C:\> Get-UnifiedGroup | Ft Alias,*URL* -auto

Alias                           CalendarUrl InboxUrl PeopleUrl PhotoUrl SharePointSiteUrl
-----                           ----------- -------- --------- -------- -----------------
TestDL-Regular
MicrosoftPowerShellBook                                                 https://scoles.sharepoint.com/sites/MicrosoftPowerShellBook
```

This creates a readable output and displays the values properly in one table, auto adjusted (-auto) to condense the information displayed. FT and FL will become important tools for building reports or figuring out what properties to select from objects in Exchange.

Filtering

In addition to formatting output with FL and FT we can also filter the output. Filtering with PowerShell involves selecting or limiting the reported set of properties on an object to a meaningful subset of properties of an object that can be used or manipulated. One use case for filtering is creating reports on items in Exchange like databases, mailboxes and servers. For example, the default output of 'get-mailbox' only displays the default properties name, alias, server name and ProhibitSendQuota. While these values are relevant to the object, it's hard to create a great report off this.

Tweaking Our PowerShell Results

First we need to figure out what we want to filter or focus on. Do we want to find all mailboxes in a certain database, on a certain mail server or maybe create a list of mailboxes with a retention policy applied? Without a filter, the Get-Mailbox command will display all mailboxes in Exchange Online.

```
Get-Mailbox
```

Results look like this:

```
PS C:\> Get-Mailbox

Name                    Alias               ServerName          ProhibitSendQuota
----                    -----               ----------          -----------------
orders                  orders              by2pr0801mb1592     99 GB (106,300,440,576 bytes)
CloudShared             cloudshared         by1pr08mb1274       99 GB (106,300,440,576 bytes)
Help Desk_58be9bb90b    HelpDesk            cy1pr08mb1992       99 GB (106,300,440,576 bytes)
John Doe                johndoe             mwhpr08mb2718       99 GB (106,300,440,576 bytes)
Office 365Test          Office365Test       cy1pr0801mb1513     99 GB (106,300,440,576 bytes)
testclouduser           testclouduser       cy4pr08mb3368       99 GB (106,300,440,576 bytes)
user01                  user01              bn6pr08mb2659       99 GB (106,300,440,576 bytes)
user02                  user02              by2pr08mb1460       99 GB (106,300,440,576 bytes)
```

In order to filter results based of a certain result, 'Where' can be used as a trigger for PowerShell cmdlets. Below are two examples.

Filter for all mailboxes whose 'ServerName' property contains 'Cy4' in the name (notice the '-like' operator):

Get-mailbox | Where {$_.ServerName -Like 'Cy4*'}

```
PS C:\> Get-mailbox | Where {$_.ServerName -like 'cy4*'}

Name                     Alias                    ServerName        ProhibitSendQuota
----                     -----                    ----------        -----------------
testclouduser            testclouduser            cy4pr08mb3368     99 GB (106,300,440,576 bytes)
User11                   User11                   cy4pr08mb2488     99 GB (106,300,440,576 bytes)
What User                whatuser                 cy4pr08mb2837     99 GB (106,300,440,576 bytes)
```

Filter for all mailboxes whose 'ProhibitSendQuota' property equals 99GB (notice the -eq operator):

Get-mailbox | Where {$_.ProhibitSendQuota -eq '99 GB (106,300,440,576 bytes)'}

```
PS C:\> Get-mailbox | Where {$_.ProhibitSendQuota -eq '99 GB (106,300,440,576 bytes)'}

Name                     Alias                    ServerName        ProhibitSendQuota
----                     -----                    ----------        -----------------
orders                   orders                   by2pr0801mb1592   99 GB (106,300,440,576 bytes)
CloudShared              cloudshared              by1pr08mb1274     99 GB (106,300,440,576 bytes)
John Doe                 johndoe                  mwhpr08mb2718     99 GB (106,300,440,576 bytes)
Office 365Test           Office365Test            cy1pr0801mb1513   99 GB (106,300,440,576 bytes)
testclouduser            testclouduser            cy4pr08mb3368     99 GB (106,300,440,576 bytes)
```

The filters noticeably reduce the number of mailboxes that are reported by the PowerShell command. Contained inside the '{ }' is the criteria for the filter to work. The '$_.ServerName' part allows us to specifically pick the database property on a mailbox. Then using an operator to decide the criteria to match a particular value in the property. In the above example we are filtering the results to display only mailboxes that are on a server with the name that starts with 'cy4'. The below sample operators are all case insensitive.

Sample operators:
-eq   Equal To
-lt   Less Than
-gt   Greater Than
-ne   Not Equal To

Filtering allows a search for common criteria on a bulk basis. This is useful for migrations to make sure no mailboxes are left on old legacy Exchange server, maybe find all mailboxes with a quota configured, etc.

Splitting

Scenario #1

Call it parsing, call it whatever. Sometimes the values stored in a CSV or variable have unwanted characters or need to be separated in order to be used for the rest of the script. Let's walk through a couple of scenarios that will better explain the usefulness of the technique.

In this book we have a script that will retrieve the IP addresses of clients that connect to Exchange 2010 servers using POP3 or IMAP4. We might do this to validate if any clients are using IMAP4 or POP3 before migrating to Exchange Online. The raw data is not ideal for creating a report. The value stored in CIP column of the log file used by the POP3 or IMAP4 service looks something like this:

IP:port --> 192.168.0.43:63475

If we want to display just the IP addresses of the clients, the information after the ':' is useless to us. In order to remove this information, we'll need to get the hex code for the ":" character. The hex code will allow us to specify which character to split the variable with. A good place to look for values is http://unicodelookup.com/:

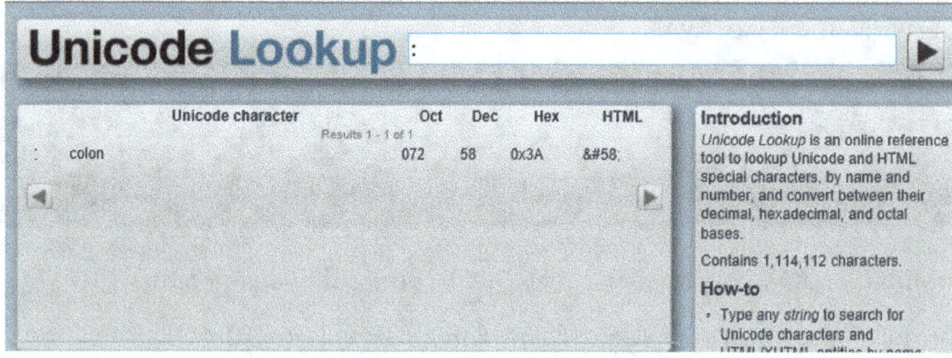

When looking for ":" we see that 0x3A is the code we will need in order to split up the value.

In Action

If we were able to work with the POP3 csv file and had a variable called $Csv that contained the value of "192.168.0.43:63475" We can use the Split command in PowerShell to split this value. To do so, we add a '.' and the word 'Split' after a variable which we can then add the character needed to split the information on.

```
$IP = $csv.Split([char]0x003A)
```

This transforms $Csv into an array of 2 values, which is stored in $IP as 192.168.0.43,63475. Once split we can chose one part of this variable and just use that information:

```
$IP[0]
```

The above variable will give the first value in its array, which is '192.168.0.43'. The port (63475) is stored as $IP[1].

Scenario #2

Using the same 'Split' cmdlet in PowerShell, let's explore another real scenario. Translating display names into aliases in Active Directory, these will then be synced to Office 365 / Exchange Online. In this scenario we know that Active Directory aliases are a combination of first and last names.

Alias	First Name	Last Name
JohnSmith	John	Smith
MichaelLarraday	Michael	Larraday

In some cases the source names use the middle initials in their name. We would have something like this:

John M. Smith
Michael G Larraday

Notice that John has a middle initial with a period and Michael does not. First we need to get a list of names and store them in the $SourceName variable:

$SourceName = (Get-MSOLUser).DisplayName

We then need to be able to account for both types of middle initials. First, let's split the name up into its three parts:

$Name = $SourceName.Split([Char]0x0020)
(The 0x0020 character is a space)

The variable $Name would look something like this for each name:

$Name = John, M., Smith
$Name = Michael, G, Larraday

Remember the data is stored like this:

$name[0] $name[1] $name[2]

$name = John, M., Smith
$name = Michael, G, Larraday

$name[0] $name[1] $name[2]

In order to get the alias, we need to add the last name to the first name and store it in the $Alias variable.

$Alias = $Name[0]+$Name[2]

This effectively ignores the middle initial which would be $name[1]:

$Alias = JohnSmith
$Alias = MichaelLarraday

Possible Complication

Like a lot of technology used in production, nothing is ever that simple. There is always some wrench thrown into the mix. In the second scenario we assume that the user will have a middle name and we will have to ignore that to create the alias. What if the user has no middle name listed in the source? What would happen?

Bob Delol

If we parsed it, we would get $Name[0] = "Bob" and $Name[1] = "Delol". There would be no $Name[2]. Now we follow the same formula before:

$Alias = $Name[0]+$Name[2]

Our results would be less than ideal:

```
$Alias = "Bob"
```

To resolve this we would need some sort of logic to handle that:

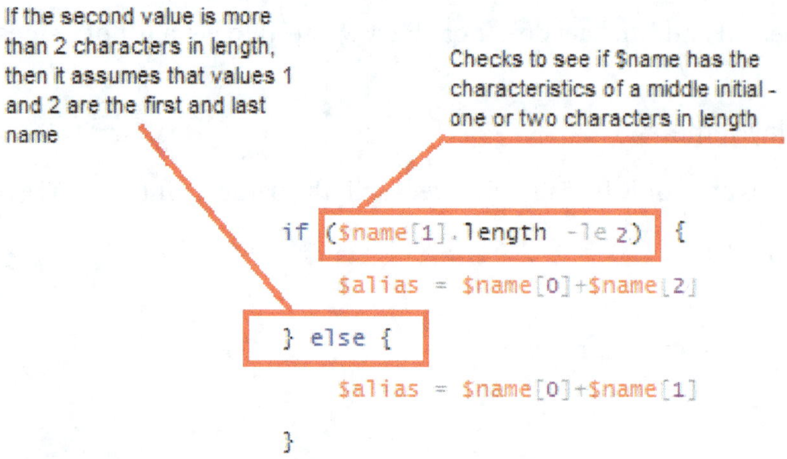

If the second value is more than 2 characters in length, then it assumes that values 1 and 2 are the first and last name

Checks to see if $name has the characteristics of a middle initial - one or two characters in length

```
if ($name[1].length -le 2) {
    $alias = $name[0]+$name[2]
} else {
    $alias = $name[0]+$name[1]
}
```

So Bob Smith would end up as "BobSmith". The rest would have their middle initial ignore as well and put together. The point of this exercise is that in real life scenarios, sometimes adjustments need to be made in order to get the results required.

Scripting in Color

Why is color important in PowerShell?

Normally, while using PowerShell, we see Black and White or Blue and White. PowerShell provides extra colors in its output for a more visual indication of the type of information presented on the console:

Examples

- Report failures in red
- Reporting success in blue or white
- Warnings reporting in yellow
- Make different code sections
- Menus can be color coded

Color Coding Examples

Reporting that a test failed: (This sample code verified that a mailbox is missing a retention policy):

```
Write-Host "The mailbox $Name does not have a retention policy" -ForegroundColor White -NoNewLine;
Write-Host "$RetentionPolicy" -ForegroundColor Red -NoNewLine
Write-Host " enabled." -ForegroundColor White
```

```
The mailbox Damian Scoles does not have a retention policy Corporate Retention Policy enabled.
```

Notice the contrast of the red with the white in the results of the commands. Also note that -NoNewLine was used as well to compress the result to one line in the output. The '-NoNewLine' option allows for us to consolidate many lines of 'Write-Host' into one. If we were to remove this switch from the above code and use this code sample:

```
Write-Host "The mailbox $Name does not have a retention policy " -ForegroundColor White
Write-Host "$RetentionPolicy" -ForegroundColor Red
Write-Host " enabled." -ForegroundColor White
```

The results would look vastly different:

```
The mailbox Damian Scoles does not have a retention policy
Corporate Retention Policy
 enabled.
```

Use care with –NoNewLine because too many lines can cause the formatting to look just as bad:

Code Sample

```
Foreach ($Name in $Names) {
    Write-Host "The mailbox $Name does not have a retention policy" -ForegroundColor White
    -NoNewLine
    Write-Host "$RetentionPolicy" -ForegroundColor Red -NoNewLine
    Write-Host " enabled." -ForegroundColor White
}
```

Results:

```
PS C:\temp> .\ProblemReport2.ps1
The mailbox CloudShared does not have a retention policy Corporate Retention Policy enabled.
The mailbox Help Desk does not have a retention policy Corporate Retention Policy enabled.
The mailbox John Doe does not have a retention policy Corporate Retention Policy enabled.
The mailbox Office 365Test does not have a retention policy Corporate Retention Policy enabled.
The mailbox Test CloudUser does not have a retention policy Corporate Retention Policy enabled.
The mailbox user01 does not have a retention policy Corporate Retention Policy enabled.
```

 As you can see, too many can cause the output to be unusable and it even carries over to the PowerShell prompt being dragged into the mess. Another example is to create a colorful menu:

```
$Menu = {
    Write-Host "    *****************************************" -ForegroundColor Cyan
    Write-Host "      License Reporting and Assignment" -ForegroundColor Cyan
    Write-Host "    *****************************************" -ForegroundColor Cyan
    Write-Host ""
    Write-Host "    (1) Report O365 Licenses" -ForegroundColor Cyan
    Write-Host "    (2) Assign licenses" -ForegroundColor Green
    Write-Host "    (3) Remove Licenses" -ForegroundColor Yellow
    Write-Host ""
    Write-Host "    (99) Exit Script" -ForegroundColor Red
}
```

While the above code sample is a bit overboard, it illustrates the technique of coloring PowerShell output:

```
    *****************************************
      License Reporting and Assignment
    *****************************************

    (1) Report O365 Licenses
    (2) Assign licenses
    (3) Remove Licenses

    (99) Exit Script
```

The key to making this work is the Invoke-Command used to display the $a variable as this colorful menu:

```
Invoke-Command -ScriptBlock $Menu
```

The ScriptBlock parameter specifies that code stored in the $a variable will execute, which is a colorful menu.

Lastly, an example of coloring would be HTML formatting. HTML color can be used, for example, in creating reports with cells of a particular mean. Red could be used to indicate an Error, yellow used to indicate a Warning and green to indicate Success. This would provide for a quick visual read of the data and allow for the recipient of the report to quickly determine what to concentrate efforts on or to troubleshoot as needed.

We could for example, check a server's patch level to see how close it is to a supportable version. Green could indicate the most recent, yellow could be for 1 to 2 CUs behind and Red could be for anything over 3 versions behind. HTML coding itself is a bit more complex, but it will covered later in the "**Chapter 18 - Reporting**".

The below code was created as sample testing code to use as a base for constructing an HTML report. The code checks the current version of Exchange Servers in an environment. If the version is current, then Green is used, Yellow means it is still supported, and its 1 or 2 CUs behind and if the server is 3 or more CUs behind, then Red is used to indicate that the server is out of the support range Microsoft has for Exchange.

Sample Code

```
$Mailboxes = Get-Mailbox
Foreach ($Mailbox in $Mailboxes) {

    #Variables
    $Rating = 0
    $RetentionPolicy = $Mailbox.RetentionPolicy
    $Quota = $Mailbox.IssueWarningQuota
    $ARchive = $Mailbox.ArchiveStatus
    $Name = $Mailbox.DisplayName

    If ($RetentionPolicy -ne $null) {
        $Rating++
    }
    If ($Quota -like '98 GB*') {
        $Rating++
    }

    If ($Archive -ne $Null) {
        $Rating++
    }

    If (($Rating -eq 0) -or ($Rating -eq 1)) {
        Write-Host "The mailbox $Name fails the base requirements check." -ForegroundColor Red
    }
    If ($Rating -eq 2) {
        Write-Host "The mailbox $Name meets a couple of requirements the base requirements check."
        -ForegroundColor Yellow
    }
```

```
    If ($Rating -eq 3) {
        Write-Host "The mailbox $Name passes the base requirements check." -ForegroundColor Green
    }
}
```

```
PS C:\> .\MailboxTestCheck.ps1
The mailbox CloudShared passes the base requirements check.
The mailbox Damian Scoles meets a couple of requirements the base requirements check.
The mailbox Discovery Search Mailbox meets a couple of requirements the base requirements check.
The mailbox Help Desk passes the base requirements check.
The mailbox John Doe passes the base requirements check.
The mailbox Office 365Test passes the base requirements check.
The mailbox Test CloudUser passes the base requirements check.
The mailbox user01 meets a couple of requirements the base requirements check.
The mailbox user02 fails the base requirements check.
The mailbox user03 fails the base requirements check.
The mailbox user04 fails the base requirements check.
```

By executing this against other servers we can test the logic without the added code for HTML. After validating the code, we can construct an HTML report that would fill in cells to correspond to the same colors listed above. A sample HTML report would look something like this:

Mailbox Requirement Check	
Name	**Tests Passed**
CloudShared	3
Damian Scoles	2
Discovery	2
Help Desk	3
John Doe	3
Office 365Test	3
Test CloudUser	3
user01	2
user02	1
user03	0
user04	1

Miscellaneous Topics

In this section we'll cover a variety of topics that are important to PowerShell in general and Exchange PowerShell specifically.

** **Note** ** When copying any code from Word, OneNote, or other editor, care should be taken with reference to quotes which do get mangled or translated wrong between copies sometimes.

Quotes

Quotes are rather important when it comes to a PowerShell script. Missing quotes can throw off your script and cause it not to run. The wrong kind of quote can prevent a PowerShell script from functioning properly. The question is what quotes are good for what.

Quotes would seem to be an innocuous part of coding PowerShell. However, they are quite important. Microsoft has a set of rules to handle quotes and should be required reading for coding in PowerShell:

https://technet.microsoft.com/en-us/library/hh847740.aspx

Single Quote (')

The single quote is the default quote to use for most, if not all quotes in PowerShell. The single quote is a literal interpretation of whatever exists between them. For example, if we take the code sample below, using a Write-Host command to display the contents of a quote, the information is who in a one to one fashion and all variables are ignored:

Example Code

```
$Score = 300
Write-Host 'My top score in bowling is $score.'
```

Results are:

```
My top score in bowling is $score.
```

As you can see, the variable was ignored with the single quote.

Double Quote (")

Double quotes will not allow a literal interpretation and will display values that are store in variables even when between the quotes.

Example Code

```
$Score = 300
Write-Host "My top score in bowling is $score."
```

Results are:

```
My top score in bowling is 300.
```

Notice the difference between the single and double quotes.

Quotes within Quotes (' " " ')

There are two ways to handle a set of quotes within quotes and prove to be quite useful in a script. One use, shown in the example below, would be to display a book title in a sentence. Without this option, the title of the book would not be displayed in double quotes:

Example 1

```
Write-Host 'The title of this book is "Practical PowerShell: Exchange Online".'
```

Results are:

```
The title of this book is "Practical PowerShell: Exchange Online".
```

Example 2

Write-Host "The title of this book is ""Practical PowerShell: Exchange Online""."

Results are the same as can be seen here:

```
The title of this book is "Practical PowerShell: Exchange Online".
```

Example 3

Write-Host 'The title of this book is 'Practical PowerShell: Exchange Online'.'

Results:

```
The title of this book is  Practical PowerShell: Exchange Online.
```

Notice the complete lack of quotes in the resulting output. So if quotes are needed, the quotes need to be correctly ordered.

In summary, start with single quotes, unless a variable or a non-literal display of information is needed then use double quotes if needed. If a variable is in between quotes, use double quotes.

Obfuscated Information

Is it possible that PowerShell would hide information when cmdlets are run querying for Exchange information? When running GET command, all available information is displayed, right? No. Not always. It depends on the command that is executed and if there is a switch to reveal more information.

Special Switches

The two switches that we need to cover are -IncludeReport. This switch can reveal a bit more detail when it comes to certain commands and are available on a few cmdlets to retrieve additional information. Here are some examples:

-IncludeReport

The '-IncludeReport' switch could be considered a verbose switch for certain PowerShell cmdlets. The most commonly used cmdlets with the -IncludeReport switch are move request commands because they pertain to migration reports generated by Exchange. Examples of this are Get-MigrationBatch, Get-MoveRequestStatistics, and Get-PublicFolderMigrationRequestStatistics.

To see what the -IncludeReport switch brings to the table, the Get-MigrationBatch is a good example. Make sure to use the Format-List option to provide the full extent of the command. Without the -IncludeReport switch, displayed would be the base set of information on the migration that is being reported by the Get-MigrationBatch:

Notice that two fields, one field called 'Report' and another called 'Reports' that are empty. If we run this one-liner:

```
SubmittedByUser              : Damian@practicalpowershell.com
OwnerId                      : NAMPR08A001.prod.outlook.com/Microsoft Exchange
OwnerExchangeObjectId        : d9c0a727-0539-4c02-b463-238e7ccb2a49
NotificationEmails           : {Damian@practicalpowershell.com}
ExcludedFolders              : {}
MigrationType                : ExchangeRemoteMove
BatchDirection               : Onboarding
Locale                       : en-US
Reports                      : {}
IsProvisioning               : False
BatchFlags                   : ReportInitial
WorkflowControlFlags         : None
AutoRetryCount               : 0
CurrentRetryCount            : 0
AllowUnknownColumnsInCsv     : False
DiagnosticInfo               :
SupportedActions             : Stop, Set, Remove
```

The Report/Reports fields will be populated and include information like this:

```
Report   : 8/30/2017 5:52:32 AM [CO2PR0801MB2277] 'NAMPR08A001.prod.outlook.com/Microsoft Exchange Hosted Organizatio
           'ExchangeRemoteMove' batch.
           8/30/2017 5:52:36 AM [BN3PR08MB1844] migration user 'backup@               ' created.
           8/30/2017 5:52:36 AM [BN3PR08MB1844] The migration batch processor ActiveMigrationJobProcessor finished wi
           migration users, which underwent the following transitions: 'StatusValidating -> 1'.
           8/30/2017 5:53:08 AM [BN3PR08MB1844] The migration batch processor ActiveMigrationJobProcessor finished wi
           migration users, which underwent the following transitions: ''.
           8/30/2017 5:53:38 AM [BN3PR08MB1844] The migration batch processor ActiveMigrationJobProcessor finished wi
           migration users, which underwent the following transitions: ''.
           8/30/2017 5:54:29 AM [BN3PR08MB1844] User 'backup@                ' failed migration: The target mailbox d
           'scoles.mail.onmicrosoft.com'.
           8/30/2017 5:54:29 AM [BN3PR08MB1844] The migration batch processor ActiveMigrationJobProcessor finished wi
           migration users, which underwent the following transitions: 'StatusSyncing -> -1, StatusFailed -> 1'.
```

While that information is good for migrations, we can reveal even more information when applying this switch to Get-MoveRequestStatistics:

```
Report      : 3/8/2016 8:35:22 AM [16-LG-EX01] '' created move request.
              3/8/2016 8:35:22 AM [16-LG-EX01] '' allowed a large amount of data loss when
              moving the mailbox (100 bad items, 0 large items).
              3/8/2016 8:39:38 AM [16-LG-EX03] The Microsoft Exchange Mailbox Replication
              service '16-LG-EX03.16-lg.local' (15.1.225.37 caps:7FFF) is examining the
              request.
              3/8/2016 8:39:43 AM [16-LG-EX03] Connected to target mailbox
              'a2595af5-babd-4608-bd27-ddf152f81a57 (Primary)', database 'Mailbox Database
              1790513196', Mailbox server '16-LG-EX03.16-lg.local' Version 15.1 (Build
              225.0).
              3/8/2016 8:39:46 AM [16-LG-EX03] Connected to source mailbox
              'a2595af5-babd-4608-bd27-ddf152f81a57 (Primary)', database 'Mailbox Database
              0794329553', Mailbox server '16-LG-EX01.16-lg.local' Version 15.1 (Build
              225.0), proxy server '16-LG-EX01.16-lg.local' 15.1.225.37
              caps:01FFBF7FFFFFCB07FFFF.
              3/8/2016 8:39:49 AM [16-LG-EX03] Request processing started.
```

As you can see, for this cmdlet, -IncludeReport is like Verbose for mailbox move requests.

Code Signing

What is it?

When a PowerShell script is signed, the code block only validates if a script has not been modified by anyone other than the original author. Code signing does not validate that the script is functional or certified. The intention of code signing is solely to make sure that the code written by the author is not modified by another scripter and passed along as the authors work.

Why Use It?

By default, PowerShell execution is restricted to Remote Signed scripts:

Remote Signed: Requires that all scripts and configuration files downloaded from the Internet be signed by a trusted publisher.

When a script is not digitally signed, the script will not run. If a script is signed, but cannot be validated, it cannot be run. Verification at this level is just one level of protection against running rogue PowerShell scripts. However, it should not be the only level of protection. Ideally, a Dev or QA environment should be used for PowerShell script testing to validate both the code signing and functionality of the script.

How to Use It

There are a few configuration options to use when configuring digital signing options in Windows PowerShell. The PowerShell cmdlet used to configure this is Set-ExecutionPolicy.

- **Restricted:** Does not load configuration files or run scripts. "Restricted" is the default execution policy.
- **AllSigned:** Requires that all scripts and configuration files be signed by a trusted publisher, including scripts that you write on the local computer.
- **RemoteSigned:** Requires that all scripts and configuration files downloaded from the Internet be signed by a trusted publisher.
- **Unrestricted**: Loads all configuration files and runs all scripts. If you run an unsigned script that was downloaded from the Internet, you are prompted for permission before it runs.
- **Bypass:** Nothing is blocked and there are no warnings or prompts.
- **Undefined:** Removes the currently assigned execution policy from the current scope. This parameter will not remove an execution policy that is set in a Group Policy scope.

In order to run a script that has not been digitally signed, you must set the Execution Policy for PowerShell scripts to Unrestricted:

```
Set-ExecutionPolicy –ExecutionPolicy Unrestricted
```

When installing a new Cumulative Update for Exchange, Microsoft recommends that command be run to prevent any issues with the installation - https://blogs.technet.microsoft.com/exchange/2015/09/15/released-september-2015-quarterly-exchange-updates/.

In some organizations, PowerShell is restricted and locked down to prevent unauthorized scripts from running. The Execution Policy for PowerShell would be set to 'Restricted' in this case. If an unsigned script with this execution policy set, you will receive an error like so:

```
PS C:\> .\prereq1.ps1
.\prereq1.4.ps1 : File C:\prereq1.ps1 cannot be loaded because running scripts is disabled on this system.
For more information, see about_Execution_Policies at http://go.microsoft.com/fwlink/?LinkID=135170.
At line:1 char:1
+ .\prereq1.4.ps1
+ ~~~~~~~~~~~~~~~
    + CategoryInfo          : SecurityError: (:) [], PSSecurityException
    + FullyQualifiedErrorId : UnauthorizedAccess
PS C:\>
```

The policy for PowerShell execution restrictions can be implemented with a GPO in the following GPO location:

```
Computer Configuration -- Policies -- Administrative Templates: Policy Definitions (ADMX) -- Windows
```

Components -- Windows PowerShell

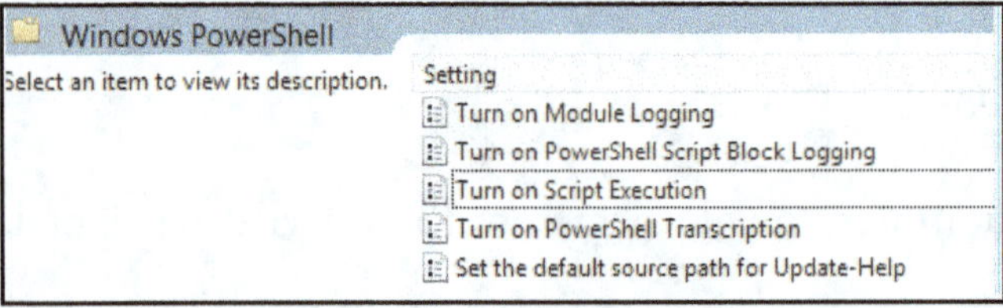

By default, this setting is not configured for the GPO:

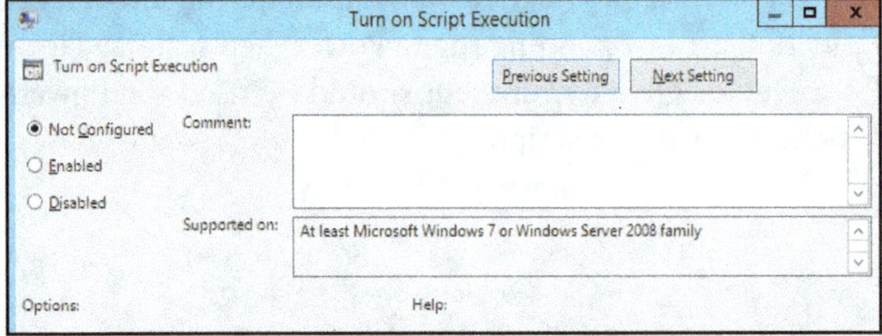

To restrict PowerShell code execution in the GPO, the setting needs to be enabled and a setting chosen:

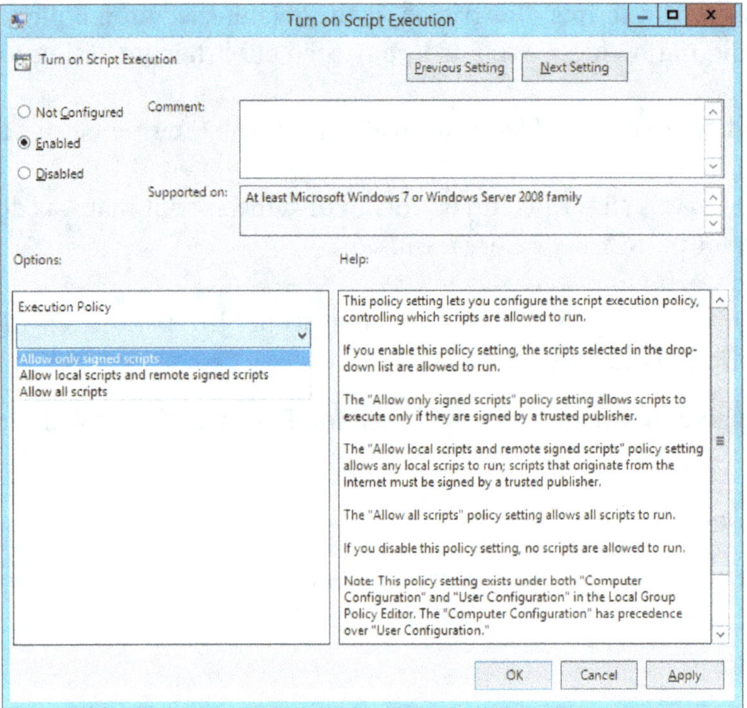

Signing Your Code

So how do you sign your scripts and what are the requirements?

Requirements – your script and a certificate to sign it with.

To sign it, the Set-AuthenticodeSignature cmdlet needs to be used. First acquire a signing certificate either from a third party or internally. Then bring up a PowerShell session in order to sign the script. One method, which was spelled out by the Scripting Guy! From Microsoft (https://blogs.technet.microsoft.com/heyscriptingguy/)is to store the certificate in a variable and then run the Set-AuthenticodeSignature cmdlet to sign the script:

```
$Cert=(dir cert:currentuser\my\ -CodeSigningCert)
Set-AuthenticodeSignature .\MyScript.ps1 $Cert –TimeStampServer "http://timestamp.globalsign.com/
scripts/timstamp.dll"
```

Using the TimeStampServer option is recommended:

```
-TimestampServer <String>
    Uses the specified time stamp server to add a time stamp to the signature. Type the URL of the time stamp server as a string.

    The time stamp represents the exact time that the certificate was added to the file. A time stamp prevents the script from failing
    if the certificate expires because users and programs can verify that the certificate was valid at the time of signing.
```

What is added to the script once it is signed?

When a script is signed, a code block is added to the end of a PowerShell script.

```
AntispamCommon.ps1 - Notepad
File  Edit  Format  View  Help

filter topN
{
  param (
    $top = 10)

  if ($script:count -lt $top)
  {
    write-output ($_)
    $script:count = $script:count + 1
  }
}

# SIG # Begin signature block
# MIIavQYJKoZIhvcNAQcCoIIarjCCGqoCAQExCzAJBgUrDgMCGgUAMGkGCisGAQQB
# gjcCAQSgwzBZMDQGCisGAQQBgjcCAR4wJgIDAQAABBAfzDtgwUsITrck0sYpfvNR
# AgEAAgEAAgEAAgEAAgEAMCEwCQYFKw4DAhoFAAQUKOZFl7KMitsRe2naqD/c+ump
# KAmgghwCMIIEwzCCA6ugAwIBAgITMwAAAG9lLVhiLBxFGKAAAAAAAbzANBgkqhkiG
# 9w0BAQUFADB3MQswCQYDVQQGEwJVUZETMBEGA1UECBMKV2FzaG1uZ3RvbjEQMA4G
# A1UEBxMHUmVkbW9uZDEeMBwGA1UEChMVTwljcm9zb2Z0IENvcnBvcmF0aW9uMSEw
# HwYDVQQDExhNaWNyb3NvZnQqVGltZS1TdGFtcCBQQ0EwHhcNMTUwMzIwMTczMjAy


# BgNVBAoTFU1pY3Jvc29mdCBDb3Jwb3JhdGlvbjEhMB8GA1UEAxMYTWljcm9zb2Z0
# IFRpbwUtU3RhbXAgUENBAhMzAAAAb2UtwG0HEUYoAAAAAABvMAkGBSsOAwIaBQCg
# XTAYBgkqhkiG9w0BCQMxCwYJKoZIhvcNAQcBMBwGCSqGSIb3DQEJBTEPFw0xNTA3
# MTAwMDIzMTRaMCMGCSqGSIb3DQEJBDEwBBSO+72hib43aVD/cYMaY9DgkEixwjAN
# BgkqhkiG9w0BAQUFAASCAQCneZqiN1u01Bo1S419v5kkIU015XBCt3jkQashnmTs
# xBFuShkfl60kqlQqzNP5k94rPX2hKFP9c7NvWB/1rXp+g4ExvcH0FhgK8/S8C5NI
# CE4Q1fgVlo4BstrUAcyvdfPerHrxeTVRfZEh1B3SCZixObTYirwJ76kzLI7P5HkZ
# 63peq8yZE+hd3c2FEYMuknrYFezosmvlnDKi8XFdwf/xlX3cbLEkviNXzItprsP1
# Z5DIJONQRkCqckzxT0nhIKJ8vQQqsLPbCCzdRDZcQ8UzFANunXFuGGWPQpn3bqj2
# beNm5c1+6i1kXwS6AJ591RmwtlikLFLtlnD2P6KjpbkI
# SIG # End signature block
```

Notice that the code signature is commented out to prevent any execution issues within the script.

For internal only scripts, a self-signed certificate can be sufficient. If the script is going to be used outside of your environment, a third party certificate must be used. The key is to use the correct kind of certificate – Class III or code-signing certificate – to generate the signature block.

3   Building Scripts

In This Chapter

- How To Begin
- Scenario One - Inactive Groups in Office 365
- Scenario Two - PowerShell and Change
- Conclusion

In the previous three chapters quite a few topics concerning PowerShell were covered, with some Exchange Online topics sprinkled into the mix. Now that some basic options have been covered let's see how these can be used in a PowerShell script and begin building your own scripts. This chapter will cover what to start with, how to add to the script, how to enhance the script, perform detailed testing and finally how to transition and use this in production with your Exchange Servers. The end result will be a working script for Exchange Online.

How to Begin

When script building, having a clear goal of what is to be accomplished is advisable. In the past programmers used various methods to build scripts. The key to our method is that we need a beginning and we need an end. This method requires a seed or first cmdlet to start with and from that we need to aim for the end goal, what could be called the purpose of the script. Let's start with a real life example.

To build a complete script, to keep the process ordered and to complete the task at hand there are a series of steps that can provide a useful guide to the process. Provided below is a series of suggested steps for creating a PowerShell script.

- Seed to start the script - usually a core concept with a corresponding PowerShell cmdlet
- Look for samples on the Internet to save time – code blocks, one-liners, routines and usage
- Loops if needed to perform iterations (Foreach, arrays, etc.) or objects in Exchange
- Define arrays if needed for the loops or other parts of the scripts
- Functions if a process is repeatable or needs to be called on from multiple parts of a script
- Export the results
- Build in some error checking or fail safes
- Commenting - top of the script - detailed description
- Commenting - document the script

> **TIP**
>
> On the first run of any new script, either the script needs to be run in a lab environment or all PowerShell cmdlets that make changes should be commented to prevent their execution. Alternatively, you can leverage the WhatIf switch to see what the cmdlet would do. However, trailing code can react as if the cmdlet failed, as the cmdlet did not actually run.

Scenario One - Inactive Groups in Office 365

This book is built on practical ways to use PowerShell and building a script in a practical manner is the goal of this sample scenario.

You are a Global Administrator in your Office 365 tenant for a medium size company. The company at one time had an Exchange server on-premises and moved to the Exchange Online about 18 months ago. Unfortunately at the time of the migration no effort was made to cleanup any old items that were no longer needed. These items include old mailboxes, Public folders, contacts and distribution groups. You have been tasked to start cleaning up any unused groups in your Exchange Online tenant. All distribution groups exist in your internal Active Directory and are currently synced to your tenant with an Azure AD Connect server.

Coding the Script

First a list of the requirements and desired outcomes should be written down and decided on before proceeding. In this scenario, IT management has done this legwork for you and provided a series of parameters for the script that will both clean-up the old distribution groups while notifying IT and responsible owners about the changes that will be made. The discussed parameters are as follows:

- All distribution lists must be examined
- Inactive distribution groups will be tracked for up to 12 months
- At 6 months on inactivity the group manager will be notified of the change, group will be hidden from the GAL
- At 12 months of inactivity, the group manager will be notified, IT will be notified and hte group will be disabled

How do we write a script that will handle these requirements? We need to be able to query this information with the script:

- Names of all the Distribution Group
- Current date
- List of groups who have received mail
- List of groups that have not received emails
- Group managers
- SMTP servers (for notifications)
- IT Email Address destination

and more....

From the above list, it looks like we will need quite a few variables to capture the data we need. First we'll start off with a date range. Message tracking in the cloud only goes so far back, so we will use an easy range of one full month in order to check for messages sent in that period:

```
# ---- VARIABLES ----
# Set time range for the message trace query
$OneMonth = ((Get-Date).AddDays(-30))
$Current = Get-Date
```

Now we'll need to define some arrays to keep track of the Distribution Groups. We need at least an Active Group array and an Inactive Group array. We'll also need an array to store all of the groups as well. Next we'll need to store all of the SMTP address for all the groups.

```
# Arrays
$ActiveGroups = @()
$ActiveGroups2 = @()
$InactiveGroups = @()
$AllGroups = @()
$Smtp = @()
```

For the next set of variables, we need to store information about the emails that will be sent out. We will need to define a To and From address, an SMTP server for relaying the mail as well as an email address for managers to contact after receiving an email about a disabled group:

```
# Variables for Emails
$From = "Notifications@Domain.Com"
$SMTPServer = "192.168.0.190"
$To = "ITGroup@Domain.Com"
$AdminAddress = "HelpDesk@Domain.Com"
```

As we progress through the script, the variable names and purpose will start to make more sense. Next, we need to prepare some credentials for connecting to Active Directory on-premises and Exchange Online. With these credentials we'll be able to make calls to the various directories and query and/ or change information.

Handling Passwords in PowerShell

In order for PowerShell to pass credentials to a remove Exchange server, like Exchange Online, we have two choices for handling passwords. First choice, and the easiest is to prompt for the password and enter it on a connection attempt. The second choice is to create a file to hold the password in a secure manner. If the script is to be run interactively, then the first option will work just fine. However, if the script is to be scheduled, then storing the password in a file for the script is the best option.

PowerShell provides two cmdlets in order to handle the process of encrypting and decrypting passwords stored in a file. The pair of cmdlets that provide this function are ConvertFrom-SecureString and ConvertTo-SecureString. First we'll need to use the ConvertFrom-SecureString cmdlet to convert a password and saving it to a file. If we review the Get-Help for ConvertFrom-SecureString, there isn't a mention of exporting to a file, only variables:

```
---------------------------- EXAMPLE 1 ----------------------------

PS C:\>$SecureString = Read-Host -AsSecureString

---------------------------- EXAMPLE 2 ----------------------------

PS C:\>$StandardString = ConvertFrom-SecureString $SecureString

---------------------------- EXAMPLE 3 ----------------------------

PS C:\>$Key = (3,4,2,3,56,34,254,222,1,1,2,23,42,54,33,233,1,34,2,7,6,5,35,43)
PS C:\>$StandardString = ConvertFrom-SecureString $SecureString -Key $Key
```

First, we'll need to create the password file to be referenced by the script. In order to do so we'll use Convert-From-SecureString which will be paired with Read-Host which will use the 'AsSecureString' switch. When paired together with the Out-File cmdlet (which will create the reference file), we can securely store the password.   The one-liner would look something like this:

```
Read-Host -AsSecureString | ConvertFrom-SecureString | Out-File C:\SecureString.txt
```

Enter a password after the cmdlet is run and a new file called SecureString.Txt is created and would look something like this:

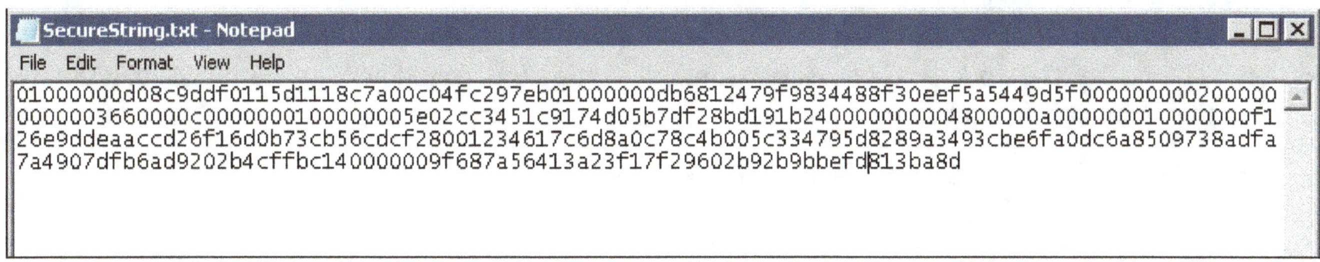

In order to use this file for credentials in PowerShell, we would want to store it the password as a variable. However, the variable is stored in a file. We can do so by using this one-liner:

```
$Password = Cat C:\SecureString-MyTenant.txt | ConvertTo-SecureString
```

** **Note** ** For obvious reasons, the file that is used to store the password should be locked down via file permissions on the server on which it is stored. If additional security is needed, we can use an Advanced Encryption Standard (AES) key to encrypt the file.

An example of this is shown in the examples of the ConvertFrom-SecureString cmdlet:

```
------------------------------- EXAMPLE 3 -------------------------------

PS C:\>$Key = (3,4,2,3,56,34,254,222,1,1,2,23,42,54,33,233,1,34,2,7,6,5,35,43)
PS C:\>$StandardString = ConvertFrom-SecureString $SecureString -Key $Key
```

In our code line for storing the password, no AES encryption was used. Now that we have the password in a secure file we can combine it with the user name and create a credential to be used for authentication. We can do this like so:

```
# Office 365 User Name and Password
$Username = "GlobalAdmin@MyTenant.OnMicrosoft.Com"
$Password = Cat C:\SecureString-MyTenant.txt | ConvertTo-SecureString
$LiveCred = New-Object -TypeName System.Management.Automation.PSCredential -Argumentlist
    $Username, $Password
```

In order to make the connection to Active Directory and Exchange Online, we'll also need to load some Power-Shell modules. These modules provide access to additional cmdlets that are needed in order to provide access to the PowerShell cmdlets we need:

```
# Load the PowerShell modules
Import-Module MSOnline
Import-Module ActiveDirectory
```

MSOnline - Used to connect to your Exchange Online tenant
ActiveDirectory - Used to access cmdlets dealing with Active Directory

If the module will not load, it may not be installed. If PowerShell 5.0 is being used, we can download the modules using the 'Install-Module' cmdlet. For example, the MSOnline one can be installed like so:

Install-Module MSOnline

https://docs.microsoft.com/en-us/powershell/azure/active-directory/install-msonlinev1?view=azureadps-1.0

For Active Directory, the workstation or server would need the RSAT Windows Feature Installed. One Windows 2012 R2, that would be done like so:

Add-WindowsFeature RSAT-AD-PowerShell,RSAT-AD-AdminCenter

https://technet.microsoft.com/en-us/library/gg413289.aspx

Connecting to Exchange Online

In order to connect we'll need two cmdlets to do so. One is the create the session and the other one will connect that session to the current PowerShell session that is executing the script. For the first part we will use the New-PS-Session cmdlet to build the session parameters for Exchange Online. The values in the one-liner are well know values that Microsoft publishes here - https://technet.microsoft.com/en-us/library/jj984289(v=exchg.160).aspx. We then store these parameters in a variable called '$Session' which will be used by the next cmdlet 'Import-PsSession'. These cmdlets are then paired like so to make the connection:

```
# Connect to Office 365
$Session = New-PSSession -ConfigurationName Microsoft.Exchange -ConnectionUri https://ps.outlook.com/powershell/ -Credential $LiveCred -Authentication Basic -AllowRedirection
Import-PSSession $Session
```

Once we have a connection to Exchange Online we can review any tracking logs for SMTP messages in the cloud. For Exchange Online, this cmdlet is Get-MessageTrace. If you are used to Exchange On-premises, this cmdlet is a bit of a departure from the Get-MessageTrackingLog cmdlet. Let's explore the examples from the Get-MessageTrace cmdlet:

Get-Help Get-MessageTrace -Examples

```
---------------------------- Example 1 ----------------------------
This example retrieves message trace information for messages sent by john@contoso.com between June 13,
2015 and June 15, 2015.

Get-MessageTrace -SenderAddress john@contoso.com -StartDate 06/13/2015 -EndDate 06/15/2015
```

From the above example we see that we can use parameters like SenderAddress, StartDate, EndDate. If we were to run just Get-MessageTrace you will find out that not the results are limited. Reviewing the description from '*Get-Help Get-MEssageTrace -Full*', we see the following:

```
PS C:\> Get-MessageTrace -StartDate 8/1/17 -EndDate 9/1/17
Invalid StartDate value. The StartDate can't be greater than 30 days from today.
    + CategoryInfo          : InvalidArgument: (:) [Get-MessageTrace], InvalidExpressionException
    + FullyQualifiedErrorId : [Server=CO2PR0801MB2277,RequestId=7e969f79-6a20-4d3f-a6f1-7d948f8ee9ab,TimeSta
   mp=9/2/2017 7:15:34 PM] [FailureCategory=Cmdlet-InvalidExpressionException] 3E276432,Microsoft.Exchange.
   Management.FfoReporting.GetMessageTrace
    + PSComputerName        : ps.outlook.com
```

You can use this cmdlet to search message data for the last 7 days. If you run this cmdlet without any parameters, only data from the last 48 hours is returned.

This statement is a bit misleading. While it is indeed true that the cmdlet will only return the last 48 hours of messages, it can actually reach back further than 7 days. Indeed, it can go back as far as 30 days:

So in order for use to use this properly, we'll need a date range that will work:

```
$OneMonth = ((Get-Date).AddDays(-30))
$Current = Get-Date
```

With this, we can construct a base one-liner that contains this date range:

```
Get-MessageTrace -StartDate $OneMonth -EndDate $Current
```

This provides a list of all the messages that have gone through in the past month:

```
Received                 Sender Address                         Recipient
                                                                Address

9/2/2017 3:06:12 PM      notifications@yammer.com               damian@prac...
9/1/2017 4:19:03 PM      damian@practicalpowershell.com         dscoles@net...
9/1/2017 2:05:04 PM      kindledirectpublishing@amazon.com      dmstork@sta...
9/1/2017 2:05:04 PM      kindledirectpublishing@amazon.com      damian@scol...
9/1/2017 2:05:04 PM      kindledirectpublishing@amazon.com      sales@pract...
8/31/2017 9:36:25 PM     info@twitter.com                       dmstork@sta...
8/31/2017 9:36:25 PM     info@twitter.com                       damian@scol...
8/31/2017 9:36:25 PM     info@twitter.com                       twitter@pra...
```

However, in the list you won't see any active groups. Why is that? That's because the messages for groups are expanded. Expanding is the act of bifurcation which splits a group into its individual parts. Luckily this information is stored separately. We need to look for messages that have a 'Status' of 'Expanded'. How do we do that?

```
Get-MessageTrace -StartDate $OneMonth -EndDate $Current -Status Expanded
```

This provides information on emails that are destined for Distribution Groups in Office 365, however, if not emails were sent in that period, no results may be found:

```
PS C:\> Get-MessageTrace -StartDate $OneMonth -EndDate $Current -status Expanded

Received              Sender Address                              Recipient Address                 Subject

9/1/2017 2:05:04 PM   kindledirectpublishing@amazon.com           sales@practicalpowershell.com     In this ...
8/31/2017 9:36:25 PM  info@twitter.com                            twitter@practicalpowershell.com   Sky Spor...
8/31/2017 3:13:18 PM  service@paypal.com                          paypal@practicalpowershell.com    Your tra...
8/31/2017 3:11:49 PM  service@paypal.com                          paypal@practicalpowershell.com    You sent...
8/31/2017 1:18:46 PM  service@paypal.com                          paypal@practicalpowershell.com    Lulu Rev...
8/31/2017 6:17:31 AM  paypal@mail.paypal.com                      paypal@practicalpowershell.com    Support ...
8/29/2017 7:47:50 PM  microsoftrewards@email.microsoftrewards.com ads@practicalpowershell.com       Damian, ...
8/28/2017 9:17:44 PM  service@paypal.com                          paypal@practicalpowershell.com    Lightnin...
8/28/2017 9:15:44 PM  info@twitter.com                            twitter@practicalpowershell.com   Dave New...
```

How can we take the above and process the results into a variable to be reference later? First, let's alphabetically sort the results by the Recipient Address, which is the SMTP address of the Distribution Group.

```
Get-MessageTrace -StartDate $OneMonth -EndDate $Current -Status Expanded | Sort-Object
RecipientAddress
```

We can further process the results by grouping the Recipient Addresses as we only need to record that at least one email was delivered to the group:

```
Get-MessageTrace -StartDate $OneMonth -EndDate $Current -Status Expanded | Sort-Object
RelatedRecipientAddress | Group-Object RecipientAddress
```

Then we can select just the name of the object and store it in a variable called '$ActiveGroups2'. We need the names so we can reference them later in a consolidate list:

```
$ActiveGroups2 += (Get-MessageTrace -StartDate $OneMonth -EndDate $Current -Status Expanded |
Sort-Object RecipientAddress | Group-Object RecipientAddress | Select-Object Name)
```

We can then consolidate the list of groups and then store the name of all the active groups in a variable called $ActiveGroups:

```
Foreach ($Line in $ActiveGroups2) {
    $ActiveGroups += $Line.Name
}
```

Next we will need a list of all mail enabled list of all groups listed in Azure AD for your Exchange Online Tenant:

```
# Get a list of all groups list in O365
$AllGroups2 = Get-DistributionGroup -Resultsize Unlimited | Select-Object -Property @
{Label="Name";Expression={$_.PrimarySmtpAddress}}
Foreach ($Line in $AllGroups2) {
    $AllGroups += $Line.Name
}
```

The use of '-Property' allows us to pick properties from object, in this case a Distribution List's Name, pulled form the Primary SMTP Address.

We now have All Groups and Active Groups stored in variables. In order to see what the differences exist between the two, we can use Compare-Object cmdlet to then store this value as $InactiveGroups2. To finish up, we need to pull out just the SMTP Address value from the group and store that in the $InactiveGroups variable for later:

```
# Find inactive groups by comparing active groups to all groups
$InactiveGroups2 = Compare-Object $ActiveGroups $AllGroups
Foreach ($Line in $InactiveGroups2) {
    $Smtp2=$Line.InputObject
    $Address=$Smtp2
    $InactiveGroups += $Address
}
```

Once we have all of the groups we can close off our PowerShell session to Office 365:

```
Get-PSSession | Remove-PSSession
```

At this point we have a know list of groups that have received email and a list of groups that have not received email. How will we keep track of these groups so that we know that a group has gone inactive after 6 months? We have some choices for tracking this information. One tracking method would be to build a CSV file to keep track of the group and its months of inactivity. A downside to this method would be file access. If this file is accidentally deleted, then all the tracking date is lost. If the file is modified, then results may be inaccurate or if the script cannot write or read the file, unintended consequences could occur. A preferred method would be to use an attribute on the group to track the value of months of inactivity. For our script we will use CustomAttribute 10. If this is used by something else in your environment, you can choose a different attribute. This way that data is stored with the object itself, one benefit is the object removed then this data is no longer relevant, the data is also available from multiple sources etc.

In order to mark a group accurately, we will start with the Active Groups which we will mark the CustomAttribute10 with a '0' as the groups are active:

```
# Set custom attribute 10 for active groups to 0
Foreach ($Line in $ActiveGroups){
    Set-DistributionGroup -Identity $Line -CustomAttribute10 0 -WarningAction SilentlyContinue
}
```

** **Note** ** The '-WarningAction' prevents an error message from being displayed. This isn't entirely necessary and is only being done to suppress a known error that occurs with this one-liner. This is a valuable tool in scripts where you know some situation could generate an error which you want to catch without alerting the user.

We will mark the Inactive Groups in a later section. Next we need to build our functions. We are building functions because the next processes will be called multiple times. Functions are self contained processes that performs distinct task. In the case of this script, we will need a function for the following tasks:

- Email Distribution Group manager for hidden groups
- Email Distribution Group manager for disabled groups
- Email IT Manager for disabled groups

Function - Email Distribution Group manager for hidden groups

The first function we need to build is one that will email a manager when a group is disabled. This function will need to perform a few tasks. We will need the email address of the manager for the Distribution Group. We will also need an appropriate email message subject and body as well as an SMTP server to relay the emails off of.

The manager of a group is a property on the Distribution Group. Lets see if we can determine the property as well as the manager on the group:

```
Get-DistributionGroup | Ft Manag*
```

```
PS C:\> Get-DistributionGroup | Ft Manag*

ManagedBy
---------
{Damian Scoles}
```

So we see that the attribute we need is ManagedBy and we are provided only a name and not an SMTP address. In order for us to email the manager, we will need the managers email address. Because in most scenarios, this script will be run from an Exchange on-premises server against mailboxes in an Office 365 tenant, we will use the Get-RemoteMailbox cmdlet to determine an email address. One other note is that some groups could be assigned more than one manager. The tricky part is pulling out the primary SMTP address while also handling multiple managers. First, we need to start with the line to start the function off with this line:

```
Function Mail-ManagerHidden ($GroupSmtpAddress) {
```

The $GroupSmtpAddress is a value we will pass later to this function. This variable will allow us to pick the correct manager to email. Next we need to get the manager of the group. The value, as we know from above, is 'ManagedBy'. This value can be gathered with a Get-DistributionGroup cmdlet. We can then store the ManagedBy value in a '$Manager' variable like so:

$Manager = ((Get-DistributionGroup $GroupSmtpAddress).ManagedBy)

Since groups can have more than one manager, we need to process each manager and query for the Primary SMTP address of the manager.

Get-Help Foreach-Object -Examples

```
-------------------------- EXAMPLE 1 --------------------------

C:\>30000, 56798, 12432 | ForEach-Object -Process {$_/1024}
-------------------------- EXAMPLE 3 --------------------------

C:\>$Events = Get-EventLog -LogName System -Newest 1000
C:\>$events | ForEach-Object -Begin {Get-Date} -Process {Out-File -Filepath Events.txt -App
putObject $_.Message} -End {Get-Date}
```

We can use these examples to build the next line. We can pipe the $Manager variable to a 'Foreach-Object' cmdlet:

$Manager | Foreach-Object {

This above line will allow us to process each manager. So if one manager is listed, then the loop runs once. If there are more, than the loop will run for each item or manager in the $Manager variable. The next line below uses the Get-Mailbox cmdlet to get information on the Manager and we'll store it in a variable called '$EmailAddresses':

$EmailAddresses = (Get-Mailbox $_).EmailAddresses

Notice the weird variable '$_'. This variable has a special purpose. Microsoft has written a great article that explains what this variable is used for:

What the Heck Is $_?

https://technet.microsoft.com/en-us/library/ee677578.aspx

Now, like most mailboxes, the manager's mailbox probably has multiple email addresses assigned to it. There could also be a SIP address used for Lync or Skype, depending on your install. In order to weed out the irrelevant information from the Primary SMTP address, we need to use the Foreach-Object cmdlet again. This cmdlet can now be used for processing each email address:

$EmailAddresses | Foreach-Object {

What values are stored in the $EmailAddresses variable? Here is a sample from a mailbox in Exchange Online:

```
smtp:JohnDoe@practicalpowershell.onmicrosoft.com
SMTP:johndoe@practicalpowershell
SPO:SPO_77932456-71bb-42ae-8a77-4ea4e460bba5@SPO_
```

Processing each of the email addresses, with the intention of looking for just the Primary SMTP address which begins with 'SMTP'. In order to do so, we need to use the $_ variable which pulls the current value from the loop. Because we are looking for an address with the capitalized characters, using -**CMatch** as the operator will allow us to find 'SMTP' and not any variation like 'Smtp' or 'smtp':

If ($_ -CMatch "SMTP*") {

If the address matches then we need to remove the 'SMTP:' in front of the address using a technique called substring. The substring allows us to remove some of the leading characters in a variable. The substring in our case needs to remove 5 characters. So if our variable has this content:

```
SMTP:Damian@PracticalPowerShell.Com
```

Then once we apply the Substring, we should get just this:

```
Damian@PracticalPowerShell.Com
```

The we can store that value in a variable called 'SMTPAddress', like so:

```
$SMTPAddress = $_.Substring(5)
```

Then we store the address. in the $SMTP array like this:

```
$SMTP += @($SMTPAddress)
```

After the first loop, if there is a second manager, the same process will occur, storing the next managers Primary SMTP address with the previous managers Primary SMTP address.

Next, we need to pull just the Distribution groups Display Name. We will use the Display Name for the notification email:

```
$DLName = (Set-DistributionGroup $GroupSmtpAddress).DisplayName
```

Then, we need to define the Body of the message. In this case, the body will contain language about what is happening, which group is affected and why this is occurring. This information van be stored in a variable called '$Body. The body is written in HTML for better formatting:

```
[string] $Body = "<strong>NOTIFICATION</strong><BR><BR>As a part of regular maintenance, IT has
decided to monitor the usage of Distribution # Lists.<BR><BR>This email is a notification that an Email
Distribution Group that you manage has been inactive for 6 months. Because of this level of inactivity,
the group has been hidden from the Global Address List. Please check this list to see if it is still valid or
not.<BR><BR>Please send an email to $AdminAddress if the list is no longer needed.  Thanks for you
assistance with this matter."
```

Last section of code for the function is the email portion. For this section we will loop through each managers SMTP address which was stored in the '$SMTP' variable.

```
Foreach ($Line in $Smtp) {
```

Then we can build up a variable called '$MessageParameters. We need this variable to contain information about the email that will be sent out. this means we will need a Subject, Body, From address, a To address and finally the SMTP server to relay the SMTP message through. The $From and $SmtpServer were defined in the beginning of the script. The Subject includes the name of the group being hidden.

```
$MessageParameters = @{
    Subject = "Distribution Group Manager Alert - Inactive Distribution Group - $DLName"
    Body = $Body
    From = $From
    To = $Line
    SmtpServer = $SmtpServer
}
```

This variable will then be used with the Send-Message cmdlet and we will also use the '-BodyAsHtml' switch which will allow thew HTML formatted Body for the message to be transmitted correctly:

```
Send-MailMessage @MessageParameters –BodyAsHtml
```

Lastly, we close off the function and put a comment here about the function ending here:

```
} # End Function Mail-ManagerHidden
```

Function - Email Distribution Group manager for disabled groups

The next function needs to send an email to a manager of a group that was disabled after 12 months. We can reuse almost all of the code from the previous function for email managers of groups that were hidden. The only real changes were the name of the function, Subject line and the body of the email message:

```
Function Mail-ManagerDisabled ($GroupSmtpAddress) {
    $Manager = ((Get-DistributionGroup $GroupSmtpAddress).ManagedBy)
    $Manager | Foreach-Object {
        $EmailAddresses = (Get-Mailbox $_).EmailAddresses
        $EmailAddresses | Foreach-Object {
            If ($_ -CMatch "SMTP*") {
                $SMTPAddress = $_.Substring(5)
                $SMTP += @($SMTPAddress)
            }
        }
    }
    $DLName = (Set-DistributionGroup $GroupSmtpAddress).DisplayName
    [string] $Body = "<strong>NOTIFICATION</strong><BR><BR>As a part of regular maintenance, IT
    has decided to monitor the usage of Distribution # Lists.<BR><BR>This email is a notification that
    an Email Distribution Group that you manage has been inactive for over 12 months. This Distribution
    group has been deleted.<BR><BR>Please send an email to $AdminAddress if you have any questions.
    Thanks for you assistance with this matter."
    Foreach ($Line in $Smtp) {
        $MessageParameters = @{
            Subject = "Distribution Group Manager Alert - Removed Distribution Group - $DLName"
            Body = $Body
            From = $From
            To = $Line
            SmtpServer = $SmtpServer
        }
        Send-MailMessage @MessageParameters –BodyAsHtml
    }
} # End Function Mail-ManagerDisabled
```

Function - Email IT Group - 12 Month Disabled

This function simply sends an email to the IT Group. Basically it is the second half of the previous functions:

```
Function EmailIT-GroupRemoval ($GroupSmtpAddress) {
    $DLName = (Get-DistributionGroup $GroupSmtpAddress).DisplayName
    [string] $Body = "<strong>NOTIFICATION</strong><BR><BR>As a part of regular maintenance this
```

```
        group was disabled.  The group has been inactive for 12 months per the DL Cleanup Script. Confirm
        that this list can be deleted and remove it from AD."
        $MessageParameters = @{
            Subject = "Distribution Group - IT Alert - Removed Distribution Group - $DLName"
            Body = $Body
            From = $From
            To = $To
            SmtpServer = $SMTPServer
        }
        Send-MailMessage @messageParameters –BodyAsHtml
    } # End Function EmailIT-GroupRemoval
```

In the last part of the script we now need to increase the value of the CustomAttribute10 property of the all of the inactive groups. For each group we need to pull the existing value into a variable, in this case $Number and then increasing that variable by 1 ($Number++) and then assigning the new value to the group:

```
# Set custom attribute 10 for inactive groups - increase by 1
# Hide or disable group
Foreach ($Line in $InactiveGroups){
    [String]$Email = $Line
    [Int]$Number = (Get-DistributionGroup -Identity $Email).CustomAttribute10
    $Number += 1
    Set-DistributionGroup -Identity $Email -CustomAttribute10 $Number
```

In this next section, we compare the value stored in the $Number variable. This variable contains the current number of months of inactivity of the group that is being processed in this loop. For the first section of code, we need to check for the $Number variable to equal 6. Notice that we are not looking for a value greater than 6, but it has to be exactly 6. That is because if the group has a CustomAttribute10 value greater than 6 should be disabled and the only other trigger point we want is 12 months of inactivity.

```
    If ($Number -eq 6) {
```

First step in the loop is to send an email to the manager using the 'Mail-ManagerHidden' function we defined earlier. Note the '$Email' variable that is listed after the function. This variable's value is passed along to the function for processing:

```
        Mail-ManagerHidden $Email
```

After the notifications are sent out, we can set a note and change the value on the group in order to make sure the change is more visible in AD Users and Computer:

```
        $Notes = "$Current - Hidden from address list due to inactive use."
        Set-Group -Identity $Email -Notes $Notes
```

Once the note has been assigned, the group is hidden and will no longer be visible in the GAL:

```
        Set-DistributionGroup -Identity $Email -HiddenFromAddressListsEnabled $True
```

After the check for groups that have a value of 6, next we need to look for any groups that the CustomAttribute10 set to 12. When a group gets to this level it means that the group has not had a single email in 12 months. This same group needs to be disabled and both the manager and IT group will be notified of this change.

```
    If ($Number -eq 12) {
```

First step in the loop is to send an email to the manager using the 'Mail-ManagerDisabled' function we defined earlier. Note the '$Email' variable that is listed after the function. This variable's value is passed along to the function for processing:

```
Mail-ManagerDisabled $Email
```

The next step in the loop is to send an email to the IT Group using the 'EmailIT-GroupRemoval' function we defined earlier. Note the '$Email' variable that is listed after the function. This variable's value is passed along to the function for processing:

```
EmailIT-GroupRemoval $Email
```

After the notifications are sent out, we can set a note and change the value on the group in order to make sure the change is more visible in AD Users and Computer:

```
$Notes = "$Current - No longer Mail Enabled due to inactive use."
Set-Group -Identity $Email -Notes $Notes
```

Once the note has been assigned, the group is disabled and will no longer be usable:

```
Disable-DistributionGroup -Identity $Email -Confirm:$False
```

This loop will now repeat until all inactive groups have been processed.

Completing the Code Section

To complete the script, the full script code would have all of these sections:

- Comment block at the top
- Variables
- Functions defined
- Query inactive groups
- Query all groups
- Email Managers
- Email IT Group
- Hide and Disable Distribution Groups

The full script is available on the TechNet Wiki for now:

https://gallery.technet.microsoft.com/Distribution-Group-Cleanup-68285e91

Conclusion

As can be seen from the above lists there are quite a few steps involved in building a script. At the end of the build process, precautions should be taken, -WhatIf should be utilized and if possible a QA/Dev environment should be used as well. This will minimize any accidents or RGE's (Resume Generating Events).

Scenario Two - PowerShell and Change

Before ending this chapter on the basics of building a script, a thought should be given to the longevity of your script…. PowerShell cmdlets change with features added, remove, deprecated and more….

Change is a constant at Microsoft. By the time you read this more PowerShell cmdlets will probably be available for Exchange Online. Other workloads in Office 365 change every month, week and day. PowerShell change is less often, but the results are no different. New editions are made, old commands deprecated and eventually removed.

Why does this matter?

As scripts are built, effort may be required to make sure the cmdlets being used are not being deprecated. Cmdlets that are being deprecated can be found in a few ways. Simply run a cmdlet in PowerShell and if the cmdlet is being deprecated a message in yellow will reveal itself. There are cmdlets still in Exchange 2016 that were listed as 'deprecated' in Exchange 2010 and 2013, so deprecated cmdlets may not always go away.

In Exchange Online the change comes quickly. PowerShell cmdlets are added. PowerShell cmdlets are removed. Often there is no notification at all. This usually comes with features being added or removed. How do we know that the cmdlets changed? One way to keep track of the changes is to connect to Exchange Online, log the number of available cmdlets and export a list of the cmdlets to a text file. This script could be run each day or scheduled to run.

Here are a couple of historical charts that map out the number of PowerShell cmdlets available for Exchange and Skype Online:

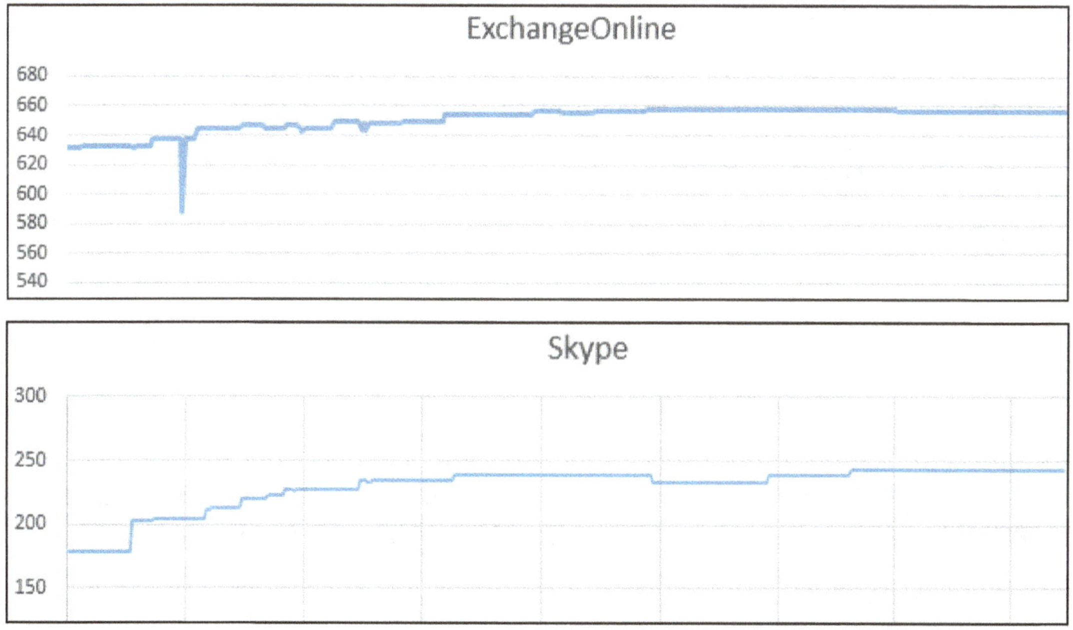

Coding the Script

Just like the first script in this chapter we will need to initiate a connection to the Exchange Online Tenant. Again, we create the credentials to be used in the connection:

```
# Office 365 User Name and Password
$Username = "GlobalAdmin@MyTenant.OnMicrosoft.Com"
$Password = Cat C:\SecureString-MyTenant.txt | ConvertTo-SecureString
$LiveCred = New-Object -TypeName System.Management.Automation.PSCredential -Argumentlist
$Username, $Password
```

Since we want to keep track of the cmdlets over time we need a place to drop the results file into. For the sake of this exercise we create a file structure like so:

```
C:\CmdletCheck - Root directory to store lists of cmdlets
C:\CmdletCheck\Historical - Store historical data
```

First step is to read in the existing CSV file that has results in it. If this is the first time a script executed, we can populate the data with a current date and a '0' to simulate the fact that there are 0 known cmdlets at this time.

```
# Read in CSC file for comparison
$CSV = Import-CSV 'C:\CmdletCheck\Historical\CurrentChart.csv'
```

Next, we can store the number of cmdlets in a variable called $ExchangeNum and it will be populated with the number found in the column ExchangeOnline in the CSV file. The $CSV variable can be read in and the current number of Exchange Online cmdlets will be stored in a variable called '$ExchangeNum':

```
Foreach ($Line in $CSV) {
    $ExchangeNum = $Line.ExchangeOnline
}
```

The CSV being utilized for the step above has the following format:

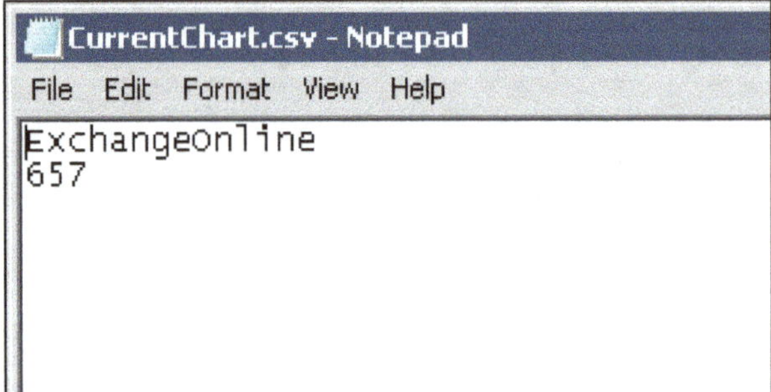

Now that we have that out of the way, it's time to connect to Office 365 and Exchange Online specifically. To do so, we need to use the New-PSSession cmdlet. What can we do with this cmdlet? Let's review the Get-Help:

```
Get-Help New-PsSession -Examples
```

```
------------------------------- EXAMPLE 11 -------------------------------

PS C:\>$so = New-PSSessionOption -SkipCACheck
PS C:\>New-PSSession -ConnectionUri https://management.exchangelabs.com/Management -SessionOption $so
 -Credential Server01\Admin01
```

Now the above is the closest of the examples included. In fact, we need a couple of other options:

Authentication - Specifies the mechanism that is used to authenticate the user's credentials - Office 365 uses 'Basic' for its default authentication.

AllowRedirection - Allows redirection of this connection to an alternate Uniform Resource Identifier (URI) - This is a required option for connecting to Office 365 because it needs to be able to redirect the session to the appropriate resource in the cloud

We will store the PowerShell session connection in a variable called $Session. This way we can use the 'Import-PS-Session' cmdlet to initiate the connection:

```
----------------------- EXAMPLE 1 -----------------------
PS C:\>$s = New-PSSession -ComputerName Server01
PS C:\>Import-PSSession -Session $s
```

Putting this together we get these two cmdlets to initial the session:

```
$Session = New-PSSession -ConfigurationName Microsoft.Exchange -ConnectionUri https://ps.outlook.
com/powershell/ -Credential $LiveCred -Authentication Basic -AllowRedirection
Import-PSSession $Session
```

After the session is connected we need to query for cmdlets that are Exchange related. How can we filter for these cmdlets? Well, let's see what cmdlets are available once we make our connection:

```
Get-Command
```

When that is typed in a seemingly endless stream of cmdlets is displayed. At the time of this writing, the total was around 3750 cmdlets. How do we get an accurate count:

```
(Get-Command).Count
```

The brackets and the '.Count' allows PowerShell the number of items that would be displayed if the entire list was show. This same method could be used again almost any variable or cmdlet that lists results.   Now, looking at the list of cmdlets, we see there are a number of modules listed.

```
Get-Command | Select-Object ModuleName -Unique
```

Well, that's great, but that provides 103 module names. None of them include the word Exchange in the name. We need to take another approach. We know that a cmdlet like 'Get-Mailbox' is an Exchange Online Cmdlet. Maybe we can get the module name from that cmdlet:

```
Get-Command Get-Mailbox
```

```
PS C:\> Get-Command Get-Mailbox

CommandType       Name              Version      Source
-----------       ----              -------      ------
Function          Get-Mailbox       1.0          tmp_ekfquvhm.cvg
```

Nice. As can be seen by the name of the module that the cmdlet is in, it appears to be a temporary module name assigned to the cmdlet. What this means is that every time we connect a PowerShell session to Exchange Online, the Module Name for Exchange Online PowerShell cmdlets will be different. What we then have to do is first query all Modules:

```
$ModuleName = (Get-Module).Name
```

To pinpoint the module for the Exchange Online Cmdlets we will check each Module until we find the module beginning with 'tmp':

```
Foreach ($Name in $ModuleName) {
    If ($Name -Like "tmp*") {
```

If the Module matches, then we can get the number of cmdlets found in Exchange Online now - notice the '.Count' at the end:

```
$NewExchangeNum = (Get-Command | Where {$_.ModuleName -eq $Name}).Count
```

Lastly, we will create a txt file that will contain all of the cmdlets from this module. The file will be named 'ExchangeOnline-<date>.txt:

```
$Service = "ExchangeOnline"
Get-command | Where {$_.ModuleName -eq $Name} | Select-ObjectName > "C:\
CmdletCheck\$Service-$Date.txt"
```

Now that we've gathered up the cmdlet names and a count of the cmdlets, we should clean up our PowerShell session to Exchange Online. Why should we clear our sessions? First, it closes the remote connection and allows us to run cmdlets on our local server. Second, it closes a potential security hole because of the direct connection to Exchange Online using a connection with administrative permissions to the tenant.

How can we close the session? Remove-PSSession:

```
-------------------------------- EXAMPLE 2 --------------------------------
PS C:\>get-pssession | remove-pssession

- or -

PS C:\>remove-pssession -session (get-pssession)

- or -

PS C:\>$s = get-pssession
PS C:\>remove-pssession -session $s
```

Using the example above we can add this code:

```
# Cleanup - Main Connection
Get-PsSession | Remove-PSSession
```

Note that the above will close ALL active sessions. For a scheduled script, this condition is acceptable as the sessions closed by this cmdlet are only the ones opened in the current script execution. It does not affect sessions outside of the PowerShell window used by the script.

Next we need to begin constructing our CSV file for storing results. We start with the first row of the chart:

```
# ReWrite the CSV File
$HeaderRow = "ExchangeOnline"
$HeaderRow > 'C:\CmdletCheck\Historical\CurrentChart.csv'
```

Add additional row to the CurrentChart.Csv spreadsheet:

```
# New numbers
$NewRow = "$NewExchangeNum"
Add-Content 'C:\CmdletCheck\Historical\CurrentChart.csv' $NewRow
```

Add additional row to the FullChart.Csv spreadsheet - Note we tag the row with the current date as well:

```
# Add row to historical data
```

```
$NewRow = "$Date,"+"$NewExchangeNum"
Add-Content 'C:\CmdletCheck\Historical\FullChart.csv' $NewRow
```

Once the CSV files are updated, we need to notify someone of the changes. First, we check to see if the new number of cmdlets ($NewExchangeNum) has changed from the previous number of cmdlets ($ExchangeNum):

```
If ($NewExchangeNum -ne $ExchangeNum) {
```

If the changes have occurred, then

```
$Change = "ExchangeOnline Cmdlets changed from $ExchangeNum to $NewExchangeNum."
Add-Content 'C:\CmdletCheck\Historical\CurrentChanges.csv' $Change
```

This next variable is set because we want to send an email out:

```
$MailRequired = 1
```

Now, if the cmdlet numbers have not changes, we user the '} Else {' code section to do so. In this section we will record no change to the new CSV file:

```
} Else {
    $NoChange = "ExchangeOnline Cmdlets did not change in number."
    Add-Content 'C:\CmdletCheck\Historical\CurrentChanges.csv' $NoChange
}
```

Once those checks complete, we can check to see of the $MailRequired variable is set to '1'. We can use 'ceq' to compare values ('ceq' stands for Case-Sensitive Comparison):

```
If ($MailRequired -ceq 1) {
```

We then set the '$Body' and '$Subject' variable for the email:

```
$Subject = "Some Office 365 PowerShell Cmdlets Changed on $EmailDate"
$Body = (Get-Content 'C:\CmdletCheck\Historical\CurrentChanges.csv') -join '<BR>'
```

Then we can send the email out with the changes that occurred.

```
Send-MailMessage -To $To -From $From -Subject $Subject -BodyAsHtml -Body $Body -SmtpServer
$SMTPServer
```

If there were no changes, and the $MailRequired is not set to 1, then we can use an '} Else {' section of code:

```
} Else {
```

We then set the '$Body' and '$Subject' variable for the email, differently then the successful email:

```
$Subject = "No Office 365 PowerShell Cmdlets Changed on $EmailDate"
$Body = "No Office 365 PowerShell Cmdlets Changed on $EmailDate."
```

Then we can send the email out with the fact no changes happened:

```
Send-MailMessage -To $To -From $From -Subject $Subject -BodyAsHtml -Body $Body -SmtpServer
$SmtpServer
}
```

Once that's complete, we can close the PS Session....

    Get-PSSession | Remove-PSSession

... and remove the CSV file we no linger need:

    Remove-Item "C:\CmdletCheck\Historical\CurrentChanges.csv"

Script Summary

In this sample, we used Send-MailMessage, If..Else, PSSession cmdlets, and more to make this happen. The key thing to remember is to add comments later once the script works. This will enable sharing of the script as well as help in troubleshooting it if there are any issues.

Script Building Conclusion

Building a script in PowerShell can take some planning and certainly takes some experimentation. An idea method would be to have some sort of test environment in order to prove out the scripts and then put it into production once the script has been vetted. Ideally the script will start with some sort of seed like mailbox information, or groups information and then expanding out to culling data points and then performing some sort of action in response to the data found. The scripts might be scheduled or run manually depending on the end purpose.

When building your scripts, make sure to take advantage of all the tools that are out there:

- PowerShell Get-Help
- Microsoft TechNet - https://technet.microsoft.com/en-us/ms376608.aspx
- Search engine - Google or Bing
- TechNet Gallery - https://gallery.technet.microsoft.com/
- GitHub - https://github.com/powershell
- MVP blog script samples

Don't ignore any help you can get from these sources. Experience will teach you that until you understand the underlying way that PowerShell operates, as well as how data could be stored in Exchange and Active Directory, it will take experimentation to get the most out of it.

What's New

In This Chapter

- Introduction
- Office 365 Roadmap
- New Features
- Rolling Out Now
- Canceled Features
- In Development
- Desktop Clients

Introduction

When you deal with on-premises servers and applications for your job and those responsibilities transfer to a cloud based solution, there certainly is some hesitation to be had. What helps is some sort of direction or information that you may not get on a timely basis with an on-premises solution. Microsoft, with their Office 365 product, has made an effort to help those administrators who support Exchange, SharePoint, Skype for Business and more and have had their responsibilities and functions moved to the cloud.

This effort has led what is collectively known as the Office 365 Roadmap. The roadmap provides an insight into the flow of features into Office 365. This includes old features, newly released features, soon to be released ones as well as ones that are in development. By providing this, an administrator can now prepare for the features that are newly released as well as soon to be released. The official site for the roadmap can be found here:

https://products.office.com/en-us/business/office-365-roadmap

In addition to the Roadmap, Microsoft also publishes the changes are published on the Dashboard for the Office 365 tenant's admin page. The publishing of the list on your tenant is a reminder that Microsoft would like you to log into your tenant at least once a day to see what changes are occurring and also to verify the health of all of your services in their cloud.

In this chapter we will talk about the changes that Microsoft is making, where they announce the changes and how this may affect your experience with PowerShell in your tenant. We will not cover the features in depth due to the sheer number of changes and modifications there are to the cloud. We will cover the changes and focus more on those that affect PowerShell in terms of new cmdlets or changes to where to access the cmdlets.

Office 365 Roadmap

Like any company who constantly enhances their product, Microsoft likes to advertise their enhancements and and features that could potentially increase a users productivity. More importantly, the Roadmap and Dashboard information is to prove that Microsoft is an innovative companies and a competitor to consider in the cloud services market. If the bundling of services in the Microsoft cloud ecosystem, known as Office 365, isn't enough of an advantage then the feature roll-out may tip the scale for potential clients.

The problem with change is not always the speed, although with any fast moving object, speed bumps do tend to occur No, the problem is visibility. If the changes are visible and end users / administrators are educated on the changes then the usage of the new features tends to increase. So what do these announcements look like?

Office Roadmap for Office 365:

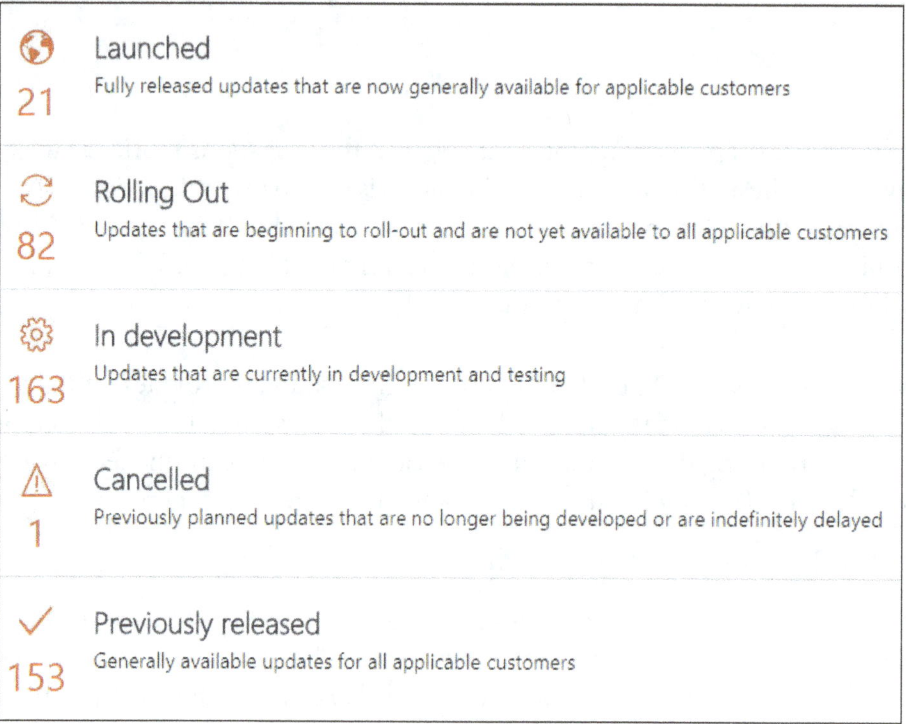

As you can see, there are quite a few features and not all of them are released yet. What's nice about the page is that we can get a quick summary of what has change, or even just want is coming in Office 365. The only part that may not help is that not all features are self-explanatory as to which workload is affected or enhanced by these feature releases.

As mentioned above, Microsoft also provides notifications of the changes that are occurring in Office 365 on the Dashboard. Simply log into your tenant at https://portal.office365.com and look on the main page. There is a 'Message Center' that lists all of the changes. If you click on this, a more detailed list will be provided. This list is a summary of not only the new features that are coming to each Office 365 Workload, but also other changes in the service itself. Not all of these changes are end user facing. Some of the changes are actually aimed at the Administrator as well.

Here is a sample of a current Dashboard as of the books publication:

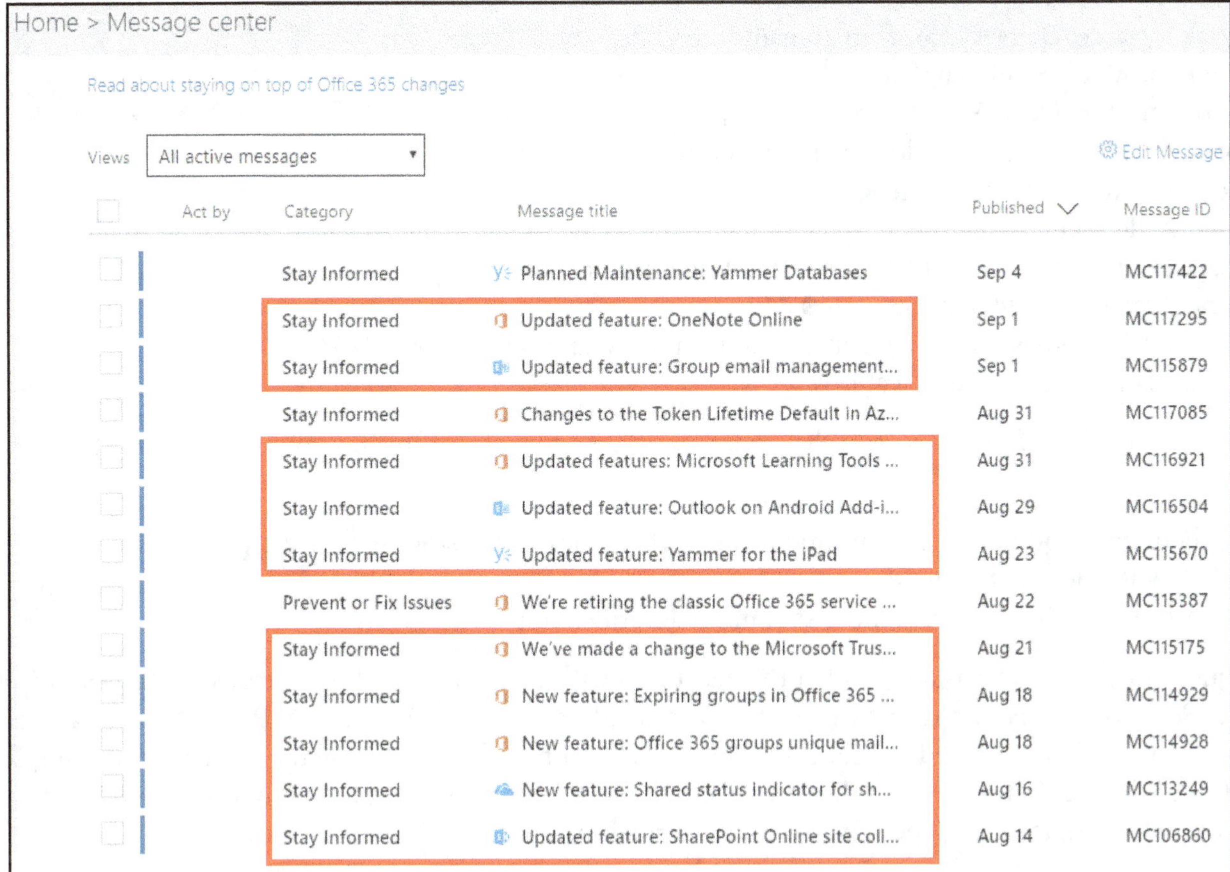

In this chapter we will analyze any features in the lists that affect Exchange Online and dig into any features that affect PowerShell for Exchange Online.

Launched Features

Launched

21

Fully released updates that are now generally available for applicable customers

Take for example the current list (as of the writing of this chapter):

- Large dictionary and unique match support in DLP policies and custom sensitive types
- Outlook for Windows: Improved add account experience
- Enhanced HIPAA protection in Office 365 DLP and Retention
- Microsoft Teams on iOS: Meeting join capabilities
- Yammer Groups Activity Reporting in O365
- Microsoft Teams on Android: Meeting join capabilities
- Office Lens: Multi page scan on Android
- Advanced Security Management – Power BI Activity Support
- Yammer iPad Relaunch

- Outlook for Windows: Improvements to OneDrive attachment handling
- Outlook for Windows: A smarter To: line
- Outlook for Mac: Delivery Confirmation and Read Receipts
- Outlook for Mac: Email templates
- Outlook for Mac: Delay Send
- Outlook for Mac: Improved add account experience
- Outlook for Mac: Favorite Folders
- DLP Policy Recommendations
- DLP alerts enhanced to provide more streamlined notifications
- General Availability of Office 365 Tasks API
- Outlook for Windows: Cloud attachment support for SharePoint Server 2016
- Microsoft Forms new grading feature

A quick analysis of these features reveals that there are quite a few of features that may be relevant to Exchange Online:

- Large dictionary and unique match support in DLP policies and custom sensitive types
- DLP Policy Recommendations
- DLP alerts enhanced to provide more streamlined notification

Now the question you may be asking is what this has to do with PowerShell and the purpose of this book? Well, it depends. Some of the features directly relate to PowerShell - changes to DLP and DLP data types - can directly affect what can be added or scoped in a DLP Transport role or it may force us to use the Security and Compliance Center (SCC). Changes in the SCC can directly affect Exchange Online because they can be inserted into the flow of email internally or externally depending on how the rules are configured.

For the first item in the above consolidate listed which deals with large dictionaries and DLP are configurable with a set of PowerShell cmdlets with a noun of 'DlpKeywordDictionary'. The caveat is that these cmdlet, like most of Microsoft's efforts with DLP, are present in the Security and Compliance Center's PowerShell. This means a different connection point to get access to these cmdlets:

```
Get-DlpKeywordDictionary
New-DlpKeywordDictionary
Remove-DlpKeywordDictionary
Set-DlpKeywordDictionary
```

Microsoft has documented this information here:

https://support.office.com/en-us/article/Create-a-keyword-dictionary-c8a95d1b-c3b6-4613-98ab-0331d1872cf3

We will cover these in depth in Chapter 11.

Rolling Out Now

⟳ Rolling Out

82   Updates that are beginning to roll-out and are not yet available to all applicable customers

In the development cycle for Office 365, before a feature is Fully Launched Reviewing the 82 features that are listed in the 'Rolling Out' section of the Roadmap, it appears that only thirteen are Exchange or Outlook related. These features are as follows:

- Meeting Poll
- Events from email
- Microsoft Bookings
- Outlook on the web: OneDrive Sharing Tips
- Outlook on the web: OneDrive Sharing Improvements
- Outlook Customer Manager - two of these
- Mailbox Plan Enhancements
- Calendar events for groups in Outlook
- Outlook for iOS and Android back-end update
- Outlook on the web: New First Run Experience
- Office 365 Groups: Invite To Join
- Focused Inbox for Outlook for Windows, Mac and web

As you can see there are quite a number of new features being added to the Exchange Online workload. These features that are in the Roll-out phase will slowly make it from the early adopters of Office 365 (First Release) to those who are on the traditional release path and not on the bleeding edge. These features will light up in a rolling upgrade of the various tenants in Office 365.

Some of these enhancements do have PowerShell components.

In addition these user facing features, the cmdlets used in Exchange Online PowerShell have also changed over time. In fact, since February 2017, Exchange Online cmdlets went from 631 to 658.

Added Cmdlets ExO

	Get-SupervisoryReviewReport	Set-TenantAnalyticsConfig
	Get-SupervisoryReviewRule	Set-UserAnalyticsConfig
Delete-QuarantineMessage	Get-SweepRule	Start-MailboxSearch
Disable-SweepRule	Invoke-ComplianceSearchActionStep	Stop-MailboxSearch
Enable-SweepRule	New-ProtectionServicePolicy	Suspend-PublicFolderMailboxMigra-tionRequest
Get-ComplianceTag	New-SafeLinksPolicy	
Get-ComplianceTagStorage	New-SweepRule	Undo-SoftDeletedUnifiedGroup
Get-DataEncryptionPolicy	Remove-CalendarEvents	Update-Recipient
Get-DataRetentionReport	Remove-SweepRule	Validate-RetentionRuleQuery
Get-DlpIncidentDetailReport	set-CASMailboxPlan	Write-AdminAuditLog
Get-MailDetailATPReport	Set-DataEncryptionPolicy	
Get-MailTrafficATPReport	Set-MigrationConfig	
Get-ReportExecutionInstance	Set-Organization	
Get-SupervisoryReviewPolicyReport	Set-ProtectionServicePolicy	
	Set-SafeLinksPolicy	
Get-SupervisoryReviewPolicyV2	Set-SweepRule	

Removed Cmdlets ExO

Get-DataRetentionReport
New-MailboxRelocationRequest
Remove-MRSRequest
Resume-MRSRequest
Set-MailboxRelocationRequest
Suspend-MRSRequest
Get-CaseHoldPolicy
Get-CaseHoldRule
Get-HoldCompliancePolicy
Get-HoldComplianceRule
Get-RetentionCompliancePolicy
Get-RetentionComplianceRule
Set-SafeLinksPolicy
Get-ClassificationRuleCollection

Canceled Features

Cancelled

4

Previously planned updates that are no longer being developed or are indefinitely delayed

Like any other software product or hosted service, feature sets can change. In the case of Microsoft's Office 365, sometimes new, desired features need to be pulled back or canceled due to deployment issues or undesirable results. As of the writing of this book, there are currently 4 canceled features. However, by the time you read this book the list could be smaller or larger. It is guaranteed to change, just like the other lists contained in this chapter.

- Admin App Launcher Customization Tools
- Outlook for iOS: Likes and Reactions
- SharePoint - News and pages: comment on news articles
- SharePoint app for Windows 10 Mobile - team news rollup

Out of these features, only the Outlook for iOS is relevant to Exchange Online and even this feature has no PowerShell component. It specifically has to do with options an end user has when it comes to emails that are displayed in Outlook Apps.

In Development

In development

163

Updates that are currently in development and testing

This set of features is Microsoft's wish list. Not all of the features here will actually exist in the cloud. Some will be removed, most will be implemented, and some will be postponed. Just remember

- Office 365 Groups: default classification and classification description
- Compliance Boundaries
- Cross premises permissions for "send on behalf of"
- Client Access Rules for Exchange Online
- Office 365 Germany: Information Rights Management and Message Encryption
- Office 365 Germany: Information Rights Management and Message Encryption
- Office 365 Germany: Usage reports in the admin center
- Office 365 Germany: Drive Shipping and Network Based Data Import for Office 365
- Removal of Safe Links Re-write for Outlook Client(s)
- Document Preview for Safe Attachments
- Safe Links in Office 365 ProPlus
- Microsoft Teams - Outlook scheduling add-in
- Groups of conditions and configurable logical operators in DLP rules
- Find and upgrade eligible Exchange Online Distribution Lists
- Distribution List owners can upgrade the DLs they own to Office 365 Groups
- Outlook on the web: Share Calendar Availability
- Office 365 Groups: naming policy in Azure Active Directory
- Recover deleted Office 365 Group from Office and Exchange admin centers
- Office 365 Groups: expiring groups
- Office 365 Advanced eDiscovery Optical Character Recognition (OCR)
- Exchange Online Protection phishing protection
- Outlook for Android: Quick Reply
- Outlook for Android: search improvements
- Outlook for Android: Draft sync
- Outlook for Android: Improved conversations
- Outlook for iOS: Draft sync
- Outlook for the web: Attach OneDrive Consumer Files
- Introducing the new Office 365 Group Card
- Change in entry point for add-ins for Outlook in Modern Conversation View
- Outlook for Windows: Improvements to Contact Card
- Outlook for Android: Set status for calendar events
- Outlook for iOS: Set status for calendar events
- Outlook for Android: new RSVP options
- Outlook for iOS: new RSVP options
- Outlook for Android: Scheduling Assistant
- Outlook for Android: Improved account and folder navigation
- Outlook for Android: Likes and Reactions
- eDiscovery Legal Hold Notices
- eDiscovery Export to compressed folder (zip file)
- eDiscovery Case Holds modernization
- Poll for a time to meet
- Outlook for iOS: search improvements
- Service Health Dashboard Update: text/ email notifications (preview)
- Outlook on the web: Sweep Enhancements
- DLP availability in sovereign cloud environments
- Outlook: Drag and drop emails into group mailbox
- Mail tile change in Office 365 App launcher

- Multi-Geo Capabilities in Office 365
- Outlook for Windows: Improved calendar attendance tracking
- Multi Geo Private Preview
- Outlook.com beta includes Calendar and People
- Outlook for iOS & Android: Create and Manage Groups
- Outlook for Mac: Create and Manage Groups
- Outlook for Windows: Redesigned conversation view

From the above list, we can see there are quite a few enhancements for Outlook whether it is for a mobile platform (iOS, Android or Windows Phone) and compliance enhancements (DLP, eDiscovery and Geo boundaries). Additionally Office Groups are being enhanced.

Desktop Clients

Most organizations use Outlook, even if the web interface from Outlook Web App is getting more and more usable for day to day operations with each version of Exchange. The following versions are supported with Exchange Online:

Outlook 2011 for MAC
Outlook 2013
Outlook 2016

https://support.office.com/en-us/article/outlook-updates-472c2322-23a4-4014-8f02-bbc09ad62213

One large caveat is coming for those who are either connecting to or thinking about connecting to Office 365 is that in 2020, the support for non-mainstream clients connecting to Office 365 will be dropped. What does this mean? Well, here are some examples of support dates for various Office suites:

Products Released	Lifecycle Start Date	Mainstream Support End Date	Extended Support End Date
Outlook 2010	7/15/2010	10/13/2015	10/13/2020
Outlook 2013	1/9/2013	4/10/2018	4/11/2023
Outlook 2016	9/22/2015	10/13/2020	10/14/2025

This effectively means that near the end of 2020 Outlook 2013 and 2016 will no longer be able to connect to Office 365. Your only option will be Outlook 2019. While this is not out quite yet from Microsoft, it has been announced for release later in 2018:

https://blogs.office.com/en-us/2017/09/26/the-next-perpetual-release-of-office/

5   Connecting to ExO

In This Chapter

- Connecting to Office 365
- UPN and Primary SMTP Address Updates

As it turns out neither Exchange Server nor Office 365 is an island unto itself. Microsoft has worked hard to construct a platform that is flexible and scalable. As such, it only makes sense to build a Hybrid interface between the two systems. Sometimes this interconnection needs PowerShell to properly manage. Exchange 2010 and Exchange 2013 both have Hybrid options which allow for Exchange on-premises to coexist with Office 365. Exchange 2016 continues this trend and allows for a Hybrid organization with Exchange Online. In fact, Microsoft has recently enhanced its Hybrid Configuration Wizard software to be independent of the Exchange Server.

When it comes to PowerShell, Exchange 2016 and Exchange Online there are lot of similarities as they are both running the same code base. Because the systems provide for different features and are coded to handle things slightly differently for a hosted versus a non-hosted environment, there will be some nuances for what is allowed on-premises versus what is allowed in the hosted Exchange Online service.

For this chapter, we assume that coexistence has been configured between Exchange on-premises and Exchange Online. Since the book is written for Exchange Online, the PowerShell cmdlets will focus on the functionality it brings. However, most of the cmdlets, scripts and one-liners will work with Exchange 2016 as well.

Notes
- If moving from a non-Exchange mail system in your local AD, install Exchange prior to installing any directory synchronization tool like Azure AD Connect.
- Make sure User Principal Names (UPN) match the Primary SMTP address when a directory sync is used.
- Installing an Exchange server in most scenarios, because using ADSI Edit to managed mail attributes is not supported.

Connecting to Office 365

Connecting PowerShell to Office 365 requires the proper version of Windows PowerShell Snap-in to handle the connection. Make sure the management computer needs to be Windows 7+ and have PowerShell 2.0 and .Net 4.5.

Office 365 has many connection points in order to manage its various services. These connection points are URLs that PowerShell uses in order to execute remote PowerShell cmdlets and scripts. Here is a sample of the connection points available (a.k.a. Connection URIs):

Service	ConnectionURI
Exchange Online	https://ps.outlook.com/powershell/
SharePoint Online	https://domainhost-admin.sharepoint.com
Security and compliance	https://ps.compliance.protection.outlook.com/powershell-liveid/

In order to connect to these services, PowerShell need additional modules in order for the connections to be successful. The current download for the Azure PowerShell module is located here -https://aka.ms/webpi-azps

The installation package is part of a larger product called 'Microsoft Web Platform Installer 5.0':

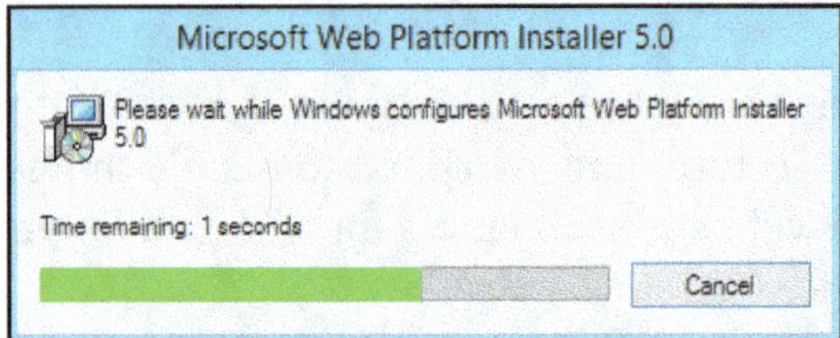

The install process for the Module is completed by clicking 'Install' and 'I Accept':

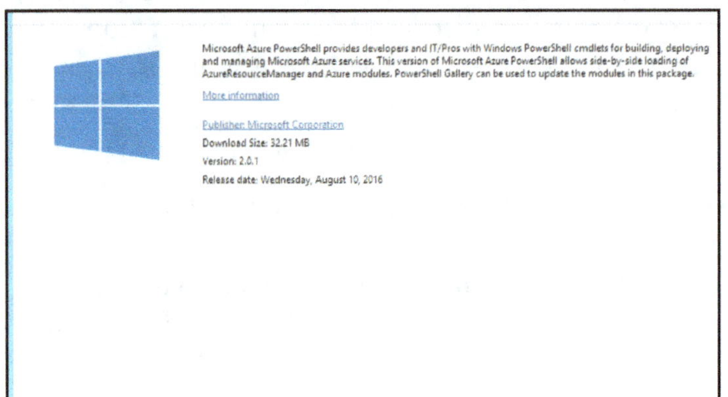

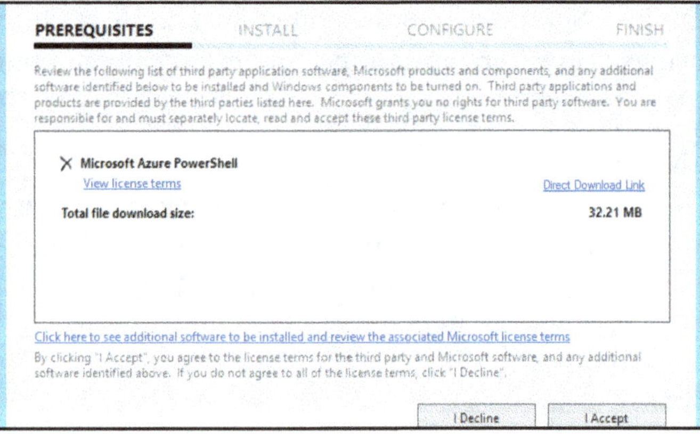

Then wait for the install to complete and click finish. The module is now installed.

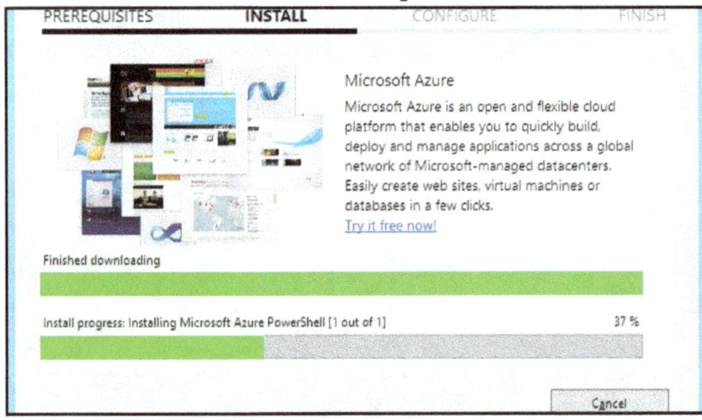

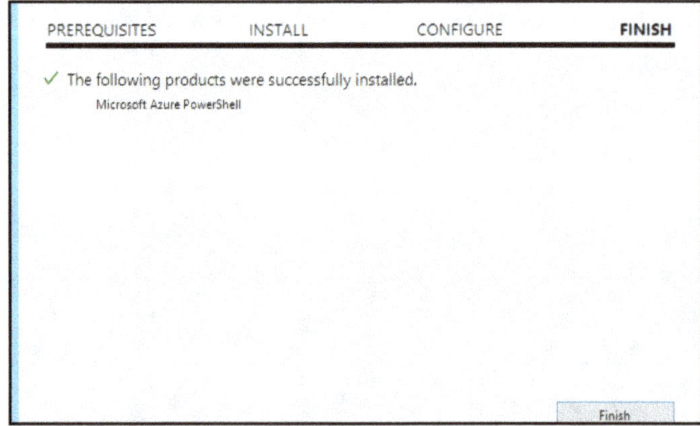

PowerShell Cmdlets

In order to connect, to Exchange Online via PowerShell, a series of cmdlets needs to be run. Make sure to start Windows PowerShell as an Administrator. First, Exchange Online credentials should be stored in a variable:

$Office365Cred = Get-Credential

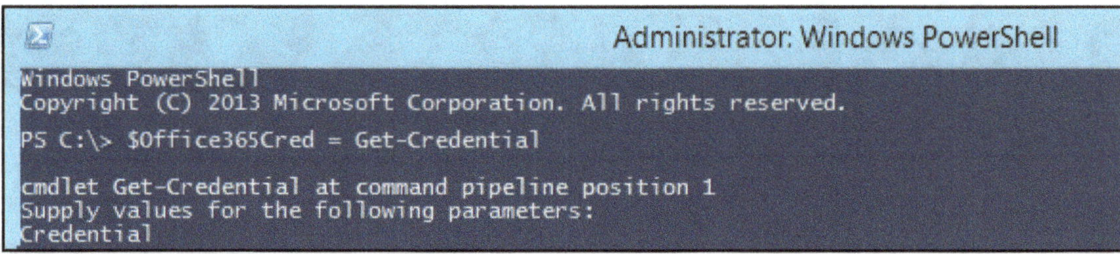

A pop-up is displayed which needs to be filled with credentials for an account with proper rights in the tenant:

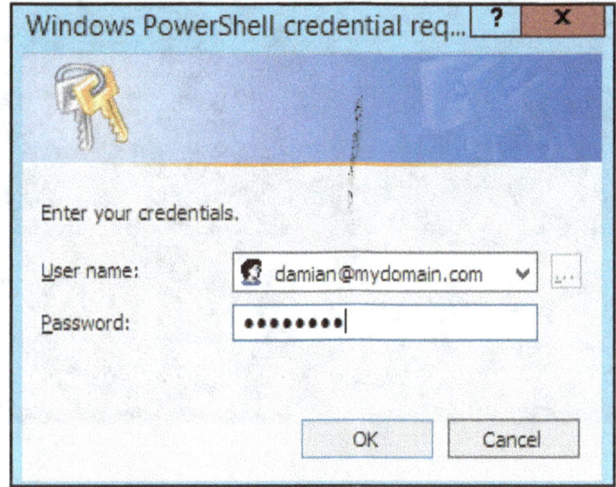

These credentials are then used as part of the PowerShell session parameters. These are again stored in a variable for a set of connection parameters:

$Session = New-PSSession -ConfigurationName Microsoft.Exchange -ConnectionUri https://ps.outlook. com/powershell/ -Credential $Office365Cred -Authentication Basic -AllowRedirection

The $Session variables are then fed into the Import-PSSession cmdlet:

Import-PSSession $Session

Once the connection has been established, PowerShell can be used to work with objects that are synced to Azure AD. The caveat is that if the object is synced from an on-premises Active Directory, then some attributes may not be manageable.

Office 365 Cmdlets

Now that a connection has been established, we need to figure out what cmdlets are available in the tenant. In PowerShell a group of cmdlets can be filtered based off the server name. For an Office 365 tenant, there is no 'server' to filter for. However, there is a name revealed after the Import-PSSession is established, in this example 'tmp_ffz2bqqb.u40', that can be queried, but this name will vary on each connect.

Cmdlets can then be found with this filter:

Get-Command | Where {$_.ModuleName -eq 'tmp_1b3asmch.buw'}

```
CommandType      Name                                  Version    Source

Function         Add-AvailabilityAddressSpace          1.0        tmp_1b3asmch.buw
Function         Add-DistributionGroupMember           1.0        tmp_1b3asmch.buw
Function         Add-MailboxFolderPermission           1.0        tmp_1b3asmch.buw
Function         Add-MailboxLocation                   1.0        tmp_1b3asmch.buw
Function         Add-MailboxPermission                 1.0        tmp_1b3asmch.buw
Function         Add-ManagementRoleEntry               1.0        tmp_1b3asmch.buw
Function         Add-PublicFolderClientPermission      1.0        tmp_1b3asmch.buw
Function         Add-RecipientPermission               1.0        tmp_1b3asmch.buw
Function         Add-RoleGroupMember                   1.0        tmp_1b3asmch.buw
Function         Add-UnifiedGroupLinks                 1.0        tmp_1b3asmch.buw
Function         Clear-ActiveSyncDevice                1.0        tmp_1b3asmch.buw
Function         Clear-MobileDevice                    1.0        tmp_1b3asmch.buw
Function         Clear-TextMessagingAccount            1.0        tmp_1b3asmch.buw
Function         Compare-TextMessagingVerificationCode 1.0        tmp_1b3asmch.buw
Function         Complete-MigrationBatch               1.0        tmp_1b3asmch.buw
Function         Delete-QuarantineMessage              1.0        tmp_1b3asmch.buw
Function         Disable-App                           1.0        tmp_1b3asmch.buw
```

Connect to Azure Active Directory

After connecting to your tenant, there is an additional connection needed using the Connect-MSOLService cmdlet. The cmdlet provides a connection to the Microsoft Azure Active Directory for your tenant. The connection allows access to user objects in your tenant. To connect, either pass stored credentials with a variable or just type in 'Connect-MSOLService' and enter credentials into the pop-up box that is presented.

Microsoft has also added a Multi-Factor Authentication (MFA) option for connecting to various PowerShell resources in Office 365. These include Exchange Online, Azure, Azure Resource Manager and more. Consider enabling this for an additional security layer for your Office 365 tenant.

   ** **Note** ** What's available for PowerShell MFA could change at any time, verify what works before trying to connect with this method.

Managing Office 365 Mailboxes from On-Premises PowerShell

In an Exchange Hybrid environment mailboxes, can exists on-premises and in the Office 365 tenant. In addition to regular mailboxes, archive mailboxes also can exist on-premises or in Office 365. The mailbox and archive mailbox can also be on the same service (Exchange or Exchange Online). PowerShell cmdlets exist to configure and manage these objects:

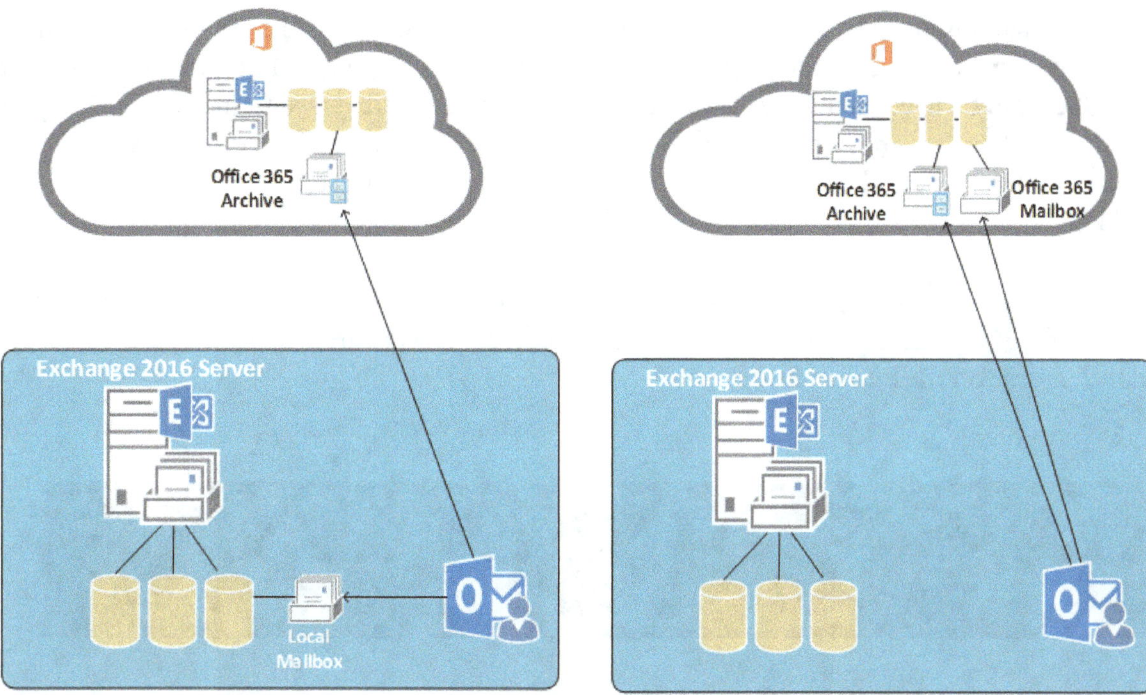

To manage the 'hybrid' environment, let's look for cmdlets on the Exchange 2016 server. What cmdlets exist that are based off a single keyword, 'Remote'? Here is a list of the cmdlets with the keyword:

Get-Command *Remote* | ft -Auto

To further narrow this down for our purposes of managing from the local server:

```
CommandType        Name                      ModuleName
-----------        ----                      ----------
Function           Disable-RemoteMailbox     16-tap-ex02.16-tap.local
Function           Enable-RemoteMailbox      16-tap-ex02.16-tap.local
Function           Get-RDRemoteApp           RemoteDesktop
Function           Get-RDRemoteDesktop       RemoteDesktop
Function           Get-RemoteDomain          16-tap-ex02.16-tap.local
Function           Get-RemoteMailbox         16-tap-ex02.16-tap.local
Function           New-RDRemoteApp           RemoteDesktop
Function           New-RemoteDomain          16-tap-ex02.16-tap.local
Function           New-RemoteMailbox         16-tap-ex02.16-tap.local
Function           Remove-RDRemoteApp        RemoteDesktop
Function           Remove-RemoteDomain       16-tap-ex02.16-tap.local
Function           Remove-RemoteMailbox      16-tap-ex02.16-tap.local
Function           Set-RDRemoteApp           RemoteDesktop
Function           Set-RDRemoteDesktop       RemoteDesktop
Function           Set-RemoteDomain          16-tap-ex02.16-tap.local
Function           Set-RemoteMailbox         16-tap-ex02.16-tap.local
```

Get-Command *remote* | Where {$_.ModuleName -eq "16-tap-ex02.16-tap.local"}

```
CommandType        Name                      ModuleName
-----------        ----                      ----------
Function           Disable-RemoteMailbox     16-tap-ex02.16-tap.local
Function           Enable-RemoteMailbox      16-tap-ex02.16-tap.local
Function           Get-RemoteDomain          16-tap-ex02.16-tap.local
Function           Get-RemoteMailbox         16-tap-ex02.16-tap.local
Function           New-RemoteDomain          16-tap-ex02.16-tap.local
Function           New-RemoteMailbox         16-tap-ex02.16-tap.local
Function           Remove-RemoteDomain       16-tap-ex02.16-tap.local
Function           Remove-RemoteMailbox      16-tap-ex02.16-tap.local
Function           Set-RemoteDomain          16-tap-ex02.16-tap.local
Function           Set-RemoteMailbox         16-tap-ex02.16-tap.local
```

Most of the cmdlets needed for managing mailboxes will have 'RemoteMailbox' in the name.

A remote mailbox is a mailbox in Office 365 whose user account is a mail enabled user that resides in Active Directory. The mailbox is recognized in the Exchange 2016 Exchange Admin Center (EAC) under Recipients - Mailboxes. PowerShell can be used to manage these mailboxes with the cmdlets we found above. To query for mailboxes in Exchange 2016 that are remote mailboxes, use the Get-RemoteMailbox cmdlet which is distinct from the Get-Mailbox cmdlet which shows only the mailboxes that are on-premises. All queries and cmdlets run against the local AD object.

When it comes to archive mailboxes, management depends on where the mailbox is. If the mailbox is on-premises and the archive is in Office 365 then the Get-Mailbox cmdlet would display the archive properties. The properties of the online archive appear on the local mailbox:

Get-Mailbox | fl Archive*

```
ArchiveGuid                   : 78ccc49c-d236-4efb-8af9-331ed1641964
ArchiveName                   : {In-Place Archive }
ArchiveQuota                  : 100 GB (107,374,182,400 bytes)
ArchiveWarningQuota           : 90 GB (96,636,764,160 bytes)
ArchiveDomain                 : domian.mail.onmicrosoft.com
ArchiveStatus                 : None
```

** **Note** **

One key factor of having archive mailboxes in the Office 365 tenant is that in order for archiving to work properly a mailbox called 'FederatedEmail.4c1f4d8b-8179-4148-93bf-00a95fa1e042' needs to exist and be accessible. If this mailbox is missing, then Hybrid mail flow could become compromised. Specifically messages that need to be delivered to an archive mailbox in Office 365 will cause the transport service on an Exchange server to crash. To fix this issue, the arbitration mailbox may need to be recreated.

Following Microsoft's article on recreating system mailboxes, make sure to run these two steps:

From the Exchange media that matches your Exchange 2016 build:

Setup.com /PrepareAD

This will create missing system mailboxes in Exchange. However these will then need to be enabled in Active Directory. Run the following cmdlet to enable the Federated mailbox (make sure to be exact on the name):

Enable-Mailbox –Arbitration "FederatedEmail.4c1f4d8b-8179-4148-93bf-00a95fa1e042"

Now messages destined for the archive mailboxes in Office 365 will be delivered.

Example 1

For this scenario, user mailboxes are moving from Exchange 2010/2013 and there is a desire or requirement to move all mailboxes. An Exchange 2016 server be used as the management server. The Hybrid Configuration Wizard is used to configure this server as the connection point between Exchange on-premises and Exchange Online. Active Directory is currently at the Windows 2008 R2 level for the domain and forest functional level. Once all of the Exchange Server 2010 servers have been patched to the latest Update Roll-up, Exchange 2016 can be installed.

The new Exchange 2016 server will now serve as the organizations "hybrid" server for the Office 365 deployment. In this example, the cmdlets for managing Office 365 mailboxes should only be used if there are issues with the moved accounts.

Cmdlets For Management
Get-RemoteMailbox
Set-RemoteMailbox
New-RemoteMailbox

What are these cmdlets used for? Get-RemoteMailbox can be used for documentation of mailboxes in Office 365. Here are some examples from Microsoft on the proper usage of these cmdlets.

Some practical examples:

```
----------------------------- Example 1 -----------------------------
This example returns a summary list of all remote mailboxes in your organization.
Get-RemoteMailbox
```

```
----------------------------- Example 2 -----------------------------
Get-RemoteMailbox -Identity laura@contoso.com | Format-List
----------------------------- Example 3 -----------------------------
Get-RemoteMailbox -Credential $Credentials
```

Example 1 would be used to get basic mailbox information:
Get-RemoteMailbox | ft SamAccountName, UserPrincipalName, RemoteRoutingAddress

```
SamAccountName  UserPrincipalName        RemoteRoutingAddress
--------------  -----------------        --------------------
Damian          Damian@domain.com        SMTP:damian@domain.onmicrosoft.com
```

Example 2 would be used to get any information on litigation, retention, and InPlace mailbox holds:
Get-RemoteMailbox|ft SamAccountName,LitigationHoldEnabled,RetentionHoldEnabled,InPlaceHolds -Auto

```
SamAccountName  LitigationHoldEnabled  RetentionHoldEnabled  InPlaceHolds
--------------  ---------------------  --------------------  ------------
Damian                                 False                 False {}
```

Example 3 covers some other critical mailbox settings:
Get-RemoteMailbox | ft SamAccountName, ArchiveState, SingleItemRecoveryEnabled, HiddenFromAddressListsEnabled -Auto

```
SamAccountName  ArchiveState  SingleItemRecoveryEnabled  HiddenFromAddressListsEnabled
--------------  ------------  -------------------------  -----------------------------
Damian          None          False                      False
```

Set-RemoteMailbox is used for changing settings on mailboxes. Perhaps the Remote Routing email address is incorrect and needs to be changed:

Set-RemoteMailbox "Damian Scoles" –RemoteRoutingAddress damian@tenant.onmicrosoft.com

New-RemoteMailbox is used for creating a mailbox that has a local Active Directory user and a mailbox in Exchange Online. Some examples by Microsoft are shown on the next page:

Get-Help New-RemoteMailbox –Examples

```
----------------------------- Example 1 -----------------------------

$Credentials = Get-Credential

Then run the New-RemoteMailbox cmdlet to create the mail user.

New-RemoteMailbox -Name "Kim Akers" -Password $Credentials.Password -UserPrincipalName kim@corp.contoso.com

After the new mail user is created, directory synchronization synchronizes the new mail user to the service and
the associated mailbox is created.

----------------------------- Example 2 -----------------------------

$Credentials = Get-Credential

Then run the New-RemoteMailbox cmdlet to create the mail user.


New-RemoteMailbox -Name "Kim Akers" -Password $Credentials.Password -UserPrincipalName kim@corp.contoso.com
-OnPremisesOrganizationalUnit "corp.contoso.com/Archive Users" -Archive
```

In practical terms, using this PS cmdlet is the simplest environment to manage from end to end as all servers are Exchange and PowerShell can be used against all servers, whether Exchange 2010, 2016 or Exchange Online.

Example 2

For this scenario, a company uses a non-Exchange Server mail system for their email system. Company employees with email may or may not have user objects in Active Directory. For a migration scenario where the company is moving to Office 365, all users in the email system will get Active Directory accounts. HR provides a list of employees in CSV format with some basic information about the employees. IT Management wants the employees listed in the CSV file to have AD object because they will have mailboxes in Office 365. The company's main corporate SMTP domain is @contoso.com. This address needs to be assigned as a UPN and the users need to have this set as their email address in Exchange as a mail user.

Exchange 2016 is installed at the latest CU release available. Once Exchange 2016 is installed, the AD accounts will be created. Once all Active Directory accounts are created, all the users in the CSV file will need to have AD accounts created, be mail enabled, accounts synchronized to Office 365, accounts converted into Remote Mailboxes in EXO, then the mailbox data can be migrated from the third-party email system to Exchange Online.

First, we need to start with the CSV file that was provided by HR. The fields and a data sample look something like this:

```
FirstName,LastName,Alias,PrimarySMTPAddress,Title
Damian,Scoles,dscoles,dscoles@contoso.com,ITGuy
David,Stork,dstork,dstork@contoso.com,ITManager
```

… and so on …

Next, a script is needed to simply add users from the CSV. A crucial component is that we need to make sure that the user account does not exist. This will be done with two verification steps - alias and user principal name. The user principal name will match the primary SMTP address.

Script # 1 - Add Users to Active Directory

First store the CSV file from HR in a variable called $csv using the Import-CSV cmdlet.

```
# Read in the CSV file
$CSV = Import-CSV "c:\downloads\Mail-System-List.csv"
```

Now that the values are stored in a $CSV variable, a loop can be created with each line of the CSV, which can be accessed with a $line variable.

```
Foreach ($Line in $Csv) {
```

With the loop started, the script will clear and set variables needed for the loop. For this script, two variables (UPN and Alias) have their values reset. Then the DisplayName variable is populated with the values of the First and Last name variables.

```
# Variable configuration / reset
$LastName = $$Line.Last
$FirstName = $Line.First
$NoAlias = $Null
$NoUPN = $Null
$DisplayName = "$FirstName $LastName"
```

Next the script needs to check for users in Active Directory using aliases. Note that the test will be performed in with Try {} Catch {} code block. If the Get-ADUser finds a user in AD then the rest of the script will be skipped because the $NoAlias variable (set to $Null at the beginning of the loop) cannot pass the test posed by 'If ($NoAlias)'. Thus the script skips to the ELSE section of the IF...ELSE code block:

```
# Verification Step One - Alias
Try {
    $User = Get-ADUser -Identity $Line.Alias -ErrorAction STOP
} Catch {
    $NoAlias = $True
}
```

If the $NoAlias variable is set to $True (no user found), then the next part of the script is initiated. Another Try {} Catch {} section is used, this time the code tries to match the UPN of a user account. If no user match is found, then $NoUPN becomes $True as well:

```
If ($NoAlias) {
    # Verification Step Two - UPN
    Try {
        $User = Get-ADUser -UserPrincipalName $Line.PrimarySMTPAddress -ErrorAction STOP
    } Catch {
        $NoUPN = $True
    }
}
```

Now if the script has passed both tests ($NoUPN = $True and $NoAlias = $True) then another Try {} Catch {} section is used to create the user. If the user is created, no error message occurs. If the creation fails, then an error message is displayed:

```
If ($NoUPN) {
  Try {
  New-ADUser -Name $Line.Alias -GivenName $FirstName -Surname -$LastName -Title $Line.Title
  -Displayname $DisplayName -ErrorAction STOP
  } Catch {
  Write-Host "Could not create the new user in Active Directory." -ForegroundColor Red
}
```

Lastly, if those tests fail, a message appears that states the user exists and a user will not be created.

```
  } Else {
    Write-Host "The user already exists in Active Directory and was not created." -ForegroundColor
    Yellow
  }
}
```

Alternative Example

If all the users that were in AD prior to running the above script were already mail enabled, and they would show up in Exchange as a mailuser, the New-MailUser cmdlet could be used instead of New-ADUser. The reason for that is New-MailUser allows for the creation of an Active Directory object (Mail User) and allow Exchange to manage it directly. This would skip the need for step one and two. The reason we are not using this method in the book is so that you, the end user of PowerShell, understand the full process of object creation from nothing to a Remote Mailbox.

Now that the users are created, we need to log onto the Exchange 2016 server to enable all user objects from the CSV as Mail Users. If you have a large Active Directory environment you may have to wait for replication to finish.

** **Note** The above script could be enhanced to make a complete report of new users created as well as a report of what users that were found in Active Directory. See the Reporting Chapter 16 for steps on how to create reports.

Part Two

For this next step we need to mail enable all users that have mailboxes in the third party messaging system. These users are all listed in the same CSV from HR. The reason we need to mail enable them is so that they can be managed from an on-premises Exchange server. After the users are mail enabled and after they are synchronized to the cloud, you can proceed to the third script which will explain how to convert a mail user to a mail enabled user.

```
Get-Help Enable-MailUser –Examples
```

```
---------------------------- Example 1 ----------------------------
This example mail-enables user John with the external email address john@contoso.com.
Enable-MailUser -Identity John –ExternalEmailAddress john@contoso.com
```

For the below script sample, the HR's CSV file is read into the $CSV variable and then a Foreach loop is used to go through each line. A Try{} Catch {} code block is used to mail enable the user and if it fails an error message is displayed.

Script # 2 - Mail Enable All Users in CSV

```
# Read in the HR CSV file
$CSV = Import-CSV "c:\downloads\Mail-System-List.csv"
Foreach ($Line in $Csv) {
   $DisplayName = "$First $Last"
   # Mail Enable the User
   Try {
      Enable-MailUser -Identity $Line.Alias -ExternalEmailAddress $Line.PrimarySMTPAddress
   } Catch {
      Write-Host "Could not mail enable the user object for $DisplayName."
   }
}
```

Results of the script:

```
[PS] C:\Downloads>.\MailEnable-Test.ps1

Name                                          RecipientType
----                                          -------------
William Tell                                  MailUser
Benjamin Franklin                             MailUser
```

For this script a couple of new cmdlets will be used for Remote Mailbox creation:

Get-Help New-MailUser –Examples

```
-------------------------- Example 1 --------------------------
New-MailUser -Name "Ed Meadows" -ExternalEmailAddress ed@tailspintoys.com -MicrosoftOnlineServicesID
ed@tailspintoys -Password (ConvertTo-SecureString -String 'P@ssw0rd1' -AsPlainText -Force)

-------------------------- Example 2 --------------------------
$password = Read-Host "Enter password" -AsSecureString
New-MailUser -Name "Ed Meadows" -ExternalEmailAddress ed@tailspintoys.com -UserPrincipalName ed@contoso
-Password $password
```

Get-Help Enable-RemoteMailbox –Examples

```
-------------------------- Example 1 --------------------------
Enable-RemoteMailbox "Kim Akers" -RemoteRoutingAddress "kima@contoso.mail.onmicrosoft.com
After the user is mail-enabled, directory synchronization synchronizes the mail-enabled user to the service and
the associated mailbox is created.

-------------------------- Example 2 --------------------------
Enable-RemoteMailbox "Kim Akers" -RemoteRoutingAddress "kima@contoso.mail.onmicrosoft.com -Archive
```

Example Summary

So what did we learn in these examples?   We learned that in order to properly manage Office 365 mailboxes that have accounts in the on-premises Active Directory, we need to satisfy a few requirements. First is that all mailboxes will need an Active Directory user account. These same Active Directory users are then mail enabled. Once they are mail enabled, they show up in the Exchange Administration Console as mail enabled users. Finally, the mail enabled users are converted to Remote Mailboxes. The last step can only be performed once the mailbox has moved off the old platform.

UPN and Primary SMTP Address Updates

In a Hybrid environment, it is sometimes necessary to change UPNs or Primary SMTP addresses. An example of this more complex Hybrid scenario, a company is consolidating email domains to a brand new SMTP domain. In doing so, the UPNs and Primary SMTP addresses for all users need to be from LittleBox.Com to BigBox.Com.

Example Script – Changing UPN and SMTP Addresses

```
# Import the AD Module
Import-Module ActiveDirectory

# Import the CSV File
$Users = Import-CSV "c:\scripting\mailboxusers.csv"
$Domain = 'BigBox.Com'

Foreach ($Line in $Users) {
        $Alias = $Line.Alias
        $Primary = $Alias+'@'+$Domain
        Get-Mailbox $Alias |Set-Mailbox -PrimarySmtpAddress $Primary -UserPrincipalName $Primary
        Get-AdUser $Alias | Set-ADUser -EmailAddress $Primary
}
```

This script needs to be run from a PowerShell console that has the Exchange Server cmdlets due to the Set-Mailbox cmdlet. This PowerShell Console can be on an Exchange Server or on a management workstation.

**** Notes ****

- Changing your users UPN should be done prior to syncing accounts to Office 365. Some features may break or have issues if these are changed post sync.
- There are some applications, internal applications for example, that may not work if the UPN is changed. Any change to a user object's UPN should be tested prior to rolling this change to all users. LDAP queries based on this property could fail and if users are logging into their workstations with their UPN they should be made aware before the change is made.
- You might have to add a UPN Suffix to your domain, but beware that you cannot add a suffix to a forest if that forest has a trust with another forest/domain with the domain name as FQDN.

6   Identity Management

In this Chapter

Introduction
Directory Synchronization
Preparing Your AD - IDFix
Install of Azure AD Connect
PowerShell and Directory Synchronization
What Needs to be Performed Where?
Licensing
Azure AD Recycle Bin

Introduction

When investing in a cloud provider like Office 365, identity management becomes a clearly important component. For this book we will cover identity management with respect to Office 365 (Azure Active Directory), Active Directory and PowerShell. There are a few ways to handle identities in Office 365 – separate directories, hybrid and cloud only directory. Each of these has its advantages and disadvantages and these should be considered before engaging in any cloud services with Office 365.

- **Separate Directories** – Internal Active Directory and Azure Active Directory are completely separate. In this environment a user maintains two different identities and possibly two different passwords.
- **Hybrid** – Internal Active Directory users and group objects are synced to Azure Active Directory. Users have one identity and possibly a shared password.
- **Cloud Only** – No on-premises Active Directory. Company is using only cloud identities for their application authentication.

For this chapter and the majority of the book, we will work with hybrid environments as this arrangement is the most commonly used. This does not mean that the concepts in this book won't translate to the other two scenarios, but there will be different ways to handle examples and scripts in this book for those scenarios. With a hybrid environment, a company can have on-premises services and services while maintaining cloud services and share a single identity source. This is certainly the biggest strength of a hybrid environment. As such its configuration should be planned and setup. The two major considerations are components that Microsoft supplies for identity management:

- **Active Directory Federation Services (ADFS)** – Can provide a login portal for Office 365 services. Allows for proxied authentication to an on-premises Active Directory. Can also be leveraged for additional application authentication beyond Office 365 as well as complicated claims rules for additional login and resource access control.
- **Directory Synchronization** – Synchronizes objects from an on-premises Active Directory to Azure Active Directory (Office 365). Can provide additional functionality, including password synchronization, password write-back, Exchange Hybrid and more. The product has also changed names many times over the years.

While ADFS can be beneficial to a company using Office 365 services we will not be discussing it for this book. Instead we will turn to directory synchronization and how it and PowerShell are used for identity management in Office 365.

Directory Synchronization

What is it?

Dirsync is the synchronization of on-premises Active Directory objects to Azure Active Directory and thus Office 365. It essentially mirrors your AD in the cloud and keeps it constantly updated. The synchronized objects in O365 can now for instance be users and groups. You choose the objects you want to synchronize. In some cases information or even objects can be synced from the cloud to onprem, depending on what options are chosen for the Azure AD Connect configuration. Objects anchored in AD, should be managed in AD. There are protections in placed that block changes to these objects in Azure AD. A good, technical deep dive can be found here:

https://dirteam.com/dave/2015/03/30/azure-active-directory-synchronization-an-introduction-part-1/

Commonly deployed with Office 365 services, directory synchronization now provides enterprises with a compelling set of features and functionality that precludes the use of ADFS. Additionally with the new Conditional Access feature, the case for using ADFS solely for Office 365 is even less compelling. However, it should be known that the feature set is continually changing over time. Microsoft provides this synchronization product that has changed from relying on ADFS to supplanting it for most configuration of Office 365.

History

Here is a brief history of the directory synchronization product and its changes over the years:

Current revision history of Directory Synchronization

https://docs.microsoft.com/en-us/azure/active-directory/connect/active-directory-aadconnect-version-history#115610

Directory Sync – First sync client for connecting your on-premises AD to BPOS. BPOS was replaced by Office 365 and DirSync continually added features with each revision. DirSync also initially started out as a 32-bit program and shifted to 64-bit prior to its replaced came into being. This product is currently out of support as of April of 2017.

Azure AD Synchronization – This was the first major revision of the directory synchronization product by Microsoft. The last version of this product was 1.0.494.0501 released in May of 2015. Its initial release was 1.0.419.0911 release in September of 2014. With such a short time line, the product It did however, add some features along the way – password sync with multiple Active Directories to Office 365, OAuth2 support, password sync. This product is currently out of support as of April of 2017.

Azure AD Connect – This is the latest iteration of the directory synchronization product. According to Microsoft, this is a product rename of the product. This renamed directory synchronization product added quite a lot of new features with its release. The current revision, at the time of the writing of this book was 1.1.640 (Sept 5, 2017). The initial release was version 1.0.8641.0 and this was released on June 2015. Additional features provided by the product – Express installation option, configuring ADFS, Upgrade from DirSync, staging mode, reduced sync interval from 3 hours to 30 min, Domain and OU filtering, scheduling of sync, PowerShell enhancements and more.

As we can see, the directory synchronization product has changed greatly over the years.

Two Phrases and Their Distinctions

When dealing with Exchange Online and Directories that support it, there tends to be some confusion among certain terms that are used for their configuration. Let's see if we can untangle the web of verbiage here.

Directory Synchronization - This process simply covers the copying of objects and properties of one directory to another directory. Usually the source of truth, at least when it comes to Office 365, is Active Directory. It could potentially be other directories, but for this book we'll assume AD. The synchronization of these objects is done irrespective of Exchange Online or Exchange on-premises or both. It is a separate process. If Exchange were not in the directory, the Directory Synchronization process would still operate and copy objects to Office 365. These objects could then be utilized to create mailboxes and be used in other work flows and services in Office 365.

Hybrid - Exchange Hybrid is the coexistence of two Exchange environments (on-premises and online). These two environments rely on the synchronization process of Azure AD Connect which is a directory synchronization process. The directory sync process not only syncs up the usual AD objects and properties, but if Exchange is installed, the synchronization process will also copy Exchange related attributes as well. Thus in Hybrid mode having Exchange on-premises and a directory synchronization server are key requirements to make it work.

Preparing Your AD - IDFIX

For Hybrid environments with an on-premises Active Directory and Azure AD, one of the key component of a user's identity is the User Principal Names (UPNs) for all users. The UPN is important for accessing resources in a Hybrid environment. Microsoft recommends that the UPN and the Primary SMTP address match (and SIP for those who use Skype for Business on-premises or Online). This recommendation is so that the end user does not experience pop-ups and is able to connect to resources without issue.

In order to validate or verify that this is correctly configured, Microsoft provides a tool called IdFix. This utility will analyze the various attributes in Active Directory and determine if there are any potential issues with connecting to an Office 365 tenant. The tool can be downloaded from here as of the writing of this book:

https://www.microsoft.com/en-us/download/details.aspx?id=36832

Any errors that are found by this tool should be remediated prior to a directory sync tool being installed and syncing data to Office 365 – Azure AD Connect for example. Once the tool is downloaded, it can be run just by double-clicking on the executable:

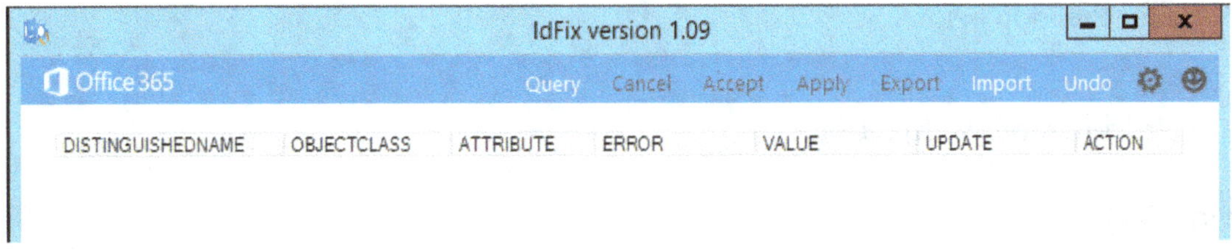

Click Query to see if there are any issues that need to be resolved:

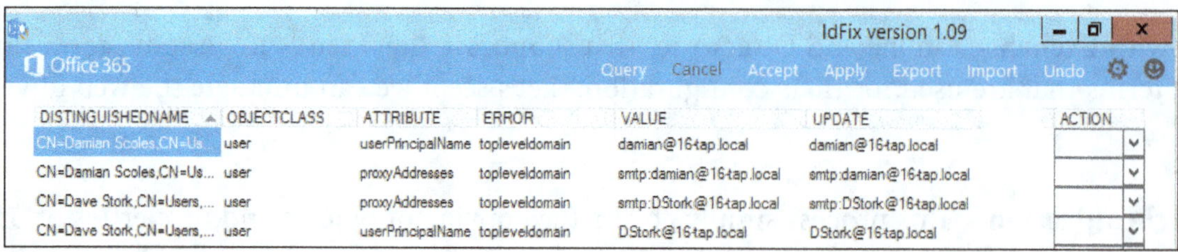

Although IdFix can fix a lot of things by itself, for this example we will export these results as a CSV. Simply click 'Export' and select a location to export the results to a CSV file. Since IdFix can export the results in a CSV format, the CSV file can be used with PowerShell later. The CSV file can be used as a data source for correcting user issues with PowerShell.

Let's take the IdFix CSV file and use it to correct any user objects with an invalid User Principal Name. The script needs to read in the CSV file, run a loop to process all the entries and correct only those invalid entries matching that criteria. The CSV file contains the following fields [As seen above]:

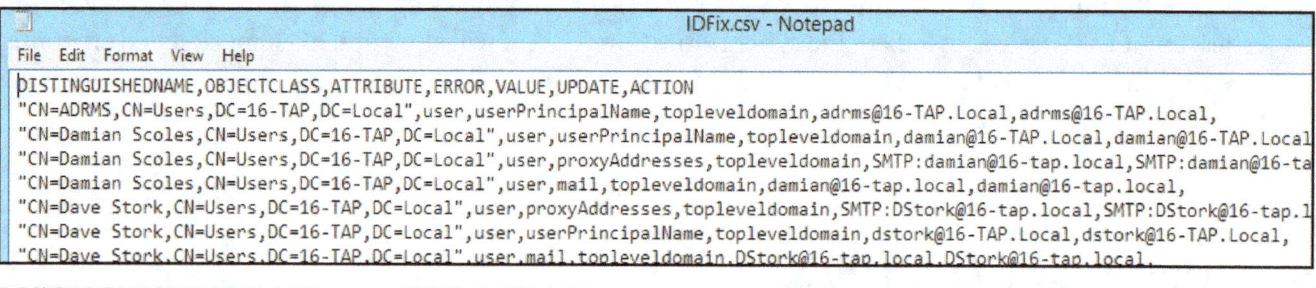

DISTINGUISHEDNAME	OBJECTCLASS	ATTRIBUTE
ERROR	VALUE	UPDATE
ACTION		

For the below example, the UserPrincipalName needs to be updated to match the primary SMTP address:

Example Script – Fix UserPrincipalName

This code section will start an error log file and populate header information of the file:

```
# Get date for the file name
$Date = Get-Date -Format "MM.dd.yyyy-hh.mm-tt"
# Create a file for errors
$ErrorFileName = "C:\Downloads\IdFix\$date-Errors.txt"
$ScriptErrors = "This is the error file for problems creating or modifying users on $date.`r
`n-------------------------------------------------------------- `r`n" | Out-File -FilePath $ErrorFileName
```

The CSV file is imported for the loop below:

```
# Import the CSV File
$Csv = Import-Csv "c:\downloads\idfix\idfix.csv"

Foreach ($Line in $Csv) {
```

First, only lines with the ObjectClass of 'User' to proceed:

```
If ($Line.ObjectClass-eq "User") {
```

Then, examining the same line, the script looks for an 'Attribute' value of UserPrincipalName and allows it to proceed:

```
If ($Line.Attribute -eq "UserPrincipalName") {
```

This section verifies the identity of the user, so that the correct mailbox can be modified:

```
$User = $Line.DistinguishedName
Try {
    $Address = (Get-Mailbox $user -ErrorAction STOP).PrimarySmtpAddress
} Catch {
    $ScriptErrors = "User $User mailbox was not found." | Out-File -FilePath $ErrorFileName
}
```

Sets the Primary SMTP address to be applied to the user to correct the error:

```
$PrimarySMTPAddress = $Address.Address
```

This code section sets the user properties correctly to fix the issues found in the IdFix report:

```
Try {
    Set-ADUser -Identity $User -UserPrincipalName $PrimarySmtpAddress
} Catch {
    $ScriptErrors = "Unable to change the UPN for the user $user" | Out-File -FilePath $ErrorFileName
}
```

Post script run, an IdFix query is run again:

DISTINGUISHEDNAME ▲	OBJECTCLASS	ATTRIBUTE	ERROR	VALUE	UPDATE
CN=Damian Scoles,CN=Us...	user	proxyAddresses	topleveldomain	smtp:damian@16-tap.local	smtp:damian@16-tap.local
CN=Dave Stork,CN=Users,...	user	proxyAddresses	topleveldomain	smtp:DStork@16-tap.local	smtp:DStork@16-tap.local

For the next error on the list, there is an issue with one of the defined proxy addresses that are on all accounts in Active Directory. To change this, the default address policy may need to be removed and then the offending proxy address can be removed.

Example Script – Remove Bad SMTP Addresses

The purpose of the script is to query only users that have ProxyAddress issues (as found in the CSV file from IdFix). After those values are filtered, the script will attempt to remove the offending SMTP address from the ProxyAddresses on a user account. Any errors encountered will be appended to a log file for later review. The script code is below.

This section grabs the current date and stores the value in a particular format in the $Date variable:

```
# Get date for the file name
$Date = Get-Date -Format "MM.dd.yyyy-hh.mm-tt"
```

A logging file gets created, with a unique name and is populated with a header for reference:

```
# Create a file for errors
$ErrorFileName = "C:\Downloads\IdFix\$date-ProxyErrors.txt"
$ScriptErrors = "This is the error file for problems creating or modifying users on $Date.`r
`n---------------------------------------------------------------- `r`n" | Out-File -FilePath $ErrorFileName
```

Then the IdFix CSV file is imported into the $CSV variable:

```
# Import the CSV File
$Csv = Import-Csv "c:\downloads\idfix\idfix.csv"
```

This loop has some complicated steps and each will be reviewed and split for clarity. First the $CSV file is used for a Foreach loop, with each line in the CSV loaded into the $Line variable:

```
Foreach ($Line in $Csv) {
```

Since the script is for user objects only, the first IF…THEN loop is started to filter for only user objects:

```
If ($Line.OBJECTCLASS -eq "User") {
```

Since the script then looks for the ProxyAddresses issues, another IF…THEN loop is started to filter for this:

```
If ($Line.Attribute -eq "ProxyAddresses") {
```

Variables are set for the loop, two are pulled from the $CSV and one is $Null for each loop. The $BadSMTP address variable will store the value that needs to be removed. The reset of these variables is to make sure no data is retained for each loop:

```
$Fail = $Null
$User = $Line.DISTINGUISHEDNAME
$BadSMTP = $Line.Value
```

In order to remove an address, the EmailAddressPolicyEnabled value needs to be $False.

```
Try {
    $PolicyApplied = (Get-Mailbox $User -ErrorAction STOP).EmailAddressPolicyEnabled
} Catch {
    $ScriptErrors = "User $user mailbox was not found." | Out-File -FilePath $ErrorFileName
}
```

If the Policy is enabled, this loop will set the 'EmailAddressPolicyEnabled' value to $False, in preparation for removing the bad SMTP Address:

```
If ($PolicyApplied) {
    # Email Address is applied - Remove the policy and then remove the address
    Try {
        Set-Mailbox $User -EmailAddressPolicyEnabled $False -ErrorAction STOP
    } Catch {
        $ScriptErrors = "The EmailAddressPolicyEnabled property for $user cannot be changed." | Out-File
        -FilePath $ErrorFileName
        $Fail = $True
    }
}
```

The next IF…ELSE code section looks to see if the policy change failed. If it did not, then the address can be removed. To remove the value, first a Get-ADUser cmdlet needs to be used with the –identity and –property parameters. The results of this cmdlet are piped ('|') to a Set-ADUser cmdlet. Notice that there is a –Remove parameter. This allows PowerShell to remove a particular value from a property on an AD Object.

```
If ($Fail -ne $True) {
    Try {
        Get-ADUser -identity $User -property * | Set-ADUser -remove @{'ProxyAddresses' = $BadSMTP}
    } Catch {
        $ScriptErrors = "Cannot remove $BadSMTP from the mailbox of $User." | Out-File -FilePath
        $ErrorFileName
    }
}
```

The purpose of this code section is to make the change if the EmailAddressPolicy is NOT enabled by default. The code is separate because there are no blockers to removing a bad Proxy Address:

```
} Else {
    # Email Address is not applied - Remove the address
    Try {
        Get-ADUser -identity $User -property * | Set-ADUser -Remove @{'ProxyAddresses' = $BadSMTP}
    } Catch {
        $ScriptErrors = "Cannot remove $BadSMTP from the mailbox of $User." | Out-File -FilePath
        $ErrorFileName
    }
}
```

Note in the Try..Catch code, there's code to export an error message to a logging file. No output should be seen if the script runs successfully. If IdFix is run again, the proxy address errors should be gone. If they are not, check the logging file for details.

New IdFix Query – very clean, error count is low after these two scripts were run:

DISTINGUISHEDNAME ▲	OBJECTCLASS	ATTRIBUTE	ERROR	VALUE	UPDATE
CN=Migration.8f3e7716-20...	user	userPrincipalName	topleveldomain	Migration.8f3e7716-2011-43e4-96b1-aba62d229136@16-TAP.Local	Migration.8f3e7716-2011-43e4-9

Install of Azure AD Connect

You can download the latest version of Azure AD Connect from Microsoft here - https://www.microsoft.com/en-us/download/details.aspx?id=47594. Once downloaded, the installation process can take us in two different directions – Express or Custom. Let's explore our options with the installation process:

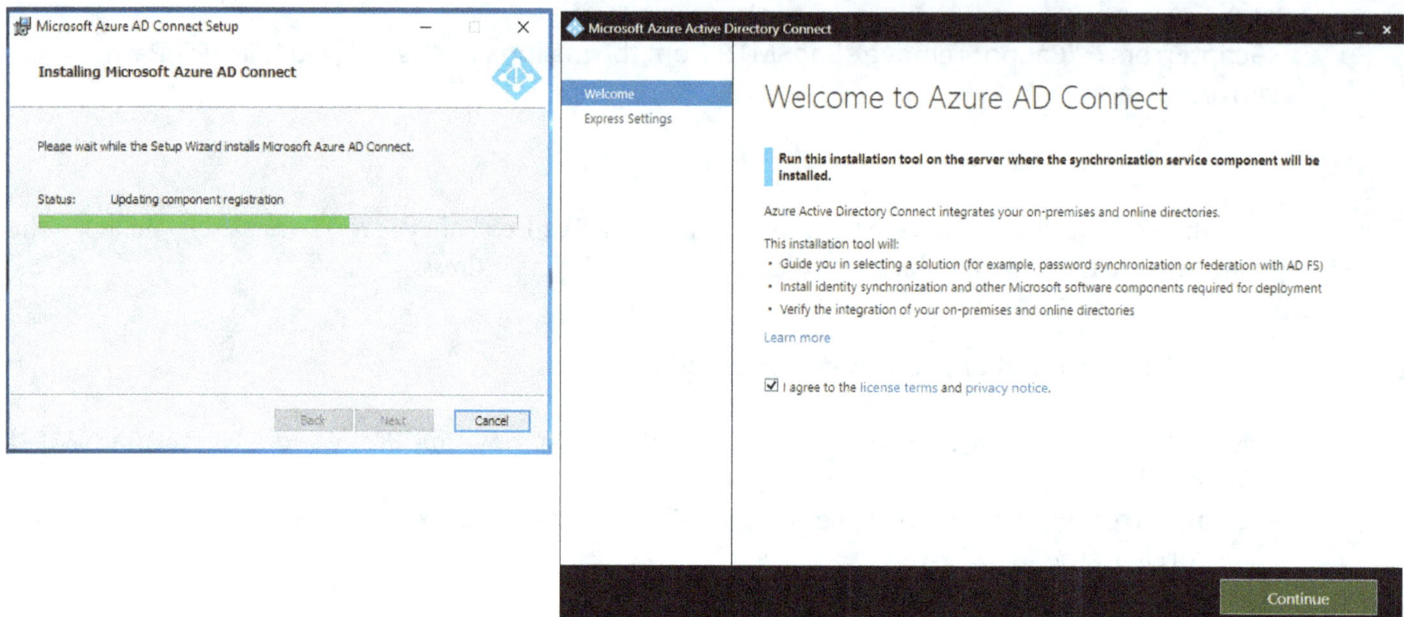

Option 1 – Express Installation

This method allows for a quick install of the directory synchronization product and allow the quickest and easiest setup. This option is great if advanced features are not required or the environment is not complex.

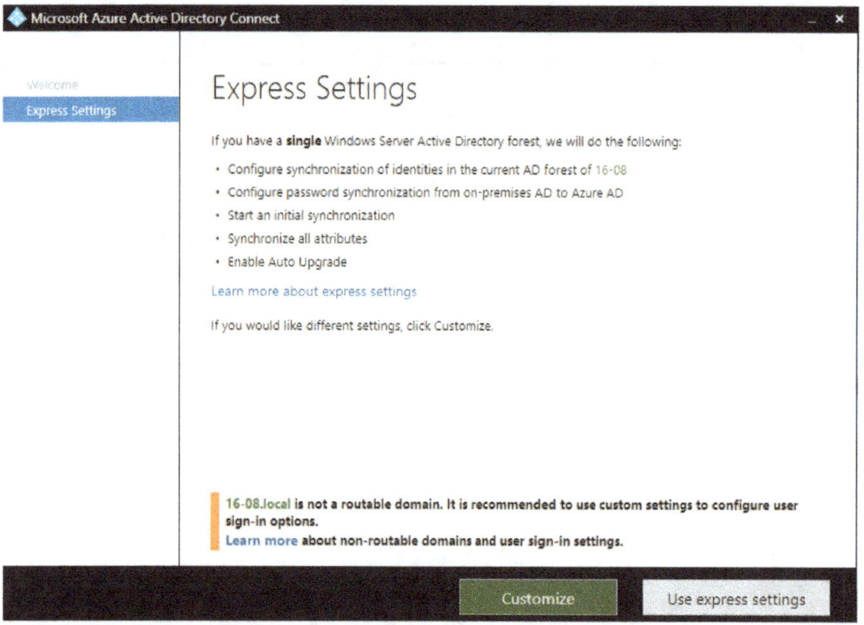

Option 2 – Customize

This installation option allows for a more complex installation process and the availability to choose (or not to choose) some of the more advanced options available with the directory synchronization.

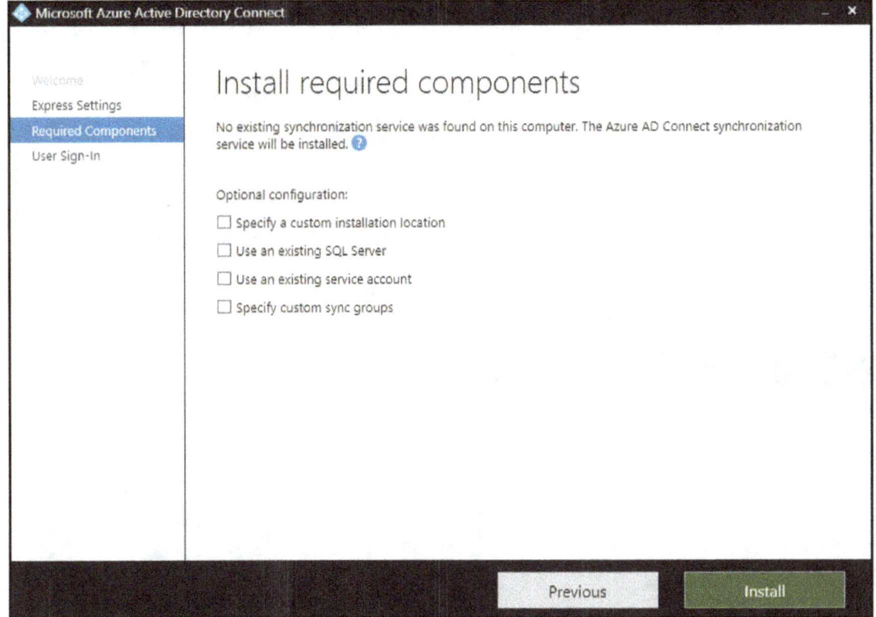

If you are unsure what these options mean, click on the blue question mark at the top, which will bring up a web link with an explanation of the options which goes to this website - http://go.microsoft.com/fwlink/?Link-ID=530302. It is obvious that we can change the plain vanilla settings by changing:

- **Custom Installation location** - Where Azure AD Connect is installed (maybe we want it on the D drive).
- **SQL** - Use a SQL server instead of using the Windows Database (recommended for larger installations).
- **Service Account** - Use a pre-created service account instead of the service account the wizard will create for you. Make sure to check the requirements for this account before selecting it as an option.
- **Sync Group** - Specify your own group names instead of using the four that are created by the Azure AD Connect wizard.

For this installation example, we'll leave it plain vanilla for this stage.

Wait for the installation to complete:

We are then provided a list of sign-in choices:

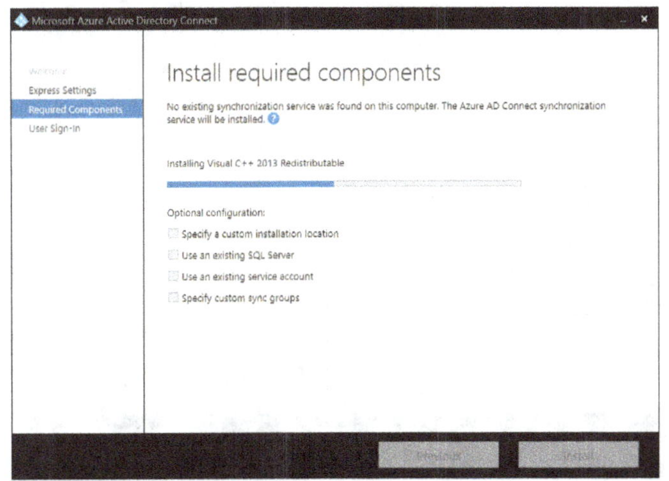

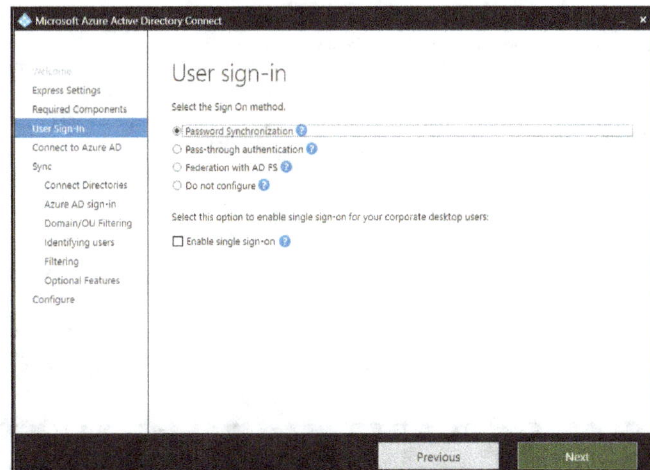

Each method of authentication is different and the option chosen would depend on your environment:

- **Password Synchronization** - Default option. User password synced to Office 365. User authenticate with the same password they use on-premises.
- **Pass-Through Authentication** - Azure AD uses your internal Active Directory to authenticate users.
- **Federation with ADFS** - Allows for a federated sign-in where corporate users do not need to re-enter their password.
- **Single Sign-On** - Users connect to their cloud services using SSO while on a corporate network.
- **Do Not Configure** - You control the federated authentication system (i.e. third party federation).

For our example, we will use Password Synchronization, but Pass-Through Authentication would work as well.

After choosing that, we'll need to connect to our Office 365 Tenant:

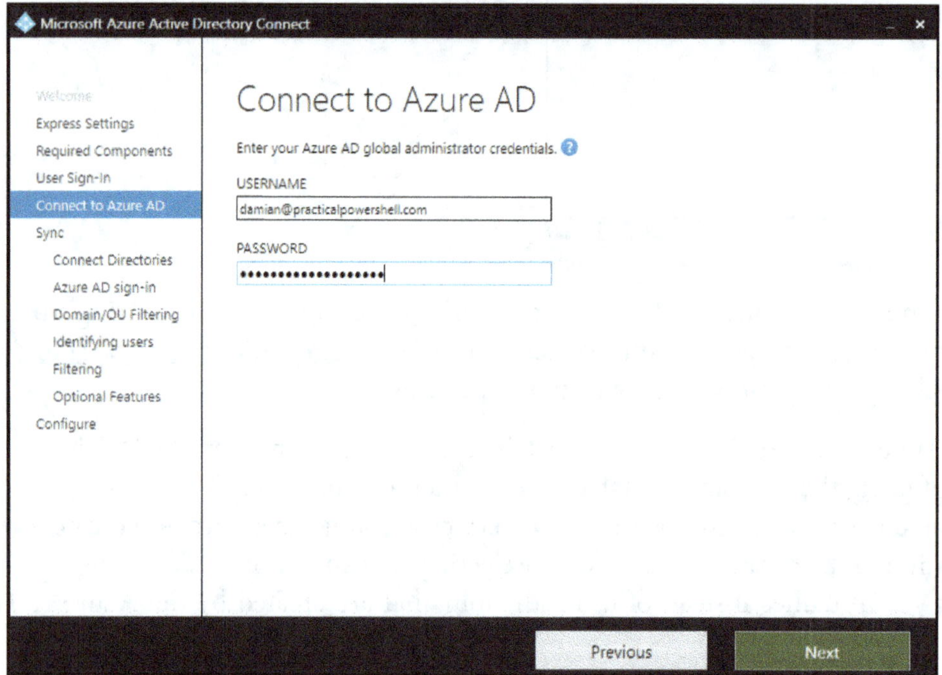

Then we'll need connect to Active Directory as our source directory:

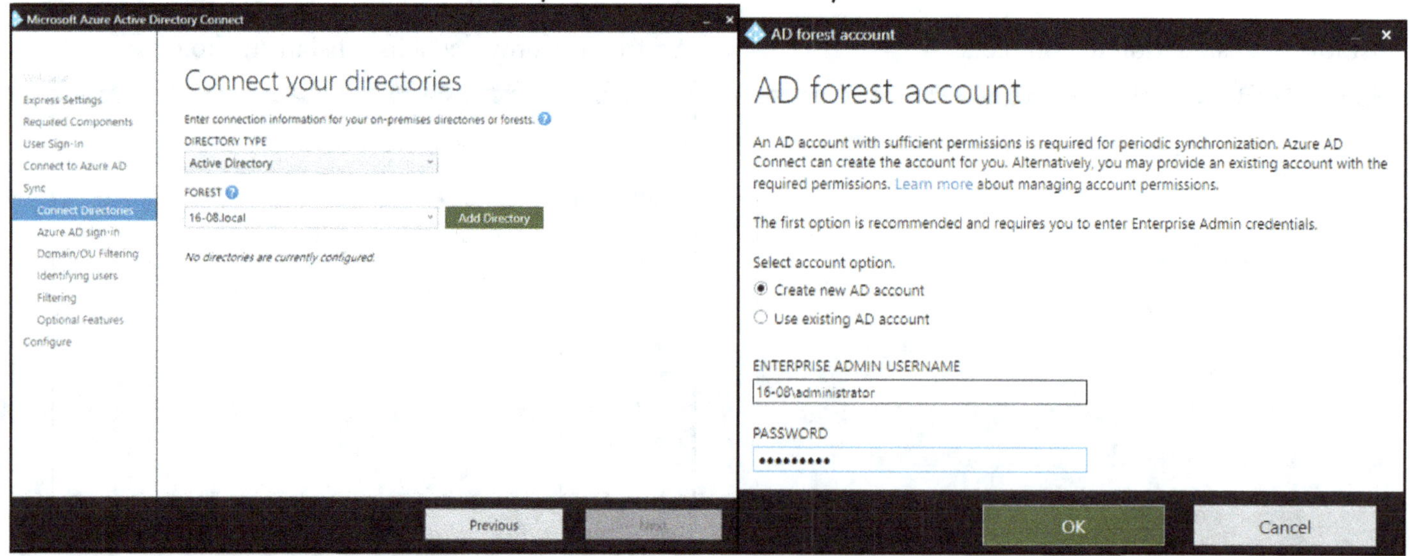

When entering the Forest Name, there are some considerations that need to be made. For flat directories, with no Root and Child domains to worry about, the default domain that is populated will suffice for the configuration of this page. However, if you have a more complex environment, you will need to choose the correct configuration for your environment. Azure AD Connect will connect to the Root Domain if it exists when setting up. If there are objects in the Root that do not need to be synchronized, these can be filtered out by choosing which partitions to synchronize.

Clicking OK and then Next will add the source directory. We need to choose an attribute for the user name and a user's User Principal Name (UPN) is typically used:

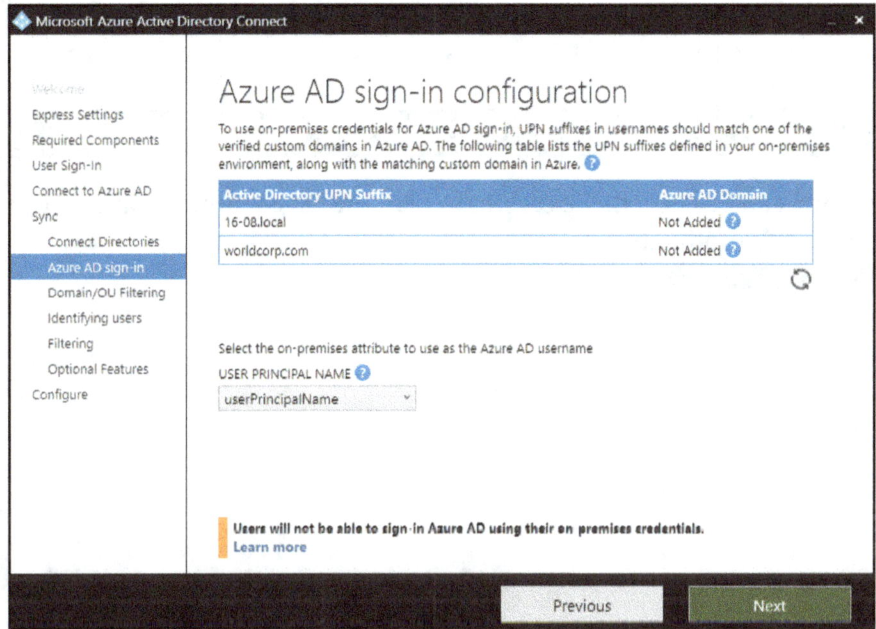

Then we can choose what OU's to sync. On the left we sync all OUs, on the right we have only some OUs selected:

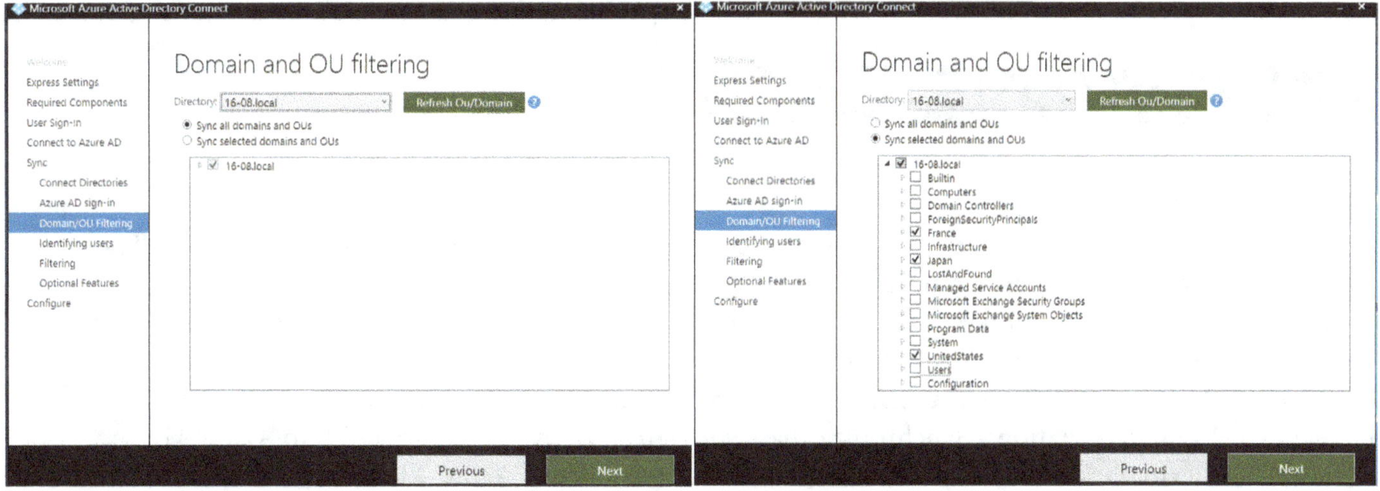

Choose your unique identifier (defaults shown):   Keep defaults for production or change for testing only:

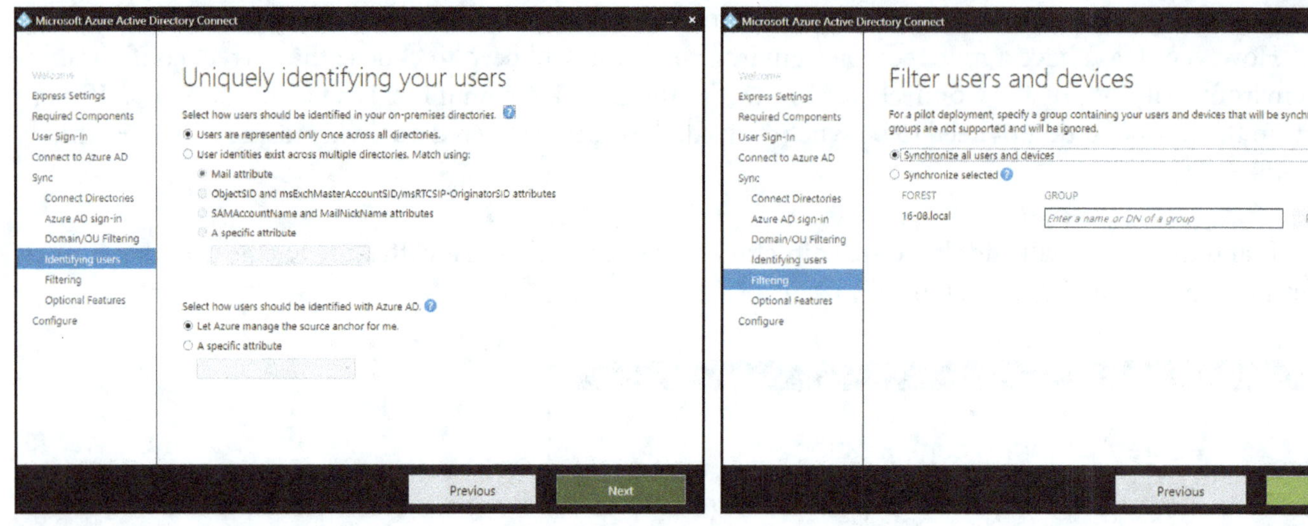

Lastly, a long list of optional features for Office 365 can be chosen. Be careful to read the list as some are in preview and may not work as expected or may be removed or modified:

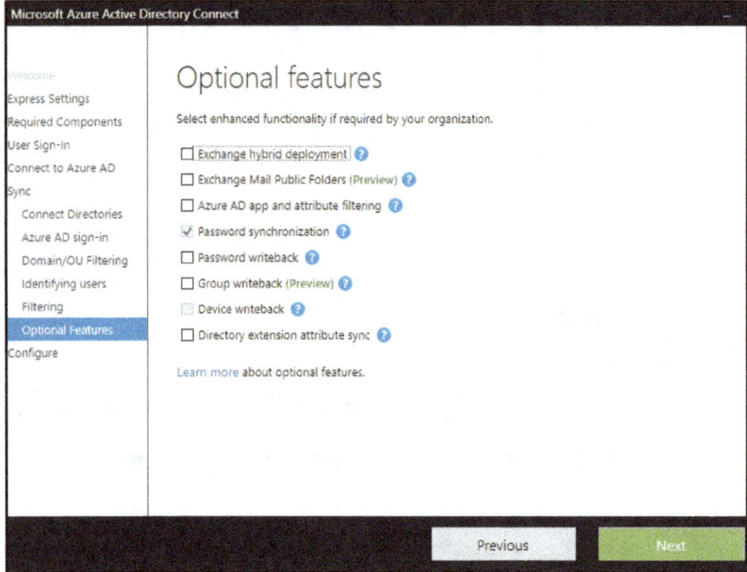

Brief explanation of the options:

- **Exchange hybrid deployment** - Allows for coexistence of Exchange and Exchange Online as well as synchronizing relevant Exchange attributes to Azure Active Directory (AD).
- **Exchange Mail Public Folders (Preview)** - Enables the synchronization of relevant attributes for Mail Enabled Public Folders to Exchange Online.
- **Azure AD app and attribute filtering** - Allows for custom attribute synchronization.
- **Password synchronization** - Synchronizes passwords from Active Directory (AD) to Azure AD.
- **Password writeback** - Enables password changes that are made in Azure AD will synchronize to an on-premises AD.
- **Group writeback (preview)** - Office 365 groups that are created will be synchronized with AD.
- **Device writeback** - Devices that are registered in Azure AD will be written back to AD.
- **Directory extension attribute sync** - Custom attributes that are on objects synced to the cloud can sync.

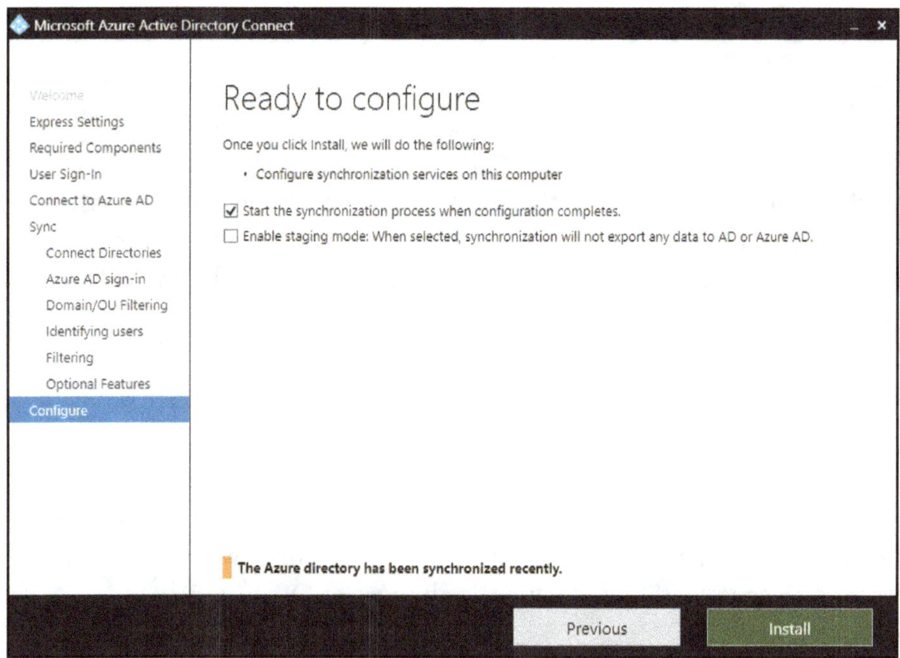

PowerShell and Directory Synchronization

Now that we've reviewed the basics of directory synchronization, let's cover the part that matters, specifically for this book, PowerShell. So what can we do with PowerShell with respect to Identity Management, Office 365 and in the end Exchange Online? Simply put, a lot:

- Change AD attributes that are synced to Office 365 and revealed in Exchange Online
- Modify the synchronization schedule
- Initial a full or delta sync process
- Modify cloud attributes
- <Other AD Stuff> - Add stuff here
- Add/Remove objects to be synced to the cloud

What complicates things from here from a PowerShell perspective and general management perspective for Identities and Office 365 is that we can run PowerShell for these tasks in three different places. These 'management spaces' are Active Directory, Azure AD Connect and Azure Active Directory:

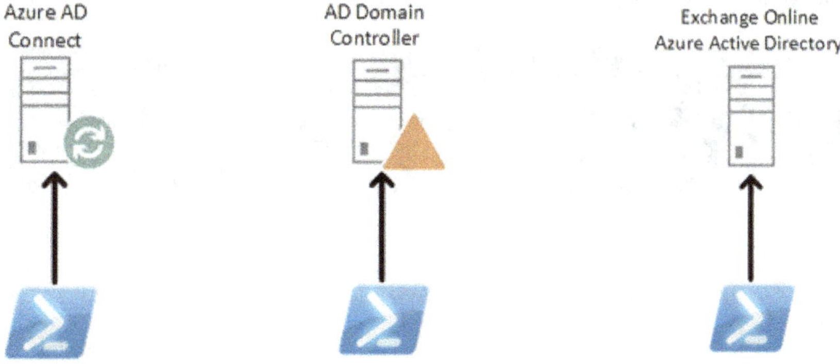

But aren't all of these aligned, synced and in the end, one and the same? The short answer is yes, and no. Each of these spaces has its specific purpose and places and this should be thought of as such.

What Needs to be Performed Where?

Active Directory

Active Directory is a good place to start because it is known as the Source of Authority in a synced environment. This means that all identities and objects originate in Active Directory. Users, Groups and more sync from Active Directory to your Azure AD Tenant (Office 365). Be sure to realize that not all attributes will sync with Office 365. Check out the Microsoft documentation on this here:

https://docs.microsoft.com/en-us/azure/active-directory/connect/active-directory-aadconnectsync-attributes-synchronized

Key attributes we can sync and manipulate in Active Directory are the User Principal Name, email addresses, password, and more. Let's see how we can make those changes. After we make the changes we will switch modes to the Azure AD Connect server processes and use PowerShell to sync the changes to Office 365.

Unlike most PowerShell cmdlets, this one produces a list of information instead of reporting the data in a table format:

```
PS C:\> Get-ADSyncConnector


ConnectorTypeName                : Extensible2
Identifier                       : b891884f-051e-4a83-95af-2544101c9083
Version                          : 18
InternalVersion                  : 1
FormatVersion                    : 1
Name                             : scoles.onmicrosoft.com - AAD
Description                      :
CreationTime                     : 10/13/2016 5:20:38 PM
LastModificationTime             : 7/25/2017 7:22:06 PM
Partitions                       : {default}
RunProfiles                      : {Full Import, Full Synchronization, Delta Import, Delta Synchroniz
ComponentProvisioningMappings    : {}
PasswordManagementSettings       : Microsoft.IdentityManagement.PowerShell.ObjectModel.ConnectorPassw
Schema                           : Microsoft.IdentityManagement.PowerShell.ObjectModel.Schema
AllParameterDefinitions          : {UserName, Password}
ConnectivityParameters           : {UserName, Password}
GlobalParameters                 : {}
CapabilityParameters             : {}
SchemaParameters                 : {}
ObjectInclusionList              : {contact, device, group, user}
AttributeInclusionList           : {accountEnabled, alias, alternativeSecurityId, altRecipient...}
AnchorConstructionSettings       : {Microsoft.IdentityManagement.PowerShell.ObjectModel.ConnectorAnch
                                   Microsoft.IdentityManagement.PowerShell.ObjectModel.ConnectorAncho
```

To get a table view, we would have to add a '| Ft' to the cmdlet, like so:

```
PS C:\> Get-ADSyncConnector | ft

ConnectorTypeNam Identifier            Version InternalVersion    FormatVersion Name
e
---------------- ----------            ------- ---------------    ------------- ----
Extensible2      b891884f-051e...           18               1                1 scoles.onmicr...
AD               beb5059c-4203...        34708               0                1 MEDIEVAL.LOCAL
```

New Object Creation

Creating objects can be performed with either AD Users and Computers (ADUC) or with PowerShell. If you are creating users in bulk then PowerShell will be the most efficient method. Singular user creation is often better left to ADUC, the exception being if you have a script that reads in a list of user attributes, perhaps from a CSV file, and can create objects from the data it contains. First, let's see how we can create local AD user accounts:

```
Get-Help New-ADUser -Examples
```

```
------------------------ EXAMPLE 1 ------------------------

C:\PS>New-ADUser GlenJohn -Certificate (new-object System.Security.Cryptography.X509Certificates.X509Certificate
-ArgumentList "export.cer")

------------------------ EXAMPLE 2 ------------------------

C:\PS>New-ADUser GlenJohn -OtherAttributes @{title="director";mail="glenjohn@fabrikam.com"}

------------------------ EXAMPLE 3 ------------------------

C:\PS>New-ADUser GlenJohn -Type iNetOrgPerson -Path "DC=AppNC" -server lds.Fabrikam.com:50000
```

The examples provided are rather basic. Most organizations would like their users to have good display names, aliases, base passwords, maybe address information, phone number and more. We can do all of this via PowerShell.

Example

A good example of this is a company that uses a third party HR application that keeps track of all of their employees. The same application exports a list of new employees on a weekly basis so that IT can create the accounts before new employees start working there. The export has a known list of fields and IT has a PowerShell script. In the CSV file there are a series of fields included - Display Name, Alias, First Name, Last Name, Office, Department, Title, Street Address, City, State, Zip Code and Office Number. The password is stored in a secure file that can be referenced by PowerShell.

We can store the password and CSV files in variables for later use:

```
$Password = Cat C:\SecureString.Txt | ConvertTo-SecureString
$CSV = Import-CSV \\FS-01\HR\NewEmployees.csv
```

Once those are stored, we can use a Foreach loop that will then insert the new employees information onto a new AD User account:

```
New-ADUser -Name $Displayname -SamAccountName $UserID -GivenName $FirstName -surname
$lastname -DisplayName $Displayname -Office $Office -Department $Department -Title $Title
-StreetAddress $StreetAddress -City $City -State $State -PostalCode $ZipCode -AccountPassword
$Password -path $OrgUnit -OfficePhone $WorkNumber
```

Once the user is created the object will be synchronized to Azure AD when the Azure AD Synchronization process runs. If the object needs to be synced immediately, a manual process via PowerShell may be run.

Modify

For modifying AD objects we use the Set-ADUser cmdlet. AD user objects have dozens of attributes we need to make sure that what we are modifying will make it to Exchange Online.

Get-Help Set-ADUser -Examples

```
------------------------ EXAMPLE 1 ------------------------

C:\PS>Set-ADUser AntonioA1 -HomePage 'http://fabrikam.com/employees/AntonioA1' -LogonWorkstations
'AntonioA1-DSKTOP,AntonioA1-LPTOP'

------------------------ EXAMPLE 2 ------------------------

C:\PS>Get-ADUser -Filter 'Name -like "*"' -SearchBase 'OU=HumanResources,OU=UserAccounts,DC=FABRIKAM,DC=COM'
-Properties DisplayName | % {Set-ADUser $_ -DisplayName ($_.Surname + ' ' + $_.GivenName)}

------------------------ EXAMPLE 3 ------------------------

C:\PS>Set-ADUser GlenJohn -Replace @{title="director";mail="glenjohn@fabrikam.com"}
```

Let's explore what we can do with manipulating user object properties.

Example

Let's change the offices for a couple of users. One of them works in Chicago, IL and the other works in Barneveld, Netherlands.

Set-ADUser Damian -Office 'Chicago'
Set-ADUser Dave -Office 'Barneveld'

We can then verify these changes with a Get-ADUser and perhaps using the 'Filter' parameter to look for specific offices:

Get-ADUser -Filter {Office -eq 'Chicago'}

```
DistinguishedName   : CN=Damian Scoles,CN=Users,DC=AAD,DC=LOCAL
Enabled             : True
GivenName           : Damian
Name                : Damian Scoles
ObjectClass         : user
ObjectGUID          : 90ba0b4d-15bc-43e6-9b74-1bc051743bb7
SamAccountName      : damian
SID                 : S-1-5-21-1816188163-520225533-903613565-1107
Surname             : Scoles
UserPrincipalName   : damian@PracticalPowerShell.Com
```

Get-ADUser -Filter {Office -eq 'Barneveld'}

```
DistinguishedName   : CN=Dave Stork,CN=Users,DC=AAD,DC=LOCAL
Enabled             : True
GivenName           : Dave
Name                : Dave Stork
ObjectClass         : user
ObjectGUID          : e1591617-3f62-4eb2-884c-6af0e9b77a7b
SamAccountName      : Dave
SID                 : S-1-5-21-1816188163-520225533-903613565-1108
Surname             : Stork
UserPrincipalName   : Dave@PracticalPowerShell.Com
```

Again, do not forget that for user objects that are synced to Azure AD, not all properties that we can manipulate are actually synced to the cloud. However, when it comes to Exchange Online and using Active Directory to build a GAL, most attributes that you will modify will sync to your Azure AD Tenant.

Another common attribute to modify on-premises is the users User Principal Name. The UPN is potentially a very important attribute for your users in Exchange Online. This attribute is typically used as the login for accessing Exchange Online, which can match the users' Primary SMTP address. If you any users with login issues, this is one attribute to check for first.

Removing Objects

A directory is only as good as the objects that are present in it. If there are objects that are no longer needed or reference users that no longer work for an organization, then we can remove them with PowerShell. Again this can be singular or en masse, preferably with a CSV file.

PowerShell

In order to remove user objects we can use the Remove-ADUser cmdlet. Remember that if this account is removed from Active Directory it will no longer be in sync with the corresponding object in Office 365. The object will be placed in the Azure AD Recycle Bin (See pg. 116 for more information). If the object is restored, then the matching object in Azure AD will also be restored (within 30 days). Now let's remove some objects:

Remove-ADUser

```
---------------------------- EXAMPLE 1 ----------------------------

C:\PS>Remove-ADUser  -Identity GlenJohn
---------------------------- EXAMPLE 2 ----------------------------

C:\PS>Search-ADAccount  -AccountDisabled | where {$_.ObjectClass -eq 'user'} | Remove-ADUser
---------------------------- EXAMPLE 3 ----------------------------

C:\PS>Remove-ADUser  -Identity "CN=Glen John,OU=Finance,OU=UserAccounts,DC=FABRIKAM,DC=COM"
```

Example

If we have some users who have left an organization:

```
$Users = Import-CSV \\FS-01\HR\EmployeeRemoval.CSV
Foreach ($User in $Users) {
   $Exist = $True
   $Identity = $Users.Identity
   Remove-ADUser -Identity $Identity
   Try {
      $Exist = Get-ADUser -Identity $Identity -ErrorAction STOP
   } Catch {
      $Exist = $False4po
   }
   If ($exist -eq $Fasle) {
      Write-Host "User $Identity has been successfully removed."
   } Else {
      Write-Host "The user has not been removed." -ForegroundColor Yellow
   }
}
```

Azure Active Directory Connect

After Active Directory, the next service to work with is the Azure AD Connect server we installed earlier in the chapter. In this section we will deal with PowerShell and the directory synchronization cmdlets available on the server.

In order to begin, we will need to open up Windows PowerShell. After opening it, we need to verify the module is loaded.

```
Get-Module
```

```
PS C:\> Get-Module

ModuleType  Name                            ExportedC

Manifest    Microsoft.PowerShell.Management  {Add-Comp
Manifest    MSOnline                         {Add-Mso
```

We do not see ADSync listed, then we make sure to run 'Import-Module ADSync'. This cmdlet will load the PowerShell cmdlets for Azure AD Connect. Notice the changes below:

```
PS C:\> Get-Module

ModuleType  Name                            Exported

Binary      ADSync                           {Add-ADS
Manifest    Microsoft.PowerShell.Management  {Add-Com
Manifest    MSOnline                         {Add-Mso
```

What cmdlets are available to us once this PowerShell module is loaded? We can find these with this one-liner:

```
Get-Command | Where {$_.ModuleName -eq 'AdSync'}
```

Total cmdlets available:

```
(Get-Command | where {$_.ModuleName -eq 'AdSync'}).Count
```

The above one-liner provides output that we have 92 cmdlets available.

Sync Schedule Adjustment

First, let's work with the basics of the AD Sync Scheduler. We can find the initial settings with the Get-ADSyncScheduler:

```
PS C:\> Get-ADSyncScheduler

AllowedSyncCycleInterval            : 00:30:00
CurrentlyEffectiveSyncCycleInterval : 00:30:00
CustomizedSyncCycleInterval         :
NextSyncCyclePolicyType             : Delta
NextSyncCycleStartTimeInUTC         : 10/10/2017 6:03:41 AM
PurgeRunHistoryInterval             : 7.00:00:00
SyncCycleEnabled                    : True
MaintenanceEnabled                  : True
StagingModeEnabled                  : False
SchedulerSuspended                  : False
SyncCycleInProgress                 : False
```

Notice the default sync cycle is indeed 30 minutes as per Microsoft's change from the original three hours in a previous version of the tool. Also notice that the Staging Mode is not configured, no sync is in progress nor is the scheduler paused.   There are some settings that we can configure for the sync scheduler itself. Consider these requirements.

- The updates need to occur on a much faster basis and increased from 30 minutes to 15 minutes.
- The run history needs to be kept for 30 days instead of the typical 7 days.

Unfortunately the PowerShell cmdlet needed to configure these settings has no usable examples:

```
Get-Help Set-ADSyncScheduler –Examples
```

```
NAME
    Set-ADSyncScheduler

ALIASES
    None


REMARKS
    None
```

To adjust the schedule, we can use a on-line like the following, which adjusts the purge interval from 7 days to 30 days and Sync Cycle interval down to 15 minutes, from 30 minutes:

```
Set-ADSyncScheduler -PurgeRunHistoryInterval 30.00:00:00 -CustomizedSyncCycleInterval 00:15:00
```

```
PS C:\> Set-ADSyncScheduler –PurgeRunHistoryInterval 30.00:00:00 –CustomizedSyncCycleInterval 00:15:00

The value for the customized sync interval is lower than the allowed value.
Requested new interval = 00:15:00  Allowed interval = 00:30:00
Scheduler will still run at the allowed sync interval even after successful execution of this cmdlet.

Are you sure you want to continue?
[Y] Yes  [N] No  [S] Suspend  [?] Help (default is "Y"): y
WARNING: The sync interval you provided will only become effective after a sync cycle.You can choose to wait for the automatic
sync cycle to happen in next 30.00 minutes, or you can manually start a sync cyle by running Start-ADSyncSyncCycle cmdlet.
PS C:\> _
```

We can then verify the changes with 'Get-ADSyncScheduler:'

```
CurrentlyEffectiveSyncCycleInterval  : 00:30:00
CustomizedSyncCycleInterval          : 00:15:00
NextSyncCyclePolicyype               : Delta
NextSyncCycleStartTimeInUTC          : 10/10/2017 6:33:45 AM
PurgeRunHistoryInterval              : 30.00:00:00
SyncCycleEnabled                     : True
MaintenanceEnabled                   : True
StagingModeEnabled                   : False
SchedulerSuspended                   : False
```

After 30 minutes, these changes will then go into effect and your synchronizations will be 15 minutes apart instead of 30 minutes.

Modifying the scheduler for the directory synchronization is just one part of the scheduler. We can also kick off full syncs and delta syncs with PowerShell as well. This is a common task for migrations when changes are made to user's information, new users are created in Active Directory or possible an additional distribution group needs to sync for the Office 365 tenant. In this case, we'll need to manually initiate the sync process using a single PowerShell cmdlet:

```
Start-ADSyncSyncCycle
```

What examples do we have for this cmdlet? None. However, if we review the full Get-Help of the cmdlet, we see this near the top:

```
NAME
    Start-ADSyncSyncCycle

SYNTAX
    Start-ADSyncSyncCycle [[-PolicyType] <SynchronizationPolicyType> {Unspecified |
    Delta | Initial}] [[-InteractiveMode] <bool>]  [<CommonParameters>]
```

When it comes to PowerShell cmdlets, this one has one of the fewest if not the fewest configurable options. If we would like to start a sync based on just recent changes, we can use a policy type of 'Delta':

Start-ADSyncSyncCycle –PolicyType Delta

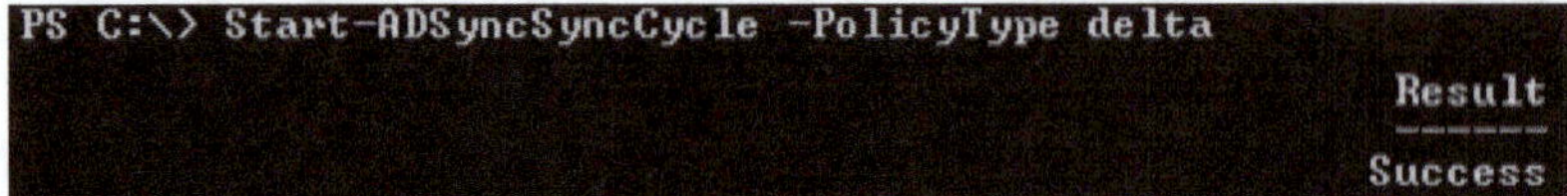

And Azure AD Connect will show the connections being made:

Name	Profile Name	Status	Start Time	End Time
ADDomain.Com	Export	success	10/11/2017 7:40:54 PM	10/11/2017 7:40:55 PM
tenant.onmicrosoft.com-AAD	Export	success	10/11/2017 7:40:33 PM	10/11/2017 7:40:53 PM
tenant.onmicrosoft.com-AAD	Delta Synchronization	success	10/11/2017 7:40:31 PM	10/11/2017 7:40:32 PM
ADDomain.Com	Delta Synchronization	success	10/11/2017 7:40:29 PM	10/11/2017 7:40:30 PM
tenant.onmicrosoft.com-AAD	Delta Import	success	10/11/2017 7:40:17 PM	10/11/2017 7:40:26 PM
ADDomain.Com	Delta Import	success	10/11/2017 7:40:16 PM	10/11/2017 7:40:16 PM
ADDomain.Com	Export	success	10/11/2017 7:10:52 PM	10/11/2017 7:10:53 PM

** **Note** ** The 'ADDomain.Com' refers to the FQDN used in your on-premises AD while the 'tenant.onmicrosoft.com' refers to your Office 365 default domain.

However, if we need to perform a full sync, for example if there is a problem with a delta sync or there is a need to force a fuller sync, we can use the 'Initial' Policy Type:

Start-ADSyncSyncCycle –PolicyType Initial

If it is successful, the PowerShell window should show this:

Azure AD Connect – Connectors

Connectors are what allows objects and attributes to sync between the two environments. One syncs objects from your on-premises Active Directory to Azure AD and the other syncs Azure AD to your on-premises Active Directory. Installing Azure AD Connect should create both of these connectors.

PowerShell

Let's start with the Get-*Connector* cmdlets with the thought of exploring what is available to modify before adding or changing existing connectors. This will allow for a non-destructive examination of the environment.

```
Get-Command Get*connector* | Where {$_.ModuleName -eq 'ADSync'}
```

```
CommandType    Name                                               ModuleName
-----------    ----                                               ----------
Cmdlet         Get-ADSyncConnector                                 ADSync
Cmdlet         Get-ADSyncConnectorHierarchyProvisioningDNComponent ADSync
Cmdlet         Get-ADSyncConnectorHierarchyProvisioningMapping     ADSync
Cmdlet         Get-ADSyncConnectorHierarchyProvisioningObjectClass ADSync
Cmdlet         Get-ADSyncConnectorParameter                        ADSync
Cmdlet         Get-ADSyncConnectorPartition                        ADSync
Cmdlet         Get-ADSyncConnectorPartitionHierarchy               ADSync
Cmdlet         Get-ADSyncConnectorRunStatus                        ADSync
Cmdlet         Get-ADSyncConnectorStatistics                       ADSync
Cmdlet         Get-ADSyncConnectorTypes                            ADSync
Cmdlet         Get-ADSyncSchedulerConnectorOverride                ADSync
```

The first cmdlet will display information on the two connectors involved in the Azure AD Connector process of directory synchronization:

```
Get-ADSyncConnector | ft
```

```
ConnectorTypeName Identifier                           Version InternalVersion FormatVersion Name
----------------- ----------                           ------- --------------- ------------- ----
Extensible2       b891884f-051e-4a83-95af-2544101c9083       1               1           1 OnlineExchangeBook.onmi...
AD                720faf5e-2407-464e-a43a-c9aff1967a5b       8               0           1 AAD.LOCAL
```

Notice that the top one is for our Azure AD tenant and AAD.LOCAL is for our on-premises AD. Now we can also review the configuration of several items when it comes to our Azure AD Connect server. Some examples are - connector details, rules and server configuration.

The first is the easiest and is a variation of the last PowerShell cmdlet we ran. First, we will look at the connector for our local Active Directory to Office 365:

```
Get-ADSyncConnector -Name AAD.LOCAL
```

```
ConnectorTypeName              : AD
Identifier                     : 720faf5e-2407-464e-a43a-c9aff1967a5b
Version                        : 8
InternalVersion                : 0
FormatVersion                  : 1
Name                           : AAD.LOCAL
Description                    :
CreationTime                   : 12/16/2017 5:56:40 AM
LastModificationTime           : 12/16/2017 5:57:00 AM
Partitions                     : {AAD.LOCAL}
RunProfiles                    : {Full Import, Full Synchronization, Delta Import, Delta Synchronization...}
ComponentProvisioningMappings  : {}
Schema                         : Microsoft.IdentityManagement.PowerShell.ObjectModel.Schema
AllParameterDefinitions        : {}
ConnectivityParameters         : {forest-login-domain, forest-login-user, password, forest-name...}
GlobalParameters               : {Connector.GroupFilteringGroupDn}
CapabilityParameters           : {}
SchemaParameters               : {}
ObjectInclusionList            : {computer, contact, container, domainDNS...}
AttributeInclusionList         : {adminDescription, assistant, c, cn...}
AnchorConstructionSettings     : {}
ListName                       :
CompanyName                    :
Type                           : AD
Subtype                        :
ExtensionConfiguration         : Microsoft.IdentityManagement.PowerShell.ObjectModel.ConnectorExtensionConfiguration
PasswordHashConfiguration      : <password-hash-sync-config><enabled>1</enabled><target>{B891884F-051E-4A83-95AF-2544101
                                 C9083}</target></password-hash-sync-config>
AADPasswordResetConfiguration  :
```

Notice the detail in the connector. There are a couple of properties above that can be expanded. The way we can tell is that we something like *'Microsoft.IdentityManagement.PowerShell.ObjectModel....'*. This means that there are more details that can be expanded, like so:

```
(Get-ADSyncConnector -Name AAD.LOCAL).Schema
```

```
Identifier           : 00000000-0000-0000-0000-000000000000
ObjectTypes          : {msDFSR-Content, device, msWMI-IntRangeParam, samServer...}
AttributeTypes       : {Name:attributeSecurityGUID Type:Binary MultiValued:False, Name:msDS-FilterContainers
                       Type:String MultiValued:True, Name:legacyExchangeDN Type:String MultiValued:False,
                       Name:cOMProgID Type:String MultiValued:True...}
IsConnectorSchema    : True
IntrinsicAttributes  : {Name:dn Type:String MultiValued:False, Name:msIdm-ObjectCustomData Type:String
                       MultiValued:False}
AllDNComponents      : {}
```

We can also dig into the server configuration and dump a series of files using the ' Get-ADSyncServerConfigura-tion' cmdlet (note this cannot be used to restore an Azure AD Connect Server):

```
Get-ADSyncServerConfiguration -path c:\Download\Export
```

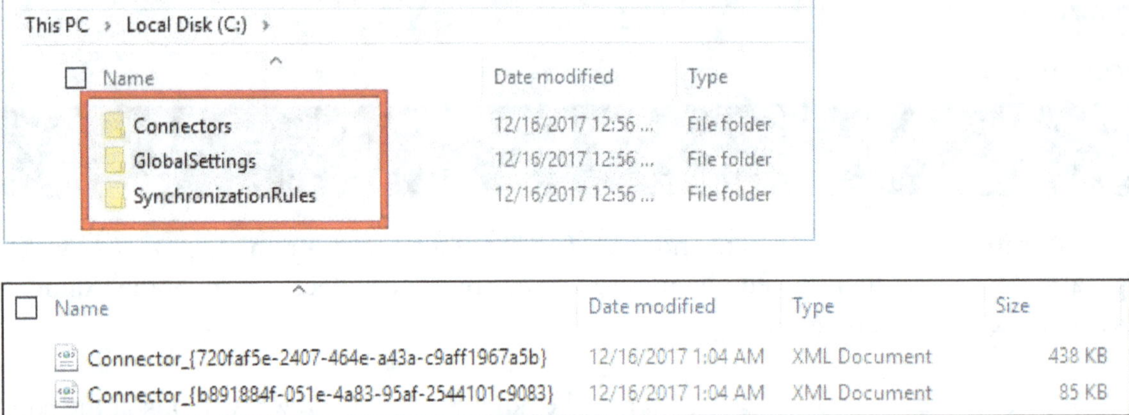

Lastly, we can export or review our rules as well with Get-ADSyncRule. The rules contain a lot of information and we can create a basic table of these rules like this:

```
Get-ADSyncRule |Ft
```

```
Identifier                           InternalId                           Name
----------                           ----------                           ----
d3f9498a-bfeb-4752-a137-dc0185f30ebf d3f9498a-bfeb-4752-a137-dc0185f30ebf In from AAD - User Join
b5b2f5c4-0562-499f-b8ac-159a71e5d7d4 b5b2f5c4-0562-499f-b8ac-159a71e5d7d4 Out to AAD - User ExchangeOnline
953e6c8e-6f5b-4a09-8642-73ef8346d45a 953e6c8e-6f5b-4a09-8642-73ef8346d45a Out to AAD - User LyncOnline
1215f7cd-9b83-4286-8961-e7a4e9d0176d 1215f7cd-9b83-4286-8961-e7a4e9d0176d Out to AAD - User SharePointOnline
8a708140-dd80-45f6-8875-b8581a1148fa 8a708140-dd80-45f6-8875-b8581a1148fa Out to AAD - Contact ExchangeOnline
3ef9f7c7-6c9f-44cc-9029-57ba4cd87107 3ef9f7c7-6c9f-44cc-9029-67ba4cd87107 Out to AAD - Contact SharePointOnline
a19533b6-187c-4838-be75-0b063bf3c635 a19533b6-187c-4838-be75-0b063bf3c635 Out to AAD - Group Join
c994d0b3-4d85-41ba-8921-638a7ba62e6f c994d0b3-4d85-41ba-8921-638a7ba62e6f Out to AAD - Group ExchangeOnline
5b51f5ac-eb9a-4fd3-807a-a8f2b0c098c1 5b51f5ac-eb9a-4fd3-807a-a8f2b0c098c1 Out to AAD - Group SharePointOnline
65e35432-0554-4bff-9b3a-c6a0075f8afb 65e35432-0554-4bff-9b3a-c6a0075f8afb In from AAD - Contact Join
df2afd59-cba1-4457-b761-34218738b70b df2afd59-cba1-4457-b761-34218738b70b In from AAD - Group Join
83fb9ec2-a62a-4ae0-9985-d24740d2a534 83fb9ec2-a62a-4ae0-9985-d24740d2a534 In from AAD - User NGCKey
06d37554-d537-4512-9c84-1e103d895a7c 06d37554-d537-4512-9c84-1e103d895a7c Out to AAD - User AzureRMS
5982c026-314f-4f28-a27b-a175c08a0216 5982c026-314f-4f28-a27b-a175c08a0216 Out to AAD - User Join
7073f0e6-f5f2-4138-b9a5-71d39c2ed172 7073f0e6-f5f2-4138-b9a5-71d39c2ed172 Out to AAD - User Identity
b4992e49-d422-4ce6-b64c-8f974ea91c60 b4992e49-d422-4ce6-b64c-8f974ea91c60 Out to AAD - User DynamicsCRM
2df63f43-b635-4099-9949-d6465b4279c7 2df63f43-b635-4099-9949-d6465b4279c7 Out to AAD - User Intune
c6fcfd30-a2d3-45bd-bb21-5615ab3a89d1 c6fcfd30-a2d3-45bd-bb21-5615ab3a89d1 Out to AAD - Contact Join
7231d454-9b01-4353-a3d6-777e4bca77de 7231d454-9b01-4353-a3d6-777e4bca77de Out to AAD - Contact Identity
f93886e1-d3d3-4072-bbd6-fc71339c907c f93886e1-d3d3-4072-bbd6-fc71339c907c Out to AAD - Contact DynamicsCRM
3d6b34fe-389c-4e22-8b06-9a34f46e1dc8 3d6b34fe-389c-4e22-8b06-9a34f46e1dc8 Out to AAD - Contact Intune
71b73c46-399a-4e72-af54-968043594649 71b73c46-399a-4e72-af54-968043594649 Out to AAD - Contact LyncOnline
524e1a9b-f6b7-49f0-b409-2a028b779bf1 524e1a9b-f6b7-49f0-b409-2a028b779bf1 Out to AAD - Contact AzureRMS
01fe57d3-ecf5-4f92-ab3e-8e5b4ef89829 01fe57d3-ecf5-4f92-ab3e-8e5b4ef89829 Out to AAD - Group Identity
a32f3f1e-8fce-4d97-ad15-d808ac4c3d92 a32f3f1e-8fce-4d97-ad15-d808ac4c3d92 Out to AAD - Group DynamicsCRM
65a52197-6431-4786-beea-e555db6eba88 65a52197-6431-4786-beea-e555db6eba88 Out to AAD - Group Intune
f72da3c0-d7c6-4f6e-86e9-ef5995a8ff74 f72da3c0-d7c6-4f6e-86e9-ef5995a8ff74 Out to AAD - Group LyncOnline
04e0bc86-62a6-46be-abdf-fc5ba891b6f5 04e0bc86-62a6-46be-abdf-fc5ba891b6f5 Out to AAD - Group AzureRMS
ce1a39f6-8687-40fa-8669-4f8039a211cf ce1a39f6-8687-40fa-8669-4f8039a211cf Out to AAD - User OfficeProPlus
0944998d-0fd7-4e3b-898b-0abafccea6a8 0944998d-0fd7-4e3b-898b-0abafccea6a8 In from AAD - Device Common
f24495d3-e42e-4dba-a532-fd43ecbc58fa f24495d3-e42e-4dba-a532-fd43ecbc58fa Out to AAD - Device Join SOAInAD
c0d06dbc-b809-4b23-a260-4a83f2ca7c0b c0d06dbc-b809-4b23-a260-4a83f2ca7c0b In from AD - User Join
f9f9d40d-675b-4d4d-973f-86b94677b5fe f9f9d40d-675b-4d4d-973f-86b94677b5fe In from AD - InetOrgPerson Join
eda3d821-dfdd-4e6f-be6a-8ef4d8e34f6b eda3d821-dfdd-4e6f-be6a-8ef4d8e34f6b In from AD - User AccountEnabled
fd49d788-4cdd-4a25-a12c-78bea21a5d66 fd49d788-4cdd-4a25-a12c-78bea21a5d66 In from AD - InetOrgPerson AccountEnabled
5dfce29d-2dc3-4722-b279-272477a8c0b0 5dfce29d-2dc3-4722-b279-272477a8c0b0 In from AD - User Common
11835c40-0c62-4935-87a0-65ac5ef1f2b0 11835c40-0c62-4935-87a0-65ac5ef1f2b0 In from AD - InetOrgPerson Common
```

It is important to note that the previous rule list contains the default rules created by the Azure AD Connect installation process. Custom rules can be added and existing rules can be modified. However, because of the nature of the default rules, this is not recommended as you could do some damage to your Office 365 Tenant.

Further reading on modifying these rules:
https://social.msdn.microsoft.com/Forums/SqlServer/en-US/c5189e16-a219-445e-9a17-d02937bda27f/azure-ad-connect-staging?forum=WindowsAzureAD

A more detailed version of the rule can be displayed with a one-liner like this:

```
Get-ADSyncRule -Identifier d3f9498a-bfeb-4752-a137-dc0185f30ebf | Fl
```

```
Identifier               : d3f9498a-bfeb-4752-a137-dc0185f30ebf
InternalId               : d3f9498a-bfeb-4752-a137-dc0185f30ebf
Name                     : In from AAD - User Join
Version                  : 1
Description              :
ImmutableTag             : Microsoft.IdentityManagement.PowerShell.ObjectModel.ImmutableTag
Connector                : b891884f-051e-4a83-95af-2544101c9083
Direction                : Inbound
Disabled                 : False
SourceObjectType         : user
TargetObjectType         : person
Precedence               : 111
PrecedenceAfter          : 00000000-0000-0000-0000-000000000000
PrecedenceBefore         : 00000000-0000-0000-0000-000000000000
LinkType                 : Join
EnablePasswordSync       : False
JoinFilter               : {Microsoft.IdentityManagement.PowerShell.ObjectModel.JoinConditionGroup}
ScopeFilter              : {Microsoft.IdentityManagement.PowerShell.ObjectModel.ScopeConditionGroup}
AttributeFlowMappings    : {Destination:accountEnabled FlowType:Direct Expression:  ValueMergeType: Update,
                           Destination:cloudAnchor FlowType:Direct Expression:  ValueMergeType: Update,
                           Destination:cloudSourceAnchor FlowType:Expression Expression: ImportedValue("sourceAnchor")
                           ValueMergeType: Update, Destination:countryCode FlowType:Direct Expression:
                           ValueMergeType: Update...}
SoftDeleteExpiryInterval : 00:00:00
SourceNamespaceId        : b891884f-051e-4a83-95af-2544101c9083
TargetNamespaceId        : cc31d470-9786-447f-8594-40abe13f9f78
VersionAgnosticTag       : Microsoft.InfromAADUserJoin.
TagVersion               : 5
IsStandardRule           : True
IsLegacyCustomRule       : False
JoinHash                 : [sourceAnchor=sourceAnchor CS=True]
```

As we can see, these can dig in and get some good detail on our sync rules for Azure AD Connect with PowerShell.

Licensing

Another case for using PowerShell in managing your Office 365 tenant is mass licensing manipulation. While the Portal for your tenant will allow for mass changes, the manipulation that it is capable is also limited. Only 100 accounts can be modified at any one time. If there is a need to adjust more at one time, then PowerShell is required to make the changes successful. PowerShell is especially useful if more complex changes are required – licensing determined by groups or granular licensing is needed.

** **Note** ** There is one more method to license users in bulk. This method is called Group Based Licensing. Basically using the Azure AD Console you can add and remove licenses for a group of users based on their group membership. The below code breaks down how licenses can be applied to users in an individual manner.

First and foremost, what PowerShell cmdlets are available for these changes? Make sure a connection is opened up via the Windows PowerShell Azure Module – connect to the tenant and then the MSOL Service.

```
Get-Command *licen*
```

```
CommandType          Name
-----------          ----
Function             Get-LicenseVsUsageSummaryReport
Cmdlet               New-MsolLicenseOptions
Cmdlet               New-MsolLicenseOptions
Cmdlet               Set-MsolUserLicense
Cmdlet               Set-MsolUserLicense
```

Starting with the first cmdlet can provide some information about license usage:

```
Get-LicenseVsUsageSummaryReport | ft -Auto
```

Date	TenantGuid	Workload	NonTrialEntitlements	TrialEntitlements	ActiveUsers
9/7/2016 12:00:00 AM		EXO	395	0	0
9/7/2016 12:00:00 AM		LYO	375	0	0
9/7/2016 12:00:00 AM		SPO	375	0	3
9/7/2016 12:00:00 AM		Yammer	375	0	1

Where would licensing be stored? Maybe the information is stored in the properties of a user account in Azure AD. To get all the properties from a user account in Azure AD, the Get-MSOLUser cmdlet can be used for this:

```
Get-MsolUser -UserPrincipalName damian@domain.com | fl
```

Deep in the properties for this user we can see that there is an Enterprise License installed for the tenant this user account is in:

```
LastName                          : Scoles
LicenseReconciliationNeeded       : False
Licenses                          : {Domain:ENTERPRISEPACK}
```

However, the licenses assigned are not granular and we need to find out what options can be set via PowerShell. Cutting to the chase, the cmdlet needed is not as obvious:

```
Get-MsolAccountSku
```

The cmdlet only has one parameter "TenantID" and one example, which is just the base cmdlet. What information will this provide us?

```
ExtensionData    : System.Runtime.Serialization.ExtensionDataObject
AccountName      : Domain
AccountObjectId  : a59a9dcf-a1c7-4dfa-b98c-d9b0fc4a8fd2
AccountSkuId     : Domain:ENTERPRISEPACK
ActiveUnits      : 375
ConsumedUnits    : 63
LockedOutUnits   : 0
ServiceStatus    : {Microsoft.Online.Administration.ServiceStatus, Microsoft.Online.Administration.ServiceStatus,
                   Microsoft.Online.Administration.ServiceStatus, Microsoft.Online.Administration.ServiceStatus...}
SkuId            : 6fd2c87f-b296-42f0-b197-1e91e994b900
SkuPartNumber    : ENTERPRISEPACK
```

Notice the information in the red rectangle, the information is repeating and not detailed. PowerShell has a tendency to oversimplify values when it cannot display them properly. That is the same case here. We will use PowerShell on the ServiceStatus value to reveal all of its contents. Also note the 'AccountSkuId' property listed above. This value will provide us a way to dig into what license types that are available to us in PowerShell.

First, capture the field in a variable:

```
$ServiceStatus = (Get-MsolAccountSku | Where {$_.SkuPartNumber -eq "ENTERPRISEPACK"}).ServiceStatus
```

Then display the variable in a table format:

The license options are then applied to the user account:

```
Set-MsolUserLicense –User $Upn –LicenseOptions $LicenseOptions
$Status = (Get-MsolUser -User $Upn).Licenses[0].ServiceStatus
```

After the script completes, the current licensing options for the user account can be verified with PowerShell first:

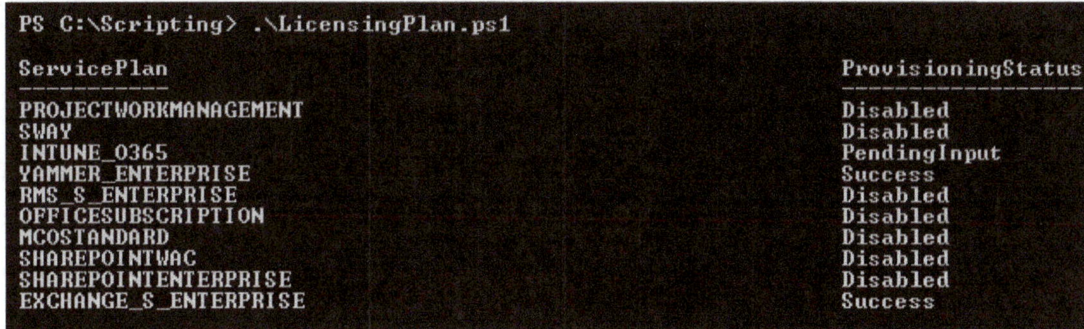

The results can also be verified in the Office 365 console:

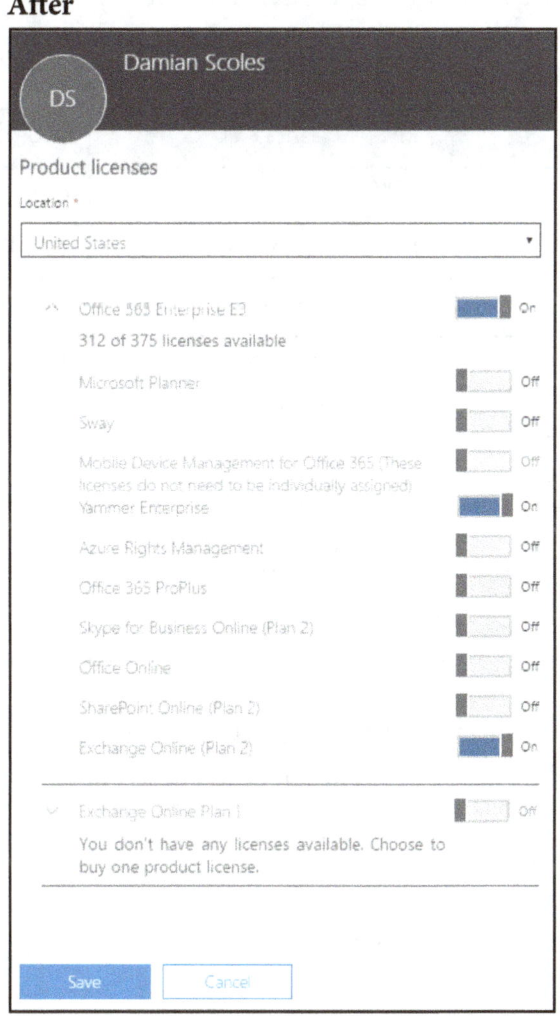

Why is this the solution? Unfortunately the licensing for Office 365 does not work in a cumulative manner or allow the option to choose which options to enable. For Office 365, Microsoft requires the licensing to be applied in a subtractive manner. For example with an E3 license (previous page) there are essentially 10 sub-licenses. By default, assigning an E3 license will enable all of these sub-licenses. However, if there are users that are only required to have Exchange Online, the other nine need to be disabled and instead of just enabling the Exchange Online license.

** **Note** ** Available features change all the time, the screen shots above are illustrative only.

The option to select and unselect license options is important as need changes, user roles change, and organizational apps needs change and so on. Being able to add or remove individual licenses are important for maintaining strict access to apps that may only be necessary for a particular user's job function.

It should also be noted that the above methodology is aimed at limiting access of end users to services that an enterprise may not way to roll out to every user. The code could then be used to add services once a user population has been properly trained in how to use a particular service like Sway or Planner for some examples.

Sample Script 2

Take the same scenario where licenses need to be adjusted. IT management has decided that there will be licensing tiers to make sure that users only have access to applications that are required for them to do their jobs. The list of requirements is divided into four different licensing groups. Here are the requirements (by group):

Warehouse	Marketing	InfoWorkers	IT
EXCHANGE_S_ENTERPRISE	SWAY	INTUNE_O365	PROJECTWORKMANAGEMENT
SHAREPOINTWAC	YAMMER_ENTERPRISE	YAMMER_ENTERPRISE	SWAY
	RMS_S_ENTERPRISE	RMS_S_ENTERPRISE	INTUNE_O365
	OFFICESUBSCRIPTION	OFFICESUBSCRIPTION	YAMMER_ENTERPRISE
	MCOSTANDARD	MCOSTANDARD	RMS_S_ENTERPRISE
	SHAREPOINTWAC	SHAREPOINTWAC	OFFICESUBSCRIPTION
	SHAREPOINTENTERPRISE	SHAREPOINTENTERPRISE	MCOSTANDARD
	EXCHANGE_S_ENTERPRISE	EXCHANGE_S_ENTERPRISE	SHAREPOINTWAC
			SHAREPOINTENTERPRISE
			EXCHANGE_S_ENTERPRISE

In order to make this work properly, Active Directory Groups need to be assigned and then the licensing can be applied in a per group manner. First, the group assignment needs to occur in order to prepare for assigning licenses on a per group basis.

Sample Source CSV File

```
SamAccountNameGroup
Administrator,IT
Guest,Warehouse
Krbtgt,Marketing
Damian,IT
```

Sample Script Code

```powershell
# Read Users from CSV list
$Users = Import-Csv "c:\Scripting\GroupsToUsers.csv"

Foreach ($Line in $Users) {
   # 'normalize' variables
   $Member = $Line.SamAccountName
   $Group = $Line.Group

   # Add user to the group listed in the CSV file
   Try {
      Add-ADGroupMember -Identity $Group -Member $Member -ErrorAction STOP
      Write-Host "Successfully added $Member to the group $Group." -ForegroundColor Cyan
   } Catch {
      Write-Host "Could not add $Member to the group $Group." -ForegroundColor Yellow
   }
}
```

When run, the users are added to their respective groups:

```
PS C:\Scripting> .\UsersToGroups.ps1
Successfully added Administrator to the group IT.
Successfully added Guest to the group warehouse.
Successfully added krbtgt to the group Marketing.
Successfully added damian to the group IT.
Successfully added dstork to the group IT.
Successfully added tuser01 to the group Marketing.
Successfully added tuser02 to the group warehouse.
Successfully added adrms to the group IT.
Successfully added jton to the group Marketing.
Successfully added jforth to the group Marketing.
Successfully added jwithers to the group Marketing.
Successfully added GlenJohn to the group IT.
Successfully added wtell to the group Marketing.
Successfully added bfranklin to the group warehouse.
```

Now the groups have been populated, the disabled plans can be created – one per AD group:

```powershell
# Disabled Options for Warehouse workers
$DisabledOptionsWH = @()
$DisabledOptionsWH += "SWAY"
$DisabledOptionsWH += "YAMMER_ENTERPRISE"
$DisabledOptionsWH += "RMS_S_ENTERPRISE"
$DisabledOptionsWH += "OFFICESUBSCRIPTION"
$DisabledOptionsWH += "MCOSTANDARD"
$DisabledOptionsWH += "SHAREPOINTENTERPRISE"
$DisabledOptionsWH += "EXCHANGE_S_ENTERPRISE"
$DisabledOptionsWH += "SHAREPOINTENTERPRISE"
$DisabledOptionsWH += "PROJECTWORKMANAGEMENT"
```

```
# Disabled Options for Marketing
$DisabledOptionsMKT = @()
$DisabledOptionsMKT += "PROJECTWORKMANAGEMENT"

# Disabled Options for Information Workers
$DisabledOptionsIW = @()
$DisabledOptionsIW += "PROJECTWORKMANAGEMENT"
$DisabledOptionsIW += "SWAY"

# Disabled Options for Information Technology
# None - all active at this time
```

After the licensing options are configured, the user lists need to be created so that licenses can be assigned by group membership:

```
# Store group members into variables
$IW = Get-ADGroup "IT" | Get-AdGroupMember
$Marketing = Get-ADGroup "Marketing" | Get-AdGroupMember
$Warehouse = Get-ADGroup "Warehouse" | Get-AdGroupMember
```

Next the connection to Office 365 need to be established:

```
# Connect to Office 365
Write-Host "Enter the password for Office 365 administrative rights." -ForegroundColor Cyan
Read-Host -SecureString | ConvertFrom-SecureString | Out-File "c:\scripting\securestring.txt"
$Password = cat "c:\scripting\securestring.txt" | ConvertTo-SecureString
$UserName = "<UPN of Global Admin>"
$O365Cred = New-Object -TypeName System.Management.Automation.PSCredential -ArgumentList $Username, $Password
$Session = New-PSSession -ConfigurationName Microsoft.Exchange -ConnectionUri https://ps.outlook.com/powershell/ -Credential $O365Cred -Authentication Basic -AllowRedirection
Import-PSSession $Session
```

Then a connection to the Microsoft Azure Active Directory tenant needs to be established:

```
# Connect to MSOL Service
Connect-MsolService -Credential $O365Cred
```

After all the connections are made (Office 365 and MSOL Service) and the variables are populated with the users to be configured for proper licensing, a licensing code block will be run for each group (a repeat of previous code):

```
# Set licensing for Information Workers
Foreach ($Line in $IW) {

    # Set variables
    $Upn = $Line.UserPrincipalName
    $Location = (Get-MsolUser -UserPrincipalName $Upn).UsageLocation
    $Licensed = (Get-MsolUser -UserPrincipalName $Upn).IsLicensed

    # Set location to United States
```

```
    If ($Location -eq $Null) {
        Set-MsolUser -UserPrincipalName $Upn -UsageLocation "US"
    }

    # Assign full license to start with
    If ($Licensed -eq $False) {
        Set-MsolUserLicense -UserPrincipalName $Upn -AddLicenses "<tenantname>:ENTERPRISEPACK"
    }

    # Remove 'excess' license options
    $LicenseOptions = New-MsolLicenseOptions –AccountSkuId "<tenantname>:ENTERPRISEPACK" –
    DisabledPlans $DisabledOptions
    Set-MsolUserLicense –User $Upn –LicenseOptions $LicenseOptions
}
```

Repeat the same code above, simply switching out this one line for each group to be configured:

```
Foreach ($Line in $IW) {
```

Which becomes:

```
Foreach ($Line in $Marketing) {
```

And:

```
Foreach ($Line in $Warehouse) {
```

Now all users have their licensing configured per IT Management. Again, this code is for assigning licenses manually with PowerShell and does not rely on Azure AD Group Based Licensing.

Azure AD Recycle Bin

Azure AD has a Recycle Bin (similar to on-premises Active Directory) for objects that are removed from the tenant. These objects stay in the Recycle Bin for 30 days and then the objects are removed permanently. There are no direct PowerShell cmdlets (like Get-RecycleBin) for the Recycle Bin in Office 365. In order to find objects, the Get-MSOLUser cmdlet has a switch for this:

```
-ReturnDeletedUsers [<SwitchParameter>]
    If set, only users in the recycling bin will be deleted.

    Required?                         false
    Position?                         named
    Default value
    Accept pipeline input?            false
    Accept wildcard characters?       false
```

The 'ReturnDeletedUsers' will provide a list of users that were removed and are now awaiting for permanent deletion:

```
UserPrincipalName          DisplayName          isLicensed
-----------------          -----------          ----------
jdoe@domain.com            John Doe             False
hcastille@domain.com       Harold Castille      True
bhope@domain.com           Bob Hope             False
thill@domain.com           Thomas Hill          False
```

These same users can be removed with the Remove-MSOLUsers. Let's go through the process for an Office 365 tenant. Users that were recently deleted can be found in the Deleted Users tab under Users in the Office 365 interface:

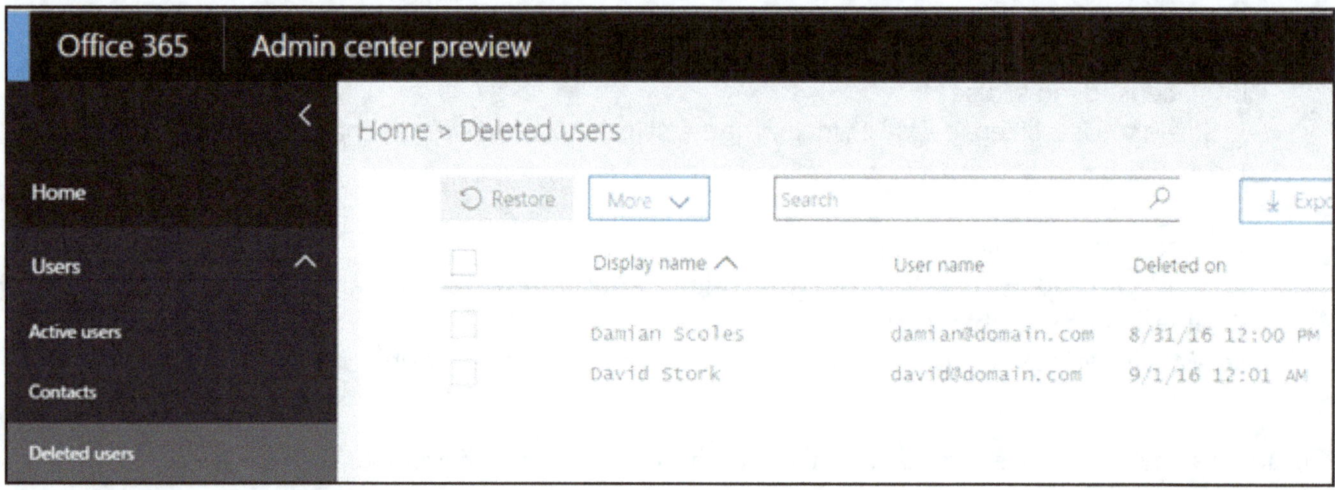

In order to properly remove users from the Recycle Bin, we first need the UPN and Object ID. The UPN is needed to verify which user will be deleted while the Object ID is actually used by PowerShell to remove the users [Don't forget to run Connect-MSOLService first]:

```
Get-MsolUser -ReturnDeletedUsers | Select UserPrincipalName, ObjectId
```

```
UserPrincipalName        Objectid
-----------------        --------
jdoe@domain.com          105856af-663a-49a8-bdad-efe8947ef70a
hcastille@domain.com     1b0ed587-4cf4-4e46-b5c5-5efab200007c
bhope@domain.com         866e6c23-629d-4239-aed9-c731173811dc
thill@domain.com         98fab817-b97b-436e-8854-47638b1af079
```

Example 1

Removing only one user from the Recycle Bin can be done with a one-liner. The only criteria needed as mentioned above, is the ObjectID from the list of objects in the Recycle Bin.

```
Remove-MsolUser -RemoveFromRecycleBin -ObjectId 98fab817-b97b-436e-8854-47638b1af079
```

```
PS C:\> Remove-MsolUser -RemoveFromRecycleBin -ObjectId 98fab817-b97b-436e-8854-47638b1af0

Confirm
Continue with this operation?
[Y] Yes  [N] No  [S] Suspend  [?] Help (default is "Y"): y
```

Then verify that the user is removed:

```
Get-MsolUser -ReturnDeletedUsers | select UserPrincipalName, ObjectId
```

```
UserPrincipalName        Objectid
-----------------        --------
jdoe@domain.com          105856af-663a-49a8-bdad-efe8947ef70a
hcastille@domain.com     1b0ed587-4cf4-4e46-b5c5-5efab200007c
bhope@domain.com         866e6c23-629d-4239-aed9-c731173811dc
```

Example 2

Removing all users in the Recycle Bin requires a query to get the objects stored in the Recycle Bin and then a cmdlet to remove these objects. Is this example the ObjectID does not need to be specified as we are removing all items.

Get-MsolUser -ReturnDeletedUsers | Remove-MsolUser -RemoveFromRecycleBin

```
PS C:\> Get-MsolUser -ReturnDeletedUsers | Remove-MsolUser -RemoveFromRecycleBin

Confirm
Continue with this operation?
[Y] Yes  [N] No  [S] Suspend  [?] Help (default is "Y"): y

Confirm
Continue with this operation?
[Y] Yes  [N] No  [S] Suspend  [?] Help (default is "Y"): y

Confirm
Continue with this operation?
[Y] Yes  [N] No  [S] Suspend  [?] Help (default is "Y"): y
```

Then verify that the user is removed:

Get-MsolUser -ReturnDeletedUsers | select UserPrincipalName, ObjectId

```
PS C:\> Get-MsolUser -ReturnDeletedUsers | select UserPrincipalName, ObjectId
PS C:\> _
```

Result – empty Recycle Bin.

In This Chapter

- Client Access
- Outlook Web Access (OWA)
- GAL Segmentation
  - Enable Address Book Policy Routing
  - Create Recipient Filter
  - Create Address Lists
  - Create Global Address List (GAL) and Offline Address Book (OAB)
  - Create a New Address Book Policy
- Accepted Domains
- POP3 and IMAP4
- Client Access Rules

For Exchange Online, configuration does not involve any of the normal server configuration that would normally need to be completed for an on-premises server. Instead we need to focus on features that can be enabled, configured and modified with PowerShell. These elements are crucial to a successful and good experience for your end users.

With a hosted Exchange environment we need to look at things like granting access to certain protocols or a user. This could mean configuring all mailboxes to connect via only ActiveSync, OWA and MAPI while blocking all users from connecting over IMAP or POP3. We can also control the experience users have with OWA and ActiveSync with policies that are built-in or ones we create new and apply to users on Exchange Online.

We will also explore Address Lists Segregation which allows different users to see different sets of users in Outlook. Typical use of this feature would be for large corporations looking to limit an address book by regions or perhaps a company with many subsidiaries would want to isolate some user look ups in their GAL.

POP3 and IMAP for will covered as they are offered as part of the Office 365 suite of connection protocols and some Line of Business applications still require these protocols. We'll explore what can be configured in a hosted Exchange environment for these two protocols.

Client Access

End user access is key to a functional messaging system. This goes for Exchange servers as well. Access for clients comes in the form of OWA, Outlook and ActiveSync. For this chapter we will cover OWA, Outlook Anywhere and MAPI over HTTP. These items need to be configured before clients begin to connect to the Exchange 2016 servers.

Client Access Mailbox

There is a subset of cmdlets that we can use to control certain parts of the client access experience for users. These cmdlets will allow us to control protocols and settings associated with those protocols. We can control the settings for POP3, MAPI behavior, EWS and overall which protocols are even allowed.

PowerShell

What cmdlets are available for the CASMailbox phrase?

    Get-Command *CASMailbox*

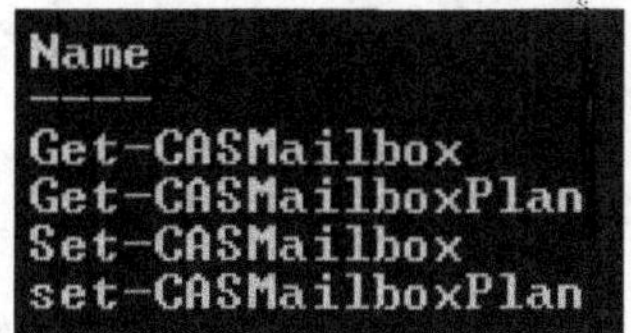

We can see there are cmdlets for Get and Set, but we also have an interesting pair of cmdlets for a CAS Mailbox Plan. We will see what these do a little later on.

First let's review the Get-CASMailbox cmdlet and see what it provides for us:

    Get-CASMailbox Damian

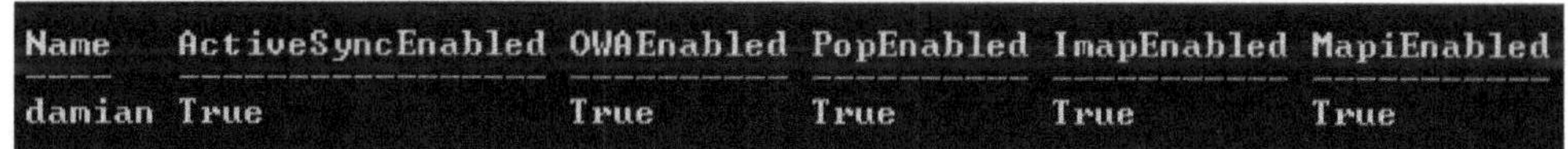

Name	ActiveSyncEnabled	OWAEnabled	PopEnabled	ImapEnabled	MapiEnabled
damian	True	True	True	True	True

- **ActiveSyncEnabled** - This allows a connection to the mailbox from a device that uses ActiveSync
- **OWAEnabled** - Web mail access via your favorite browser over Port 443
- **POPEnabled** - by default this allows a secure POP3 connection on Port 995
- **IMAPEnabled** - enabled by default as well for IMAP4 access on Port 993
- **MAPIEnabled** - This was the standard protocol for access via Outlook clients

From the Get-CASMailbox cmdlet we can see that there are five main protocols listed and in the case of this one mailbox, they are all enabled. As we can see here all of these protocols/access methods are enabled by default for mailboxes in Office 365. The same methods can all be disabled or enabled depending on the needs of the organization.

The Get-CASMailbox | Ft provides a pretty basic view and we will explore later how we can use this as a reference for the Set-CASMailbox to alter what protocol a mailbox can be accessed with.

Now image that we would like to see a more detailed view of these CAS protocols and the settings for one mailbox:

Get-CASMailbox Damian | FL

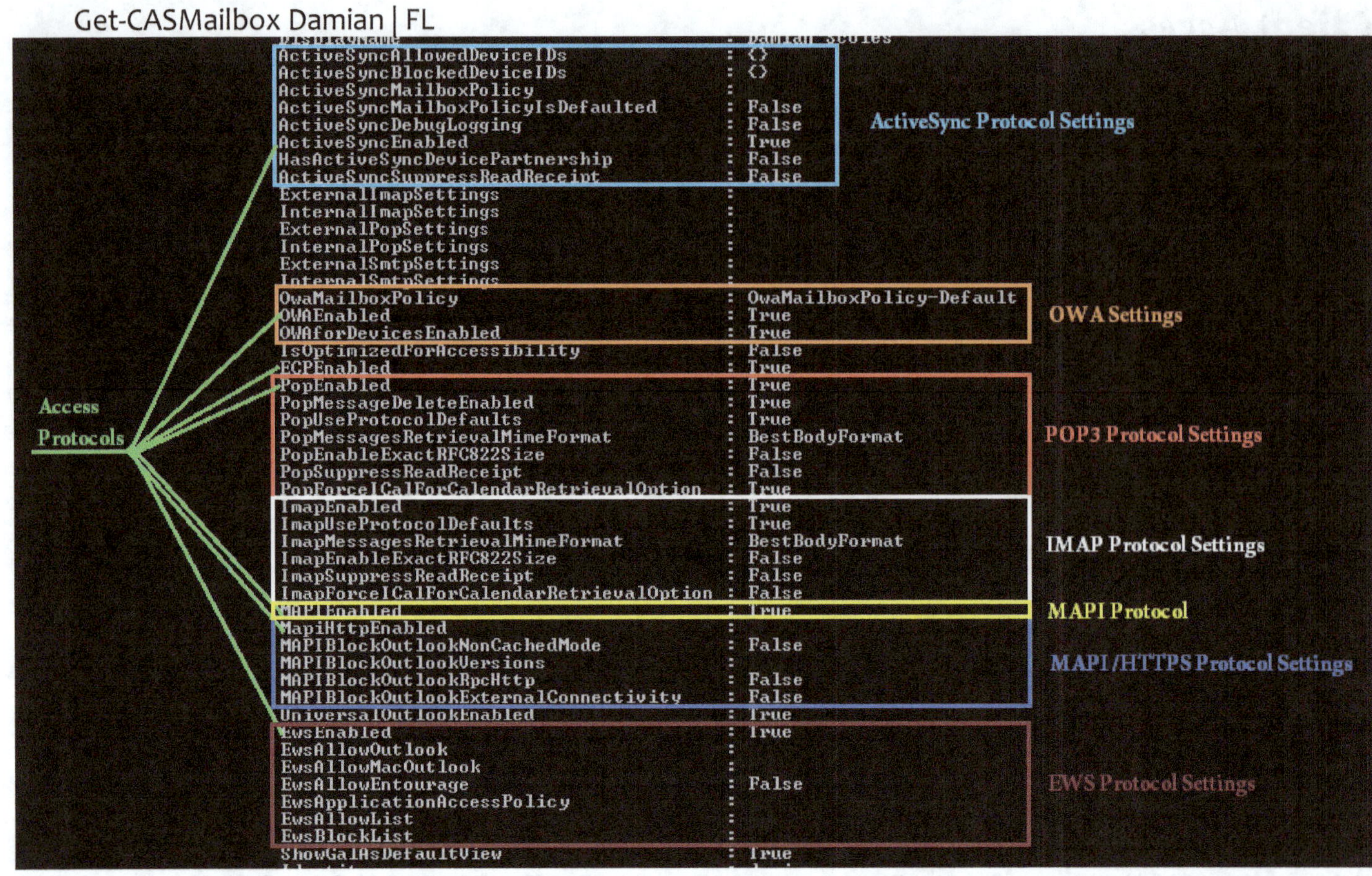


```
DisplayName                              : Damian Scoles
ActiveSyncAllowedDeviceIDs               : {}
ActiveSyncBlockedDeviceIDs               : {}
ActiveSyncMailboxPolicy                  :
ActiveSyncMailboxPolicyIsDefaulted       : False
ActiveSyncDebugLogging                   : False
ActiveSyncEnabled                        : True
HasActiveSyncDevicePartnership           : False
ActiveSyncSuppressReadReceipt            : False
ExternalImapSettings                     :
InternalImapSettings                     :
ExternalPopSettings                      :
InternalPopSettings                      :
ExternalSmtpSettings                     :
InternalSmtpSettings                     :
OwaMailboxPolicy                         : OwaMailboxPolicy-Default
OWAEnabled                               : True
OWAforDevicesEnabled                     : True
IsOptimizedForAccessibility              : False
ECPEnabled                               : True
PopEnabled                               : True
PopMessageDeleteEnabled                  : True
PopUseProtocolDefaults                   : True
PopMessagesRetrievalMimeFormat           : BestBodyFormat
PopEnableExactRFC822Size                 : False
PopSuppressReadReceipt                   : False
PopForceICalForCalendarRetrievalOption   : True
ImapEnabled                              : True
ImapUseProtocolDefaults                  : True
ImapMessagesRetrievalMimeFormat          : BestBodyFormat
ImapEnableExactRFC822Size                : False
ImapSuppressReadReceipt                  : False
ImapForceICalForCalendarRetrievalOption  : False
MAPIEnabled                              : True
MapiHttpEnabled                          :
MAPIBlockOutlookNonCachedMode            : False
MAPIBlockOutlookVersions                 :
MAPIBlockOutlookRpcHttp                  : False
MAPIBlockOutlookExternalConnectivity     : False
UniversalOutlookEnabled                  : True
EwsEnabled                               : True
EwsAllowOutlook                          :
EwsAllowMacOutlook                       :
EwsAllowEntourage                        : False
EwsApplicationAccessPolicy               :
EwsAllowList                             :
EwsBlockList                             :
ShowGalAsDefaultView                     : True
```

As we can see there are quite a few properties we can adjust for each of the protocol methods as well as revealing a couple more - EWS and MAPI/HTTPS.

One common task for these protocols is to decide what access we would want to provide for the users. Do we want all users to access OWA, ActiveSync, MAPI, MAPI over HTTPS, POP, IMAP and so on?

Scenario

You have a new IT manager who has decided that she would like to secure access to Office 365 mailboxes. She has asked the Help Desk and Administrators to figure out what protocols are in use and to lock down those that are not. After investigating here is the recommendation that is presented to the IT Manager:

In Use: ActiveSync, MAPI/HTTPS, ECP, OWA
Not In Use: POP, IMAP, MAPI

The IT Manager wants to now restrict these protocols for all mailboxes in Office 365. Because the Get-CASMailbox cmdlet was use to pull the protocol types, it is decided that the Set-CASMailbox cmdlet be used to restrict access:

Get-Help Set-CASMailbox -Examples

```
----------------------- Example 1 -----------------------
Set-CASMailbox adam@contoso.com -OWAEnabled $false -PopEnabled $false

----------------------- Example 2 -----------------------
Set-CASMailbox adam@contoso.com -ActiveSyncDebugLogging $true -ActiveSyncMailboxPolicy Managemen

----------------------- Example 3 -----------------------
Set-CASMailbox tony@contoso.com -DisplayName "Tony Smith" -MAPIBlockOutlookRpcHttp $true
```

Reviewing the examples it looks like each protocol can be specified in the Set-CASMailbox cmdlet. As all mailboxes will be affected, the Get-Mailbox cmdlet should be piped into the Set-CASMailbox cmdlet like this:

Get-Mailbox | Set-CASMailbox -PopEnabled $False -IMAPEnabled $False -MAPIEnabled $False

Once the changes are made, we can check with a Get-Mailbox cmdlet, which will show the following:

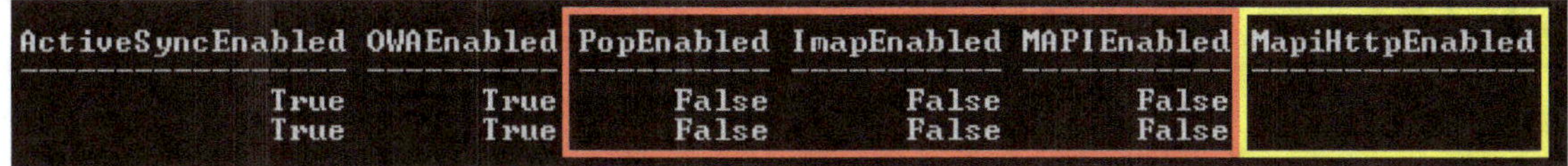

Notice that the protocols that were disabled, now show 'False' as expected. However, notice the last protocol 'MapiHTTPEnabled'. No value is displayed for this protocol. When reviewing the Get-Help for Set-CAS-Mailbox, what we find is that the 'MAPIHTTPEnabled' parameter for Set-CASMailbox, only works in Exchange 2016. The MAPI over HTTPs is set to be 'the' protocol to connect to Office 365 (it may be by the time you read this) and it is not configurable at this point either.

In some scenarios you may want to block access to a protocol like MAPI over HTTPS or RPC over HTTPs and this can be done with Client Access Rules, which is covered at the end of this chapter.

Another set of parameters that are commonly configured are 'OWA Mailbox Policy' and 'ActiveSyncDebugLogging'. The first is used to set a policy that applies to mailboxes for when they access their mailboxes via OWA. The second can be used to help diagnose ActiveSync connection issues.

Example - OWA Mailbox Policy

If we've configured an OWA Mailbox Policy called 'Company OWA Policy' we can apply this like so:

Set-CASMailbox Damian -OwaMailboxPolicy

We can also apply the same policy to multiple mailboxes or all mailboxes depending on the needs within PowerShell.

Example - ActiveSync Debug Logging

Mobile access to email has become more important year after year. Whether you connect with an Windows Phone, iPhone or Android sometimes issues occur where the connection cannot be made. So we can turn on some logging and send that to an email address for further diagnostics. The setting for a single mailbox can be initiated by turning on ActiveSync Debug Logging:

Set-CASMailbox Damian -ActiveSyncDebugLogging $True

After the troubleshooting is complete, make sure to turn this setting off:

Set-CASMailbox Damian -ActiveSyncDebugLogging $True

*-CASMailboxPlan Cmdlets

In addition to the CAS Mailbox cmdlets, there is also a set of CAS Mailbox Plan cmdlets. Let's explore what these cmdlets can be used for. First, the two cmdlets:

```
Name
----
Get-CASMailboxPlan
set-CASMailboxPlan
```

What information can get from just the 'Get' cmdlet:

Get-CASMailboxPlan | Ft

```
RunspaceId                              ActiveSyncMailboxPolicy ActiveSyncDebugLogging ActiveSyncEnabled ActiveSyncSuppres
                                                                                                          sReadReceipt
----------                              ----------------------- ---------------------- ----------------- -----------------
d5c8a543-fb9e-48f8-ab1c-efbf769da61f                                            False              True             False
d5c8a543-fb9e-48f8-ab1c-efbf769da61f                                            False              True             False
d5c8a543-fb9e-48f8-ab1c-efbf769da61f                                            False              True             False
d5c8a543-fb9e-48f8-ab1c-efbf769da61f                                            False              True             False
```

Well the results from the cmdlet are far from ideal. First, where is the name?

Get-CasMailboxPlan | Ft Name

```
Name

ExchangeOnline-1c3fca3a-6d76-46ae-b71e-ce4b1dfd468c
ExchangeOnlineDeskless-b6b400da-3a01-40b0-a349-595dbae06834
ExchangeOnlineEnterprise-124f6119-7869-40e4-90a6-14e20837d794
ExchangeOnlineEssentials-4f90387b-2a8b-4891-a7b1-03ff753632a5
```

Notice that the names are a little more descriptive. The plans also correspond to the licensing that is assigned or can be assigned to users to enable certain features in Exchange Online. A chart of the licensing can be found here:

https://msdn.microsoft.com/en-us/library/dd229067(v=exchsrvcs.149).aspx

Let's examine the 'ExchangeOnlineEnterprise' license which corresponds to an E3 licenses in Office 365:

Get-CASMailboxPlan ExchangeOnlineEnterprise-124f6119-7869-40e4-90a6-14e20837d794 | Fl

```
ActiveSyncMailboxPolicy            :
ActiveSyncDebugLogging             : False
ActiveSyncEnabled                  : True
ActiveSyncSuppressReadReceipt      : False
DisplayName                        : ExchangeOnlineEnterprise
ECPEnabled                         : True
ImapEnabled                        : True
ImapUseProtocolDefaults            : True
ImapMessagesRetrievalMimeFormat    : BestBodyFormat
ImapEnableExactRFC822Size          : False
ImapProtocolLoggingEnabled         : False
ImapSuppressReadReceipt            : False
ImapForceICalForCalendarRetrievalOption : False
MAPIEnabled                        : True
MapiHttpEnabled                    :
MAPIBlockOutlookNonCachedMode      : False
MAPIBlockOutlookVersions           :
MAPIBlockOutlookRpcHttp            : False
MAPIBlockOutlookExternalConnectivity : False
OwaMailboxPolicy                   : OwaMailboxPolicy-Default
OWAEnabled                         : True
OWAforDevicesEnabled               : True
PopEnabled                         : True
PopMessageDeleteEnabled            : True
PopUseProtocolDefaults             : True
PopMessagesRetrievalMimeFormat     : BestBodyFormat
PopEnableExactRFC822Size           : False
PopProtocolLoggingEnabled          : False
PopSuppressReadReceipt             : False
PopForceICalForCalendarRetrievalOption : True
RemotePowerShellEnabled            : True
EwsEnabled                         : True
EwsAllowOutlook                    :
EwsAllowMacOutlook                 :
EwsAllowEntourage                  :
EwsApplicationAccessPolicy         :
EwsAllowList                       :
```

If we remember the settings revealed with 'Get-CASMailbox' cmdlet, a lot of the available properties here are similar. We would also notice that there are some missing properties as well. For example, settings that appear to apply to a single user are not included in the CAS Mailbox plan - ActiveSyncAllowedDeviceIDs, ActiveSync-BlockedDeviceIDs, ActiveSyncMailboxPolicyIsDefaulted and HasActiveSyncSuppressReadReceipt. However, all the other settings included in the CAS Mailbox planned can be applies en masse to all mailboxes with a certain license applied to them. A practical approach to this would be to use the plan configuration to globally change the protocols allowed or change settings that need to be set for all mailboxes in Exchange Online. In the case of the next example, we are reducing the protocols allowed for any mailbox with an E3 license:

```
Set-CASMailboxPlan 'ExchangeOnlineEnterprise-124f6119-7869-40e4-90a6-14e20837d794' -PopEnabled
$False -IMAPEnabled $False -MAPIEnabled $False
```

Now, while we can make these changes, there are some parameters that are not allowed and are restricted to Microsoft:

```
-PopEnableExactRFC822Size (<$true | $false>
    This parameter is reserved for internal Microsoft use.

    Required?                        false
    Position?                        Named
    Default value
    Accept pipeline input?           False
    Accept wildcard characters?      false
```

In the case of Set-CASMailboxPlan, over 30 parameters are for Microsoft use only. While it would be nice to configure these plans to make the changes global, Microsoft would prefer these changes not be made without their guidance. These parameters can also be verified on the TechNet page for this cmdlet:

https://technet.microsoft.com/en-us/library/mt492754(v=exchg.160).aspx

Outlook Web Access (OWA)

Outlook Web Access (OWA) is the web client that is typically used by users who don't need all of the capabilities of Outlook, do not use Outlook enough to justify a license, mobile users and road-warriors. Like Exchange on-premises, Exchange Online has policy and settings that can be applied to affect the users experience for OWA as on-premises you could also configure the OWA virtual directories to achieve the same effect.

Configuring OWA in Exchange Online is limited to configuring OWA Mailbox Policies. All other configuration options are left behind the scenes:

```
Get-command *owa*

Name
----
Get-OwaMailboxPolicy
New-OwaMailboxPolicy
Remove-OwaMailboxPolicy
Set-OwaMailboxPolicy
```

Let's start with the Get-OWAMailboxPolicy to see what we have available for configuration:

```
PS C:\> Get-OwaMailboxPolicy | Ft Name

Name
----
OwaMailboxPolicy-Default
```

We can see from the results, we have a default policy and nothing else defined. We can dig into more details with the Format-List options like so:

```
Get-OWAMailboxPolicy OWAMailboxPolicy-Default | Fl
```

```
WacEditingEnabled                                    : True
PrintWithoutDownloadEnabled                          : True
DropboxAttachmentsEnabled                            : True
BoxAttachmentsEnabled                                : True
OneDriveAttachmentsEnabled                           : True
GoogleDriveAttachmentsEnabled                        : True
ThirdPartyAttachmentsEnabled                         : True
ClassicAttachmentsEnabled                            : True
ReferenceAttachmentsEnabled                          : True
SaveAttachmentsToCloudEnabled                        : True
InternalSPMySiteHostURL                              :
ExternalSPMySiteHostURL                              :
DirectFileAccessOnPublicComputersEnabled             : True
DirectFileAccessOnPrivateComputersEnabled            : True
WebReadyDocumentViewingOnPublicComputersEnabled      : True
WebReadyDocumentViewingOnPrivateComputersEnabled     : True
ForceWebReadyDocumentViewingFirstOnPublicComputers   : False
ForceWebReadyDocumentViewingFirstOnPrivateComputers  : False
WacViewingOnPublicComputersEnabled                   : True
WacViewingOnPrivateComputersEnabled                  : True
ForceWacViewingFirstOnPublicComputers                : False
ForceWacViewingFirstOnPrivateComputers               : False
ActionForUnknownFileAndMIMETypes                     : Allow
WebReadyFileTypes                                    : {.xlsx, .pptx, .docx, .xls...}
WebReadyMimeTypes                                    : {application/vnd.openxmlformats-officedocument.presentationml.pr
                                                       esentation, application/vnd.openxmlformats-officedocument.wordpr
                                                       ocessingml.document, application/vnd.openxmlformats-officedocume
                                                       nt.spreadsheetml.sheet, application/vnd.ms-powerpoint...}
WebReadyDocumentViewingForAllSupportedTypes          : True
WebReadyDocumentViewingSupportedMimeTypes            : {application/msword, application/vnd.ms-excel,
                                                       application/x-msexcel, application/vnd.ms-powerpoint...}
WebReadyDocumentViewingSupportedFileTypes            : {.doc, .dot, .rtf, .xls...}
```

The above is a small sample of the available properties that are included in the default OWA Mailbox Policy. This is quite different from what is available in the Exchange Admin Center:

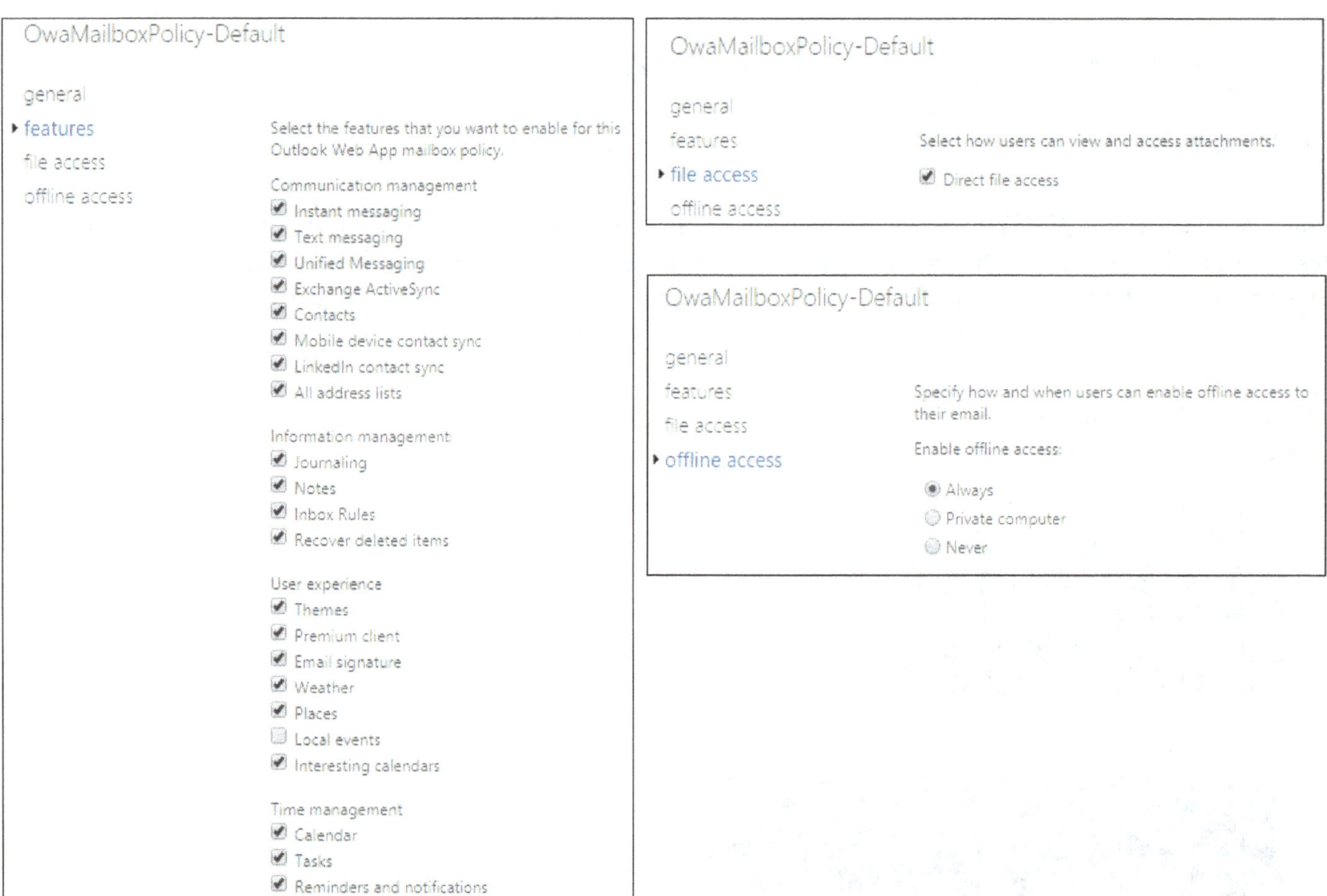

The web based access to the OWA Mailbox Policy allows access to some common features like File Access and

Offline Access. This is perhaps easy to configure in the Exchange Admin Center. As we can see, by default we have one OWA Mailbox Policy which is by default applied to all mailboxes as they are created:

Get-Mailbox | Get-CASMailbox | Ft DisplayName,OWAMailboxPolicy

```
PS C:\Get-Mailbox | get-casmailbox| ft DisplayName,OWAMailboxPolicy

DisplayName                     OwaMailboxPolicy
-----------                     ----------------
Damian Scoles                   OwaMailboxPolicy-Default
John Doe                        OwaMailboxPolicy-Default
```

These two users have the default OWA Mailbox policy assigned to them. By default a lot of options are enabled and this may or may not be the desired result. The provided options in the GUI may not be the options we need to tweak for our user population. As such, we can use PowerShell to make these changes and produce a policy that is what we need. For example, we would like to turn off some of the cloud options for attachments for these users:

```
PrintWithoutDownloadEnabled           : True
DropboxAttachmentsEnabled             : True
BoxAttachmentsEnabled                 : True
OneDriveAttachmentsEnabled            : True
GoogleDriveAttachmentsEnabled         : True
ThirdPartyAttachmentsEnabled          : True
ClassicAttachmentsEnabled             : True
ReferenceAttachmentsEnabled           : True
SaveAttachmentsToCloudEnabled         : True
```

From the above screenshot we can see we have some interesting options that are on by default. Let's adjust these so that there are no cloud attachment options enabled. We can do so by disabled Dropbox, Google and Box as available options, like so:

Set-OwaMailboxPolicy OwaMailboxPolicy-Default -DropboxAttachmentsEnabled $False -BoxAttachmentsEnabled $False -GoogleDriveAttachmentsEnabled $False

Now we have this as a result:

```
PrintWithoutDownloadEnabled           : False
DropboxAttachmentsEnabled             : False
BoxAttachmentsEnabled                 : False
OneDriveAttachmentsEnabled            : True
GoogleDriveAttachmentsEnabled         : False
ThirdPartyAttachmentsEnabled          : True
ClassicAttachmentsEnabled             : True
ReferenceAttachmentsEnabled           : True
SaveAttachmentsToCloudEnabled         : True
```

For this example, OneDrive is still enabled as this will be part of our Office 365 tenant, controlled with Office 365 security processes and thus considered safe for attaching to emails.

There are some properties of the OWA Mailbox Policies that are considered a 'MultiValuedProperty'. What this means is that the property contains multiple values and needs to be treated a bit differently then other properties which are single value ones. What does that mean? Let's review one example - 'BlockedFileTypes'. This property contains 88 file types. These 88 are the default file types that are blocked by Exchange Online. What if we need to add a value or extension? First, don't do this:

Set-OwaMailboxPolicy OwaMailboxPolicy-Default -BlockedFileTypes '.txt'

That will set the property to just '.txt'. The other 88 default file types will be wiped out. So, don't do that, unless that was your intent. In order to add a value, we'll need to store all 88 file types in a variable, add the new one to that variable and then apply that variable to the 'BlockedFileTypes' variable. To do so, we run a set of PowerShell cmdlets like so:

Sample Code to Add Blocked File Types

```
#Variable Definition
$CurrentFileTypes = @()
$CurrentFileTypes = (Get-OwaMailboxPolicy).BlockedFileTypes
$OWAPolicyName = 'OwaMailboxPolicy-Default'
$Loop = 0

# Get New File Types
Write-Host ' '
Write-Host 'How many new file types do you want to add? ' -NoNewLine -ForegroundColor Yellow
$Number = Read-Host
Write-Host '------------------------------------------' -ForegroundColor Yellow
Write-Host ' '
Do {
    Write-Host 'File type to add: ' -NoNewLine -ForegroundColor Green
    $Type = Read-Host
    $CurrentFileTypes += $Type
    $Loop++
} While ($Loop -lt $Number)

# Add File Types
Write-Host ' '
Write-Host 'Adding file types now.' -ForegroundColor Yellow
Write-Host ''
Set-OwaMailboxPolicy -Identity $OWAPolicyName -BlockedFileTypes $CurrentFileTypes
Write-Host ' '
Write-Host 'Done adding file types.' -ForegroundColor Cyan
```

The above script allows for use input which allows for this to be run at any time in the future. Here is what a sample run would look like if we wanted to add some custom file types:

```
How many new file types do you want to add? 2
--------------------------------------------------

File type to add: .tyt
File type to add: .klk

Adding file types now.....

Done adding file types.
```

Now, what if we wanted to do the reverse and remove the file type specified? How would we code for that? The easiest cmdlet to use to remove items is Compare-Object. Compare-Object will allow PowerShell to look at the entire contents of a variable looking for a particular string.

Sample Code to Remove Blocked File Types

```
#Variable Definition
$CurrentFileTypes = @()
```

```
$Remaining = @()
$NewFileTypes = @()
$CurrentFileTypes = (Get-OwaMailboxPolicy).BlockedFileTypes
$OWAPolicyName = 'OwaMailboxPolicy-Default'
$Loop = 0

# Get New File Types
Write-Host ' '
Write-Host 'How many new file types do you want to Remove? ' -NoNewLine -ForegroundColor Red
$Number = Read-Host
Write-Host '-------------------------------------------' -ForegroundColor Red
Write-Host ' '
Do {
   Write-Host 'File type to remove: ' -NoNewLine -ForegroundColor Yellow
   $Type = Read-Host
   $Remaining = (Compare-Object -ReferenceObject $CurrentFileTypes -DifferenceObject $Type).
   InputObject
   $Loop++
} While ($Loop -lt $Number)

# Any remaining file types will be stored in $NewFileTypes variable
$NewFileTypes = $Remaining

# Add File Types
Write-Host ' '
Write-Host 'Removing file types now.' -ForegroundColor Red
Write-Host ''
Set-OwaMailboxPolicy -Identity $OWAPolicyName -BlockedFileTypes $NewFileTypes
Write-Host ' '
Write-Host 'Done removing file types.' -ForegroundColor Red
```

Sample removal of a custom file type:

```
How many new file types do you want to Remove? 1
-------------------------------------------

File type to remove: .unf

Removing file types now.

Done removing file types.
```

Now that we have an OWA Mailbox Policy configured we can assign them to our mailboxes in an Exchange Tenant. Typically there is one default OWA Mailbox Policy that is set for 99% of the mailboxes in an organization. We can verify what is already present with this one-liner:

```
Get-Mailbox | Get-CASMailbox | ft DisplayName,OWAMailboxPolicy
```

Which provides this for results:

```
DisplayName                OwaMailboxPolicy
-----------                ----------------
Damian Scoles              OwaMailboxPolicy-Default
John Doe                   OwaMailboxPolicy-Default
```

If we've created more that one OWA policy we can assign it with the Set-CASMailbox cmdlet. An example of this would be if there is a separate policy for IT, C level executives and the rest of the company. In this case, we can assign the different policies to different people. Before assigning policies, verify the policies that are available:

```
PS C:\> Get-OwaMailboxPolicy | ft Name

Name
----
OwaMailboxPolicy-Default
IT OWA Policy
C-Level OWA Policy
```

Now that we have the names available, we can assign the policies:

Set-CASMailbox Damian -OwaMailboxPolicy 'IT OWA Policy'

Set-CASMailbox John.Doe -OwaMailboxPolicy 'C-Level OWA Policy'

After assigning the OWA Mailbox Policies make sure to verify the changes:

```
DisplayName                OwaMailboxPolicy
-----------                ----------------
Damian Scoles              IT OWA Policy
John Doe                   C-Level OWA Policy
```

The last option we have for OWA Mailbox Policies is removal. If there are excess policies or policies that need to be removed because they are no longer needed, we can remove them as well with the Remove-OWAMailboxPolicy. Remember to change the OWA Mailbox Policy for any users who are assigned to this policy otherwise you will experience an error like so:

```
PS C:\> Remove-OwaMailboxPolicy 'C-Level OWA Policy'

Confirm
Are you sure you want to perform this action?
Removing Outlook Web App mailbox policy "C-Level OWA Policy".
[Y] Yes  [A] Yes to All  [N] No  [L] No to All  [?] Help (default is "Y"): y
Couldn't delete mailbox policy C-Level OWA Policy because it is associated with users.
    + CategoryInfo          : WriteError: (C-Level OWA Policy:OwaMailboxPolicy) [Remove-O
   eAss...PolicyException
    + FullyQualifiedErrorId : [Server=CY4PR13MB1350,RequestId=94971d08-54dd-4dc1-bd4d-c27
   8:08:56 PM] [FailureCategory=Cmdlet-CannotDeleteAssociatedMailboxPolicyException] F6EA
   gement.Tasks.RemoveOwaMailboxPolicy
    + PSComputerName        : ps.outlook.com
```

GAL Segmentation

GAL Segmentation is the concept of separate address lists that are limited access wise to sets of users. Think of a company that has many subsidiaries. Users in the parent company have access to all the information of their subsidiaries. However, each subsidiary may not necessarily have the same access. When it comes to Exchange Online, we may want to isolate these entities so they only see their own address lists. This is just one use case for the GAL Segmentation feature in Exchange Online. In order to configure this, we'll need to perform these steps:

- Enable Address Book Policy Routing
- Create Recipient Filter
- Create Address Lists
- Create Global Address List (GAL) and Offline Address Book (OAB)
- Create a new Address Book Policy

Microsoft's official guidance is listed below and applies generally to Office 365 and Exchange 2013+:

https://technet.microsoft.com/en-us/library/hh529948(v=exchg.150).aspx

Enable Address Book Policy Routing

The first step down the road of GAL Segmentation is the enabling of Email Address Book Policy routing. This setting can be changed with the Set-TransportConfig cmdlet available in Exchange Online. If we review the Get-Help for Set-TransportConfig, we see there is a parameter that will allow the configuration of that setting:

```
Get-Help Set-TransportConfig -Full
```

```
-AddressBookPolicyRoutingEnabled <$true | $false>
    The AddressBookPolicyRoutingEnabled parameter controls how recipients are resolved in an organization that
    uses address book policies to create separate virtual organizations within the same Exchange organization.
    Specifically, the global address list <GAL> that's specified in the user's address book policy controls how
    recipients are resolved. When the value of this parameter is $true, users that are assigned different GALs
    appear as external recipients. When the value of this parameter is $false, users that are assigned different
    GALs appear as internal recipients.

    The default value is $false. Note that this parameter has no effect if your organization doesn't use address
    book policies, or if the address book policy routing agent isn't installed and enabled. Also note that
    changing the value of this parameter may take up to 30 minutes to take effect. For more information about
    address book policies, see Address book policies in Exchange 2016.

    Required?                   false
    Position?                   Named
    Default value
    Accept pipeline input?      False
    Accept wildcard characters? false
```

Using the related 'Get' cmdlet, we can verify that this is disabled by default:

```
Get-TransportConfig | fl AddressBookPolicyRoutingEnabled
```

```
PS C:\> Get-TransportConfig | fl AddressBookPolicyRoutingEnabled

AddressBookPolicyRoutingEnabled : False
```

We can now configure this for true and move on to the next step:

```
Set-TransportConfig -AddressBookPolicyRoutingEnabled $True
```

Create Recipient Filter

In order to construct a valid address book that is usable for a particular group of users, we will need to decide what users will be placed in that Address Book. A common method is to use a distribution group. For our example configuration we will have one distribution group per subsidiary, one distribution group for the main company and one distribution group for all mailboxes in the entire company.

Example

For this scenario there is a company call Railroad Holdings, Inc. This company had five subsidiaries - West Coast Trains, East Coast Trolleys, British Railway, Great Railroad Company and Subway Car Corp. In order to create these distribution groups and keep them up to date, we'll use the New-DynamicDistributionGroup:

```
Get-Help New-DynamicDistributionGroup -Examples
```

```
------------------------- Example 1 -------------------------

New-DynamicDistributionGroup -Name "Marketing Group" -IncludedRecipients "MailboxUsers,MailContacts"
-ConditionalDepartment "Marketing","Sales"

------------------------- Example 2 -------------------------

New-DynamicDistributionGroup -Name "Washington Management Team" -RecipientFilter ((RecipientType -eq
'UserMailbox') -and (Title -like 'Director*' -or Title -like 'Manager*') -and (StateOrProvince -eq 'WA'))
-RecipientContainer "North America"
```

In this example, users in each subsidiary company will have their CustomAttribute10 set to the company that they work for. Each group will thus be created based on this criteria.

Company
Railroad Holdings, Inc
West Coast Trains
East Coast Trolleys
British Railway
Great Railroad Company
Subway Car Corp.

Here is the code to create each DDL:

```
New-DynamicDistributionGroup -Name 'All - Railroad Holdings, Inc' -RecipientFilter {CustomAttribute10 -eq 'Railroad Holdings, Inc.'}
New-DynamicDistributionGroup -Name 'All - West Coast Trains' -RecipientFilter {CustomAttribute10 -eq 'West Coast Trains'}
New-DynamicDistributionGroup -Name 'All - East Coast Trolleys' -RecipientFilter {CustomAttribute10 -eq 'All - East Coast Trolleys'}
New-DynamicDistributionGroup -Name 'All - British Railway' -RecipientFilter {CustomAttribute10 -eq 'All - British Railway'}
New-DynamicDistributionGroup -Name 'All - Great Railroad Company' -RecipientFilter {CustomAttribute10 -eq 'All - Great Railroad Company'}
New-DynamicDistributionGroup -Name 'All - Subway Car Corp.' -RecipientFilter {CustomAttribute10 -eq 'All - Subway Car Corp.'}
```

Sample creation of one of the above Dynamic Distribution Groups:

```
PS C:\> New-DynamicDistributionGroup -Name 'All - East Coast Trolleys' -RecipientFilter
{CustomAttribute10 -eq 'All - East Coast Trolleys'}

Name                          ManagedBy
----                          ---------
All - East Coast Trolleys
```

Create Address Lists

Before we begin to configure new Address Lists for Exchange Online, we need to make sure the correct permissions are applied. As Microsoft states on Tech Net - *"In Exchange Online, the *-AddressList cmldets are only available in the Address Lists management role.* **By default** *in Exchange Online, the Address List role* **isn't assigned to any role groups**. *To use any cmdlets that require the Address List role, you need to add the role to a role group."* This means that before we begin, we need to assign this permission to the admin user we use to configure Exchange with.

We can see the role we need to assign by checking it with the Get-ManagementRole cmdlet:

```
PS C:\> Get-ManagementRole a*

Name                          RoleType
----                          --------
ArchiveApplication            ArchiveApplication
Address Lists                 AddressLists
ApplicationImpersonation      ApplicationImpersonation
Audit Logs                    AuditLogs
```

We need to create a Role Group and assign this Management Role to it:

```
PS C:\> New-RoleGroup "Address Lists" -Roles "Address Lists"

Name             AssignedRoles    RoleAssignments                                        Ma
----             -------------    ---------------                                        --
Address Lists    {Address Lists}  {OnlineExchangeBook.onmicrosoft.com\Address Lists-Address Lists} {O
```

After creating the Role Group, we now assign this group to a user to manage lists:

```
PS C:\> New-ManagementRoleAssignment -Name 'Address Lists' -Role 'Address Lists' -User Damian

Name             Role             RoleAssigneeName     RoleAssigneeType     AssignmentMethod
----             ----             ----------------     ----------------     ----------------
Address Lists    Address Lists    damian               User                 Direct
```

Remember to close your PowerShell session to Exchange Online after adding this Role Group and then reconnect. Otherwise the new Address List cmdlets will not be available. Now that we have the correct permissions, we can review the default Address Lists with this cmdlet:

Get-AddressList

```
Name                     DisplayName              RecipientFilter
----                     -----------              ---------------
All Contacts             All Contacts             ((Alias -ne $null) -and (((ObjectCategory -like 'perso
All Distribution Lists   All Distribution Lists   ((Alias -ne $null) -and (ObjectCategory -like 'group')
All Rooms                All Rooms                ((Alias -ne $null) -and (((RecipientDisplayType -eq '(
All Users                All Users                ((Alias -ne $null) -and ((((((ObjectCategory -like ')
All Groups               All Groups               ((Alias -ne $null) -and (RecipientTypeDetailsValue -e
Public Folders           Public Folders           ((Alias -ne $null) -and (ObjectCategory -like 'publicl
Offline Global Address...Offline Global Address...((Alias -ne $null) -and ((((((((((ObjectClass -eq 'us
```

What other Address List cmdlets are available?

Get-Command *AddressList

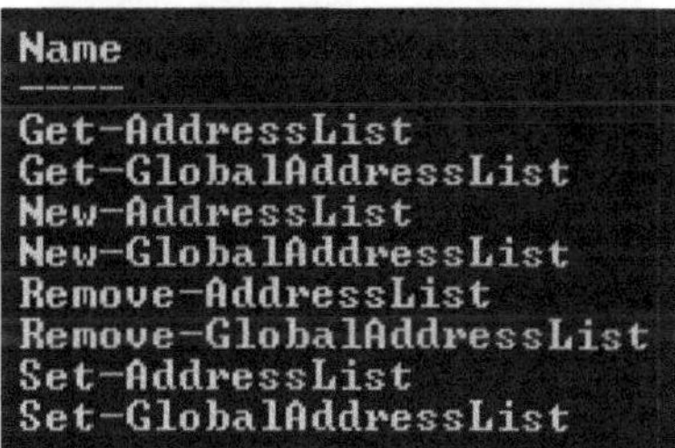

```
Name
----
Get-AddressList
Get-GlobalAddressList
New-AddressList
New-GlobalAddressList
Remove-AddressList
Remove-GlobalAddressList
Set-AddressList
Set-GlobalAddressList
```

For creating new Address Lists, it looks like the 'New-AddressList' is the cmdlet we'll need. Let's first review the examples for the cmdlet:

```
------------------------- Example 1 -------------------------
New-AddressList -Name MyAddressList -RecipientFilter (((RecipientType -eq 'MailboxUser') -and ((StateOrProvince
-eq 'Washington') -or (StateOrProvince -eq 'Oregon'))))
------------------------- Example 2 -------------------------
New-AddressList -Name MyAddressList2 -ConditionalStateOrProvince Washington -IncludedRecipients MailboxUsers
------------------------- Example 3 -------------------------
New-AddressList -Name "AL_AgencyB" -RecipientFilter (((RecipientType -eq 'MailboxUser') -and (CustomAttribute15
-like *AgencyB*))
```

None of the above examples exactly match our scenario. We will use Example 1, match the Recipient Type as a user mailbox and the distinguished name of the group we used as well. First, we need to get the distinguished name of the group:

```
$DDN = (Get-DynamicDistributionGroup 'All - Railroad Holdings, Inc').DistinguishedName
```

After that we can then use the $DDN value in our recipient filter as one of the criteria for adding users to the Address List:

```
New-AddressList -Name "All - Railroad Holdings" -RecipientFilter "RecipientType -eq 'UserMailbox'
-And MemberOfGroup -eq '$DDN'" -DisplayName "All - Railroad Holdings"
```

Now we have one Address list. We will need to do the same for each Dynamic Distribution Group. We can even do a loop to process each of these:

```
#Define Groups to be used for the Address Lists
$Groups = "All - Railroad Holdings","All - West Coast Trains","All - East Coast Trolleys","All - British Railway","All - Great Railroad Company","All - Subway Car Corp"

Foreach ($Group in $Groups) {
    $DDN = (Get-DynamicDistributionGroup $Group).DistinguishedName
    New-AddressList -Name $Group -RecipientFilter "RecipientType -eq 'UserMailbox' -and MemberOfGroup -eq '$DDN'" -DisplayName $Group
    #Clear $DDN variable
    $DDN = $Null
}
```

With a successful run we see each Address List's creation:

```
Name                        DisplayName              RecipientFilter

All - West Coast Trains     All - West Coast Trains   ((RecipientType -eq 'UserMailbox') -and (MemberOfGroup -eq 'CN=A...
All - East Coast Trolleys   All - East Coast Trolleys ((RecipientType -eq 'UserMailbox') -and (MemberOfGroup -eq 'CN=A...
All - British Railway       All - British Railway     ((RecipientType -eq 'UserMailbox') -and (MemberOfGroup -eq 'CN=A...
All - Great Railroad C...   All - Great Railroad C... ((RecipientType -eq 'UserMailbox') -and (MemberOfGroup -eq 'CN=A...
All - Subway Car Corp.      All - Subway Car Corp.    ((RecipientType -eq 'UserMailbox') -and (MemberOfGroup -eq 'CN=A...
```

Verifying the lists are available:

```
Name                        DisplayName              RecipientFilter

All - West Coast Trains     All - West Coast Trains   ((RecipientType -ec
All - East Coast Trolleys   All - East Coast Trolleys ((RecipientType -ec
All - British Railway       All - British Railway     ((RecipientType -ec
All - Great Railroad C...   All - Great Railroad C... ((RecipientType -ec
All Contacts                All Contacts              ((Alias -ne $null)
All Distribution Lists      All Distribution Lists    ((Alias -ne $null)
All Rooms                   All Rooms                 ((Alias -ne $null)
All Users                   All Users                 ((Alias -ne $null)
All Groups                  All Groups                ((Alias -ne $null)
Public Folders              Public Folders            ((Alias -ne $null)
Offline Global Address...   Offline Global Address... ((Alias -ne $null)
All - Subway Car Corp.      All - Subway Car Corp.    ((RecipientType -ec
All - Railroad Holdings     All - Railroad Holdings   ((RecipientType -ec
```

Create Global Address List (GAL) and Offline Address Book (OAB)

Now that we have our Dynamic Distribution Groups and Address Lists created, we can configure the two most important parts of this exercise - a new GAL and a new OAB for each subsidiary. Let's see what PowerShell cmdlets are available to us for each of these tasks.

Global Address List (GAL)

Get-Command *GlobalAddressList

```
Name
----
Get-GlobalAddressList
New-GlobalAddressList
Remove-GlobalAddressList
Set-GlobalAddressList
```

Examples for New-GlobalAddressList:

Get-Help New-GlobalAddressList -Examples

```
-------------------------- Example 1 --------------------------
New-GlobalAddressList -Name "NewGAL"

-------------------------- Example 2 --------------------------

New-GlobalAddressList -Name GAL_AgencyB -RecipientFilter ((((RecipientType -eq "UserMailbox") -and
(CustomAttribute15 -eq "AgencyB")))
```

We will follow the second example a bit in our code below:

```
$DDN = (Get-DynamicDistributionGroup 'All - Railroad Holdings, Inc').DistinguishedName
New-GlobalAddressList -Name 'Railroad Holdings GAL' -RecipientFilter "MemberOfGroup -eq '$DDN'"

$DDN = (Get-DynamicDistributionGroup 'All - West Coast Trains').DistinguishedName
New-GlobalAddressList -Name 'West Coast Trains GAL' -RecipientFilter "MemberOfGroup -eq '$DDN'"

$DDN = (Get-DynamicDistributionGroup 'All - East Coast Trolleys' ).DistinguishedName
New-GlobalAddressList -Name 'East Coast Trolleys GAL' -RecipientFilter "MemberOfGroup -eq '$DDN'"

$DDN = (Get-DynamicDistributionGroup 'All - British Railway').DistinguishedName
New-GlobalAddressList -Name 'British Railway GAL' -RecipientFilter "MemberOfGroup -eq '$DDN'"

$DDN = (Get-DynamicDistributionGroup 'All - Great Railroad Company').DistinguishedName
New-GlobalAddressList -Name 'Great Railroad Company GAL' -RecipientFilter "MemberOfGroup -eq '$DDN'"

$DDN = (Get-DynamicDistributionGroup 'All - Subway Car Corp.').DistinguishedName
New-GlobalAddressList -Name 'Subway Car Corp GAL' -RecipientFilter "MemberOfGroup -eq '$DDN'"
```

We can verify the GAL's were created:

```
PS C:\> Get-GlobalAddressList

Name                              RecipientFilter
----                              ---------------
Great Railroad Company GAL        MemberOfGroup -eq 'CN=All - Great Railroad Company,OU=OnlineExchange...
Subway Car Corp GAL               MemberOfGroup -eq 'CN=All - Subway Car Corp.,OU=OnlineExchangeBook.o...
Corporate GAL                     MemberOfGroup -eq 'CN=All - Railroad Holdings\, Inc,OU=OnlineExchang...
Default Global Address List       ((Alias -ne $null) -and (((ObjectClass -eq 'user') -or (ObjectClass ...
West Coast Trains GAL             MemberOfGroup -eq 'CN=All - West Coast Trains,OU=OnlineExchangeBook....
East Coast Trolleys GAL           MemberOfGroup -eq 'CN=All - East Coast Trolleys,OU=OnlineExchangeBoo...
British Railway GAL               MemberOfGroup -eq 'CN=All - British Railway,OU=OnlineExchangeBook.on...
```

Offline Address Book

To create a new Offline Address Book, we need to find the relevant cmdlets:

Get-Command *OfflineAddress*

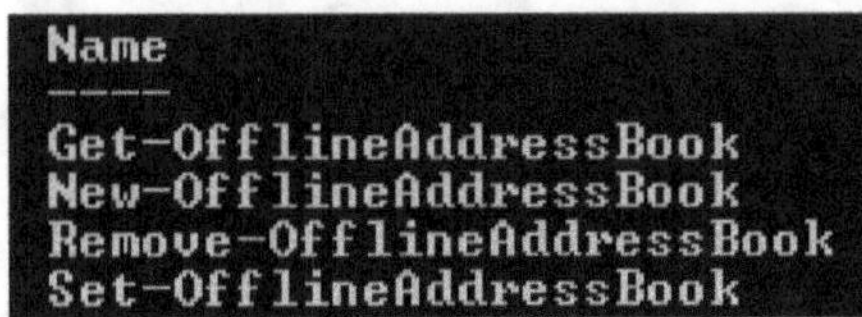

```
Name
----
Get-OfflineAddressBook
New-OfflineAddressBook
Remove-OfflineAddressBook
Set-OfflineAddressBook
```

Get-Help New-OfflineAddressBook -Examples

```
--------------------------- Example 1 ---------------------------
New-OfflineAddressBook -Name "Contoso Executives OAB" -AddressLists "Default Global Address List","Contoso
Executives Address List" -GlobalWebDistributionEnabled $true
```

Now that we have some examples to use, we'll create our new ones, one for each GAL we created before. This way we now have a GAL and OAB per company. For our example, we'll need six new Offline Address Books.

New-OfflineAddressBook -Name "Railroad Holdings OAB" -AddressLists 'All - Railroad Holdings'
New-OfflineAddressBook -Name "West Coast Trains OAB" -AddressLists 'All - West Coast Trains'
New-OfflineAddressBook -Name "East Coast Trolleys OAB" -AddressLists 'All - East Coast Trolleys'
New-OfflineAddressBook -Name "British Railway OAB" -AddressLists 'All - British Railway'
New-OfflineAddressBook -Name "Great Railroad Company OAB" -AddressLists 'All - Great Railroad Company'
New-OfflineAddressBook -Name "Subway Car Corp OAB" -AddressLists 'All - Subway Car Corp.'

We can verify our Offline Address Books are available:

```
PS C:\> Get-OfflineAddressBook

Name                          Versions    AddressLists
----                          --------    ------------
Great Railroad Company OAB    {Version4}  {\All - Subway Car Corp.}
Default Offline Address Book  {Version4}  {\Offline Global Address List}
Subway Car Corp OAB           {Version4}  {\All - Subway Car Corp.}
Corporate OAB                 {Version4}  {\All - Railroad Holdings}
West Coast Trains OAB         {Version4}  {\All - West Coast Trains}
East Coast Trolleys OAB       {Version4}  {\All - Railroad Holdings}
British Railway OAB           {Version4}  {\All - British Railway}
```

Create a New Address Book Policy

We've now created many objects in Exchange Online to get here - Dynamic Distribution Groups, Address Lists, Global Address Lists and Offline Address Lists. At this point we are ready to configure the segmentation piece. First part of this is to create an Address Book Policy that will contain the Offline Address Book, Global Address List and Address Lists. One of the surprise items for the creation of an Address Book Policy is the requirement for a Rooms List. So if you are in the process of creating Address Book Policies, make sure to have a rooms list ready.

New-AddressBookPolicy -Name 'Corporate ABP' -AddressLists 'All - Railroad Holdings' -GlobalAddressList "\Corporate GAL" -OfflineAddressBook "\Corporate OAB" -RoomList 'All Rooms'
New-AddressBookPolicy -Name 'West Coast Trains ABP' -AddressLists 'All - West Coast Trains' -GlobalAddressList "\West Coast Trains GAL" -OfflineAddressBook "\West Coast Trains OAB" -RoomList 'West Coast Trains Rooms'
New-AddressBookPolicy -Name 'East Coast Trolleys ABP' -AddressLists 'All - East Coast Trolleys' -GlobalAddressList "\East Coast Trolleys GAL" -OfflineAddressBook "\East Coast Trolleys OAB" -RoomList

```
'East Coast Trolleys Rooms'
New-AddressBookPolicy-Name'BritishRailwayABP'-AddressLists'All-BritishRailway'-GlobalAddressList
"\British Railway GAL" -OfflineAddressBook "\British Railway OAB" -RoomList 'British Railway Rooms'
New-AddressBookPolicy -Name 'Great Railroad Company ABP' -AddressLists 'All - Great Railroad
Company' -GlobalAddressList "\Great Railroad Company GAL" -OfflineAddressBook "\Great Railroad
Company OAB" -RoomList 'Great Railroad Company Rooms'
New-AddressBookPolicy -Name 'Subway Car Corp ABP' -AddressLists 'All - Subway Car Corp.'
-GlobalAddressList "\Subway Car Corp GAL" -OfflineAddressBook "\Subway Car Corp OAB" -RoomList
'Subway Car Corp Rooms'
```

After the Address Book Policies are created, we need to assign the Address Book Policy (ABP) to user's mailboxes. Now, in the previous pages where we created our Address Lists, you'll note that we used the 'CustomAttribute10' to identify which company a user is in and use that to assign the ABP:

```
Get-Mailbox -Filter {CustomAttribute10 -eq 'Railroad Holdings, Inc.'} | Set-Mailbox -AddressBookPolicy
'Corporate ABP'
Get-Mailbox -Filter {CustomAttribute10 -eq 'West Coast Trains'} | Set-Mailbox -AddressBookPolicy 'West
Coast Trains ABP'
Get-Mailbox -Filter {CustomAttribute10 -eq 'East Coast Trolleys'} | Set-Mailbox -AddressBookPolicy 'East
Coast Trolleys ABP'
Get-Mailbox -Filter {CustomAttribute10 -eq 'British Railway'} | Set-Mailbox -AddressBookPolicy 'British
Railway ABP'
Get-Mailbox -Filter {CustomAttribute10 -eq 'Great Railroad Company'} | Set-Mailbox -AddressBookPolicy
'Great Railroad Company ABP'
Get-Mailbox -Filter {CustomAttribute10 -eq 'Subway Car Corp'} | Set-Mailbox -AddressBookPolicy
'Subway Car Corp ABP'
```

We can verify that the attribute and the ABP are correct for all users:

```
DisplayName                 CustomAttribute10          AddressBookPolicy

Damian Scoles               Railroad Holdings, Inc.    Corporate ABP
John Doe                    West Coast Trains          West Coast Trains ABP
Larry Simmons               East Coast Trolleys        East Coast Trolleys ABP
Pete Blanket                British Railway            British Railway ABP
Phish Master                Great Railroad Company     Great Railroad Company ABP
Ron Don                     Subway Car Corp            Subway Car Corp ABP
```

Accepted Domains

Accepted domains are the SMTP domains that your Exchange Online will accept email for. By default the only domain defined is the default Microsoft define domain - 'Tenant.OnMicrosoft.Com'. When it comes to PowerShell there isn't a lot we can do. Unlike Exchange on-premises where we configure these domains in Exchange instead. These domains are available because they were configured globally for Office 365.

PowerShell

```
Get-Command *accepted*
```

```
CommandType    Name                   Version    Source

Function       Get-AcceptedDomain     1.0        tmp_gscmapld.4hu
Function       Set-AcceptedDomain     1.0        tmp_gscmapld.4hu
```

Okay. So we can review Accepted Domains currently present in Office 365 and we can configure existing ones. However, we cannot add, remove or do much with Accepted Domains in Exchange Online. Let's review what the commands we can use, starting with the Get-AcceptedDomain cmdlet:

```
Get-AcceptedDomain | Ft -Auto
```

```
Name                                     DomainName                               DomainType     Default
----                                     ----------                               ----------     -------
OnlineExchangeBook.mail.onmicrosoft.com  OnlineExchangeBook.mail.onmicrosoft.com  Authoritative  False
OnlineExchangeBook.onmicrosoft.com       OnlineExchangeBook.onmicrosoft.com       Authoritative  True
```

That at least provided a quick list of defined Accepted Domains in Exchange Online. We can still use Format-List in order to get more detailed information on the domain.

```
Get-AcceptedDomain | Fl
```

```
DomainName                        : OnlineExchangeBook.onmicrosoft.com
CatchAllRecipientID               :
DomainType                        : Authoritative
MatchSubDomains                   : False
AddressBookEnabled                : True
Default                           : True
EmailOnly                         : False
ExternallyManaged                 : False
AuthenticationType                : Managed
LiveIdInstanceType                : Business
PendingRemoval                    : False
PendingCompletion                 : False
FederatedOrganizationLink         : Federation
MailFlowPartner                   :
OutboundOnly                      : False
PendingFederatedAccountNamespace  : False
PendingFederatedDomain            : False
IsCoexistenceDomain               : False
PerimeterDuplicateDetected        : False
IsDefaultFederatedDomain          : False
EnableNego2Authentication         : False
InitialDomain                     : True
```

Now we can see some value to the Get-AcceptedDomain cmdlet. However, while information is revealed, reviewing the Set-AcceptedDomain cmdlet reveals that not much can be changed by the Office 365 Admin. Let's first start with a sample usage of the cmdlet:

```
Get-Help Set-AcceptedDomain -Examples
```

```
______________________ Example 1 ______________________
Set-AcceptedDomain -Identity Contoso -MakeDefault $true
```

If we review the available parameters for Set-AcceptedDomain, there are only four that we can use and they are circled in red in the below screenshot:

```
-Identity <AcceptedDomainIdParameter>
-AddressBookEnabled <$true | $false>              This parameter is available only in on-premises Exchange 2016.
-DomainType <Authoritative | ExternalRelay | InternalRelay>
-EnableNego2Authentication <$true | $false>       This parameter is reserved for internal Microsoft use.
-MakeDefault <$true | $false>                     This parameter is available only in on-premises Exchange 2016.
-MatchSubDomains <$true | $false>
-Name <String>                                    This parameter is available only in on-premises Exchange 2016.
-OutboundOnly <$true | $false>                    This parameter is available only in the cloud-based service.
-PendingCompletion <$true | $false>               This parameter is reserved for internal Microsoft use.
-PendingRemoval <$true | $false>                  This parameter is reserved for internal Microsoft use.
```

So in reality we can change the Domain Type, if Subdomains are allowed and if the domain is simply a relay domain for internal emails.

POP3 and IMAP4

POP3 and IMAP4 protocols are common connection protocols for clients other than Outlook. The protocols are also commonly used by applications and programs to scrape a mailboxes information and or messages. How can these properties be utilized? Let's take a scenario where a company has put in place a policy that restricts the use of certain protocols in Exchange Online. IT wants to restrict POP3 and IMAP access. There is a small subset of users that require the use of these protocols and IT wants to limit IMAP and POP protocols. Lastly, we need to accomplish these goals with PowerShell and it needs to be scalable.

Where To Start

Each protocol will have two groups of users – those that have access and those that do not. The first step would be to group users that should have access as this group will be the easiest to build and maintain rather than trying to maintain a group of those to block access to a resource. In Active Directory, create a group called "POP3 Access" and another called "IMAP Access". We then add users who will have access to these resources, using Active Directory Users and Computers.

Now that the groups are populated with users a script will be needed to enforce these access conditions. What is needed in order to build the script?

1. Need to store this user list in a variable to determine access or use the group name in the script as the determining factor for access in the script.
2. What access should be granted or denied depending on members?
3. What commands can we use to query this information in Exchange?
4. What commands can we use to add or remove access to the resource?
5. How often do we would want to reinforce this action?

PowerShell Cmdlet Determination

Storing the names of users who need access or using the group name?

Using a group name is far easier than storing the list of names. The reason to do this is if PowerShell were to cycle through each mailbox to determine access, it would be easier to see if they are a member of a group (single comparison) versus comparing a list of uses (multiple comparisons). The single comparison method is much faster.

What access should be granted or denied depending on group membership?

In this case, the requirement was to allow certain user's access to POP3 and block all other users from using POP3. Going back to the Get-CASMailbox cmdlet, 'OWA Enabled' is an option that can be configured on a mailbox. Get CASMailbox has a set-command for changing settings – Set-CASMailbox. Not knowing what options that can be configured, we can run a 'Get-Help Set-CASMailbox –Full' to see what options can be changed, while specifically looking for POP3 and IMAP4:

```
[PS] C:\>Get-Help Set-CASMailbox -Full

NAME
    Set-CASMailbox

SYNOPSIS
    This cmdlet is available in on-premises Exchange Server 2016 and in the cloud-based service.
    Some parameters and settings may be exclusive to one environment or the other.

    Use the Set-CASMailbox cmdlet to configure client access settings on a mailbox. For example,
    you can configure settings for Microsoft Exchange ActiveSync, Microsoft Outlook, Outlook on
    the web, POP3, and IMAP4.

    For information about the parameter sets in the Syntax section below, see Exchange cmdlet
    syntax.

SYNTAX
    Set-CASMailbox -Identity <MailboxIdParameter> [-ActiveSyncAllowedDeviceIDs
    <MultiValuedProperty>] [-ActiveSyncBlockedDeviceIDs <MultiValuedProperty>]
    [-ActiveSyncDebugLogging <$true | $false>] [-ActiveSyncEnabled <$true | $false>]
    [-ActiveSyncMailboxPolicy <MailboxPolicyIdParameter>] [-Confirm [<SwitchParameter>]]
    [-DisplayName <String>] [-DomainController <Fqdn>] [-ECPEnabled <$true | $false>]
    [-EmailAddresses <ProxyAddressCollection>] [-EwsAllowEntourage <$true | $false>]
    [-EwsAllowList <MultiValuedProperty>] [-EwsAllowMacOutlook <$true | $false>] [-EwsAllowOutlook
    <$true | $false>] [-EwsApplicationAccessPolicy <EnforceAllowList | EnforceBlockList>]
    [-EwsBlockList <MultiValuedProperty>] [-EwsEnabled <$true | $false>] [-IgnoreDefaultScope
    <SwitchParameter>] [-ImapEnabled <$true | $false>] [-ImapEnableExactRFC822Size <$true |
    $false>] [-ImapForceICalForCalendarRetrievalOption <$true | $false>]
    [-ImapMessagesRetrievalMimeFormat <TextOnly | HtmlOnly | HtmlAndTextAlternative |
    TextEnrichedOnly | TextEnrichedAndTextAlternative | BestBodyFormat | Tnef>]
    [-ImapSuppressReadReceipt <$true | $false>] [-ImapUseProtocolDefaults <$true | $false>]
    [-IsOptimizedForAccessibility <$true | $false>] [-MAPIBlockOutlookExternalConnectivity <$true
    | $false>] [-MAPIBlockOutlookNonCachedMode <$true | $false>] [-MAPIBlockOutlookRpcHttp <$true
    | $false>] [-MAPIBlockOutlookVersions <String>] [-MAPIEnabled <$true | $false>]
    [-MapiHttpEnabled <$true | $false>] [-Name <String>] [-OWAEnabled <$true | $false>]
    [-OWAforDevicesEnabled <$true | $false>] [-OwaMailboxPolicy <MailboxPolicyIdParameter>]
    [-PopEnabled <$true | $false>] [-PopEnableExactRFC822Size <$true | $false>]
    [-PopForceICalForCalendarRetrievalOption <$true | $false>] [-PopMessagesRetrievalMimeFormat
    <TextOnly | HtmlOnly | HtmlAndTextAlternative | TextEnrichedOnly |
    TextEnrichedAndTextAlternative | BestBodyFormat | Tnef>] [-PopSuppressReadReceipt <$true |
```

Looking closely at the options we see IMAPEnabled and POPEnabled. Both have two settings - $True and $False. We can set these values for each mailbox in Exchange Online.

It is worth noting here that if you have used Exchange on-premises you will see the lack of IMAP and POP PowerShell cmdlets that could be used to configure these settings. For example if we run 'Get-Command *IMAP*' Wee see that there are three cmdlets we can choose from:

    Get-ImapSubscription
    New-ImapSubscription
    Set-ImapSubscription

These cmdlets can be used for ingestion purposes and are not intended for use as client protocol settings. This means that we are indeed limited to the Set-CASMailbox cmdlet as show above. Now, there are configurable options beyond simply enabling the protocol on a per mailbox or a global basis with the cmdlet:

- ImapForceICalForCalendarRetrievalOption
- ImapMessagesRetrievalMimeFormat
- ImapSuppressReadReceipt
- ImapUseProtocolDefaults

However, as we can see by the available options, these are not related to how a client connects to Office 365 with the IMAP protocol. In order for a client to connect, it must be configured according to Microsoft's official documentation on this - https://technet.microsoft.com/en-us/library/dn551174(v=exchg.150).aspx.

With the base command figured out, the next step is to use these cmdlets to set the access for all mailboxes or for some mailboxes based off of group membership. How can group membership be verified?

What commands can we use to query this information in Exchange?

First, we need to store the group name in a variable:

```
$POPGroup = Get-MSOLGroup -All | Where-Object {$_.DisplayName -eq "POP3 Access"}
$IMAPGroup = Get-MSOLGroup -All | Where-Object {$_.DisplayName -eq "IMAP Access"}
```

Then we can get a list of users in that group:

```
$POPAccess = Get-MSOLGroupMember -GroupObjectId $PopGroup.ObjectId -All | Select-Object
-ExpandProperty DisplayName
$IMAPAcess = Get-MSOLGroupMember -GroupObjectId $ImapGroup.ObjectId -All | Select-Object
-ExpandProperty DisplayName
```

** **Note** ** These cmdlets need to be run after a connection to the MSOL Service has been made.

What commands can we use to add or remove access to the resource?

As discussed above, one PowerShell cmdlet and two parameters will allow for the changing of access to IMAP or POP:

```
Set-CASMailbox –IMAPEnabled $True
Set-CASMailbox –POPEnabled $True
```

$False would be used to disable access to those not in these groups.

Putting It Together

Then, using the names of the groups stored in $MemberOf, check for any groups that match our POP3 Access groups and then set POP3access:

```
If ($MemberOf -Like "*POP3 Access*") { Set-CasMailbox $Alias –POPEnabled $True}
```

Putting these pieces together, we can create a script like this: (note we are excluding the Discovery mailbox as well)

```
# Group Names
$POPGroup = Get-MSOLGroup -All | Where-Object {$_.DisplayName -eq "POP3 Access"}
$IMAPGroup = Get-MSOLGroup -All | Where-Object {$_.DisplayName -eq "IMAP Access"}
# Group Membership
$POPAccess = Get-MSOLGroupMember -GroupObjectId $PopGroup.ObjectId -All | Select-Object
-ExpandProperty DisplayName
$IMAPAccess = Get-MSOLGroupMember -GroupObjectId $ImapGroup.ObjectId -All | Select-Object
-ExpandProperty DisplayName
# Set POP Access - Remove all and then set those allowed
```

```
Get-Mailbox | Set-Mailbox -POPEnabled $False
Foreach ($Mailbox in $POPAccess) {
    Set-CASMailbox $Mailbox -POPEnabled $True
}
# Set IMAP Access - Remove all and then set those allowed
Get-Mailbox | Set-Mailbox -IMAPEnabled $False
Foreach ($Mailbox in $POPAccess) {
    Set-CASMailbox $Mailbox -POPEnabled $True
}
```

Prior to running the above script, validate who has the setting enabled or disabled: (*note what mailboxes are disabled*)

Name	ActiveSyncEnabled	OWAEnabled	PopEnabled
Administrator	True	True	False
extest_628b03ba937b4	True	True	False
John Larson	True	True	False
Richard Kohen	True	True	False

After the script is run, ONLY John and Richard would get POP3 access, all others remain disabled ($False) because they are members of the correct group.

Name	ActiveSyncEnabled	OWAEnabled	PopEnabled
Administrator	True	True	False
extest_628b03ba937b4	True	True	False
John Larson	True	True	True
Richard Kohen	True	True	True

For the IMAP configuration, we would also see something similar:

Before the script:

Name	ActiveSyncEnabled	OWAEnabled	PopEnabled	ImapEnabled	MapiEnabled
Administrator	True	True	False	False	True
extest_628b03ba937b	True	True	False	False	True
John Larson	True	True	True	False	True
Richard Kohen	True	True	True	False	True

After the script:

Name	ActiveSyncEnabled	OWAEnabled	PopEnabled	ImapEnabled	MapiEnabled
Administrator	True	True	False	True	True
extest_628b03ba937b4	True	True	False	False	True
John Larson	True	True	True	True	True
Richard Kohen	True	True	True	False	True

How often we would want reinforce this action?

Once the script is created, we would then need to decide how and when to enforce these settings. Running the script weekly and daily would be ideal from a restrictive access view. The script can be deployed as a cleanup tool or enforcement tool using the Windows scheduler, setting up jobs to handle these changes on a weekly or daily basis.

Client Access Rules

What is it?

Client Access Rules are specifically designed to control access to Exchange Online by allowing or blocking different types of client connections. These rules are similar to Transport Rules that we would use to control the flow of email in Exchange Online. We can control whether MAPI is allowed, PowerShell connections allowed and also control these by group or user just for some examples of what is allowed. Now, these rules are different from Conditional Access as Client Access Rules controls authentication for Exchange Online whereas Conditional Access can control access to other workloads beyond Exchange as well as determining MFA requirements for those apps.

When it comes to PowerShell and Office 365 one thing is for sure, change is constant. Nothing can be more revealing than looking at some of the new cmdlets that are appearing in the various workloads for Office 365. For this article, we are covering a series of cmdlets that were released in January of 2018 for Exchange Online. These cmdlets are all centered around the new 'Client Access Rule' concept:

- Get-ClientAccessRule
- New-ClientAccessRule
- Remove-ClientAccessRule
- Set-ClientAccessRule
- Test-ClientAccessRule

Microsoft documentation on this feature:

https://technet.microsoft.com/en-us/library/mt842508(v=exchg.150).aspx

Cmdlet Review

The cmdlets provided begin with a full set of verbs and by this I mean we have Get, Set, New, Remove and Test. If you have not created any Client Access Rules, then there are none to begin with. Running Get-ClientAccessRule will show no results when run for the first time. In order to create our first rule, we'll need to use the New-ClientAccessRule cmdlet. We can review the Get-Help -Examples for this cmdlet first:

```
------------------------------ Example 1 ------------------------------

This example creates a new client access rule named Block ActiveSync that blocks access for
Exchange ActiveSync clients, except for clients in the IP address range 192.168.10.1/24.


New-ClientAccessRule -Name "Block ActiveSync" -Action DenyAccess -AnyOfProtocols
ExchangeActiveSync -ExceptAnyOfClientIPAddressesOrRanges 192.168.10.1/24
```

There are quite a few options available for tweaking the control of access to your environment. Here are some useful parameters or the New-ClientAccessRule cmdlet:

- **Action** – Can allow or deny access based on other criteria .
- **AnyOfAuthenticationTypes** – Authentication types that are valid for control are – AdfsAuthentication, BasicAuthentication, CertificateBasedAuthentication, NonBasicAuthentication and OAuthAuthentication
- **AnyOfClientIPAddressesOrRanges** – Define single IP or IP Ranges as a criteria for the rule.
- **AnyOfProtocols** – Allow or block various access protocols to Exchange Online – ExchangeActiveSync, Ex-

changeAdminCenter, ExchangeWebServices, IMAP4, OfflineAddressBook, OutlookAnywhere, OutlookWebApp, POP3, PowerShellWebServices, RemotePowerShell and REST

- **ExceptAnyOfAuthenticationTypes** – Exceptions to the Client Access Rule authentication protocols – AdfsAuthentication, BasicAuthentication, CertificateBasedAuthentication, NonBasicAuthentication and OAuthAuthentication
- **ExceptAnyOfClientIPAddressesOrRanges** – This parameter can be a single IP, an IP range and / or CIDR IP with subnet.
- **ExceptAnyOfProtocols** – The reverse of the 'AnyOfProtocols' setting, but with the same protocols – ExchangeActiveSync, ExchangeAdminCenter, ExchangeWebServices, IMAP4, OfflineAddressBook, OutlookAnywhere, OutlookWebApp, POP3, PowerShellWebServices, RemotePowerShell and REST
- **ExceptUsernameMatchesAnyOfPatterns** – Allows the rule to look at one or more user names to match and apply access rights.
- **Scope** – The parameter scopes the rule to either End-User connections or all connections made to the service.
- **UsernameMatchesAnyOfPatterns** – Pattern match user names instead of specifying an exact match.
- **UserRecipientFilter** – Filters the rule based on recipient properties – City, Company, CountryOrRegion, CustomAttribute1-15, Department, Office, PostalCode, StateOrProvince and StreetAddress.

Creating a Rule

So what can we actually accomplish with the above parameters? We can create rules that are targeted – blocking a particular user or group of users or we can create more broadly target rules that affect all users. With these rules we can decide how we want users to connect to Exchange Online.

> ** **NOTE** ** All of these controls are available via PowerShell only. Hopefully something will be added to the Exchange Admin Center for Exchange Online in order to facilitate this for those adverse to PowerShell.

Let's tackle some scenarios and create rules based on these scenarios:

Example One

In this scenario we want to create two different Client Access Rules. One is to block all access to Exchange Online unless the users is on a corporate subnet and if they are a member of a particular group. The second rule will allow members of IT to connect no matter where they are.

Rule One

```
New-ClientAccessRule -Name 'Corporate Policy' -UserRecipientFilter {CustomAttribute11 -eq 'InternalOnly'} -AnyOfClientIPAddressesOrRanges '10.0.0.0/24' -Action AllowAccess
```

Rule Two

```
New-ClientAccessRule -Name 'IT Access Policy' -UserRecipientFilter {CustomAttribute11 -eq 'ITDept'} -Action AllowAccess
```

Notice that when the rules are created, we are provided with a warning about the rule taking effect in 24 hours, for the first rule, and an hour subsequently after that.

```
PS C:\> New-ClientAccessRule -Name 'Corporate Policy' -UserRecipientFilter {CustomAttribute11 -e
q 'InternalOnly'} -AnyOfClientIPAddressesOrRanges '10.0.0.0/24' -Action AllowAccess

Confirm
Are you sure you want to perform this action?
Creating Client Access Rule Corporate Policy - Modifying rules incorrectly may result in blocking
access to your tenant for both administrators and users. Please ensure that your ruleset always
allows some access to PowerShell so that you can administer the tenant and modify Client Access
Rules.
[Y] Yes  [A] Yes to All  [N] No  [L] No to All  [?] Help (default is "Y"): y
WARNING: Please note: your first rule may take up to 24 hours to be implemented. Any rule after the
 first one may take up to an hour to be implemented.

Name                  Priority Enabled DatacenterAdminsOnly
----                  -------- ------- --------------------
Corporate Policy 1             True    False
```

We can verify the rules were created correctly with Get-ClientAccessRule:

```
PS C:\> Get-ClientAccessRule

Name                  Priority Enabled DatacenterAdminsOnly
----                  -------- ------- --------------------
Corporate Policy 1             True    False
IT Access Policy 2             True    False
```

Detailed look at one of the rules:

```
Priority                                    : 1
Enabled                                     : True
DatacenterAdminsOnly                        : False
Action                                      : AllowAccess
AnyOfClientIPAddressesOrRanges              : {10.0.0.0/24}
ExceptAnyOfClientIPAddressesOrRanges        : {}
AnyOfSourceTcpPortNumbers                   : {}
ExceptAnyOfSourceTcpPortNumbers             : {}
UsernameMatchesAnyOfPatterns                : {}
ExceptUsernameMatchesAnyOfPatterns          : {}
UserIsMemberOf                              : {}
ExceptUserIsMemberOf                        : {}
AnyOfAuthenticationTypes                    : {}
ExceptAnyOfAuthenticationTypes              : {}
AnyOfProtocols                              : {}
ExceptAnyOfProtocols                        : {}
UserRecipientFilter                         : CustomAttribute11 -eq 'InternalOnly'
Scope                                       : All
```

Example Two

In this next example, we need to block access for any user to POP, IMAP and OWA:

```
New-ClientAccessRule -Name 'Block Protocols' -AnyOfProtocols Pop,Imap,OutlookWebApp -Action
DenyAccess
```

Notice there are no parameters for users or attributes or any other checks. Simply blocks these forms of access from your Exchange Online Tenant. Use rules like this carefully. Test it out to make sure it meets your company's needs.

Example Three

For this last example we need to block all PowerShell access to the tenant for users with a Custom Attribute 10 of 'NoPowerShell':

```
New-ClientAccessRule -Name 'Block PowerShell Access' -UserRecipientFilter {CustomAttribute11
-eq 'RemotePowerShell'} -AnyOfProtocols PowerShellWebServices, RemotePowerShell -Action
DenyAccess
```

Make sure to test this rule prior to moving it into production.

Testing Rules

This one is rather interesting and you need possibly more variables for input than you may have put into your rule to begin with. For example, if we were to test any of the sample rules that are shown previously, we need to provide the Test cmdlet with at least this information:

- Protocol
- RemoteAddress
- AuthenticationType
- RemotePort
- User

Sample run from the Test cmdlet:

```
PS C:\> Test-ClientAccessRule -Protocol OutlookWebApp -RemoteAddress 206.100.100.1 -Authenticati
onType BasicAuthentication -RemotePort 443 -User damian@OnlineExchangeBook.onmicrosoft.com

Identity            Name                 Action
--------            ----                 ------
Block Protocols     Block Protocols      DenyAccess
```

A successful test of an 'AllowAccess' rule would look like this:

```
PS C:\> Test-ClientAccessRule -Protocol ExchangeActiveSync -RemoteAddress '10.0.0.1' -Authentica
tionType BasicAuthentication -RemotePort 443 -User damian@OnlineExchangeBook.onmicrosoft.com

Identity            Name                 Action
--------            ----                 ------
Corporate Policy    Corporate Policy     AllowAccess
```

Key thing is to know the criteria you are testing for because if you do not get any results back from the Test-ClientAccessRule cmdlet, then you are not providing the correct data or test person in the cmdlet.

Removing Client Access Rules

The easiest of the cmdlet is the one for removing rules. All we need is the name of a rule and we can remove it. First, let's check the rules we have so we can get the right name:

```
Name                        Priority Enabled DatacenterAdminsOnly
----                        -------- ------- --------------------
Corporate Policy            1        True    False
IT Access Policy            2        True    False
Block Protocols             3        True    False
Block PowerShell Access     4        True    False
```

Sample removal:

Remove-ClientAccessRule 'Block PowerShell Access'

```
PS C:\> Remove-ClientAccessRule 'Block PowerShell Access'

Confirm
Are you sure you want to perform this action?
Removing Client Access Rule Block PowerShell Access - Modifying rules incorrectly may result in
blocking access to your tenant for both administrators and users. Please ensure that your ruleset
always allows some access to PowerShell so that you can administer the tenant and modify Client
Access Rules.
[Y] Yes  [A] Yes to All  [N] No  [L] No to All  [?] Help (default is "Y"): y
```

Final Thoughts on Client Access Rules

Before implementing these rules, make sure you layout the intention and can match the PowerShell cmdlet settings to what you are allowing or blocking in Exchange Online. Blocking certain authentication protocols, for example, could have unintended consequences. Test before pushing out to production users. Be especially careful with restricting PowerShell access as you could lock everyone out and then you won't be able to work with your tenant with PowerShell any more.

8   Users

In This Chapter

- Types of Objects
- Creating Users
- Enabling Mailbox
- Deleting Users
- Modifying Users
- Converting Types
- Reporting

There is a saying in IT that the perfect network doesn't have any pesky users. While it's true admin work would be much easier without users, it completely defeats the purpose of having a network at all. In fact, users should be a key focus point of your network because they are the ones that create the company and make sure it is creating revenue. Which in turn pays for the network and your salary; at least in most cases.

So, users are fundamental in your network and obviously, the topic of this chapter. In this chapter, we will discuss creating and managing users along with all the secondary configuration options that will benefit your users, network and your admin responsibilities.

While the Exchange Admin Center offers a great deal of configuration options regarding the creation, management, etc. of users, you will hopefully see the major benefits of PowerShell when requiring bulk creation and changes. Knowing what is possible with Exchange Management Shell (EMS) might have some impact on how best to provision your users, your use of attributes and other conventions. It might be prudent to review those practices.

Types of Objects

There are different types of objects that this chapter will address:

- User Mailbox
- Mail Enabled User
- Mail Contact
- Resource Mailbox
- Archive Mailbox
- Public Folder Mailbox
- Shared Mailbox
- Remote Mailbox

A **User Mailbox** is an AD user with a mailbox. This is different from a **Mail User** that can log in, but has no mailbox, and will only forward to another email address. A **Mail Contact** is an object that represents an email address in another environment, but is not security enabled and therefore cannot login.

Resource Mailboxes have a disabled user account, like a User Mailbox they also have a calendar but it is designed for resource reservations like rooms and/or equipment. There are two types of resource mailboxes: Room and Equipment. These have a few different attributes and additional features to support planning meetings or equipment information.

A **Shared Mailbox** has a disabled user account. The idea is that normal user mailboxes get permission to access email and send as that mailbox, with all the data stored in that mailbox and not across different mailboxes. Useful for general email addresses like info@company.com etc., in which several people require access and send permissions.

With Modern Public Folders introduced in Exchange Server 2013, the infrastructure has changed radically and Public Folder data is no longer stored in a separate database, but in **Public Folder Mailboxes** in mailbox databases. The user experience has not changed however.

An **Archive Mailbox** is an additional mailbox linked to the user's primary mailbox, with the distinct difference that the Archive mailbox is only available via Outlook Desktop (ProPlus) and Outlook Web App (OWA) edition when connected to Exchange. This means that no offline access is available per design, it is meant primarily as a PST replacement.

Creating Users

To explain the intricacies of creating users who will be able to send and receive email, we should look a little into how Azure Active Directory (AAD) works and how Exchange Online leverages it.

Mailbox or Mail Enabled User

There are two kinds of users possible, mailbox or mail enabled. The first is a user account that can be authenticated by the Azure Active Directory and has a mailbox connected to it. This means the user can send and receive email, manage calendars, contacts, etc. All that information is stored in Exchange Online.

A mail enabled user (or mail user for short) can also be authenticated by the Azure Active Directory, but does not have a mailbox. Their user object does have an email address and a forwarding address, most likely to a mailbox in another environment (i.e partner company). If anyone sends an email to this user, Exchange will forward the email to the forwarding address. For instance, if you are an IT consultant with multiple customers, it's reasonable to not have to maintain multiple mailboxes. This way users of each environment can find you in the Address List and send email, you on the other hand will get all email in one mailbox depending on your forwarding address. Nice to know: that will also limit the need for Exchange Online Licenses.

New Mailbox

You can directly create a new mailbox without the need to create an Azure Active Directory user first, it will be automatically created. However, the options available to you are mostly limited to things related to Exchange, for instance a home path cannot be configured in the same action. You will probably need to configure the user with MSOL cmdlets if so required.

> ** **Note** ** If your environment is synced, creating users and mailboxes with New-MSOLUSer is not a recommended process. Instead the objects (user account and remote mailbox) should be initiated from your on-premises Exchange and Active Directory servers. If your environment is not synced and is cloud-only, then using New-MSOLUSer is the appropriate course of action as this will be the only way to create new objects in Exchange Online.

Use the following command to create a MSOL User object as the first step to creating a mailbox, we need to use the New-MSOLUser cmdlet:

```
New-MsolUser -UserPrincipalName Dom.Rigel@Contoso.Com -DisplayName "Dom Rigel" -FirstName "Dom" -LastName "Rigel" -UsageLocation "US"
```

> ** **Note** ** When using spaces in the Name field, you are required to use quotation marks if there is a space. The UserPrincipalName should obviously be valid for the Domain (you might need to add UPN suffixes) and preferably should correspond to the primary SMTP address the account will be using.

You can define the password via a prompt:

```
$SecurePassword = Read-Host -Prompt "Enter password" -AsSecureString
```

or a pre-determined value:

```
$PlainPassword = "Th1sSho4ldB3Secr3t"
$SecurePassword = $PlainPassword | ConvertTo-SecureString -AsPlainText -Force
```

In both cases the passwords must adhere to the password policy in place. The first method is fine for single changes. The latter is ideal for bulk additions of mailboxes. Obviously, you can also define a randomly generated unique password for each new mailbox, which is from a security perspective preferable.

Once a user is created, it needs to be licensed for Exchange Online. See Chapter 6 for those details. Once the user is assigned a license, it does take a period of time for the mailbox to be created in Exchange Online. Once it is, you will be able to work with it in the Exchange Admin Center or Exchange PowerShell.

To define FirstName, LastName etc. at account creation:

```
Set-MsolUser Dom. Rigel@Contoso.Com -FirstName Dom -LastName Rigel
```

In order to configure additional parameters for a mailbox we can use the 'Set-Mailbox' cmdlet. This cmdlet has a few parameters we can use to configure a mailbox:

PrimarySmtpAddress – Which defines the primary SMTP address or reply address for that mailbox. Do note that when using this parameter, the Email Address Policy (EAP) setting EmailAddressPolicyEnabled is set to $False which means no EAP is applied on this account. This can be useful if you don't want this account to have all the

SMTP addresses applied from an EAP, for instance with Shared Mailboxes. Or this mailbox will be used for a very specific purposes requiring only the set address. It is worth noting that creating and utilizing EAPs requires an on-premises Exchange server as this option is not available in Exchange Online.

AccountDisabled – When creating the mailbox and logon account, security policies might dictate you to disable the Active Directory account until it's ready for use (maybe additional security settings are required) or when the actual user is allowed to use it. For these circumstance, you can use this switch, but no value is required (i.e. $False isn't needed).

There are several types of policies available in Exchange, you can set specific (custom) policies with the following aptly named policy parameters:

- ActiveSyncMailboxPolicy
- AddressBookPolicy
- RetentionPolicy
- RoleAssignmentPolicy
- SharingPolicy

Name, DisplayName, FirstName, LastName are all values that have a special relationship together. These values are used by other users or even admins to identify the correct mailbox to the real-world user. Especially in large organizations it is prudent to have a good naming convention in place, also planning for all deviations that will happen. No naming convention will incorporate every possible situation, especially if your users have very different cultural naming standards and practices.

FirstName and LastName were already discussed, but it still important to point out that these values can be used in your Email Address Policy. So, even though they are not mandatory, it might help with your Email Address Policies or help your users find the correct person within Exchange Online.

You can further specify the user's Office and Phone parameters. These are, by default, visible in address lists etc., so make sure that privacy regulations in your country/region are followed. Note that you can filter based on Office locations when using RecipientFilter with many Exchange cmdlets.

Furthermore, not even all Exchange related values can be set when creating the mailbox, it is highly likely that you must use other cmdlets to completely configure the mailbox account to your organizations requirements and/or liking.

Enabling Mailbox

If your user(s) already have an Active Directory account, some parameters are already configured via other means. This way you only must concentrate on Exchange specific attributes and thus cmdlet parameters.

You can mailbox enable a user with at least these parameters:

```
Enable-Mailbox -Identity Sjon.Lont
```

In this case Identity can be the Name, Display Name or other types of values, that can uniquely identify the target user account. Note that when not specifying other parameters the default values are used, the same when using the New-Mailbox cmdlets.

The cmdlet further behaves the same as the New-Mailbox cmdlet, with the distinct difference the AD account and the mandatory values are already provided.

Enabling Archive Mailbox

You can enable the Archive Mailbox on an existing mailbox user with an archive switch:

    Enable-Mailbox Dom.Rigel -Archive -ArchiveName "Dom Rigel Archive"

The ArchiveName specifies the name that identifies the Archive mailbox, otherwise the default naming is used, which is "In-Place Archive – " before the mailbox display name.

You can also create a new mailbox immediately with an archive by adding the -Archive switch to New-Mailbox or Enable-Mailbox.

The default archive quota and archive quota warning are 100 GB and 100 GB. These values cannot be changed in either the Admin Center or via PowerShell. However, we can adjust the archive and make it into an AutoExpanding archive if we have the proper licenses. This can be done with this command:

    Enable-Mailbox Dom.Rigel -AutoExpandingArchive

Do not forget to apply the appropriate Retention Policy, which can be specified when Archive enabling the user with the -RetentionPolicy parameter.

New Mail Contacts

Mail enabled contacts are a way to create entries in the Global Address List that users can use to email often used addresses outside of your environment. For instance, if you have a Shared Service Desk supplier, you can create a mail contact with a recognizable name and an internal email address which also contains a forwarding address.

To create a contact:

    New-MailContact -Name "Richard Deck" -ExternalEmailAddress R.Deck@Outlook.Com

Note that the contact will get an SMTP address according Email Address Policy settings, however the ExternalE-mailAddress is the primary address and all email sent to the contact will be forwarded to the external address.

To delete a contact:

    Remove-MailContact "Richard Deck"

Deleting Users

There are two options: deleting the mailbox or deleting the user account including the mailbox. It depends on your own requirements and situations which of the two options is valid.

To remove the mailbox and NOT the user:

```
Disable-Mailbox -Identity Dom.Rigel -PermanentlyDisable
```

** **Note** ** This only works if the user does not have an assigned Exchange License. In order to remove a mailbox without removing the user, the license for Exchange would have to be removed. See Chapter 6 for how to change licenses for users.

To remove the mailbox AND the user:

```
Remove-Mailbox -Identity Dom.Rigel -Confirm:$False
```

Alternatively, it's also possible to change the type of a user mailbox to Shared to keep the data and email flow available. See later in this chapter on how to do this.

Modifying Users

There is one constant, and that is that things change. This is definitely the case for users. A lot can be changed via Exchange PowerShell and it's probable that a lot of settings are never changed or will require being changed.

But when it comes to modifying mailbox users, there are several things to consider. Most importantly, there is no single cmdlet that can modify everything on a mailbox. You must use the correct cmdlet for the required changes you want to make.

For an overview of all the attributes that (might) be subject to any modification, see the Reporting section later in this chapter. In that overview the Get-* cmdlets are used, but obviously to change the attributes you should use the Set-* variant or in some cases (like permissions) the option to use Add-* or Remove-* is also an option.

It's not the goal of this book to review every possible modification available, we will show what we feel are the most important and common modifications.

User

The user object is where it all starts, whether it has a mailbox or is only mail-enabled. You can change the UPN of a user in the cloud, or maybe change the Display Name. To change a UserPrincipalName, there is a command called 'Set-MsolUserPrincipalName' like so:

```
Set-MsolUserPrincipalName -UserPrincipalName user@contoso.com -NewUserPrincipalName johns@contoso.com
```

** **Note** ** Don't forget to connect to the MSOL service with either Connect-MSOLService or Connect-EX-OPSSession (MultiFactor) before running these cmdlets.

There are a few other cmdlets that can be used to manipulate user accounts and we can find them again with the Get-Command technique:

```
Get-Command *MsolUser*
```

Which provides us with a short list of cmdlets:

```
Get-MsolUser
Get-MsolUserByStrongAuthentication
Get-MsolUserRole
New-MsolUser
Remove-MsolUser
Restore-MsolUser
Set-MsolUser
Set-MsolUserLicense
Set-MsolUserPassword
Set-MsolUserPrincipalName
```

Mailbox

There are several cmdlets that configure options on a (user) mailbox, most of those features are set with Set-Mailbox. There are other cmdlets that set other very specific settings, so if this cmdlet doesn't provide what you want to change you might have to use another cmdlet.

Why not in one cmdlet? Some of the settings control specific user settings that a user should have access to. Because of that everything is controlled in one way or another with PowerShell and Role Based Access Control (RBAC), it's sometimes easier to have a separate cmdlet for specific settings that are also configurable by users. It makes it easier to control those permissions (via Role Assignments with RBAC).

Settings on the mailbox include some email flow control such as addresses, forwarding or size/delivery restrictions, storage or quota settings and some policies. Others include junk email handling, OWA configuration (including features other than what is set via OWA Mailbox policies) and regional settings.

We will discuss some cmdlets in more detail below, in a per cmdlet way instead of a per scenario way.

Set-Mailbox

One example to change the email flow settings is to set a forwarding address to another user:

```
Set-Mailbox -Identity Gene.Ricks@Contoso.Com -DeliverToMailboxAndForward:$True
-ForwardingAddress Ann.Ples@Contoso.Com
```

Above we set this to an SMTP address, for which there must be a matching mail object for it; a mailbox, mail user or mail contact. If you needed to forward a message to an external SMTP address the ForwardingSmtpAddress property would be set instead.

With delivery restrictions, you can control what email is accepted or not.

```
Set-Mailbox -Identity Gene.Ricks@Contoso.Com -RequireSenderAuthenticationEnabled:$True
-AcceptMessagesOnlyFromSendersOrMembers @('Ann.Ples@Contoso.Com')
```

-RejectMessagesFromSendersOrMembers @('Mike.Soft@Contoso.Com')

With RequireSenderAuthenticationEnabled only accounts in your Exchange Online Tenant can email this mailbox (this is enabled for distribution groups by default). You can also configure users or groups to be accepted or rejected explicitly, in this example email from Ann Ples is accepted and from Mike Soft is rejected. Note that those are multi-valued properties.

Another setting is the mailbox quota's, mainly the IssueWarningQuota, ProhibitSendQuota and ProhibitSendReceiveQuota settings. There are also quota's when using auditing and Litigation/In-Place hold, but the principle is the same. The big difference is that most mailboxes will use the default Database quota settings, but in case you need to override those settings you have to set them on the mailbox:

Set-Mailbox-IdentityGene.Ricks@Contoso.Com-IssueWarningQuota'10737418240'-ProhibitSendQuota '11811160064' -ProhibitSendReceiveQuota '12884901888'

In this example the mailbox quotas are respectively 10GB, 11GB and 12GB, the normal input is in MB (megabytes) however you can explicitly state whether you use MB or GB etc.:

Set-Mailbox -Identity Gene.Ricks@Contoso.Com -IssueWarningQuota 10GB

If you require to retain deleted items longer than the default 14 days that are a mailbox default:

Set-Mailbox -Identity Gene.Ricks@Contoso.Com -UseDatabaseRetentionDefaults:$false -RetainDeletedItemsFor '30'

In this example the database retention defaults are disabled; the deleted items are retained for user recovery for 31 days. There is a limit in Exchange Online for the RetainDeletedItemsFor value and that is 30. If we try to set it greater than 30, then we get an error like so:

```
PS C:\> Set-Mailbox -Identity Damian -UseDatabaseRetentionDefaults:$false -RetainDeletedItemsFor '32'
The operation on mailbox "damian" failed because it's out of the current user's write scope. The value of properties
'RetainDeletedItemsFor' exceeds the maximum allowed for user 'damian' with license 'BPOS_S_Enterprise'.
    + CategoryInfo          : InvalidOperation: (damian:ADObjectId) [Set-Mailbox], InvalidOperationException
    + FullyQualifiedErrorId : [Server=CY4PR13MB1350,RequestId=27b218de-57d6-45b0-8494-1bbabdcebbbc,TimeStamp=12/7/2017
   3:11:38 AM] [FailureCategory=Cmdlet-InvalidOperationException] 4D104F39,Microsoft.Exchange.Management.RecipientTa
  sks.SetMailbox
    + PSComputerName        : ps.outlook.com
```

For setting additional SMTP addresses see example Adding/Removing an email address later in this chapter.

Set-MailboxAutoReplyConfiguration

Configures Out of Office (OOF) replies, including scheduling, inside and outside organization message. Basically, every possible setting the user can set. See Enabling and configure Out of Office settings by the admin for an example.

Set-MailboxJunkEmailConfiguration

Configure the User Junk folder with specifics in addition to what the user has configured via OWA/Outlook.

Set-MailboxJunkEmailConfiguration -Identity Gene.Ricks@Contoso.Com -TrustedSendersAndDomains fabrikam.com

The above will add the fabrikam.com domain as a trusted sender and Exchange will handle those domains differently (however if you have valid spam filtering software, their settings probably take precedence).

Set-MailboxRegionalConfiguration

Configures regional settings on a specific mailbox, such as time zone, date format, language etc.. Users will be prompted the first time they log in OWA or it will be configured depending on the client. However, as an admin you can provision these settings.

See Setting Regional setting in this chapter for an example.

OWA

There are some settings specifically for OWA. The user can change these settings, but as in other similar examples it might be required to provision some settings for users.

```
Set-MailboxMessageConfiguration
```

Configures the behavior of OWA for a specific mailbox. For instance; the automatic addition of a signature, always show the 'From:' field when composing messages, conversation order and whether ReplyAll is the default response:

```
Set-MailboxMessageConfiguration -Identity Gene.Ricks@Contoso.Com -AutoAddSignature
$True -AlwaysShowFrom $True -ConversationSortOrder ChronologicalNewestOnTop
-IsReplyAllTheDefaultResponse $False
```

Set-MailboxSpellingConfiguration

Set the spelling language in OWA, force check before sending the email and whether to ignore uppercase and mixed digits:

```
Set-MailboxSpellingConfiguration  -Identity  Gene.Ricks@Contoso.Com  -CheckBeforeSend  $True
-IgnoreUpperCase $True -IgnoreMixedDigits $True -DictionaryLanguage Dutch
```

Calendar

Calendar settings can be changed to affect the way calendar invites are processed or to set timezones for instance. While you can configure calendar settings for user mailboxes during provisioning, you will likely have to perform these actions more often for Room and Equipment Mailboxes as users can change most of these settings themselves.

Set-MailboxCalendarConfiguration

Can change calendar configurations and is available to the user, but also the admins so they can provision certain settings for the users. Such as WorkDays/WorkingHours, the first week of the year, timezones and such. Some customization are for OWA only as Outlook (or other clients) have their own settings that supersede these.

```
Set-MailboxCalendarConfiguration -Identity Gene.Ricks@Contoso.Com –WeekStartDay Monday
```

Sets the first day of the week to Monday, instead of the default Sunday.

Set-MailboxCalendarFolder

This cmdlet is only relevant when sharing a calendar with a federated Exchange organization or when Internet

Publishing is allowed. You can reset the published URLs, change the date range of what is published and disable the sharing. You can only do this for you own mailbox, unless you change the Role Assignment.

```
Set-MailboxCalendarFolder administrator:\Calendar -PublishEnabled $True -DetailLevel Limited
```

Set-CalendarProcessing

The cmdlet Set-CalenderProcessing configures the way Exchange will handle meeting requests. As previously stated, users can configure these settings themselves and some settings are not relevant for user mailboxes. However, they are for Room and Equipment mailboxes which can turn them into automatic booking systems. You can use the same principal for inactive mailboxes, previously owned by users and setting to refuse every meeting request.

```
Set-CalendarProcessing    -Identity    Auditorium    -ProcessExternalMeetingMessages    $True
-AutomateProcessing AutoAccept -AddOrganizerToSubject $True -AddAdditionalResponse $True
-AdditionalResponse "Your request has been accepted."
```

This example configures the Room mailbox Auditorium to process External meeting requests (coming from outside of the Exchange organization), automatically accepts the requests, changes the Subject to the name of the organizer and will reply with a customized response to the organizer.

You can set additional options like whether users can set a reoccurring meeting, maximum meeting duration and delegates that have to give approval.

Client Access

All client access related settings are performed with Set-CASMailbox. You can disable/enable and configure specific protocols, such as IMAP/POP or OWA, ActiveSync and Exchange Web Services (EWS). Basically, everything mailbox client connection related (with the exception of SMTP) can be configured.

```
Set-CASMailbox -Identity Gene.Ricks@Contoso.Com -PopEnabled $False -ImapEnabled $False
-EwsAllowEntourage $False -ActiveSyncEnabled $False
```

In this example, POP, IMAP and ActiveSync are disabled and EWS Entourage support (an Outlook for MacOS predecessor) is not allowed. Note that IMAP and POP are default enabled, but the service is by default disabled on every Exchange server. Thus, if an application or user requires either one of the protocols the services must be enabled and started. It's a best practice to disable these protocols or to not publish the ports to the Internet as a way of increasing security.

Policies

Policies are an easy way to ensure users get the right configuration and is preferable to changing each specific user. There are several policies available:

- OWA Mailbox
- Retention
- RoleAssignmentPolicy
- SharingPolicy
- Mobile Device

OWA Mailbox policies regulate the Outlook Web App capabilities available to the user, the default has every feature enabled. For instance, Offline Mode is one often disabled feature in the default policy or other custom policies.

Retention policies give users and admins the option to regulate the retention of items in their mailbox or specific folders. When the mailbox is Archive enabled Retention policies (with the "Move to Archive") are commonly used, but an Archive mailbox is not required for their use.

Role assignments are part of Role Based Access Control (RBAC), the security model within Exchange. These policies regulate what users can carry out what actions on what objects, such as updating a distribution group for instance.

Sharing policies regulate sharing of calendar information within federated Exchange organizations or via Internet Calendar Publishing.

Mobile Device policies configure the security settings and features on connected mobile devices, via Exchange ActiveSync or the Outlook for iOS/Android app. Most commonly a mandatory PIN is set via these policies.

Obviously to assign or to change policies, the policies must exist. Assigning or changing the assigned policy on a mailbox is done via the Set-Mailbox or Set-CASMailbox cmdlet:

OWA Mailbox policy:

    Set-CASMailbox -Identity Gene.Ricks@Contoso.Com -OwaMailboxPolicy NoOfflineOWA

Retention Policy:

    Set-Mailbox -Identity Gene.Ricks@Contoso.Com -RetentionPolicy AutoCleanDeletedItems

Role Assignment policy:

    Set-Mailbox -Identity Gene.Ricks@Contoso.Com -RoleAssignmentPolicy EditSubsetGroups

Sharing policy:

    Set-Mailbox -Identity Gene.Ricks@Contoso.Com -SharingPolicy InternetSharing

ActiveSync Mailbox policy:

    Set-CASMailbox -Identity Gene.Ricks@Contoso.Com -ActiveSyncMailboxPolicy HighSecurity

See Chapter 9 for more information on managing non-user objects. For Mobile Device policies check Chapter 15.

Permissions

These are different levels of permissions possible on Exchange mailboxes:

- Full Access
- Send As
- Send On Behalf
- Folder Permissions

To add Full Access permissions, use Add-MailboxPermission:

```
Add-MailboxPermission -user Mike.Soft -identity Ann.Ples -AccessRights FullAccess -InheritanceType All
-Automapping $False
```

In this case Mike Soft will be granted full access on Ann Ples' Mailbox, additionally this permission will be granted to all folders within the mailbox. The setting Automapping controls whether Ann's mailbox is automatically added in Mike's Outlook (via AutoDiscover), in this case by setting it to $false it will not. When the Automapping feature is not configured it is default True (which is also the case when using the Exchange Admin Center). This will not grant Send-As permissions, that is actually a recipient based permission and can be set via:

```
Add-RecipientPermission -Identity Ann.Ples -Trustee Mike.Soft -AccessRights 'Send As'
```

In this example user Mike has been granted Send As permissions to Ann's Mailbox. Do note that Mike has to change the 'From:' value in Outlook to Ann's email address. In cases where it is required that the actual sender is still visible, Send on Behalf is the best option. This must be configured with the Set-Mailbox cmdlet:

```
Set-Mailbox –Identity Ann.Ples -GrantSendOnBehalfTo Mike.Soft
```

In this example Mike has been granted Send on Behalf permissions. As with Send-As, Mike must change the 'From:' value in Outlook to make use of this permission. However, the recipient will now see the actual sender even if replies are sent back to the main mailbox (Ann's). In some cases, Full Access is too broad therefore it is good to be able to set permissions on specific folders. Folder Permissions are set via the user itself in Outlook or OWA, but admins can use:

```
Add-MailboxFolderPermission -Identity Ann.Ples:\Inbox -User Mike.Soft -AccessRights Owner
```

In this example, Mike gets Owner permissions on the Inbox folder inside Ann's Mailbox. There are quite a lot of different permissions possible, be sure to read up on them at TechNet. Note that the Calendar folder has two additional permission roles specifically for availability visibility.

Additional information - https://technet.microsoft.com/en-us/library/dd298062(v=exchg.160).aspx

In this example, the Add-MailboxFolderPermission was used which adds permissions and lets previously set (not inherited) permissions as is. Use the Set-MailboxFolderPermission to edit previously assigned permissions, and Remove-MailboxFolderPermissions to remove permissions.

```
[PS] C:\>Add-MailboxFolderPermission -Identity Ann.Ples:\Inbox -User GeneRicks -AccessRights Owner

FolderName          User                AccessRights        SharingPermissionFlags
----------          ----                ------------        ----------------------
Inbox               Gene Ricks          {Owner}


[PS] C:\>Set-MailboxFolderPermission -Identity Ann.Ples:\Inbox -User GeneRicks -AccessRights Editor
[PS] C:\>Get-MailboxFolderPermission -Identity Ann.Ples:\Inbox

FolderName          User                AccessRights        SharingPermissionFlags
----------          ----                ------------        ----------------------
Inbox               Default             {None}
Inbox               Anonymous           {None}
Inbox               Gene Ricks          {Editor}


[PS] C:\>Remove-MailboxFolderPermission -Identity Ann.Ples:\Inbox -User GeneRicks

Confirm
Are you sure you want to perform this action?
Removing mailbox folder permission on "Ann.Ples:\Inbox" for user "Gene Ricks".
[Y] Yes  [A] Yes to All  [N] No  [L] No to All  [?] Help (default is "Y"):
[PS] C:\>
[PS] C:\>Get-MailboxFolderPermission -Identity Ann.Ples:\Inbox

FolderName          User                AccessRights        SharingPermissionFlags
----------          ----                ------------        ----------------------
Inbox               Default             {None}
Inbox               Anonymous           {None}
```

Note that the Well-Known folders (like Inbox, Calendar, Sent Items etc.) will change with regional settings set by the user (via OWA) or by language settings of Outlook when first connecting to their Mailbox. This might pose a challenge if you want to automate specific settings on those Well-Known folders. Luckily the FolderType is a constant and that value will tell you what kind of folder it is. Custom made folders (a second calendar for instance) have the folder type of "User Created". Use the following PowerShell one-liner in order to find the specific name of the Well-Known Calendar folder:

```
Get-Mailbox <Mailbox>|Get-MailboxFolderStatistics|Where {$_.FolderType -eq "Calendar"}
```

The value of the FolderType can be Inbox, Contacts, Sent Items, Deleted Items etc.. You can list this for a specific mailbox with:

```
Get-Mailbox <mailbox> |Get-MailboxFolderStatistics| Select FolderType
```

Often Requested Changes

Below is a comprehensive list of often performed changes.

Enabling and configure Out of Office settings by the admin

Even with all the options available to a user to configure the Out of Office (OOF, which is an abbreviation for Out of Facility, harking back to early Exchange years when its predecessor was used internally), you might get requests to set this. Luckily this is relatively easily done:

```
Set-MailboxAutoReplyConfiguration -Identity Ann.Ples -AutoReplyState Enabled -InternalMessage "I'm currently out of office."
```

This is the simplest configuration, there are options to set a message for external users (i.e. not in the Exchange organization), setting a time period when the OOF status has to be enabled, automatically declining meeting request etc. Basically, every setting available to the user, when using a recent version of Outlook or OWA. However, for an admin this example will probably be sufficient in most cases.

Regional Setting

In some cases you want to set regional settings for a user, so that the user has an even more fluid first logon experience and isn't bothered by questions about language etc.. Especially valid if your organization is set in a single language region etc..

You can set the specific regional settings with:

```
Set-MailboxRegionalConfiguration -Identity "Hans de Vries" -Language nl-nl -DateFormat "dd-MM-yy" -LocalizeDefaultFolderName -TimeZone "W. Europe Standard Time"
```

In this example the user will have Netherlands Dutch language settings in OWA and in Outlook, the LocalizeDefaultFolderName parameter will change the well known folders like Inbox and Calendar to the localized versions (respectively 'Postvak IN' and 'Kalender' in this case). The latter could be important when you have scripts to set Calendar folder permissions or require to migrate to a non-Exchange environment via PST. Furthermore, the date format has been set to correspond with the region and the time zone has been set to West Europe.

Adding/Removing an Email Address

Even with Email Address Policies it is possible that the naming convention doesn't provide the required SMTP address. Or the account requires additional SMTP addresses or the user changed his or her name.

> ** **Note** ** Don't forget that modifying properties of an object while connected to Exchange Online Power-Shell is only supported for cloud only objects.

You can add email addresses with the Set-Mailbox cmdlet with the EmailAddresses parameter. However, if you use this parameter the value will replace all of the configured address (only to be added again by the Email Address Policy). Therefore you need to use a little different syntax:

```
Set-Mailbox Ann.Ples -EmailAddresses @{Add="smtp:Ann.Ples@Contoso.Com"}
```

In this example the Ann.Ples@Contoso.Com address is added to other addresses on the Ann Ples mailbox. Note the small caps type "smtp". If you change this to capital letters, this will become the Primary SMTP address. However, this could be overruled by any active Email Address Policy.

Removing an email address is achieved by using Remove instead of Add:

```
Set-Mailbox Ann.Ples -EmailAddresses @{Remove="smtp:Ann.Ples@Contoso.Com"}
```

In both cases, other SMTP addresses configured on the mailbox are not removed.

Converting Mailbox Types

There are times you might have to change the type of the (user) object to another; types being user, resource or shared. Sometimes, converting a mail user to a full mailbox enabled user is required or when mergers have been completed Linked mailboxes might have to be converted to user mailboxes. This quickly summarizes the options and some of the things you should consider.

Converting Mail User to User Mailbox

There are situations that might require you to convert a mail user to a mailbox user.

In order to convert a Mail User into a Mailbox, you will need to assign an Exchange Online License. First, you will need to create the Mail User in Office 365:

```
PS C:\> New-MailUser -Name 'Pete Blanket' -ExternalEmailAddress PBlanket@Outlook.Com -MicrosoftOnlineServicesID pbla
nket@OnlineExchangeBook.onmicrosoft.com

cmdlet New-MailUser at command pipeline position 1
Supply values for the following parameters:
Password: ********

Name                                        RecipientType
----                                        -------------
Pete Blanket                                MailUser
```

Converting User Mailbox to Shared Mailbox

This might be useful when a person leaves the organization, but you are required to keep the data intact due to legal and/or compliance regulations. By converting the mailbox from user mailbox to shared, you disable the AD account (lowering the risk of breaches), give access to others within the company and you are still able to keep the mail flow intact.

** **Note** ** Shared mailboxe do not require an Exchange Online license, unless a Legal Hold is put in place.

You can convert mailbox types with the Set-Mailbox cmdlet:

```
Set-Mailbox -Identity PeteBlanket -Type Shared
```

You can change the type of mailboxes to Resources (Room, Equipment), Shared or User Mailboxes in this way with the Set-Mailbox cmdlet. Valid values are:

- Regular
- Room
- Equipment
- Shared

When changing the type of the mailbox, do not forget that additional configuration specifics for the new mailbox type is required depending on your organizational needs.

Reporting

In this section, we will give some attention towards reporting on user mailboxes. This is discussed in more depth in Chapter 18 - Reporting, but there are some specifics that warrant a mention in this chapter.

General Remarks

It's prudent to check with every update if there are any new commands or new attributes exposed in the Get cmdlets. Especially when new features are added, you'd expect to find some way of configuring those features. However, as Exchange is developed with Office 365 (or specifically Exchange Online) in mind you might encounter attributes that are of no use in the cloud (or vice versa). You can ignore those.

When you have a lot of objects, do not forget to add the -ResultSize parameter to your cmdlet preferably with "Unlimited" as a value, otherwise only 1,000 objects are returned. You will get a warning, but within a script you might miss that and it could result in incomplete processing or reporting of your environment. For testing purposes, you could use this to limit the number of objects returned and thus speed up your script.

```
WARNING: By default, only the first 1000 items are returned. Use the ResultSize parameter to specify the number of
items returned. To return all items, specify "-ResultSize Unlimited". Be aware that, depending on the actual number of
items, returning all items can take a long time and consume a large amount of memory. Also, we don't recommend storing
the results in a variable. Instead, pipe the results to another task or script to perform batch changes.
```

Cmdlets

Let's see the relevant cmdlets, what kind of information they reveal and in some instances, some extra useful information. Do note that some cmdlets are not that obvious. Check the screenshots for some formatting suggestions, some -Identity fields are sometimes a bit more complex than just adding user identity values. Also, some cmdlets show more interesting information when you pipe the cmdlet to Format-List (FL in short), this has been used in the examples but is not required when using a script (as PowerShell returns objects not text).

Get-MsolUser

Lists attributes such as phone, address names etc. from Active Directory users, whether they are mail- or mailbox enabled or not. The focus is the Active Directory user object rather than the mailbox.

```
Get-MsolUser -Identity Damian@OnlineExchangeBook.OnMicrosoft.Com | Fl
```

```
ExtensionData                               : System.Runtime.Serialization.ExtensionDataObject
AlternateEmailAddresses                     :
AlternateMobilePhones                       : {}
AlternativeSecurityIds                      : {}
BlockCredential                             : False
City                                        :
CloudExchangeRecipientDisplayType           : 1073741824
Country                                     : US
Department                                  :
DirSyncProvisioningErrors                   : {}
DisplayName                                 : Damian Scoles
Errors                                      :
Fax                                         :
FirstName                                   : Damian
ImmutableId                                 :
IndirectLicenseErrors                       : {}
IsBlackberryUser                            : False
IsLicensed                                  : True
LastDirSyncTime                             :
LastName                                    : Scoles
LastPasswordChangeTimestamp                 : 12/6/2017 6:37:28 AM
LicenseReconciliationNeeded                 : False
Licenses                                    : {OnlineExchangeBook:ENTERPRISEPACK}
LiveId                                      : 1003BFFDA6AA7561
MSExchRecipientTypeDetails                  :
MobilePhone                                 :
ObjectId                                    : ce59bace-e444-4ade-940d-ddbb3754d3c3
Office                                      :
OverallProvisioningStatus                   : Success
PasswordNeverExpires                        :
PasswordResetNotRequiredDuringActivate      :
PhoneNumber                                 : 630-299-9473
PortalSettings                              : PortalSettings
PostalCode                                  :
PreferredDataLocation                       :
PreferredLanguage                           : en
ProxyAddresses                              : {SMTP:damian@OnlineExchangeBook.onmicrosoft.com}
ReleaseTrack                                :
ServiceInformation                          : {}
SignInName                                  : damian@OnlineExchangeBook.onmicrosoft.com
SoftDeletionTimestamp                       :
State                                       :
StreetAddress                               :
StrongAuthenticationMethods                 : {}
StrongAuthenticationPhoneAppDetails         : {}
StrongAuthenticationProofupTime             :
StrongAuthenticationRequirements            : {}
StrongAuthenticationUserDetails             :
StrongPasswordRequired                      :
StsRefreshTokensValidFrom                   : 12/6/2017 6:37:28 AM
Title                                       :
UsageLocation                               : US
UserLandingPageIdentifierForO365Shell       :
UserPrincipalName                           : damian@OnlineExchangeBook.onmicrosoft.com
UserThemeIdentifierForO365Shell             :
UserType                                    : Member
ValidationStatus                            : Healthy
WhenCreated                                 : 12/6/2017 6:37:29 AM
```

Get-Mailbox

Lists mailbox enabled objects, these can be of RecipientTypeDetail UserMailbox, Shared, Linked, Room or Equipment. The focus of this cmdlet is settings directly related to the mailbox functionality. Most interesting attributes are those related to quotas of not only the user mailbox but all kinds of quotas, mailflow handling, auditing, and the custom attributes.

```
Get-Mailbox -Identity Damian@OnlineExchangeBook.OnMicrosoft.Com | Fl

RunspaceId                             : 223be553-ccd2-4a1c-9a00-4427470d894d
Database                               : NAMPR13DG085-db010
MailboxProvisioningConstraint          :
IsMonitoringMailbox                    : False
MailboxRegion                          :
MailboxRegionLastUpdateTime            :
MessageCopyForSentAsEnabled            : False
MessageCopyForSendOnBehalfEnabled      : False
MailboxProvisioningPreferences         : {}
UseDatabaseRetentionDefaults           : False
RetainDeletedItemsUntilBackup          : False
DeliverToMailboxAndForward             : True
IsExcludedFromServingHierarchy         : False
IsHierarchyReady                       : True
IsHierarchySyncEnabled                 : True
HasSnackyAppData                       : False
LitigationHoldEnabled                  : False
SingleItemRecoveryEnabled              : True
RetentionHoldEnabled                   : False
EndDateForRetentionHold                :
StartDateForRetentionHold              :
RetentionComment                       :
RetentionUrl                           :
LitigationHoldDate                     :
LitigationHoldOwner                    :
ElcProcessingDisabled                  : False
ComplianceTagHoldApplied               : False
WasInactiveMailbox                     : False
DelayHoldApplied                       : False
InactiveMailboxRetireTime              :
OrphanSoftDeleteTrackingTime           :
LitigationHoldDuration                 : Unlimited
ManagedFolderMailboxPolicy             :
RetentionPolicy                        : Default MRM Policy
AddressBookPolicy                      :
CalendarRepairDisabled                 : False
ExchangeGuid                           : 79fbc71d-49a4-487f-b21b-ffc7e5dd6072
MailboxContainerGuid                   :
UnifiedMailbox                         :
MailboxLocations                       : {1;160cf56c-28eb-49a5-88f4-22b8848cdb18;MainArchive;namprd13.prod.outlook.com;
                                         3d023dda-cbfd-465f-8211-af56b1593230, 1;79fbc71d-49a4-487f-b21b-ffc7e5dd6072;P
                                         rimary;namprd13.prod.outlook.com;3d023dda-cbfd-465f-8211-af56b1593230}
AggregatedMailboxGuids                 : {}
ExchangeSecurityDescriptor             : System.Security.AccessControl.RawSecurityDescriptor
ExchangeUserAccountControl             : None
AdminDisplayVersion                    : Version 15.20 (Build 302.2)
MessageTrackingReadStatusEnabled       : True
ExternalOofOptions                     : External
ForwardingAddress                      : john.doe
ForwardingSmtpAddress                  :
RetainDeletedItemsFor                  : 30.00:00:00
IsMailboxEnabled                       : True
Languages                              : {}
OfflineAddressBook                     :
ProhibitSendQuota                      : 11 GB (11,811,160,064 bytes)
ProhibitSendReceiveQuota               : 12 GB (12,884,901,888 bytes)
RecoverableItemsQuota                  : 30 GB (32,212,254,720 bytes)
RecoverableItemsWarningQuota           : 20 GB (21,474,836,480 bytes)
CalendarLoggingQuota                   : 6 GB (6,442,450,944 bytes)
DowngradeHighPriorityMessagesEnabled   : False
ProtocolSettings                       : {IMAP4§0§§§§§§§§§§§, POP3§0§§§§§§§§§§§§1, RemotePowerShell§1,
                                         MAPI§1§0§§§§0§§§§§0...}
RecipientLimits                        : 500
ImListMigrationCompleted               : False
SiloName                               :
IsResource                             : False
IsLinked                               : False
IsShared                               : False
IsRootPublicFolderMailbox              : False
LinkedMasterAccount                    :
ResetPasswordOnNextLogon               : False
ResourceCapacity                       :
ResourceCustom                         : {}
ResourceType                           :
RoomMailboxAccountEnabled              :
SamAccountName                         : damia511622036315638
SCLDeleteThreshold                     :
SCLDeleteEnabled                       :
SCLRejectThreshold                     :
SCLRejectEnabled                       :
SCLQuarantineThreshold                 :
SCLQuarantineEnabled                   :
SCLJunkThreshold                       :
SCLJunkEnabled                         :
AntispamBypassEnabled                  : False
ServerLegacyDN                         : /o=ExchangeLabs/ou=Exchange Administrative Group
                                         (FYDIBOHF23SPDLT)/cn=Configuration/cn=Servers/cn=MWHPR1301MB2078
ServerName                             : mwhpr1301mb2078
UseDatabaseQuotaDefaults               : False
IssueWarningQuota                      : 10 GB (10,737,418,240 bytes)
RulesQuota                             : 256 KB (262,144 bytes)
Office                                 :
UserPrincipalName                      : damian@OnlineExchangeBook.onmicrosoft.com
UMEnabled                              : False
MaxSafeSenders                         :
MaxBlockedSenders                      :
NetID                                  : 1003BFFDA6AA7561
ReconciliationId                       :
WindowsLiveID                          : damian@OnlineExchangeBook.onmicrosoft.com
MicrosoftOnlineServicesID              : damian@OnlineExchangeBook.onmicrosoft.com
```

```
RoleAssignmentPolicy                          : Default Role Assignment Policy
DefaultPublicFolderMailbox                    :
EffectivePublicFolderMailbox                  :
SharingPolicy                                 : Default Sharing Policy
RemoteAccountPolicy                           :
MailboxPlan                                   : ExchangeOnlineEnterprise-124f6119-7869-40e4-90a6-14e20837d794
ArchiveDatabase                               : NAMPR13DG005-db010
ArchiveGuid                                   : 160cf56c-28eb-49a5-88f4-22b8848cdb18
ArchiveName                                   : {In-Place Archive -Damian Scoles}
JournalArchiveAddress                         :
ArchiveQuota                                  : 100 GB (107,374,182,400 bytes)
ArchiveWarningQuota                           : 90 GB (96,636,764,160 bytes)
ArchiveDomain                                 :
ArchiveStatus                                 : Active
ArchiveState                                  : Local
AutoExpandingArchiveEnabled                   : False
DisabledMailboxLocations                      : False
RemoteRecipientType                           : None
DisabledArchiveDatabase                       :
DisabledArchiveGuid                           : 00000000-0000-0000-0000-000000000000
QueryBaseDN                                   :
QueryBaseDNRestrictionEnabled                 : False
MailboxMoveTargetMDB                          :
MailboxMoveSourceMDB                          :
MailboxMoveFlags                              : None
MailboxMoveRemoteHostName                     :
MailboxMoveBatchName                          :
MailboxMoveStatus                             : None
MailboxRelease                                :
ArchiveRelease                                :
IsPersonToPersonTextMessagingEnabled          : False
IsMachineToPersonTextMessagingEnabled         : True
UserSMimeCertificate                          : {}
UserCertificate                               : {}
CalendarVersionStoreDisabled                  : False
ImmutableId                                   :
PersistedCapabilities                         : {BPOS_S_Enterprise}
SKUAssigned                                   : True
AuditEnabled                                  : False
AuditLogAgeLimit                              : 90.00:00:00
AuditAdmin                                    : {Update, Move, MoveToDeletedItems, SoftDelete...}
AuditDelegate                                 : {Update, SoftDelete, HardDelete, SendAs...}
AuditOwner                                    : {UpdateFolderPermissions}
WhenMailboxCreated                            : 12/6/2017 12:52:02 AM
SourceAnchor                                  :
UsageLocation                                 : United States
IsSoftDeletedByRemove                         : False
IsSoftDeletedByDisable                        : False
IsInactiveMailbox                             : False
IncludeInGarbageCollection                    : False
WhenSoftDeleted                               :
InPlaceHolds                                  : {}
GeneratedOfflineAddressBooks                  : {}
AccountDisabled                               : False
StsRefreshTokensValidFrom                     : 12/6/2017 12:37:28 AM
DataEncryptionPolicy                          :
Extensions                                    : {}
HasPicture                                    : False
HasSpokenName                                 : False
IsDirSynced                                   : False
AcceptMessagesOnlyFrom                        : {john.doe}
AcceptMessagesOnlyFromDLMembers               : {}
AcceptMessagesOnlyFromSendersOrMembers        : {john.doe}
AddressListMembership                         : {\Offline Global Address List, \All Users, \Mailboxes(VLV), \All
                                                Mailboxes(VLV)...}
AdministrativeUnits                           : {}
Alias                                         : damian
ArbitrationMailbox                            :
BypassModerationFromSendersOrMembers          : {}
OrganizationalUnit                            : nampr13a006.prod.outlook.com/Microsoft Exchange Hosted
                                                Organizations/OnlineExchangeBook.onmicrosoft.com
CustomAttribute1                              :
CustomAttribute10                             :
CustomAttribute11                             :
CustomAttribute12                             :
CustomAttribute13                             :
CustomAttribute14                             :
CustomAttribute15                             :
CustomAttribute2                              :
CustomAttribute3                              :
CustomAttribute4                              :
CustomAttribute5                              :
CustomAttribute6                              :
CustomAttribute7                              :
CustomAttribute8                              :
CustomAttribute9                              :
ExtensionCustomAttribute1                     : {}
ExtensionCustomAttribute2                     : {}
ExtensionCustomAttribute3                     : {}
ExtensionCustomAttribute4                     : {}
ExtensionCustomAttribute5                     : {}
DisplayName                                   : Damian Scoles
EmailAddresses                                : {SPO:SPO_de374a39-6500-4a91-b3e7-dc0b95f8a6b5@SPO_29368d28-0dc7-46c2-80f4-0ccb
                                                8ae2c65f, SIP:damian@OnlineExchangeBook.onmicrosoft.com,
                                                SMTP:damian@OnlineExchangeBook.onmicrosoft.com}
GrantSendOnBehalfTo                           : {john.doe}
ExternalDirectoryObjectId                     : ce59bace-c444-4ade-940d-ddbb3754d3c3
HiddenFromAddressListsEnabled                 : False
LastExchangeChangedTime                       :
LegacyExchangeDN                              : /o=ExchangeLabs/ou=Exchange Administrative Group
                                                (FYDIBOHF23SPDLT)/cn=Recipients/cn=2724c10509f34a6da6e9a0f080a40633-damian
MaxSendSize                                   : 35 MB (36,700,160 bytes)
MaxReceiveSize                                : 36 MB (37,748,736 bytes)
ModeratedBy                                   : {}
ModerationEnabled                             : False
PoliciesIncluded                              : {}
PoliciesExcluded                              : {{26491cfc-9e50-4857-861b-0cb8df22b5d7}}
EmailAddressPolicyEnabled                     : False
PrimarySmtpAddress                            : damian@OnlineExchangeBook.onmicrosoft.com
RecipientType                                 : UserMailbox
RecipientTypeDetails                          : UserMailbox
RejectMessagesFrom                            : {}
RejectMessagesFromDLMembers                   : {}
RejectMessagesFromSendersOrMembers            : {}
RequireSenderAuthenticationEnabled            : True
SimpleDisplayName                             :
SendModerationNotifications                   : Always
UMDtmfMap                                     : {reversedPhone:3749992036, emailAddress:326426,
                                                lastNameFirstName:726537326426, firstNameLastName:326426726537}
WindowsEmailAddress                           : damian@OnlineExchangeBook.onmicrosoft.com
MailTip                                       :
MailTipTranslations                           : {}
```

Get-MailboxAutoReplyConfiguration

Configuration of the Out of Office (OOF) replies, including scheduling, and inside and outside organization message. Basically, every possible setting the user (or an admin) has set. With this you can check whether an OOF has been set.

```
Get-MailboxAutoReplyConfiguration -Identity Gene.Ricks@Contoso.Com
```

```
RunspaceId                          : 223be553-ccd2-4a1c-9a00-4427470d894d
AutoDeclineFutureRequestsWhenOOF    : False
AutoReplyState                      : Disabled
CreateOOFEvent                      : False
DeclineAllEventsForScheduledOOF     : False
DeclineEventsForScheduledOOF        : False
EventsToDeleteIDs                   :
EndTime                             : 12/8/2017 12:00:00 AM
ExternalAudience                    : All
ExternalMessage                     :
InternalMessage                     :
DeclineMeetingMessage               :
OOFEventSubject                     :
StartTime                           : 12/7/2017 12:00:00 AM
MailboxOwnerId                      : Gene Ricks
Identity                            : Gene Ricks
IsValid                             : True
ObjectState                         : Unchanged
```

Get-CalendarProcessing

Display the way Exchange will process meeting invites on the mailbox at hand. In most cases for user mailboxes the default settings will be adequate, however for Room, Equipment and maybe Shared mailboxes changes may be required. Due to privacy regulations, it might be required to remove the subject of a meeting from a room mailbox. Or you want to limit the way users are booking a meeting with a room mailbox.

```
Get-CalendarProcessing -Identity Gene.Ricks@Contoso.Com | fl
```

```
RunspaceId                          : 223be553-ccd2-4a1c-9a00-4427470d894d
AutomateProcessing                  : AutoUpdate
AllowConflicts                      : False
BookingWindowInDays                 : 180
MaximumDurationInMinutes            : 1440
AllowRecurringMeetings              : True
EnforceSchedulingHorizon            : True
ScheduleOnlyDuringWorkHours         : False
ConflictPercentageAllowed           : 0
MaximumConflictInstances            : 0
ForwardRequestsToDelegates          : True
DeleteAttachments                   : True
DeleteComments                      : True
RemovePrivateProperty               : True
DeleteSubject                       : True
AddOrganizerToSubject               : True
DeleteNonCalendarItems              : True
TentativePendingApproval            : True
EnableResponseDetails               : True
OrganizerInfo                       : True
ResourceDelegates                   : {}
RequestOutOfPolicy                  : {}
AllRequestOutOfPolicy               : False
BookInPolicy                        : {}
AllBookInPolicy                     : True
RequestInPolicy                     : {}
AllRequestInPolicy                  : False
AddAdditionalResponse               : False
AdditionalResponse                  :
RemoveOldMeetingMessages            : True
AddNewRequestsTentatively           : True
ProcessExternalMeetingMessages      : False
RemoveForwardedMeetingNotifications : False
MailboxOwnerId                      : Gene Ricks
Identity                            : Gene Ricks
```

Get-MailboxCalendarConfiguration

This cmdlet shows the configuration of the calendar specific settings, such as the time zone, working hours and such. You could use this to check whether users are correctly provisioned per their actual regional location or other considerations.

Most of these features influence Outlook Web App, although some are also valid for other clients. The EventsFromEmailEnabled* and Weather* settings are for Exchange online only (as some other features which are mention on the TechNet page for this cmdlet).

Note that this cmdlet does not change any calendar processing settings. See Get-CalendarProcessing for those settings.

```
Get-MailboxCalendarConfiguration -Identity Gene.Ricks@Contoso.Com | Fl
```

```
RunspaceId                               : 223be553-ccd2-4a1c-9a00-4427470d894d
WorkDays                                 : Weekdays
WorkingHoursStartTime                    : 08:00:00
WorkingHoursEndTime                      : 17:00:00
WorkingHoursTimeZone                     : Pacific Standard Time
WeekStartDay                             : Monday
ShowWeekNumbers                          : False
FirstWeekOfYear                          : FirstDay
TimeIncrement                            : ThirtyMinutes
RemindersEnabled                         : True
ReminderSoundEnabled                     : True
DefaultReminderTime                      : 00:15:00
WeatherEnabled                           : FirstRun
WeatherUnit                              : Default
WeatherLocations                         : {}
WeatherLocationBookmark                  : 0
DefaultMeetingDuration                   : 30
AgendaMailEnabled                        : False
SkipAgendaMailOnFreeDays                 : True
DailyAgendaMailSchedule                  : Default
AgendaMailIntroductionEnabled            : True
EventsFromEmailEnabled                   : True
EventsFromEmailDelegateChecked           : False
EventsFromEmailShadowMailboxChecked      : False
ReportEventsCreatedFromEmailEnabled      : True
CreateEventsFromEmailAsPrivate           : True
FlightEventsFromEmailEnabled             : True
DiningEventsFromEmailEnabled             : True
HotelEventsFromEmailEnabled              : True
RentalCarEventsFromEmailEnabled          : True
EntertainmentEventsFromEmailEnabled      : True
PackageDeliveryEventsFromEmailEnabled    : False
InvoiceEventsFromEmailEnabled            : True
UseBrightCalendarColorThemeInOwa         : False
CalendarFeedsPreferredLanguage           :
CalendarFeedsPreferredRegion             :
CalendarFeedsRootPageId                  :
ConversationalSchedulingEnabled          : True
IsMailboxSectionEnabled                  : True
IsCalendarSectionEnabled                 : True
IsWorkingHoursSectionEnabled             : True
LocalEventsEnabled                       : FirstRun
LocalEventsLocation                      :
AgendaPaneEnabled                        : True
Identity                                 : Gene Ricks
```

Get-MailboxCalendarFolder

The cmdlet shows settings specifically targeted at sharing or publishing Calendar folder data of the user. It shows the period that data is visible, including the detail level for anonymous users. This is only the case when the calendar is shared, which is defined by the PublishEnabled attribute and the existence of publishing URLs.

```
Get-MailboxCalendarFolder -Identity Gene.Ricks@Contoso.Com:\Calendar
```

```
RunspaceId                        : 223be553-ccd2-4a1c-9a00-4427470d894d
Identity                          : Gene Ricks:\Calendar
PublishEnabled                    : False
PublishDateRangeFrom              : ThreeMonths
PublishDateRangeTo                : ThreeMonths
DetailLevel                       : LimitedDetails
SearchableUrlEnabled              : False
PublishedCalendarUrl              :
PublishedICalUrl                  :
ExtendedFolderFlags               : ExchangePublishedCalendar
CalendarSharingFolderFlags        : None
CalendarSharingOwnerSmtpAddress   :
CalendarSharingPermissionLevel    : Null
SharingLevelOfDetails             : None
SharingPermissionFlags            : None
SharingOwnerRemoteFolderId        : AAA=
LastAttemptedSyncTime             : 01/02/0001 00:00:00
LastSuccessfulSyncTime            : 01/02/0001 00:00:00
IsValid                           : True
ObjectState                       : Changed
```

The same user now with a shared calendar:

```
RunspaceId                        : 223be553-ccd2-4a1c-9a00-4427470d894d
Identity                          : Gene Ricks:\Calendar
PublishEnabled                    : True
PublishDateRangeFrom              : ThreeMonths
PublishDateRangeTo                : ThreeMonths
DetailLevel                       : LimitedDetails
SearchableUrlEnabled              : False
PublishedCalendarUrl              : http://outlook.office365.com/owa/calendar/79fbc71d49a4487fb21bffc
                                    7e5dd6072@OnlineExchangeBook.onmicrosoft.com/3ed26c2e01194f5caa4b
                                    6d5b89ffe0de103472916113708089252/calendar.html
PublishedICalUrl                  : http://outlook.office365.com/owa/calendar/79fbc71d49a4487fb21bffc
                                    7e5dd6072@OnlineExchangeBook.onmicrosoft.com/3ed26c2e01194f5caa4b
                                    6d5b89ffe0de103472916113708089252/calendar.ics
ExtendedFolderFlags               : ExchangePublishedCalendar
CalendarSharingFolderFlags        : None
CalendarSharingOwnerSmtpAddress   :
CalendarSharingPermissionLevel    : Null
SharingLevelOfDetails             : None
SharingPermissionFlags            : None
SharingOwnerRemoteFolderId        : AAA=
LastAttemptedSyncTime             : 01/02/0001 00:00:00
LastSuccessfulSyncTime            : 01/02/0001 00:00:00
IsValid                           : True
```

Get-MailboxFolder

View information on folders in your own mailbox.

```
Get-MailboxFolder Damian:\Inbox | Fl
```

```
PS C:\> Get-MailboxFolder Damian:\Inbox | Fl

RunspaceId                : 9ad6a38d-fd12-42e0-9bc4-9b9e8114c0d9
Name                      : Inbox
Identity                  : damian:\Inbox
ParentFolder              : damian:\
FolderStoreObjectId       : LgAAAAAHDC2POPk+RbUOQxp8hiH0AQC3MDdN6NBeTbIx9ZBl/izjAAAAAAEMAAAB
FolderSize                : 18501
HasSubfolders             : False
FolderClass               : IPF.Note
FolderPath                : {Inbox}
AssociatedDumpsterFolders :
DefaultFolderType         : Inbox
ExtendedFolderFlags       : Normal
MailboxOwnerId            : damian
IsValid                   : True
ObjectState               : Unchanged
```

Do note that you require the correct permissions on the mailbox, otherwise an error will be show stating that the mailbox doesn't exist. It's already trying to get information on the root folder and because you don't have access it will think it doesn't exist.

The default permissions are set via the Role Based Access Control role MyBaseOptions, this means that even an administrator can only use this cmdlet on their own mailbox, but will get this error when trying to query others. This obviously limits the use of this cmdlet for reporting.

```
The specified mailbox  Gene.Ricks@Contoso.Com\Inbox doesn't exist.
    + CategoryInfo          : NotSpecified: (:) [Get-MailboxFolder], ManagementObjectNotFoundExcep
   tion
    + FullyQualifiedErrorId : [Server=L16-EX01,RequestId=93e85a5d-0e0e-4210-b8dd-16577b1fd465,T
   imeStamp=12/17/2016 3:04:26 PM] [FailureCategory=Cmdlet-ManagementObjectNotFoundException] 701B
   F26B,Microsoft.Exchange.Management.StoreTasks.GetMailboxFolder
    + PSComputerName        : L16-EX01.LAb2016.Com
```

Get-MailboxFolderPermission

Used to view folder permissions within mailboxes. You must specify the correct folder path, which for the default/well-known folders in Exchange is dependent on the regional settings of the mailbox that create these folders at first login. So, the default Calendar folder might be named different in Spanish.

Also, note that the Calendar folder permissions have additional AccessRights available, AvailabilityOnly and LimitedDetails. Both influence the visibility of specific information of meetings (subject and location is also shown with LimitedDetails).

Get-MailboxFolderPermission -Identity Gene.Ricks@Contoso.Com:\Inbox

```
[PS] C:\>Get-MailboxFolderPermission -Identity Gene.Ricks@contoso.com:\Inbox

FolderName              User                    AccessRights
----------              ----                    ------------
Inbox                   Default                 {None}
Inbox                   Anonymous               {None}


[PS] C:\>Get-MailboxFolderPermission -Identity Gene.Ricks@contoso.com:\Calendar

FolderName              User                    AccessRights
----------              ----                    ------------
Calendar                Default                 {AvailabilityOnly}
Calendar                Anonymous               {None}
```

Get-MailboxFolderStatistics

View information on specific folders in a mailbox. This includes the folder size and number of items. For more information, you can add the -IncludeAnalysis switch, which can help with troubleshooting. It will return values that would otherwise remain empty, the reason being that it can take a while for the analysis to complete. The values however, can help with troubleshooting or reporting.

Get-MailboxFolderStatistics -Identity Gene.Ricks@Contoso.Com -FolderScope Inbox -IncludeAnalysis

This would result into something like this excerpt:

```
TopSubject                      : [Outlook junk mail report] isthis sapm is this spam?
TopSubjectSize                  : 30.29 KB (31,015 bytes)
TopSubjectCount                 : 1
TopSubjectClass                 : REPORT.IPM.Note.NDR
TopSubjectPath                  : \Top of Information Store\Inbox
TopSubjectReceivedTime          : 12/9/2016 1:02:52 AM
TopSubjectFrom                  : Microsoft Outlook
TopClientInfoForSubject         : \ \
TopClientInfoCountForSubject    : 1
```

Another parameter that might provide useful information for troubleshooting or reporting is the IncludeOldestAndNewestItems parameter. As the name suggests, you will then receive more information on the oldest and newest items in the specified mailbox.

```
Get-MailboxFolderStatistics -Identity Gene.Ricks@Contoso.Com -FolderScope Inbox
-IncludeOldestAndNewestItems
```

This would result into this:

```
RunspaceId                              : 9ad6a38d-fd12-42e0-9bc4-9b9e8114c0d9
Date                                    : 12/6/2017 9:16:46 AM
CreationTime                            : 12/6/2017 9:16:46 AM
LastModifiedTime                        : 12/7/2017 5:24:52 AM
Name                                    : Inbox
FolderPath                              : /Inbox
FolderId                                : LgAAAAHDC2POPk+RbUOQxp8hiH0AQC3MDdN6NBeTbIx9ZB1/izjAAAAAAEMAAAB
FolderType                              : Inbox
ContentFolder                           : True
ContentMailboxGuid                      : 79fbc71d-49a4-487f-b21b-ffc7e5dd6072
RawContentMailboxGuid                   :
Movable                                 : False
RecoverableItemsFolder                  : False
AssociatedIPMFolderPath                 :
ContainerClass                          :
Flags                                   :
TargetQuota                             : User
StorageQuota                            : Unlimited
StorageWarningQuota                     : Unlimited
ItemsInFolder                           : 10
DeletedItemsInFolder                    : 0
FolderSize                              : 18.07 KB (18,501 bytes)
ItemsInFolderAndSubfolders              : 10
DeletedItemsInFolderAndSubfolders       : 0
FolderAndSubfolderSize                  : 18.07 KB (18,501 bytes)
CurrentSchemaVersion                    : 0.175
OldestItemReceivedDate                  :
NewestItemReceivedDate                  :
OldestDeletedItemReceivedDate           :
NewestDeletedItemReceivedDate           :
OldestItemLastModifiedDate              :
NewestItemLastModifiedDate              :
OldestDeletedItemLastModifiedDate       :
NewestDeletedItemLastModifiedDate       :
ManagedFolder                           :
DeletePolicy                            :
ArchivePolicy                           :
TopSubject                              :
TopSubjectSize                          : 0 B (0 bytes)
TopSubjectCount                         : 0
TopSubjectClass                         :
TopSubjectPath                          :
TopSubjectReceivedTime                  :
TopSubjectFrom                          :
TopClientInfoForSubject                 :
TopClientInfoCountForSubject            : 0
SearchFolders                           :
AuditAuxMailboxGuid                     :
AuditFolderStubSize                     :
LastMovedTimeStamp                      :
Identity                                : Gene.Ricks\Inbox
IsValid                                 : True
ObjectState                             : New
```

Note that you do not supply a folder path, but rather a folder type with the FolderScope parameter. With this all folders of the same type are returned and not just one specific folder.

Valid input values for FolderScope are:

All	Calendar
Contacts	ConversationHistory
DeletedItems	Drafts
Inbox	JunkEmail

Journal	LegacyArchiveJournals
ManagedCustomFolder	NonIpmRoot
Notes	Outlook
Personal	RecoverableItems
RssSubscriptions	SentItems
SyncIssues	Tasks

The ManagedCustomFolder value returns output for all managed custom folders. The RecoverableItems value returns output for the Recoverable Items folder and the Deletions, DiscoveryHolds, Purges, and Versions subfolders. Also see TechNet. If you require information regarding statistics of the whole mailbox, see Get-MailboxStatistics.

Get-MailboxJunkEmailConfiguration

Use this cmdlet to see the User Junk Mail folder configuration for a specific mailbox, including any blocked or trusted email addresses or domains. This can be useful to determine whether your central anti-spam solutions requires some tweaking.

```
Get-MailboxJunkEmailConfiguration -Identity Gene.Ricks@Contoso.Com
```

In this case the user has blocked a Wingtoys address.

```
RunspaceId                    : 9ad6a38d-fd12-42e0-9bc4-9b9e8114c0d9
Status                        : IsPresent, IsEnabled
Enabled                       : True
TrustedListsOnly              : False
ContactsTrusted               : False
TrustedSendersAndDomains      : {fabrikam.com}
BlockedSendersAndDomains      : {henk@wingtoys.com}
TrustedRecipientsAndDomains   : {fabrikam.com}
MailboxOwnerId                : Gene Ricks
Identity                      : Gene Ricks
IsValid                       : True
ObjectState                   : Unchanged
```

** **Note** ** Realize that with Exchange Online Protection, these settings can require an additional step in troubleshooting messages ending up in the Junk Mail folder. See this Microsoft article on this:

https://support.office.com/en-us/article/prevent-email-from-being-marked-as-spam-in-eop-and-office-365-74aaade0-efc0-46ac-b949-f2d1d59256fa

Get-MailboxMessageConfiguration

Shows the configuration of Outlook Web App for a specific mailbox.

```
Get-MailboxMessageConfiguration -Identity Gene.Ricks@Contoso.Com
```

```
RunspaceId                          : 9ad6a38d-fd12-42e0-9bc4-9b9e8114c0d9
AfterMoveOrDeleteBehavior           : OpenNextItem
NewItemNotification                 : All
EmptyDeletedItemsOnLogoff           : False
AutoAddSignature                    : True
AutoAddSignatureOnReply             : False
SignatureText                       :
SignatureHtml                       :
AutoAddSignatureOnMobile            : True
SignatureTextOnMobile               :
UseDefaultSignatureOnMobile         : True
DefaultFontName                     : Calibri
DefaultFontSize                     : 3
DefaultFontColor                    : #000000
DefaultFontFlags                    : Normal
AlwaysShowBcc                       : False
AlwaysShowFrom                      : True
DefaultFormat                       : Html
ReadReceiptResponse                 : DoNotAutomaticallySend

PreviewMarkAsReadBehavior           : OnSelectionChange
PreviewMarkAsReadDelaytime          : 5
ConversationSortOrder               : ChronologicalNewestOnTop
ShowConversationAsTree              : False
HideDeletedItems                    : False
SendAddressDefault                  :
EmailComposeMode                    : Inline
CheckForForgottenAttachments        : True
AreFlaggedItemsPinned               : False
IsReplyAllTheDefaultResponse        : False
KeyboardShortcutsMode               : Owa
LinkPreviewEnabled                  : True
ShowPreviewTextInListView           : True
ShowUpNext                          : True
GlobalReadingPanePosition           : Right
IsFavoritesFolderTreeCollapsed      : False
IsMailRootFolderTreeCollapsed       : False
MailFolderPaneExpanded              : True
IsHashtagTreeCollapsed              : False
IsGroupsTreeCollapsed               : False
GroupSuggestionDismissalCount       : 0
GroupSuggestionDismissalDate        :
ShowSenderOnTopInListView           : True
ShowReadingPaneOnFirstLoad          : False
NavigationPaneViewOption            : Default
AllOwaConfiguration                 :
PreferAccessibleContent             : False
MailboxOwnerId                      : Gene Ricks
Identity                            : Gene Ricks
IsValid                             : True
ObjectState                         : Unchanged
```

Get-MailboxPermission

Shows the permissions set on the specific mailbox. Note that these are not permissions on the subsequent folders. The IsInherited column indicates whether the permission is inherited from a higher source from the Azure Active Directory (AAD) configuration as Mailbox permissions are actually AAD permissions.

```
Get-MailboxPermission -Identity Gene.Ricks@Contoso.Com
```

Identity	User	AccessRights	IsInherited	Deny
Gene Ricks	NT AUTHORITY\SELF	{FullAccess, ReadPermission}	False	False
Gene Ricks	NAMPRD13\Administ...	{FullAccess}	True	True
Gene Ricks	NAMPRD13\Domain A...	{FullAccess}	True	True
Gene Ricks	NAMPRD13\Enterpri...	{FullAccess}	True	True
Gene Ricks	NAMPRD13\Organiza...	{FullAccess}	True	True
Gene Ricks	NT AUTHORITY\SYSTEM	{FullAccess}	True	False
Gene Ricks	NT AUTHORITY\NETW...	{ReadPermission}	True	False
Gene Ricks	NAMPRD13\Administ...	{FullAccess, DeleteItem, ReadPermission, ChangePermissio...	True	False
Gene Ricks	NAMPRD13\Domain A...	{FullAccess, DeleteItem, ReadPermission, ChangePermissio...	True	False
Gene Ricks	NAMPRD13\Enterpri...	{FullAccess, DeleteItem, ReadPermission, ChangePermissio...	True	False
Gene Ricks	NAMPRD13\Organiza...	{FullAccess, DeleteItem, ReadPermission, ChangePermissio...	True	False
Gene Ricks	NAMPRD13\Public F...	{ReadPermission}	True	False
Gene Ricks	NAMPRD13\Exchange...	{FullAccess, ReadPermission}	True	False
Gene Ricks	NAMPRD13\Exchange...	{FullAccess, DeleteItem, ReadPermission, ChangePermissio...	True	False
Gene Ricks	NAMPRD13\Managed ...	{ReadPermission}	True	False
Gene Ricks	S-1-5-21-15893167...	{ReadPermission}	True	False
Gene Ricks	PRDTSB01\JitUsers	{ReadPermission}	True	False

If you require only the permissions of a specific user, you can use the -User parameter.

Get-MailboxPermission -Identity Gene.Ricks@Contoso.Com -User Administrator

```
Identity             User                 AccessRights                                              IsInherited Deny
--------             ----                 ------------                                              ----------- ----
Gene Ricks           NAMPRD13\Administ... {FullAccess}                                              True        True
Gene Ricks           NAMPRD13\Administ... {FullAccess, DeleteItem, ReadPermission, ChangePermissio... True       False
```

In some cases, you only want to report on non-inherited permissions i.e. directly assigned mailbox permissions, which are the permissions set if you use Exchange cmdlets. You can do that by filtering using the Where cmdlet.

Get-MailboxPermission -Identity Gene.Ricks@Contoso.Com | Where {$_.IsInherited -eq $False}

```
Identity             User                 AccessRights                    IsInherited  Deny
--------             ----                 ------------                    -----------  ----
Gene Ricks           NT AUTHORITY\SELF    {FullAccess, ReadPermission}    False        False
```

Get-MailboxRegionalConfiguration

Use this cmdlet to extract regional settings on a specific mailbox, such as timezone, date format, language etc..

Get-MailboxRegionalConfiguration -Identity Gene.Ricks@Contoso.Com | fl

```
RunspaceId                              : c8ca4800-9430-4aea-aeab-a740cc956b4c
DateFormat                              : M/d/yyyy
Language                                : en-US
DefaultFolderNameMatchingUserLanguage   : False
TimeFormat                              : h:mm tt
TimeZone                                : W. Europe Standard Time
Identity                                : Gene Ricks
IsValid                                 : True
ObjectState                             : New
```

The *DefaultFolderNameMatchingUserLanguage* indicates whether the default (or Well-Known folders such as Inbox) are localized, if True, those folders names are in the language indicated. This has an impact when you use specific cmdlets that target specific folders, for instance folder permissions.

Get-MailboxSpellingConfiguration

Retrieve spelling configuration set by the user for Outlook Web App.

Get-MailboxSpellingConfiguration -Identity Gene.Ricks@Contoso.Com

```
RunspaceId           : c8ca4800-9430-4aea-aeab-a740cc956b4c
CheckBeforeSend      : False
DictionaryLanguage   : EnglishUnitedStates
IgnoreUppercase      : False
IgnoreMixedDigits    : False
Identity             : Gene Ricks
IsValid              : True
ObjectState          : New
```

Get-MailboxStatistics

Will show you statistics of a specific mailbox, such as the database name, size, number of items, the last logged on user etc. (although if this interests you, you should turn on auditing on those mailboxes for more detail information).

```
Get-MailboxStatistics -Identity Gene.Ricks@Contoso.Com | fl
```

```
letedItemCount                 : 0
emCount                        : 392
talDeletedItemSize             : 0 B (0 bytes)
talItemSize                    : 1.189 MB (1,246,709 bytes
ssageTableTotalSize            : 1.75 MB (1,835,008 bytes)
ssageTableAvailableSize        : 512 KB (524,288 bytes)
tachmentTableTotalSize         : 0 B (0 bytes)
tachmentTableAvailableSize     : 0 B (0 bytes)
herTablesTotalSize             : 1.125 MB (1,179,648 bytes
herTablesAvailableSize         : 320 KB (327,680 bytes)
Encrypted                      : False
```

Retrieve client access settings on a specific mailbox such as what kind of protocols are enabled on this mailbox and the specific configuration of these protocols:

```
Get-CASMailbox -Identity Gene.Ricks@Contoso.Com
```

Name	ActiveSyncEnabled	OWAEnabled	PopEnabled	ImapEnabled	MapiEnabled
Gene Ricks	False	True	False	False	True

```
Get-CASMailbox -Identity Gene.Ricks@Contoso.Com | Fl
```

```
RunspaceId                            : c8ca4800-9430-4aea-aeab-a740cc956b4c
EmailAddresses                        : {SPO:SPO_de374a39-6500-4a91-b3e7-dc0b95f8a6b5@SPO_29368d28-0dc7-46c2-80f4-0cc
                                        b8ae2c65f, SIP:Gene.Ricks@OnlineExchangeBook.onmicrosoft.com
                                        SMTP:Gene.Ricks@OnlineExchangeBook.onmicrosoft.com}
LegacyExchangeDN                      : /o=ExchangeLabs/ou=Exchange Administrative Group
                                        (FYDIBOHF23SPDLT)/cn=Recipients/cn=2724c10509f34a6da6e9a0f080a40633-Gene.Ricks
LinkedMasterAccount                   :
PrimarySmtpAddress                    : Gene.Ricks@OnlineExchangeBook.onmicrosoft.com
SamAccountName                        : damia511622036315638
ServerLegacyDN                        : /o=ExchangeLabs/ou=Exchange Administrative Group
                                        (FYDIBOHF23SPDLT)/cn=Configuration/cn=Servers/cn=MWHPR1301MB2078
ServerName                            : mwhpr1301mb2078
DisplayName                           : Gene Ricks
ActiveSyncAllowedDeviceIDs            : {}
ActiveSyncBlockedDeviceIDs            : {}
ActiveSyncMailboxPolicy               : Default
ActiveSyncMailboxPolicyIsDefaulted    : True
ActiveSyncDebugLogging                : False
ActiveSyncEnabled                     : False
HasActiveSyncDevicePartnership        : False
ActiveSyncSuppressReadReceipt         : False
ExternalImapSettings                  :
InternalImapSettings                  :
ExternalPopSettings                   :
InternalPopSettings                   :
ExternalSmtpSettings                  :
InternalSmtpSettings                  :
OwaMailboxPolicy                      : OwaMailboxPolicy-Default
OWAEnabled                            : True
OWAforDevicesEnabled                  : True
IsOptimizedForAccessibility           : False
ECPEnabled                            : True
PopEnabled                            : False
PopMessageDeleteEnabled               : True
PopUseProtocolDefaults                : True
PopMessagesRetrievalMimeFormat        : BestBodyFormat
PopEnableExactRFC822Size              : False
PopSuppressReadReceipt                : False
PopForceICalForCalendarRetrievalOption : True
ImapEnabled                           : False
ImapUseProtocolDefaults               : True
ImapMessagesRetrievalMimeFormat       : BestBodyFormat
ImapEnableExactRFC822Size             : False
ImapSuppressReadReceipt               : False
ImapForceICalForCalendarRetrievalOption : False
MAPIEnabled                           : True
MapiHttpEnabled                       :
MAPIBlockOutlookNonCachedMode         : False
MAPIBlockOutlookVersions              :
MAPIBlockOutlookRpcHttp               : False
MAPIBlockOutlookExternalConnectivity  : False
UniversalOutlookEnabled               : True
EwsEnabled                            : True
EwsAllowOutlook                       :
EwsAllowMacOutlook                    :
EwsAllowEntourage                     : False
EwsApplicationAccessPolicy            :
EwsAllowList                          :
EwsBlockList                          :
ShowGalAsDefaultView                  : True
Identity                              : Gene Ricks
IsValid                               : True
ExchangeVersion                       : 0.20 (15.0.0.0)
```

Non-User Objects

In This Chapter

- Shared Mailboxes
- Resource Mailboxes
- Public Folder Mailboxes
- Distribution Groups
- Group Moderation
- Office 365 Groups
- Putting It All Together

In the previous chapter, we covered user mailboxes and their management with PowerShell. While most Exchange Online operations involve these user mailboxes, there are other non-user objects that need to be managed as well. These objects serve a variety of purposes in Exchange Online and include objects like Shared Mailboxes, Resource Mailboxes, Public Folder Mailboxes and Distribution Groups.

Shared Mailboxes provide a common mailbox for a group of users to access. They also provide a common address for sending emails out as a single email address. They can be used by departments as a shared inbox or calendar for departmental operations.

Resource Mailboxes can be used for various reasons, from rooms, to equipment to other resources that an organization may want to keep track of. Examples of resources are Rooms and Equipment mailboxes. Room Lists can also be created and managed with PowerShell.

Public Folder Mailboxes are used by Exchange Online to store Public Folder data. Gone are the days of Public Folder databases with SMTP replicas and separate management. Public folders in Exchange Online are easier to manage and control with PowerShell or with the Exchange Online interface.

Distribution Groups are used for mass mailing, for updates meant for a group or for granting access to a group of people to mail objects in Exchange Online. With PowerShell we can manipulate the characteristics of these groups, add and remove members and more. Groups can also be moderated to control the flow of messages and to prevent information overload or improper emails from being sent to groups.

Office 365 Groups are a metamorphosis of the current Distribution Groups. This type of group provides more than just mail flow like Distribution Groups. A newly created group adds something in SharePoint, Exchange, One Note, and Planner. We'll explore the Exchange Online side of these groups.

Shared Mailboxes

Shared Mailboxes are commonly used by organizations as either a central place for group emails to be delivered or as a single mailbox to be used as a public customer facing presence where a group of users can send as a single user. Some examples are Customer Service mailboxes like 'Help Desk' where the customers are internal users and 'Support' where the clients are external people that have purchased a company's product. Another user would be a 'Faxes' mailbox that would be used as a central location for all faxes coming into an organization that could be received and then forwarded on to the appropriate internal recipients. Additionally a shared mailbox could be used for solely a group calendar which for example could be used by marketing management and users to keep track of when people will be in the office or maybe when marketing events are occurring.

PowerShell

Like the previous chapter explained, creating a new user in PowerShell is done using the New-Mailbox PowerShell cmdlet. When creating a new shared mailbox, a special parameter needs to be used in order for the mailbox to be designated as a shared mailbox. The '-Shared' parameter is all that is needed in order for this to occur.

Example

In this example, the IT Manager has decided he wants the Help Desk to respond to emails from a single mailbox so that all communications are funneled through a central mailbox. The manager wants this because this ensures that end users reply to the Help Desk emails and not individuals. Because schedules for Help Desk workers vary greatly, a central mailbox will allow for other Help Desk employees to be able to pick up an existing case if the original Help Desk employee was off work due to scheduling or sickness.

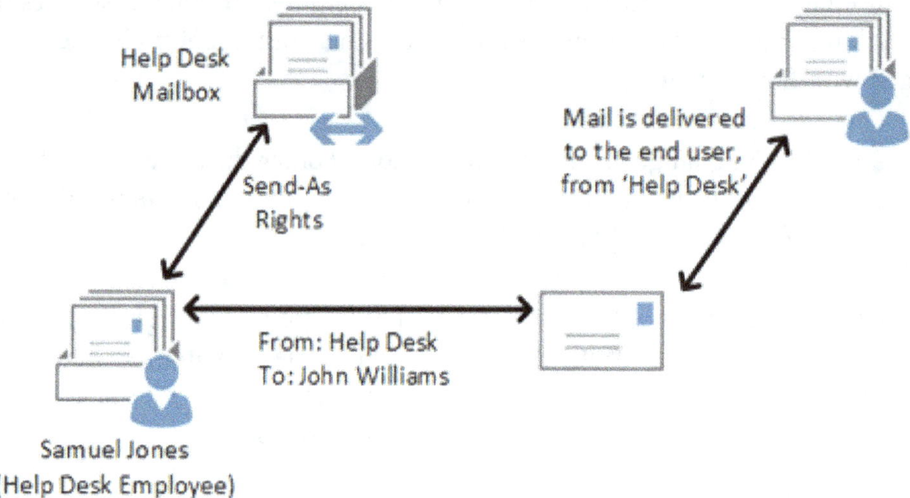

Now we need to create the mailbox and then assign Full Mailbox and Send-As rights to all users in the Help Desk Active Directory group. First, let's create the shared mailbox:

```
New-Mailbox -Shared -Name "Help Desk" -DisplayName "Help Desk"
```

```
Name         Alias        ServerName        ProhibitSendQuota
----         -----        ----------        -----------------
Help Desk    HelpDesk     mwhpr08mb3581     99 GB (106,300,440,576 bytes)
```

The Help Desk shared mailbox is now in Exchange Online and we need to assign rights to the mailbox for the Help Desk users to be able to send as the shared mailbox. For this part, there are two options for assigning the correct permissions for the Help Desk users. Either the rights can be assigned on a per-user or a per-group basis. For a group like the Help Desk, it would be more appropriate to use a group as the Help Desk group is likely to have a higher turnover rate than other groups. The other reason to use a group is that it is far easier to assign rights with groups than users. That way when a new Help Desk user is hired, in order to grant rights to the Shared Mailbox, all the admin has to do is to add the user to the group instead of using PowerShell to assign the rights.

PowerShell

How can permissions be added to mailboxes in Exchange via PowerShell? First, let's check for appropriate PowerShell cmdlets with the 'Permissions' keyword in them:

```
Get-Command *Permission*

CommandType          Name
-----------          ----
Function             Add-MailboxFolderPermission
Function             Add-MailboxPermission
Function             Add-PublicFolderClientPermission
Function             Add-RecipientPermission
Function             Get-MailboxFolderPermission
Function             Get-MailboxPermission
Function             Get-PublicFolderClientPermission
Function             Get-RecipientPermission
Function             Remove-MailboxFolderPermission
Function             Remove-MailboxPermission
Function             Remove-PublicFolderClientPermission
Function             Remove-RecipientPermission
Function             Set-MailboxFolderPermission
```

As we can see above, there are a few cmdlets that are useful for manipulating mailbox permissions. In particular, the Add-MailboxPermission cmdlet looks like what we need to handle this. Reviewing the examples for the cmdlet, Example 3 appears to be what is needed for this example.

```
-------------------------- Example 3 --------------------------
Add-MailboxPermission -Identity JeroenC -User 'Mark Steele' -AccessRights FullAccess -InheritanceType All
-AutoMapping $false
```

Now if the Help Desk users are all in a group called "Help Desk Users", we can first add the FullAccess permission as seen above to the Help Desk Mailbox:

```
Add-MailboxPermission –Identity "Help Desk" –User "Help Desk" –AccessRights FullAccess –
InheritanceType All
```

** **Note** ** The group needs to be a security type group, not a distribution type group. The object needs to be either pre-created in a non-synced environment or a synced object if you have Azure AD Connect in place.

The 'InheritanceType' parameter is used to make sure the permissions are applied to all folders in the mailbox. We now need to assign the Send-As permissions. However, the Add-MailboxPermission cmdlet does not have an option for that. The available permissions are:

FullAccess	ExternalAccount	DeleteItem
ReadPermission	ChangePermission	ChangeOwner

Notice that Send-As is not included in the above list. So if this is not a mailbox level permission, where else can rights be assigned? In Office 365 we need to use a cmdlet called 'Add-RecipientPermission' cmdlet like so:

Add-RecipientPermission -Identity 'Help Desk' -Trustee 'Help Desk Users' -AccessRights 'SendAs'

Now users from the Help Desk can send as the Help Desk and not themselves:

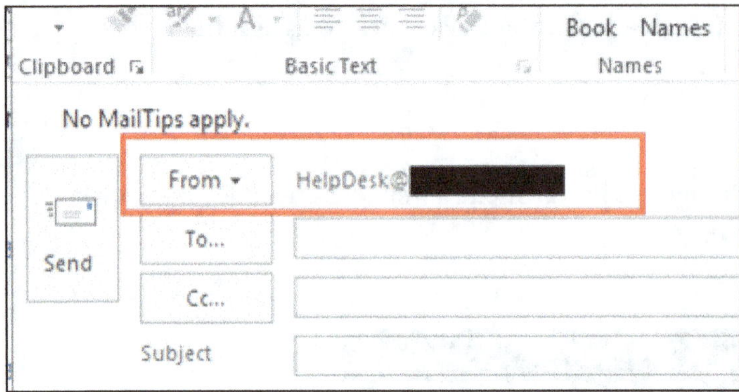

Example

In another scenario, the IT Department has received a request to produce a list of all shared mailboxes and a list of who has permissions for each mailbox. The rights that should be reported on are Send-As and Full Mailbox permissions. As we saw from the previous example, assigning these rights requires different PowerShell cmdlets (Add-ADPermission, Add-MailboxPermission and Add-RecipientPermission). We can safely assume that there are multiple cmdlets needed to query these. One more criteria we need to consider – whether or not the right was assigned directly (not inherited) by an Administrator or if the right was inherited and not assigned by an admin. From the request, it appears there is no distinction, just a report of the rights that are assigned on a mailbox. As such we will just look for 'Full Access' and 'Send-As' permission on the mailbox.

Let's start with the mailbox permission set with Add-MailboxPermission. From the previous page (top) we see a cmdlet called Get-MailboxPermission. For this environment, we will use a mailbox called "Help Desk" which has these permissions assigned to it, as our way to work out our PowerShell for all mailboxes.

First, let's see what PowerShell can reveal to us:

Get-Mailbox 'Help Desk' | Get-MailboxPermission | FT -Auto

```
Identity          User                                                       AccessRights
--------          ----                                                       ------------
Help Desk_58be9bb90b  NT AUTHORITY\SELF                                      {FullAccess, ReadPermission}
Help Desk_58be9bb90b  NT AUTHORITY\SELF                                      {FullAccess, ExternalAccount, ReadPermission}
Help Desk_58be9bb90b  damian0365@scoles.onmicrosoft.com                      {FullAccess}
Help Desk_58be9bb90b  Damian8192@scoles.onmicrosoft.com                      {FullAccess}
Help Desk_58be9bb90b  NAMPRD08\Administrator                                 {FullAccess}
Help Desk_58be9bb90b  NAMPRD08\Domain Admins                                 {FullAccess}
Help Desk_58be9bb90b  NAMPRD08\Enterprise Admins                             {FullAccess}
Help Desk_58be9bb90b  NAMPRD08\Organization Management                       {FullAccess}
Help Desk_58be9bb90b  NAMPRD08\BY2PR08CA0004$                                {FullAccess}
Help Desk_58be9bb90b  NT AUTHORITY\SYSTEM                                    {FullAccess}
Help Desk_58be9bb90b  NT AUTHORITY\NETWORK SERVICE                           {ReadPermission}
Help Desk_58be9bb90b  NAMPRD08\Administrator                                 {FullAccess, DeleteItem, ReadPermission, ChangeP...
Help Desk_58be9bb90b  NAMPRD08\Domain Admins                                 {FullAccess, DeleteItem, ReadPermission, ChangeP...
Help Desk_58be9bb90b  NAMPRD08\Enterprise Admins                            {FullAccess, DeleteItem, ReadPermission, ChangeP...
Help Desk_58be9bb90b  NAMPRD08\Organization Management                       {FullAccess, DeleteItem, ReadPermission, ChangeP...
Help Desk_58be9bb90b  NAMPRD08\Public Folder Management                      {ReadPermission}
Help Desk_58be9bb90b  NAMPRD08\Exchange Servers                             {FullAccess, ReadPermission}
Help Desk_58be9bb90b  NAMPRD08\Exchange Trusted Subsystem                    {FullAccess, DeleteItem, ReadPermission, ChangeP...
Help Desk_58be9bb90b  NAMPRD08\Managed Availability Servers                  {ReadPermission}
Help Desk_58be9bb90b  NAMPRD08\BY2PR08CA0004$                                {FullAccess, DeleteItem, ReadPermission, ChangeP...
Help Desk_58be9bb90b  S-1-5-21-1589316702-2032257147-3807288276-5106         {ReadPermission}
Help Desk_58be9bb90b  PRDTSB01\JitUsers                                      {ReadPermission}
```

From that one-liner we don't see the permissions assigned to the mailbox. Remember how we applied the Send-As permission with the Add-RecipientPermission? Well there is a corresponding cmdlet to query this with 'Get-RecipientPermission' to display those explicit rights:

```
Get-Mailbox "Help Desk" | Get-RecipientPermission
```

```
Identity    Trustee                         AccessControlType AccessRights Inherited
--------    -------                         ----------------- ------------ ---------
Help Desk   NT AUTHORITY\SELF               Allow             {SendAs}     False
Help Desk   damian@practicalpowershell.com  Allow             {SendAs}     False
Help Desk   HelpDesk@practicalpowershell.com Allow            {SendAs}     False
```

Now we can also go back to the Get-MailboxPermission cmdlet to filter down the results a bit. We need to remove any Organizational admins, NT Authority accounts and generally filter it down to users and groups that you care about. This one-liner should about do it:

```
Get-Mailbox "Help Desk" | Get-mailboxPermission | Select-Object Identity,User,AccessRights | Where {($_.User -NotLike "*SELF") -And ($_.User -NotLike "NT Auth*") -And ($_.User -NotLike "NAMPRD*")}
```

```
Identity             User                                   AccessRights
--------             ----                                   ------------
Help Desk_58be9bb90b damian0365@practicalpowershell.com     {FullAccess}
Help Desk_58be9bb90b Damian@practicalpowershell.com         {FullAccess}
Help Desk_58be9bb90b PRDTSB01\JitUsers                      {ReadPermission}
```

One of the filters that was use, filters for users like like NAMPRD. This abbreviation is specific to mailboxes in Noth AMerica and thus this filter will vary per region in Office 365. Notice at the bottom of the list there is a 'JitUsers'. This is a Built In group from Office 365. JIT stands for Just In Time Administration. If you want to exclude that from the list, you can use this:

```
Get-Mailbox "Help Desk" | Get-mailboxPermission | Select-Object Identity,User,AccessRights | Where {($_.User -NotLike "*SELF") -And ($_.User -NotLike "NT Auth*") -And ($_.User -NotLike "NAMPRD*") -and ($_.User -NotLike '*JITUsers')}
```

```
Identity             User                                   AccessRights
--------             ----                                   ------------
Help Desk_58be9bb90b damian0365@practicalpowershell.com     {FullAccess}
Help Desk_58be9bb90b Damian@practicalpowershell.com         {FullAccess}
```

Resource Mailboxes

There are two types of Resource Mailboxes in Exchange Online – Room and Equipment. The room mailbox is generally used to designate rooms that will be used by more than two people for meeting purposes. Whether these are large or small conference rooms, stand up only spaces or maybe even the lunch room, the purpose of a room mailbox is to provide a central scheduling place for users within Exchange. Calendars on room mailboxes operate differently than calendars for regular users and can be tweaked to handle different booking scenarios (AutoBooking and restricted hours) in an organization. A resource mailbox is generally used for items that can be checked out for a certain time period like projects, or TVs or maybe even vehicles for a company.

Equipment Mailboxes

Examples of equipment mailboxes are projectors, cars, laptops and more. By creating a mailbox in Exchange your users will be able to use their own mailbox calendar to book or request the booking of equipment that may be used for example in a client presentation. By its definition equipment should be portable or something that one of your users can transport.

Example

For this example we have a sale department with a hundred sales people that constantly travel to client sites to help present new products or to inform potential clients about the services your company provides. These sales people use a series of projectors for their presentations. The projectors range from the small travel projectors to the larger, more professional and higher quality projectors. The sales people and IT management would like to create these as objects in Exchange so that the sales people can check them out. The idea is that instead of constantly asking about the availability of equipment, the sales people would be able to confirm availability and schedule meetings with the equipment to secure the projects for a certain amount of hours / days.

Some of the projectors (the larger ones) require the approval of Sales Managers. The reason is that the larger projectors are expensive company property and need to be properly tracked. Some have gone missing over the years due to mismanagement.

PowerShell

Creating a mailbox for the projects is the same as creating a user mailbox, with the exception of a –Equipment parameter being added to designate the mailbox as an equipment mailbox:

```
New-Mailbox –Name "Portable Projector 1" –Equipment
```

```
Name                        Alias               ServerName          ProhibitSendQuota
----                        -----               ----------          -----------------
Portable Projector 1        PortableProjector1  cy4pr0801mb3795     99 GB (106,300,440,576 bytes)
```

Now that the mailbox is in Exchange we can modify some settings. For the smaller projectors, we need to make sure that they are available for AutoBooking and restrict to only be bookable by the Sales Department. How do we do this? Set-CalendarProcessing. This cmdlet can be used with any mailbox. It is especially useful for Equipment, Shared and Room mailboxes.

Let's review some examples from the cmdlet:

```
------------------------------- Example 1 ----------------------------
Set-CalendarProcessing -Identity "Conf 212" -AutomateProcessing AutoAccept -DeleteComments $true
-AddOrganizerToSubject $true -AllowConflicts $false
```

From these examples, we can use the bottom example for our cmdlet to enable resource mailbox scheduling and make sure to include this parameter:

```
–AutomateProcessing AutoAccept
```

The request also stated that only users in the Sales Department can reserve the equipment. Reviewing examples from the same cmdlet we see that there is an option to do this as well:

```
------------------------------- Example 6 ----------------------------
Set-CalendarProcessing -Identity "Car 53" -AutomateProcessing AutoAccept -BookInPolicy
"ayla@contoso.com","tony@contoso.com"
```

Reviewing Get-Help for Set-CalendarProcessing, the BookInPolicy states that:

"The BookInPolicy parameter specifies a comma-separated list of users who are allowed to submit in-policy meeting requests to the resource mailbox. Any in-policy meeting requests from these users are automatically approved."

By default all users should be blocked from automatically booking a room. Putting together the two parameters, we get:

```
Set-CalendarProcessing "Portable Projector 1" –AutomateProcessing AutoAccept –BookInPolicy "Sales Dept"
```

Now when someone from the Sales Department wants to book this projector they can. Now, if we want to restrict all projectors with the word 'Projector' in the name to just the Sales Department we first need a way to get a list of all of these projectors:

```
Get-Mailbox -Filter {(RecipientTypeDetails -eq "EquipmentMailbox") -and (Name -Like "*projector*")}
```

The '–filter' parameter allows for the result set of 'Get-Mailbox' to be shrunk to only mailboxes that are Equipment and have 'projector' in the name.

Equipment Mailbox Management

When all the equipment mailboxes are created, a report on the equipment mailboxes can be generated with:

```
Get-Mailbox -Filter {RecipientTypeDetails -eq "EquipmentMailbox"}
```

Or:

```
Get-Mailbox -RecipientTypeDetails EquipmentMailbox
```

Using the above one-liner, we can now perform mass manipulation on a group of mailboxes based solely on the type of mailbox specified. For example, we can change the calendar processing for this. First, let's see what the default setting is on this new mailbox we created:

```
Get-Mailbox -Filter {RecipientTypeDetails -eq "EquipmentMailbox"} | Get-CalendarProcessing
```

```
Identity                                                      AutomateProcessing
--------                                                      ------------------
Portable Projector 1                                          AutoUpdate
```

Now if we want to change the setting to be AutoAccept using this one-liner, we can use this example:

```
-------------------------- Example 3 --------------------------
Set-CalendarProcessing -Identity "5th Floor Conference Room" -AutomateProcessing AutoAccept -AllBookInPolicy $true
```

Which gives us syntax we can apply with our filter above:

```
Get-Mailbox -Filter {RecipientTypeDetails -eq "EquipmentMailbox"} | Set-CalendarProcessing -AutomateProcessing AutoAccept
```

Room Mailboxes

Room mailboxes are by far the most used and configured of the resource mailboxes in Exchange. Room mailboxes need more care and maintenance to get them into useful order. Rooms can be large or small and designated as such in the capacity property. They can even be organized into lists. Let's see what we can do with rooms with PowerShell.

Example

Take for example a large organization that has a dozen locations in the US and Asia. Each of these locations has dozens of rooms. IT Management has been given the directive to create a series of rooms for each location. The naming of the rooms needs to be easy for end users to interpret which location and / or what floor a room is on. Groups of rooms should also be created if possible in order to help the end user find an appropriate room or even just an available room in a quick manner. First, we need to create all of the rooms. For this scenario we will use this list of locations:

US	Asia
Orlando	Tokyo
Dallas	Taipei
San Diego	Seoul
Denver	Shanghai
New York	Singapore
Seattle	Hong Kong

For the sake of this book, we will concentrate on one site in the US and one site in Asia to work on creating and configuring these rooms per management's requirements. We will use PowerShell to create the rooms and then configure booking options for each room. In order to facilitate the creation of the rooms, a CSV file is prepopulated with details such as the region the room it's in, what city, the floor the room is on, a description, capacity and phone number. The same CSV file is below:

```
Region,City,Floor,Description,Capacity,Phone
US,Orlando,1,SW,20,"+1 (407) 220-1212"
US,Orlando,1,SE,20,"+1 (407) 220-1213"
US,Orlando,1,NW,20,"+1 (407) 220-1214"
US,Orlando,1,NE,25,"+1 (407) 220-1215"
US,Orlando,1,Large,50,"+1 (407) 220-1216"
US,Orlando,2,SW,20,"+1 (407) 220-2212"
US,Orlando,2,SE,15,"+1 (407) 220-2213"
US,Orlando,2,NW,20,"+1 (407) 220-2214"
US,Orlando,2,NE,20,"+1 (407) 220-2215"
US,Orlando,2,Large,40,"+1 (407) 220-2216"
US,Orlando,3,SW,20,"+1 (407) 220-3212"
US,Orlando,3,SE,20,"+1 (407) 220-3213"
US,Orlando,3,NW,20,"+1 (407) 220-3214"
US,Orlando,3,NE,20,"+1 (407) 220-3215"
US,Orlando,3,Small,5,"+1 (407) 220-3216"
US,Orlando,4,SW,15,"+1 (407) 220-4212"
US,Orlando,4,SE,15,"+1 (407) 220-4213"
US,Orlando,4,NW,25,"+1 (407) 220-4214"
US,Orlando,4,NE,20,"+1 (407) 220-4215"
US,Orlando,4,Small,10,"+1 (407) 220-4216"
US,Orlando,5,Amphitheater,100,"+1 (407) 220-5212"
US,Orlando,5,"Standing Room",75,"+1 (407) 220-5213"
US,Orlando,5,NW,25,"+1 (407) 220-5214"
US,Orlando,6,Executive,10,"+1 (407) 220-6212"
Asia,Seoul,10,SW,15,+82-02-505-1212
Asia,Seoul,10,SE,15,+82-02-505-1213
Asia,Seoul,10,NW,15,+82-02-505-1214
Asia,Seoul,10,NE,15,+82-02-505-1215
Asia,Seoul,10,Large,30,+82-02-505-1216
Asia,Seoul,10,Small,5,+82-02-505-1217
Asia,Seoul,15,SW,20,+82-02-505-2212
Asia,Seoul,15,SE,15,+82-02-505-2213
Asia,Seoul,15,NW,20,+82-02-505-2214
Asia,Seoul,15,NE,15,+82-02-505-2215
Asia,Seoul,15,Large,50,+82-02-505-2216
Asia,Seoul,16,SW,15,+82-02-505-3212
Asia,Seoul,16,SE,15,+82-02-505-3213
```

Now that a list of rooms is stored in a CSV file we can create a script that will read each line in the CSV file and create a room based off this information.

Sample Script

First section reads in the CSV we created above:

```
$Rooms = Import-CSV C:\Scripting\RoomList.csv
```

Next, using a Foreach loop, the $Rooms variable is looped to go through each line:

```
Foreach ($Room in $Rooms) {
   $Region = $Room.Region
   $City = $Room.City
   $Floor = $Room.Floor
   $Location = "$Region-$City"
   $Capacity = $Room.Capacity
   $Phone = $Room.Phone
   $Description = $Room.Description
   $Roomname = "$City"+"-Floor-"+"$Floor"+"-"+"$Description"
```

Once the variable and values for the room are set, the New-Mailbox cmdlet is used to create the rooms as needed in the organization:

```
# Create mailbox with criteria from CSV file
   New-Mailbox -Room -Name $RoomName -Phone $Phone -ResourceCapacity $Capacity -Office
   $Location
}
```

A sample run shows the rooms being created:

Name	Alias	ServerName	ProhibitSendQuota
Orlando-Floor-1-SW	Orlando-Floor-1-SW	mwhpr0801mb3673	99 GB (106,300,440,576 bytes)
Orlando-Floor-1-SE	Orlando-Floor-1-SE	cy4pr0801mb3777	99 GB (106,300,440,576 bytes)
Orlando-Floor-1-NW	Orlando-Floor-1-NW	dm5pr08mb3468	99 GB (106,300,440,576 bytes)
Orlando-Floor-1-NE	Orlando-Floor-1-NE	cy4pr08mb3479	99 GB (106,300,440,576 bytes)
Orlando-Floor-1-Large	Orlando-Floor-1-L...	cy4pr0801mb3828	99 GB (106,300,440,576 bytes)
Orlando-Floor-2-SW	Orlando-Floor-2-SW	cy4pr08mb3575	99 GB (106,300,440,576 bytes)
Orlando-Floor-2-SE	Orlando-Floor-2-SE	mwhpr0801mb3739	99 GB (106,300,440,576 bytes)
Orlando-Floor-2-NW	Orlando-Floor-2-NW	dm5pr08mb3561	99 GB (106,300,440,576 bytes)
Orlando-Floor-2-NE	Orlando-Floor-2-NE	mwhpr08mb3344	99 GB (106,300,440,576 bytes)
Orlando-Floor-2-Large	Orlando-Floor-2-L...	cy4pr08mb3574	99 GB (106,300,440,576 bytes)
Orlando-Floor-3-SW	Orlando-Floor-3-SW	dm5pr0801mb3830	99 GB (106,300,440,576 bytes)
Orlando-Floor-3-SE	Orlando-Floor-3-SE	mwhpr0801mb3755	99 GB (106,300,440,576 bytes)
Orlando-Floor-3-NW	Orlando-Floor-3-NW	dm5pr0801mb3655	99 GB (106,300,440,576 bytes)
Orlando-Floor-3-NE	Orlando-Floor-3-NE	cy4pr0801mb3811	99 GB (106,300,440,576 bytes)
Orlando-Floor-3-Small	Orlando-Floor-3-S...	mwhpr0801mb3657	99 GB (106,300,440,576 bytes)
Orlando-Floor-4-SW	Orlando-Floor-4-SW	bn3pr0801mb1058	99 GB (106,300,440,576 bytes)
Orlando-Floor-4-SE	Orlando-Floor-4-SE	mwhpr08mb3503	99 GB (106,300,440,576 bytes)
Orlando-Floor-4-NW	Orlando-Floor-4-NW	cy4pr0801mb3778	99 GB (106,300,440,576 bytes)
Orlando-Floor-4-NE	Orlando-Floor-4-NE	mwhpr08mb3568	99 GB (106,300,440,576 bytes)
Orlando-Floor-4-Small	Orlando-Floor-4-S...	mwhpr0801mb3740	99 GB (106,300,440,576 bytes)
Orlando-Floor-5-Amphit...	Orlando-Floor-5-A...	mwhpr08mb3375	99 GB (106,300,440,576 bytes)
Orlando-Floor-5-Standi...	Orlando-Floor-5-S...	cy4pr0801mb3779	99 GB (106,300,440,576 bytes)
Orlando-Floor-5-NW	Orlando-Floor-5-NW	mwhpr0801mb3722	99 GB (106,300,440,576 bytes)
Orlando-Floor-6-Executive	Orlando-Floor-6-E...	mwhpr0801mb3739	99 GB (106,300,440,576 bytes)
Seoul-Floor-10-SW	Seoul-Floor-10-SW	dm2pr0801mb1037	99 GB (106,300,440,576 bytes)
Seoul-Floor-10-SE	Seoul-Floor-10-SE	mwhpr0801mb3802	99 GB (106,300,440,576 bytes)
Seoul-Floor-10-NW	Seoul-Floor-10-NW	dm5pr0801mb3736	99 GB (106,300,440,576 bytes)
Seoul-Floor-10-NE	Seoul-Floor-10-NE	cy4pr0801mb3716	99 GB (106,300,440,576 bytes)
Seoul-Floor-10-Large	Seoul-Floor-10-Large	bn6pr08mb3554	99 GB (106,300,440,576 bytes)
Seoul-Floor-10-Small	Seoul-Floor-10-Small	dm5pr0801mb3701	99 GB (106,300,440,576 bytes)
Seoul-Floor-15-SW	Seoul-Floor-15-SW	mwhpr08mb3517	99 GB (106,300,440,576 bytes)

Room Lists

Once rooms have been created in Exchange, a new feature can be used called Room Lists. Think of Room Lists as groups of rooms that are logically put together by location.

PowerShell

Let's start out by looking for cmdlets that we can use to manage these lists. As a forewarning, it's not located where you think:

    Get-Command *Room*
    Get-Command *List*

Neither reveal any useful information. So how do I get the right cmdlet? Use a Search Engine.

Search Terms: Exchange PowerShell Room Lists

So according to the results list above, a Room List can be created as part of a Distribution Group creation. Reviewing the Get-Help for New-DistributionGroup you will see the 'RoomList' parameter:

```
-RoomList <SwitchParameter>
    The RoomList switch specifies that all members of this distribution group are room mailboxes. You don't need
    to specify a value with this switch.

    You can create a distribution group for an office building in your organization and add all rooms in that
    building to the distribution group. Room list distribution groups are used to generate a list of building
    locations for meeting requests in Outlook 2010 or later. Room lists allow a user to select a building and get
    availability information for all rooms in that building, without having to add each room individually.
```

So the Room List parameter allows for a group of rooms to be stored as members of a Distribution Group and seen by the client as a grouping of Rooms.

PowerShell

Using the rooms we created above, let's see if we can create a list of all room mailboxes in Orlando. Now, it would be nice if the New-DynamicDistributionGroup had a switch for Room Lists, but it does not. So any rooms added will be a manual process.

First, we can store all Rooms that start with Orlando in a variable called $Members:

```
$Members = Get-Mailbox -Filter {Name -Like "Orlando*"} | Where {$_.RecipientTypeDetails
-eq"RoomMailbox"} | select -ExpandProperty Alias
```

After that, a new Distribution Group can be created with the –RoomList parameter and members added from the $Members variable:

```
New-DistributionGroup -Name "Orlando Meeting Rooms" -DisplayName "Orlando Meeting Rooms"
-RoomList -Members $Members
```

Verifying that the group has all the room mailboxes in it:

```
Get-DistributionGroupMember -Identity "Orlando Meeting Rooms"
```

Now when a new meeting is created and 'Add Rooms' is chosen, the List appears instead of each individual room:

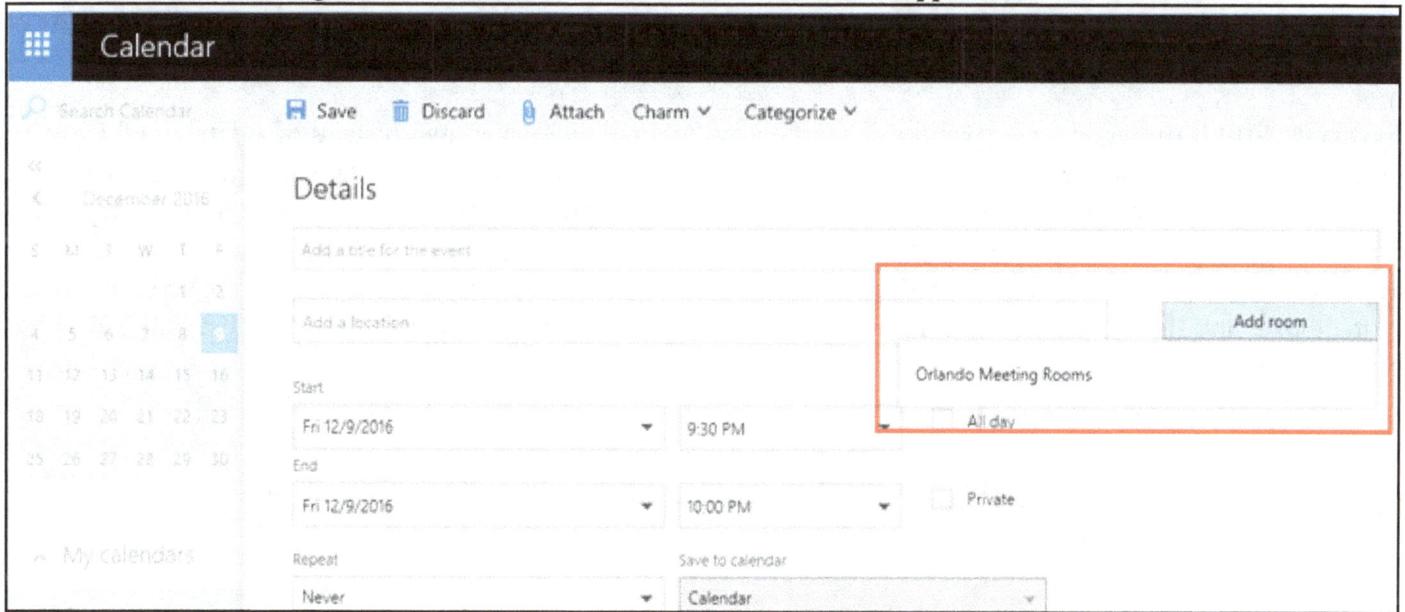

New room lists will begin to populate and display when the 'Add Rooms' button is used:

Clicking on the Seoul Room List, a list of available rooms appears for the user:

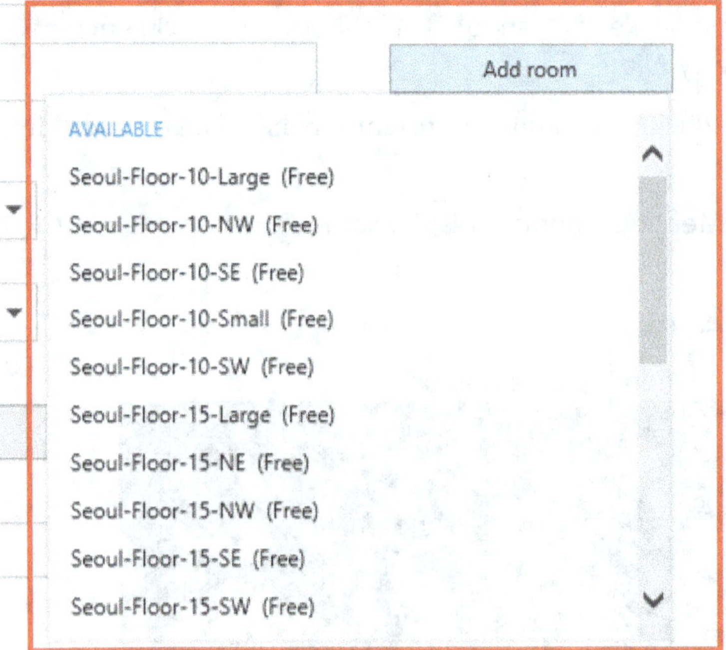

Room Lists can become very useful in organizations with either a lot of rooms, or a highly organized set of rooms and their names. Regular Distribution Groups can also be converted into Room Lists as well.

Public Folder Mailboxes

Exchange 2013 introduced a new paradigm for the way Public Folders operate. Instead of a database for Public Folders, a series of mailboxes in a regular mailbox database store all the Public Folder data, including the hierarchy. The reasoning was that Public Folder replication was notoriously problematic and used SMTP to make copies on other Public Folder Databases. This had the potential to clog up SMTP queues. Exchange Online takes the same approach. If you are creating Public Folder content in Exchange Online, then you will need to create Public Folder mailboxes and then Public Folders. Either Exchange on-premises or Exchange Online can host Public Folders, but not both.

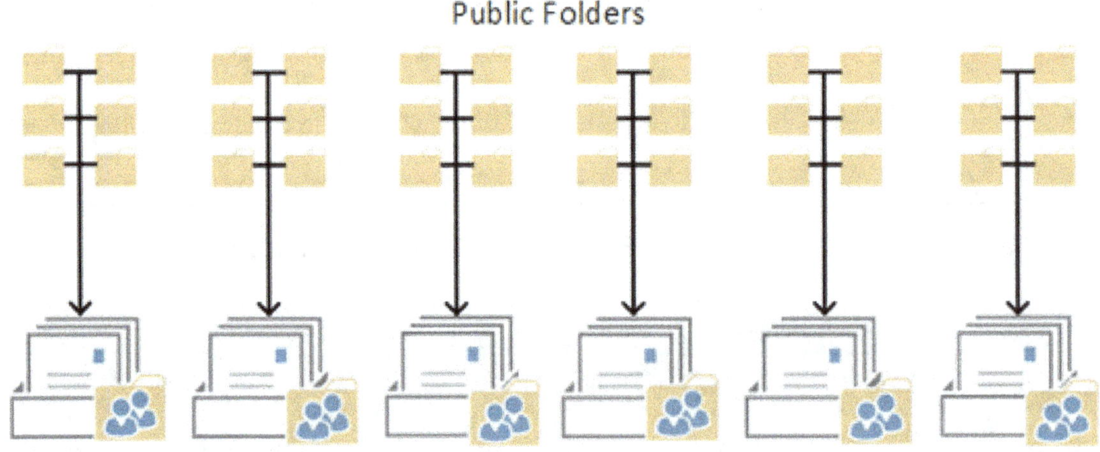

PowerShell

First, we'll explore what PowerShell cmdlets are available for Public Folders:

Get-Command *PublicFolder*

```
CommandType          Name
-----------          ----
Function             Add-PublicFolderClientPermission
Function             Disable-MailPublicFolder
Function             Enable-MailPublicFolder
Function             Get-MailPublicFolder
Function             Get-PublicFolder
Function             Get-PublicFolderClientPermission
Function             Get-PublicFolderItemStatistics
Function             Get-PublicFolderMailboxDiagnostics
Function             Get-PublicFolderMailboxMigrationRequest
Function             Get-PublicFolderMailboxMigrationRequestStatistics
Function             Get-PublicFolderMigrationRequest
Function             Get-PublicFolderMigrationRequestStatistics
Function             Get-PublicFolderStatistics
Function             New-PublicFolder
Function             New-PublicFolderMigrationRequest
Function             New-SyncMailPublicFolder
Function             Remove-PublicFolder
Function             Remove-PublicFolderClientPermission
Function             Remove-PublicFolderMigrationRequest
Function             Remove-SyncMailPublicFolder
Function             Resume-PublicFolderMailboxMigrationRequest
Function             Resume-PublicFolderMigrationRequest
Function             Set-MailPublicFolder
Function             Set-PublicFolder
Function             Set-PublicFolderMailboxMigrationRequest
Function             Set-PublicFolderMigrationRequest
Function             Suspend-PublicFolderMailboxMigrationRequest
Function             Suspend-PublicFolderMigrationRequest
Function             Update-PublicFolderMailbox
```

What we see from the above is that there is no direct cmdlet for creating a Public Folder mailbox. We know that Public Folders require Public Folder mailboxes, so what about the New-Mailbox cmdlet? Is there a parameter for this?

Get-Help New-Mailbox –Full

```
-PublicFolder <SwitchParameter>
    The PublicFolder switch specifies that the mailbox is a public folder mailbox. You don't need to specify a
    value with this switch.

    This switch is required only if you're creating a public folder mailbox.

    Public folder mailboxes are specially designed mailboxes that store the hierarchy and content of public
    folders. The first public folder mailbox created in your Exchange organization is called the primary hierarchy
    mailbox. It contains the writeable copy of the hierarchy of public folders for the organization and public
    folder content. There can be only one writeable copy of the public folder hierarchy in your organization. All
    other public folder mailboxes are called secondary public folder mailboxes and contain a read-only copy of the
    hierarchy and the content for public folders.
```

Public Folder mailboxes can be created with a simple one-liner that requires only two parameters – the first is '-PublicFolder' and the second is '-name':

New-Mailbox –PublicFolder –Name "Public Folder 1"

```
Name                    Alias               ServerName        ProhibitSendQuota
----                    -----               ----------        -----------------
Public Folder 1         PublicFolder1       cy4pr0801mb3697   99 GB (106,300,440,576 bytes)
```

To verify that the mailbox was created, simple run:

Get-Mailbox -PublicFolder

```
Name                           Alias                  ServerName      ProhibitSendQuota
----                           -----                  ----------      -----------------
PFTest                         PFTest                 dm5pr08mb2522   49.5 GB (53,150,220,288 bytes)
Public Folder 1                PublicFolder1          cy4pr0801mb3697 99 GB (106,300,440,576 bytes)
```

Once mailboxes have been created, Public Folder(s) can be created in order to store data. The cmdlet we need is New-PublicFolder. What examples are provided by Microsoft?

```
---------------------- Example 1 ----------------------
New-PublicFolder -Name Marketing
---------------------- Example 2 ----------------------
New-PublicFolder -Name FY2013 -Path \Legal\Cases
---------------------- Example 3 ----------------------
New-PublicFolder -Name Support -Mailbox North_America
```

First, we will create a Root Public Folder to hold other Public Folders for the IT Department.

New-PublicFolder -Name 'IT Department' -Path '\'

Then we can create sub-Public Folders under the root of 'IT Department'.

New-PublicFolder -Name 'Testing' -Path '\IT Department'

You can keep creating folders like, or via a script, as needed.

Distribution Groups

Distribution Groups in Exchange Online come in two different varieties – Dynamic and Static. Static groups are ones where the membership needs to be added or removed manually with PowerShell, Exchange EAC or Active Directory Users and Computers. A Dynamic Distribution Group builds its membership based on a set of criteria you define and thus the members that appear in the group are dynamic. This means that, based on the criteria for a group, if a user no longer meets that criteria, the user does not appear as a member of the group. If a user object is modified to meet the criteria again, it will then appear as a member of the group again. The distinction is also important in PowerShell as there exists two different sets of cmdlets for each group type.

PowerShell

First, let's review what cmdlets are available for distribution groups (dynamic or regular):

Get-Command *Distribution*

```
CommandType     Name
-----------     ----
Function        Add-DistributionGroupMember
Function        Get-DistributionGroup
Function        Get-DistributionGroupMember
Function        Get-DynamicDistributionGroup
Function        Get-EligibleDistributionGroupForMigration
Function        New-DistributionGroup
Function        New-DynamicDistributionGroup
Function        Remove-DistributionGroup
Function        Remove-DistributionGroupMember
Function        Remove-DynamicDistributionGroup
Function        Set-DistributionGroup
Function        Set-DynamicDistributionGroup
Function        Update-DistributionGroupMember
Function        Upgrade-DistributionGroup
```

Now that we have a list of PowerShell cmdlets to use, let's use the New-DistributionGroup cmdlet to create some groups for Exchange:

Get-Help New-DistributionGroup –Examples

```
-------------------------- Example 1 --------------------------

New-DistributionGroup -Name Managers"Managers" -Type "Security"
You use the Add-DistributionGroupMember cmdlet to add members after you create the group.

-------------------------- Example 2 --------------------------

New-DistributionGroup -Name "ITDepartment" -Members
chris@contoso.com,michelle@contoso.com,laura@contoso.com,julia@contoso.com
```

The examples given by PowerShell are rather basic and if more options are desired, then make sure to run:

Get-Help New-DistributionGroup -Full

Some sample options that can be chosen for the group are:

RequireSenderAuthenticationEnabled – This parameter determines if only internal users can send emails to the group or if external senders are allowed.
MemberJoinRestriction – If the group membership needs to be controlled, use this option to set 'ApprovalRequired' which will allow the membership to be managed.
MemberDepartRestriction – Conversely, the opposite of the above option, this is for users wishing to leave a group, the same controls can be put into place as those wishing/needing to join a group.
ManagedBy – Assigns a user the role of managing the group for approvals, removals, approve moderation requests and more.

Management

In Exchange, Distribution Groups can be used for many purposes. Whether they are used to represent parts of a company (e.g. All Users, North American Users and Paris Users). Or for a specific notification for IT (e.g. Alerts), they all need to be managed and maintained. In most organizations there will be group sprawl with groups going unused or forgotten and even completely emptied of all users without removal. Proper management and pruning of these extraneous groups allows for more efficient management. For the scenario below we'll explore a couple of items that can be managed for groups.

Example

In this scenario, we have an environment that has grown from Exchange 2000 and steadily updated Exchange and have now migrated to Exchange Online. The company has also grown from 50 users to well over 2,000 users through organic growth and acquisitions. Now the messaging team has decided to do some cleanup. There are 1,000 distribution groups that have been created over the past 15 years by various administrators. No one in the organization can say for sure which groups are needed and which are not.

In this scenario, we need to evaluate two criteria – number of members in a group and if any emails have gone to the group. The first is relatively easy as we simply need to query each group to see if it contains members. For the second, determining mail flow to groups requires a bit of legwork and keeping track of active groups. From the list of cmdlets above, we see there is a cmdlet specifically for distribution group members. What do the examples for this cmdlet provide to help us query for empty groups:

```
----------------------- Example 1 -----------------------
Get-DistributionGroupMember -Identity "Marketing USA"
```

Not much to go on with the included examples for the cmdlet. However, when the cmdlet is run against a distribution group in Exchange, it reveals the members of that particular group. For our scenario, we have 1,000 distribution groups to query and get members from. This will require each group name to be piped from Get-DistributionGroup to the Get-DistributionGroupMember cmdlet in a Foreach loop. Two loops will be needed as each group type (dynamic and regular) need to be handled separately.

To determine which groups are empty, we first need to get a complete list of groups and store the groups in a variable:

```
$DistributionGroups = Get-DistributionGroup -ResultSize Unlimited
```

Once a list of groups is stored in $DistributionGroups we can now go through each group in a Foreach loop:

```
Foreach ($Group in $DistributionGroups) {
```

Notice the naming of variables was done for ease of keeping track of the current context, whether it's all groups ($DistributionGroups) or the current group in the list ($Group). In addition, we'll use a variable as a counter to keep track of distribution groups with no members ($N) – we'll set this to 0 before the Foreach loop.

For the next line we query the current Distribution Group in the loop for members:

```
$Members = Get-DistributionGroupMember -Identity $Group.DisplayName
```

Then, using an IF statement, the $Empty variable is checked to see if it is empty:

```
If ($Members -eq $Null) {
```

If this variable has no value assigned, then no members were found that are in the current group. This is reported to the PowerShell window with the Write-Host statement. The $N++ is an incremental counter:

```
Write-Host "The group $Group is an empty Distribution Group." -ForegroundColor Yellow
$N++
```

At the very end of the script we'll check to see if $N is equal to zero and if it is, then no empty groups have been found:

```
If ($N -eq 0) {
    Write-Host "No empty Distribution Groups were found." -ForegroundColor Cyan
}
```

If there are no empty groups, then the script will report that:

```
    -- Empty Distribution Group report --

  No empty Distribution Groups were found.



    -- Empty Dynamic Distribution Group report --

  No empty Dynamic Distribution Groups were found.
```

When there are groups present with no members, the script will report them like so:

```
-- Empty Distribution Group report --

The group Sales Dept is an empty Distribution Group.
```

Dynamic Groups require a slightly different tactic. The line that queries for members has to be different because a dynamic group doesn't have actual members, virtual membership is calculated at query time for these groups.

Regular group members
```
$Members = Get-DistributionGroupMember -Identity $Group.DisplayName
```

Dynamic group members
```
$GroupDetails = Get-DynamicDistributionGroup $Group.DisplayName
$Members = Get-Recipient -RecipientPreviewFilter $GroupDetails.RecipientFilter
```

Note, the RecipientFilter is used to find all recipients that match the filter on the dynamic group.

Complete Script Code – Empty Distribution Groups

```
# Get a list of all empty distribution groups
$DistributionGroups = Get-DistributionGroup -ResultSize Unlimited
Write-Host "-- Empty Distribution Group report --" -ForegroundColor Green
Write-Host " "
$N = 0

 Foreach ($Group in $DistributionGroups) {
    $Members = Get-DistributionGroupMember -Identity $Group.DisplayName
    If ($Members -eq $Null) {
       Write-Host "The group $Group is an empty Distribution Group." -ForegroundColor Yellow
       $N++
    }
}

If ($N -eq 0) {
    Write-Host "No empty Distribution Groups were found." -ForegroundColor Cyan
}

Script Code – Empty Dynamic Distribution Groups

CLS
$DynamicDistribution = Get-DynamicDistributionGroup
Write-Host "-- Empty Dynamic Distribution Group report --" -ForegroundColor Green
Write-Host " "
$N = 0

Foreach ($Group in $DynamicDistribution) {
    $Members = Get-Recipient -RecipientPreviewFilter $Group.RecipientFilter
    If ($Members -eq $Null) {
```

```
      Write-Host "The group $Group is an empty Dynamic Distribution Group." -ForegroundColor Yellow
      $N++
   }
}

If ($N -eq 0) {
   Write-Host "No empty Dynamic Distribution Groups were found." -ForegroundColor Cyan
}
```

Get-MessageTrace

If you are used to tracking messages for emails in Exchange on-premises, then you will have to retrain yourself for tracking messages for Exchange Online. This is because you don't have direct access to the log files, using Get-MessageTrackingLog, and instead have to use the Get-MessageTrace cmdlet. The Get-MessageTrace cmdlet behaves different because of these environmental differences. What we also discover is that because of what would appear to be throttling, adjustments may need to be made in how messages are traced based on the size and email volume of your environment.

First we need to review what Get-MessageTrace can do and what is available in the Get-Help for the cmdlet.

```
Get-Help Get-MessageTrace -Examples
```

```
------------------------------------ Example 1 ------------------------------------

Get-MessageTrace -SenderAddress john@contoso.com -StartDate 06/13/2015 -EndDate 06/15/2015
```

Not too complicated. However, if we review the full help for the cmdlet there are a couple of options that appear peculiar at first. These are '-Page' and -'PageSize':

-Page

The Page parameter specifies the page number of the results you want to view. Valid input for this parameter is an integer between 1 and 1,000. The default value is 1.

-PageSize

The PageSize parameter specifies the maximum number of entries per page. Valid input for this parameter is an integer between 1 and 5,000. The default value is 1,000.

Each of these refers to how many results that can be pulled from the logs. This means by default, we can pull 1 full 'page' of results which provides up to 1,000 results. Other cmdlets in Exchange / Exchange Online have a '-ResultSize' parameter that could potentially be set to 'Unlimited'. However, there is no parameter for MessageTrace for Get-MessageTrace. As such, we need to use the 'Page' and 'PageSize' parameters to provide a larger result set. How can we do this? A sample trace for all messages from myself (Damian@PracticalPowershell.Com) to an external recipient (Ryan.Simmons@Gmail.Com) for the past month, could be done like so:

```
Get-MessageTrace -SenderAddress 'Damian@PracticalPowerShell.Com' -RecipientAddress 'Ryan.Simmons@Gmail.Com' -StartDate '11/03/2017' -EndDate '12/03/2017'
```

** **Note** ** With Get-MessageTrace, we are limited to a max total of 30 days of data to pull results from.

On a relatively quiet tenant with a low number of messages, this might succeed. However, what you will find is that if the mail system is rather active, the search only actually reviews a very small portion of messages. For example, a university with 30,000 people with an EDU tenant might have students sending three emails a day on average and that gives us 90,000 potential emails per day. Imagine the limitations of 1,000 emails now. There is no way to review all of these emails with the default 'pagesize' and 'pages'.

What can we do to handle this number of messages? First we'll use the 'page' and 'pagesize' parameters to provide a larger window to review messages. The default 'pagesize' is 2,000 and has a maximum value of 5,000. For this PowerShell sample code we'll use 5,000:

```
$PageSize = 5000
```

Now we'll set the initial page to 1 since we'll want to start at the first page of results:

```
$Page = 1
```

We'll need a date range of a month, just like the first trace we ran above.

```
$StartDate = '11/03/17 12:01AM'
$EndDate = '12/03/17 11:59PM'
```

Using these parameters in a real world scenario we can examine how many messages were filtered as SPAM by EOP before they get delivered to these same 30,000 EDU users. For this I will run a loop of results. The other caveat you will find is that there is a maximum of 200 pages that can be examined as well. For a small environment that may not be an issue, but for a larger environment, it might make the date range a bit of an issue depending on number of messages processed.

In the below script, we use the values from the variables above and place them into a '# Variable Block' at the top of the script.

```
# Variable Block
$Page = 1
$PageSize = 5000
$TotalCount = 0
$Start = '11/29/17 12:01AM'
$End = '12/03/17 11:59PM'
```

A 'Do...While' loop is used to handle the 200 page limit. Inside the loop a Get-MessageTrace is run against each 'page' of 5,000 messages. Two variables are used, one ($Results) is used for filtering all messages for Spam and the second variable ($Results2). The $Count variable is used to keep track of the total number of Spam messages. We also are filtering the results for a specific Status property value of 'FilteredAsSpam'.

```
Do {
    $N = 1
    $Results = Get-MessageTrace -StartDate $Start -EndDate $End -Page $Page -PageSize $PageSize |
    Where {$_.Status -eq 'FilteredAsSpam'}
    $Results2 = Get-MessageTrace -StartDate $Start -EndDate $End -Page $Page -PageSize $PageSize

    If ($Results2 -eq $Null) {
```

```
    $Page = 201
  } Else {
    $Results2[0].Received
    $Count = $Results.Count
    Write-Host "Found $Count SPAM messages." -ForegroundColor Cyan
    Write-Host "Page Number - $Page" -ForegroundColor Yellow
    $Page++
  }
} While ($Page -lt 200)
```

When run against a large amount of messages, expect to see results like this:

```
Sunday, December 3, 2017 11:58:31 PM          $Results2[0].Received
Found 819 SPAM messages.                      $Count
Page Number - 1                               Number of Pages
Sunday, December 3, 2017 9:18:48 PM
Found 858 SPAM messages.
Page Number - 2
Sunday, December 3, 2017 6:24:57 PM
Found 1080 SPAM messages.
Page Number - 3
Sunday, December 3, 2017 4:09:40 PM
Found 1029 SPAM messages.
Page Number - 4
Sunday, December 3, 2017 2:23:11 PM
Found 1113 SPAM messages.
Page Number - 5
```

Notice there is about a two hour time difference between the pages, with hundreds of messages found between the timestamps. Another reason for the date/timestamp is to allow us to narrow down a date range if we need to. The difficulty becomes how to work with the two hundred page limit. If we know that each page is two hours and that there is a two hundred page limit, that means that we can work with a four hundred hour window for the script. Thats about a two week window.

This method could be used to find any sort of messages or even a lack of messages if we need to filter for a reverse scenario of missing messages.

Group Moderation

Emails to groups sometimes need to be moderated. Examples of this moderation occur with groups that contain C level management which may not want emails from just anyone in the company. Dynamic Groups such as 'All Employees' are also ones that should be controlled to prevent mass emails of 'ReplyAll' which can cause havoc or even embarrassment in the organization. Depending on the size of the organization, message approvers could be a single individual or a group of users responsible for this task.

PowerShell

To see what can be done in PowerShell, we can review the Get-Help for the Set-DistributionGroup:

Get-Help Set-DistributionGroup

```
SYNTAX
    Set-DistributionGroup -Identity <DistributionGroupIdParameter> [-AcceptMessagesOnlyFrom <MultiValuedProperty>]
    [-AcceptMessagesOnlyFromDLMembers <MultiValuedProperty>] [-AcceptMessagesOnlyFromSendersOrMembers
    <MultiValuedProperty>] [-Alias <String>] [-ArbitrationMailbox <MailboxIdParameter>]
    [-BypassModerationFromSendersOrMembers <MultiValuedProperty>] [-BypassNestedModerationEnabled <$true | $false>]
    [-BypassSecurityGroupManagerCheck <SwitchParameter>] [-Confirm <SwitchParameter>] [-CreateDTMFMap <$true |
    $false>] [-CustomAttribute1 <String>] [-CustomAttribute10 <String>] [-CustomAttribute11 <String>]
    [-CustomAttribute12 <String>] [-CustomAttribute13 <String>] [-CustomAttribute14 <String>] [-CustomAttribute15
    <String>] [-CustomAttribute2 <String>] [-CustomAttribute3 <String>] [-CustomAttribute4 <String>]
    [-CustomAttribute5 <String>] [-CustomAttribute6 <String>] [-CustomAttribute7 <String>] [-CustomAttribute8
    <String>] [-CustomAttribute9 <String>] [-DisplayName <String>] [-DomainController <Fqdn>] [-EmailAddresses
    <ProxyAddressCollection>] [-EmailAddressPolicyEnabled <$true | $false>] [-ExpansionServer <String>]
    [-ExtensionCustomAttribute1 <MultiValuedProperty>] [-ExtensionCustomAttribute2 <MultiValuedProperty>]
    [-ExtensionCustomAttribute3 <MultiValuedProperty>] [-ExtensionCustomAttribute4 <MultiValuedProperty>]
    [-ExtensionCustomAttribute5 <MultiValuedProperty>] [-ForceUpgrade <SwitchParameter>]
    [-GenerateExternalDirectoryObjectId <SwitchParameter>] [-GrantSendOnBehalfTo <MultiValuedProperty>]
    [-HiddenFromAddressListsEnabled <$true | $false>] [-IgnoreDefaultScope <SwitchParameter>] [-IgnoreNamingPolicy
    <SwitchParameter>] [-MailTip <String>] [-MailTipTranslations <MultiValuedProperty>] [-ManagedBy
    <MultiValuedProperty>] [-MaxReceiveSize <Unlimited>] [-MaxSendSize <Unlimited>] [-MemberDepartRestriction <Closed
    | Open | ApprovalRequired>] [-MemberJoinRestriction <Closed | Open | ApprovalRequired>] [-ModeratedBy
    <MultiValuedProperty>] [-ModerationEnabled <$true | $false>] [-Name <String>] [-PrimarySmtpAddress <SmtpAddress>]
    [-RejectMessagesFrom <MultiValuedProperty>] [-RejectMessagesFromDLMembers <MultiValuedProperty>]
    [-RejectMessagesFromSendersOrMembers <MultiValuedProperty>] [-ReportToManagerEnabled <$true | $false>]
    [-ReportToOriginatorEnabled <$true | $false>] [-RequireSenderAuthenticationEnabled <$true | $false>]
    [-ResetMigrationToUnifiedGroup <SwitchParameter>] [-RoomList <SwitchParameter>] [-SamAccountName <String>]
    [-SendModerationNotifications <Never | Internal | Always>] [-SendOofMessageToOriginatorEnabled <$true | $false>]
    [-SimpleDisplayName <String>] [-UMDtmfMap <MultiValuedProperty>] [-WhatIf <SwitchParameter>] [-WindowsEmailAddress
    <SmtpAddress>] [<CommonParameters>]
```

From the above list of parameters we see there are two parameters for handling moderation of distribution groups. Reviewing the detailed description of these parameters we can get an understanding of what they are used for:

```
-ModeratedBy <MultiValuedProperty>
    The ModeratedBy parameter specifies one or more moderators for this recipient. A moderator
    approves messages sent to the recipient before the messages are delivered. A moderator
    must be a mailbox, mail user, or mail contact in your organization. You can use any value
    that uniquely identifies the moderator.
```

```
-ModerationEnabled <$true | $false>
    The ModerationEnabled parameter specifies whether moderation is enabled for this
    recipient. Valid value are:

    * $true Moderation is enabled for this recipient. Messages sent to this recipient must be
      approved by a moderator before the messages are delivered.
    * $false Moderation is disabled for this recipient. Messages sent to this recipient are
      delivered without the approval of a moderator. This is the default value.
    You use the ModeratedBy parameter to specify the moderators.
```

Combined, these two values enable control of message flow to a particular group. Below is an example of how to configure moderation on a Distribution Group called 'Sales Dept':

```
Set-DistributionGroup "Sales Dept" -ModerationEnabled $true -ModeratedBy "Damian"
```

Note that when this is set, a Mail Tip might be displayed for users in OWA or Outlook depending on other configuration settings:

Messages sent to Sales Dept are moderated. They may be rejected or delayed. Remove recipient

Controlling Group Mail Flow

If moderators are not desired, other controllers can be put in place such as restricting who can send to the group or if external senders can send to an internal group.   Restrictions as to who can send to the group or who are blocked from sending to the group can also be set if so desired.

To control these settings we can review the list of parameters from the last section. The appropriate settings are as follows:

AcceptMessagesOnlyFrom	AcceptMessagesOnlyFromDLMembers
AcceptMessagesOnlyFromSendersOrMembers	RejectMessagesFrom
RejectMessagesFromDLMembers	RejectMessagesFromSendersOrMembers

Depending on what the desired restrictions are for a group, we can pick from the above list to configure these restrictions.

Example 1

Take for example a company that has a group specifically for Sales. The Sales Department would like to restrict emails so that only users within the Sale Group can email the Sales Group distribution list. From the above parameters, it appears that either 'AcceptMessagesOnlyFrom' or 'AcceptMessagesOnlyFromDLMembers' would work. However, the restriction is for only group members so 'AcceptMessagesOnlyFromDLMembers' would be the ideal option for this scenario. Reviewing the parameter from Get-Help we can see that this acts like an Access Control List (ACL) on a distribution group:

```
-AcceptMessagesOnlyFromDLMembers <MultiValuedProperty>
    The AcceptMessagesOnlyFromDLMembers parameter specifies who is allowed to send messages to
    this recipient. Messages from other senders are rejected.
```

```
Set-DistributionGroup "Sales Dept" –AcceptMessagesOnlyFromDLMembers "Sales Dept"
```

Prior to a message being sent to the group from someone outside the group they will now receive a Mail Tip:

You don't have permission to send to Sales Dept. Remove recipient

The end user also received an NDR:

Delivery has failed to these recipients or groups:

Sales Dept (SalesDept@Domain.Com)
Your message couldn't be delivered because you don't have permission to send to this distribution list. Ask the owner of the distribution list to grant you permission and then try again.

Users in the Sales Department group will not receive a Mail Tip and will be the only ones who can send to this distribution group.

Example 2

In another example a group has been created for C Level Executives and the directive from IT Management is that only direct reports may send emails to this new group. The group is called 'Company Executives' for this example.

We can then use PowerShell to get a list of the direct reports for each C Level executive:

First, we clear the array variable we will use to store the users allowed to send to this group:

```
$TeamMembers = @()
```

Next store the group name in a variable for use in the script:

```
$Group = "Company Executives"
```

Then all the members of the group are also stored in a variable. In order to do this, we use the Get-Distribution-Group and feed this to the Get-DistributionGroupMember command to get the members of $Group:

    $Members = Get-DistributionGroup $Group | Get-DistributionGroupMember

Then a Foreach loop will read through each line in $Members to get all members and their direct reports:

    Foreach ($Member in $Members) {

Within this loop, we first get the DistinguishedName of each member and add it to $TeamMembers:

    $TeamMembers += $Member.DistinguishedName

Next, the DistinguishedName of all users with that manager are added to $TeamMembers:

    $TeamMembers += (Get-User -Properties * -Filter {Manager -eq $Member.DistinguishedName}).
    DistinguishedName
    }

With the $TeamMembers variable now storing all members of the group, their direct reports, and the loop finished, we need to remove any duplicates from $TeamMembers:

    $TeamMembers = $TeamMembers | Select -Unique

Then the AcceptMessagesOnlyFrom parameter is set for the group with the $DirectReports:

    Set-DistributionGroup $Group -AcceptMessagesOnlyFrom $DirectReports

Once set, we can verify the users are correctly configured:

    Get-DistributionGroup $Group | FT AcceptMessagesOnlyFrom

```
AcceptMessagesOnlyFrom
----------------------
{John Doe, Damian Scoles}
```

Office 365 Groups

Office 365 Groups are the latest iteration of Distribution Groups with a twist. The group is not solely used in Exchange Online and functions similarly to Site Mailboxes from on-premises Exchange in that the historical content is accessible by a group of user. The group provides access to shared Yammer, SharePoint, Planner and Exchange resources. Make sure to verify licensing before activating this feature in Exchange Online.

The Group will be available for Outlook and OWA users. With either platform the group will allow be greater interaction, sharing and features than a typical Distribution List as it isn't all about email any more. More features are linked to a group to enhance their experience together as a group.

To make the most use of these new groups, great a test group and pilot them out to make that the features make sense before a roll-out to end users in your environment.

PowerShell

Office 365 Groups have their own set of PowerShell cmdlets, but the noun used for the cmdlets is not an obvious one. That's because we need to look for cmdlets with the phrase 'UnifiedGroup' in them. A Unified Group is an Office 365 Group.

Get-Command *UnifiedGroup*

```
Name
----
Add-UnifiedGroupLinks
Get-UnifiedGroup
Get-UnifiedGroupLinks
New-UnifiedGroup
Remove-UnifiedGroup
Remove-UnifiedGroupLinks
Set-UnifiedGroup
Undo-SoftDeletedUnifiedGroup
```

By default, there are no Unified or Office 365 Groups in your Exchange Online tenant. That can be verified with the Get-UnifiedGroup cmdlet. Since we have not groups to explore initially, let's create a group so we can that review the object in Exchange Online.

Get-Help New-UnifiedGroup -Examples

```
----------------------------- Example 1 -----------------------------

New-UnifiedGroup -DisplayName "Engineering Department" -Alias engineering
```

Following the above basic example, we get this result while creating a group for the IT Department:

```
PS C:\> New-UnifiedGroup -DisplayName 'IT Department' -Alias ITDepartment

Name                     Alias            ServerName        AccessType
----                     -----            ----------        ----------
IT Department_cc617b9f15 ITDepartment     cy4pr13mb1350     Public
```

Great! Now we have an Office 365 Group. What Next? Let's check out it's properties:

```
ExchangeGuid                         : d22a2e5f-a78b-4429-91e8-a5dc5fc1e016
FileNotificationsSettings            :
GroupSKU                             : Default
HiddenGroupMembershipEnabled         : False
InboxUrl                             :
IsExternalResourcesPublished         : True
IsMailboxConfigured                  : True
Language                             : en-US
MailboxProvisioningConstraint        :
ManagedByDetails                     : {damian}
Notes                                :
PeopleUrl                            :
PhotoUrl                             :
ProvisioningOption                   :
ServerName                           : cy4pr13mb1350
SharePointSiteUrl                    :
SharePointDocumentsUrl               :
SharePointNotebookUrl                :
SubscriptionEnabled                  : True
WelcomeMessageEnabled                : True
ConnectorsEnabled                    : True
IsMembershipDynamic                  : False
Classification                       :
GroupPersonification                 :
YammerEmailAddress                   :
GroupMemberCount                     : 1
MailboxRegion                        :
GroupExternalMemberCount             : 0
AllowAddGuests                       : True
WhenSoftDeleted                      :
EmailAddresses                       : {SMTP:ITDepartment@OnlineExchangeBook.onmicrosoft.com}
PrimarySmtpAddress                   : ITDepartment@OnlineExchangeBook.onmicrosoft.com
Name                                 : IT Department_cc617b9f15
DisplayName                          : IT Department
RequireSenderAuthenticationEnabled   : True
ModerationEnabled                    : False
```

In the properties there are a lot of options that could prove useful for this Office 365, depending on what the purpose of the group is, however these are not all exposed on PowerShell as of the writing of this book.

- Hidden
- Moderation settings

Converting Existing Group to Office 365 Group

As of the writing of this book, Microsoft is pushing to convert regular distribution groups to Office 365 groups:

This isn't necessarily a good or bad thing. Microsoft is a software company that would like it's end users to use all the features it spends time and money to create. The higher visibility will drive some customers to adopt this feature. However, the push to convert existing groups to Office 365 Groups may not be the wisest choices or even a necessary choice. A modern way to enable collaborate within organization groups. Office 365 Groups achieve this with the following elements:

- Shared inbox
- Shared files library
- Shared calendar
- Shared OneNote notebook
- Guest access
- Content is discoverable
- Self-Service creation

As we can see, groups can be upgraded from the GUI with a couple of options. We can also do this with PowerShell. How can we do this? First we need to find groups that can be upgraded:

```
Get-EligibleDistributionGroupForMigration
```

```
DisplayName      PrimarySmtpAddress                                    WhenChanged
-----------      ------------------                                    -----------
Help Desk Users  HelpDeskUsers@OnlineExchangeBook.onmicrosoft.com  12/1/2017 4:13:37 PM
```

If we had more than one group, it would show in this list above.   Upgrade-DistributionGroup -DLIdentities @ ('TestGroup@OnlineExchangeBook.onmicrosoft.com')

```
RunspaceId                    : 79493651-1abf-4bdb-bc39-2e11db72b056
dlIdentity                    : HelpDeskUsers@OnlineExchangeBook.onmicrosoft.com
ErrorReason                   :
ExternalDirectoryObjectId     : e7c91e06-6a7a-42f3-8d9a-d9e547924509
SuccessfullySubmittedForUpgrade : True
Identity                      :
IsValid                       : True
```

That's all it takes to convert an existing Distribution Group to an Office 365 Group.

Putting It All Together

Combining some knowledge from Chapter 8 and this chapter, we'll write a script that can provide a useful reporting script on mailboxes and groups within Exchange Online. Let's take a typical environment that has user, shared, room, equipment and public folder mailboxes. There are also regular and dynamic distribution groups. You'd like to have a quick report that was generated by PowerShell that was able to display the number of mailboxes of each type, number of groups by type and the sizes of each mailbox category.

In the below script, we can use Get-Mailbox, Get-DistributionGroup, Get-DynamicDistributionGroup and Get-MailboxStatistics to do this. For finding each mailbox type, we look for a value called "RecipientTypeDetails". Why use that? Because it provides the mailbox differentiation information we need.

Script Code

This first section uses the 'Get-Mailbox' cmdlet to get a list of mailboxes. The '-filter' parameter allows for a filter based on one mailbox property, which in our case is 'RecipientTypeDetails'. This attribute was chosen because it stores the type of mailbox the object is. Next, the ().Count bracket is used in order to get a count of whatever is returned from within the parentheses:

```powershell
# Get mailbox and group counts per type
$DistributionGroupCount = (Get-DistributionGroup).Count
$DynDistributionGroupCount = (Get-DynamicDistributionGroup).Count
$AllMailboxCount = (Get-Mailbox).Count
$UserMailboxCount = (Get-Mailbox -Filter {RecipientTypeDetails -eq "UserMailbox"}).Count
$SharedMailboxCount = (Get-Mailbox -Filter {RecipientTypeDetails -eq "SharedMailbox"}).Count
$PublicFolderMailboxCount = (Get-Mailbox -PublicFolder).Count
$EquipmentMailboxCount = (Get-Mailbox -Filter {RecipientTypeDetails -eq "EquipmentMailbox"}).Count
$RoomMailboxCount = (Get-Mailbox -Filter {RecipientTypeDetails -eq "RoomMailbox"}).Count
```

For this last section of the script a visual report will be displayed in the PowerShell window which will give mailbox and group counts as well as the sizes of each type of mailbox in Exchange:

```powershell
Write-Host "Number of Mailboxes found:" -ForegroundColor Green
Write-Host "------------------------" -ForegroundColor Green
Write-Host "User Mailboxes: $UserMailboxCount." -ForegroundColor White
Write-Host "Shared Mailboxes: $SharedMailboxCount." -ForegroundColor White
Write-Host "Room Mailboxes: $RoomMailboxCount." -ForegroundColor White
Write-Host "Equipment Mailboxes: $EquipmentMailboxCount." -ForegroundColor White
Write-Host "Public Folder Mailboxes: $PublicFolderMailboxCount." -ForegroundColor White
Write-Host " " # Blank line for formatting
```

```
Write-Host "Number of Distribution Groups" -ForegroundColor Green
Write-Host "Distribution Groups: $DistributionGroupCount." -ForegroundColor White
Write-Host "Dynamic Distribution Groups: $DynDistributionGroupCount." -ForegroundColor White
Write-Host " " # Blank line for formatting
```

A quick run of the script generates a little concise report for Exchange:

```
Number of Mailboxes found:
---------------------------
User Mailboxes: 26.
Shared Mailboxes: 3.
Room Mailboxes: 1.
Equipment Mailboxes: 1.
Public Folder Mailboxes: 1.

Number of Distribution Groups
Distribution Groups: 8.
Dynamic Distribution Groups: 3.
```

10   Mail Flow

In This Chapter

- Mail Flow Connectors
- Message Tracing
- Transport Rules
- Accepted Domains

The flow of e-mail is THE most important part of Exchange Online. Without proper mail flow, the proper function Exchange Online in an organization breaks down. Potential problems with Exchange that would interrupt mail flow are Internet connection issues or Office 365 Service Issues. Being able to properly configure, maintain and troubleshoot SMTP in the messaging system is key.

The Exchange Admin Center (EAC) provides a way to configure mail flow features like send and receive connectors, transport rules, journaling and message traces. However, the EAC is limited in many ways and some configuration options REQUIRE the use of PowerShell as no option is offered through EAC. Examples of this are usually found in the expanded control of connectors and Centralize Transport settings in Office 365.

This chapter will cover the various parts of Exchange Online mail flow from what the components are, the cmdlets used to configure them as well as cmdlets used to troubleshoot mail flow issues that could come up.

Mail Flow Connectors

If you have a Hybrid configuration, the SMTP connectors can be key to making mail flow functional in Exchange Online. By default there are no connectors for sending and receiving email in Exchange Online. This may seem strange for anyone who has managed Exchange on-premises before, but it will make sense once we dive deeper into it. By default there is a no need to configure a Send Connector as email will flow outbound via internal mechanisms that are built into your Exchange Online tenant.

Let's explore the PowerShell cmdlets that can manage, report or modify connectors in Exchange:

```
Get-Command *connector*
Name
----
Get-InboundConnector
Get-IntraOrganizationConnector
Get-OutboundConnector
Get-OutboundConnectorReport
New-InboundConnector
New-IntraOrganizationConnector
New-OutboundConnector
Remove-InboundConnector
Remove-IntraOrganizationConnector
Remove-OutboundConnector
Set-InboundConnector
Set-IntraOrganizationConnector
Set-OutboundConnector
Validate-OutboundConnector
```

By default, a brand new tenant has no connectors that will show with the Get-*Connector cmdlets:

Get-InboundConnector
Get-IntraOrganizationConnector
Get-OutboundConnector

No connectors exist by default:

```
PS C:\> Get-InboundConnector
PS C:\> Get-IntraOrganizationConnector
PS C:\> Get-OutboundConnector
```

So what does this mean for your Office 365 Tenant? How does mail even flow without connectors? By default Exchange Online Protection (EOP) handles the connections for Inbound and Outbound traffic. Microsoft provides good documentation on this here:

https://blogs.technet.microsoft.com/ucando365talks/2014/02/25/exchange-online-protection-reporting-customization-and-support-options-streamlining-for-your-organization-emergency-notes/

That begs the question, if mail will flow to and from your Exchange Online tenant, why would we need to configure a connector in Exchange Online? There are a few scenarios that would require specific connectors created. One of these is Exchange Hybrid. If you have an Exchange Server, or other mail system, that is on-premises and you are transitioning to Office 365, then you will need connectors. Inbound and outbound connectors will probably both be needed in order to configure Hybrid with the legacy mail server. If running Exchange on-premises with Exchange Online, utilize the Hybrid Configuration Wizard to configure these options.

Another scenario is if journaling is configured, the end point for the journaled messages may require a specific connector. This connector would possibly use smart host settings, authentication and more. Another scenario would be if you require the connection to use Transport Layer Security (TLS) and if a TLS connection could not be established, then the connection would not be made and email not delivered. Banks and other institutions could require this. This is otherwise known as a mandatory TLS connection.

Example

For this example, we would like to route email from our on-premises mail server which is not an Exchange server and thus no Hybrid connector will be created. From the connector cmdlets, it looks like the *InboundConnector noun is the one we need for this scenario. First, we can review the Get-Help on the cmdlet:

```
-------------------------- Example 1 --------------------------
New-InboundConnector -Name "Contoso Inbound Connector" -SenderDomains *.contoso.com
-SenderIPAddresses 192.168.0.1/25 -RestrictDomainstoIPAddresses $true

-------------------------- Example 2 --------------------------
New-InboundConnector -Name "Contoso Inbound Secure Connector" -SenderDomains *.contoso.com
-SenderIPAddresses 192.168.0.1/25 -RestrictDomainstoIPAddresses $true -RequireTLS $true
-TlsSenderCertificateName *.contoso.com
```

A sample connector can be created like so:

```
New-InboundConnector -Name 'Inbound Mail Connector' -ConnectorType 'OnPremises'
-ConnectorSource 'Default' -Enabled:$True -CloudServicesMailEnabled:$True
-TlsSenderCertificateName 'mail.scolesfamily.net' -SenderDomains @('*') -RequireTls:$True
-RestrictDomainsToCertificate:$True -RestrictDomainsToIPAddresses:$False
```

Notice these parameters:

ConnectorType - this is the source of the traffic, in our case an on-premises mail server
CloudServicesMailEnabled - default setting, allows for cross-premises message header tags

Example

In this example we are taking an on-premises connector that is used to force a TLS connection to a particular banking institution. The connector has a couple of parameters that we need to copy to the new one in Exchange Online:

SMTP SmartHost - mail.bankinstitute.net
Domains - (a list of 50+ domains...)

The original connector has quite a few domains, so using PowerShell to store this in a variable and then pass this along to the Exchange Online connector would be the best way to do so.

Let's review what the cmdlet, New-OutboundConnector, has for examples:

```
----------------------------- Example 1 -----------------------------
New-OutboundConnector -Name "Contoso Outbound Connector" -RecipientDomains *.contoso.com
-TlsSettings DomainValidation -TlsDomain *.contoso.com
```

The above example does not include our need for adding a list of domains for the connector, but if we review the full help for the cmdlet, we see we can use 'RecipientDomains' for this. There is also an option called 'SmartHost' where we can specify the remote destination for emails that match this connector:

```
# Store all domains in a $Domains variable
$Spaces = (Get-SendConnector "Bank Institution Connector").AddressSpaces
$Domains = @()
Foreach ($Space in $Spaces) {
    $Domains += $Space.Address
}

# Connect to Office 365
$LiveCred = Get-Credential
$Session = New-PSSession -ConfigurationName Microsoft.Exchange -ConnectionUri https://ps.outlook.com/powershell/ -Credential $LiveCred -Authentication Basic -AllowRedirection
Import-PSSession $Session

# Configure new Send-Connector
New-OutboundConnector -Name "Banking" -ConnectorSource Default -ConnectorType Partner -TlsSettings DomainValidation -TlsDomain *.bankinstitute.net -Enabled $True -SmartHost mail.bankinstitute.net -RecipientDomains $Domains -UseMxRecord $False
```

Some additional parameters to cover here:

TLSDomain - The domain(s) to be secured by this connector. If an email is set to a domain on the list, the email will be routed through this connector.
TLSSettings - The connector will verify the FQDN of the target server's certificate and that it matches the domain in the TLSDomain parameter.

Now we have a connector in Exchange Online that uses TLS to server mail.bankinstitute.net and if no TLS connection can be made the connection will fail and no mail will be transported. If the connection succeeds, all mail will be transported securely. The connection between the servers is now secure, however, no security is applied directly to the message like S/MIME or IRM.

Removing Connectors

Removing an existing connector is sometimes needed after a service is retired or internal mail servers are removed. PowerShell provides a cmdlet that allows for the removal of a connector. To find out about this cmdlet, use the Get-Help:

Get-Help Remove-InboundConnector -Examples

```
------------------------------- Example -------------------------------
Remove-InboundConnector "Contoso Inbound Connector"
```

Get-Help Remove-OutboundConnector -Examples

```
------------------------------- Example 1 -------------------------------
Remove-OutboundConnector "Contoso Outbound Connector"
```

Using the above examples, we can write a small one-liner to remove any old or test connectors that are no longer needed. To remove the connector, the Remove-ReceiveConnector needs an identity of the connector to be removed. The help file also provides information on what comprises an appropriate identity for the Receive Connector.

```
-Identity <InboundConnectorIdParameter>
    The Identity parameter specifies the Inbound connector you want to remove.
```

Remove-ReceiveConnector "BOA"

```
PS C:\> Remove-OutboundConnector "BOA"

Confirm
Are you sure you want to perform this action?
Removing OutboundConnector "BOA".
[Y] Yes  [A] Yes to All  [N] No  [L] No to All  [?] Help (default is "Y"): y
```

Connector Reporting

In practical terms, a report on connectors would be good for overall Exchange Online documentation and not much else. A report like this would be just another page in an environment's documentation, providing a comprehensive look at the servers. Connectors, both Outbound and Inbound, have quite a few properties that could be documented. Cherry picking properties is not advisable because a missed property could cause an issue on a rebuild of a connector. So, a simple way to document a connector is to export all settings to a text file.

Example - Documenting One Connector

```
Get-OutboundConnector | fl > 'C:\Documentation\OutboundConnector.txt'
```

Part of the Receive-ApplicationRelay.txt file:

```
RunspaceId                      : ef4b5f62-a50e-41ba-890c-e4a349d83f5a
Enabled                         : True
UseMXRecord                     : False
Comment                         :
ConnectorType                   : Partner
ConnectorSource                 : Default
RecipientDomains                : {bankers.net, bankwithus.net, banking.com, bankinstitute.net...}
SmartHosts                      : {mail.bankinstitute.net}
TlsDomain                       : *.bankinstitute.net
TlsSettings                     : DomainValidation
IsTransportRuleScoped           : False
RouteAllMessagesViaOnPremises   : False
CloudServicesMailEnabled        : False
AllAcceptedDomains              : False
TestMode                        : False
LinkForModifiedConnector        : 00000000-0000-0000-0000-000000000000
ValidationRecipients            :
IsValidated                     : False
LastValidationTimestamp         :
AdminDisplayName                :
ExchangeVersion                 : 0.1 (8.0.535.0)
Name                            : Banking
```

Example – Document All Connectors

```
$Inbound = (Get-InboundConnector).Name
Foreach ($Connector in $Inbound) {
  Try {
    Get-InboundConnector -Identity $Connector -ErrorAction STOP | fl > 'C:\Documentation\
    InboundConnector.txt'
    Write-Host "The Inbound Connector $Connector has been documented." -ForegroundColor Cyan
  } Catch {
    Write-Host "The Inbound Connector $Connector has not been documented." -ForegroundColor
    Red
  }
}
 $Connector = $Null
$Outbound = (Get-OutboundConnector).Name
Foreach ($Connector in $Outbound) {
  Try {
    Get-OutboundConnector -Identity $Connector -ErrorAction STOP | fl > 'C:\Documentation\
    OutboundConnector.txt'
    Write-Host "The Outbound Connector $Connector has been documented." -ForegroundColor
    Cyan
  } Catch {
    Write-Host "The Outbound Connector $Connector has not been documented." -ForegroundColor
    Red
  }
}
```

Using the Try and Catch along with Foreach loops the above script will document all Send and Receive Connectors. There is also some visual feedback as to which connectors are properly documented and which ones are not. Below is the visual output from the script:

```
PS C:\> .\ConnectorDoc.ps1
The Inbound Connector Inbound Mail Connector has been documented.
The Outbound Connector Banking has been documented.
PS C:\>
```

Centralized Mail Transport

One of the options when configuring Hybrid with Exchange Online and Exchange On-Premises is a concept called Centralized Mail Transport. Centralized Mail Transport routes all emails from your Office 365 mailboxes to your on-premises servers before sending them to the Internet. The reason an organization would do this is if there is an internal processing that is needed for all messages in an environment - journaling, Data Loss Prevention (DLP), etc. - that would necessitate all emails to flow back to an on-premises servers. Inbound messages that are directed to your Exchange Online tenant will also pass through Exchange:

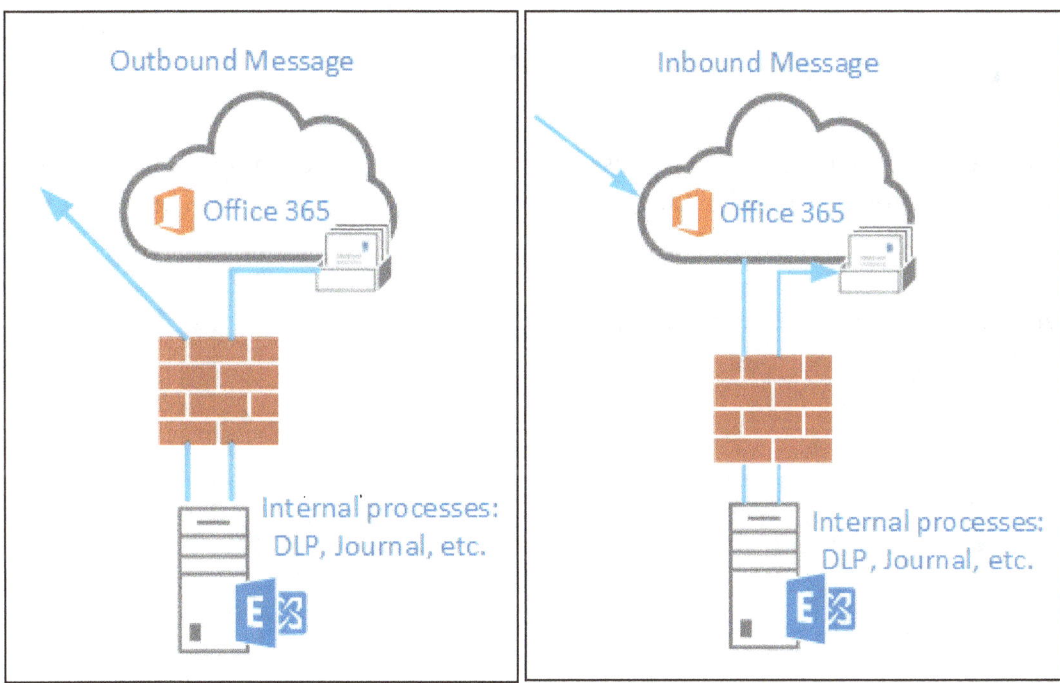

Adding Centralized Mail Transport

There are two ways to add this to your tenant. One is to use the Hybrid Configuration Wizard and the other is to use PowerShell to change 'RouteAllMessagesViaOnPremises' settings in order to turn it on. This setting is a property on the Outbound Connector that was created by the Hybrid Connector. In most cases this property will be off and only because Microsoft does not recommend it for most organizations and turns it off by default. If, however, we need this setting to be true, we simply need to run the following:

```
Set-OutboundConnector 'Hybrid Mail Flow Outbound Connector' -RouteAllMessagesViaOnPremises
$True
```

** **Note** ** Make sure you have good reason to turn on Centralized Mail Routing as it does indeed affect the way emails are routed in your environment.

Removing Centralized Mail Transport

In order to remove this setting, we need to configure the property to the opposite value, like the below example:

```
Set-OutboundConnector 'Hybrid Mail Flow Outbound Connector' -RouteAllMessagesViaOnPremises $False
```

** **Note** ** One caveat to turning this on is that if there is an issue with the mail from between on-premises and Exchange Online, messages could queue up and eventually fail.

Message Tracing

In Office 365, tracking down a message requires the use of Message Trace PowerShell cmdlets. A good introduction to this was provided in Chapter 9. Please refer to page 187 for more information on how to track down a message.

Transport Rules

Transport Rules can be used for so many purposes. These rules are usually created in the EAC, however, there are some rules that are easier to create in PowerShell due to the amount of options available. Let's start with what is available outside of PowerShell.

Within the EAC there are some pre-canned templates for Transport Rules:

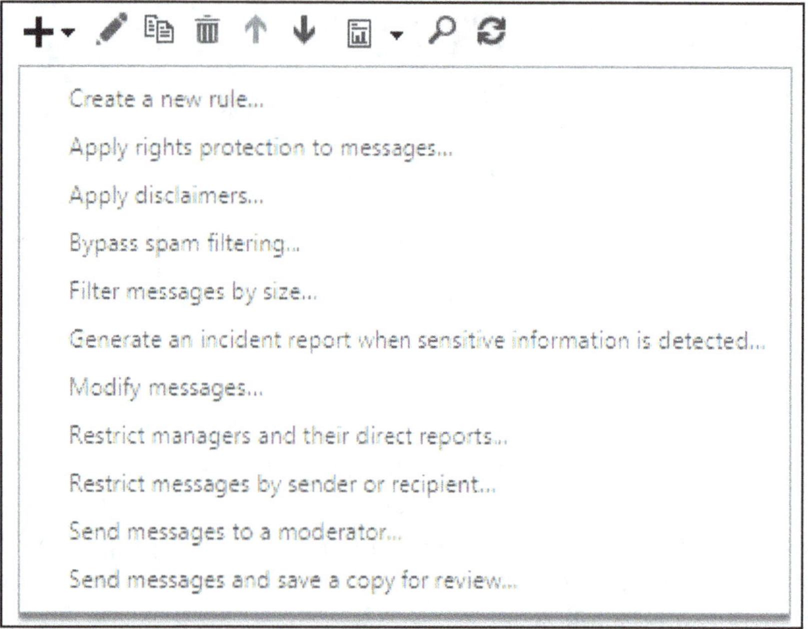

While these rule templates make life easier for making certain rules, PowerShell provides for additional configuration options not available in the web interface. With this thought in mind, this section will cover the Transport Rule PowerShell cmdlets. First, start with what cmdlets are available for Transport Rules:

Get-Command –Noun TransportRule

```
CommandType          Name
-----------          ----
Function             Disable-TransportRule
Function             Enable-TransportRule
Function             Get-TransportRule
Function             New-TransportRule
Function             Remove-TransportRule
Function             Set-TransportRule
```

** **Note** ** In the above PowerShell cmdlet, a difference technique is used to find a cmdlet. The term we are searching for in the PowerShell cmdlet is in the noun (right of the hyphen) portion of the PowerShell cmdlet. We can use the '-Noun' parameter to find cmdlets with the 'TransportRule' phrase in the noun.

Let's now examine these cmdlets in the context of some real-world scenarios.

Example 1

In this scenario the legal department has requested a disclaimer to be placed at the bottom of each email. The disclaimer has to contain text that was provided. Other requirements for the disclaimer are that it must only be applied once to a message, it can be applied to only external emails, it needs to be in HTML format and contain images that provide link backs to the company's Facebook sites. PowerShell can be used to create a Disclaimer rule:

New-TransportRule -SentToScope 'NotInOrganization' -ApplyHtmlDisclaimerLocation 'Append' -ApplyHtmlDisclaimerText 'This email is for its intended recipient. If you are not the recipient, please delete this email immediately.' -ApplyHtmlDisclaimerFallbackAction 'Wrap' -Name 'Legal Required Disclaimer' -StopRuleProcessing:$false -Mode 'Enforce' -RuleErrorAction 'Ignore' -SenderAddressLocation 'Header' -ExceptIfSubjectOrBodyContainsWords 'This email is for its intended recipient'

$Logo = '
<div style="color:#675C53; letter-spacing: 2px; line-height: 125%;"><a href="https://www.facebook.com"> <img src="https://www.facebookbrand.com/img/assets/asset.f.logo.lg.png "></a>
</div>'

New-TransportRule -Name 'FaceBook_logo' -Comments 'Contoso Signature - Logo' -FromMemberOf 'signature@contoso.com' -ApplyHtmlDisclaimerText $Logo -ApplyHtmlDisclaimerLocation Append -ApplyHtmlDisclaimerFallbackAction Wrap -ExceptIfSubjectOrBodyContainsWords 'This email is for its intended recipient' -Enabled $False -Priority 10

Example 2

Your company has decided to block all ZIP attachments in emails from external senders. The rule should also send the original email to an email address of "Damian@OnlineExchangeBook.onmicrosoft.com" and delete it prior to delivery.

New-TransportRule -Name "ZIP Block" -AttachmentNameMatchesPatterns zip
-GenerateIncidentReport "Damian@OnlineExchangeBook.onmicrosoft.com"
-IncidentReportContent AttachOriginalMail -DeleteMessage $True -SetAuditSeverity Medium

Options needed for this new Transport Rule:

AttachmentNameMatchesPatterns - the name of the attachment to be found with the rule - in this case it will be 'zip'
GenerateIncidentReport - destination email address for incident reports when the rule matches its criteria
IncidentReportContent - specifies the message properties that are included in the incident report
SetAuditSeverity - defines a severity assigned to the message and logged into the message tracking logs

Incident report looks like the below image, notice the Rule Hit at the bottom of the screenshot for 'ZIP Block'. Below is an example of real spam being blocked because of the ZIP attachment:

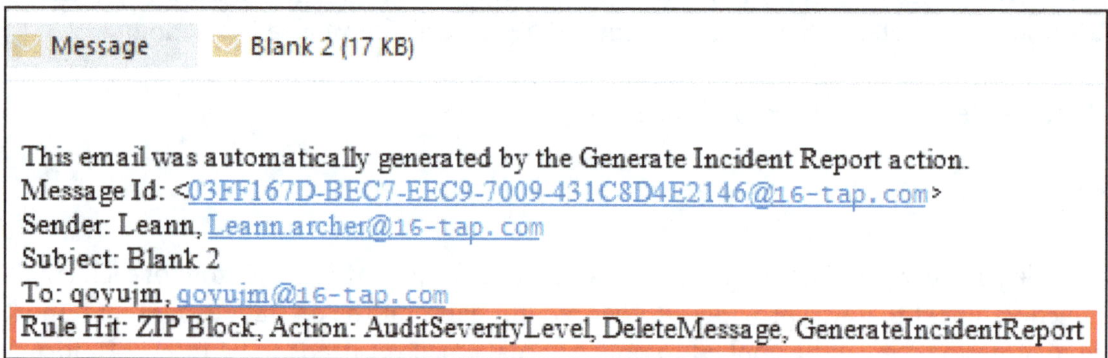

The original email is an attachment in this case 'Blank 2' is the original message with the ZIP file.

Accepted Domains

Accepted Domains are domains for which Exchange will answer SMTP deliveries for. If a domain is not defined and an email delivery is attempted for that domain, it will not be delivered. Defining these domains is important. In addition to defining the domain, it is also ideal to have Postmaster email addresses defined as well:

PowerShell

```
Get-Command *accepted*
```

Notice there is no option here for adding an Accepted Domain for routing email through Exchange. Why is this missing from Exchange Online? It's because the domain needs to be added to the MSOL connection point via New-MsolDomain first. Then the added domain can be manipulated within Exchange Online PowerShell.

** **Note** ** A new connection to MSOL can be initiated in PowerShell from any location that has the MSOnline PowerShell module available.

Once connected, a simple one-liner like the one below can be used to add an unverified domain to your tenant:

```
New-MsolDomain -Name OnlinePowerShellBooks.Com
```

One the domain is verified we can now work with it in Exchange Online. One thing you will notice is that the domain is not set to the default, which would be needed to change the default domain from the current default to the correct external domain:

```
Set-AcceptedDomain -Identity OnlinePowerShellBooks.Com -MakeDefault $True
```

Other Domain types are 'ExternalRelay' and 'InternalRelay'. The ExternalRelay one allows emails to exit Exchange and be delivered to an Internet destination. While the InternalRelay type allows for only local relay, possibly to another internal mail server.

Postmaster Check

RFC 822 specifies that the Postmaster address be valid for an organization. The standard does not specify whether or not the email address is attached to one mailbox or simply as an alias for any number of mailboxes in Exchange. To find a mailbox that has the Postmaster@Domain.Com address attached to it, simply use the Get-Mailbox cmdlet:

RFC stands for Request for Comments. These documents are considered to be official documents by the IETF and ISOC. First created in 1969 as an informal process for keeping track of changes in ARPANET, they eventually morphed into a set of standards that are to be adhered to for system interoperability on the Internet.

```
Get-Mailbox Postmaster@domain.com
```

If a mailbox is found, then this requirement from RFC 822 has been satisfied. However, what if there is more than one domain in the environment? First, a list of accepted domains is needed:

```
Get-Command –Noun AcceptedDomain
```

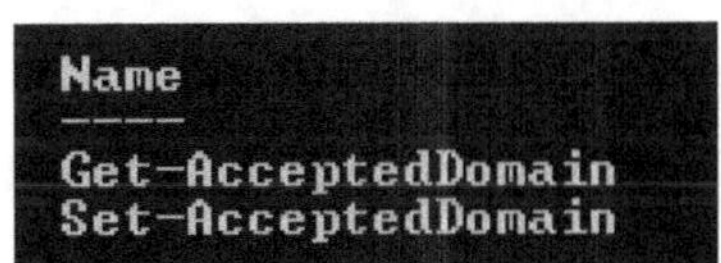

From the above results we can choose Get-AcceptedDomain as our seed cmdlet. As always, make sure to store the output from the Get-AcceptedDomain cmdlet with a variable. However, in this scenario the script does not need all information about an accepted domain, only the name of the domain is needed. How do we get this property? Well, let's examine the output of Get-AcceptedDomain cmdlet:

Name	DomainName	DomainType	Default
OnlineExchangeBook.mail.onm...	OnlineExchangeBook.mail.onm...	Authoritative	False
OnlineExchangeBook.onmicros...	OnlineExchangeBook.onmicros...	Authoritative	True

From that cmdlet, the property is appropriately name 'Domain Name'. So, using a variable for store, the Get-AcceptedDomain cmdlet and the 'DomainName' property, the following one-liner is assembled:

```
$AcceptedDomains = (Get-AcceptedDomain).DomainName
```

For processing more than one domain, a Foreach loop will be used:

```
Foreach ($Domain in $AcceptedDomains) { }
```

Now, for each domain, the verification check is for 'postmaster@domain.com'. In order to do this, first the script needs to assemble the postmaster address:

```
$Postmaster = 'Postmaster@'+$Domain
```

Now with the correct address, the script can check for a mailbox with this address. The Get-Mailbox cmdlet is the best option for this. All that is needed is the email address, which was just assembled for the Postmaster mailbox:

```
$Check = Get-Mailbox $Postmaster
```

However, what if the mailbox does not exist? There will be a need for error handling. In order to do so, results from a Get-Mailbox cmdlet for the constructed Postmaster address are stored in a variable. If the variable is empty, then a negative response is written to the screen. If the Postmaster mailbox is found, a positive response is displayed.

```
$Check = Get-Mailbox $Postmaster -ErrorAction SilentlyContinue
If (!$Check) {
    Write-Host $Postmaster" does not exist." -ForegroundColor Yellow
} Else {
    Write-Host $Postmaster" does exist." -ForegroundColor Cyan
}
```

Assemble all the code together to get this:

```
$AcceptedDomains = (Get-AcceptedDomain).DomainName
Foreach ($Domain in $AcceptedDomains) {
    $PostMaster = 'Postmaster@'+$Domain
    $Check = Get-Mailbox $Postmaster -ErrorAction SilentlyContinue
    If (!$Check) {
        Write-Host $Postmaster" does not exist." -ForegroundColor Yellow
    } Else {
        Write-Host $Postmaster" does exist." -ForegroundColor Cyan
    }
}
```

In the below testing, the two domains listed in Exchange do not have a Postmaster address defined and thus generate yellow text, a warning to add these addresses.

```
Postmaster@OnlineExchangeBook.mail.onmicrosoft.com does not exist.
Postmaster@OnlineExchangeBook.onmicrosoft.com does not exist.
```

To rectify this, either create a Postmaster mailbox that has both these aliases assigned to it, create one Postmaster mailbox per domain or add the aliases to an existing account, preferably in IT.

Removing An Accepted Domain

In order to remove an accepted domain, simply remove the domain from MSOL after connecting to your MSOL service.

```
Remove-MsolDomain -DomainName OnlinePowerShellBooks.Com -Force
```

The 'Force' switch is optional and will forcibly remove the domain even if there are dependencies on the domain.

11   Mail Flow - Compliance

In This Chapter

- Message Hygiene
- Data Loss Prevention
- Journaling
- Azure Information Protection
- Office 365 Message Encryption

In the previous chapter we covered some of the basics of Simple Mail Transport Protocol (SMTP) in Exchange Online and how we can work with it in PowerShell. This chapter will cover the more advanced components of SMTP in Exchange Online – message hygiene, Data Loss Prevention (DLP), Journaling and Rights Management. Additional tasks that can be done with PowerShell may require additional licensing in Exchange. Some of the features talked about may need additional licensing in order to utilize them in Office 365.

This chapter covers enterprise level features that are more likely to be used by larger messaging environments. Generally larger environments dictate more strict compliance requirements rather than smaller environments. Legal departments tend to be larger and more structured with policies in place for protecting all forms of communication and email is heavily regulated.

DLP is an interesting feature that was introduced into Exchange Server 2013, continued in Exchange Server 2016 as well as Exchange Online. This features allows for more advanced transport rules for processing emails containing potentially sensitive information in them. Additional knowledge of Regular Expressions (RegEx) and compliance regulations may be needed in order to make the most of this feature. RegEx allows for more complex transport criteria.

The Journaling feature is a feature commonly used in Exchange. Typically Journaling is used for compliance, business continuity or discovery purposes. Messages can only be journaled to a destination external to Office 365. This is a key component to keep in mind if you are moving to Office 365 from Exchange on-premises.

Rights Management is a particularly interesting feature that also requires some licensing outside of Exchange Online. While Rights Management will be covered with respect to Exchange Online and will include the requisite background services and configuration. We will set up policies and then apply them to emails only.

Lastly, we'll cover Message Hygiene which entails configuring Exchange Online Protection, DMARC, DKIM, SPF and more.

Message Hygiene

Message Hygiene is a nebulous topic, but one of importance from an administration and user perspective. According to some sources, 60% of all email is SPAM, making this an important component of any mail system. For administrators reducing the amount of Spam or malware that enters Exchange makes for less supports calls, fixing or troubleshooting issues with email. For the end user, a reduced amount of bad messages makes for a better experience. In this chapter will cover external controls, Malware filters and Exchange Online Protection (EOP).

External Controls

In order to block Spam prior to the message being delivered to any Exchange Mailbox, there are some additional things we can enable to help control Message Hygiene.

- **Domain Key Identified Mail (DKIM)** – Allows a recipient of a message to verify the sender of the message. Requires a third party product like PowerMTA, DkimX or a DKIM Transport / Signing Agent. Signs the email with a digital signature that is verifiable with via the signers public key.
- **Domain Message Authentication Reporting & Conformance (DMARC)** – A Special TXT DNS record used by servers on how to handle DKIM or SPF failures and where those failures are reported.
- **Sender Policy Framework (SPF) Record** – A special DNS record that provides a list of valid SMTP servers for your domain.
- **Exchange Online Protection (EOP)** – Built-in service for providing Message Hygiene for Exchange Online.

  ** **Note** ** Only one of the above can be configured with PowerShell, but these items should be on your list to begin protecting Exchange Online. SPF and DMARC both require external DNS records to be configured. A good article on this can be found by Microsoft - https://blogs.technet.microsoft.com/fasttrack-tips/2016/07/16/spf-dkim-dmarc-and-exchange-online/.

For DKIM, there are options to configure this feature either in the Exchange Admin Center or with PowerShell. For PowerShell we can see what cmdlets are available first:

Get-Command *DKIM*

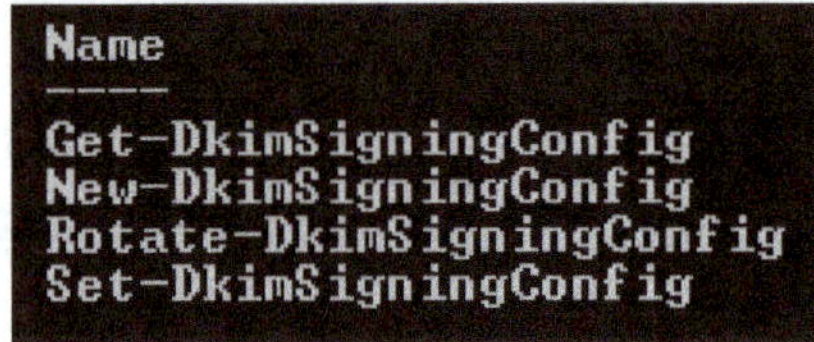

We can review the default configuration for DKIM:

Get-DkimSigningConfig

More information about the actual DKIM configuration can be revealed using Format-List (FL) instead of the default Format-Table (FT).

Get-DkimSigningConfig | Fl

Some of the most important pieces of the configuration are listed in the red square:

```
RunspaceId                    : a675230f-47dc-4f9e-aa99-70d94d9d94fe
Domain                        : OnlineExchangeBook.onmicrosoft.com
AdminDisplayName              :
Selector1KeySize              : 1024
Selector1CNAME                : selector1-OnlineExchangeBook-onmicrosoft-com._domainkey.OnlineExchan
                                geBook.onmicrosoft.com
Selector1PublicKey            : v=DKIM1; k=rsa; p=MIGfMA0GCSqGSIb3DQEBAQUAA4GNADCBiQKBgQCprpQr9EQVdl
                                rKMdOoCzRW4YWC8wTJhKOgjRSdghi8Q/S6Qf02VG69Jo2ul55rEzdn3bqDMj+pw74eU0
                                L7Zhv1Qx/JnDJi2pRIDGz5szgNmmsAL14rGHqeuU3gxvUKyFFXUo2LW0xaBZm/ZVlu7b
                                ZbmCDsCzYVSeEvzZrxdexLtQIDAQAB;
Selector2KeySize              : 1024
Selector2CNAME                : selector2-OnlineExchangeBook-onmicrosoft-com._domainkey.OnlineExchan
                                geBook.onmicrosoft.com
Selector2PublicKey            : v=DKIM1; k=rsa; p=MIGfMA0GCSqGSIb3DQEBAQUAA4GNADCBiQKBgQCwgwTKtSeBn0
                                aFdnLgQbLTqxQUGQWQ2AHLVkfZ5UxyLo4LCArs7LSOo3Wg3i7sXPVn0LRKi7+189q89W
                                mb/dn+tUcHiA0FhqIyYFDj8NbKUAcz4Mcw0bu+9vALiUq40fjp6MO2B6D9AiYVcYq8T+
                                /hrxcHM5fNM8yl0S84hYIcqwIDAQAB;
Enabled                       : True
IsDefault                     : True
HeaderCanonicalization        : Relaxed
BodyCanonicalization          : Relaxed
Algorithm                     : RsaSHA256
NumberOfBytesToSign           : All
IncludeSignatureCreationTime  : True
IncludeKeyExpiration          : False
KeyCreationTime               : 12/6/2017 8:02:32 AM
LastChecked                   : 12/6/2017 8:02:32 AM
RotateOnDate                  : 12/6/2017 8:02:32 AM
SelectorBeforeRotateOnDate    : selector2
```

Enabling DKIM for a domain is quick and easy:

```
Set-DkimSigningConfig -Enabled:$True -Identity 'PracticalPowerShell.com'
```

Make sure you have created your two CNAME records that are needed for proper DKIM operation.

Exchange Online Protection

Beyond the external control above, Exchange Online also provides it's own anti-malware / anti-virus service called Exchange Online Protection or EOP. EOP provides layers of protection, some are configurable in your specific tenant, while many others are inherent to the service and are not exposed for configuration purposes. Similar to how other third-party providers will scan messages as they arrive at their servers, EOP will scan messages looking for known payloads, attack patterns and more. The configurable portion of EOP allows for these types of filtering:

- **Malware** - configure notifications and how to handle certain file types.
- **Connection Filters** - consists of IP Allow and IP Block lists for controlling who can send email to you.
- **Spam Filters** - provides quite a few configurable options like Bulk SPAM controls, domain/email block and allow lists, international SPAM controls, as well as a set of more advanced controls.
- **Outbound SPAM** - configure notifications if outbound SPAM is detected.

Now that we know the available configurable options for EOP, how do we modify or configure these settings with PowerShell?

PowerShell

First off, we'll start with the Malware Filter configuration:

```
Get-Command *MalwareFilter*

Name
----
Disable-MalwareFilterRule
Enable-MalwareFilterRule
Get-MalwareFilterPolicy
Get-MalwareFilterRule
New-MalwareFilterPolicy
New-MalwareFilterRule
Remove-MalwareFilterPolicy
Remove-MalwareFilterRule
Set-MalwareFilterPolicy
Set-MalwareFilterRule
```

In Exchange Online, the Malware configuration consists of two parts, Malware Filter Policy and Malware Filter Rules. The Rules roll up and can be associated with a Policy in order to be applied. There are no requirements to use the Malware Filter Rules as we can see that none are provided in a brand new tenant.

Malware Filter Policies

In a brand new tenant, there are no defined Malware Rules in EOP. If we were to run 'Get-MalwareFilterRule', no results would be returned. However, there is a default policy, the same one you see in the Exchange Admin Center, and the 'Get-MalwareFilterPolicy | Fl' cmdlet will display that configuration:

```
CustomAlertText                        :
AdminDisplayName                       :
CustomInternalSubject                  :
CustomInternalBody                     :
CustomExternalSubject                  :
CustomExternalBody                     :
CustomFromName                         :
CustomFromAddress                      :
InternalSenderAdminAddress             :
ExternalSenderAdminAddress             :
BypassInboundMessages                  : False
BypassOutboundMessages                 : False
Action                                 : DeleteMessage
IsDefault                              : True
CustomNotifications                    : False
EnableInternalSenderNotifications      : False
EnableExternalSenderNotifications      : False
EnableInternalSenderAdminNotifications : False
EnableExternalSenderAdminNotifications : False
EnableFileFilter                       : False
FileTypes                              : {ace, ani, app, docm...}
ZapEnabled                             : True
ExchangeVersion                        : 0.20 (15.0.0.0)
Name                                   : Default
```

We can configure this Malware Filter Policy using PowerShell, so let's review some examples of this configuration:

```
Get-Help Set-MalwareFilterPolicy -Examples

-------------------------- Example 1 --------------------------

Set-MalwareFilterPolicy -Identity "Contoso Malware Filter Policy" -Action DeleteMessage
 -EnableInternalSenderAdminNotifications $true -InternalSenderAdminAddress admin@contoso.com

-------------------------- Example 2 --------------------------

$FileTypesAdd = Get-MalwareFilterPolicy -Identity Default | select -Expand FileTypes

$FileTypesAdd += "com","bat"
Set-MalwareFilterPolicy -Identity Default -EnableFileFilter $true -FileTypes $FileTypesAdd
```

Example

Management has decided they would like to change the way malware messages are processed by EOP. First they would like to have Administrators notified when a malware messages is detected. Next, if the sender is internal, they would like to notify that user if a malware message was sent from their account. Lastly they would like to notify an external sender if their message contained malware as well. How can we do this? First, we would need to review the full Get-Help for the Set-MalwareFilterPolicy cmdlet.

Parameters we can use:

First step is to allow custom notifications, set a From address and a display name for that address:

```
-CustomNotifications $True
-CustomFromAddress ITAdmins@PracticalPowerShell.Com
-CustomFromName 'Big Box IT Admins'
```

Next, we have the internal message notifications for any messages sent by your Exchange Online mailboxes. We will enable notifications to administrators, the sender (internal), which admin email address to use and a custom subject and body for the notification.

```
-EnableInternalSenderAdminNotifications $True
-EnableInternalSenderNotifications $True
-InternalSenderAdminAddress ITAdmins@PracticalPowerShell.Com
-CustomInternalBody 'Dear user, you have recently sent out a message that contains malware. Please contact the IT Department.'
-CustomInternalSubject 'Malware detected!'
```

Next, we have the external message notifications for any messages sent to your Exchange Online mailboxes. We will enable notifications to administrators, the sender (external), which admin email address to use and a custom subject and body for the notification.

```
-EnableExternalSenderAdminNotifications $True
-EnableExternalSenderNotifications $True
-ExternalSenderAdminAddress ITAdmins@PracticalPowerShell.Com
-CustomExternalBody 'Dear sender, you have recently sent out a message that contains malware. Please contact our IT Department @ ITAdmins@PracticalPowerShell.Com'
-CustomExternalSubject 'Malware detected!'
```

Combining all of the options makes for one very long one-liner:

```
Set-MalwareFilterPolicy Default -CustomNotifications $True -CustomFromAddress ITAdmins@PracticalPowerShell.Com -CustomFromName 'Big Box IT Admins' -EnableInternalSenderAdminNotifications $True -EnableInternalSenderNotifications $True -InternalSenderAdminAddress ITAdmins@PracticalPowerShell.Com -CustomInternalBody 'Dear user, you have recently sent out a message that contains malware. Please contact the IT Department.' -CustomInternalSubject 'Malware detected!' -EnableExternalSenderAdminNotifications $True -EnableExternalSenderNotifications $True -ExternalSenderAdminAddress ITAdmins@PracticalPowerShell.Com -CustomExternalBody 'Dear sender, you have recently sent out a message that contains malware. Please contact our IT Department @ ITAdmins@PracticalPowerShell.Com' -CustomExternalSubject 'Malware detected!'
```

These changes should then be verified:

```
AdminDisplayName                              :
CustomInternalSubject                         : Malware detected!
CustomInternalBody                            : Dear user, you have recently sent out a message that
                                                contains malware.  Please contact the IT Department.
CustomExternalSubject                         : Malware detected!
CustomExternalBody                            : Dear sender, you have recently sent out a message that
                                                contains malware.  Please contact our IT Department @
                                                ITAdmins@PracticalPowerShell.Com
CustomFromName                                : Big Box IT Admins
CustomFromAddress                             : ITAdmins@PracticalPowerShell.Com
InternalSenderAdminAddress                    : ITAdmins@PracticalPowerShell.Com
ExternalSenderAdminAddress                    : ITAdmins@PracticalPowerShell.Com
BypassInboundMessages                         : False
BypassOutboundMessages                        : False
Action                                        : DeleteMessage
IsDefault                                     : True
CustomNotifications                           : True
EnableInternalSenderNotifications             : True
EnableExternalSenderNotifications             : True
EnableInternalSenderAdminNotifications        : True
EnableExternalSenderAdminNotifications        : True
EnableFileFilter                              : False
FileTypes                                     : {ace, ani, app, docm...}
```

Malware Filter Rules

To enhance the Malware Policies there are Malware Rules that can add to the Policies. Rules can be used like Access Control Lists (ACLs) and determine who is affected by a particular Malware Policy by blocking or allowing particular accounts or groups.

Get-Help New-MalwareFilterRule -Examples

```
------------------------ Example 1 ------------------------
New-MalwareFilterRule -Name "Contoso Recipients" -MalwareFilterPolicy "Contoso Malware Filter
Policy" -RecipientDomainIs contoso.com
```

Example

In the previous example we configured notifications for emails that were detected as malware. The notifications were configured for any internal or external message and there were no restrictions placed on which mailboxes this would apply to and thus all mailboxes are affected. What if we wanted to restrict this policy to the IT department only, possibly for testing before putting the Malware Policy into production. If we review the full Get-Help for the New-MalwareFileRule we see one option that we can use:

-SentToMemberOf
-MalwareFilterPolicy

This enabled us to create the rule, assign it to the policy and then apply it only to the IT Admins group (with the provided SMTP address):

New-MalwareFilterRule -Name "IT Admin Testing Rule" -SentToMemberOf ITAdmins@
PracticalPowerShell.Com -MalwareFilterPolicy Default

** **Note** ** You cannot apply a Malware Filter Rule to the Default Malware Filter Policy.

Connection Filters

Connection Filters are used to specifically block or allow certain email server IPs from connecting to your Office 365 tenant. These types of filters are good for either allowing a trusted source, like a partner organization, to connect or to block a server that is either currently sending Spam to your tenant or has done so in the past. Microsoft already has extensive lists for blocked IPs due to its own internal parameters. You are more likely to use an allow IP connections than block when using EOP.

PowerShell

In order to configure these settings, we first need to find the cmdlets needed in PowerShell that will allow us to do so. We'll use the noun phrase 'ConnectionFilter' to find the relevant cmdlets:

```
Get-Command *ConnectionFilter*
```

```
Name
Get-HostedConnectionFilterPolicy
New-HostedConnectionFilterPolicy
Remove-HostedConnectionFilterPolicy
Set-HostedConnectionFilterPolicy
```

First, if we run the Get-HostedConnectionFilterPolicy we see that the default policy is not configured with any settings:

```
AdminDisplayName        :
IsDefault               : True
IPAllowList             : {}
IPBlockList             : {}
EnableSafeList          : False
DirectoryBasedEdgeBlockMode : Default
Identity                : Default
Id                      : Default
IsValid                 : True
```

Now let's review some examples for configuring this filter:

```
Get-Help Set-HostedConnectionFilterPolicy -Examples
```

```
-------------------------- Example 1 --------------------------
Set-HostedConnectionFilterPolicy "Contoso Connection Filter Policy" -IPAllowList
192.168.1.10,192.168.1.23 -IPBlockList 10.10.10.0/25,172.17.17.0/24

-------------------------- Example 2 --------------------------
Set-HostedConnectionFilterPolicy "Contoso Connection Filter Policy" -IPAllowList
@{Add="192.168.2.10","192.169.3.0/24","192.168.4.1-192.168.4.5";Remove="192.168.1.10"}
```

Example

Engineers on the Messaging Team have been tracking the IP connections made by SMTP servers and were able to connect Spam and Malware attacks by these bad IPs. On the reverse side the Messaging Team also has a list of known good SMTP servers from clients, partners and other sources. They are now in the process of preparing EOP as their new protection service before they move mailboxes to their new Exchange Online tenant.

In order to configure the IP Allow and IP Block lists, we need to run the Set-HostedConnectionFilterPolicy cmdlet in order to do so. Here is a sample of what they would need to configure:

```
Set-HostedConnectionFilterPolicy Default -IPAllowList 64.34.23.43,23.100.100.1 -IPBlockList
64.34.23.44,23.100.100.2
```

We can verify the settings have been applied:

```
Get-HostedConnectionFilterPolicy Default
```

```
RunspaceId                        : 792cf214-33a1-464d-bf35-3f50
AdminDisplayName                  :
IsDefault                         : True
IPAllowList                       : {23.100.100.1, 64.34.23.43}
IPBlockList                       : {23.100.100.2, 64.34.23.44}
EnableSafeList                    : False
DirectoryBasedEdgeBlockMode       : Default
Identity                          : Default
```

After applying these settings, one of the engineers realized they had their lists mixed, how can they reverse the settings? First we'll wipe out all settings to ensure no duplicates or odd values are retained:

```
Set-HostedConnectionFilterPolicy Default -IPAllowList $Null -IPBlockList $Null
Get-HostedConnectionFilterPolicy Default
```

```
IsDefault                         : True
IPAllowList                       : {}
IPBlockList                       : {}
EnableSafeList                    : False
DirectoryBasedEdgeBlockMode       : Default
Identity                          : Default
```

```
Set-HostedConnectionFilterPolicy Default -IPBlockList 64.34.23.43,23.100.100.1 -IPAllowList 64.34.23.44,23.100.100.2
Get-HostedConnectionFilterPolicy Default
```

```
AdminDisplayName                  :
IsDefault                         : True
IPAllowList                       : {23.100.100.2, 64.34.23.44}
IPBlockList                       : {23.100.100.1, 64.34.23.43}
EnableSafeList                    : False
DirectoryBasedEdgeBlockMode       : Default
Identity                          : Default
```

Spam Filter

The Spam Filters in Exchange Online are quite varied and can be a bit confusing. Trying to find PowerShell cmdlets for configuring these settings can be confusing as well. That is because there is no cmdlet that is listed as a Spam Filter cmdlet. How do we find the cmdlet for it? We use the 'Show Command Logging' feature that we covered in Appendix B. By using that and changing one setting in the Spam Filter we see that changing the Spam Filter requires the 'Set-HostedContentFilterPolicy' cmdlet. Let's see what other cmdlets we have that share the same noun phrase:

```
Get-Command *HostedContentFilter*
```

```
Name
----
Disable-HostedContentFilterRule
Enable-HostedContentFilterRule
Get-HostedContentFilterPolicy
Get-HostedContentFilterRule
New-HostedContentFilterPolicy
New-HostedContentFilterRule
Remove-HostedContentFilterPolicy
Remove-HostedContentFilterRule
Set-HostedContentFilterPolicy
Set-HostedContentFilterRule
```

Looks like we have a lot of configuration cmdlets to choose from to make adjustments to the Spam Filter. Similar to the Malware Policies and Rules we covered earlier in the chapter, the Spam Filter has Rules and Policies as well.

So we can configure more Rules and Policies depending on our need. Let's start out with the default Spam Filter Policy to see what is configured and what we can configure with PowerShell.

Get-HostedContentFilterPolicy

```
Name      SpamAction   HighConfidenceSpamAction  IsDefault
----      ----------   ------------------------  ---------
Default   MoveToJmf    MoveToJmf                 True
```

So we have one Spam Policy that we can configure called 'Default'. Let's review this in more detail:

Get-HostedContentFilterPolicy | Fl

```
RunspaceId                                    : f81f6f03-f259-40bc-9665-1927b37e233d
AdminDisplayName                              :
AddXHeaderValue                               :
ModifySubjectValue                            :
RedirectToRecipients                          : {}
TestModeBccToRecipients                       : {}
FalsePositiveAdditionalRecipients             : {}
QuarantineRetentionPeriod                     : 15
EndUserSpamNotificationFrequency              : 3
TestModeAction                                : None
IncreaseScoreWithImageLinks                   : On
IncreaseScoreWithNumericIps                   : Off
IncreaseScoreWithRedirectToOtherPort          : Off
IncreaseScoreWithBizOrInfoUrls                : Off
MarkAsSpamEmptyMessages                       : Off
MarkAsSpamJavaScriptInHtml                    : Off
MarkAsSpamFramesInHtml                        : Off
MarkAsSpamObjectTagsInHtml                    : Off
MarkAsSpamEmbedTagsInHtml                     : Off
MarkAsSpamFormTagsInHtml                      : Off
MarkAsSpamWebBugsInHtml                       : Off
MarkAsSpamSensitiveWordList                   : Off
MarkAsSpamSpfRecordHardFail                   : Off
MarkAsSpamFromAddressAuthFail                 : Off
MarkAsSpamBulkMail                            : On
MarkAsSpamNdrBackscatter                      : Off
IsDefault                                     : True
LanguageBlockList                             : {}
RegionBlockList                               : {}
HighConfidenceSpamAction                      : MoveToJmf
SpamAction                                    : MoveToJmf
EnableEndUserSpamNotifications                : False
DownloadLink                                  : False
EnableRegionBlockList                         : False
EnableLanguageBlockList                       : False
EndUserSpamNotificationCustomFromAddress      :
EndUserSpamNotificationCustomFromName         :
EndUserSpamNotificationCustomSubject          :
EndUserSpamNotificationLanguage               : Default
EndUserSpamNotificationLimit                  : 0
BulkThreshold                                 : 7
AllowedSenders                                : {}
AllowedSenderDomains                          : {}
BlockedSenders                                : {}
BlockedSenderDomains                          : {}
ZapEnabled                                    : True
InlineSafetyTipsEnabled                       : True
BulkSpamAction                                : MoveToJmf
PhishSpamAction                               : MoveToJmf
Identity                                      : Default
Id                                            : Default
IsValid                                       : True
```

As we can see from the screenshot above of a brand new tenant, there are a lot of settings that are off and not set. These are off for a reason as turning them on could potentially block legitimate emails if you do not understand what the settings do. However, there is a provided mechanism for testing settings as some of the parameters have possible values of On, Off and Test. This last one is important if there is some uncertainty as to what the setting will do in production. Microsoft provides a good description of these options and their effects on filtering here:

https://technet.microsoft.com/en-us/library/jj200684(v=exchg.150).aspx

** **Note** ** There are a couple of these settings in the Spam Filter that show 'MoveToJmf':

```
HighConfidenceSpamAction      : MoveToJmf
SpamAction                    : MoveToJmf

BulkSpamAction                : MoveToJmf
PhishSpamAction               : MoveToJmf
```

The 'MoveToJmf' setting is just an abbreviated 'Move To Junk Mail Filter'; though it isn't clear why this had to be abbreviated for this property.

Example

Let's say we want to configure our Spam Filter to test a few parameters. To help analyze the impact of the change, we need to set the 'TestModeAction' parameter to either 'AddXHeader' or 'BccMessage Redirect'. This will allow us to either tag the message with a X-Header we can track or to have a copy of the message sent to a certain address for analysis. For this example we will use an X-Header and change the MarkAsSpamFormTagsInHtml, MarkAsSpamFramesInHtml and MarkAsSpamEmbedTagsInHtml parameters all to 'Test'.

    Set-HostedContentFilterPolicy Default -MarkAsSpamFormTagsInHtml Test -MarkAsSpamFramesInHtml
    Test -MarkAsSpamEmbedTagsInHtml Test -TestModeAction BccMessage -TestModeBccToRecipients
    Damian@PracticalPowerShell.Com

Now if a message matches any of these settings, a copy will be BCC'd to the email address specified in the 'TestModeBccToRecipients' parameter in our cmdlet.

Outbound Spam

Exchange Online Protection has an interesting feature that looks for Outbound Spam for your Exchange Online tenant. While the feature is useful, there isn't a lot we can configure. We can notify some admins of the emails that are outbound Spam or we can add some BCC recipients to the message. There isn't much else to this particular feature.

PowerShell

There aren't a lot of configuration settings and thus not a lot of PowerShell cmdlets available to configure it. Let's take a look at what we can do:

    Get-Command *HostedOutbound*

So, we can Get and we can Set out Outbound Spam settings. First we can check to see what is set by default on the Outbound Spam configuration:

    Get-HostedOutboundSpamFilterPolicy | Fl

```
RunspaceId                                    : f81f6f03-f259-40
AdminDisplayName                              :
NotifyOutboundSpamRecipients                  : {}
BccSuspiciousOutboundAdditionalRecipients     : {}
BccSuspiciousOutboundMail                     : False
NotifyOutboundSpam                            : False
ExchangeVersion                               : 0.20 (15.0.0.0)
Name                                          : Default
```

Now that we see what our defaults are, let's look to configure this feature with the Set cmdlet that is available to us:

Get-Help Set-HostedOutboundSpamFilterPolicy -Examples

```
---------------------------- Example 1 ----------------------------
Set-HostedOutboundSpamFilterPolicy Default -NotifyOutboundSpam $true
-NotifyOutboundSpamRecipients chris@contoso.com
```

Sample Scenario

Take for example an organization that is worried about Spam being sent outbound from their organization and would like have the administrators of Exchange Online notified if outbound Spam does get sent. For us to do so, we need to configure two parameters:

- NotifyOutboundSpam - This is by default set to 'False', so no notifications are sent
- NotifyOutboundSpamRecipients - This property is blank because the first one is set to False

We just need a recipient for notifications and then we can configure the Outbound Spam settings:

```
Set-HostedOutboundSpamFilterPolicy Default -NotifyOutboundSpam $True
-NotifyOutboundSpamRecipients 'Damian@PracticalPowerShell.Com'
```

We can run the 'Get-HostedOutboundSpamFilterPolicy | Fl' one-liner to verify our configuration worked:

```
RunspaceId                                   : f81f6f03-f259-40bc-9665-1927b37e23
AdminDisplayName                             :
NotifyOutboundSpamRecipients                 : {Damian@PracticalPowerShell.Com}
BccSuspiciousOutboundAdditionalRecipients    : {}
BccSuspiciousOutboundMail                    : False
NotifyOutboundSpam                           : True
ExchangeVersion                              : 0.20 (15.0.0.0)
Name                                         : Default
```

Using Transport Rules for Spam Protection

In addition to using EOP and other features in Exchange Online, a more rudimentary method still exists for blocking unwanted emails - Transport Rules. While this may seem like an inelegant solution, using transport rules to control SPAM is used by many corporations today. These Transport Rules could be simple or complex, depending on the desired results. As a starting point we can use an article written by Microsoft on the subject:

https://technet.microsoft.com/en-us/library/dn720438(v=exchg.150).aspx

The above article provides us with some examples of what can be done, however these are done in the EAC and not in PowerShell. Referring back to Chapter 10's section on Transport Rules, we can construct some rules to control SPAM using techniques like RegEx.

Data Loss Prevention

Data Loss Prevention (DLP) is a growing feature request among many types of organizations. The draw for these companies is that the DLP provides another line of defense for loss of corporate sensitive data. Key among features built into Exchange Server's DLP are the predefined sensitive data types provided by Microsoft and that DLP can be customized for an environment with templates and policy tips. For the end user, DLP is invisible for some scenarios, for example when administrators are testing rules, when a DLP policy stops a message from either reaching the end user or exiting Exchange DLP is only visible when a Policy Tip is configured to make the end user aware of the information that was being sent out.

** **Note** ** DLP requires at least an E3 license in order to use in Exchange Online. A bigger note is that DLP may eventually be pulled from Exchange Online and you will only be able to configure this in the Security and Compliance Center.

Features of DLP

- 40 Sensitive Data Types
- Policy Tips – for OWA and Outlook
- Document Fingerprinting
- Coordinates with Transport Rules
- Customization – Templates
- 'Test Mode' – without affecting users

DLP PowerShell

First, we'll start with the cmdlets that are available for DLP:

```
Get-Command *DLP*
```

```
Export-DlpPolicyCollection
Get-DlpCompliancePolicy
Get-DlpComplianceRule
Get-DlpComplianceRuleV2
Get-DlpDetailReport
Get-DlpDetectionsReport
Get-DlpIncidentDetailReport
Get-DlpKeywordDictionary
Get-DlpPolicy
Get-DlpPolicyTemplate
Get-DlpSensitiveInformationTypeRulePackage
Get-DlpSiDetectionsReport
Get-MailDetailDlpPolicyReport
Import-DlpPolicyCollection
New-DlpPolicy
Remove-DlpPolicy
Set-DlpPolicy
```

Exchange Online has no DLP policies defined by default. This can be verified with 'Get-DLPPolicy' on a brand new Exchange Online tenant.

DLP Templates

DLP Templates are one of the building blocks for DLP in Exchange Online. To begin with the process, first use a Template that is custom created or a Microsoft Template. A DLP Policy is built based on that Template and then the DLP Policy is used in a Transport Rule.

With Exchange Online, Microsoft has included a few DLP Templates to speed up deployment of DLP:

```
Get-DlpPolicyTemplate | Ft –Auto
```

```
Name                                                         Publisher Version
----                                                         --------- -------
U.S. Personally Identifiable Information (PII) Data           Microsoft 15.0.3.0
U.S. Gramm-Leach-Bliley Act (GLBA)                           Microsoft 15.0.3.0
PCI Data Security Standard (PCI DSS)                         Microsoft 15.0.3.0
Japan Financial Data                                         Microsoft 15.0.3.0
U.K. Financial Data                                          Microsoft 15.0.3.0
France Financial Data                                        Microsoft 15.0.3.0
U.S. Financial Data                                          Microsoft 15.0.3.0
Japan Personally Identifiable Information (PII) Data         Microsoft 15.0.3.0
U.K. Personally Identifiable Information (PII) Data          Microsoft 15.0.3.0
France Personally Identifiable Information (PII) Data        Microsoft 15.0.3.0
Germany Personally Identifiable Information (PII) Data       Microsoft 15.0.3.0
Germany Financial Data                                       Microsoft 15.0.3.0
Canada Health Information Act (HIA)                          Microsoft 15.0.3.0
Canada Personal Information Protection Act (PIPA)            Microsoft 15.0.3.0
Canada Personal Information Protection Act (PIPEDA)          Microsoft 15.0.3.0
Canada Personal Health Act (PHIPA) – Ontario                Microsoft 15.0.3.0
Canada Personal Health Information Act (PHIA) – Manitoba     Microsoft 15.0.3.0
U.K. Personal Information Online Code of Practice (PIOCP)    Microsoft 15.0.3.0
U.K. Data Protection Act                                     Microsoft 15.0.3.0
U.K. Privacy and Electronic Communications Regulations      Microsoft 15.0.3.0
U.K. Access to Medical Reports Act                          Microsoft 15.0.3.0
Japan Protection of Personal Information                     Microsoft 15.0.3.0
U.S. Health Insurance Act (HIPAA)                            Microsoft 15.0.3.0
France Data Protection Act                                   Microsoft 15.0.3.0
```

Creating Custom DLP Templates can be done with PowerShell or with an XML editor as there is no option to do so in the EAC. Whichever way the template is created it can be imported into Office 365 with PowerShell. The surprise here for anyone working with this on-premises is that in Office 365, this functionality has been removed from Exchange Online and is now only in the Security and Compliance Center.

Times have changed. The XML file is no longer something we can import into Exchange Online. With Microsoft's emphasis on the Security and Compliance Center and the de-emphasis of the crossover features in Exchange Online, this would seem to be a natural progression. If we attempt to connect to Exchange Online and import the new data type with the New-ClassificationRuleCollection, we see that this function has been neutered and unusable:

```
PS C:\> New-ClassificationRuleCollection -FileData ([Byte[]]$(Get-Content -Path "C:\_Technical\F
ormattedSSN.xml" -Encoding Byte -ReadCount 0))
Custom sensitive information types are now managed from the Security & Compliance Center
PowerShell using the New-DlpSensitiveInformationTypeRulePackage,
Set-DlpSensitiveInformationTypeRulePackage, Get-DlpSensitiveInformationTypeRulePackage, and
Remove-DlpSensitiveInformationTypeRulePackage cmdlets. Learn more at https://aka.ms/dlpcustomtypes.
    + CategoryInfo          : InvalidOperation: (:) [New-ClassificationRuleCollection], Classifica
```

So what to do? We need to connect PowerShell to the Security and Compliance Center. We need to run these three lines in PowerShell:

```
$LiveCred = Get-Credential
$Session = New-PSSession -ConfigurationName Microsoft.Exchange -ConnectionUri https://ps.compliance.protection.outlook.com/powershell-liveid/ -Credential $LiveCred -Authentication Basic -AllowRedirection
Import-PSSession $Session
```

```
PS C:\> $LiveCred = Get-Credential

cmdlet Get-Credential at command pipeline position 1
Supply values for the following parameters:
Credential

PS C:\> $Session = New-PSSession -ConfigurationName Microsoft.Exchange -ConnectionUri https://ps.compliance.prote
shell-liveid/ -Credential $LiveCred -Authentication Basic -AllowRedirection
WARNING: Your connection has been redirected to the following URI:
"https://nam05b.ps.compliance.protection.outlook.com/powershell-liveid?PSVersion=5.1.14409.1005 "
PS C:\temp\XMLScript> Import-PSSession $Session
WARNING: The names of some imported commands from the module 'tmp_t2zmsder.a1s' include unapproved verbs that migh
find the commands with unapproved verbs, run the Import-Module command again with the Verbose parameter. For a lis

ModuleType Version    Name                      ExportedCommands
---------- -------    ----                      ----------------
Script     1.0        tmp_t2zmsder.a1s          {Add-ComplianceCaseMember, Add-eDiscoveryCaseAdmin, Add-
```

Once connected to the Security and Compliance Center we can now check out how to do the same tasks we used to do in Exchange Online. First we can use the information from the error message to find the new cmdlets:

```
Get-Command *DlpSensitiveInformationType*
```

```
Name
----
Get-DlpSensitiveInformationType
Get-DlpSensitiveInformationTypeRulePackage
New-DlpSensitiveInformationTypeRulePackage
Remove-DlpSensitiveInformationTypeRulePackage
Set-DlpSensitiveInformationTypeRulePackage
```

So, now that we have the correct cmdlets, how do we add the data type in the new Security and Compliance Center?

```
Get-Help New-DlpSensitiveInformationTypeRulePackage -Examples
```

From the above example, we see that an XML file is needed in order to create/import a DLP Template into Exchange. Creating an XML file takes a bit of time and is somewhat complicated. These XML files can be created with a PowerShell script that has a series of questions. This script was written by one of the authors of the book and can be found here:

https://justaucguy.wordpress.com/2015/01/27/dlp-custom-xml-generation-script/

In practical terms, creating a one-off XML file is easier if you can use the Microsoft help and TechNet pages that are provided. Skipping forward, assuming an XML file has been created (BigBox-PII.XML) we can import the template using the example above for guidance.

```
$Directory = "C:\XmlScript\ConfidentialInformation.xml"
New-DlpSensitiveInformationTypeRulePackage -FileData ([Byte[]]$(Get-Content -Path $Directory -Encoding Byte -ReadCount 0))
```

Once the template is created, we can proceed to the creating of a DLP Policy based off of this template. There is no real limit to the number of templates that can be created. The advantage of a custom XML for a custom template is that a RegEx query can be used to query for custom criteria – bank account numbers, custom card numbers, etc. The process for DLP rules is the same from here on whether the XML file is a custom or predefined template.

DLP Policies

DLP policies are built off of either the built-in templates provided by Microsoft (see above) or custom templates like the one created in the example on this page. Transport Rules use DLP policies as matching criteria for SMTP messages traversing through Exchange Online. Pre-canned templates exist for more common data types (financial data for Canada, UK or the US).

Creating a new DLP Policy with PowerShell requires the 'New-DLPPolicy' cmdlet. Here is an example of the cmdlet:

```
Get-Help New-DlpPolicy –Examples
```

```
------------------------------ Example 1 ------------------------------

This example creates a new DLP policy named Contoso PII with the following values:

The DLP policy is enabled and set to audit only.

The DLP policy is based on the existing "U.S. Personally Identifiable Information (PII) Data"
DLP policy template.
New-DlpPolicy –Name "Contoso PII" -Template "U.S. Personally Identifiable Information (PII)
Data"
```

Other options that are available for configuring a new DLP Policy that should be considered are:

- **Mode <Audit | AuditAndNotify | Enforce>** - How the policy notifies the end users
- **State <Enabled | Disabled>** - Policies are enabled by default

Sample Policy creations of these two new DLP Policies will be based off of an existing Microsoft templates ("Japan Financial Data") and a template we created in the previous section ("Big Box PII"):

```
New-DlpPolicy -Name "Big Box Personal Info" -Template "Big Box PII"
New-DlpPolicy -Name "Japanese Subsidiary Finance Data" -Template "Japan Financial Data"
```

The Japanese DLP Policy did generate a notification when it was created:

```
WARNING: The rule contains NotifySender action with an option that may reject the message. In case
the message gets rejected, other actions won't be applied.
```

Once created, verifying the policies is the next step:

```
Get-DlpPolicy | ft -Auto
```

```
Name                                     Publisher      State    Mode
----                                     ---------      -----    ----
Japanese Subsidiary Finance Data Microsoft              Enabled  Audit
Big Box PII                              Data Big Box   Enabled  Audit
```

Now there are two DLP policies that can be called by Transport Rules to affect messages that meet the policy's criteria.

Policy Tips

Policy Tips are like any other Exchange Tips (MailTips is one example) that provide a visual indicator of a problem or something that the end user (the message sender) should be aware of. DLP Policy Tips will work in either Outlook or OWA. For Outlook, make sure that the latest version of Outlook 2013 or 2016 are used in order to get the most out of the tips. Outlook can cache DLP information and any changes that are made may show up immediately. Previous versions of Outlook do not work with Policy Tips, nor a standalone installation of Outlook.

** **Note** ** Policy tips do not work if the full Office Suite is also not installed. Standalone Outlook will not work with Policy Tips - https://support.microsoft.com/en-us/kb/2823263.

With regards to PowerShell and Policy Tips, the wording of the tip can be customized and the tip can be turned on or off depending on the scenario. For example, a DLP Policy, tied to a Transport Rule that looks for sensitive data, can be flagged for 'Testing with no Policy Tips'. To configure the rule, we need to look at options for this rule ('mode' parameter):

```
Get-Help Set-TransportRule –Full
```

```
-Mode <Audit | AuditAndNotify | Enforce>
    The Mode parameter specifies in which mode this rule will operate. Valid values include:

    * Audit The rule is turned on, and what would have happened if the rule was enforced is
      logged in message tracking logs. Exchange doesn't take any action that impacts the
      delivery of the message.
    * AuditAndNotify The rule is turned on, and it operates the same way it would in Audit
      mode, but notifications are also enabled.
    * Enforce The rule is turned on, and all actions specified in the rule are taken.
    The default value is Enforce.

    Required?                    false
    Position?                    Named
    Default value
    Accept pipeline input?       False
```

Using the switch '-Mode Audit' and no Policy Tips would be visible to the end user. For either '-Mode AuditAnd-Notify' or '-Mode Enforce', policy tips would be visible in the mail client if a message matches the rule (and the associated DLP Policy). Policy Tips can also be customized. If, instead of the pre-canned tips, there is a need for a custom message for end users, these can be done with PowerShell. First, what cmdlets are available:

```
Get-Command *PolicyTip*

CommandType     Name
-----------     ----
Function        Get-PolicyTipConfig
Function        New-PolicyTipConfig
Function        Remove-PolicyTipConfig
Function        Set-PolicyTipConfig
```

First, we start with what is already configured for Policy Tips:

```
Get-PolicyTipConfig
```

As expected, no results are to be found. We will need to create our own set of Policy Tips to notify end users with these custom messages.

```
Get-Help New-PolicyTipConfig –Examples
```

The most important parameter is '-Value' as it determines what the end message will be provided to the end user. Notice that the second example provides a URL for the end user. This might be more appropriate if there is a fully fleshed out policy for these restricted attachments or PII. When creating a new Policy Tip, the name of the tip needs to reference two criteria: the locale and the action to be performed. A working example for the English language would be:

```
-Name "en\NotifyOnly"
```

If for example the wrong name is chosen, then a lot of errors are generated:

```
Name must be in the form locale\action where action can be: "zh-CHS, en, fr, de, ja, zh-CHT, it,
ko, pt, ru, es, ar, cs, da, nl, fi, el, he, hu, no, pl, pt-PT, sv, tr, ro, th, fil-PH, hi, id, lv,
ms, uk, vi, bg, hr, et, lt, sr, sk, sl, eu, ca, zh-HK, fa, gl, is, kk, sr-Cyrl-CS, ur, af, sq,
am-ET, hy, as-IN, bn-IN, bn-BD, bs-Cyrl-BA, bs-Latn-BA, ka, gu, ha-Latn-NG, ig-NG, iu-Latn-CA,
ga-IE, xh-ZA, zu-ZA, kn, km-KH, qut-GT, rw-RW, sw, kok, ky, lo-LA, lb-LU, mk, ms-BN, ml-IN, mt-MT,
mi-NZ, mr, ne-NP, nn-NO, or-IN, ps-AF, pa, quz-PE, nso-ZA, tn-ZA, si-LK, ta, tt, te, uz, cy-GB,
wo-SN, yo-NG" and locale can be: "NotifyOnly, RejectOverride, Reject, Url". If action is URL,
then name must be "Url" with no locale.
    + CategoryInfo          : InvalidArgument: (:) [New-PolicyTipConfig], NewPolicyTipConfigInvali
   dNameException
    + FullyQualifiedErrorId : [Server=CY4PR13MB1350,RequestId=f270388e-bd26-463b-bd99-e68cd8c6ba60
   ,TimeStamp=1/12/2018 5:52:01 AM] [FailureCategory=Cmdlet-NewPolicyTipConfigInvalidNameExceptio
   n] 899BB49D,Microsoft.Exchange.Management.PolicyNudges.NewPolicyTipConfig
    + PSComputerName        : ps.outlook.com
```

A complete cmdlet would look like this:

```
New-PolicyTipConfig -Name en\NotifyOnly -Value 'This message contains private information that should not be shared outside of this company.'
```

To verify the cmdlet worked:

```
Get-PolicyTipConfig | ft –Auto
```

```
Identity       Value
--------       -----
en\NotifyOnly This message contains private information that should not be shared outside of thi...
```

Other possible actions are RejectOverride and Reject. Reject will block the message completely whereas RejectOverride allows for an override if the user puts "Override" in the subject line of the message.

New-PolicyTipConfig -Name en\RejectOverride -Value 'This message contains private information that should not be shared outside of this company.'

Document Fingerprinting

DLP's Document Fingerprinting feature allows for DLP to search for very specific content that is sent through e-mail, in this case a matching attachment. The fingerprint is basically a hash of the properties of the document in question. The document itself is not stored in Exchange. Outlook will also evaluate a document locally and the document is not sent over the wire between Exchange and Outlook. The process is similar to creating a template, with the source being a document to import. Then build Transport Rules around the document to restrict, allow or log when a rule processes the e-mail. Below is a scenario which will provide a better idea as to what can be done with this, and what PowerShell can provide.

Scenario

HR has some confidential forms that are to be used internally by the company. They've provided IT with three forms that need to prevent from being emailed to anyone external to the organization. First, place a copy of the document on the Exchange server so that it can be imported for creating the DLP Policy. Any form or document to be 'fingerprinted' should be blank so that no information interferes with the evaluation.

For PowerShell cmdlets, start with Get-Content (used to store the file in a variable) and then use New-FingerPrint to create the fingerprint based off the content from the Get-Content variable. Follow this by creating a new Data Classification to be used by Transport Rules later.

There are three forms to be protected:

- EmployeePII-Form.docx
- Employee-Review-2016.docx
- Termination-RequestForm.docx

Next, store the document content in a variable in preparation for Transport Rules to use the content. Let's walk through the process of taking these documents and creating Transport Rules to handle them:

Import each individual document into a separate variable to be used by New-Fingerprint:

```
$HRDoc1 = Get-Content "C:\Documents\HR\EmployeePII-Form.docx" -Encoding Byte
$HRDoc2 = Get-Content "C:\Documents\HR\Employee-Review-2016.docx" -Encoding Byte
$HRDoc3 = Get-Content "C:\Documents\HR\Termination-RequestForm.docx" -Encoding Byte
```

Notice that the documents are encoded as a 'byte' type document. According to the help file on the 'Get-Help' cmdlet, there are a few data types that can be used:

ASCII, BigEndianUnicode, Byte, String, Unicode, UTF7, UTF8 and Unknown.

In choosing a Word document (which is a binary file) we need to choose 'byte' for the encoding to properly ingest the hash from the file. The 'Get-Content' cmdlet does have other parameters, but for the purposes of fingerprinting itself, no others are required. Simply put in a location of the file and what encoding to use for the document for fingerprinting and store that in a variable.

Create a fingerprint based off the document stored in each variable:

    $HRDoc1_Fingerprint = New-Fingerprint -FileData $HRDoc1 -Description "Employee PII Form"
    $HRDoc2_Fingerprint = New-Fingerprint -FileData $HRDoc2 -Description "Employee Review 2016"
    $HRDoc3_Fingerprint = New-Fingerprint -FileData $HRDoc3 -Description "Termination Request Form"

** No cmdlet can query Fingerprints that were created, to see the fingerprints raw data, you can simply 'dump' the variable contents to the PowerShell window:

    $HRDoc1_Fingerprint | fl


```
Description   : Employee PII Form
ShingleCount  : 20
Value         : fz382n/99+z//vdfsu/9Rv/G3/7G+vZT11Pu/v/v+//F2s9v/td9//X6sxN/dtfbz6rv3v/+9fy6U9f8W/9/9v/+3sr9xsf7+2d/Xt/P
                919/bM+K/7//3ePvktyX/cff/3f3/H92/Preiu/+3/N//XXs/27v3vrX/ftdW39O/leb//9275517ebj375/+/5ff17/9/
                x8f9TtX7f/9u/etv/7//b9b6//67F+7e//5/7LP9f7//3vt37/p5f+fvs1/v//GTH//rd38919/v7v/Mf/7v/v6q1s3//+
                vv3o/fvur/n3/+dTz67039bc1/qf/7r+v/P/TnHs0u377/3m3/9//PbM5do6/c76f+7+yu93j9/XvN3bk9w7////72//619
                Pf3v///6//uyv10x00z+Xn87Nrv7vXe3fydF3/c/qrb3X9//1eP//3eu+z/9n/M17x/f8//58/T7H/+vn/W+ut/7+fUuH
                9kP37Kn991P7U++eD//7/M7j3md97O/PxueW738//e78f924y91//n897293/P3/xdrbW/1W/e5/v5NT//992/+azPr/35n
                3Nrv/v/P5uudX3/978//vf6q5sO58+vn+uzPR/9DxPrde7pf996P+f3u+//ez/vX/1/9U+36//9/259/+9fu+s///Z/Tv/
                S/99/tf8n9/rZ61919/P+u/v//6zy/Hu5fvnZ3//79//37vff/7nzcb6/e9/f/Zjf27vzrl/f04f/85/z80/2eba8u7WR+
                uzus/392/Wb/ulv/9ez/3jr/3pr9Vv//x97/995D7//T7P9b/z//XLOT9szr6btfj/9r/+/Oc+7z7Nza/frfy8Tf/z0b/1
                3bx/v/+T7+9/TN3b19P/7n/97fr/dv/u+//3/7Eb2/3HQ7WX0+3jzZ79e//P95L/eP2+/9/78zfevszfo+m23PTa/+7Hd3
                vlefy+9/++9/396KrH/90//0f/z/9/9+nRvrycP572//fn/9z8rr5+h9bX/9RvW4zd77d+ZDj//fvJ/df/z9bv/e/f7d+/
                78//Rtv/f1v/zN7e/Nov//3b7n33x3///vqj+8+eff3/Z/H8/87+9837a//uitEX785L/9/bf37/ftMzS///fLvL/3+67n3
                +/79/+/ut8u+3//76v//X/+///3/Pf38nv1fW/t//mf/91/77u792/175sf/3p3z/vv02sZH/fp/v/f//1//vdvM+3/Pr3
                ffz/+Gv/8/n/9rpf9/z/zu/9fv+r/7Gzf3bN+v7+f+y9U/f3f//t+9NT+3fHb//+c+x7/Z/Jf73Z1/9mPH39dv/O37f/ftX83/vv73/s
                t+/9Rv73/dv9//7//3fvut/HxN/9z5r93d7//s/+/3z/d/d70/3r79db+vf/dv92795/P+/6v/uU2/v/17x/fv/T5/p/e8v/x/r75/93
                /Uv1/P9v/33P6Wr/783//+vn3/razObP/fj7/7Pb/Xab7ubLf7/3H//e/97/f37/t9x/9vvf+///R978//b/dv/+/h/b50bxtrc/vtv
                txd/9tz/zpre3+/P/r5/P8za31t/9/O38+/v/2/9/6r/9+76+t+r/33/3+rfb8f6+99/duvv3o77dx//1/zHzfp3+te613/9bzzkz/
                /opu/f/b7/f//O/n1xPU2n9/f3399k//3nt/7s//u937/X93f35z7P7a++zf+Pz/9fz/7n/+/Ufv/1//1tt/PXv/y//v/75/z/++397L
                f9y//97b/2y+f8/ae/30vlv///9////078706n9c//9//iz/8e6RG9+e+/+T+wv/v8uTX//bmXv/7t/bd/7/bu/O+2f91v/+u/fn2197
                t9n2zPbz/XuDyZ/Nf37vzvTaL///3v/Pa/9/zn97rX27/P/2x/uv/75f//bUvP24z8p/f/66f261n+99/fzf+y/9fz1/H/2/3/9+/v8
                /73Pnvv/1N//zF//72f//dX83fvu38/0f8zv76Ptk/zn359zxt7f7v3sfz3/P3/+f/b3/n9M//7/fn/9j+vP+g//29vX+v
                37h/PWr9j9nxv95Lf///7t6us1v/f///+H39Un99dfzW3vtnff7/d50f/2zvb/9H7+/7/1v///+7//X6/9z/d+Tf7+7fi/z9v5N//3vu
                dez//v9Xvv/9dn+9++99/MbH7frPyrObqn1//dT/97/7e3/+08+6d5P5//zeyu/Ok937/5Le/33vf+/Oz5p/fs+uf3723v/ef25/++/u
                19x//P5H19+737/XS///7t/M6+/1+/n9av272Xfu9v/zzfPs/+//zv//xuPd2n/vi/r//9Xf37fn99bt5f//+/ef/v91v9nj//9+Prf
                ++fr5/9v/2e5+/nsq//vzvf+51f3M9be3t730/T/0+n/Zvtfa/+off7b+v/9U3v//3/9Rvt//45/f3+9P/29/87n+1/03/1unbOf////
                f7/e24vrtvz+///e9v/dvP98///Pjv7qkft//P3m7s6D2f9//3z/f19b1t+Us3/s/39/v87Hf/64//9/f96610//8v7v9/9u/+a3F/9G
                79//9n9fdex/W/7f///eQ1/b93c=
```


The New-Fingerprint cmdlet has even less options than the Get-Content cmdlet and examples from the cmdlet use only the two parameters chosen above – FileData and Description. FileData references the document stored in the variable.

Now that the Fingerprint has been created, it can be used by the New-DataClassification cmdlet to create a data classification for a Transport Rule:

    New-DataClassification -Name "HR Confidential Form 1" -Fingerprints $HRDoc1_Fingerprint
    -Description "Message contains confidential employee information."

    New-DataClassification -Name "HR Confidential Form 2" -Fingerprints $HRDoc2_Fingerprint
    -Description "Message contains confidential employee information."

    New-DataClassification -Name "HR Confidential Form 3" -Fingerprints $HRDoc3_Fingerprint
    -Description "Message contains confidential employee information."

The New-DataClassification cmdlet can be used to create individual classifications or it can group multiple Fingerprints together into one classification as the parameter used for this is 'Fingerprints' not 'Fingerprint'. Make sure to separate multiple Fingerprints with a comma.

    ** **Note** ** Document Fingerprints can also be added to existing data classifications using the Set-DataClassification cmdlet and the –Fingerprints parameter:

    Set-DataClassification -Name "HR Confidential Form 3" -FingerPrints $HRDoc3_Fingerprint

To verify the Fingerprints were successful in being converted to an Exchange Data Classifications, run the following:

Get-DataClassification

```
Name                                    LocalizedName                           Publisher               ClassificationType
----                                    -------------                           ---------               ------------------
Croatia Identity Card Number            Croatia Identity Card Number            Microsoft Corporation               Entity
Czech National Identity Card Number     Czech National Identity Card Number     Microsoft Corporation               Entity
Greece National ID Card                 Greece National ID Card                 Microsoft Corporation               Entity
South Africa Identification Number      South Africa Identification Number      Microsoft Corporation               Entity
HR Confidential Form 1                  HR Confidential Form 1                   16-TAP                         Fingerprint
HR Confidential Form 2                  HR Confidential Form 2                   16-TAP                         Fingerprint
HR Confidential Form 3                  HR Confidential Form 3                   16-TAP                         Fingerprint
```

Notice the header fields of Invariant Name, Localized Name, Publisher and Classification Type. The other Data Classification entries show the Publisher to be Microsoft and the Classification Type to be Entity. Can we change ours to something more meaningful? First, what other cmdlets are available for Data Classifications:

Get-Command *DataClass*

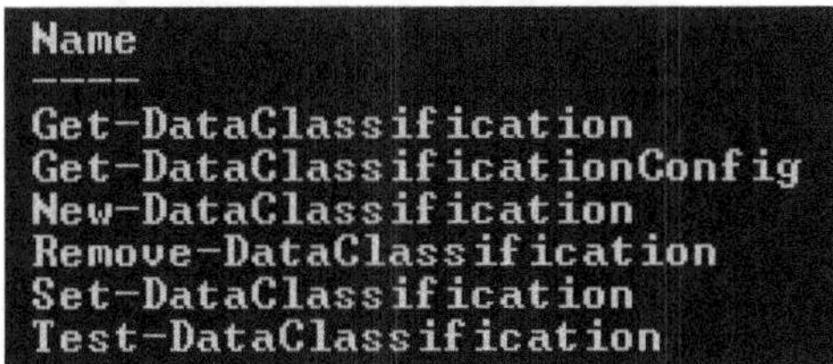

```
Name
----
Get-DataClassification
Get-DataClassificationConfig
New-DataClassification
Remove-DataClassification
Set-DataClassification
Test-DataClassification
```

Upon reviewing the parameters for these cmdlets reveals that this cannot be changed. The Classification type is set once a Fingerprint is used. The publisher simply matches the name of the server it was created on.

Continuing on the Fingerprints are created and stored as new Data Classifications. This Data Classification can be used by a Transport Rule to block these emails (and their attachments) from leaving Exchange.

New-TransportRule -Name 'Notify :External Recipient BigBox confidential' -RejectMessageReasonText 'This file is restricted and may not be emailed outside the company.' -NotifySender $Null -Mode Enforce -SentToScope NotInOrganization -MessageContainsDataClassification @{Name=' HR Confidential Form 1'}

New-TransportRule -Name 'Notify :External Recipient BigBox confidential #2' -RejectMessageReasonText 'This file is restricted and may not be emailed outside the company.' -NotifySender $Null -Mode Enforce -SentToScope NotInOrganization -MessageContainsDataClassification @{Name=' HR Confidential Form 2'}

New-TransportRule -Name 'Notify :External Recipient BigBox confidential #3' -RejectMessageReasonText 'This file is restricted and may not be emailed outside the company.' -NotifySender $Null -Mode Enforce -SentToScope NotInOrganization -MessageContainsDataClassification @{Name=' HR Confidential Form 3'}

Verify Transport Rules were created:

Get-TransportRule

```
Name                                            State     Mode      Priority  Comments
----                                            -----     ----      --------  --------
Notify :External Recipient BigBox confide...    Enabled   Enforce   3
Notify :External Recipient BigBox confide...    Enabled   Enforce   4
Notify :External Recipient BigBox confide...    Enabled   Enforce   5
```

How does this work in practice? First, a message created in OWA is created with one of the three HR documents attached and addresses to an external recipient:

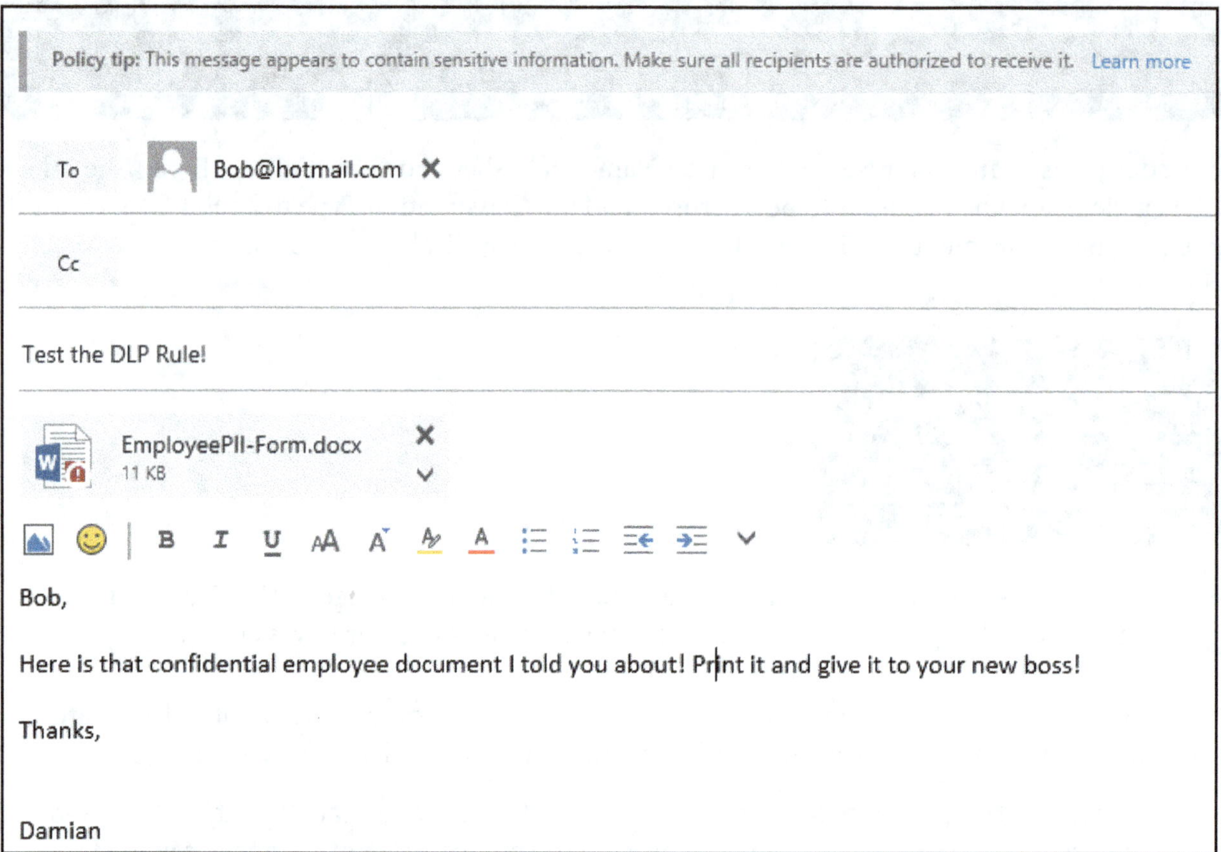

Notice the Policy Tip at the top of the email as well as the fact that the document itself has a red exclamation point to indicate that it has been recognized by its content. If a user is unsure why this is occurring, there is a 'Learn More' button at the top which provides this tidbit (as well as an option for feedback). The option shown is based on which Action was chosen in the Policy Tip.

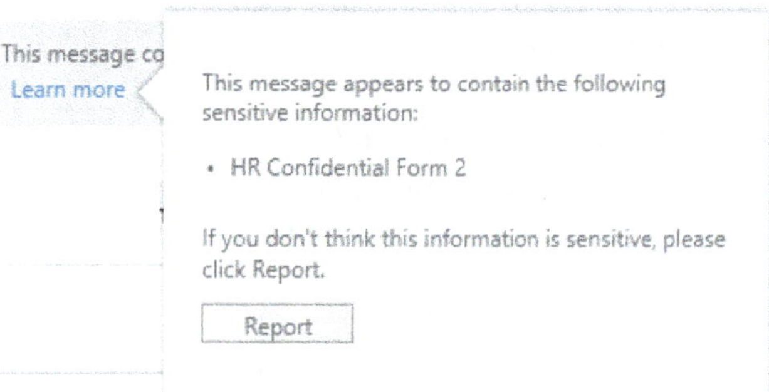

After the message is sent, an NDR is generated:

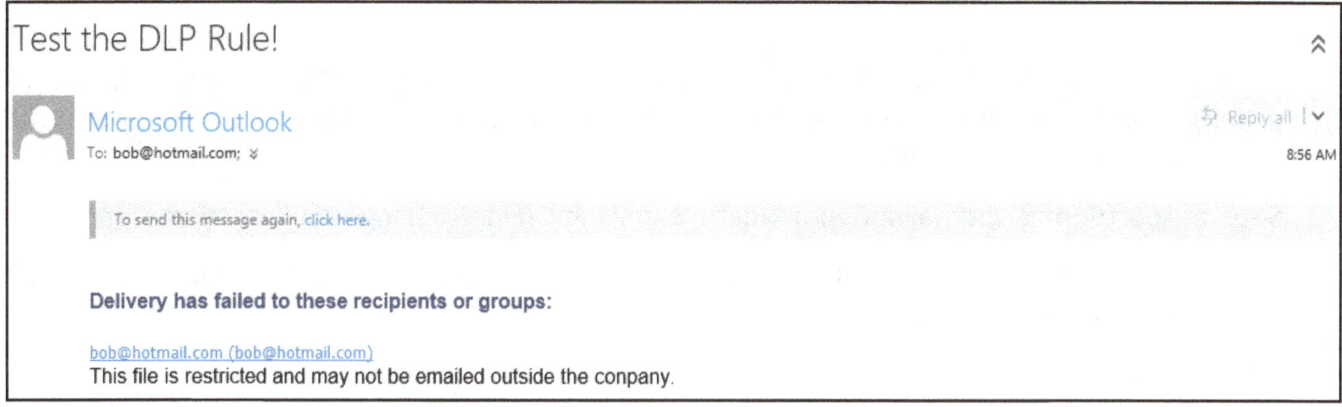

Going back to PowerShell, how can these DLP flagged messages be tracked? There are three cmdlets that may be of use to us:

```
Get-DlpDetailReport
Get-DlpDetectionsReport
Get-DlpIncidentDetailReport
```

What other ways can the Document Fingerprinting feature be used? Maybe in a set of documents that should never leave HR or be sent in email or some intellectual property documents (patent forms) that should never leave R&D or never even be sent through email. These scenarios can also be controlled via the Document Fingerprinting feature. Each scenario should be created with its own unique fingerprint, data classification and Transport Rules to keep track of each particular scenario in a company. This will make troubleshooting much easier if issues or discrepancies occur (document is updated or message is or is not delivered).

Journaling

Journaling is the process of making a copy of an email and storing it in a location routed via an email address. A message can be journaled to a local database or an external service. Either method is supported using the Journaling Rule cmdlets below. Messages can be journaled for compliance or for business continuity. Business continuity is one of the features external services tote as a reason to use their product.

**** Note ** Journaling in Office 365 must use an external recipient.**

PowerShell

For journaling, a small subset of cmdlets is available for managing Journal Rules in Exchange Server 2016:

```
Get-Command *journ*
```

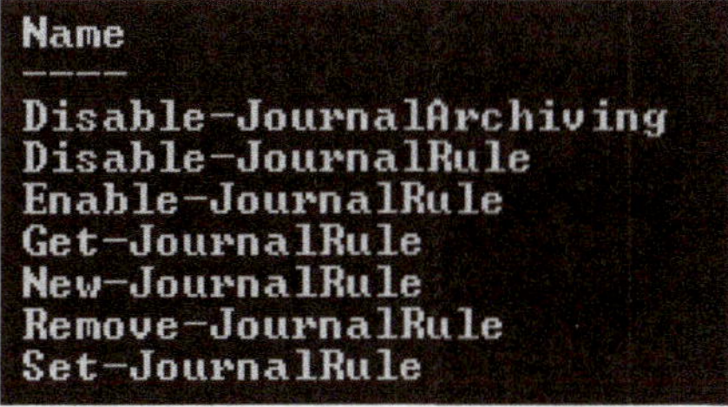

By default, there are no Journal rules configured by default which can be confirmed by running 'Get-JournalRule' in a new Exchange Server environment.

** **Note** ** Before a Journal Rule is creates, we also need to configure where Non-Delivery Reports (NDR) go for Journal reports that cannot be delivered to their destination. This setting can be configured with the 'Set-TransportConfig' cmdlet like so:

Set-TransportConfig -JournalingReportNdrTo 'damian@OnlineExchangeBook.onmicrosoft.com'

Now we can begin exploring PowerShell Journaling, create some Journaling rules using the 'New-JournalRule' cmdlet. See below for an example:

New-JournalRule

Commonly Used Options

JournalEmailAddress - The recipient address of the journaled message (external only)
Name - Name of the new Journal Rule
Enabled <$True | $False> - Whether the rule is enabled or not
Recipient <SmtpAddress>
Scope <Internal | External | Global>
- Global - Global rules process all email messages that pass through a Transport service.
- This includes email messages that were already processed by the external and internal rules.
- Internal - Internal rules process email messages sent to and received by recipients in your organization.
- External - External rules process email messages sent to recipients or from senders outside your organization.

Sample One-Liner

New-JournalRule -Name "CFO Journaling" -JournalEmailAddress "BigBoxJournal@ThirdPartyDomain.Com" -Recipient SeanSmith@BigBox.Com -Enabled $True

```
Name                 : CFO Journaling
Recipient            : SeanSmith@BigBox.Com
JournalEmailAddress  : BigBoxJournal@ThirdPartyDomain.Com
Scope                : Global
Enabled              : True
```

Example Usage

As the email administrator of the legal department determined that with a new implementation of Exchange Online, all messages need to be journaled. The reason for the Journaling is to comply with the current government regulations for email retention.

New-JournalRule -Name "All Messages" -JournalEmailAddress "BigBoxJournal@ThirdPartyDomain.Com" -Scope Global -Enabled $True

```
Name                 : All Messages
Recipient            :
JournalEmailAddress  : BigBoxJournal@ThirdPartyDomain.Com
Scope                : Global
Enabled              : True
```

Script Scenario

You work for a company with 12,000 users. There are offices all over the world with major concentrations of users in the US and Europe. There are different compliance requirements for the different regions.

All the users from Europe need to be journaled for new compliance regulations, separate from current archiving and business continuity of the US branch. The users are in three different countries and the legal department wants each group to be journaled to a country specific journaling provider - one for each country. Your IT manager wants separate rules and a way to track the configuration. HR provides a complete list of users to help verify that the correct employees are being journaled.

Here are the steps that need to be taken in order to make this possible:

- Configure a recipient to receive NDRs that could potentially be generated if the journaled message is not delivered
- Identify users with the correct CustomAttribute1 value based on their country
- Create a Journal rule for the particular country and use the group created in the previous step

The creation of the group is critical because the rules use that as a basic for determining which users to journal where.

CSV File Format

```
Mailbox,CustomAttribute
Damian,1
DStork,2
TestUser01,3
TUser02,1
```

Script

First we need to create some Dynamic Distribution Groups so that we can apply the Journal Rules for everyone in that group:

```
# Create Dynamic list of users and a Journal Rule that uses that group
New-DynamicDistributionGroup -Name GermanyJournaling -RecipientFilter {(CustomAttribute1 -eq "1")}
$Smtp = ((Get-DynamicDistributionGroup GermanyJournaling).PrimarySmtpAddress).Address

New-JournalRule -Name "Journaling for Germany mailboxes" -JournalEmailAddress "Journaling-Germany" -Scope Global -Recipient $Smtp -Enabled $True

# Create Dynamic list of users and a Journal Rule that uses that group
New-DynamicDistributionGroup -Name ItalyJournaling -RecipientFilter {(CustomAttribute1 -eq "2")}
$Smtp = ((Get-DynamicDistributionGroup ItalyJournaling).PrimarySmtpAddress).Address
```

```
New-JournalRule -Name "Journaling for Italy mailboxes" -JournalEmailAddress "Journaling-Italy"
-Scope Global -Recipient $Smtp -Enabled $True

# Create Dynamic list of users and a Journal Rule that uses that group
New-DynamicDistributionGroup -Name PolandJournaling -RecipientFilter {(CustomAttribute1 -eq "3")}
$Smtp = ((Get-DynamicDistributionGroup PolandJournaling).PrimarySmtpAddress).Address

New-JournalRule -Name "Journaling for Poland mailboxes" -JournalEmailAddress "Journaling-Poland"
-Scope Global -Recipient $smtp -Enabled $True
```

Sample Output

```
Name                        : Journaling for Germany mailboxes
Recipient                   :
JournalEmailAddress         : Journaling-Germany-BigCorp@theexternalhoster.com
Scope                       : Global
Enabled                     : True
```

With the above setup, any email that goes to a user who is in the Dynamic Distribution List for a particular country will have their messages journaled to a external journaling provider for their locality.

Journaling Verification

Now that the Journaling is in place, how can we verify that Journaling is working as expected? There are a few places where we can verify the proper operation of the Journaling setup can be verified – contents of the Journaling mailbox (check with the external hosting service), Message Trace or Mailbox Statistics:

Message Trace

Following in the footsteps of Chapter 10, a review of message traces can provide information on how many messages are getting delivered to a Journaling mailbox like so:

```
Get-Messagetrace-StartDate3/1/18-EndDate3/9/18|where{$_.SenderAddress-like'MicrosoftExchange*'}
| ft Received,SenderAddress,Subject,Status
```

** **Note** ** Like a lot of queries in Exchange, using the correct date format is important. The date is in the US format of MM/DD/YY. If another format is used like YY/MM/DD, an error message will be generated:

```
Cannot process argument transformation on parameter 'StartDate'. Cannot convert value "18/2/3" to type
"System.DateTime". Error: "String was not recognized as a valid DateTime."
    + CategoryInfo          : InvalidData: (:) [Get-MessageTrace], ParameterBindin...mationException
    + FullyQualifiedErrorId : ParameterArgumentTransformationError,Get-MessageTrace
    + PSComputerName        : ps.outlook.com
```

A successful search will generate these results:

```
Received             Sender Address                                                              Subject          Status
--------             --------------                                                              -------          ------
3/6/2018 7:16:11 AM MicrosoftExchange329e71ec88ae4615bbc36ab6ce41109e@ExchangeOnlineBook.onmicrosoft.com Design Document Delivered
3/6/2018 7:15:41 AM MicrosoftExchange329e71ec88ae4615bbc36ab6ce41109e@ExchangeOnlineBook.onmicrosoft.com Client Needs    Delivered
3/6/2018 7:11:54 AM MicrosoftExchange329e71ec88ae4615bbc36ab6ce41109e@ExchangeOnlineBook.onmicrosoft.com test journaling Delivered
```

Reporting on Journaling Rules

Knowing what rules are in place can be important if there is a need to troubleshoot a Journaling process, especially if there is an external product or process that is analyzing these messages. Understanding what destination email address is being used to journal for what recipient(s). 'Get-JournalRule' is the cmdlet to provide the needed information:

```
Get-JournalRule | ft Name, JournalEmailAddress, Scope, Enabled –Auto
```

```
Name                          JournalEmailAddress                                  Scope   Enabled
----                          -------------------                                  -----   -------
Journaling for Germany mailboxes Journaling-Germany-BigCorp@TheExternalHoster.Com  Global  True
Journaling for Italy mailboxes   Journaling-Italy-BigCorp@IT-Journaling.Com        Global  True
Journaling for Poland mailboxes  Journaling-Poland-BigCorp@SMTP-Jounrnal.Com       Global  True
```

Disabling Rules

Why disable a Journaling Rule? Normally the disabling of Journaling Rules is done when the original need has past or a new rule needs to be created or if a different destination server or to who to journal. The Disable-Journal cmdlet is the cmdlet for the job. First we need to use the Get-JournalRule on the rule to be disabled and then pipe '|' that journal rule to the 'Disable-JournalRule' cmdlet:

```
Get-JournalRule "Journaling for Germany mailboxes" | Disable-JournalRule
```

```
Confirm
Are you sure you want to perform this action?
Disabling journal rule "Journaling for Germany mailboxes".
[Y] Yes  [A] Yes to All  [N] No  [L] No to All  [?] Help (default is "Y"): y
```

After disabling the rule, verify that the rule is disabled:

```
Get-JournalRule
```

```
Name                : Journaling for Germany mailboxes
Recipient           :
JournalEmailAddress : Journaling-Germany-BigCorp@theExternalHoster.com
Scope               : Global
Enabled             : False
```

Enabled is now set to 'False'.

If the rule needs to be re-enabled, simply use the same process as the Disable-JournalRule:

```
Get-JournalRule "Journaling for Germany mailboxes" | Enable-JournalRule
```

This cmdlet does not provide any feedback, only by running Get-JournalRule will you be able to verify if the rule is enabled again.

Removing Rules

Removing a rule is similar to disabling the Journaling Rule – use the Get-JournalRule and pass that information along to the Remove-JournalRule:

```
Get-JournalRule "Journaling for Germany mailboxes" | Remove-JournalRule
```

```
Confirm
Are you sure you want to perform this action?
Removing journal rule "Journaling for Germany mailboxes".
[Y] Yes  [A] Yes to All  [N] No  [L] No to All  [?] Help (default is "Y"): y
```

Azure Information Protection

Rights Management in Exchange 2016 relies on Active Directory Right Management Services (ADRMS) as an additional security feature that can be added. Exchange refers to RMS as Information Rights Services or IRM.

Rights Management for Exchange Online is now known as Azure Information Protection (AIP). For the customer, Exchange Online and AIP do not require any physical servers, just licensing is needed to activate scenarios. In this scenario we need to turn on a few items, configure some settings and then we'll be able to start working with the Rights Management service and protect emails that pass through Exchange Online.

Rights Management - this is the general concept of protecting messages sent from Exchange (online or on-premises) to external or internal recipients and controlling what actions can be performed on the messages. These actions could include encrypting the messages, prevent the message from being forwarded or

Azure Information Protection (AIP) - AIP is the Office 365 iteration of Rights Management and it can be applied to Exchange Online messaging. In addition, we can also configure AIP to apply templates and rules against other workloads in Office 365.

As we review AIP and Exchange Online, you will see references to older terminology like IRM for PowerShell cmdlets. Just remember that the end goal is to protect emails within Exchange Online.

First, we need to enable the Rights Management feature in our tenant. This feature is off by default and enabling it will open up a couple of features being discussed in this chapter - Azure Information Protection and Office 365 Message Encryption.

In order to enable this feature we need to perform a few steps:

(1) Enable Rights Management

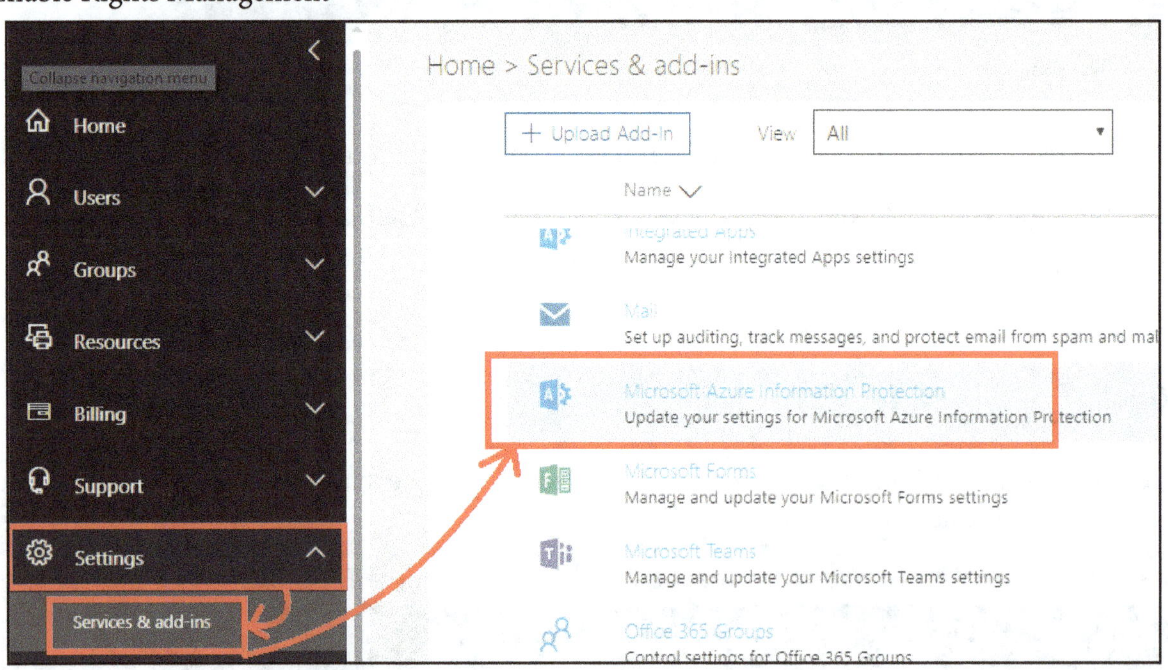

Once we pull up Azure Information Protection, we get a small window to the right:

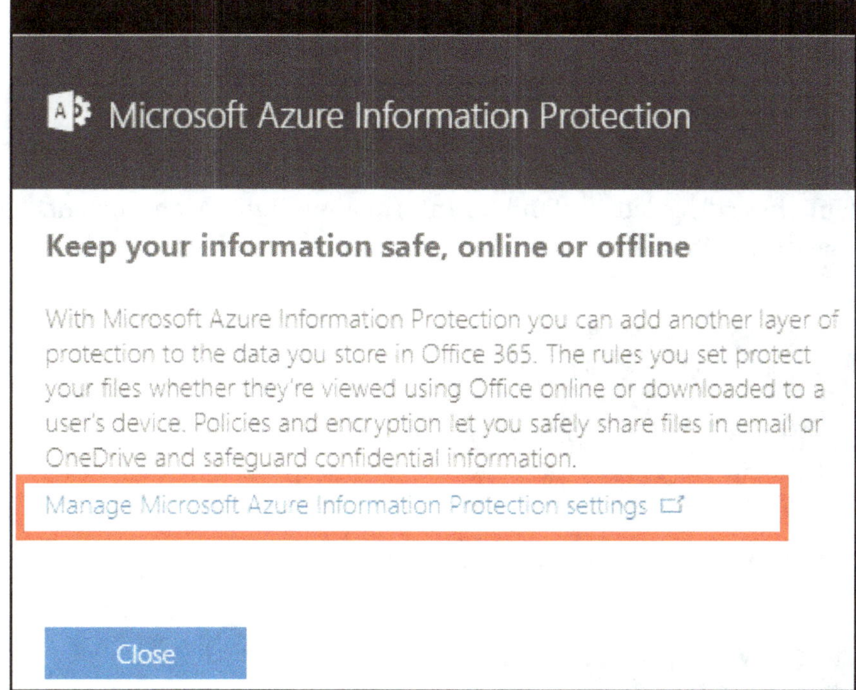

This link will then take us to your Azure Portal and specifically to the Rights Management controls:

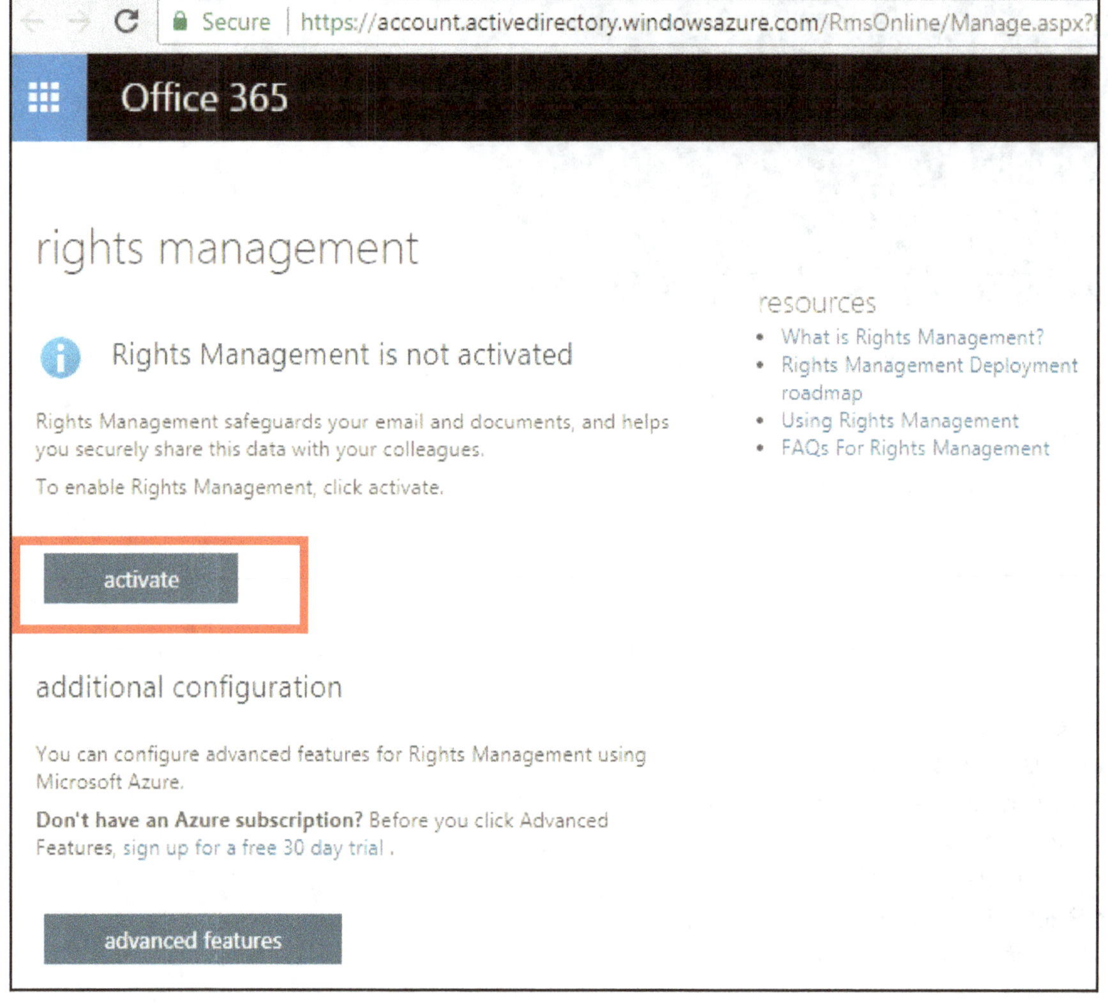

For Information Protection we should also log into our Windows Azure portal to enable the Azure Information Protection feature. Once we have our tenant prepared we can dive into the PowerShell side of AIP.

PowerShell

First, in Exchange Online, we have some cmdlets that we can use to verify the Rights Management configuration. We'll start with cmdlets with 'IRM' in them, these three letters stand for Information Rights Management. As we'll see below, there are only three cmdlets that deal with this feature.

Get-Command *irm*

```
CommandType          Name
-----------          ----
Alias                irm -> Invoke-RestMethod
Function             Get-IRMConfiguration
Function             Set-IRMConfiguration
Function             Test-IRMConfiguration
```

From the above, we will explore the current IRM configuration in Exchange Online:

Get-IRMConfiguration

```
InternalLicensingEnabled           : False
ExternalLicensingEnabled           : True
AzureRMSLicensingEnabled           : False
TransportDecryptionSetting         : Optional
JournalReportDecryptionEnabled     : True
SimplifiedClientAccessEnabled      : False
ClientAccessServerEnabled          : True
SearchEnabled                      : True
EDiscoverySuperUserEnabled         : True
RMSOnlineKeySharingLocation        :
RMSOnlineVersion                   :
ServiceLocation                    :
PublishingLocation                 :
LicensingLocation                  : {}
```

Notice that by default that IRM is enabled for client access on the Exchange server. However notice that only External Licensing is enabled and that the IRM configuration is not published. Below is a list of parameters that can be configured for IRM:

Get-Help Set-IRMConfiguration -Full

Parameters

ClientAccessServerEnabled <$true | $false> - this option turns on IRM for OWA and ActiveSync
Confirm [<SwitchParameter>]
DomainController <Fqdn>
EDiscoverySuperUserEnabled <$true | $false> -
ExternalLicensingEnabled <$true | $false> - enable or disable IRM for messages sent to external recipients
Force <SwitchParameter>
InternalLicensingEnabled <$true | $false> -
JournalReportDecryptionEnabled <$true | $false>
LicensingLocation <MultiValuedProperty>

```
PublishingLocation <Uri>
RefreshServerCertificates <SwitchParameter>
RMSOnlineKeySharingLocation <Uri>
SearchEnabled <$true | $false>
TransportDecryptionSetting <Disabled | Optional | Mandatory>
```

When further customizing the IRM configuration, the following setting should also be considered:

eDiscoverySuperUserEnabled – If this is set to true, users with eDiscovery privileges can access IRM protected emails.
SearchEnabled – On by default, it enables OWA to search for IRM messages.
InternalLicensingEnabled – Allows for the use of RMS on internal emails.
JournalReportDecryptionEnabled – If journaling is present in Exchange, any IRM messages that are journaled have an unencrypted copy stored with the Journal message.

For a scenario where internal messages should be protected by IRM and legal needs to perform legal discovery on emails that are IRM protected, the IRM configuration should be updated like so:

```
Set-IRMConfiguration –eDiscoverySuperUserEnabled $True –InternalLicensingEnabled $True
```

Once configured, RMS is ready to use internally and templates and configuration within RMS should be configured. Both internal and external licensing can be enabled in the same configuration if need be.

```
Set-IRMConfiguration -InternalLicensingEnabled $True -ExternalLicensingEnabled $False
```

In addition to configuring the IRM settings, the same settings can be tested / verified using the Test-IRMConfiguration cmdlet. To test the configuration for external recipients, the following syntax can be used:

```
Test-IRMConfiguration -Recipient damian@geek.com -Sender damian@BigCorp.Com
```

The test will go through a series of steps:

```
Results : Checking Exchange Server ...
             - PASS: Exchange Server is running in Datacenter.
          Loading IRM configuration ...
             - PASS: IRM configuration loaded successfully.
          Retrieving RMS Certification Uri ...
             - PASS: RMS Certification Uri:
          https://8180295c-35df-414c-bb1c-244750534d06.rms.na.aadrm.com/_wmcs/certification.
          Verifying RMS version for
          https://8180295c-35df-414c-bb1c-244750534d06.rms.na.aadrm.com/_wmcs/certification ...
             - PASS: RMS Version verified successfully.
```

And a final result at the end:

```
OVERALL RESULT: PASS with warnings on disabled features
```

In order to apply an Information Protection template to an email, we need to create one. These can only be created in the Security and Compliance Center and published for use by Exchange in this console. This is outside our scope, however you can find more about these AIP templates here:

https://docs.microsoft.com/en-us/information-protection/deploy-use/configure-policy-templates

PowerShell

To now apply the AIP Template to an email. This requires a new Transport Rule which will specify the criteria needed to trigger it, like any other Transport Rule, and then an AIP Template is set to apply to these messages.

```
Get-Help New-TransportRule -Full
```

From here we can see there is an option called 'ApplyRightsProtectionTemplate' which will be useful for applying an AIP template. We also have conditions like 'SentToScope', 'SubjectMatchPatterns' and From. In our sample, we can apply an 'AIP Template' called 'Highly Confidential \ All Employees'. We will also pick a from address as well as a sent to an external email address and we get this:

```
New-TransportRule -From @([Microsoft.Exchange.Management.ControlPanel.PeopleIdentity])
-SentToScope 'NotInOrganization' -SubjectMatchesPatterns @('"Highly Confidential"')
-ApplyRightsProtectionTemplate 'Highly Confidential \ All Employees' -Name 'Highly Confidential
- AIP' -StopRuleProcessing:$False -Mode 'Enforce' -Comments ' ' -RuleErrorAction 'Ignore'
-SenderAddressLocation 'Header'
```

So in order to apply AIP to messages, create an AIP Template we need an AIP Template and a corresponding Transport Rule to protect messages.

Outlook Protection Rules

Transport Rules can be created to utilize RMS to protected messages in Exchange Online. However, Outlook Protection Rules will protect messages at the Outlook level even before the email has left the Outlook client. These rules are created in Exchange Online and downloaded to the Outlook client via Exchange Web Services (EWS). This means that when an email is sent via Outlook and an Outlook Protection Rule has been applied, the message is already protected before it enters the Transport pipeline and on to its destination. The end-user will also know this has occurred whereas a Transport Rule would be invisible to the end user as it's applied in flight instead of in the client.

PowerShell

Let's review the PowerShell cmdlets for Outlook Protection Rules:

```
Get-Command *OutlookProt*
```

```
CommandType         Name
-----------         ----
Function            Disable-OutlookProtectionRule
Function            Enable-OutlookProtectionRule
Function            Get-OutlookProtectionRule
Function            New-OutlookProtectionRule
Function            Remove-OutlookProtectionRule
Function            Set-OutlookProtectionRule
```

Like many other protections in Exchange, there are no Outlook Rules by default which can be verified with the Get-OutlookProtectionRule cmdlet. In order to get started let's review the New-OutlookProtectionRule examples:

```
Get-Help New-OutlookProtectionRule –Examples
```

```
------------------------ Example 1 ------------------------

This example applies the AD RMS template Template-Contoso to messages sent to the SMTP address Joe@contoso.com.
New-OutlookProtectionRule -Name "Project Contoso" -SentTo Joe@contoso.com -ApplyRightsProtectionTemplate
"Template-Contoso"
```

Other parameters to consider when working with Outlook Protection Rules are –ApplyRightsProtectionTemplate,

SentTo, SentToScope, UserCanOverride and Enabled. A sample command would look like this:

```
New-OutlookProtectionRule -Name "R and D" -SentTo Sam@HotMail.Com
-ApplyRightsProtectionTemplate "Big Box – Outlook Rule 1" -UserCanOverride $False
```

Mobile Protection

Mobile protection via IRM is enabled when the 'ClientAccessServerEnabled' setting is configured for $True:

```
Set-IRMConfiguration –ClientAccessServerEnabled $True
```

Now ActiveSync devices can be protected as well. Microsoft also recommends that certain settings for the Microsoft ActiveSync policy should also be configured:

DevicePasswordEnabled - $True
RequireDeviceEncryption - $True
AllowNonProvisionableDevices - $False

Depending on the name of the ActiveSync policy being applied to your mobile devices, the one-liners to make these changes might be a bit different. In the case below, we will modify the default policy to these settings:

```
Get-MobileDeviceMailboxPolicy | Where {$_.IsDefault -eq "True"} | Set-MobileDeviceMailboxPolicy
-PasswordEnabled $True -RequireDeviceEncryption $True -AllowNonProvisionableDevices $False
```

If IRM is not enabled on the mobile device policy, that should be enabled as well:

```
Get-MobileDeviceMailboxPolicy | Where {$_.IsDefault -eq "True"} | Set-MobileDeviceMailboxPolicy –
IRMEnabled $True
```

Mobile devices users can now perform the following actions:

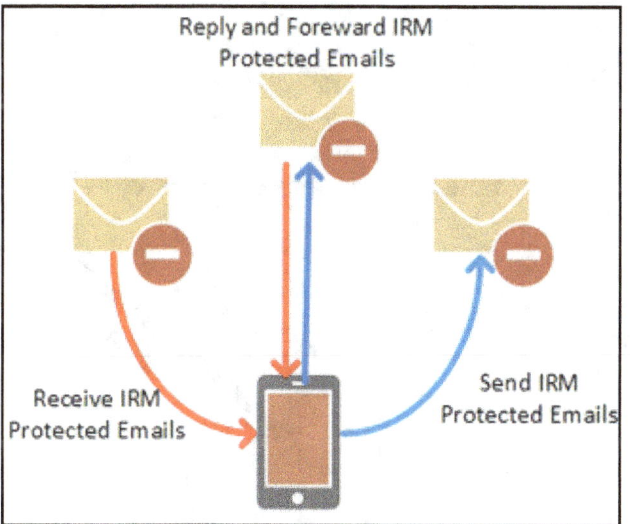

Same Message Tracking applies to mobile devices as would have been present with OWA and Outlook client emails.

Office 365 Message Encryption (OME)

Another useful feature that is built into Exchange Online is the encryption feature. This feature allows us to configure the secure sending of emails to external recipients without the worry or risk of its interception and deciphering its contents. How is that possible? It's because the message never truly leaves Exchange Online. All that is sent is a link to the email for the intended recipient to validate and then access.

As with all thing Microsoft and especially Exchange Online, the OME process now contains a potential enhancement in the form of AIP. The new experience changes the experience for those using and receiving encrypted messages. Some considerations for this new method:

Licensing considerations

The original OME is included in E3 licenses and can also be purchased separately for tenants that do not use E3. AIP is also included in subscriptions with E3 making the usage of it an easy move for those using OME now. If, however, you do not have an E3 subscription, AIP can be purchased as a separate line item and there are additional license levels if a company needs the more advance functionality it provides:

https://azure.microsoft.com/en-us/pricing/details/information-protection/

Microsoft Guidance on OME and AIP:

https://support.office.com/en-us/article/Set-up-new-Office-365-Message-Encryption-capabilities-built-on-top-of-Azure-Information-Protection-7ff0c040-b25c-4378-9904-b1b50210d00e

OME in Motion:

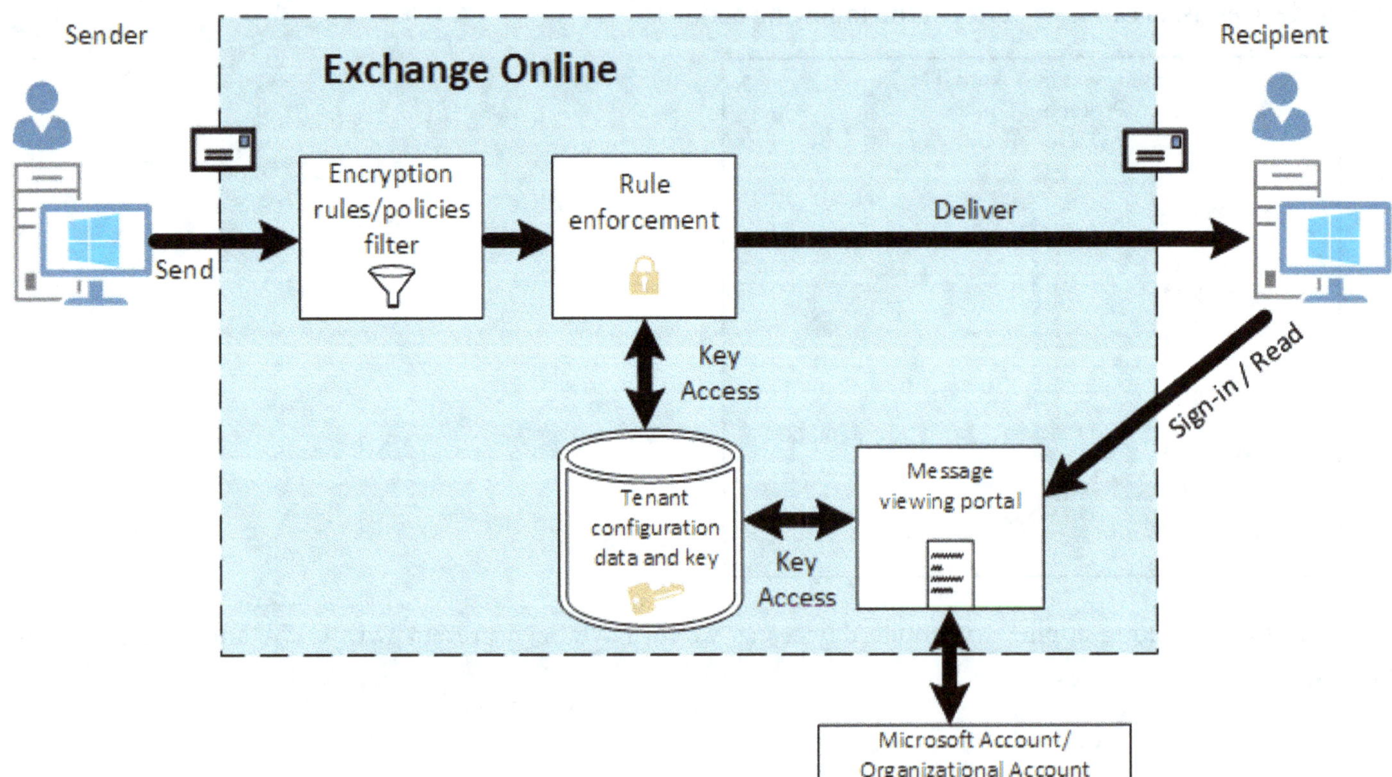

In order to set up Office 365 Message Encryption we need to perform these tasks:

(1) Enable Rights Management (See the previous Azure Information Protection section).
(2) PowerShell Configuration

First step is to set an RMS key location. If you are in North America, we can use the below one-liner:

```
Set-IRMConfiguration -RMSOnlineKeySharingLocation https://sp-rms.na.aadrm.com/TenantManagement/ServicePartner.svc
```

If you are in a different part of the world, refer to this chart from Microsoft for your ' RMSOnlineKeySharingLocation' value:

Location	RMS key sharing location
North America	https://sp-rms.na.aadrm.com/TenantManagement/ServicePartner.svc
European Union	https://sp-rms.eu.aadrm.com/TenantManagement/ServicePartner.svc
Asia	https://sp-rms.ap.aadrm.com/TenantManagement/ServicePartner.svc
South America	https://sp-rms.sa.aadrm.com/TenantManagement/ServicePartner.svc
Office 365 for Government	https://sp-rms.govus.aadrm.com/TenantManagement/ServicePartner.svc1

Next we need to import the configuration from RMS Online:

```
Import-RMSTrustedPublishingDomain -RMSOnline -Name "RMS Online"
```

Next we can test to make sure all is set up correctly:

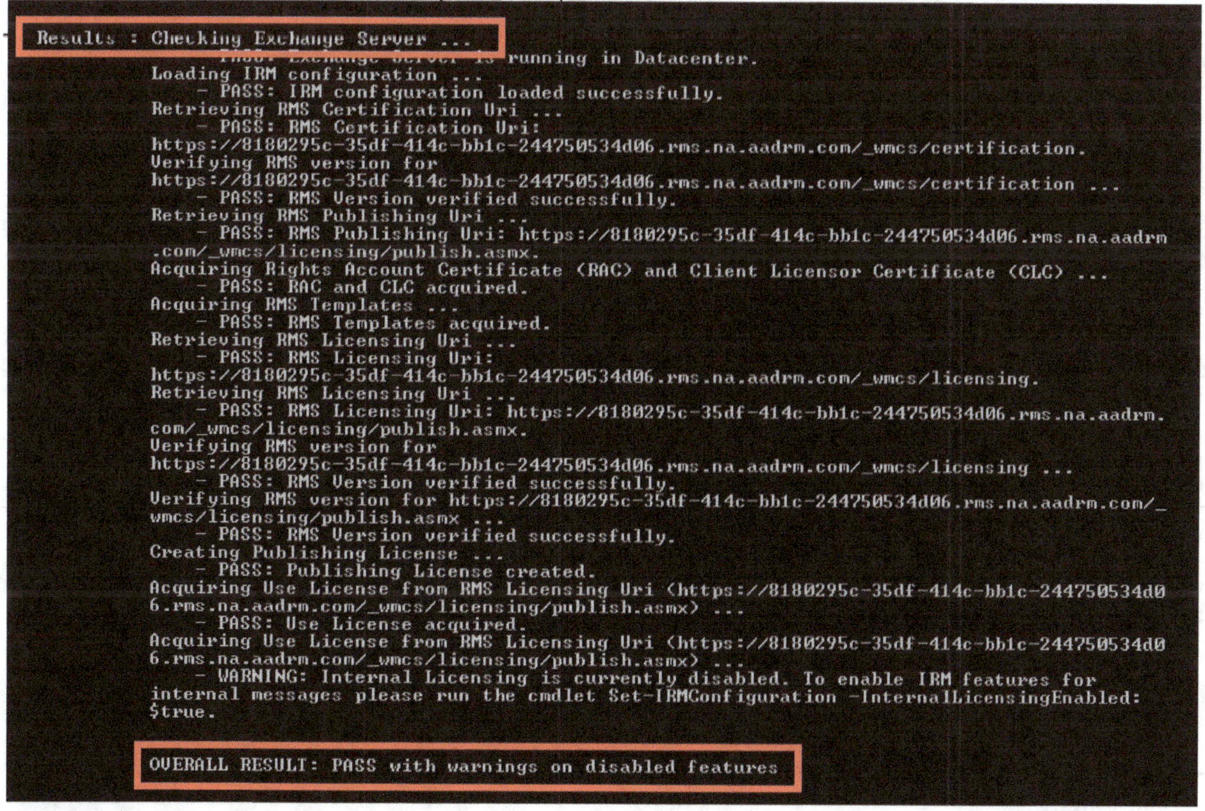

```
Results : Checking Exchange Server ...
          - PASS: Exchange Server is running in Datacenter.
Loading IRM configuration ...
          - PASS: IRM configuration loaded successfully.
Retrieving RMS Certification Uri ...
          - PASS: RMS Certification Uri:
https://8180295c-35df-414c-bb1c-244750534d06.rms.na.aadrm.com/_wmcs/certification.
Verifying RMS version for
https://8180295c-35df-414c-bb1c-244750534d06.rms.na.aadrm.com/_wmcs/certification ...
          - PASS: RMS Version verified successfully.
Retrieving RMS Publishing Uri ...
          - PASS: RMS Publishing Uri: https://8180295c-35df-414c-bb1c-244750534d06.rms.na.aadrm
.com/_wmcs/licensing/publish.asmx.
Acquiring Rights Account Certificate (RAC) and Client Licensor Certificate (CLC) ...
          - PASS: RAC and CLC acquired.
Acquiring RMS Templates ...
          - PASS: RMS Templates acquired.
Retrieving RMS Licensing Uri ...
          - PASS: RMS Licensing Uri:
https://8180295c-35df-414c-bb1c-244750534d06.rms.na.aadrm.com/_wmcs/licensing.
Retrieving RMS Licensing Uri ...
          - PASS: RMS Licensing Uri: https://8180295c-35df-414c-bb1c-244750534d06.rms.na.aadrm.
com/_wmcs/licensing/publish.asmx.
Verifying RMS version for
https://8180295c-35df-414c-bb1c-244750534d06.rms.na.aadrm.com/_wmcs/licensing ...
          - PASS: RMS Version verified successfully.
Verifying RMS version for https://8180295c-35df-414c-bb1c-244750534d06.rms.na.aadrm.com/_
wmcs/licensing/publish.asmx ...
          - PASS: RMS Version verified successfully.
Creating Publishing License ...
          - PASS: Publishing License created.
Acquiring Use License from RMS Licensing Uri (https://8180295c-35df-414c-bb1c-244750534d0
6.rms.na.aadrm.com/_wmcs/licensing/publish.asmx) ...
          - PASS: Use License acquired.
Acquiring Use License from RMS Licensing Uri (https://8180295c-35df-414c-bb1c-244750534d0
6.rms.na.aadrm.com/_wmcs/licensing/publish.asmx) ...
          - WARNING: Internal Licensing is currently disabled. To enable IRM features for
internal messages please run the cmdlet Set-IRMConfiguration -InternalLicensingEnabled:
$true.


OVERALL RESULT: PASS with warnings on disabled features
```

Next we enable licensing for internal usage:

```
Set-IRMConfiguration -InternalLicensingEnabled $True
```

Lastly we verify the configuration is in place:

```
Get-IRMConfiguration
```

```
InternalLicensingEnabled          : True
ExternalLicensingEnabled          : True
AzureRMSLicensingEnabled          : False
TransportDecryptionSetting        : Optional
JournalReportDecryptionEnabled    : True
SimplifiedClientAccessEnabled     : False
ClientAccessServerEnabled         : True
SearchEnabled                     : True
EDiscoverySuperUserEnabled        : True
RMSOnlineKeySharingLocation       : https://sp-rms.na.aadrm.com/TenantManagement/ServicePartner.svc
RMSOnlineVersion                  :
ServiceLocation                   : https://8180295c-35df-414c-bb1c-244750534d06.rms.na.aadrm.com/_wmc
                                    s/certification
PublishingLocation                : https://8180295c-35df-414c-bb1c-244750534d06.rms.na.aadrm.com/_wmc
                                    s/licensing/publish.asmx
LicensingLocation                 : {https://8180295c-35df-414c-bb1c-244750534d06.rms.na.aadrm.com/_wm
                                    cs/licensing}
```

Transport Rules

Microsoft has made many improvements in this area and we will cover the new options available for the end user as well as other configuration options that are available. In the past it used to be required that Exchange Online Transport Rules would need to be created in order to make OME work properly. However we now have a 'Protect' button in Outlook on the Web for Exchange Online and the Outlook client also has the RMS protection plug-in that can also be used to protect the messages. This is what is currently what is available in Outlook on the Web:

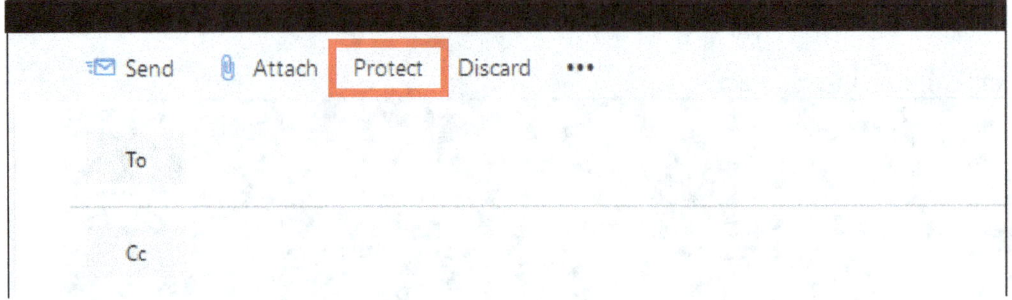

PowerShell

In order for Message Encryption to work for all users we'll need to create a pair of Transport Rules. One rule will encrypt the message to external senders while the other will decrypt replies from external sources if the message is encrypted.

Encrypt

New-TransportRule -SentToScope 'NotInOrganization' -SubjectContainsWords @('Encrypt') -ApplyOME:$True -Name 'Message Encryption - Sensitive' -StopRuleProcessing:$false -Mode 'Enforce' -Comments '' -RuleErrorAction 'Ignore' -SenderAddressLocation 'Header'

Decrypt

For decryption we simply look for any message from an external sender and remove any encryption that may have been applied.

New-TransportRule -FromScope 'NotInOrganization' -RemoveOME:$true -Name 'Remove Decryption - External Sender' -StopRuleProcessing:$False -Mode 'Enforce' -Comments '' -RuleErrorAction 'Ignore'

-SenderAddressLocation 'Header'

Branding

The last configuration item we can do for Office 365 Encrypted Messages is to change the branding or look of the messages that are sent.

Get-Command *OMECon*

So we have the usual Get and Set cmdlet pair for the OME configuration. Let's see what the default OME configuration is:

Get-OMEConfiguration

```
RunspaceId           : 792cf214-33a1-464d-
Image                :
ImageUrl             :
EmailText            :
PortalText           :
DisclaimerText       :
BackgroundColor      :
OTPEnabled           : True
SocialIdSignIn       : True
```

We can see that all of the values we need for branding are currently blank. How do we make them 'un-blank'?

For the logo specified below, make sure you are aware of size limitations:

```
n the recipient.  Delete this if it was not addressed to you."
The size of the supplied image is larger than the allowed maximum of 40 KB. Please provide an
image that is smaller than 40 KB.
    + CategoryInfo          : InvalidArgument: (:) [Set-OMEConfiguration], LocalizedException
    + FullyQualifiedErrorId : [Server=CY4PR13MB1350,RequestId=334f2005-d729-4e43-9765-40688090ebba
    ,TimeStamp=1/16/2018 3:41:37 PM] [FailureCategory=Cmdlet-LocalizedException] 24D50385,Microsof
```

We can configure a sample OME configuration with this one-liner:

Set-OMEConfiguration -Identity "Big Box OME Configuration" -Image (Get-Content "C:\BigBoxLogo.Jpg" -Encoding byte) -Emailtext "Encrypted message from the Big Box Corporation." -PortalText "Big Box Corporation secure email portal." -DisclaimerText "This message is intended only for the recipient. Delete this if it was not addressed to you."

Basically this cmdlet configures a few features for your Message Encryption in Office 365:

```
PS C:\> Get-OMEConfiguration

RunspaceId              : 8f02f991-a6df-4feb-ab26-aff9b807115f
Image                   : {137, 80, 78, 71...}
ImageUrl                : https://e4eomev2branding.blob.core.windows.net/f39b5e86-2806-40cc-ace0-3c
                          2a0140585a/logo.png
EmailText               : Encrypted message from the Bog Box Corporation.
PortalText              : Big Box Corporation secure email portal.
DisclaimerText          : This message is intended only for the recipient.  Delete this if it was
                          not addressed to you.
BackgroundColor         :
OTPEnabled              : True
SocialIdSignIn          : True
ClientEncryptionEnabled : True
ExpirationOptionEnabled : True
Identity                : OME Configuration
IsValid                 : True
ObjectState             : Unchanged
```

- **Image** - Placed at the bottom of the encrypted email
- **Email Text** - Part of the message body for the encrypted email

- **Portal Text** - What the recipient sees
- **Disclaimer Text** - More information about the encrypted message

One thing to remember about the configuration is that we can configure multiple OME configurations and apply them to different people and thus have different ways of enabling encryption in Exchange Online.

Now if we were to send an email, with the subject line of 'Encrypt', then the message will be encrypted and the recipient of this message will see the following:

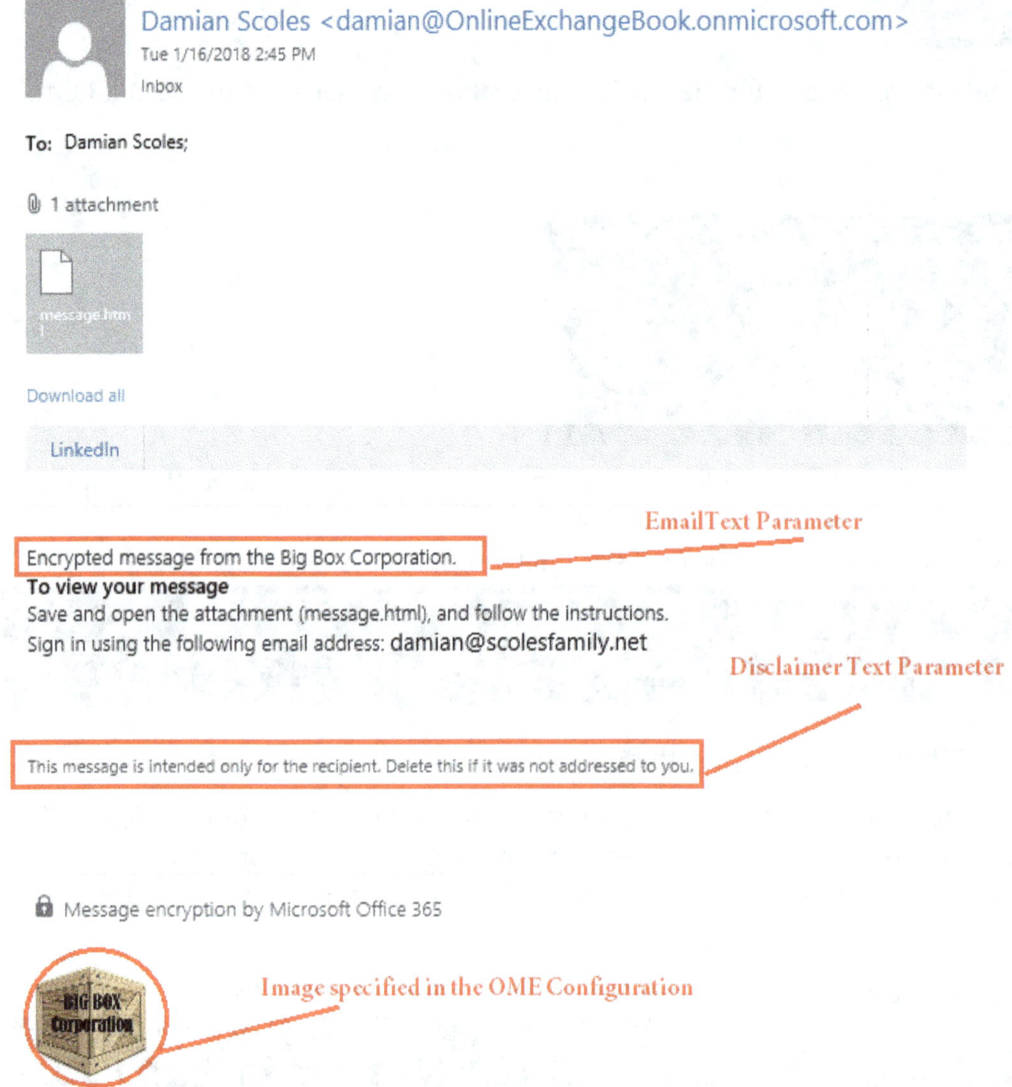

The PortalText shows up when trying to open the email and the email portal email looks like:

This we now have a branded experience for our encrypted messaging.

12 Security and Compliance Center

In This Chapter
- Security and Compliance Center
- Connecting with PowerShell
- Permissions
- Classifications - Labels and DLP
- Search and Investigation

Due to the nature of Office 365, there are overlaps between features as well as unique apps that do not appear on-premises. The Security and Compliance Center from Microsoft is the new central point of administration for compliance and other features for Office 365. Overlap between SCC and Exchange Online rests on items like eDiscovery and holds on mailboxes.

In this chapter we'll cover the basics of the Security and Compliance Center (SCC) interface which is Microsoft attempt at consolidating numerous security features and functions into one interface. This console touches up many workloads in Office 365, but we will concentrate on those that directly affect Exchange Online. this means that some functions and good features will not be covered.

Later we'll take a deep dive into PowerShell for the SCC. That way the interfaces for interacting with the SCC will make more sense. The cases we create, the holds that are put in place and more will then be visible in the SCC and allow for downloading or further manipulation. Because of the consolidation, PowerShell management also has to be consolidated and therefor there is a specific PowerShell URL for SCC.

In SCC we have Classifications and Labels in order to tag or designate items for policies. Classifications are ways of identifying objects or items to apply policies to. These classifications are like Exchange Retention Policies and Tags. There are three parts to the concept of labels - Label, Label Policy and Retention Rule. These three work together to create automatically applied labels or ones that are available to end users.

Data Loss Prevention - just like Exchange Online, there is a DLP module in the SCC that covers a broader set of workloads. However, the general idea is still there in the sense that we are now trying to protect data in SharePoint and OneDrive in addition to Exchange Online.

Search and Investigation - eDiscovery, content searches and mailbox holds can be done from here. Companies with Exchange Online tenants will want to learn these features as they are the future for these Exchange Online functions.

Security and Compliance Center

The Security and Compliance Center (SCC) is an effort by Microsoft to create a centralized place for processes like eDiscovery, Compliance Management, DLP and more. The central console will tap into many of the workloads that exist separately now in Office 365. These workloads include Exchange Online, SharePoint, OneDrive and more. Features that currently exist in these workloads are being pulled into the SCC.

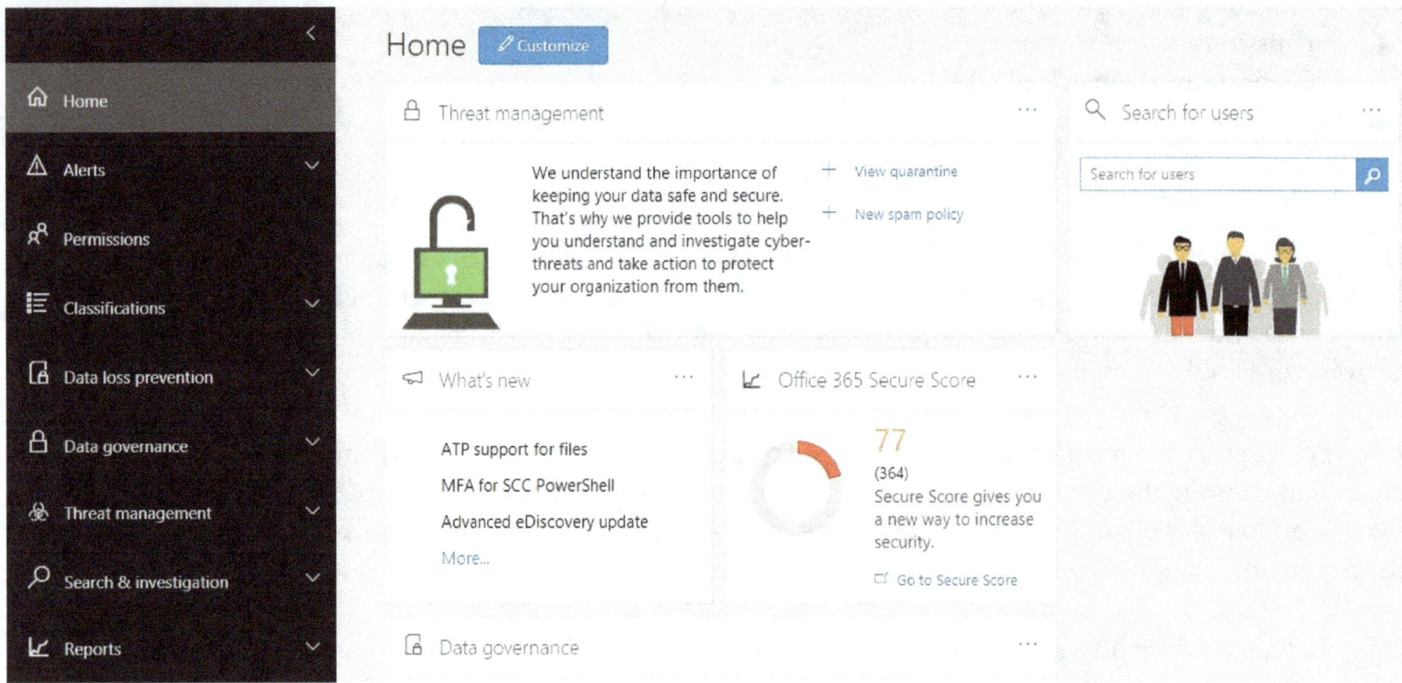

For Exchange Online, workloads that are handled or can be handled in the SCC include items like eDiscovery of mailbox content, mailbox holds, DLP and more. Some of these features were to be transitioned earlier in 2017 but are taking longer to actual move to the SCC. In the end, it is better to prepare for this change rather than creating your processes in Office 365 only.

Reviewing the SCC console we see that there are a few options available to us right off the bat. These options are:

- **Permissions** - Where to grant access to individual users in your tenant. The roles included here include specialized roles like Compliance Admin, Security Reader and Reviewer. Assign permissions carefully.
- **Classifications** - This tab deals with retention labels and sensitive information types.
- **Data Loss Prevention** - Puts controls in place that control access to sensitive data and how it is accessed or disbursed.
- **Data Governance** - Provides a way to control data for importing, archiving, retention and journaling.
- **Threat Management** - Cover ATP Safe Links and Safe Attachments, Anti-Malware, Anti-Spam and DKIM.
- **Search and Investigation** - Construct Content Searches, review Audit Logs, perform eDiscovery searches and access Office 365 Cloud App Security (E5 licenses).
- **Reports** - Review reports, schedule reports and download reports.

Connecting with PowerShell

Earlier in the book we explained how a connection could be made to remote PowerShell for Exchange Online. The Security and Compliance Center also has its own connection point. As such, we can use a PowerShell window to make a connection to our tenant's Security and Compliance Center and make changes, modifications or simply do some reporting via this console.

What we know is that the SCC has it's own remote PowerShell connection point and we can connect to it like so:

```
$LiveCred = Get-Credential
$Session = New-PSSession -ConfigurationName Microsoft.SCC -ConnectionUri https://ps.compliance.
protection.outlook.com/powershell-liveid/ -Credential $LiveCred -Authentication Basic
-AllowRedirection
Import-PSSession $Session
```

The only difference between connecting to the SCC and Exchange Online is the 'ConnectionUri':

ps.compliance.protection.outlook.com vs. ps.outlook.com

The connection should look something like this in PowerShell:

```
cmdlet Get-Credential at command pipeline position 1
Supply values for the following parameters:
Credential
WARNING: Your connection has been redirected to the following URI:
"https://nam05b.ps.compliance.protection.outlook.com/powershell-liveid?PSVersion=5.1.14409.1012 "
WARNING: The names of some imported commands from the module 'tmp_eg2khs5g.iho' include unapproved
verbs that might make them less discoverable. To find the commands with unapproved verbs, run the
Import-Module command again with the Verbose parameter. For a list of approved verbs, type
Get-Verb.

ModuleType Version      Name                                ExportedCommands

Script     1.0          tmp_eg2khs5g.iho                    {Add-ComplianceCaseMember, Add-eDiscoveryC
```

Once connected we can now run cmdlets specific to the Security and Compliance Center. Notice the Module Name listed above - 'tmp_eg2khs5g.iho'. This is the temporary module name that will be associated with all SCC specific cmdlets. On the next connection, this name should be different.

If the Module Name is always changing, how would we be able to query just those cmdlets and know what is available in that session? First, let's see what modules are loaded when we've connected to the SCC:

```
Get-Module
```

```
ModuleType Version      Name

Manifest   3.1.0.0      Microsoft.PowerShell.Management
Manifest   3.0.0.0      Microsoft.PowerShell.Security
Manifest   3.1.0.0      Microsoft.PowerShell.Utility
Script     1.0          tmp_eg2khs5g.iho
```

Notice that the Module type for the SCC module is a 'Script'. No other loaded module is of this type. Another common attribute we can work off of is the name. Even thought the name will change, it has at least one consistency and that is the name will always begin with 'tmp_'. So if we were to run a filter like so, we would find all cmdlets for the loaded SCC module:

```
Get-Command | Where {$_.ModuleName -Like 'tmp_*'}
```

To see how effective this is, let's see how many cmdlets are available for the entire SCC connection and only those that are specific to the SCC module:

```
(Get-Command).Count
(Get-Command | Where {$_.ModuleName -like 'tmp_*'}).Count
```

```
PS C:\> (Get-Command).Count
4056
PS C:\> (Get-Command | Where {$_.ModuleName -like 'tmp_*'}).Count
158
```

Permissions

Like other services in your Office 365 tenant, controlling who has access and who has access to what in the SCC is an important aspect of managing the SCC. These assignments will be important as the data that can be pulled from the SCC can be highly sensitive and confidential. We cover a similar set of Management Roles, Role Groups and Role Assignment. First, let's review what roles are available and what they mean in the context of the SCC.

Get-ManagementRole

```
Name                                    RoleType
----                                    --------
View-Only Retention Management          ViewOnlyRetentionManagement
Export                                  Export
RMS Decrypt                             RmsDecrypt
Manage Alerts                           ManageAlerts
Role Management                         RoleManagement
View-Only Manage Alerts                 ViewOnlyManageAlerts
Supervisory Review Administrator        SupervisoryReviewAdmin
View-Only Device Management             ViewOnlyDeviceManagement
Organization Configuration             OrganizationConfiguration
DLP Compliance Management               DLPComplianceManagement
Review                                  Review
Disposition Management                  DispositionManagement
View-Only DLP Compliance Management     ViewOnlyDLPComplianceManagement
RecordManagement                        RecordManagement
Audit Logs                              AuditLogs
Security Reader                         SecurityReader
Security Administrator                  SecurityAdmin
Preview                                 Preview
Service Assurance View                  ServiceAssuranceView
Search And Purge                        SearchAndPurge
View-Only Audit Logs                    ViewOnlyAuditLogs
Compliance Administrator                ComplianceAdmin
Device Management                       DeviceManagement
Compliance Search                       ComplianceSearch
Case Management                         CaseManagement
Retention Management                    RetentionManagement
View-Only Record Management             ViewOnlyRecordManagement
View-Only Recipients                    ViewOnlyRecipients
Hold                                    Hold
```

As we can see from the above list, there are quite a few Management Roles which are the individual rights that can be assigned to end users or preferably to Role Groups which are then assigned to end-users. Roles Groups are preferable because they allow for more than one Management Role to be assigned to a user or group of users at a time. Built-In Role Groups have a list of Management Roles that are preassigned for convenience. Let's review what Role Groups we have available in the SCC:

Get-RoleGroup

```
Name                        AssignedRoles
----                        -------------
Reviewer                    {FFO.extest.microsoft.com/Microsoft Exc
SecurityAdministrator       {FFO.extest.microsoft.com/Microsoft Exc
ComplianceAdministrator     {FFO.extest.microsoft.com/Microsoft Exc
OrganizationManagement      {FFO.extest.microsoft.com/Microsoft Exc
SupervisoryReview           {FFO.extest.microsoft.com/Microsoft Exc
TenantAdmins                {}
ServiceAssuranceUser        {FFO.extest.microsoft.com/Microsoft Exc
eDiscoveryManager           {FFO.extest.microsoft.com/Microsoft Exc
SecurityReader              {FFO.extest.microsoft.com/Microsoft Exc
```

These same groups are the ones that are exposed in the GUI for the SCC Permissions page.   What is a little hard to work with is the column of values titled 'AssignedRoles'. Trying to parse this takes a bit and if you were to examine all the properties for one Role Group, it makes it easier to decide how to extract a particular Role Groups Management Roles that are assigned to it.

Take for example the eDiscoveryManager Role Group. Let see what properties are available:

```
RunspaceId                  : c70e1d52-409d-4792-a4b0-a5138367fe6e
ManagedBy                   : {}
RoleAssignments             : {FFO.extest.microsoft.com/Microsoft Exchange Hosted Organizations/Onli
                              Manager, FFO.extest.microsoft.com/Microsoft Exchange Hosted Organizati
                              Manager, FFO.extest.microsoft.com/Microsoft Exchange Hosted Organizati
                              Manager, FFO.extest.microsoft.com/Microsoft Exchange Hosted Organizati
                              Manager...}
Roles                       : {FFO.extest.microsoft.com/Microsoft Exchange Hosted Organizations/Onli
                              FFO.extest.microsoft.com/Microsoft Exchange Hosted Organizations/Onlin
                              FFO.extest.microsoft.com/Microsoft Exchange Hosted Organizations/Onlin
                              FFO.extest.microsoft.com/Microsoft Exchange Hosted Organizations/Onlin
DisplayName                 : eDiscovery Manager
ExternalDirectoryObjectId   :
Members                     : {}
SamAccountName              :
Description                 : Perform searches and place holds on mailboxes, SharePoint Online sites
RoleGroupType               : Standard
LinkedGroup                 :
Capabilities                : {}
LinkedPartnerGroupId        :
LinkedPartnerOrganizationId :
Identity                    : FFO.extest.microsoft.com/Microsoft Exchange Hosted
                              Organizations/OnlineExchangeBook.onmicrosoft.com/Configuration/eDiscov
Id                          : FFO.extest.microsoft.com/Microsoft Exchange Hosted
                              Organizations/OnlineExchangeBook.onmicrosoft.com/Configuration/eDiscov
IsValid                     : True
ExchangeVersion             : 0.10 (14.0.100.0)
Name                        : eDiscoveryManager
DistinguishedName           : CN=eDiscoveryManager,CN=Configuration,CN=OnlineExchangeBook.onmicrosof
                              Organizations,DC=FFO,DC=extest,DC=microsoft,DC=com
Guid                        : 84d7d9bc-f1b4-aeba-6fc8-bc86ef251075
ObjectCategory              :
ObjectClass                 : {group}
WhenChanged                 : 1/16/2018 8:45:47 AM
WhenCreated                 : 12/6/2017 12:40:42 AM
WhenChangedUTC              : 1/16/2018 2:45:47 PM
WhenCreatedUTC              : 12/6/2017 6:40:42 AM
OrganizationId              : FFO.extest.microsoft.com/Microsoft Exchange Hosted Organizations/Onlin
                              FFO.extest.microsoft.com/Microsoft Exchange Hosted Organizations/Onlin
```

Notice in the results, the field 'AssignedRoles' does not appear, but we have two to content with 'RoleAssignments' and 'Roles'. The properties are different.

Digging further into this Role Group, we'll specifically look at the 'Roles' property as the roles are ones we can then pick apart to see what is assigned to the Role Group in total.

    (Get-RoleGroup 'ediscoveryManager').Roles

This provides us a list of roles (with VERY long names):

```
FFO.extest.microsoft.com/Microsoft Exchange Hosted Organizations/OnlineExchangeBook.onmicrosoft.com/Export
FFO.extest.microsoft.com/Microsoft Exchange Hosted Organizations/OnlineExchangeBook.onmicrosoft.com/RMS Decrypt
FFO.extest.microsoft.com/Microsoft Exchange Hosted Organizations/OnlineExchangeBook.onmicrosoft.com/Review
FFO.extest.microsoft.com/Microsoft Exchange Hosted Organizations/OnlineExchangeBook.onmicrosoft.com/Preview
FFO.extest.microsoft.com/Microsoft Exchange Hosted Organizations/OnlineExchangeBook.onmicrosoft.com/Compliance Search
FFO.extest.microsoft.com/Microsoft Exchange Hosted Organizations/OnlineExchangeBook.onmicrosoft.com/Case Management
FFO.extest.microsoft.com/Microsoft Exchange Hosted Organizations/OnlineExchangeBook.onmicrosoft.com/Hold
```

Taking the first one, we know the right is 'Export' for short. This is a Management Role and we can pick it apart like this:

```
Get-ManagementRole 'Export'
```

```
Name    RoleType
----    --------
Export  Export
```

Not very descriptive, so we'll add a 'Fl' at the end and get this:

```
RunspaceId                   : e35eb26c-f7f3-49a7-9c41-5c2ea24860fe
RoleEntries                  : {}
RoleType                     : Export
ImplicitRecipientReadScope   : Organization
ImplicitRecipientWriteScope  : Organization
ImplicitConfigReadScope      : None
ImplicitConfigWriteScope     : None
IsRootRole                   : True
IsEndUserRole                : False
MailboxPlanIndex             :
Description                  : Lets people export the mailbox and site content that was returned from a search.
Parent                       :
IsDeprecated                 : False
```

Now we have a description of that particular role. Now, if want to automatically pull this information and get the Management Role descriptions for each under one Role Group, we can do so with this script:

```
$Roles = (Get-RoleGroup 'eDiscoveryManager').Roles
Foreach ($Role in $Roles) {
    $RoleName = $Role.Split([char]0x002F)
    $Name = $RoleName[3]
    $Description = (Get-ManagementRole $Name).Description
    Write-Host $Name -NoNewline -ForegroundColor Green
    Write-Host ': '$Description -ForegroundColor White
}
```

A successful run reveals the descriptions from each Management Role in the 'eDiscovery Manager' Role Group:

```
Export:   Lets people export the mailbox and site content that was returned from a search.
RMS Decrypt:   Lets people decrypt RMS-protected content when exporting search results.
Review:   Lets people use Office 365 Advanced eDiscovery to track, tag, analyze, and test documents
that are assigned to them.
Preview:   Lets people view a list of items that were returned from a content search. They'll also b
e able to open each item from the list to view its contents.
Compliance Search:   Lets people perform searches across mailboxes and get an estimate of the result
s.
Case Management:   Lets people create, edit, delete, and control access to eDiscovery cases.
Hold:   Lets people place content in mailboxes, sites, and public folders on hold. When on hold, a c
opy of the content is stored in a secure location. Content owners will still be able to modify or de
lete the original content.
```

To apply this to any role, we simply need to replace the Role Group listed on the first line with the one we are needing information on. Expanding upon that, we can even use a loop for each Role Group and pull out the Management Roles if we so desired.

Being able to figure out who has what role assigned to them can be accomplished with the Get-RoleGroupMember

-Identity cmdlet that is available. By default the only group that should contain a member is the TenantAdmins group that is listed here. This group is also known as the Global Admins for your tenant. With the default setup we have a blank slate with which to assign rights to the SCC.

```
Add-RoleGroupMember eDiscoveryManager -Member 'Damian Scoles'
```

We can then verify that the user is added correctly:

```
PS C:\> Get-RoleGroupMember eDiscoveryManager

Name              RecipientType
----              -------------
Damian Scoles     MailUser
```

Removing a role member is just as easy as adding one:

```
Remove-RoleGroupMember eDiscoveryManager -Member 'Damian Scoles'
```

```
PS C:\> Remove-RoleGroupMember eDiscoveryManager -Member 'Damian Scoles'

Confirm
Are you sure you want to perform this action?
Removing the member "Damian Scoles" from the role group "eDiscoveryManager".
[Y] Yes  [A] Yes to All  [N] No  [L] No to All  [?] Help (default is "Y"): y
```

Classifications - Labels and DLP

When it comes to working with data on an automatic basis, we need to provide some sort of system or information that these processes can work with. In the case of Office 365 and Exchange Online, these processes are DLP and Transport Rules. The bits of information that can be fed to these processes are Labels and Sensitive Information Types. We can originate this information from two places - Exchange Online Admin console and the other is the Security and Compliance Center. While we have covered the Exchange Online Admin Center version of this, we also need to cover the SCC because that is where Microsoft is investing for the future of data protection that will include Exchange Online as well.

When reviewing the console for the SCC, we see that we can use two methods for data classification. We can use Labels or we can use Sensitive Information Types. If you are familiar with Retention Policies and Tags, then you will understand the concept of Labels and Label Policies. These follow a similar set of rules, with a twist. While Sensitive Information Types can be used in Exchange Transport Rules, Labels are applied in a more automatic fashion to the content in Office 365.

Labels

Labels are used to define what we want to tag. These Labels can be used to control content that gets tagged. This could include emails, SharePoint data and OneDrive data in your Office 365 tenant. We will cover this topic from the perspective of Exchange Online only. When we dig a bit deeper into Labels, we find that there are three components to successfully apply them to content in your tenant - Compliance Tags, Compliance Rules and Compliance Policies.

Make sure to read this article on how Labels are applied, in terms of timing, for each workload in Office 365:

https://support.office.com/en-us/article/overview-of-labels-af398293-c69d-465e-a249-d74561552d30

PowerShell

First, let's see what we can find for PowerShell cmdlets when it comes to creating Labels for the SCC.

Get-Command *label*

Hmmm.... no results found. ? How are we going to create Labels? Well, let's go to our favorite search engine to see what we can find:

Search Terms: PowerShell Security Compliance Center Labels

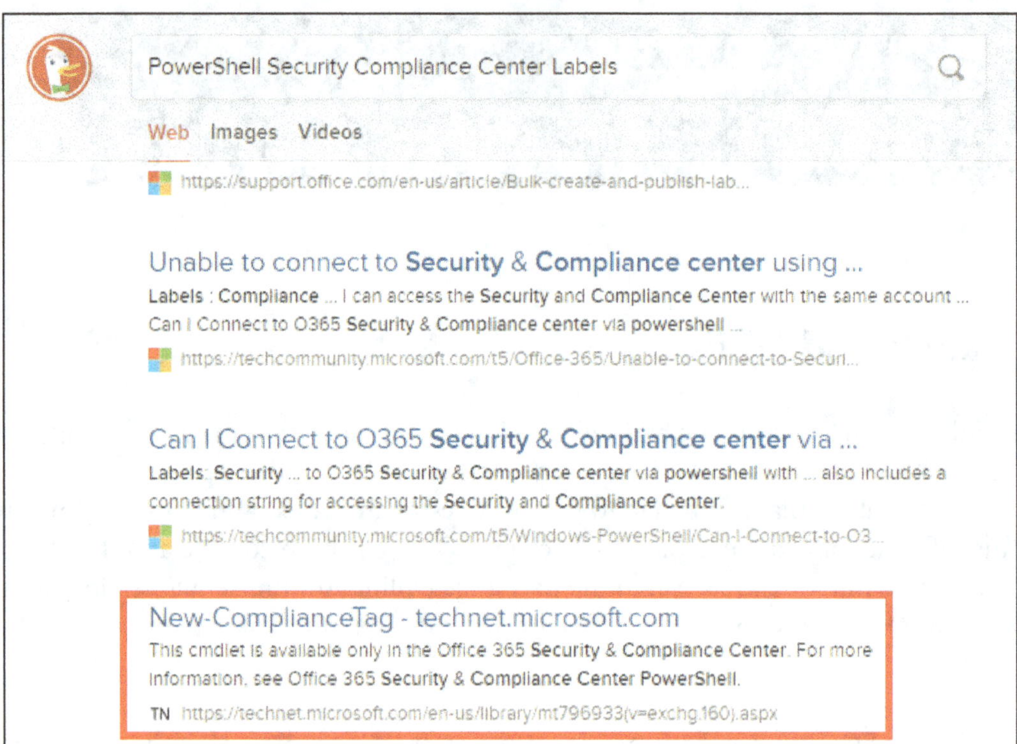

Notice the reference to one PowerShell cmdlet here, New-ComplianceTag. Sounds promising. Let's take a look in PowerShell help to see what it can do:

```
PS C:\> get-help New-ComplianceTag -Full

NAME
    New-ComplianceTag

SYNOPSIS
    This cmdlet is available only in the Office 365 Security & Compliance Center. For more
    information, see Office 365 Security & Compliance Center PowerShell.

    Use the New-ComplianceTag cmdlet to create labels in the Security & Compliance Center. Labels
    apply retention settings to content.

    For information about the parameter sets in the Syntax section below, see Exchange cmdlet
    syntax.
```

Some cmdlet examples:

```
------------------------------ Example 1 ------------------------------
New-ComplianceTag -Name "HR Content" -RetentionAction Keep -RetentionDuration 1825
-RetentionType ModificationAgeInDays
```

Common parameters used with Compliance Tags:

- **IsRecordLabel** - Can tag content permanently or not. Once tagged a Record Label cannot be removed.
- **RetentionAction** - Decided if the content is kept, deleted or keepanddelete.
- **Retention Duration** - How long will the item be retained.
- **RetentionType** - CreationAgeInDays, EventAgeInDays, ModificationAgeInDays, TaggedAgeInDays.

Labels can be used by the end user once they are published in Outlook, SharePoint and OneDrive. The workloads the tag can be created for are not customizable. It will apply to all of these workloads. However, we can use Label Policies to restrict the end workload that the Label applies to.

Example

We can create a retention tag for confidential emails that would allow us to keep the emails for up to seven years. A sample Label would be created like this:

    New-ComplianceTag -Name Confidential -RetentionAction Keep -RetentionDuration 2555 -RetentionType ModificationAgeInDays

Now we need to restrict this just to Exchange Online. In order to do so, we need to use a cmdlet called 'New-RetentionCompliancePolicy'.

    New-RetentionCompliancePolicy -Name 'Exchange 7 Years' -ExchangeLocation All

Then we can publish the Labels with the Compliance Rule cmdlet:

    New-RetentionComplianceRule -Policy 'Exchange 7 Years' -PublishComplianceTag 'Confidential'

More information on publishing these Labels and Policies can be found here:

https://support.office.com/en-us/article/bulk-create-and-publish-labels-by-using-powershell-8986701b-ffa1-46ec-8fd0-8f7e81d5b25f

Now we have a Label and Label Policy that is this together with a Compliance Rule that will allow users to assign a seven year Label on their emails. We used the 'All' designation for ExchangeLocations which means all mailboxes will see this Label.

Sensitive Information Types

Built In

As with Exchange Online, the Security and Compliance Center has built-in Sensitive Information Types that we can use right away. We can take a quick peak at the names of some of the policies like so:

Get-DlpSensitiveInformationType

```
Name                                                      Publisher              Type
----                                                      ---------              ----
U.S. / U.K. Passport Number                               Microsoft Corporation  Entity
EU Debit Card Number                                      Microsoft Corporation  Entity
Credit Card Number                                        Microsoft Corporation  Entity
Japan Passport Number                                     Microsoft Corporation  Entity
U.S. Social Security Number (SSN)                         Microsoft Corporation  Entity
Australia Medical Account Number                          Microsoft Corporation  Entity
U.K. National Insurance Number (NINO)                     Microsoft Corporation  Entity
France Passport Number                                    Microsoft Corporation  Entity
Japan Bank Account Number                                 Microsoft Corporation  Entity
U.S. Individual Taxpayer Identification Number (ITIN)     Microsoft Corporation  Entity
Spain Social Security Number (SSN)                        Microsoft Corporation  Entity
Japan Driver's License Number                             Microsoft Corporation  Entity
ABA Routing Number                                        Microsoft Corporation  Entity
SWIFT Code                                                Microsoft Corporation  Entity
Canada Social Insurance Number                            Microsoft Corporation  Entity
Australia Driver's License Number                         Microsoft Corporation  Entity
Japan Resident Registration Number                        Microsoft Corporation  Entity
Drug Enforcement Agency (DEA) Number                      Microsoft Corporation  Entity
U.S. Bank Account Number                                  Microsoft Corporation  Entity
German Driver's License Number                            Microsoft Corporation  Entity
Poland Identity Card                                      Microsoft Corporation  Entity
Japan Social Insurance Number (SIN)                       Microsoft Corporation  Entity
Sweden National ID                                        Microsoft Corporation  Entity
Australia Tax File Number                                 Microsoft Corporation  Entity
German Passport Number                                    Microsoft Corporation  Entity
Chile Identity Card Number                                Microsoft Corporation  Entity
Australia Passport Number                                 Microsoft Corporation  Entity
Australia Bank Account Number                             Microsoft Corporation  Entity
Israel National ID                                        Microsoft Corporation  Entity
France Driver's License Number                            Microsoft Corporation  Entity
```

The above is a partial list of the available types. The number of types appears to be greater than that of Exchange Online. How many are there? Let's do a '.Count' for all of these types

(Get-DlpSensitiveInformationType).count

What we find is that there are 82 Sensitive Information Types in the SCC, compared to only 40 DLP Policy Templates in Exchange Online. We can pull from the above list when constructing Transport Rules or using them in the SCC for applying them to other workloads like SharePoint and OneDrive.

Custom

In addition to the built-in Sensitive Information Types, we can add our own custom ones. Custom data types could be used to track bank routing information, social security numbers, credit cards, confidential phases and more. Let's review the PowerShell cmdlets that we can use to make these new types:

Get-Command *DlpSensitiveInformation*

```
Name
----
Get-DlpSensitiveInformationType
Get-DlpSensitiveInformationTypeRulePackage
New-DlpSensitiveInformationTypeRulePackage
Remove-DlpSensitiveInformationTypeRulePackage
Set-DlpSensitiveInformationTypeRulePackage
```

First we will start with the creation of some new Sensitive Information Types. Here is the sole example from this cmdlet:

Get-Help New-DlpSensitiveInformationTypeRulePackage -Examples

```
-------------------------- Example 1 --------------------------

This example imports the sensitive information type rule package C:\My Documents\External
Sensitive Info Type Rule Collection.xml.

    New-ClassificationRuleCollection -FileData ([Byte[]]$(Get-Content -Path "C:\My
    Documents\External Sensitive Info Type Rule Collection.xml" -Encoding Byte -ReadCount 0))
```

Notice the highlighted section that refers to the use of an XML file for the new data type. Microsoft does not provide a link here on how to create such an XML file, but if you search the Internet, you will be able to find this handy link:

https://aka.ms/dlpcustomtypes

This link takes us to a page explaining how to create an XML file that can be used against custom scenarios. Creating an XML file takes a bit of time and is somewhat complicated. These XML files can be created with a PowerShell script that has a series of questions. This script was written by one of the authors of the book and can be found here:

https://justaucguy.wordpress.com/2015/01/27/dlp-custom-xml-generation-script/

In practical terms, creating a one-off XML file is easier if you can use the Microsoft help and TechNet pages that are provided. Skipping forward, assuming an XML file has been created (ConfidentialInformation.Xml) we can import the template using the example above for guidance.

```
$FullDirectory = "C:\xmlscript\ConfidentialInformation.xml"
New-DlpSensitiveInformationTypeRulePackage -FileData ([Byte[]]$(get-content -Path $FullDirectory
-Encoding Byte -ReadCount 0))
```

When run successfully, we should see a good result like so:

```
PS C:\>  New-DlpSensitiveInformationTypeRulePackage -FileData ([Byte[]]$(get-content -Path
$fulldirectory -Encoding Byte -ReadCount 0))


Invariant Name    Localized Name    Publisher  Encrypted
-------------     -------------     ---------  ---------
KeywordSearch-CI  KeywordSearch-CI             False
```

Which we can then verify as well, post-creation:

```
PS C:\> Get-DlpSensitiveInformationTypeRulePackage

Invariant Name         Localized Name         Publisher               Encrypted Exportable
-------------          -------------          ---------               --------- ----------
Microsoft Rule Package Microsoft Rule Package Microsoft Corporation   False     True
KeywordSearch-CI       KeywordSearch-CI       Cummins                 False     True
```

In order to use these we need to create Transport Rules in Exchange Online. Connect to Exchange Online via PowerShell first, as we explained in Chapter 5. Once connected we can create a Transport Rule, like we did in Chapter 10. In this case however, we need to reference the DLP information. In this case we need the 'Message-ContainsDataClassifications' parameter:

```
-MessageContainsDataClassifications <Hashtable[]>
    This parameter specifies a condition or part of a condition for the rule. The name of the
    corresponding exception parameter starts with ExceptIf.

    In on-premises Exchange, this condition is only available on Mailbox servers.

    The MessageContainsDataClassifications parameter specifies a condition that looks for
    sensitive information types in the body of messages, and in any attachments.

    This parameter uses the syntax
    @(<SensitiveInformationType1>),@(<SensitiveInformationType2>),..... For example, to look
    for content that contains at least two credit card numbers, and at least one ABA routing
    number, use the value @(Name="Credit Card Number"; minCount="2"),@(Name="ABA Routing
    Number"; minCount="1").

    For a list of sensitive information types available, see Sensitive information types in
    Exchange 2016.

    You can specify the notification options by using the NotifySender parameter.
```

A sample rule, using one of the Sensitive Information Types we just defined, would look like this:

```
New-TransportRule -SentToScope 'NotInOrganization' -MessageContainsDataClassifications
@(Name="KeywordSearch-CI";mincount = '1') -ModerateMessageByUser @([Microsoft.
Exchange.Management.ControlPanel.PeopleIdentity]) -Name 'Sent to scope Outside the
organization' -StopRuleProcessing:$False -Mode 'Enforce' -Comments '' -RuleErrorAction 'Ignore'
-SenderAddressLocation 'Header'
```

This Transport Rule will look for our criteria and if there is a match once or more in the email, then it will trigger the rule above.

Search and Investigation

Searching for content, exporting content and holding content are all part of the Search and Investigation piece. If you need to perform these types of functions for Exchange Online, the optimal place to do that now is in the SCC. These types of actions will eventually be removed or at the very least deprecated from Exchange Online. The reason for that again is consolidation. From the SCC, an eDiscovery Manager can now search multiple workloads in Office 365 with ease. For the scenarios and cmdlets provided in this book, we will concentrate on Exchange Online only.

Compliance Searches

Reviewing the cmdlets for the SCC, we don't see any specific to Content Searches. However, there are cmdlets that deal with Compliance Searches. If we review the help for the New-ComplianceSearch cmdlet, we'll see that there is a parameter for content searches:

```
------------------------------ Example 2 ------------------------------

This example creates a new compliance search named Hold-Tailspin Toys that searches all member
of the distribution group named Research Department. Because the search uses the
ContentMatchQuery parameter, only messages that match the query are searched.

New-ComplianceSearch -Name "Hold-Tailspin Toys" -ExchangeLocation "Research Department"
-ContentMatchQuery "'Patent' AND 'Project Tailspin Toys'"
```

Content queries can be constructed with the Keyword Query Language (KQL) which can be referenced here:

https://docs.microsoft.com/en-us/sharepoint/dev/general-development/keyword-query-language-kql-syntax-reference

Compliance Cases

Now, if your legal needs are a bit more complex, or if you have searches and holds that need to be held together as groups, we can use Compliance Cases to assist us with this task. A Case is a holder for the searches that you've created. These can be convenient in a legal sense because we can group together multiple Compliance Searches into one Compliance Case. Organizing them in this way will make it easier for a legal team to pull information from one source instead of having to comb through a lot of informational sources.

PowerShell

```
Get-Help New-ComplianceCase -Examples
```

```
------------------------------- Example 1 -------------------------------
New-ComplianceCase -Name "Fabrikam Litigation"
```

Not much to go on here. Let's review the parameters that are available to us in the full Get-Help for this cmdlet. We have these parameters - Name, Confirm, Description, Domain Controller, Sources and WhatIf. Most of these parameters are 'reserved for internal Microsoft use'. This means that the Compliance Case is purely just a holder and the only way to associate searches with a case, is to first create the case and then specify this case in the creation of a new Compliance Search. In fact we see this in the help for the New-ComplianceSearch:

```
-Case <String>
    The Case parameter specifies the name of an eDiscovery case that the new compliance search
    will be associated with. If the value contains spaces, enclose the value in quotation
    marks.
```

Let's walk though an example so that we can build a case and then associates some searches with it.

Example

Your company, Bib Box, Inc. is currently involved in a legal case where a client is suing because some of the boxes you provided were too small compare to the specs that were provided by their engineers and confirmed by your company's R&D department. The manager of the company's compliance department is asking for all of the content from the mailboxes of R&D members as well as a couple of salespeople that were involved in the deal. In order to keep track of this better, the searches need to be stored in their own case. The reasoning for the last decision is that there are currently two other legal cases in-progress now and they need to be kept secret.

First create the case:

```
New-ComplianceCase -Name 'BigBox-vs-FastBox'
```

Now that we have case, we can create our compliance searches we can define all mailboxes and store them in a variable to be called later:

```
$Mailboxes = 'John Bean','Tyrone Smith','Han Francis'
```

For each mailbox we'll create the same search and associate it with the same case we created earlier:

```
Foreach ($Mailbox in $Mailboxes) {
    New-ComplianceSearch
}
```

A successful run will show all three of the content searches created, but not started:

```
Name          RunBy JobEndTime Status
----          ----- ---------- ------
John Bean                      NotStarted
Tyrone Smith                   NotStarted
Han Francis                    NotStarted
```

If we try to run Get-ComplianceSearch after these are created it would appear that none were, because we get a blank response from PowerShell:

```
PS C:\> Get-ComplianceSearch
PS C:\>
```

In order to find the cases, we need to specifically reference them:

```
Get-ComplianceSearch 'John Bean'
Get-ComplianceSearch 'Tyrone Smith'
Get-ComplianceSearch 'Han Francis'
```

We see again that these are not started. To start them, we need to use the' Start-ComplianceSearch' cmdlet:

```
Get-ComplianceSearch 'John Bean' | Start-ComplianceSearch
Get-ComplianceSearch 'Tyrone Smith' | Start-ComplianceSearch
Get-ComplianceSearch 'Han Francis' | Start-ComplianceSearch
```

Now we have searches running in the background and available to our legal team for our example legal case.

In This Chapter

- Layered Security
  - Management Roles
  - Management Role Entries - Granular Permissions
  - Management Role Groups
  - Special Management Role Groups
  - Default User Role
- Impersonation
- Management Scopes
- Auditing
  - Admin Audit Logs
  - Mailbox Audit Logs

Layered Security

Ingrained in the coding of Exchange Online are layers of security that are used to prevent unauthorized access to various areas of Exchange like mailbox data, configuration and more. The ecosystem of security consists of multiple layers that enable a complex setup with administrators given access to all, some or none of Exchange. Typically the security layers concern more of the administration side of Exchange, however, some conditions can also be applied to user access as well.

Management Role Groups are a special type of Security Group that contains Universal Security Groups, other Role Groups and users which are also known as Role Group Members. Group members can be added and removed to fit the needs of an organization. Exchange Management Roles are assigned to the groups. Management Role Scopes are also assigned to control what rights a Role Group member can exercise within Exchange.

Management Role Entries are the individual rights that can be assigned or grouped into Management Roles. A Management Role Entry usually consists of a single PowerShell script or cmdlet and the relevant parameters that can be accessed by a Management Role.

Management Roles are groups of Management Role Entries and are grouped logically to help an administrator perform a certain task. These roles are assigned to Role Groups as part of this arrangement.

Impersonation is the act of a user or service account accessing another user's mailbox as if they were the owner of the mailbox. This right is typically assigned to an application that needs to process email in a user's mailbox or perform some specialized task like mailbox migrations.

Auditing is the process of keeping track of changes. In the case of Exchange we have auditing for Admin changes PowerShell or EAC as well as auditing for mailbox access. Auditing can be monitored and reports generated for compliance and security requirements for an organization. Admin Audit logging is on by default while mailbox access logging is not. Check your region privacy settings before enabling the mailbox features.

In this chapter we will cover these topics in-depth and as they relate to PowerShell.

Management Roles

Permissions for managing Exchange are broken down into a concept called Management Roles. Each of these roles can be assigned to a user in order to allow that person to configure those portions of Exchange. Role Groups are security groups within Exchange to which the Management Roles are assigned to so that a member of this Role Group has the rights granted to it. Role Groups in Exchange vary from a Read Only Admins all the way up to the Organization Management Group which has most of the Management Roles in Exchange. Let's explore these Management Roles and then Role Groups in order to get a better idea of how security is layered in Exchange 2016.

PowerShell

Let's explore what cmdlets are available for Management Role management in PowerShell:

```
Get-Command *ManagementRole*
```

This provides us with a short list of cmdlets:

Add-ManagementRoleEntry	Remove-ManagementRole
Get-ManagementRole	Remove-ManagementRoleAssignment
Get-ManagementRoleAssignment	Remove-ManagementRoleEntry
Get-ManagementRoleEntry	Set-ManagementRoleAssignment
New-ManagementRole	Set-ManagementRoleEntry
New-ManagementRoleAssignment	

If we need to get a list of available Management Roles, we can use this simple cmdlet:

```
Get-ManagementRole
```

When run, a long list of management roles is provided:

Address Lists	My Custom Apps	Org Custom Apps
ApplicationImpersonation	My Marketplace Apps	Org Marketplace Apps
Audit Logs	My ReadWriteMailbox Apps	Organization Client Access
Compliance Admin	MyBaseOptions	Organization Configuration
Data Loss Prevention	MyContactInformation	Organization Transport Settings
Distribution Groups	MyAddressInformation	Public Folders
E-Mail Address Policies	MyMobileInformation	Recipient Policies
Federated Sharing	MyPersonalInformation	Remote and Accepted Domains
Information Rights Management	MyDistributionGroupMembership	Reset Password
Journaling	MyDistributionGroups	Retention Management
Legal Hold	MyMailSubscriptions	Role Management
Mail Enabled Public Folders	MyMailboxDelegation	Security Admin
Mail Recipient Creation	MyProfileInformation	Security Group Creation and Membership
Mail Recipients	MyDisplayName	Security Reader
Mail Tips	MyName	Team Mailboxes
Mailbox Import Export	MyRetentionPolicies	Transport Hygiene
Mailbox Search	MyTeamMailboxes	Transport Rules
Message Tracking	MyTextMessaging	UM Mailboxes
Migration	MyVoiceMail	UM Prompts
Move Mailboxes	O365SupportViewConfig	Unified Messaging

User Options	LegalHoldApplication	TeamMailboxLifecycleApplication
View-Only Audit Logs	MailboxSearchApplication	UserApplication
View-Only Configuration	MeetingGraphApplication	
View-Only Recipients	OfficeExtensionApplication	
ArchiveApplication	SendMailApplication	

What can we determine about each of these Management Roles with just PowerShell? We know that it is possible to get a list of the roles with Get-ManagementRole, now we need to run that cmdlet against the role to determine important information about the Management Role. We can also limit the scope of the output to just RoleEntries:

(Get-ManagementRole 'Legal Hold').RoleEntries

```
SetHoldOnMailboxes
GetHoldOnMailboxes
GetDiscoverySearchConfiguration
(Microsoft.Exchange.Management.PowerShell.E2010) Write-AdminAuditLog -Comment -Confirm -ErrorAction
 -ErrorVariable -OutBuffer -OutVariable -WarningAction -WarningVariable -WhatIf
(Microsoft.Exchange.Management.PowerShell.E2010) Start-AuditAssistant -Identity
(Microsoft.Exchange.Management.PowerShell.E2010) Set-UnifiedAuditSetting -ErrorAction -ErrorVariable
 -Identity -OutBuffer -OutVariable -WarningAction -WarningVariable
(Microsoft.Exchange.Management.PowerShell.E2010) Set-MailboxSearch -Confirm -Description -ErrorActio
n -ErrorVariable -Force -Identity -InPlaceHoldEnabled -ItemHoldPeriod -Name -OutBuffer -OutVariable
 -SourceMailboxes -WarningAction -WarningVariable -WhatIf
(Microsoft.Exchange.Management.PowerShell.E2010) Set-Mailbox -AccountDisabled -Confirm -ElcProcessin
gDisabled -Force -Identity -InactiveMailbox -LitigationHoldDate -LitigationHoldDuration -LitigationH
oldEnabled -LitigationHoldOwner -RecalculateInactiveMailbox -RemoveDelayHoldApplied -RetentionCommen
t -RetentionPolicy -RetentionUrl -SingleItemRecoveryEnabled -StsRefreshTokensValidFrom
```

Notice that there are a series of PowerShell cmdlets listed in the value of the 'RoleEntries' on the Management Role. After the PowerShell cmdlets are listed, a little more information about the cmdlet is revealed:

```
RoleType                      : LegalHold
ImplicitRecipientReadScope    : Organization
ImplicitRecipientWriteScope   : Organization
ImplicitConfigReadScope       : OrganizationConfig
ImplicitConfigWriteScope      : None
IsRootRole                    : True
IsEndUserRole                 : False
MailboxPlanIndex              :
Description                   : This role enables administrators to configure whether data within a
                                mailbox should be retained for litigation purposes in an
                                organization.
Parent                        :
IsDeprecated                  : False
AdminDisplayName              :
ExchangeVersion               : 0.12 (14.0.451.0)
Name                          : Legal Hold
DistinguishedName             : CN=Legal Hold,CN=Roles,CN=RBAC,CN=Configuration,CN=sct-15_20_323_4-ms
                                online-bpos_s_2caf9,CN=ConfigurationUnits,DC=namprd13,DC=prod,DC=outl
                                ook,DC=com
Identity                      : Legal Hold
```

Can we get a better list from the 'Role Entries' property of the Management Role? With some work, yes we can. For an Exchange 2016 Server, which is what Exchange Online is currently based on, it takes one cmdlet to list these Role Entries. However, in Exchange Online it's a bit of a mess:

```
PS C:\> (Get-ManagementRole 'Legal Hold').RoleEntries
SetHoldOnMailboxes
GetHoldOnMailboxes
GetDiscoverySearchConfiguration
(Microsoft.Exchange.Management.PowerShell.E2010) Write-AdminAuditLog -Comment -Confirm -Er
(Microsoft.Exchange.Management.PowerShell.E2010) Start-AuditAssistant -Identity
(Microsoft.Exchange.Management.PowerShell.E2010) Set-UnifiedAuditSetting -ErrorAction -Err
(Microsoft.Exchange.Management.PowerShell.E2010) Set-MailboxSearch -Confirm -Description -
Buffer -OutVariable -SourceMailboxes -WarningAction -WarningVariable -WhatIf
(Microsoft.Exchange.Management.PowerShell.E2010) Set-Mailbox -AccountDisabled -Confirm -El
uration -LitigationHoldEnabled -LitigationHoldOwner -RecalculateInactiveMailbox -RemoveDel
-StsRefreshTokensValidFrom
(Microsoft.Exchange.Management.PowerShell.E2010) Remove-MailboxSearch -Confirm -ErrorActio
```

Notice that the information is in a bit of a jumble and we first get the PowerShell module - *Microsoft.Exchange.Management.PowerShell.E2010*, then the cmdlet - *'Write-AdminAuditLog'* and then the switches.

This output cannot be formatted with Format-Table or Format-List. What can we do? Well, we can use '-Split' to separate out values. For this output, all of the items are separated by a space. This means we can parse out the line by splitting it by space. The name of the cmdlet is always in the second column and we can reference it as the [1] value in an array. Here is the PowerShell code to do so:

```powershell
$ManagementRole = 'Legal Hold'
$RoleEntries = (Get-ManagementRole $ManagementRole).RoleEntries
Write-Host 'Cmdlet: ' -ForegroundColor White -NoNewline
Write-Host "$ManagementRole" -ForegroundColor Green
Write-Host ''
Write-Host 'Role Name' -ForegroundColor Cyan
Write-Host '----------' -ForegroundColor Cyan
Write-Host ''
Foreach ($Role in $RoleEntries) {
    $Content = $Role -Split ' '
    $RoleName = $Content[1]
    $RoleName
}
```

This code does have some extra bits, but it produces output we can read and interpret:

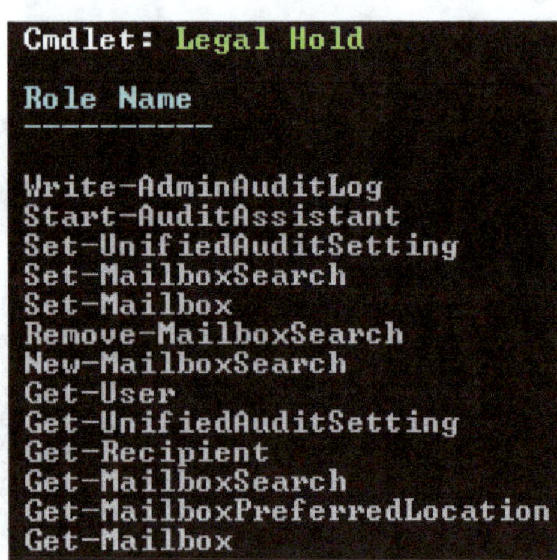

We can manipulate the code above to check any cmdlet we want. For example, if we wanted cmdlets or 'Team Mailboxes' we would replace the Role in the first variable and re-run the script:

```powershell
$ManagementRole = 'Team Mailboxes'
```

New Management Role

There are a lot of default Management Roles provided with Exchange Online. These existing roles may not be granular enough or encompassing enough depending on what the needs of the role are. For example we can create a new Management Role that is essentially a modified version of Help Desk Role Group. The original Role Group has three Management Roles assigned to it:

> Help Desk
>
> Members of this management role group can view and manage the configuration for individual recipients and view recipients in an Exchange organization. Members of this role group can only manage the configuration each user can manage on his or her own mailbox. Additional permissions can be added by assigning additional management roles to this role group.
>
> Assigned Roles
>
> Reset Password
> User Options
> View-Only Recipients

Let's say we need a Role that can run all cmdlets having to deal with mailboxes. First, we need all of the cmdlets available:

```
Get-Command *Mailbox
```

Disable-Mailbox	Get-UMMailbox	Set-SiteMailbox
Disable-UMMailbox	New-Mailbox	Set-UMMailbox
Enable-Mailbox	New-SchedulingMailbox	Test-SiteMailbox
Enable-UMMailbox	New-SiteMailbox	Undo-SoftDeletedMailbox
Get-CASMailbox	Remove-Mailbox	Update-PublicFolderMailbox
Get-GroupMailbox	Set-CASMailbox	Update-SiteMailbox
Get-Mailbox	Set-GroupMailbox	
Get-SiteMailbox	Set-Mailbox	

We can call this new Management Role something like 'Mailbox Management'. When providing just a name and the Role Entries, we receive an error about not providing a parent for the Management Role:

```
New-ManagementRole 'Mailbox Management'
```

```
cmdlet New-ManagementRole at command pipeline position 1
Supply values for the following parameters:
Parent:
Cannot process argument transformation on parameter 'Parent'. Cannot convert value "" to type
"Microsoft.Exchange.Configuration.Tasks.RoleIdParameter". Error: "Parameter values of type
Microsoft.Exchange.Configuration.Tasks.RoleIdParameter can't be empty. Specify a value, and try
again.
Parameter name: identity"
    + CategoryInfo          : InvalidData: (:) [New-ManagementRole], ParameterBindin...mationExcep
   tion
    + FullyQualifiedErrorId : ParameterArgumentTransformationError,New-ManagementRole
    + PSComputerName        : ps.outlook.com
```

The parent value is another Management Role that this new Management Role is based off of. In our case, we can speculate that these cmdlets are available in Recipient Management. So if we specify this as the parent, we can run the cmdlet successfully:

```
New-ManagementRole -Name 'Mailbox Management' -EnabledCmdlets Disable-Mailbox,Disable-
UMMailbox,Enable-Mailbox,Enable-UMMailbox,Get-CASMailbox,Get-GroupMailbox,Get-Mailbox,Get-
SiteMailbox,Get-UMMailbox,New-Mailbox,New-SchedulingMailbox,New-SiteMailbox,Remove-
Mailbox,Set-CASMailbox,Set-GroupMailbox,Set-Mailbox,Set-SiteMailbox,Set-UMMailbox,Test-
```

SiteMailbox,Undo-SoftDeletedMailbox,Update-PublicFolderMailbox,Update-SiteMailbox -parent 'Mail Recipients'

This would normally work right off the bat for an on-premises Exchange server. However, in the cloud, a tweak needs to be made because the above will generate an error message unless a customization has been made:

```
The command you tried to run isn't currently allowed in your organization. To run this command,
you first need to run the command: Enable-OrganizationCustomization.
    + CategoryInfo          : NotSpecified: (:) [New-ManagementRole], InvalidOperatio...ontextExce
   ption
    + FullyQualifiedErrorId : [Server=CY4PR13MB1350,RequestId=f019cece-03c9-4825-8eb4-5714a2621a32
   ,TimeStamp=12/13/2017 3:28:59 AM] [FailureCategory=Cmdlet-InvalidOperationInDehydratedContextE
   xception] 5822E75B,Microsoft.Exchange.Management.RbacTasks.NewManagementRole
    + PSComputerName        : ps.outlook.com
```

So what exactly is the Enable-OrganizationCustomization cmdlet and what does it do?

```
DESCRIPTION
    In the Microsoft datacenters, certain objects are consolidated to save space. When you use
    Exchange Online PowerShell or the Exchange admin center to modify one of these objects for the
    first time, you may encounter an error message that tells you to run the
    Enable-OrganizationCustomization cmdlet.

    Here are some examples of when you might see this:

    * Creating a new role group or creating a new management role assignment.
    * Creating a new role assignment policy or modifying a built-in role assignment policy.
    * Creating a new Outlook on the web mailbox policy or modifying a built-in Outlook on the web
      mailbox policy.
    * Creating a new sharing policy or modifying a built-in sharing policy.
    * Creating a new retention policy or modifying a built-in retention policy.
    Note that you are only required to run the Enable-OrganizationCustomization cmdlet once in
    your Exchange Online organization. If you attempt to run the cmdlet again, you'll get an error.

    You need to be assigned permissions before you can run this cmdlet. Although all parameters
    for this cmdlet are listed in this topic, you may not have access to some parameters if
    they're not included in the permissions assigned to you. To see what permissions you need, see
    the "Organization configuration" entry in the Feature permissions in Exchange Online topic.
```

We can simply run this cmdlet without any switches if we want and it will allow us to add these roles:

```
Enable Configuration Customizations for Organization
    Creating built-in Exchange Roles
    [ooooooooooooooooooooo                                                              ]
```

** **Note** ** The reason this needs to be done is that the tenant is in a dehydrated state or tiny tenant mode. Microsoft does this for their own management reason. So when an admin runs into this issue in PowerShell, they can rehydrate their tenant with the Enable-OrganizationConfiguration cmdlet.

https://blogs.technet.microsoft.com/rmilne/2015/02/27/office-365-command-you-tried-to-run-isnt-currently-allowed-due-to-dehydration/

What we find out is that the list of cmdlets we assigned are not actually provided to the new Management Role:

```
PS C:\> New-ManagementRole -Name 'Mailbox Management' -EnabledCmdlets Disable-Mailbox,Disable-UMMai
lbox,Enable-Mailbox,Enable-UMMailbox,Get-CASMailbox,Get-GroupMailbox,Get-Mailbox,Get-SiteMailbox,Get
-UMMailbox,New-Mailbox,New-SchedulingMailbox,New-SiteMailbox,Remove-Mailbox,Set-CASMailbox,Set-Group
Mailbox,Set-Mailbox,Set-SiteMailbox,Set-UMMailbox,Test-SiteMailbox,Undo-SoftDeletedMailbox,Update-Pu
blicFolderMailbox,Update-SiteMailbox -parent 'Mail Recipients'


Name                      RoleType
----                      --------
Mailbox Management        MailRecipients
```

To verify this worked, we use the script we wrote previously to check the built-in roles and we see that the new Management Role was created correctly:

```
Management Role: Mailbox Management

Role Name
---------

Disable-Mailbox
Enable-Mailbox
Get-CASMailbox
Get-GroupMailbox
Get-Mailbox
Get-SiteMailbox
New-Mailbox
Set-CASMailbox
Set-GroupMailbox
Set-Mailbox
```

Notice that the UMMailbox cmdlets are not listed, nor are the Update or Test cmdlets. This is because the 'Mail Recipients' Management Roles does not have these defined. In order to get the full set, we would need a Management Role with more cmdlets to choose from.

Remove Management Role

Creating Management Roles can help tailor the way Exchange is used in a particular environment. One thing that tends to get lost is cleanup of custom created items in Exchange. If for example a Management Role was created for a custom purpose, removing a role is easier than creating it. If we have the name of the role, we simply need to run the Remove-ManagementRole cmdlet to do so:

```
Remove-ManagementRole 'Mailbox Management'
```

```
[PS] C:\>Remove-ManagementRole 'Mailbox Management'

Confirm
Are you sure you want to perform this action?
Removing the "Mailbox Management" management role object.
[Y] Yes  [A] Yes to All  [N] No  [L] No to All  [?] Help (default is "Y"): y
```

Management Role Entries - Granular Permissions

Permissions required for Exchange Online PowerShell cmdlets can also be examined as granularly as the PowerShell cmdlets themselves. Each cmdlet has a set of roles or permissions that are allowed to run them. In 99% of cases where specific rights may need to be assigned, using the built in roles and other security features is the best method to do so. However, it may be unclear as to what PowerShell cmdlets are allowed to be run once a particular Management Role has been assigned. How can we figure out what cmdlets are allowed to be run per a particular Management Role?

PowerShell

How can we do this? Let's start by using your favorite search engine to find the information:

Search Terms: PowerShell cmdlet permissions:

Examining the page, we see that Microsoft has provides a cmdlets in order to find permissions for a cmdlet or even a parameter on a cmdlet:

Get-ManagementRoleEntry -Identity *\<Cmdlet>

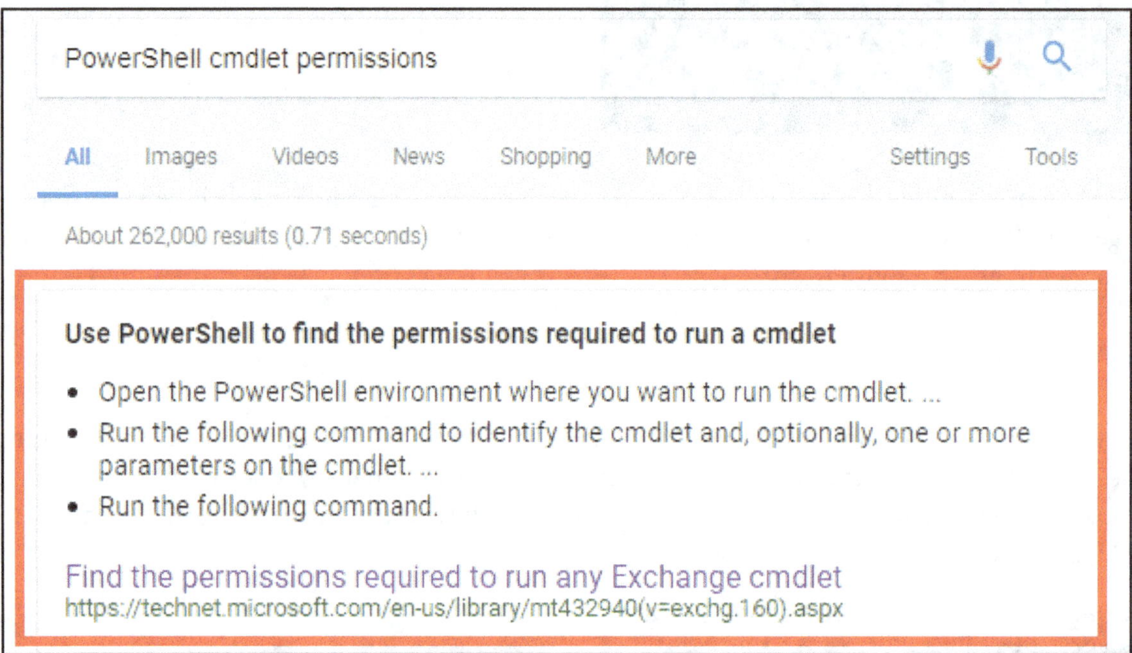

Let's use the code provided to see what permissions are required to run a few cmdlets. First, we will compare the Management Roles available for the Get-Mailbox and New-Mailbox PowerShell cmdlets. We see that the Roles that are allowed to run the Get-Mailbox cmdlet and there are quite a few (below is a partial list):

Get-ManagementRoleEntry -Identity *\Set-Mailbox

```
Name              Role                    Parameters
----              ----                    ----------
Set-Mailbox       Audit Logs              {AuditAdmin, AuditDelegate, AuditEnable...
Set-Mailbox       Legal Hold              {AccountDisabled, Confirm, ElcProcessin...
Set-Mailbox       Mail Recipients         {AcceptMessagesOnlyFrom, AcceptMessages...
Set-Mailbox       Mailbox Management      {AcceptMessagesOnlyFrom, AcceptMessages...
Set-Mailbox       MyBaseOptions           {AcceptMessagesOnlyFrom, AcceptMessages...
Set-Mailbox       MyMailboxDelegation     {GrantSendOnBehalfTo, Identity}
Set-Mailbox       MyProfileInformation    {DisplayName, Identity, SimpleDisplayName}
Set-Mailbox       MyDisplayName           {DisplayName, Identity, SimpleDisplayName}
Set-Mailbox       Public Folders          {DefaultPublicFolderMailbox, Identity, ...
Set-Mailbox       Reset Password          {Identity, RoomMailboxPassword}
Set-Mailbox       Retention Management    {AccountDisabled, ElcProcessingDisabled...
Set-Mailbox       UM Mailboxes            {Confirm, CreateDTMFMap, ErrorAction, E...
Set-Mailbox       User Options            {AcceptMessagesOnlyFrom, AcceptMessages...
```

Then if we review the entries for the New-Mailbox cmdlet:

Get-ManagementRoleEntry -Identity *\New-Mailbox

```
Name              Role                     Parameters
----              ----                     ----------
New-Mailbox Mail Enabled Public Folders    {HoldForMigration, IsExcludedFromServingHierarchy, Name,...
New-Mailbox Mail Recipient Creation        {ActiveSyncMailboxPolicy, Alias, Archive, Confirm...}
New-Mailbox Mail Recipients                {EnableRoomMailboxAccount}
New-Mailbox Public Folders                 {HoldForMigration, IsExcludedFromServingHierarchy, Name,...
New-Mailbox Retention Management           {EnableRoomMailboxAccount}
```

In this last example, we can see that there is only one role for the New-MailboxImportRequest cmdlet:

Get-ManagementRoleEntry -Identity *\New-MailboxImportRequest

```
[PS] C:\>Get-ManagementRoleEntry -Identity *\New-MailboxImportRequest

Name                          Role                  Parameters
----                          ----                  ----------
New-MailboxImportRequest      Mailbox Import Export {AcceptLargeDataLoss
```

Each of these roles can be assigned directly to a user or a user could be assigned a Management Role that includes this particular role. How to we find what Management Role has the role that allows access to these cmdlets? From the same link shown on page 267, we can use a set of cmdlets to display the Management Role that has the permission that had access to a cmdlet:

```
$Perms = Get-ManagementRole -Cmdlet <Cmdlet>
$Perms | Foreach {Get-ManagementRoleAssignment -Role $_.Name -Delegating $false | Format-Table
-Auto Role,RoleAssigneeType,RoleAssigneeName}
$Perms
```

For a real world example we can use the New Mailbox cmdlet :

```
$Perms = Get-ManagementRole -Cmdlet New-Mailbox
$Perms | Foreach {Get-ManagementRoleAssignment -Role $_.Name -Delegating $false | Format-Table
-Auto Role,RoleAssigneeType,RoleAssigneeName}
$Perms
```

```
Role                         RoleAssigneeType  RoleAssigneeName
----                         ----------------  ----------------
Mail Enabled Public Folders  RoleGroup         Organization Management

Role                         RoleAssigneeType  RoleAssigneeName
----                         ----------------  ----------------
Mail Recipient Creation      RoleGroup         Organization Management
Mail Recipient Creation      RoleGroup         Recipient Management

Role                         RoleAssigneeType  RoleAssigneeName
----                         ----------------  ----------------
Mail Recipients              RoleGroup         Organization Management
Mail Recipients              RoleGroup         Recipient Management

Role                         RoleAssigneeType  RoleAssigneeName
----                         ----------------  ----------------
Public Folders               RoleGroup         Organization Management

Role                         RoleAssigneeType  RoleAssigneeName
----                         ----------------  ----------------
Retention Management         RoleGroup         Compliance Management
Retention Management         RoleGroup         Organization Management
Retention Management         RoleGroup         Records Management
```

Parsing the results above by eliminating the duplicate entries above, we can refine this to five Management Roles which have permission to run the 'New-Mailbox' cmdlet:

> Organization Management
> Recipient Management
> Public Folder Management
> Compliance Management
> Records Management

Management Role Groups

In order to help administrator Exchange Online, Microsoft has provided a set of standard Management Role Groups for us to use. These Role Groups include very limited rights groups all the way up to a full administrator Role Group. The array of groups allows for a range of Administrative Access to Exchange Online and allows us to follow a model of least permissions when granting access to users. We can limit what a user has access to with these generalized Role Groups. If the groups are not sufficient, they can also be modified as needed, duplicated or modified to fit a specific need.

PowerShell

How do we find these Management Role Groups in Exchange Online? Let's see what cmdlets have the keywords 'rolegroup':

> Get-Command *RoleGroup

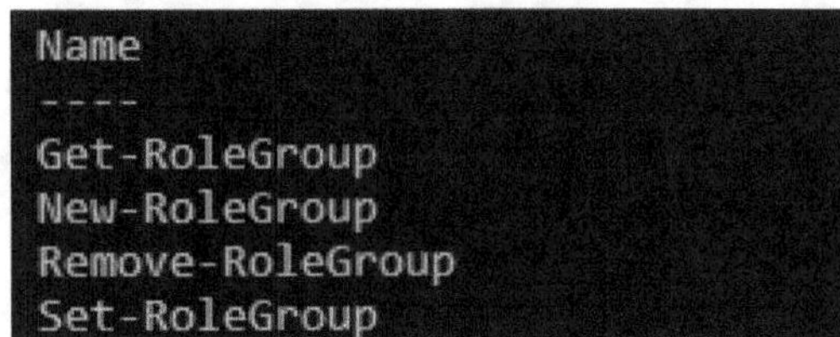

We can use Get-RoleGroup to see what groups are available in Exchange:

> Get-RoleGroup

```
Name                                          AssignedRoles
----                                          -------------
Organization Management                       {Address Lists, ApplicationImpersonation, Arch...
Recipient Management                          {Distribution Groups, Mail Recipient Creation,...
View-Only Organization Management             {View-Only Configuration, View-Only Recipients}
UM Management                                 {UM Mailboxes, UM Prompts, Unified Messaging}
Help Desk                                     {Reset Password, User Options, View-Only Recip...
Records Management                            {Audit Logs, Journaling, Message Tracking, Ret...
Discovery Management                          {Legal Hold, Mailbox Search}
Hygiene Management                            {Transport Hygiene, View-Only Configuration, V...
Compliance Management                         {Audit Logs, Compliance Admin, Data Loss Preve...
Security Reader                               {Security Reader}
Security Administrator                        {Security Admin}
TenantAdmins_-254864124                       {}
RIM-MailboxAdminse11e8bd7cda743038cd8ebef53c43706  {ApplicationImpersonation}
```

What's interesting about the list is that we can see the group names as well as the Management Roles ('Assigned Roles') assigned to those groups in the list. We see that Organization Management has the most roles assigned, while a Role Group like 'Security Reader' and 'Security Administrator' both only have one Management Role assigned to it. Let's dig a little deeper into these Role Groups: how to create them, how to modify them and how to assign them to users.

Special Management Role Groups

Within the menagerie of Management Roles in Exchange Online there are a few that are more special than others. These roles allow the user assigned these roles to perform special tasks or be able to do almost anything in Exchange. These three roles were picked as they are some of the most commonly assigned roles. The roles mentioned are Import/Export PST, eDiscovery, and Organization Admin. We'll explore what these roles are designated for and how to assign them to a user. While exploring the assignment, we can also examine what PowerShell cmdlets are available to the role.

Assigning Via PowerShell

All of these roles can be configured in the Exchange Admin Center (EAC), however, since this is a PowerShell book we will review how to do this in PowerShell. At the start of the chapter, we got a list of PowerShell cmdlets that handle Management Roles. One of cmdlets is called 'New-ManagementRoleAssignment' which will allow us to assign a Management Role to a mailbox. Let's see what examples we can cull from Get-Help:

```
------------------------- Example 1 -------------------------
New-ManagementRoleAssignment -Role "Mail Recipients" -SecurityGroup "Tier 2 Help Desk"

------------------------- Example 2 -------------------------
New-ManagementRoleAssignment -Role "MyVoiceMail" -Policy "Sales end-users"
```

We can also assign the role directly to a mailbox using the 'User' parameter:

```
New-ManagementRoleAssignment -Role <Role to Assign> -User <user>
```

Now let's walk through these three roles to see what they are and how to assign them to users.

Organization Admin

The Organizational Admin role is one of the most important, if not the most important, Management Role in Exchange. As an Organizational Admin, the user assigned this role is allowed to perform almost any task in Exchange – from adding mailboxes, configuring Transport Rules, adding Exchange Servers and many other maintenance tasks. In PowerShell, an Organizational Admin would be able to run about 99% of all the cmdlets available. Outside of these abilities, there are a few that a user assigned to this role are not assigned.

The role we need to assign is called 'Organization Management':

```
Add-RoleGroupMember "Organization Management" -Member 'Damian'
```

After we assign the role, how do we determine who has this role? We might need to remove extra names or even add additional users to help manage Exchange. We can do that with the example code below:

```
Get-RoleGroupMember 'Organization Management'
```

Import/Export PST

This is one Management Role that is not granted to the Organization Admin Management Role Group. This role grants the user permission to perform the following tasks:

Import PST files into a user's mailbox
Export email from a mailbox to a PST file

For our examples, we will first assign the role to an Administrator:

New-ManagementRoleAssignment -Role "Mailbox Import Export" -User 'JSmith'

```
[PS] C:\>New-ManagementRoleAssignment -Role "Mailbox Import Export" -User 'JSmith'

Name                           Role            RoleAssigneeName   RoleAssigneeType   AssignmentMethod   E
                                                                                                       e

----                           ----            ----------------   ----------------   ----------------   --
Mailbox Import Export-John ... Mailbox Import... John Smith         User               Direct
```

In the second example we can also assign the role to a group of users who will manage the import process for a company:

New-ManagementRoleAssignment -Role "Mailbox Import Export" -SecurityGroup 'PSTManagement'

```
[PS] C:\>New-ManagementRoleAssignment -Role "Mailbox Import Export" -SecurityGroup 'PSTManagement'

Name                           Role            RoleAssigneeName   RoleAssigneeType   AssignmentMethod   EffectiveUs
                                                                                                       e

----                           ----            ----------------   ----------------   ----------------   -----------
Mailbox Import Export-PSTMa... Mailbox Import... PSTManagement      SecurityGroup      Direct
```

Without the assignment of this role, the cmdlets available for import are not visible:

```
[PS] C:\>Get-Command *ImportRequest
[PS] C:\>
```

Once the role is assigned, we can see the cmdlets needed for PST import:

```
[PS] C:\>Get-Command *ImportRequest

CommandType     Name
-----------     ----
Function        Get-MailboxImportRequest
Function        New-MailboxImportRequest
Function        Remove-MailboxImportRequest
Function        Resume-MailboxImportRequest
Function        Set-MailboxImportRequest
Function        Suspend-MailboxImportRequest
```

Discovery Management Role Group

In addition to the Import/Export Role, eDiscovery is also not a Management Role that is provided to the Organization Management Role Group. This means that if you have an eDiscovery administrator that handles these tasks or a legal department that handles the eDiscovery process, they will need this role assigned to them. Without this, there are cmdlets that cannot be run without it.

Reviewing the EAC, we see that the Discovery Management Role has two Assigned Roles. We also see that by default, the same role has no members assigned to it:

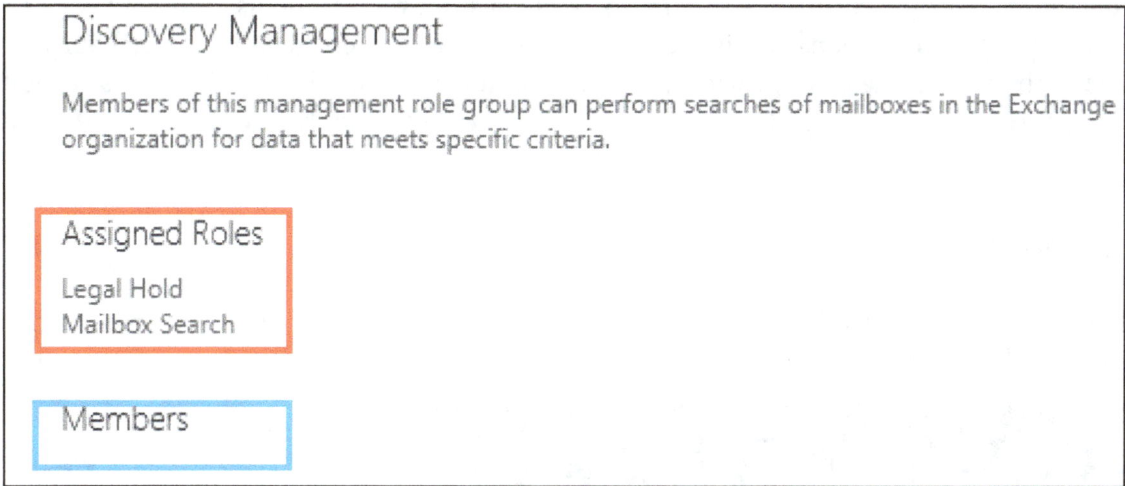

eDiscovery Management Roles

Legal Hold - This role allows a user to determine if emails should be retained for litigation purposes. These holds can be placed for a period or for an indefinite time as well.

Mailbox Search - Allows the holder of this role to search the contents of one of more mailboxes in the organization.

PowerShell

Discovery Management cmdlets are based off of the noun 'MailboxSearch' and using these keywords, we find that there are four cmdlets available to do searches:

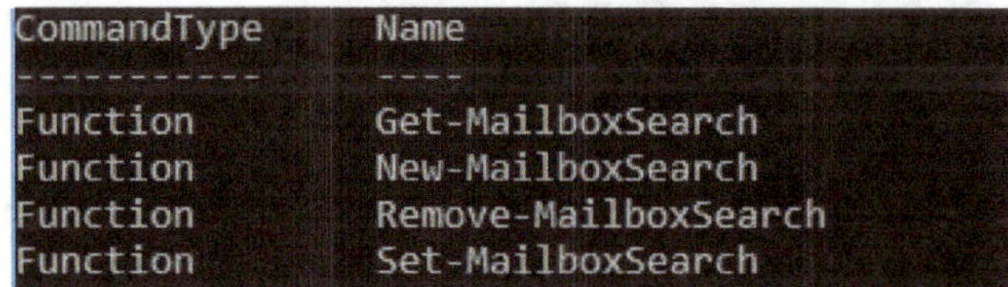
```
CommandType     Name
-----------     ----
Function        Get-MailboxSearch
Function        New-MailboxSearch
Function        Remove-MailboxSearch
Function        Set-MailboxSearch
```

We can verify that Discovery Management does have permission to use these cmdlets like so:

```
Name             Role           Parameters
----             ----           ----------
Set-MailboxSearch Legal Hold     {Confirm, Description, ErrorAction, ErrorVariable...}
Set-MailboxSearch Mailbox Search {AllPublicFolderSources, AllSourceMailboxes, Confirm, Descripti...

PS C:\> Get-ManagementRoleEntry -Identity *\Remove-MailboxSearch | FT -Auto
Name             Role           Parameters
----             ----           ----------
Remove-MailboxSearch Legal Hold     {Confirm, ErrorAction, ErrorVariable, Identity...}
Remove-MailboxSearch Mailbox Search {Confirm, ErrorAction, ErrorVariable, Identity...}
```

Custom Role Groups

In addition to the built in Management Role, we can also create custom roles to be used in Exchange Online. These roles can be simply modified versions of existing roles or brand new ones created for a special purpose. The first method is usually the easiest one to work with depending on the role requirements. For this section we'll first examine the Help Desk Management Role which is one of the more commonly utilized or modified roles in Exchange.

Help Desk Management Role

In Exchange, Help Desk is considered a Role Group. So in order to find out what roles are assigned to this Role Group, we can start with the Get-RoleGroup cmdlet:

```
PS C:\> Get-RoleGroup 'Help Desk'

Name        AssignedRoles
----        -------------
Help Desk   {Reset Password, User Options, View-Only Recipients}
```

Default User Role

In addition to the administration/management security roles in Exchange, there is also a Default User Role assigned to users with mailboxes.

PowerShell

What PowerShell cmdlets are used to handle this assignment to the mailbox? First, let's review what is in the EAC:

To find PowerShell cmdlets that can configure this policy, we can use keywords from within that red box above.

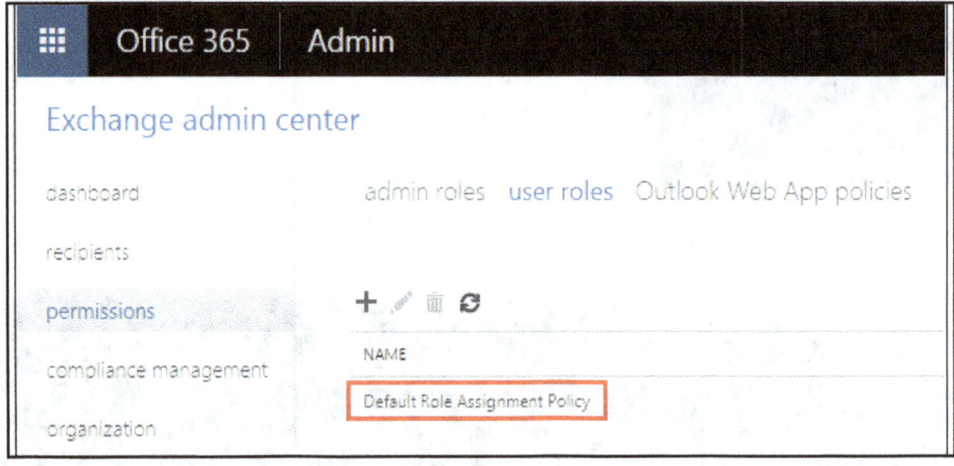

Here is what we can try:

```
Get-Command *RoleAssignmentPolicy

Get-RoleAssignmentPolicy
New-RoleAssignmentPolicy
```

Remove-RoleAssignmentPolicy
Set-RoleAssignmentPolicy

We can check to see what is assigned to the role:

Get-RoleAssignmentPolicy

```
RunspaceId          : 787c33c4-c0de-4979-bc94-96de5eb80d50
IsDefault           : True
Description         : This policy grants end users the permission to set their options in Outlook on
                      the web and perform other self-administration tasks.
RoleAssignments     : {MyTeamMailboxes-Default Role Assignment Policy, My Custom Apps-Default Role
                      Assignment Policy, My Marketplace Apps-Default Role Assignment Policy, My
                      ReadWriteMailbox Apps-Default Role Assignment Policy...}
AssignedRoles       : {MyTeamMailboxes, My Custom Apps, My Marketplace Apps, My ReadWriteMailbox
                      Apps...}
AdminDisplayName    :
ExchangeVersion     : 0.11 (14.0.509.0)
Name                : Default Role Assignment Policy
DistinguishedName   : CN=Default Role Assignment Policy,CN=Policies,CN=RBAC,CN=Configuration,CN=Onlin
                      eExchangeBook.onmicrosoft.com,CN=ConfigurationUnits,DC=NAMPR13A006,DC=PROD,DC=O
                      UTLOOK,DC=COM
Identity            : Default Role Assignment Policy
Guid                : d19e2ff9-2c06-40c0-b7a7-bf2a1894ab8e
ObjectCategory      : NAMPR13A006.PROD.OUTLOOK.COM/Configuration/Schema/ms-Exch-RBAC-Policy
ObjectClass         : {top, msExchRBACPolicy}
WhenChanged         : 12/12/2017 9:34:35 PM
WhenCreated         : 12/12/2017 9:34:35 PM
```

Taking a specific look at the assigned Roles and Role Assignments with these PowerShell cmdlets:

(Get-RoleAssignmentPolicy).AssignedRoles | FT Name

```
MyTeamMailboxes
My Custom Apps
My Marketplace Apps
My ReadWriteMailbox Apps
MyBaseOptions
MyContactInformation
MyMailSubscriptions
MyProfileInformation
MyRetentionPolicies
MyTextMessaging
MyVoiceMail
MyDistributionGroupMembership
MyDistributionGroups
```

(Get-RoleAssignmentPolicy).RoleAssignments | Ft Name

```
MyTeamMailboxes-Default Role Assignment Policy
My Custom Apps-Default Role Assignment Policy
My Marketplace Apps-Default Role Assignment Policy
My ReadWriteMailbox Apps-Default Role Assignment Policy
MyBaseOptions-Default Role Assignment Policy
MyContactInformation-Default Role Assignment Policy
MyMailSubscriptions-Default Role Assignment Policy
MyProfileInformation-Default Role Assignment Policy
MyRetentionPolicies-Default Role Assignment Policy
MyTextMessaging-Default Role Assignment Policy
MyVoiceMail-Default Role Assignment Policy
MyDistributionGroupMembership-Default Role Assignment Pol
MyDistributionGroups-Default Role Assignment Policy
```

We can also, by extension, also see what is assigned to user mailboxes by looking specifically for this property of the mailbox object in Exchange:

Get-Mailbox | Ft DisplayName,RoleAssignmentPolicy

```
DisplayName                    RoleAssignmentPolicy
-----------                    --------------------
Damian Scoles                  Default Role Assignment Policy
John Doe                       Default Role Assignment Policy
```

What exactly can we do with this information? First, a quick look at the EAC and the User Roles tab:

If we edit the 'Default Role Assignment Policy' we can see that some items are checked, others are not:

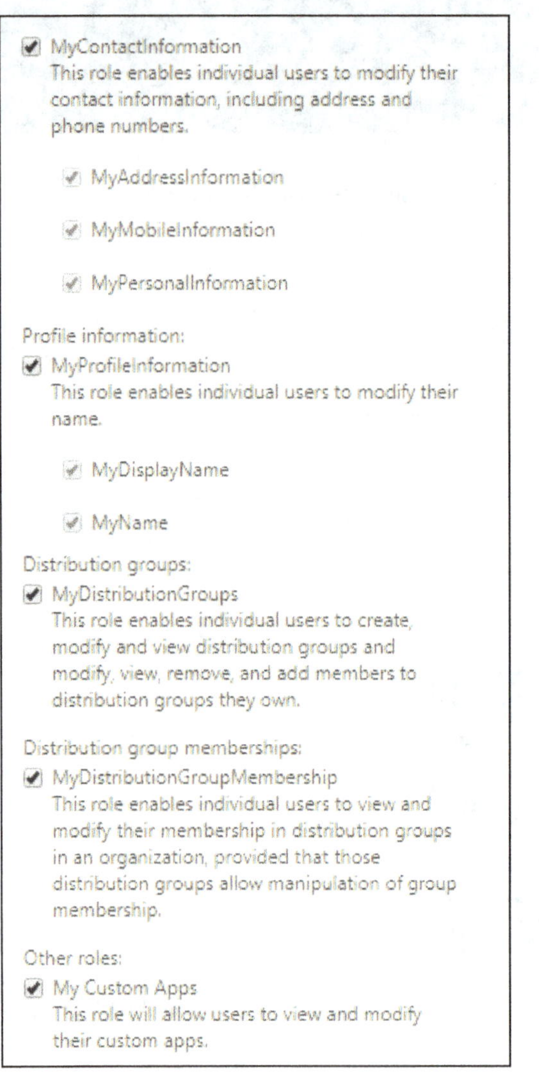

We can see that the average user can modify their profile information, distribution groups, retention policy information and more however, the ability to manage some mailbox delegation is blocked. These values can be changed within the EAC or via PowerShell. Any Role Assignment Policies that exist in Exchange Online cannot be modified to change the existing Assigned Roles. In order to accomplish this, we will need to create a new policy and set it as default.

Let's take the scenario where the users will be allowed to see their own Retention Tags. The default Role Assignment Policy does not allow for this. We will have to use the New-RoleAssignmentPolicy to handle this. Let's see what our options are by looking at the examples:

Get-Help New-RoleAssignmentPolicy -Examples

The most relevant example is this one:

```
-------------------------- Example 3 --------------------------

New-RoleAssignmentPolicy -Name "Limited End User Policy" -Roles "MyPersonalInformation",
"MyDistributionGroupMembership", "MyVoiceMail" -IsDefault
```

If we are looking to add to the default policy, then we need to grab the existing set, add the new right and then apply it to this cmdlet above:

New-RoleAssignmentPolicy –Name 'Modified Default' –Roles "MyTeamMailboxes", "MyDistributionGroupMembership", "My Custom Apps", "My Marketplace Apps", "My ReadWriteMailbox Apps", "MyBaseOptions", "MyContactInformation", "MyTextMessaging", "MyVoiceMail", "MyRetentionPolicies","MyMailboxDelegation"

The cmdlet successfully runs and produces this output:

```
PS C:\> New-RoleAssignmentPolicy –Name 'Modified Default' –Roles "MyTeamMailboxes", "MyDistributionG
roupMembership", "My Custom Apps", "My Marketplace Apps", "My ReadWriteMailbox Apps", "MyBaseOptions
", "MyContactInformation", "MyTextMessaging", "MyVoiceMail", "MyRetentionPolicies","MyMailboxDelegat
ion"


RunspaceId             : 787c33c4-c0de-4979-bc94-96de5eb80d50
IsDefault              : False
Description            :
RoleAssignments        : {OnlineExchangeBook.onmicrosoft.com\MyTeamMailboxes-Modified Default,
                         OnlineExchangeBook.onmicrosoft.com\MyDistributionGroupMembership-Modified
                         Default, OnlineExchangeBook.onmicrosoft.com\My Custom Apps-Modified Default,
                         OnlineExchangeBook.onmicrosoft.com\My Marketplace Apps-Modified Default...}
AssignedRoles          : {MyTeamMailboxes, MyDistributionGroupMembership, My Custom Apps, My
                         Marketplace Apps...}
AdminDisplayName       :
ExchangeVersion        : 0.11 (14.0.509.0)
Name                   : Modified Default
DistinguishedName      : CN=Modified Default,CN=Policies,CN=RBAC,CN=Configuration,CN=OnlineExchangeBook.
                         onmicrosoft.com,CN=ConfigurationUnits,DC=NAMPR13A006,DC=PROD,DC=OUTLOOK,DC=COM
Identity               : Modified Default
Guid                   : 56447b07-a337-4c1b-9196-6206e18a97c5
ObjectCategory         : NAMPR13A006.PROD.OUTLOOK.COM/Configuration/Schema/ms-Exch-RBAC-Policy
ObjectClass            : {top, msExchRBACPolicy}
WhenChanged            : 12/13/2017 8:21:28 AM
WhenCreated            : 12/13/2017 8:21:28 AM
WhenChangedUTC         : 12/13/2017 2:21:28 PM
WhenCreatedUTC         : 12/13/2017 2:21:28 PM
OrganizationId         : NAMPR13A006.PROD.OUTLOOK.COM/Microsoft Exchange Hosted
                         Organizations/OnlineExchangeBook.onmicrosoft.com - NAMPR13A006.PROD.OUTLOOK.COM
                         /ConfigurationUnits/OnlineExchangeBook.onmicrosoft.com/Configuration
Id                     : Modified Default
OriginatingServer      : DM5PR13A006DC03.NAMPR13A006.PROD.OUTLOOK.COM
IsValid                : True
ObjectState            : Changed
```

We can change the policy to the fault with the Set-RoleAssignmentPolicy:

Get-RoleAssignmentPolicy 'Modified Default' | Set-RoleAssignmentPolicy -IsDefault

Which provides these results:

```
PS C:\> Get-RoleAssignmentPolicy 'Modified Default' | Set-RoleAssignmentPolicy -IsDefault

Confirm
Changing the default "RoleAssignmentPolicy" to "Modified Default". This will change the current
default policy into a non-default policy. Do you want to continue?
[Y] Yes  [A] Yes to All  [N] No  [L] No to All  [?] Help (default is "Y"): y
PS C:\>
```

Impersonation

Impersonation is the security feature in Exchange that allows for a user or a service to impersonate the end user while accessing a particular mailbox. This permission can be granted to permit a user access to all mailboxes, but it can also be scoped to limit the access to certain mailboxes. Typical uses for Impersonation are:

- **Migrations** - Allowing a service or application full access to all mailboxes to move them to another location
- **Line of Business Applications** - Many of these applications typically requires the configuration of an account with impersonation rights

With the advent of Exchange 201x, Microsoft's Role Based Access Control (RBAC) changed the way Impersonation is configured, Exchange Online includes this change as well. Impersonation is a Management Role that gets assigned. As we learned above, we can assign a Management Role with the New-ManagementRoleAssignment. For a sample configuration, we can use this cmdlet to assign the ApplicationImpersonation Role to a migration service account that an application server will use to move mailboxes to another Exchange Server in a different Active Directory Forest:

New-ManagementRoleAssignment -Name 'MigrationService' -Role ApplicationImpersonation -User MigrationService

```
PS C:\> New-ManagementRoleAssignment -Name 'MigrationService' -Role ApplicationImpersonation -User M
igrationService

Name                            Role            RoleAssigneeN  RoleAssigneeT  AssignmentMet  EffectiveUse
                                                ame            ype            hod            rName
----                            ----            -------------  -------------  -------------  ------------
MigrationService                Applicatio...   MigrationS...  User           Direct
```

Once assigned, the application now has full access to all the user mailboxes.

Removing Impersonation

The Management Role can be assigned as long as it is needed for the application to operate correctly. Once the need is no longer there, this same role assignment can be removed from the user account. We can use the Remove-ManagementRoleAssignment cmdlet to do that. If we combine the Get-ManagementRoleAssignment with the Remove cmdlet, we can remove the role assignment:

Get-ManagementRoleAssignment 'MigrationService' | Remove-ManagementRoleAssignment

```
PS C:\> Get-ManagementRoleAssignment 'MigrationService' | Remove-ManagementRoleAssignment

Confirm
Are you sure you want to perform this action?
Removing the "MigrationService" management role assignment object. The following properties were
configured: management role "ApplicationImpersonation", role assignee "MigrationService", delegation
type "Regular", recipient write scope "Organization", and configure write scope "None".
[Y] Yes  [A] Yes to All  [N] No  [L] No to All  [?] Help (default is "Y"): y
PS C:\>
```

Reporting Impersonation

We can use PowerShell to produce a report of who has been assigned that role. We can do this with the 'Get-ManagementRoleAssignment' cmdlet. We can use this to see who has been assigned the 'ApplicationImpersonation' Management Role:

Get-ManagementRoleAssignment | where {$_.Role -eq 'ApplicationImpersonation'}

The output for this cmdlet is a bit messy:

```
PS C:\> Get-ManagementRoleAssignment | where {$_.Role -eq 'ApplicationImpersonation'}

Name                          Role          RoleAssigneeN RoleAssigneeT AssignmentMet EffectiveUse
                                            ame           ype           hod           rName
----                          ----          ------------- ------------- ------------- ------------
ApplicationImpersonation-RI... Applicatio... RIM-Mailbo... RoleGroup     Direct        All Group...
ApplicationImpersonation-Or... Applicatio... Organizati... RoleGroup     Direct        All Group...
```

We can clean this up and just produce a table with the name of the role and who is assigned like so:

Get-ManagementRoleAssignment | where {$_.Role -eq 'ApplicationImpersonation'} | Ft
Role,RoleAssigneeName

```
PS C:\> Get-ManagementRoleAssignment | where {$_.Role -eq 'ApplicationImpersonation'} | Ft Role,Role
AssigneeName

Role                     RoleAssigneeName
----                     ----------------
ApplicationImpersonation RIM-MailboxAdminse11e8bd7cda743038cd8ebef53c43706
ApplicationImpersonation Organization Management
```

From this report we see there are only two roles assigned at the moment. If a user were assigned the right, the user would be listed in the results from that cmdlet. A non-owner mailbox access report would be able to determine if these rights were used.

Management Scopes

While some application service accounts need full access, it is possible that an application would only need access to a small subset of the available mailboxes in Exchange. The limiting of this range is called a Management Scope. A Management Scope is a filter that creates the restriction of where to apply the Impersonation Role.

PowerShell

Let's see what cmdlets are available by using Get-Command:

Get-Command *ManagementScope

As we can see, we can create, remove, modify and display any Management Scope in Exchange Online. By Default there are no defined Management Scopes that we can use. We will have to create a Management Scope and then assign this Management Scope to a Management Role, like 'ApplicationImpersonation'. Let's review the available options for the 'New-ManagementScope' cmdlet:

Get-Help New-ManagementScope -Examples

```
-------------------------- Example 1 --------------------------
New-ManagementScope -Name "Mailbox Servers 1 through 3" -ServerList MailboxServer1, MailboxServer2,
MailboxServer3

-------------------------- Example 2 --------------------------
New-ManagementScope -Name "Redmond Site Scope" -ServerRestrictionFilter {ServerSite -eq
"CN=Redmond,CN=Sites,CN=Configuration,DC=contoso,DC=com"}

-------------------------- Example 3 --------------------------
New-ManagementScope -Name "Executive Mailboxes" -RecipientRoot "contoso.com/Executives"
-RecipientRestrictionFilter {RecipientType -eq "UserMailbox"}
```

Scenario

A company called ABC, Corp has a subsidiary whose mailboxes are in the cloud with the parent companies mailboxes. ABC, Corp wants the subsidiary to only be able to manage their own mailboxes. The want to assign a role to someone on the subsidiaries Help Desk. The subsidiary has a different SMTP domain and this will be used for filtering

```
New-ManagementScope -Name 'Domain 1' -RecipientRestrictionFilter {PrimarySMTPAddress -Like '*@
OnlineExchangeBook.onmicrosoft.com'}
```

We can then create a Management Role Assignment (taken from a previous example):

```
New-ManagementRoleAssignment -Name 'HelpDesk-Subsidiary' -Role MailboxManagement –User
HelpDesk
```

Once we have the scope and the role, we can now use the Set-ManagementRoleAssignment to apply the scope to the role:

```
Set-ManagementRoleAssignment -Identity 'HelpDesk' -CustomRecipientWriteScope 'Domain 1'
```

Now the Help Desk account is limited in its MailboxManagement rights to just the mailboxes with the Primary smtp addresses with '@OnlineExchangeBook.onmicrosoft.com' in them.

Auditing

It seems like a lifetime ago, but there was once a time when there wasn't an express need to audit the system administrator or email administrator. They were the trusted IT support people who handled the thankless job of maintaining the servers in corporate datacenters. With the advent of multiple compliance based standards, the auditing of the actions of an administrator have become important. Microsoft recognized this in Exchange 2010 with Admin Audit Logging.

Admin Audit Logs

Admin Audit Logging is in a way self-explanatory. Basically the actions of an Administrator in Exchange are being tracked in a way that can be audited and searched for possible misdeeds. This includes login attempts without permission or even a bad configuration. The log can be dumped for examination by a third party, examined in the Exchange Admin Center or even just simply displayed to the screen.

PowerShell

What PowerShell cmdlets are available for this part of Exchange's security mechanisms? Well, let's find out:

```
Get-Command *AdminAudit*
```

This provides a short list of cmdlets:

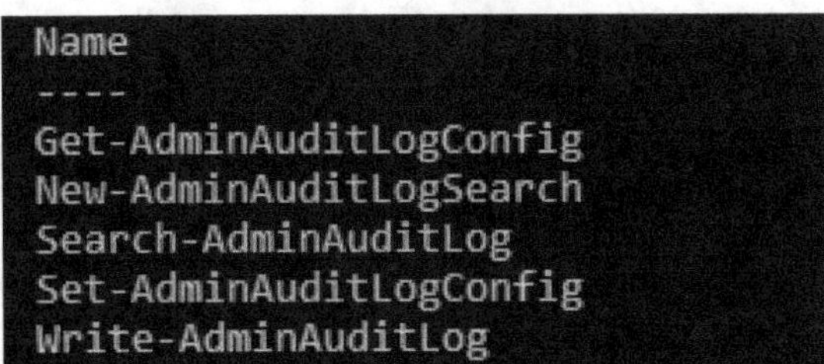

Let's start off with reviewing what the Admin Audit Log is configured for:

Get-AdminAuditLogConfig

```
AdminAuditLogEnabled             : True
LogLevel                         : None
TestCmdletLoggingEnabled         : False
AdminAuditLogCmdlets             : {*}
AdminAuditLogParameters          : {*}
AdminAuditLogExcludedCmdlets     : {}
AdminAuditLogAgeLimit            : 90.00:00:00
LoadBalancerCount                : 3
RefreshInterval                  : 10
PartitionInfo                    : {}
UnifiedAuditLogIngestionEnabled  : False
UnifiedAuditLogFirstOptInDate    :
AdminDisplayName                 :
ExchangeVersion                  : 0.10 (14.0.100.0)
Name                             : Admin Audit Log Settings
DistinguishedName                : CN=Admin Audit Log Settings,CN=Global Settings,CN=Configuration,C
                                   N=OnlineExchangeBook.onmicrosoft.com,CN=ConfigurationUnits,DC=NAM
                                   PR13A006,DC=PROD,DC=OUTLOOK,DC=COM
Identity                         : Admin Audit Log Settings
Guid                             : cc8688e8-0c15-411d-8551-8387f50a4dfc
ObjectCategory                   : NAMPR13A006.PROD.OUTLOOK.COM/Configuration/Schema/ms-Exch-Admin-A
                                   udit-Log-Config
ObjectClass                      : {top, msExchAdminAuditLogConfig}
WhenChanged                      : 12/12/2017 9:34:55 PM
WhenCreated                      : 12/12/2017 9:34:26 PM
WhenChangedUTC                   : 12/13/2017 3:34:55 AM
WhenCreatedUTC                   : 12/13/2017 3:34:26 AM
OrganizationId                   : NAMPR13A006.PROD.OUTLOOK.COM/Microsoft Exchange Hosted
                                   Organizations/OnlineExchangeBook.onmicrosoft.com - NAMPR13A006.PR
                                   OD.OUTLOOK.COM/ConfigurationUnits/OnlineExchangeBook.onmicrosoft.
                                   com/Configuration
Id                               : Admin Audit Log Settings
```

Notice that the log age limit is 90 days, plenty of time to generate reports from and get history from as well. Two other parameters are important - AdminAuditLogCmdlets and AdminAuditLogParameters which refer to all cmdlets and all parameters. In most scenarios, the 'LogLevel' setting of 'None' is sufficient, however, the LogLevel can also be configured as 'Verbose'. The Verbose LogLevel setting also adds two additional bits of information:

ModifiedProperties (old and new)
ModifiedObjectResolvedName properties

What has changed with the Admin Audit Log over the past versions is the addition of the UnifiedAuditLog parameters. These two parameters link Exchange On-premises and Exchange Online. Only one can be configured. The UnifiedAuditLogIngestionEnabled parameter can be set to True or False. The default is False, which only audits and allows searches of Exchange On-Premises servers. If the setting is configured for True, the Admin Audit Logs for Office 365 are recorded in Office 365 and searches will be allowed after the fact. Other configurable parameters for the Admin Audit Log are:

AdminAuditLogCmdlets
AdminAuditLogParameters
AdminAuditLogExcludedCmdlets

The auditable cmdlets and parameters can be fine-tuned if that is desired, but to get a true sense of what an admin is doing the default configuration is the way to go. The third parameter 'AdminAuditLogExcludedCmdlets' allows for exclusions from the entirety of what is defined in the first two cmdlets. For example, if all cmdlets are chosen '*' to be audited, one could exclude certain cmdlets that may not be important like running Get-MessageTrackingLog or any Get cmdlets as well. This would allow for a more fine-tuned set of Admin Audit Logs.

Lastly, the amount of time included in the logs can also be adjusted from the default of 90 days. If the value is set for 0, all the logs are purged. Setting a number less than the default will truncate what is available in the Admin Audit Log as well.

Searching the Admin Audit Log

You will notice that there are two cmdlets for handling searches of the Admin Audit Log:

```
New-AdminAuditLogSearch
Search-AdminAuditLog
```

So which of these cmdlets are we supposed to use for searching the logs? Let's review some examples from these two cmdlets to compare the two:

```
Get-Help New-AdminAuditLogSearch -Full
```

```
------------------------------ Example 1 ------------------------------

New-AdminAuditLogSearch -Name "Mailbox Quota Change Audit" -Cmdlets Set-Mailbox -Parameters
UseDatabaseQuotaDefaults, ProhibitSendReceiveQuota, ProhibitSendQuota -StartDate 01/24/2015 -EndDate 02/12/2015
-StatusMailRecipients david@contoso.com, chris@contoso.com

------------------------------ Example 2 ------------------------------

New-AdminAuditLogSearch -ExternalAccess $true -StartDate 07/25/2015 -EndDate 10/24/2015 -StatusMailRecipients
admin@contoso.com,pilarp@contoso.com -Name "Datacenter admin audit log"
```

```
Get-Help Search-AdminAuditLog -Full
```

```
------------------------------ Example 1 ------------------------------
Search-AdminAuditLog -Cmdlets Set-Mailbox -Parameters UseDatabaseQuotaDefaults, ProhibitSendReceiveQuota,
ProhibitSendQuota -StartDate 01/24/2015 -EndDate 02/12/2015 -IsSuccess $true

------------------------------ Example 2 ------------------------------
Search-AdminAuditLog -Cmdlets New-RoleGroup, New-ManagementRoleAssignment

------------------------------ Example 3 ------------------------------
Search-AdminAuditLog -ExternalAccess $true -StartDate 09/17/2015 -EndDate 10/02/2015
```

Reviewing the two cmdlets, the help reveals a small different between the two cmdlets. The first one, New-Admin-AuditLogSearch cmdlet examples both include the 'StatusMailRecipients' parameter and the parameter is required for the cmdlet. Thus the only way to get the results is via an email. This email is generated and delivered within a period of 15 minutes.

New-AdminAuditLogSearch

A sample run shows the status of the report and information to be gathered:

```
PS C:\> New-AdminAuditLogSearch -StartDate 11/01/17 -EndDate 12/15/17 -StatusMailRecipients dami
an@OnlineExchangeBook.onmicrosoft.com


RunspaceId              : 4902ae07-3dfd-4c29-a9a7-2da78b7bbb6d
Cmdlets                 : {}
Parameters              : {}
ObjectIds               : {}
UserIds                 : {}
Name                    : Search20171214{28f15b89-2ed9-497c-8372-36db2ac3252e}
StartDateUtc            : 11/1/2017 12:00:00 AM
EndDateUtc              : 12/15/2017 12:00:00 AM
StatusMailRecipients    : {damian@OnlineExchangeBook.onmicrosoft.com}
CreatedBy               : NAMPR13A006.PROD.OUTLOOK.COM/Microsoft Exchange Hosted
                          Organizations/OnlineExchangeBook.onmicrosoft.com/damian
ExternalAccess          :
QueryComplexity         : 0
Identity                : 6ad9ad7d-81c4-4db4-a0a9-8d58d9c119ee
IsValid                 : True
ObjectState             : New
```

After the cmdlet is run, the results will be emailed to the Administrator's mailbox:

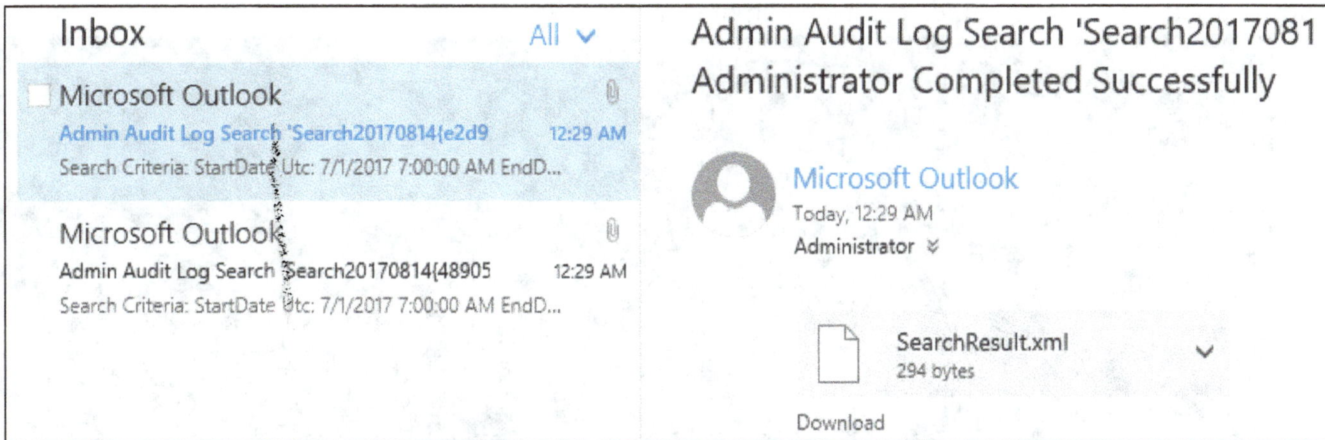

The XML report will look something like this:

```xml
<?xml version="1.0" encoding="UTF-16"?>
- <SearchResults>
    - <Event OriginatingServer="16-05-EX01 (15.01.0669.032)" ExternalAccess="false" ObjectModified="d78992db-e612-46fb-956b-64f9a60858
      AdminAuditLogSearch" Caller="Administrator@16-05.Local">
      - <CmdletParameters>
          <Parameter Value="7/1/2017 12:00:00 AM" Name="StartDate"/>
          <Parameter Value="8/31/2017 12:00:00 AM" Name="EndDate"/>
          <Parameter Value="administrator@16-05.local" Name="StatusMailRecipients"/>
        </CmdletParameters>
      </Event>
    - <Event OriginatingServer="16-05-EX01 (15.01.0669.032)" ExternalAccess="false" ObjectModified="747e6502-ec35-48c2-8763-82e622250a
      AdminAuditLogSearch" Caller="Administrator@16-05.Local">
      - <CmdletParameters>
          <Parameter Value="7/1/2017 12:00:00 AM" Name="StartDate"/>
          <Parameter Value="8/1/2017 12:00:00 AM" Name="EndDate"/>
          <Parameter Value="administrator@16-05.local" Name="StatusMailRecipients"/>
        </CmdletParameters>
      </Event>
    - <Event OriginatingServer="16-05-EX01 (15.01.0669.032)" ExternalAccess="false" ObjectModified="MigrationService" Succeeded="true" Run[
      ManagementRoleAssignment" Caller="Administrator@16-05.Local">
      - <CmdletParameters>
          <Parameter Value="MigrationService" Name="Identity"/>
        </CmdletParameters>
      </Event>
    - <Event OriginatingServer="16-05-EX01 (15.01.0669.032)" ExternalAccess="false" ObjectModified="MigrationService" Succeeded="true" Run[
      ManagementRoleAssignment" Caller="Administrator@16-05.Local">
      - <CmdletParameters>
          <Parameter Value="MigrationService" Name="Name"/>
          <Parameter Value="ApplicationImpersonation" Name="Role"/>
          <Parameter Value="MigrationService" Name="User"/>
        </CmdletParameters>
      </Event>
```

We can see the cmdlets, parameters, when it was run and by whom. If there are certain criteria that needs to be found, it can be pulled out via PowerShell or an XML editor depending on the need and volume of the reports. The cmdlet does have some limitations (https://technet.microsoft.com/en-us/library/ff459243(v=exchg.160).aspx):

'After the New-AdminAuditLogSearch cmdlet is run, the report is delivered to the mailboxes you specify within 15 minutes. The log is included as an XML attachment on the report email message. The maximum size of the log that can be generated is 10 megabytes (MB).'

Search-AdminAuditLog

Below is a sample run of the cmdlet and the output it can produce:

```
PS C:\temp> Search-AdminAuditLog -StartDate 11/22/17

RunspaceId              : 4902ae07-3dfd-4c29-a9a7-2da78b7bbb6d
ObjectModified          : john.smit
CmdletName              : Remove-Mailbox
CmdletParameters        : {Identity}
ModifiedProperties      : {}
Caller                  : damian@OnlineExchangeBook.onmicrosoft.com
ExternalAccess          : False
Succeeded               : True
Error                   :
RunDate                 : 12/6/2017 5:16:57 PM
OriginatingServer       : CY4PR13MB1350 (15.20.0302.000)
Identity                : AAMkADM0MjA3Nz11LWZjZjQtNGZjNS1iODE2LTJhY2FlNzhmYTBjYwBGAAAAAADso6EVTVN7Tb+iOW
                          cWF3ZFBwBjg6dugHC/T5kN6nS3WwMbAAAAAAEVAABjg6dugHC/T5kN6nS3WwMbAAAD6/hAAA=
IsValid                 : True
ObjectState             : New

RunspaceId              : 4902ae07-3dfd-4c29-a9a7-2da78b7bbb6d
ObjectModified          : damian
CmdletName              : Enable-Mailbox
CmdletParameters        : {Identity, Archive}
ModifiedProperties      : {}
Caller                  : damian@OnlineExchangeBook.onmicrosoft.com
ExternalAccess          : False
Succeeded               : True
```

Like any other screen output, the results can be exported to an XML file for future examination like so:

Search-AdminAuditLog -StartDate <start date> -EndDate <end date> -resultsize 25000 | Export-Clixml <file name>

The more practical of the two for further analysis is the Search-AdminAuditLog as the file can be placed in a central location for analysis. A sample XML file looks like this:

```xml
<Objs Version="1.1.0.1" xmlns="http://schemas.microsoft.com/powershell/2004/04">
  <Obj RefId="0">
    <TN RefId="0">
      <T>Deserialized.Microsoft.Exchange.Management.SystemConfigurationTasks.AdminAuditLogEvent</T>
      <T>Deserialized.Microsoft.Exchange.Data.ConfigurableObject</T>
      <T>Deserialized.System.Object</T>
    </TN>
    <ToString>Microsoft.Exchange.Management.SystemConfigurationTasks.AdminAuditLogEvent</ToString>
    <Props>
      <S N="ObjectModified">damian</S>
      <S N="CmdletName">Set-Mailbox</S>
      <Obj N="CmdletParameters" RefId="1">
        <TN RefId="1">
          <T>Deserialized.Microsoft.Exchange.Data.MultiValuedProperty`1[[Microsoft.Exchange.Data.Admi
          <T>Deserialized.Microsoft.Exchange.Data.MultiValuedPropertyBase</T>
          <T>Deserialized.System.Object</T>
        </TN>
        <LST>
          <Obj RefId="2">
            <TN RefId="2">
              <T>Deserialized.Microsoft.Exchange.Data.AdminAuditLogCmdletParameter</T>
              <T>Deserialized.System.Object</T>
            </TN>
            <ToString>LitigationHoldEnabled</ToString>
            <Props>
              <S N="Name">LitigationHoldEnabled</S>
              <S N="Value">True</S>
            </Props>
          </Obj>
          <Obj RefId="3">
            <TNRef RefId="2" />
            <ToString>LitigationHoldDuration</ToString>
            <Props>
              <S N="Name">LitigationHoldDuration</S>
              <S N="Value">365.00:00:00</S>
            </Props>
          </Obj>
```

Mailbox Audit Logs

Mailbox auditing logging is set on a per mailbox basis. The logging will capture the mailbox access by mailbox owners, delegates and administrators. The types of access that are logged can also be configured with PowerShell. Let's explore how we can configure the logging and examine the logs with PowerShell.

PowerShell

What PowerShell cmdlets are available for this part of Exchange's security mechanisms? Well, let's find out:

Get-Command *MailboxAudit*

```
[PS] C:\>Get-Command *MailboxAudit*

CommandType      Name
-----------      ----
Function         Get-MailboxAuditBypassAssociation
Function         New-MailboxAuditLogSearch
Function         Search-MailboxAuditLog
Function         Set-MailboxAuditBypassAssociation
```

Mailbox Audits are not pre-configured, but are similar to how we ran the searches of the Admin Audit Logs in the previous section. First, we need to enable the auditing on the mailboxes we want to track. We can set this on a per mailbox basis or on a global basis to track all mailboxes in Exchange. The cmdlet we need for this is Set-Mailbox.

Mailbox Auditing Default Settings

What options are needed in order to configure this?   First, we can start with:

Get-Help Set-Mailbox -Full

We can review the parameters with the 'Audit' keyword in it like these:

AuditAdmin - What is logged when an administrator accesses a mailbox
AuditDelegate - What delegate rights are audited when accessed
AuditEnabled - Whether or not mailbox auditing is enabled
AuditLog - Microsoft only parameter, do not set without support
AuditLogAgeLimit - The number of days the log is kept for with 90 days set as the default
AuditOwner - Rights that are audited for a mailbox owner

Let's review the default settings on mailboxes to see values to change to allow accurate auditing of a mailbox:

Get-Mailbox | fl *audit*

```
AuditEnabled      : False
AuditLogAgeLimit  : 90.00:00:00
AuditAdmin        : {Update, Move, MoveToDeletedItems, SoftDelete, HardDelete, FolderBind, SendAs,
                    SendOnBehalf, Create}
AuditDelegate     : {Update, SoftDelete, HardDelete, SendAs, Create}
AuditOwner        : {}

AuditEnabled      : False
AuditLogAgeLimit  : 90.00:00:00
AuditAdmin        : {Update, Move, MoveToDeletedItems, SoftDelete, HardDelete, FolderBind, SendAs,
                    SendOnBehalf, Create}
AuditDelegate     : {Update, SoftDelete, HardDelete, SendAs, Create}
AuditOwner        : {}
```

Notice that auditing is not enabled for either mailbox. Also notice what actions are audited for Admins as well as what actions are auditing for mailbox delegates. An age limit of 90 days is configured for the audit logs. There also is no set owner for the mailbox auditing.

Configuring Mailbox Auditing

** **Note** ** Before we get too deep into mailbox auditing in Exchange Online make sure to review your local and/or regional privacy laws to make sure this will work for you without breaking the law.

Adding mailbox auditing involves using the Set-Mailbox cmdlet. First, the auditing needs to be enabled on the mailbox needs to be audited:

```
[PS] C:\>Get-Mailbox Damian | Set-Mailbox -AuditEnabled $True
[PS] C:\>Get-Mailbox Dave | Set-Mailbox -AuditEnabled $True
[PS] C:\>
```

After auditing is enabled, we can adjust settings like the length the logs are kept, with the default being 90 days. For example we can adjust the length like 120 and 150 days:

```
[PS] C:\>Get-Mailbox Dave | Set-Mailbox -AuditLogAgeLimit 120.00:00:00
[PS] C:\>Get-Mailbox Damian | Set-Mailbox -AuditLogAgeLimit 150.00:00:00
[PS] C:\>
```

Once done, we can verify the changes:

Get-Mailbox | FT Audit*

This provides these results:

```
AuditEnabled       : True
AuditLogAgeLimit   : 150.00:00:00
AuditAdmin         : {Update, Move, MoveToDeletedItems, SoftDelete, HardDelete, FolderBind, SendAs,
                     SendOnBehalf, Create}
AuditDelegate      : {Update, SoftDelete, HardDelete, SendAs, Create}
AuditOwner         : {}

AuditEnabled       : True
AuditLogAgeLimit   : 120.00:00:00
AuditAdmin         : {Update, Move, MoveToDeletedItems, SoftDelete, HardDelete, FolderBind, SendAs,
                     SendOnBehalf, Create}
AuditDelegate      : {Update, SoftDelete, HardDelete, SendAs, Create}
AuditOwner         : {}
```

Once the auditing is enabled, we can now generate searches of these logs.

Searching the Mailbox Audit Log

You will notice that there are two methods in order to search these generated logs:

Search-MailboxAuditLog
New-MailboxAuditLogSearch

So which of these cmdlets are we supposed to use for searching the logs? Let's review some examples from these two cmdlets to compare the two:

Search-MailboxAuditLog

```
---------------------- Example 1 ----------------------
Search-MailboxAuditLog -Identity kwok -LogonTypes Admin,Delegate -StartDate 1/1/2015 -EndDate 12/31/2015
 -ResultSize 2000

---------------------- Example 2 ----------------------
Search-MailboxAuditLog -Mailboxes kwok,bsmith -LogonTypes Admin,Delegate -StartDate 1/1/2015 -EndDate
12/31/2015 -ResultSize 2000

---------------------- Example 3 ----------------------
Search-MailboxAuditLog -Identity kwok -LogonTypes Owner -ShowDetails -StartDate 1/1/2016 -EndDate
3/1/2016 | Where-Object {$_.Operation -eq "HardDelete"}
```

New-MailboxAuditLogSearch

```
---------------------- Example 1 ----------------------
New-MailboxAuditLogSearch "Admin and Delegate Access" -Mailboxes "Ken Kwok","April Stewart" -LogonTypes
Admin,Delegate -StartDate 1/1/2015 -EndDate 12/31/2015 -StatusMailRecipients auditors@contoso.com

---------------------- Example 2 ----------------------
New-MailboxAuditLogSearch -ExternalAccess $true -StartDate 09/01/2015 -EndDate 10/24/2015
 -StatusMailRecipients admin@contoso.com
```

Reviewing the two cmdlets, the help reveals a small difference between the two cmdlets. The first one, the New-MailboxAuditLogSearch cmdlet, both examples include the 'StatusMailRecipients' parameter and the parameter is required for the cmdlet. Thus the only way to get the results is via an email. This email is generated and delivered within a period of 15 minutes.

Search-MailboxAuditLog

A sample run of this cmdlet shows how it displays the results to the PowerShell window:

```
[PS] C:\>Search-MailboxAuditLog -StartDate 8/1/17
Creating a new session for implicit remoting of "Search-MailboxAuditLog" command...
[PS] C:\>
```

No results? That's because no mailboxes have had the Audit Logging setting enabled. This is an expected result. If we had enabled the logging on a mailbox and there was some sort of activity, we would see this instead:

```
[PS] C:\>Search-MailboxAuditLog -Identity Dave


RunspaceId                  : ad48ccec-dff6-487e-bdb6-18b4bf057bd0
MailboxGuid                 : dab7b892-2bfc-409c-a408-b10acf62bfc6
MailboxResolvedOwnerName    : Dave Stork
LastAccessed                : 8/15/2017 1:58:10 PM
Identity                    : Dave Stork
IsValid                     : True
ObjectState                 : New
```

We can also export this to an XML like so:

Search-MailboxAuditLog -Identity Damian -StartDate 11/23/17 -EndDate 12/13/17 | Export-Clixml c:\temp\test.xml


```xml
<?xml version="1.0"?>
<Objs xmlns="http://schemas.microsoft.com/powershell/2004/04" Version="1.1.0.1">
  <Obj RefId="0">
    <TN RefId="0">
      <T>Microsoft.Exchange.Data.Directory.Management.MailboxAuditLogRecord</T>
      <T>Microsoft.Exchange.Data.ConfigurableObject</T>
      <T>System.Object</T>
    </TN>
    <ToString>Microsoft.Exchange.Data.Directory.Management.MailboxAuditLogRecord</ToString>
    <Props>
      <S N="MailboxGuid">dab7b892-2bfc-409c-a408-b10acf62bfc6</S>
      <S N="MailboxResolvedOwnerName">Dave Stork</S>
      <DT N="LastAccessed">2017-08-15T13:58:10-05:00</DT>
      <Obj RefId="1" N="Identity">
        <TN RefId="1">
          <T>Microsoft.Exchange.Data.Directory.Management.MailboxAuditLogRecordId</T>
          <T>Microsoft.Exchange.Data.ObjectId</T>
          <T>System.Object</T>
        </TN>
        <ToString>16-08.local/Users/Dave Stork</ToString>
        <MS>
          <BA N="SerializationData">AAEAAAD/////AQAAAAAAAAMAgAAAGVNaWNyb3NvZnQuRXhjaGFuZ2UuR(
        </MS>
      </Obj>
      <B N="IsValid">true</B>
      <Obj RefId="2" N="ObjectState">
        <TN RefId="2">
          <T>Microsoft.Exchange.Data.ObjectState</T>
          <T>System.Enum</T>
          <T>System.ValueType</T>
          <T>System.Object</T>
        </TN>
        <ToString>New</ToString>
        <I32>0</I32>
      </Obj>
    </Props>
```


New-MailboxAuditLogSearch

A sample run shows the status of the report and information to be gathered:

```
PS C:\> New-MailboxAuditLogSearch -Mailboxes john.doe -StartDate 11/29/17 -EndDate 12/14/17 -Sta
tusMailRecipients damian@OnlineExchangeBook.onmicrosoft.com


RunspaceId            : 4902ae07-3dfd-4c29-a9a7-2da78b7bbb6d
Mailboxes             : {NAMPR13A006.PROD.OUTLOOK.COM/Microsoft Exchange Hosted
                        Organizations/OnlineExchangeBook.onmicrosoft.com/john.doe}
LogonTypes            : {Admin, Delegate}
Operations            : {}
ShowDetails           : False
HasAttachments        :
ConsumerMailbox       : False
Name                  : Search20171214{72f9a9cb-5fb7-4641-8479-041e17f3915d}
StartDateUtc          : 11/29/2017 12:00:00 AM
EndDateUtc            : 12/14/2017 12:00:00 AM
StatusMailRecipients  : {damian@OnlineExchangeBook.onmicrosoft.com}
CreatedBy             : NAMPR13A006.PROD.OUTLOOK.COM/Microsoft Exchange Hosted
                        Organizations/OnlineExchangeBook.onmicrosoft.com/damian

ExternalAccess        :
QueryComplexity       : 0
Identity              : 405f264c-12e5-43c5-a09b-94e485273a99
IsValid               : True
ObjectState           : New
```

Same as the previous cmdlet when no audit logging is enabled. Below is what would be expected if Audit Logging were enabled:

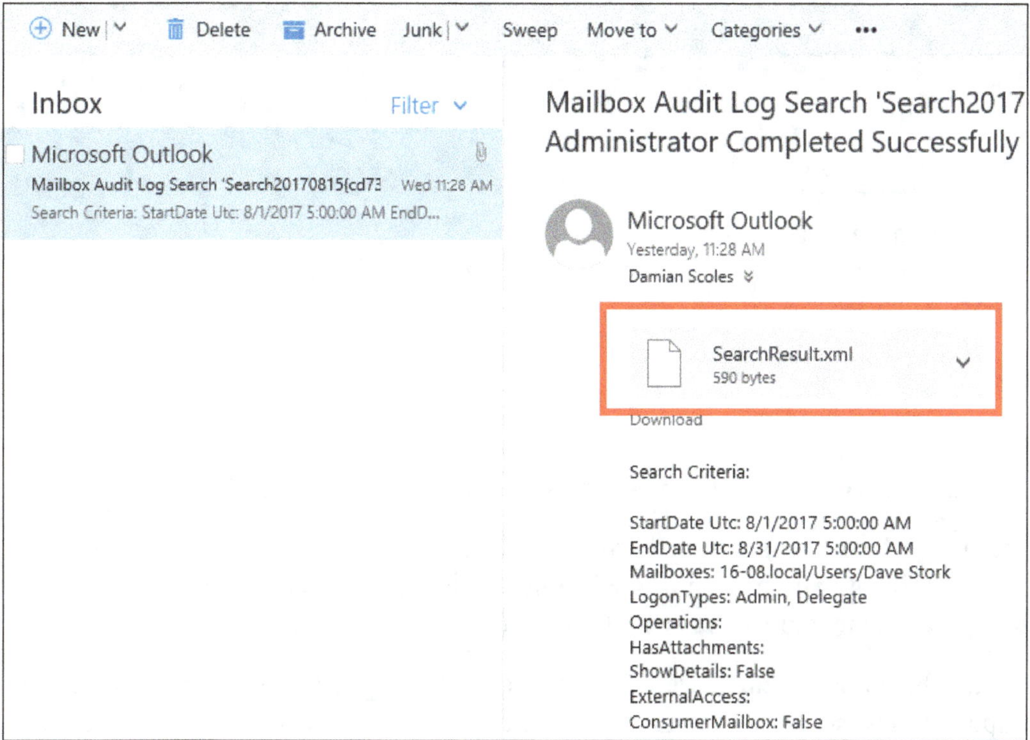

XML looks like this:

```xml
<?xml version="1.0" encoding="UTF-16"?>
- <SearchResults>
    <Event LastAccessed="2017-08-15T13:58:10-05:00" Owner="Dave Stork" MailboxGuid="dab7b892-2bfc-409c-a408-b10acf62bfc6"/>
  </SearchResults>
```

** **Note** ** It should be a good practice to audit Shared and Room mailboxes on a regular basis, while keeping regional privacy laws in consideration.

Migrations

In This Chapter

- Introduction
- Basics (Migrations from On-Premises)
- Checking Migration Status and Reports
- Public Folder Migrations

Introduction

Migrations when it comes to Exchange Online typically involves a couple different scenarios:

- Migration to Exchange Online from an on-premises solution (Exchange, Lotus Notes, etc.)
- Migration from Exchange Online to an on-premises solution (Exchange, Lotus Notes, etc.)
- Migration from Exchange Online tenant to Exchange Online tenant

With respect to PowerShell and Exchange Online, we will cover some very specific scenarios and not all of the scenarios above. For example, the last scenario, a tenant to tenant migration, is typically done with third party tools and beyond setting up users, mailboxes, etc, there really isn't anything else special that PowerShell can do for us in that scenario.

** **Note** ** Tenant to Tenant migrations will be a feature of Office 365 in the future.

With new versions of Exchange, we now have mailbox moves that can be synced (without completing the migration) to the destination Exchange Server or Exchange Online. With the advent of larger mailboxes this is a rather important advancement. Otherwise it could mean that a migration would take too long to perform in a single big bang, meaning that you have to migrate mailboxes in stages and maintain a coexistence environment until the last mailbox has been moved. It was also a major step towards making Office 365 more accessible to migrate to and more flexible for Microsoft on managing servers and databases.

Note that a mailbox is not locked during the data copy to Office 365 and the user can still access email via their various clients. However, there is an option that is still available, called -ForceOffline switch in the New-MoveRequest cmdlet. You shouldn't have to use it under normal conditions, however from time to time a mailbox is fickle and can only move via an Offline move.

Now, most of the move mailbox options are available from within the Exchange Admin Center in one way or another. But in our experience, EAC is probably fine for simple migrations or the incidental move of one mailbox. If you migrate your server environment from one major build to another, it's almost impossible to ignore PowerShell. Those migrations are far more complex and full of caveats, that it almost always requires the use of custom PowerShell cmdlets and scripts.

But, before delving more into the PowerShell of (Online) Mailbox moves we shall explain the fundamentals of Mailbox moves.

Basics (Migrations from On-Premises)

Although Exchange 2016 creates Migration Batches (more on that later) automatically even when moving one single mailbox, the basis of a mailbox migration is the New-MoveRequest cmdlet. The name is telling; you request the system to move a mailbox. Why is that? Well, it could be the source or more importantly the target server is not in good health before or during the move. The Mailbox Replication service (present on each server in 2016) can decide that the move is too impactful or too risky and stalls the move.

Exchange is responsible for a successful mailbox move to be not to impactful on client experience, due to performance loss (a move does cost extra resources) and preventing data loss during a move.

Another benefit is that the moves can be stopped or synced at any time. This is possible since all move requests are stored in arbitration mailboxes (system mailboxes, hidden from normal view) for processing at any time. Or when a move fails for whatever reason, if you can resolve the issue you can restart the (online) move again. Or you could temporarily suspend any moves when you perceive any issues in your Exchange environment and after resolving those issues, continue at your leisure.

This means the mailbox migrations are a lot more robust and flexible for admins than in previous versions of Exchange (2007 and earlier). You can prepare, pre-stage the data and if necessary troubleshoot your migration long before completing the mailbox moves to the target servers. That moment that is traditionally prone to errors and requiring some aftercare normally. With online mailbox moves, these efforts will often be limited to client issues, rather than (also) server issues.

Migration Batch

As mentioned previously when using the web based Exchange Admin Center, even when you move one single mailbox it will create a Migration Batch. Migration Batches are bulk mailbox moves, which makes those bulk moves more easy to handle: Stopping or suspending them will stop/suspend all moves that are a part of the batch.

Before we create an actual Migration Batch, we need to create a connection point that Exchange Online can use to pull the mailbox data from Exchange on-premises. This connection point is called a Migration Endpoint. The Migration Endpoint consists of a web address (accessible over the Internet) and a set of credentials with which to authenticate with this endpoint. Let's review what cmdlets are available for Migration Endpoints:

Get-Command *MigrationEndpoint

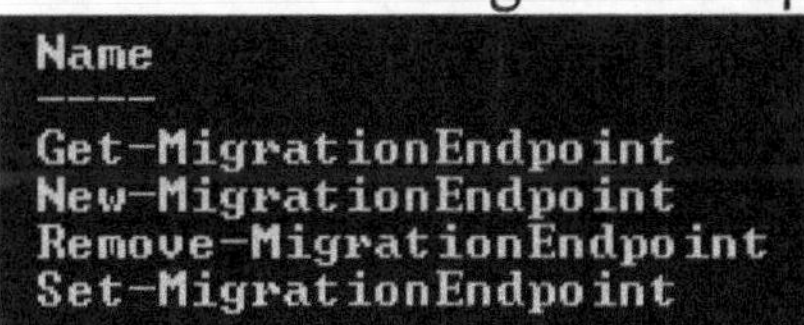

```
Name

Get-MigrationEndpoint
New-MigrationEndpoint
Remove-MigrationEndpoint
Set-MigrationEndpoint
```

As we can see from the list above, we have our typical PowerShell verbs associated with the MigrationEndpoint noun phrase. Now we can review the examples from the New-MigrationEndpoint:

```
--------------------------- Example 1 ---------------------------

New-MigrationEndpoint -Name Endpoint1 -ExchangeRemoteMove -Autodiscover -EmailAddress
tonysmith@contoso.com -Credentials (Get-Credential contoso\tonysmith)

--------------------------- Example 2 ---------------------------

New-MigrationEndpoint -Name Endpoint2 -ExchangeRemoteMove -RemoteServer MRSServer.contoso.com
-Credentials (Get-Credential Contoso.com\Administrator)
```

```
New-MigrationEndpoint -Name MRSEndpoint -ExchangeRemoteMove -RemoteServer Exchange.
MyDomain.Com -Credentials (Get-Credential MyDomain.Com\Administrator)
```

```
Identity      EndpointType         RemoteServer
MRSEndpoint  ExchangeRemoteMove  Exchange.MyDomain.Com
```

Once we have our Migration Endpoint created, we can now work on creating a Migration Batch for moving a mailbox to Office 365.

Creating a most basic new batch:

```
New-MigrationBatch -Name BatchMove01 -SourceEndpoint MRSEndpoint -TargetDeliveryDomain
PracticalPowerShell.onmicrosoft.com -CSVData ([System.IO.File]::ReadAllBytes("C:\scripting\batch01.
csv")) -NotificationEmails damian@practicalpowershell.com
```

The parameter Local indicates a move to an Exchange Online tenant. The Name is the identifier and CSVData is a CSV file with the mailboxes required to move with this Migration Batch. Also in the line are the SourceEndpoint (where Exchange Online connects to move data). The only column required in the CSV is "EmailAddress", where each mailbox to be migrated should have at least their email address listed, one per line. For information on the format of the input CSV file see:

https://technet.microsoft.com/en-US/library/ms.exch.eac.LearnMoreMigrationImportCsv(EXCHG.150).aspx?v=15.20.428.14&l=1&s=BPOS_S_E15_0

So, that's the basic command, but let's take a look at the other often used cmdlets and parameters. To know what's already present as a Migration Batch, you'd have to list them with Get-MigrationBatch:

```
PS C:\> Get-MigrationBatch

Identity      Status     Type                TotalCount
--------      ------     ----                ----------
BatchMove01  Stopped  ExchangeRemoteMove  1
BatchMove02  Stopped  ExchangeRemoteMove  1
```

With the AutoComplete parameter, you can tell Exchange that the mailboxes in the Migration Batch may be completed immediately when all the data has been moved of a specific mailbox. With the parameter AutoStart the batch will start at creation, if you do not use this you will have to start the batch manually with:

```
Start-MigrationBatch -Identity "<batchname>"
```

```
PS C:\> Get-MigrationBatch

Identity      Status     Type                TotalCount
--------      ------     ----                ----------
BatchMove01  Syncing   ExchangeRemoteMove  1
BatchMove02  Starting  ExchangeRemoteMove  1
```

You can see the status has (eventually) changed to Syncing, after starting the Migration Batch.

In optimal situations, there are no corrupt items in mailboxes, however based on years of experience there can be many unexpected corruptions that may make an object unreadable or unable to be migrated. Sometimes you can repair those objects, but it is not always practical. Luckily you can configure the Migration Batch to accept a number of corrupt items that will be skipped and thus lost, with the BadItemLimit parameter.

Not only can corrupt items stall a mailbox move, also large items that are over the set MaxReceiveSize value in the organization can halt a move. The LargeItemLimit specifies the number of "violations" that are acceptable, but note that those items are not migrated and thus this can also lead to data/items being lost. You could consider increasing the MaxReceiveSize (and MaxSendSize), using Set-TransportConfig, in the organization or probably better these specific values on the mailbox in the source Exchange environment. Mailbox limits, like these, will stay in effect after the migration, because they are stored in the AD and replicated to Office 365 or the target forest normally. The BadItemLimit and LargeItemLimit parameters are available in the Exchange Admin Center as well, but if you require the use of Exchange PowerShell, these parameters are often a good practice to include. Note that the LargeItemLimit parameter is not valid for local moves, those within the same Exchange organization. Both the BadItemLimit and LargeItemLimit can lead to data loss, so use these parameters with care.

Example of the BadItemLimit parameter:

```
New-MigrationBatch -Name BatchMove01 -SourceEndpoint MRSEndpoint -TargetDeliveryDomain
PracticalPowerShell.onmicrosoft.com -CSVData ([System.IO.File]::ReadAllBytes("C:\scripting\batch01.
csv")) -AutoStart -BadItemLimit 10 -NotificationEmails damian@practicalpowershell.com
```

When your environment contains Archive mailboxes in Exchange Server, it might be required to move the primary mailbox separate from the Archive mailbox, you can configure that with the PrimaryOnly or ArchiveOnly parameter. For instance, when you require only Archive mailboxes moved:

```
New-MigrationBatch -Name BatchMove01 -SourceEndpoint MRSEndpoint -TargetDeliveryDomain
PracticalPowerShell.onmicrosoft.com -CSVData ([System.IO.File]::ReadAllBytes("C:\scripting\batch01.
csv")) -AutoStart -BadItemLimit 10 -NotificationEmails damian@practicalpowershell.com -ArchiveOnly
```

Whenever you don't use AutoComplete with your Migration Batch, the batch will automatically synchronize each mailbox every 24 hours. If for whatever reason you do not want this to happen (you expect some performance issues during those synchronization moments for instance), you should use parameter AllowIncrementalSyncs with the value $False. Note that this will result in a longer completion duration which lowers the benefits of an online move.

There are guidelines for the CSV files in order to work correctly with Migration Batches. One requirement is a column with header EmailAddress that will contain the (primary) SMTP address of the mailbox you want to move. Other columns are optional, but when configured will overrule the settings made with MigrationBatch cmdlets. Optional column names are: BadItemLimit and/or MailboxType. For MailboxType this will determine whether the primary, archive mailbox or both are moved (with the values PrimaryOnly, ArchiveOnly and PrimaryAndArchive).

A valid CSV would look like this:

```
EmailAddress, BadItemLimit, MailboxType
Manager@contoso.com, 10, PrimaryAndArchive
Admin1@contoso.com, 20, Primary
```

In this example, the Manager's primary mailbox will be with a Bad Item Limit of ten while the Admin's primary mailbox will be moved, the Archive mailboxes will remain on it's current location and twenty bad items are accepted.

If you get CSV files with some extra columns with attributes not used for mailbox migrations, you could use AllowUnknownColumnsInCsv in order to let Exchange ignore those and only focus on the Identity values.

For those who require regular updates, via email, on the status of the Migration Batch, use the NotificationEmails parameter. It's a multi-valued string and entries should be delimited with commas. Like so:

```
-NotificationEmails admin1@contoso.com, manager@contoso.com
```

Did you forgot a parameter or do you need to change a specific value? Know that you can change certain parameter values of existing Migration Batches with Set-MigrationBatch. For instance:

```
Set-MigrationBatch -Identity Batch01 -BadItemLimit 10 -AllowIncrementalSyncs $False
```

Not all values can be changed, for a full overview of the available Set-MigrationBatch parameters check out: https://technet.microsoft.com/en-us/library/jj218662(v=exchg.160).aspx.

For a full overview of the New-MigrationBatch parameters, what they do and when you should use them check out this page: https://technet.microsoft.com/en-us/library/jj219166(v=exchg.160).aspx.

Other Migration Batch cmdlets are:

Start-MigrationBatch

- Starts a previously defined Migration Batch.
- https://technet.microsoft.com/en-us/library/jj219165(v=exchg.160).aspx

Stop-MigrationBatch

- Stops a Migration Batch immediately, although already migrated (and potentially completed) mailboxes are left untouched.
- https://technet.microsoft.com/en-us/library/jj219168(v=exchg.160).aspx

Complete-MigrationBatch

- Finalizes the mailbox migration process. After this command has been entered, a last incremental synchronization will be performed and after that the user client will use the new mailbox location.
- https://technet.microsoft.com/en-us/library/jj218648(v=exchg.160).aspx

Remove-MigrationBatch

- Removes a non-running or completed Migration Batch. You can only have 100 Migration Batches at a time, so at some point it may be required to clean up old batches.
- https://technet.microsoft.com/en-us/library/jj219167(v=exchg.160).aspx

Get-MigrationConfig

- Too see the maximum number of batches or concurrent migrations.

Set-MigrationConfig

- To change migration configuration settings, such as the maximum number of batches. You can change that from 100 to 200 with:

```
Set-MigrationConfig -MaxNumberOfBatches 200
```

Move Requests

Migration Batches create the actual move requests, the actual objects that controls each mailbox move. The batch is there to easily manage move requests in bulk. However, knowing how to control separate move requests is paramount in most successful mailbox migrations.

First, a simple Move Request command in Exchange PowerShell would look like:

```
New-MoveRequest damian@practicalpowershell.com -Remote -RemoteHostName mail.
Practicalpowershell.com -TargetDeliveryDomain practicalpowershell.onmicrosoft.com
-RemoteCredential -$LiveCred -BadItemLimit 10 -SuspendWhenReadyToComplete
```

In this case the Identity value can be different, but we tend to use the Active Directory User Principal Name (UPN) or the primary email address (often they are the same). They are both unique values, user friendly and most objects have an attribute with either of them.

The Move Request will be queued immediately and when the source server is ready the move will begin. During this time the user can still work up until the last percentages. On those last moments, the mailbox moved is finalized; its locked so further changes can't be made to it, the last changes are performed and synchronized, and changes are made in both the source and target Active Directory, if different. There are also a couple of different ways to delay the move finalization that are covered later.

Depending on your source and target destination, the user may have to restart Outlook after their mailbox move is finalized, in order for the Outlook profile to be updated to the new target environment. When users are prompted to restart Outlook was changed with Exchange 2013. With 2013 and higher (including Exchange Online), the server name value stored in Outlook is actually a unique identifier based on the Mailbox ID and the AD domain name and no longer a "server" name. This way Outlook does not have to be restarted as that ID will never change and clients should be connecting to normally a single normally load balanced DNS entry that can point to any Exchange 2016 server. For mailboxes being moved from Exchange 2010 or 2013, the Outlook protocol may also be updated from MAPI/RPC to a HTTPS based connection, using Outlook Anywhere. MAPI over HTTP is the new default protocol for connecting to Exchange Online.

Do note, that you cannot manage Move Requests not part of a Migration Batch via the Exchange Admin Center, so you will have to use Exchange PowerShell to manage the mailbox moves done directly with New-MoveRequest.

This principle of Online Mailbox moves makes migrations a lot more flexible and less prone to risks. For instance, to create a Move Request that will be suspended before it completes, add the SuspendWhenReadyToComplete switch:

```
New-MoveRequest damian@practicalpowershell.com -Remote -RemoteHostName mail.
Practicalpowershell.com -TargetDeliveryDomain practicalpowershell.onmicrosoft.com
-RemoteCredential -$LiveCred -SuspendWhenReadyToComplete
```

It will stop the progress at 95%. This value is not an actual representation of the amount of data migrated, it's just Exchange's internal way of telling you it's practically done. By default, the Move Request will also perform an incremental sync every 24 hours.

So, now we have a Move Request that is suspended. Can we do anything useful with it? Well, yes! With Set-MoveRequest we can change some of the parameters of the move, without stopping and restarting the move from the start! Better yet, even if the move has failed we can still change parameters and restart the move. When it's an Online move (read: from Exchange 2010 or higher) it will restart at the point of failure.

A lot of parameters available within New-MoveRequest are the same as with the New-MigrationBatch cmdlet. This is logical as the Migration Batch in its turn creates a move request per mailbox and subsequently passes on the specified parameter to the move request.

To control the amount of acceptable corrupted objects, before a move fails, you use BadItemLimit with an integer indicating how many failed objects are acceptable. If you have a value of 51 or higher (meaning you accept skipping 50 corrupted objects before the mailbox move fails and stops), you have to add the additional AcceptLargeDataLoss switch otherwise the move will fail. This is an additional safety measure to prevent you from accidentally accepting a data loss of more than 50 items.

In addition, the LargeItemLimit should be used to indicate the number of objects that are allowed to be skipped, that are larger than the message receive limits set on the target. The default message size limit is only valid for mailboxes that inherit the default database limits on the target database, otherwise message size limits set on the mailbox will be used. Another possible reason for failure, is when there are items already in the mailbox that exceed the limits, which existed before specific mailbox item size limits were set.

An alternative to the LargeItemLimit parameter is the AllowLargeItems switch, which is specific for move requests and is not available with Migration Batches. When the AllowLargeItems switch has been added to a New-MoveRequest, Exchange will move all items that exceed the size limits set on target databases or mailbox limits. Both AllowLargeItems and LargeItemLimit should not be used together, the LargeItemLimit will cause the move to fail once the threshold specified has been reached even with the AllowLargeItems switch included. So you cannot use both parameters at the same time since this will result in a failed mailbox move when not expected.

If you have Archive mailboxes you can also control the migration of the primary or archive mailbox separate from each other. The same switches and parameters that control these behaviors are also present. For a description see our section within New-MigrationBatch. The switches and parameters are:

- ArchiveOnly
- PrimaryOnly

Every Migration Batch will have a name, but move requests can also have a Batch name defined by using the parameter BatchName. This is a way to easily bulk manage multiple similar move requests. For instance, if you create multiple Move Requests with the same Batch name, you can reference that parameter value. For instance, you've created multiple move requests like so:

```
New-MoveRequest damian@practicalpowershell.com -Remote -RemoteHostName mail.
Practicalpowershell.com -TargetDeliveryDomain practicalpowershell.onmicrosoft.com
-RemoteCredential -$LiveCred -BatchName "Logistics"

New-MoveRequest dave@practicalpowershell.com -Remote -RemoteHostName mail.
Practicalpowershell.com -TargetDeliveryDomain practicalpowershell.onmicrosoft.com
-RemoteCredential -$LiveCred "Logistics"
```

Now you can find them via:

    Get-MoveRequest -BatchName "Logistics"

Subsequently you can pipe the output to other cmdlets, for instance Get-MoveRequestStatistics:

    Get-MoveRequest -BatchName "Logistics" | Get-MoveRequestStatistics

If you've created a Migration Batch, the move request batch name attribute does not correspond exactly with the Migration Batch name value. To give distinction between move requests created via a Migration Batch or a manual action, Migration Batches have the batch name prepended with "MigrationService:". So, if you have any need to investigate specific move requests created via a Migration Batch with the name "Batch01", you could use the following syntax:

    Get-MoveRequest -BatchName "MigrationService:Batch01"

Obviously, you can pipe this to other commands. In this case:

    Get-MoveRequest -BatchName "MigrationService:Batch01" | Get-MoveRequestStatistics

Another way to influence the impact of your mailbox moves after initial pre-staging has completed, is the frequency of incremental synchronizations. The default value is every 24 hours. The format looks like, where dd:hh:mm:ss stands for days (dd), hours (hh), minutes (mm) and seconds (ss):

    New-MoveRequest -Identity "<Mailbox ID>" **-IncrementalSyncInterval <dd.hh:mm:ss>** -Remote
    -RemoteHostName   mail.Practicalpowershell.com   -TargetDeliveryDomain   practicalpowershell.
    onmicrosoft.com -RemoteCredential -$LiveCred

For instance, you create a move request and set it to sync every 12 hours with the IncrementalSyncInterval parameter:

    New-MoveRequest   -Identity   "<Mailbox   ID>"   **-IncrementalSyncInterval   00.12:00:0** -Remote
    -RemoteHostName   mail.Practicalpowershell.com   -TargetDeliveryDomain   practicalpowershell.
    onmicrosoft.com -RemoteCredential -$LiveCred

Normally adjusting the interval is probably not required, however it makes sense if you want specific batches to be started and completed after specific moments in time. You can adjust the sync frequency to suit your needs. You can schedule the start time of a move request with the parameter StartAfter and you can also schedule the completion of a move with the parameter CompleteAfter.

The date value format is dependent on the regional settings of the server and specifically the Short Date value. In this example the format is M/d/yyyy, which translates as 5/23/2016.

    New-MoveRequest -Identity <mailboxid> **-StartAfter 5/23/2016** -Remote -RemoteHostName
    mail.Practicalpowershell.com -TargetDeliveryDomain practicalpowershell.onmicrosoft.com
    -RemoteCredential -$LiveCred

You can also add a specific time, which uses the short time notation in your regional settings. You have to add quotes to the value when you do so:

    New-MoveRequest -Identity <mailboxid> **-CompleteAfter "6/19/2016 9:59"** -Remote
    -RemoteHostName mail.Practicalpowershell.com -TargetDeliveryDomain practicalpowershell.
    onmicrosoft.com -RemoteCredential -$LiveCred

They can also be combined into one cmdlet:

```
New-MoveRequest -Identity <mailboxid> -StartAfter 6/10/2016 -CompleteAfter "6/19/2016 9:59" –
IncrementalSyncInterval 00:01:00:00 -Remote -RemoteHostName mail.Practicalpowershell.com
-TargetDeliveryDomain practicalpowershell.onmicrosoft.com -RemoteCredential -$LiveCred
```

This will start the Move Request on the 10th of June 2016 and will complete it nine days later at 9:59 (AM in this case, a 24 hour notation was configured in regional settings). It will sync every one hour after the initial synchronization has finished.

The use of the StartAfter and CompleteAfter parameters is recommended by Microsoft. However, there is no specific technical reason to use these versus just manually completing the mailbox moves. Usage of either options to complete moves is dependent on your specific requirements. I personally like to manually perform the completion of moves, mostly because some organizations have a GO/NOGO moment just before completion. You can find the date and time short formats in Control Panel>Region:

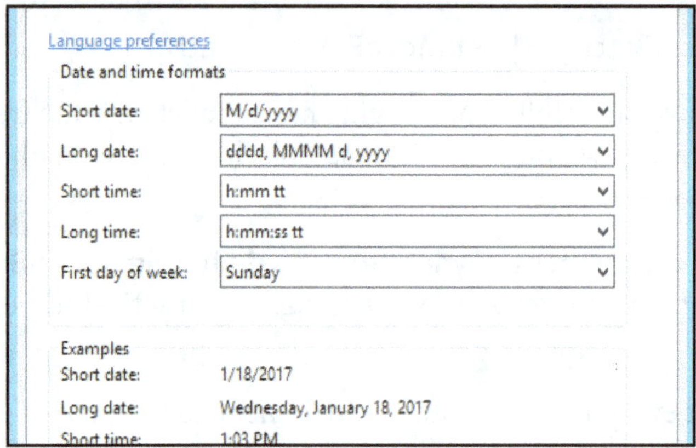

Two other switches, PreventCompletion and SuspendWhenReadyToComplete, also prevent the completion of the Move Request. Both of these switches suspend the mailbox move, at 95%, like the CompleteAfter switch. But both of these switches require manually finishing/resuming the mailbox move for it to be completed. Therefore, Microsoft recommends using the CompleteAfter switch to make sure the mailbox moves are completed at some point and not forgotten about.

If you want to create move requests, but be certain that they are not immediately queued and potentially started, you can use the Suspend switch.

When a move request has completed (with or without errors), the requests will be saved up to 30 days and then removed from the system. If you require shorter/longer duration, you can specify this with CompletedRequestAge-Limit. The value is an integer and represents the amount of days:

```
Set-MoveRequest -Identity <Mailbox ID> -CompletedRequestAgeLimit 120 -Remote
-RemoteHostName mail.Practicalpowershell.com -TargetDeliveryDomain practicalpowershell.
onmicrosoft.com -RemoteCredential -$LiveCred
```

This will retain the completed Move Request for 120 days.

In some specific cases, it is possible you cannot migrate a mailbox with an online move. In such cases, one thing that might help is to explicitly force an offline move. This will cause the mailbox to be locked as soon as the move request has reached the InProgress status. Unfortunately, this means users cannot access the mailbox until the offline mailbox move has completed.

```
New-MoveRequest -Identity <Mailbox ID> -ForceOffline -Remote -RemoteHostName mail.
Practicalpowershell.com -TargetDeliveryDomain practicalpowershell. onmicrosoft.com
-RemoteCredential -$LiveCred
```

** **Note** ** If there are issues with moving the mailbox at this point, perhaps move the mailbox to another mailbox database for Exchange on-premises, prior to moving a mailbox to Exchange Online.

For a full overview of the parameters, what they do and when you should use them check out this page: https://technet.microsoft.com/en-us/library/dd351123(v=exchg.160).aspx

Other cmdlets regarding Move Request are:

Get-MoveRequest

- Listing current Move Requests.
- https://technet.microsoft.com/en-us/library/dd335227(v=exchg.160).aspx

Remove-MoveRequest

- Removing a Move Request.
- https://technet.microsoft.com/en-us/library/dd335149(v=exchg.160).aspx

Resume-MoveRequest

- Resume a suspended Move Request. Either due to when the SuspendWhenReadyToComplete switch has been set or the Suspend-MoveRequest cmdlet.
- https://technet.microsoft.com/en-us/library/ee332320(v=exchg.160).aspx

Set-MoveRequest

- Change specific attributes of a Move Request, for instance when it has failed due to too many bad items.
- https://technet.microsoft.com/en-us/library/ee332314(v=exchg.160).aspx

Suspend-MoveRequest

- Suspending a Move Request in queue or when in progress. Restart the move with Resume-MoveRequest.
- https://technet.microsoft.com/en-us/library/ee332310(v=exchg.160).aspx

Checking Migration Status and Reports

During the mailbox move or pre-staging, you undoubtedly want to monitor the progress and catch any problematic moves. Also in this case the EAC provides basic information that might not be enough for large batch moves.

Even if using Exchange Migration Batches, each mailbox is represented by a Move Request. The Migration Batches are a way to easily manage those multiple Move Requests.

Status

To see the status of current Migration Batches, use:

Get-MigrationBatch

```
[PS] C:\>Get-MigrationBatch

Identity                      Status              Type                    TotalCount
--------                      ------              ----                    ----------
DB01 to DB02                  Completed           ExchangeLocalMove       2
Select Users                  Created             ExchangeLocalMove       3
```

That only tells us information about Migration Batches and not real info on specific mailbox statuses. You would need Get-MoveRequest for this.

In order to get statistics from a list of all Move Requests independent of their state, you can use:

Get-MoveRequest -ResultSize Unlimited | Get-MoveRequestStatistics

However, you can achieve a more granular view by adding the status:

Get-MoveRequest -ResultSize Unlimited -MoveStatus Completed | Get-MoveRequestStatistics

```
[PS] C:\>Get-MoveRequest -ResultSize Unlimited -MoveStatus Completed | Get-MoveRequestStatistics

DisplayName        StatusDetail       TotalMailboxSize          TotalArchiveSize        PercentComplete
-----------        ------------       ----------------          ----------------        ---------------
Administrator      Completed          58.47 KB (59,873 bytes)                           100
Jan Crichton       Completed          2.678 KB (2,742 bytes)                            100
```

This will show each move that has the InProgress status equal to Completed. The status options are AutoSuspended, Completed, CompletedWithWarning, CompletionInProgress, Failed, InProgress, None, Queued, and Suspended. Most are evident, however AutoSuspended are those requests that have finished the pre-staging and were given the SuspendWhenReadyToComplete parameter in the Move Request.

If you want to limit your selection to a specific Migration Batch, you can add the BatchName:

Get-MoveRequest -ResultSize Unlimited -BatchName "<batchname>" | Get-MoveRequestStatistics

Note that the BatchName value in New-MoveRequest, created directly, are different than the MigrationBatch value created by EAC and the New-MigrationBatch cmdlet, Exchange adds "MigrationService:" to the latter. So, in order to find all Move Requests from a previously created MigrationBatch use:

Get-MoveRequest -ResultSize Unlimited -BatchName "MigrationService" | Get-MoveRequestStatistics

When the job kicks off, an initialization message like so will appear:

```
DisplayName StatusDetail         TotalMailboxSize          TotalArchiveSize PercentComplete
----------- ------------         ----------------          ---------------- ---------------
Backup      WaitingForJobPickup  200.7 KB (205,479 bytes)                   0
```

If there are any issues, then they should appear using the same cmdlet. Here is an example error:

```
DisplayName StatusDetail           TotalMailboxSize          TotalArchiveSize PercentComplete
----------- ------------           ----------------          ---------------- ---------------
Backup      TransientFailureTarget 200.7 KB (205,479 bytes)  0 B (0 bytes)    95
```

Obviously, you can get it even more granular if you add the MoveStatus:

Get-MoveRequest -ResultSize Unlimited -BatchName "<batchname>" -MoveStatus Completed | Get-MoveRequestStatistics

Reporting

If there are any move requests that have failed, you need to know what the cause of the failure is. Most cases involve too many corrupt/bad items or too many large items, where the limits have been reached. Before increasing those limits, you'd probably want to know whether these are important items or not, for instance a calendar item from five years back is probably not crucial and can be skipped. But sometimes it's an important mail with attachments, you might want to try and extract that object via other means if possible (Outlook perhaps). Or you could decide to perform a New-MailboxRepairRequest on the source mailbox.

Luckily you can investigate each move requests' detailed reporting, you can retrieve that report via:

    Get-MoveRequestStatistics -Identity "<move request>" -IncludeReport

However, you won't see that report unless specifically made visible: Via piping to Format-List or (cmdlet).

Report:

    Get-MoveRequestStatistics -Identity "<move request>" -IncludeReport | Fl

```
[PS] C:\>Get-MoveRequestStatistics -Identity "Jan Crichton" -IncludeReport | FL Report

Report : 5/25/2016 5:10:44 PM [L16-EX01] '' created move request.
         5/25/2016 5:10:53 PM [L16-EX01] The Microsoft Exchange Mailbox Replication service 'L16-EX01.lab2016.com'
         (15.1.396.30 caps:03FFFF) is examining the request.
         5/25/2016 5:10:54 PM [L16-EX01] Connected to target mailbox '364180a1-ec52-44a4-a383-d570da49140b (Primary)',
         database 'DB02', Mailbox server 'L16-EX01.lab2016.com' Version 15.1 (Build 396.0).
         5/25/2016 5:10:54 PM [L16-EX01] Connected to source mailbox '364180a1-ec52-44a4-a383-d570da49140b (Primary)',
         database 'DB01', Mailbox server 'L16-EX01.lab2016.com' Version 15.1 (Build 396.0).
         5/25/2016 5:10:54 PM [L16-EX01] Request processing started.
         5/25/2016 5:10:54 PM [L16-EX01] Source mailbox information:
         Regular Items: 1, 2.678 KB (2,742 bytes)
         Regular Deleted Items: 0, 0 B (0 bytes)
         FAI Items: 0, 0 B (0 bytes)
         FAI Deleted Items: 0, 0 B (0 bytes)
         5/25/2016 5:10:54 PM [L16-EX01] Cleared sync state for request 364180a1-ec52-44a4-a383-d570da49140b due to
         'CleanupOrphanedMailbox'.
         5/25/2016 5:10:57 PM [L16-EX01] Stage: CreatingFolderHierarchy. Percent complete: 10.
```

    (Get-MoveRequestStatistics -Identity "<move request>" -IncludeReport).report

```
[PS] C:\>(Get-MoveRequestStatistics -Identity "Jan Crichton" -IncludeReport).Report|FL Entries

Entries : {5/25/2016 5:10:44 PM [L16-EX01] '' created move request., 5/25/2016 5:10:53 PM [L16-EX01] The Microsoft
          Exchange Mailbox Replication service 'L16-EX01.lab2016.com' (15.1.396.30 caps:03FFFF) is examining the
          request., 5/25/2016 5:10:54 PM [L16-EX01] Connected to target mailbox '364180a1-ec52-44a4-a383-d570da49140b
          (Primary)', database 'DB02', Mailbox server 'L16-EX01.lab2016.com' Version 15.1 (Build 396.0)., 5/25/2016
          5:10:54 PM [L16-EX01] Connected to source mailbox '364180a1-ec52-44a4-a383-d570da49140b (Primary)', database
          'DB01', Mailbox server 'L16-EX01.lab2016.com' Version 15.1 (Build 396.0)., 5/25/2016 5:10:54 PM [L16-EX01]
          Request processing started., 5/25/2016 5:10:54 PM [L16-EX01] Source mailbox information:
          Regular Items: 1, 2.678 KB (2,742 bytes)
          Regular Deleted Items: 0, 0 B (0 bytes)
          FAI Items: 0, 0 B (0 bytes)
          FAI Deleted Items: 0, 0 B (0 bytes), 5/25/2016 5:10:54 PM [L16-EX01] Cleared sync state for request
          364180a1-ec52-44a4-a383-d570da49140b due to 'CleanupOrphanedMailbox'., 5/25/2016 5:10:57 PM [L16-EX01]
          Stage: CreatingFolderHierarchy. Percent complete: 10., 5/25/2016 5:11:02 PM [L16-EX01] Initializing folder
          hierarchy from mailbox '364180a1-ec52-44a4-a383-d570da49140b (Primary)': 24 folders total., 5/25/2016
          5:11:02 PM [L16-EX01] Folder creation progress: 0 folders created in mailbox
          '364180a1-ec52-44a4-a383-d570da49140b (Primary)'., 5/25/2016 5:11:03 PM [L16-EX01] Folder hierarchy
          initialized for mailbox '364180a1-ec52-44a4-a383-d570da49140b (Primary)': 23 folders created., 5/25/2016
          5:11:03 PM [L16-EX01] Stage: CreatingFolderHierarchy. Percent complete: 10., 5/25/2016 5:11:05 PM [L16-EX01]
          Stage: CreatingInitialSyncCheckpoint. Percent complete: 15., 5/25/2016 5:11:05 PM [L16-EX01] Initial sync
          checkpoint progress: 0/24 folders processed. Currently processing mailbox
          '364180a1-ec52-44a4-a383-d570da49140b (Primary)'., 5/25/2016 5:11:05 PM [L16-EX01] Initial sync checkpoint
          completed: 23 folders processed., 5/25/2016 5:11:06 PM [L16-EX01] Stage: LoadingMessages. Percent complete:
          20....}
```

As you can see, they provide the same information. To export that to a text file, you can use the Export-Csv cmdlet:

    Get-MoveRequestStatistics -Identity "<move request>" -IncludeReport | Export-CSV -Encoding UTF8
    -Path "<filename>"

The encoding ensures any non-ASCII characters are presented correctly (such as in DisplayName values, etc.). The Path is the path and filename of the export file.

If you require bulk export of reports, a Foreach loop is required. The basic principle would be:

```
$MoveRequests = Get-MoveRequest -ResultSize Unlimited

Foreach ($MoveRequest in $MoveRequests){
(Get-MoveRequestStatistics -Identity $MoveRequest.Identity -IncludeReport).Report | Export-CSV -Encoding UTF8 -Path "$MoveRequest.txt"}
```

First all move requests are stored in a variable. Then for each request, the Get-MoveRequestStatistics cmdlet is performed on them. That cmdlet retrieves the move statistics report, which is then exported to a TXT file (in CSV format) with the DisplayName of the mailbox as a file name.

Obviously, there are variants possible, depending on your requirements. Most importantly you can select specific move requests by adding more filters. Check the beginning of the chapters on how to leverage Get-MoveRequest in order to get the reports you need. Be sure to also check out the chapter on Reporting with PowerShell.

Public Folder Migrations

Yes, Public Folders just won't die on us… Starting in Exchange 2013, the way Public Folder data is stored has changed dramatically. From a separate type of database (Public Folder Database as opposed to Mailbox Database), data is now stored in Public Folder Mailboxes inside Mailbox Databases. End-user experience hasn't changed, but the administration is somewhat different and more importantly the migration from legacy Public Folders to Modern Public Folders is very different.

Simply put, the move is akin to the Mailbox Move Request; the mailbox replication service is responsible for synchronizing Public Folder data across Public Folder mailboxes. This is initially staged online, which means users can continue to view/edit Public Folders during this stage. After the initial stage, incremental syncs are performed until the moment of switchover and a relatively short downtime of Public Folders.

The process is best described in this TechNet Article:

Use batch migration to migrate legacy public folders to Office 365 and Exchange Online:

https://technet.microsoft.com/en-us/library/dn874017(v=exchg.150).aspx

Use batch migration to migrate modern public folders to Office 365 and Exchange Online:

https://technet.microsoft.com/en-us/library/mt798260(v=exchg.160).aspx

15 # Mobile Devices

15 Mobile Devices

In This Chapter

- Mobile Device Policies
- Managing Devices
- Getting Devices for a Mailbox
- Device Wipe
- Reporting

Since the introduction of Exchange ActiveSync (EAS) in Exchange 2003 SP1, it has seen adoption over the years leading up to the current status that practically every mobile device has EAS capabilities.

There have been improvements every major build of Exchange Server, not just features but also in regards to access complacency and security. Regarding management, the adoption of PowerShell has been a welcome improvement, making admin control a lot easier than before.

To recap the whole process: A user has a device and a mailbox in Exchange Online. The user wants to access their mailbox from that device and it has EAS capabilities. The user enters his or hers email address and their corresponding password. In a lot of cases the connection is successful and a pop-up appears warning you about security policies that have to be implemented. After accepting the user can now access mail, calendar, contacts and sometime additional features like Tasks or setting the Out of Office reply.

There are variants when used with conditional access from Office 365 Mobile Device Management (MDM)/Intune or other MDM solutions or when certificate based authentication is required.

In the background, a device partnership has been made between the users' mailbox and the device, which is manageable (locking, remote wiping, etc.) belonging to the users and admin's capabilities. What is available depends on device capabilities and support.

In this chapter, we will go through device access, device policies, managing devices and some reporting. It's important to note that as with Exchange Online, some cmdlets have been renamed from ActiveSync to MobileDevice, as the focus for Microsoft seems to be the Outlook app on iOS and Android and Outlook Mail app on Windows 10, which relies on the REST API for its connection to Office 365:

https://technet.microsoft.com/en-us/library/mt465746(v=exchg.150).aspx

Mobile Device Policies

The most important thing regarding Mobile Device Policies are the specific policies that define what features are available (such as Camera, downloads from the Store, etc.) and the level of security (password policy, remote wipe options). This is configured in the Mobile Device Mailbox Policy, which is assigned to mailboxes. You can have multiple policies which can be assigned to different mailboxes. However, an assigned Mobile Device Mailbox policy will be valid for all devices that have a device partnership with that specific account; you cannot have a different policy on the same mailbox for different devices.

Managing Mobile Device Mailbox Policies

The basis of controlling devices with Exchange is the Mobile Device Mailbox policy, previously known as the Exchange ActiveSync (EAS) Mailbox policy. The policy defines specific security settings the device might have to support and implement, and the user has to accept them in order to gain access to their mailbox.

You can have multiple policies in your organization, to cater different security policies. But a user (or mailbox) can only have one policy applied, which is valid for all devices connected to the mailbox.

For those who are wondering about users that have multiple mailboxes configured on their device: the policies are applied cumulative with the most restrictive setting being applied over less restrictive settings or undefined settings.

Listing

To get a listing of current Mobile Device mailbox policies you use:

```
Get-MobileDeviceMailboxPolicy
```

You would see at least the Default policy and its values in raw output:

```
PS C:\> Get-MobileDeviceMailboxPolicy

RunspaceId                           : 4902ae07-3dfd-4c29-a9a7-2da78b7bbb6d
AllowNonProvisionableDevices         : True
AlphanumericPasswordRequired         : False
AttachmentsEnabled                   : True
DeviceEncryptionEnabled              : False
RequireStorageCardEncryption         : False
PasswordEnabled                      : False
PasswordRecoveryEnabled              : False
DevicePolicyRefreshInterval          : Unlimited
AllowSimplePassword                  : True
MaxAttachmentSize                    : Unlimited
WSSAccessEnabled                     : True
UNCAccessEnabled                     : True
MinPasswordLength                    :
MaxInactivityTimeLock                : Unlimited
MaxPasswordFailedAttempts            : Unlimited
PasswordExpiration                   : Unlimited
PasswordHistory                      : 0
IsDefault                            : True
AllowApplePushNotifications          : True
AllowMicrosoftPushNotifications      : True
AllowGooglePushNotifications         : True
AllowStorageCard                     : True
AllowCamera                          : True
RequireDeviceEncryption              : False
AllowUnsignedApplications            : True
AllowUnsignedInstallationPackages    : True
AllowWiFi                            : True
AllowTextMessaging                   : True
AllowPOPIMAPEmail                    : True
AllowIrDA                            : True
RequireManualSyncWhenRoaming         : False
AllowDesktopSync                     : True
AllowHTMLEmail                       : True
RequireSignedSMIMEMessages           : False
```

** **Note** ** The cmdlet Get-ActiveSyncMailboxPolicy does the same as Get-MobileDeviceMailboxPolicy, but is deprecated and will be removed sometime in the future.

Creating and Assigning

You can create additional Mobile Device policies via:

New-MobileDeviceMailboxPolicy -Name "VIP"

```
PS C:\> New-MobileDeviceMailboxPolicy -Name "VIP"

RunspaceId                            : 4902ae07-3dfd-4c29-a9a7-2da78b7bbb6d
AllowNonProvisionableDevices          : False
AlphanumericPasswordRequired          : False
AttachmentsEnabled                    : True
DeviceEncryptionEnabled               : False
RequireStorageCardEncryption          : False
PasswordEnabled                       : False
PasswordRecoveryEnabled               : False
DevicePolicyRefreshInterval           : Unlimited
AllowSimplePassword                   : True
MaxAttachmentSize                     : Unlimited
WSSAccessEnabled                      : True
UNCAccessEnabled                      : True
MinPasswordLength                     :
MaxInactivityTimeLock                 : Unlimited
MaxPasswordFailedAttempts             : Unlimited
PasswordExpiration                    : Unlimited
PasswordHistory                       : 0
IsDefault                             : False
AllowApplePushNotifications           : True
AllowMicrosoftPushNotifications       : True
AllowGooglePushNotifications          : True
AllowStorageCard                      : True
AllowCamera                           : True
RequireDeviceEncryption               : False
AllowUnsignedApplications             : True
AllowUnsignedInstallationPackages     : True
AllowWiFi                             : True
AllowTextMessaging                    : True
AllowPOPIMAPEmail                     : True
AllowIrDA                             : True
RequireManualSyncWhenRoaming          : False
AllowDesktopSync                      : True
AllowHTMLEmail                        : True
RequireSignedSMIMEMessages            : False
```

Without any parameters configured a default configuration will be used. You can add values at creation or adjust values after creating the policy. Example:

Set-MobileDeviceMailboxPolicy -Identity "VIP" -DeviceEncryptionEnabled $True

This will require Device Encryption on our previously created policy.

If a policy isn't required anymore, you can remove it:

Remove-MobileDeviceMailboxPolicy -Identity "VIP"

Be sure that the policy isn't assigned to any mailbox or are assigned to another policy, otherwise the mailboxes will revert to the Default policy. You can define the default Mobile Device mailbox policy in the policy itself (only one can be the default, obviously):

Set-MobileDeviceMailboxPolicy -Identity "VIP" -IsDefault $True

Assigning the MobileDevice Mailbox policy is done via Set-CASMailbox:

Set-CASMailbox JanCrichton@contoso.com -ActiveSyncMailboxPolicy "VIP"

And if required you can assign a specific policy to all mailboxes, however you could just use the Default policy. It's probably more common to have most mailboxes use the default policy and assign specific policy to specific users. One way is to use groups to determine who would require a certain policy:

```
(Get-Group -Identity "VIP").Members | Set-CASMailbox -ActiveSyncMailboxPolicy "VIP"
```

Now, this is just one possible way but it should give you an idea how to use and assign multiple Mobile Device Mailbox Policies.

> ** **Note** ** The cmdlets New-ActiveSyncMailboxPolicy, Set-ActiveSyncMailboxPolicy, Remove-ActiveSync-MailboxPolicy are the same as respectivly New-MobileDeviceMailboxPolicy, Set-MobileDeviceMailboxPolicy, Remove-MobileDeviceMailboxPolicy but are deprecated and will be removed in the future.

Best Practices

It depends on your organization and your stance on types of supported devices (non-managed or highly managed with conditional access), but most organizations agree on basic security with the below items:

Allow Non-Provisionable Devices

Allows devices to synchronize, even if it's clear that they cannot apply certain policies; for instance Device Encryption. This is basically the "Best Effort" setting; if the device supports a set feature, it has to enable it. If the device does not support a feature, it will still be allowed to sync despite possible lower security. Disable (default) when you want to have a strict adherence to the device policy. But to enable it use:

```
Set-MobileDeviceMailboxPolicy -Identity Default -AllowNonProvisionableDevices $True
```

Required Password

With this setting a password is required. This means a user has to input a password or PIN at boot time and to unlock the device. In this way, access to company data can be protected. There are different choices to be made, a numeric PIN or alphanumeric password.

```
Set-MobileDeviceMailboxPolicy -Identity Default -PasswordEnabled:$True
```

You can set the minimal amount of characters required for the PIN:

```
Set-MobileDeviceMailboxPolicy -Identity Default -MinPasswordLength 4
```

In this case the PIN has a minimum of four numbers. You can have a forced minimum password length with a maximum of 16 (so passwords need to be at least sixteen, if so configured). However, four or six are common.

What about fingerprint access? This feature is dependent on the device OS as to how that is handled. In iOS you are required to enter the PIN the first time at start up and then fingerprint authentication via TouchID is possible. With Android, it's very dependent on how it's implemented, however a lot of pattern locks weren't possible when requiring a PIN. Consider this when configuring this setting.

You can force an alphanumeric password, such as on Desktops.

```
Set-MobileDeviceMailboxPolicy -Identity Default -AlphanumericPasswordRequired:$True
```

If enabled, you can set the amount of complex characters, ranging from one to four.

```
Set-MobileDeviceMailboxPolicy -Identity Default -MinPasswordComplexCharacters 4
```

Where MinPasswordComplexCharacters can be one of the following values:

1. Digits only
2. Digits and lower case letters
3. Digits, lower case letters, and upper case letters
4. Digits, lower case letters, upper case letters, and special characters

However, on most mobiles a value of four is not very user friendly and it's not very common, but due to more combinations and complexity of these kinds of passwords it does provide extra security. But you won't make many friends with those kind of requirements (unless you'll only allow devices with a physical or large on-screen keyboard).

Other ways to increase password security, is to limit the reuse of old passwords:

```
Set-MobileDeviceMailboxPolicy -Identity Default -PasswordHistory 2
```

With two in this example the previous two passwords are remembered and blocked from being reused and with zero no passwords are remembered. Determining an ideal number is dependent on how often the device password has to change. You can control that by adding a password age limit:

```
Set-MobileDeviceMailboxPolicy -Identity Default -PasswordExpiration '90.00:00:00'
```

The value syntax is DD.HH:MM:SS, or days, hours, minutes and seconds.

As with Outlook clients, you will need to find a balance between usability and security.

Encrypted Device and Memory Card

These settings will make encryption mandatory for the device itself. Nowadays most modern mobile OS have device encryption enabled per default, but if it is not it might require the device to perform a reboot and additional configuration time. However, this will mean that the complete device is encrypted, which means any sensitive company data is secure from malicious attempts to access this when locked.

```
Set-MobileDeviceMailboxPolicy -Identity Default -RequireDeviceEncryption:$True
```

Some devices offer to extend the storage capacity via memory cards. Some OS's allow applications and their data to be moved to the memory card or data from within the app is stored on the card. When the card is not encrypted, that data is readable for anyone that has access to the card. For instance, when the device is stolen or lost. An encrypted card will prevent unintentional data leaks. However, some devices require the card to be formatted when encryption was not set initially. This could mean data loss. Warn your users when enabling this option, which you can in this way:

```
Set-MobileDeviceMailboxPolicy -Identity Default -RequireStorageCardEncryption:$True
```

Lock Device After x Minutes

Same idea with automatic locks on desktop computers, requiring users to authenticate in order to continue their session. Adds security when the device is (temporarily) left unattended or lost, narrowing the window the device and its data is accessible. With mobile devices, often a PIN is allowed for easily accessing the device. Some apps lock only the access to the app with a PIN, while most lock the whole device.

```
Set-MobileDeviceMailboxPolicy -Identity "VIP" -MaxInactivityTimeLock '00:15:00'
```

This example will lock the device after fifteen minutes of inactivity. In most cases this value is the same as the desktop lock policy, which makes sense as users are already use to those kinds of mechanism and makes explaining somewhat easier.

Wipe Device After x Failed Attempts

To prevent hammering and brute force attempts by just guessing the password and trying endlessly, this policy adds a self-destruct mechanism to the device or data in the app (depending on various mobile OS and other parameters).

```
Set-MobileDeviceMailboxPolicy -Identity "VIP" -MaxPasswordFailedAttempts 8
```

In this example the device will be wiped after eight failed attempts to access the contents of the device by trying to guess the password, this is an anti-hammering feature which can be useful when devices end up in the wrong hands. It does not require a connection to Exchange, so this will work even when the device has no Internet connection. This also means that an admin cannot override it remotely. The valid range is four to sixteen attempts.

Be sure that users are informed about this feature and its consequences when configured. Especially if the device is not company owned, it will surely contain personal data (like photos) which will most likely also be wiped. I've had cases that devices were wiped because their young children got hold of their device and pushed the screen buttons over and over, accidentally activating this feature.

Disable Camera etc.

Additional options are to disable certain hardware features of the device, such as Bluetooth, the camera or other requirements. Do note that these (and some other settings) require the use of an Exchange Enterprise Client Access License in addition to the Exchange Standard Client Access License.

This example would disable the camera (if present) on the device:

```
Set-MobileDeviceMailboxPolicy -Identity Default -AllowCamera:$False
```

In some cases, it even makes camera apps unavailable (for sure in iOS).

There are a lot more configurations possible, it depends on your requirements and the capabilities of the devices you require to adhere to these policies. Be sure to test these policies out with test devices before deploying to your users.

Managing Devices

Device Access ABQ

One of the improvements introduced in Exchange Server 2010 is Device Access Rules, sometimes referred to as ABQ which stands for Allow, Block or Quarantine.

This way it's possible to either block or quarantine specific types of devices. Perhaps a specific DeviceOS has issues (which has happened in the past with iOS 6.x for instance) or you want to limit access to devices that are supported by your organization.

With Block, devices are permanently prohibited access to Exchange; you'd have to resolve the limitation (for instance DeviceOS version due to an update) and remove the blocked partnership and try again. As with Quarantine the partnership does not have to be removed from the mailbox, just the blocking issue has to be resolved (for instance updating the device OS to a supported version).

You can add a block with New-ActiveSyncDeviceAccessRule:

```
New-ActiveSyncDeviceAccessRule -QueryString "iOS 9.0.2 13A452" -Characteristic DeviceOS
-AccessLevel Quarantine
```

As you can see, there are several parameters involved. Starting at the back is the AccessLevel; in this example the access rule will set the access level to Quarantine, other options are Allow or Block. This means that when the blocking issue has been resolved, the user can connect again without removing the partnership, resulting in a sort of temporary ban. For instance, if your organization doesn't support a certain Device OS version because of known bugs (iOS has had some in the past), you should use this option.

The Characteristic parameter can be used to configure the specific device identifier which has to be handled by the Access rule, valid values are DeviceModel, DeviceType, DeviceOS, UserAgent and XMWSLHeader. Those values can be extracted from Exchange when those devices already have made successful partnership with the Exchange mailbox, use:

```
Get-MobileDevice | Format-List DeviceOS, DeviceModel, DeviceType, DeviceUserAgent
```

Which will result in something like this:

```
PS C:\> Get-MobileDevice | Format-List DeviceOS,DeviceModel,DeviceType,DeviceUserAgent


DeviceOS          : iOS 9.0.2 13A452
DeviceModel       : iPad2C1
DeviceType        : iPad
DeviceUserAgent   : Apple-iPad2C1/1301.452

DeviceOS          : Windows Phone 10.0.10149
DeviceModel       : RM-1034_1032
DeviceType        : WP8
DeviceUserAgent   : MSFT-WP/10.0.10149

DeviceOS          : Windows Phone 8.10.14219
DeviceModel       : RM-1045_1064
DeviceType        : WP8
DeviceUserAgent   : MSFT-WP/8.10.14219
```

DeviceOS is the actual OS version and build, DeviceModel the specific model, DeviceType the major type (Android, iPad, iPhone, etc.) and finally DeviceUserAgent. DeviceUserAgent is the same as UserAgent. The XMWSL-

Header is a new characteristic and its values aren't found in Exchange. However, most of the times DeviceOS is used with ABQ. Alternatively, you could get (some) device information via Get-MobileDevice:

```
Get-MobileDevice | Ft DeviceType,DeviceModel
```

Which provides this kind of output:

```
PS C:\> Get-MobileDevice | ft devicetype,devicemodel

DeviceType        DeviceModel
----------        -----------
UniversalOutlook  NOKIA RM927_nam_vzw_100
```

Removing a device class is possible, this can be required if you want a lean list. This could be the case because you now require limited access to only a specific set of devices after allowing all device classes.

```
Remove-MobileDevice -Type 'UniversalOutlook'
```

Another option available is to change the default ActiveSync behavior with Set-ActiveSyncOrganizationSettings. You can set the default DefaultAccessLevel to Allow, Block or Quarantine. The default is Allow, setting it to Quarantine is probably the next user friendly setting. You can enable email requests via the multi valued property AdminMailRecipients, and add extra clarification in the email message users get when their devices are blocked/quarantined with OtaNotificationMailInsert (when a device update is required) and UserMailInsert (to add additional information in the notification mail).

As you can see in the above example the DeviceOS and DeviceUserAgent are version dependent. This means that you might have to add an additional rule if the DeviceOS changes. Therefore, you could focus on DeviceType if you want to regulate the different types of devices (no Windows Phone, just iPhones or something like this). However, you will probably already see some of the caveats of ABQ, if so you might want to invest in real MDM solutions.

** **Note** ** The cmdlet Get-ActiveSyncDevice does the same as Get-MobileDevice, but is being deprecated and will eventually be removed from Exchange Online.

In order to check whether there is already a Device Access Rule in place, use:

```
Get-ActiveSyncDeviceAccessRule
```

This would give you output like this (if there is a rule present):

```
RunspaceId         : c695bc75-5d5e-498b-977c-3563e3c69db0
QueryString        : iOS 9.0.2 13A452
Characteristic     : DeviceOS
AccessLevel        : Quarantine
Name               : iOS 9.0.2 13A452 (DeviceOS)
AdminDisplayName   :
ExchangeVersion    : 0.10 (14.0.100.0)
DistinguishedName  : CN=iOS 9.0.2 13A452 (DeviceOS),CN=Mobile Mailbox Settings,CN=Configuration,CN=O
                     nlineExchangeBook.onmicrosoft.com,CN=ConfigurationUnits,DC=NAMPR13A006,DC=PROD,
                     DC=OUTLOOK,DC=COM
Identity           : iOS 9.0.2 13A452 (DeviceOS)
Guid               : a7a78304-8020-497e-a6a4-adc6482b1d8f
ObjectCategory     : NAMPR13A006.PROD.OUTLOOK.COM/Configuration/Schema/ms-Exch-Device-Access-Rule
ObjectClass        : {top, msExchDeviceAccessRule}
WhenChanged        : 12/14/2017 12:02:00 PM
WhenCreated        : 12/14/2017 12:02:00 PM
WhenChangedUTC     : 12/14/2017 6:02:00 PM
WhenCreatedUTC     : 12/14/2017 6:02:00 PM
OrganizationId     : NAMPR13A006.PROD.OUTLOOK.COM/Microsoft Exchange Hosted
                     Organizations/OnlineExchangeBook.onmicrosoft.com - NAMPR13A006.PROD.OUTLOOK.COM
                     /ConfigurationUnits/OnlineExchangeBook.onmicrosoft.com/Configuration
Id                 : iOS 9.0.2 13A452 (DeviceOS)
```

In this case the access rule will Quarantine certain iPhone models.

When there is no requirement for the Device Access Rule anymore, you can remove it via:

```
Remove-ActiveSyncDeviceAccessRule -Identity "iPhone5C2 (DeviceModel)"
```

Or when the requirements change, you can change the AccessLevel to another value.

```
Set-ActiveSyncDeviceAccessRule -Identity "iPhone5C2 (DeviceModel)" -AccessLevel "Allow"
```

However, after changing this AccessLevel parameter, you might have to manually check whether all devices are now adhering to the new access level.

Default Access Level

But what if you only want to allow one specific device (because it's company owned) and block every other device? Even with multiple device access rules you cannot be certain only the specific devices have access to your Exchange organization.

Luckily you can set a default access level for mobile devices. To see the current configuration use:

```
Get-ActiveSyncOrganizationSettings
```

Which gives you an unformatted output, like below (with default values):

```
PS C:\> Get-ActiveSyncOrganizationSettings

RunspaceId                        : c695bc75-5d5e-498b-977c-3563e3c69db0
DefaultAccessLevel                : Allow
UserMailInsert                    :
AllowAccessForUnSupportedPlatform : False
AllowRMSSupportForUnenlightenedApps : False
AdminMailRecipients               : {}
OtaNotificationMailInsert         :
DeviceFiltering                   :
Name                              : Mobile Mailbox Settings
IsIntuneManaged                   : False
HasAzurePremiumSubscription       : False
OtherWellKnownObjects             : {}
AdminDisplayName                  :
ExchangeVersion                   : 0.10 (14.0.100.0)
DistinguishedName                 : CN=Mobile Mailbox Settings,CN=Configuration,CN=OnlineExchange
                                    Book.onmicrosoft.com,CN=ConfigurationUnits,DC=NAMPR13A006,DC=
                                    PROD,DC=OUTLOOK,DC=COM
Identity                          : Mobile Mailbox Settings
Guid                              : 88a2eb75-b703-41ac-aaf6-71b68c5da119
ObjectCategory                    : NAMPR13A006.PROD.OUTLOOK.COM/Configuration/Schema/ms-Exch-Mob
                                    ile-Mailbox-Settings
ObjectClass                       : {top, msExchMobileMailboxSettings}
WhenChanged                       : 12/6/2017 12:49:12 AM
WhenCreated                       : 12/6/2017 12:49:12 AM
WhenChangedUTC                    : 12/6/2017 6:49:12 AM
WhenCreatedUTC                    : 12/6/2017 6:49:12 AM
OrganizationId                    : NAMPR13A006.PROD.OUTLOOK.COM/Microsoft Exchange Hosted
                                    Organizations/OnlineExchangeBook.onmicrosoft.com - NAMPR13A00
                                    6.PROD.OUTLOOK.COM/ConfigurationUnits/OnlineExchangeBook.onmi
                                    crosoft.com/Configuration
Id                                : Mobile Mailbox Settings
```

Changing the values can be done via:

```
Set-ActiveSyncOrganizationSettings -DefaultAccessLevel Quarantine -UserMailInsert "Contact IT for access"
```

This will set the default access toward Quarantine and will send a mail to the user with additional information.

Do note, that you can then allow the specific device on a user level (without affecting other similar devices) or create a specific Device Access rule, which overrule the Organization settings. This is why if you already have users connecting with ActiveSync devices and you need to implement (or change) the default access level, in order to prevent current devices to be unable to access Exchange you have to create separate device access rules allowing those devices (if so required).

Allowing a Blocked/Quarantined Device

If a device has been blocked or quarantined, an admin can override this. You have to use the Set-CASMailbox in order to achieve this:

```
Set-CASMailbox -ActiveSyncAllowedDeviceIDs @('2FA6AB45DD32ECF337F603CBC6393ECB') -Identity JanCrichton@contoso.com
```

Identity is the UserMailbox containing the specific device and with ActiveSyncAllowedDeviceIDs you can add devices in the allowed list. This is a multi-valued property as indicated by the formatting. Take that into account when the user has multiple devices that have had a block or quarantine.

The value is the specific device ID. This is found via the Get-MobileDevice cmdlet:

```
Get-MobileDevice | ft FriendlyName, DeviceID
```

Which results into this:

Getting Devices for a Mailbox

Mobile and ActiveSync devices are easily accessible in PowerShell via Get-MobileDevice. To manage an individual device, you must have the full distinguished name (DN) path of the object. A DN can be something like:

```
damian\ExchangeActiveSyncDevicesHx§UniversalOutlook§3863B909D1CF4738B795F593DD266C4
```

If you want to get devices for a specific user, use the Get-MobileDevice command with the -Mailbox parameter added with the correct identity:

```
Get-MobileDevice -Mailbox damian@practicalpowershell.com | ft FriendlyName, DeviceID, Identity
```

Which would result into something like this:

```
FriendlyName DeviceId                          Identity
------------ --------                          --------
Lumia 929    A123A54AAF1FFF8BC014DA6BB8744D22  Damian-PP\ExchangeActiveSyncDevices\WP8§A123A54AAF1FFF8BC014...
Lumia 929    859D5F8274FD397B2C8D2469996464E6  Damian-PP\ExchangeActiveSyncDevices\WP8§859D5F8274FD397B2C8D...
```

Device Wipe

The most drastic security measure in order to prevent data leakage is of course the remote wipe. This feature has been available in EAS from the beginning and enables either the user or the admin to completely wipe the device and reset it toward a factory default. In recent years, some OSs or apps implemented a partial wipe, deleting only the account info and downloaded data for that app. Due to the rise of using your personal device for business purposes, the fact that EAS could wipe your device and all of your personal data became more and more controversial.

Some Device OS's or the app that are used only wipe the data obtained via the EAS synchronization and not for instance your precious pets or children's photos. Do note that they report a successful wipe, but do not assume that the compete device has been reset to factory defaults. Saved attachments may be present on external storage, encrypted or not encrypted (depending on device policies). So, if you need guarantees, managing your devices via ActiveSync is probably not adequate and you should investigate Mobile Device Management (MDM) such as Microsoft Intune or use the Office 365 MDM solution. There are also third party solutions like AirWatch and MobileIron.

A user can also initiate a remote wipe from webmail (OWA), but an admin can do so as well using the Clear-MobileDevice cmdlet, using the full Identity value:

```
Clear-MobileDevice -Identity "Damian-PP\ExchangeActiveSyncDevices\
WP8§A123A54AAF1FFF8BC014DA6BB8744D22" -NotificationEmailAddresses damian@
practicalpowershell.com
```

Please note that Identity defines the specific mobile device, not the mailbox ID as a user can easily have multiple (active) devices partnered with their mailbox. A notification email address is optional, but it can be a helpful indicator for the end-user as to what just happened.

The next time the device connects to Exchange Online via ActiveSync, the device notices the wipe request and will adhere according tp how the app or OS would handle it normally. This also means you get confirmation whether the wipe request was received.

Another consideration is when you want to re-introduce the previously wiped device to Exchange Online, the wipe command still stands and will wipe the device again as soon as you connect it to Exchange Online.

You can cancel the wipe request by adding the Cancel switch to the command:

```
Clear-MobileDevice -Identity "Damian-PP\ExchangeActiveSyncDevices\
WP8§A123A54AAF1FFF8BC014DA6BB8744D22" -Cancel
```

Another option is to remove the device partnership. However, if the device was lost and in the hands of a malicious person, keeping wipe request in place even will be more secure way to remove data from the device and to prevent unsolicited access to Exchange. If your credentials are compromised, the device will be wiped again immediately after they connect to Exchange (if the device still matches the same partnership, a software update might break that relationship).

****Note **** The cmdlet Clear-ActiveSyncDevice does the same as Clear-MobileDevice, but is deprecated and will be removed in a future version of Exchange. The same is valid for Get-ActiveSyncDeviceStatistics which has its equivalent in Get-MobileDeviceStatistics.

Removing a Device

There might be reasons to remove a mobile device, for instance if there are too many stale partnerships it can prevent users adding a new device; the device limit is per default 10.

You can remove the device with the same cmdlet as with removing the wipe command.

```
Remove-MobileDevice -Identity "Damian-PP\ExchangeActiveSyncDevices\
WP8§A123A54AAF1FFF8BC014DA6BB8744D22" -NotificationEmailAddresses damian@
practicalpowershell.com
```

Note: The cmdlet Remove-ActiveSyncDevice does the same as Remove-MobileDevice, but is deprecated and will be removed in a future version of Exchange.

ActiveSync Device Limit

If you are accustomed to Exchange on-premises you might be concerned about limitations on ActiveSync devices and your Exchange Online mailboxes. However, unlike Exchange on-premises, the limitations for these device connections is much greater by default. The limit currently is 100 devices:

https://technet.microsoft.com/en-au/library/exchange-online-limits.aspx#BKMK_ExchangeActiveSync_Limits

Also, there are no Throttling PowerShell cmdlets in Exchange Online, so no need to configure these settings.

Reporting

To get a feel of where your company data resides, it's common to create an overview of clients (and especially mobile devices). What kind of device types, Device OS builds, what was the last sync, etc. can be useful information to check on your BYOD implementation or perhaps even choosing a third party Mobile Device Management (MDM) solution. You may want to know what you have and whether you can manage them with a certain third-party product. Or maybe you just are a numbers geek and just want to know!

These examples tend to use Format-Table (or FT) to modify output. However, there's a lot more (potentially) useful information in the output, so check that out and experiment with it.

Types of devices/OS etc.

If you require a list of used Devicetypes (in order to build a device access rule for instance), use the following:

```
(Get-MobileDevice -ResultSize Unlimited).Devicetype | Sort-Object |Get-Unique
```

If you want a list with all devices DeviceOS's, use the following:

```
(Get-MobileDevice -ResultSize Unlimited).DeviceOS|Select $_.DeviceOS -Unique
```

The ResultSize parameter is used in case there are more than 1,000 devices connected to Exchange.

Stale partnerships (last sync)

You might want to create a list with all devices and their last successful synchronization, using this cmdlet you can:

```
Get-MobileDevice|Get-MobileDeviceStatistics|FTDeviceFriendlyName,DeviceID,LastSyncAttemptTime,
LastSuccessSync -Auto
```

This will give you all devices and their sync times. However, you might want to sort it on the sync date:

```
Get-MobileDevice|Get-MobileDeviceStatistics|Sort ($_.LastSuccessSync) | FT DeviceFriendlyName,
DeviceID, LastSyncAttemptTime, LastSuccessSync -Auto
```

Note, both of these cmdlets may take a while to produce results.

As it stands now it will be sorted with the oldest date first in the table. Note that the ResultSize hasn't been added, which might be required if you have more than a thousand devices.

Blocked/Quarantined Devices

Each device has a DeviceAccessState which shows whether the device has been Blocked or Quarantined. This makes it simple to make a list:

```
Get-Mobiledevice -Filter {DeviceAccessState -ne "Allowed"} | FT FriendlyName, DeviceAccessState,
UserDisplayName -Auto
```

In this case the Get-MobileDevice cmdlet has a filter option, so we can use it to filter out what we don't want to see. In this case Allowed devices.

Wiped Devices

This information is stored in the device statistics. To see whether devices have been successfully wiped, use this:

```
Get-MobileDevice | Get-MobileDeviceStatistics | Where {$_.Status -eq "DeviceWipeSucceeded"}
```

You can see something like this:

```
RunspaceId               : 75ebeb44-7a0c-4c1e-8909-46edbe6fee1d
FirstSyncTime            : 1/17/2017 5:43:36 PM
LastPolicyUpdateTime     : 1/17/2017 5:58:11 PM
LastSyncAttemptTime      : 1/17/2017 5:54:44 PM
LastSuccessSync          : 1/17/2017 5:54:44 PM
DeviceType               : WindowsMail
DeviceID                 : 2FA6AB45DD32ECF337F603CBC6393ECB
DeviceUserAgent          : MSFT-WIN-3/10.0.10586
DeviceWipeSentTime       : 1/17/2017 5:58:11 PM
DeviceWipeRequestTime    : 1/17/2017 5:55:09 PM
DeviceWipeAckTime        : 1/17/2017 5:58:11 PM
LastPingHeartbeat        :
RecoveryPassword         : ********
DeviceModel              : Virtual Machine
DeviceImei               :
DeviceFriendlyName       : WINDOWS10VMB
DeviceOS                 : Windows 10.0.10586
DeviceOSLanguage         : English
DevicePhoneNumber        :
MailboxLogReport         :
DeviceEnableOutboundSMS  : False
DeviceMobileOperator     : OperatorName
```

Note the different moments in time when the wipe request was requested, sent and actually performed by the device (if you trust the device or app being accurate). You can also see the Wipe requester, in this case the Administrator.

ActiveSync Enabled/Disabled Accounts

If you limit access to ActiveSync, it might be helpful to have an overview which mailboxes have this protocol (or client access protocols) enabled or not. You can see this as such:

Get-Mailbox | Get-CasMailbox -ProtocolSettings

Which will show this:

```
[PS] C:\>Get-Mailbox | Get-CasMailbox -ProtocolSettings

Name               ActiveSyncEnabled OWAEnabled        PopEnabled        ImapEnabled       MapiEnabled
----               ----------------- ----------        ----------        -----------       -----------
Administrator      True              True              True              True              True
DiscoverySear...   True              True              True              True              True
Jeff Withers       False             True              True              True              True
Damian Scoles      False             True              True              True              True
Journaling Ma...   True              True              True              True              True
```

So, to only show ActiveSync disabled accounts the syntax would be:

Get-Mailbox | Get-CASMailbox -ProtocolSettings | Where {$_.ActiveSyncEnabled -eq $False}

Which would result in:

```
[PS] C:\>Get-Mailbox | Get-CASMailbox -ProtocolSettings | Where {$_.ActiveSyncEnabled -eq $False}

Name               ActiveSyncEnabled OWAEnabled        PopEnabled        ImapEnabled       MapiEnabled
----               ----------------- ----------        ----------        -----------       -----------
Jeff Withers       False             True              True              True              True
Damian Scoles      False             True              True              True              True
Dave Stork         False             True              True              True              True
James Forth        False             True              True              True              True
Help Desk          False             True              True              True              True
```

** **Note** ** Refer to Client Access Rules for more options when it comes to controlling this.

<table><tr><td>16</td><td># Public Folders</td></tr></table>

In This Chapter

- Introduction
- Background – Legacy Public Folders
- Modern Public Folders
- Creating Public Folder Mailboxes
- Creating Public Folders
- Removing Public Folders
- Get-PublicFolder*
- Mail Enabled Public Folders
- Public Folder Permissions
- Troubleshooting

Introduction

In terms of written material, Public Folders have been written about for two decades now. It's like a relative's favorite pound cake that keeps giving, when no one wants it. For those of you lucky enough to have Public Folders, Microsoft has provided a plethora of PowerShell cmdlets to handle modern Public Folders. While the architecture has changed since the days of Public Folder Databases, the general concepts of folders, permissions, mail flow are relatively the same as previous generations. Exchange Online simply provides for a better architecture and PowerShell management than older versions of Exchange.

Background - Legacy Public Folders

In previous versions of Exchange Server (2010 and before), Public Folders existed in their own databases and its own ecosystem entirely. Replication took place via SMTP messages, along the same path that your user emails traveled.   There were lots of intricacies that needed to be paid attention to with Public Folders. Then Modern Public Folders came along and now we have mailboxes that serve up data and hierarchy. The same mailboxes reside in regular mailbox databases and when put in a DAG cluster, can be made highly available like any other mailbox/database. This is quite a change from previous versions.

Modern Public Folders

If you are starting with a new Exchange Online tenant and there are no Public Folders in play, stop now. Do not go down the road of creating Public Folders. Find another solution before venturing down this path - Teams or Office 365 Groups come to mind.   If you insist on creating Public Folders, the first part of managing Public Folders in Exchange 2016 usually begins with creating new ones. This requires the creation of Public Folder mailboxes that contain the typical Public Folder hierarchy as well as the Public Folders themselves.

If however, you insist on creating new Public Folders, then read on!

The Basics

Before we create anything, we need to review information on how Public Folders are structured in Exchange Online. Exchange 2013+ and Exchange Online Public Folders no longer have their own database. They no longer rely on SMTP messages for replicating content between copies in the environment. We have two new concepts with Public Folders - Public Folder Mailboxes and Public Folders (in the mailboxes).

In Exchange Online Public Folders have been modernized to take advantage of Exchange high availability and storage technologies of the mailbox database. The Public Folder architecture uses specially designed mailboxes to store both the hierarchy and the Public Folder content. This also means that there's no longer a Public Folder database. Public Folder replication now uses the continuous replication model. High availability for the hierarchy and content mailboxes are provided by a database availability group (DAG). While as a consumer of Exchange Online, we won't typically see this, it is still good to know how Public Folder data replication is handled.

Due to the new architecture, with Public Folders being based on mailboxes in a mailbox database where only one copy can be active at a time, there is no longer support for multi-master based replication. Like other mailbox databases, only one replica can be the active copy and all clients connect to the active copy only to get data and make changes. Therefore, special consideration is needed, in some cases where users are distributed over various networks and speeds. In Exchange Online, these copies are hidden from the administrator, but are set for high availability.

New Public Folder Replication Model

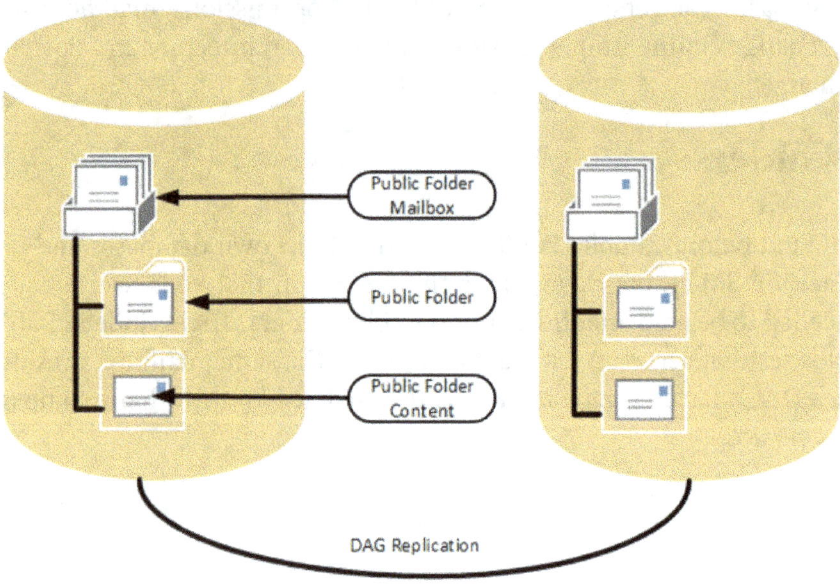

PowerShell

Let's explore Public Folders like we've done with so many other topics in this book, with PowerShell! First, we need a list of cmdlets available to us:

```
Get-Command *PublicF*
```

Add-PublicFolderClientPermission	New-SyncMailPublicFolder
Disable-MailPublicFolder	Remove-PublicFolder
Enable-MailPublicFolder	Remove-PublicFolderClientPermission
Get-MailPublicFolder	Remove-PublicFolderMigrationRequest
Get-PublicFolder	Remove-SyncMailPublicFolder
Get-PublicFolderClientPermission	Resume-PublicFolderMailboxMigrationRequest
Get-PublicFolderItemStatistics	Resume-PublicFolderMigrationRequest
Get-PublicFolderMailboxDiagnostics	Set-MailPublicFolder
Get-PublicFolderMailboxMigrationRequest	Set-PublicFolder
Get-PublicFolderMailboxMigrationRequestStatistics	Set-PublicFolderMailboxMigrationRequest
Get-PublicFolderMigrationRequest	Set-PublicFolderMigrationRequest
Get-PublicFolderMigrationRequestStatistics	Suspend-PublicFolderMailboxMigrationRequest
Get-PublicFolderStatistics	Suspend-PublicFolderMigrationRequest
New-PublicFolder	Update-PublicFolderMailbox
New-PublicFolderMigrationRequest	

That's a lot of PowerShell cmdlets indeed. So what to do with them?

Creating Public Folder Mailboxes

So in order to create Public Folders for the end user to use, we need to first create a Public Folder Mailbox. Creating this requires the use of the '-PublicFolder' switch to toggle the mailbox type to a Public Folder and not a regular user mailbox.

Example

```
New-mailbox -PublicFolder -Name 'PFMailbox01'
```

```
PS C:\> New-mailbox -PublicFolder -Name "PFMailbox01"

Name                        Alias             ServerName        ProhibitSendQuota
----                        -----             ----------        -----------------
PFMailbox01                 PFMailbox01       mwhpr1301mb2029   99 GB (106,300,440,576 bytes)
WARNING: Failed to replicate mailbox:'PFMailbox01' to the
site:'namprd13.prod.outlook.com/Configuration/Sites/MWHPR1301'. The mailbox will be available for
logon in approximately 15 minutes.
```

Depending on how much data will be put into the folders, as well as where the users are located, this will determine how many to create. For a new Exchange Online tenant, one should be sufficient at the start. However if you were moving old data over (say from Exchange 2010 on-premises), you would have to decide how big each mailbox should be, say 5 GB, 10 GB or 20 GB? If you are moving over 100 GB from Exchange 2010, you may need 5 to 20 mailboxes for that data.

Creating Public Folders

Consider this scenario:

Unlike most organizations, this scenario contains an environment bereft of Public Folders. Your manager has requested a series of Public Folders be created so that they can begin hosting content in Public Folders. He has provided a list of names and hierarchy for how he wants to store content:

Research and Development
    For Clients
    Internal Information
    Managers Only
    Future Projects

IT
    Applications
    Networking
    Servers
    Workstations

** **Note** ** Ok, we know this isn't too realistic, but it is a good start for learning how to use the cmdlets.

Remember at the beginning of the chapter we mentioned that Public Folders are now based on mailboxes? Well, this means that we need to create at least one mailbox in order to hold the Public Folders you create as well as to serve up the Public Folder hierarchy. To create a Public Folder mailbox we need to rely on the New-Mailbox cmdlet we used earlier in the book.

```
New-Mailbox 'Public Folder Mailbox 01' -PublicFolder
```

One thing to remember is that there is an inherent delay between creating the new mailbox and serving up the new Public Folder hierarchy. This is according to Microsoft:

https://blogs.technet.microsoft.com/exchange/2016/12/05/modern-public-folder-deployment-best-practices/

The delay may be up to 24 hours. This can be accelerated by manually updating the hierarchy if you so choose.

```
Update-PublicFolderMailbox -Identity 'Public Folder mailbox name' -SuppressStatus -Fullsync -InvokeSynchronizer
```

Once the Public Folder mailboxes are all created, we can then create folders for content to be placed. Let's explore the cmdlets available for creating Public Folders:

```
Get-Command *-PublicFolder

Get-PublicFolder
New-PublicFolder
Remove-PublicFolder
Set-PublicFolder
```

Most of these cmdlets are self-explanatory. For example, after creating the brand new mailboxes, we can use the New-PublicFolder cmdlet to create new folders. Let's check out the help on the cmdlet:

Get-Help New-PublicFolder -Examples

```
--------------------------- Example 1 ---------------------------
This example creates the public folder Marketing in the root of the public folder.
New-PublicFolder -Name Marketing

--------------------------- Example 2 ---------------------------
This example creates the public folder FY2013 under the existing folders \Legal\Cases. The path to the new folder
is \Legal\Cases\FY2013.
New-PublicFolder -Name FY2013 -Path \Legal\Cases

--------------------------- Example 3 ---------------------------
This example creates the public folder Support in the North_America hierarchy public folder mailbox.
New-PublicFolder -Name Support -Mailbox North_America
```

Let's take a scenario where the IT department receives requests for new Public Folders to be created. One root Public Folder per department in the company needs to be created. Under these departmental root Public Folders, other subfolders need to be created. The departments in this sample company are IT, Research, Marketing, Executive and HR.

```
New-PublicFolder -Name IT
New-PublicFolder -Name Research
New-PublicFolder -Name Marketing
New-PublicFolder -Name Executive
New-PublicFolder -Name HR
```

These one-liners create some base level (or root level) Public Folders. Now we've created our departmental folders, we need a couple of other standard Public Folders created under each one. In order to do this, we'll need to use the '-path' parameter to specify which root folders these Public Folders will be created, otherwise we'll end up creating more root Public Folders:

```
New-PublicFolder -Name Calendar -path \IT
New-PublicFolder -Name Calendar -path \Research
New-PublicFolder -Name Calendar -path \Marketing
New-PublicFolder -Name Calendar -path \Executive
New-PublicFolder -Name Calendar -path \HR
```

Now we have our Public Folder structure in place. To verify that this worked, we can use the Get-PublicFolder cmdlet. First, we can try this without the Get-Help to see what we get:

Get-PublicFolder

```
Name                                                          Parent Path
----                                                          -----------
IPM_SUBTREE
```

Ok, that isn't particularly helpful. Where are our Public Folders? Checking 'Get-Help Get-PublicFolders -Examples' does not reveal how to show all Public Folders. So how do we do this? Well, the root of all Public Folders is '\'. So let's see what that gives us:

Get-PublicFolder '\'

```
Name                                                          Parent Path
----                                                          -----------
IPM_SUBTREE
```

Still not very helpful. There are parameters for Get-PublicFolders called '-Recurse' that sounds like it allows the cmdlet to reveal all the Public Folders under the root of '\':

Get-PublicFolder '\' -Recurse

```
Name                                                         Parent Path
----                                                         -----------

IPM_SUBTREE
Executive                                                    \
Calendar                                                     \Executive
HR                                                           \
Calendar                                                     \HR
IT                                                           \
Calendar                                                     \IT
Marketing                                                    \
Calendar                                                     \Marketing
Research                                                     \
Calendar                                                     \Research
```

Looks good, but the formatting makes it hard to read. How can we reformat the results? Well, objects in Power-Shell are typically revealed with either Name, DisplayName or Identity. In the case of Public Folders, Identity is the field we need for revealing:

Get-PublicFolder '\' -Recurse | FT Identity

```
Identity
--------

\
\Executive
\Executive\Calendar
\HR
\HR\Calendar
\IT
\IT\Calendar
\Marketing
\Marketing\Calendar
\Research
\Research\Calendar
```

That list looks a little nicer and it is easier to see subfolders of the departmental root Public Folder as well. Get-Pub-licFolder can also be a useful cmdlet for documenting information about your Public Folders. How do we format the information provided by this cmdlet to make things better? Let's take for example the Research department's calendar folder and see what properties exist on the folder:

Get-PublicFolder '\Research\Calendar' |fl

```
Identity                        : \Research\Calendar
Name                            : Calendar
MailEnabled                     : False
MailRecipientGuid               :
ParentPath                      : \Research
LostAndFoundFolderOriginalPath  :
ContentMailboxName              : PFMailbox01
ContentMailboxGuid              : cc233ce3-f55f-4f16-bd0e-59caa06594df
EformsLocaleId                  :
PerUserReadStateEnabled         : True
EntryId                         : 0000000001A447390AA6611CD9BC800AA002FC45A0300900AEADACB21A444949A7D2FC6B48(
DumpsterEntryId                 : 0000000001A447390AA6611CD9BC800AA002FC45A0300900AEADACB21A444949A7D2FC6B48(
ParentFolder                    : 0000000001A447390AA6611CD9BC800AA002FC45A0300900AEADACB21A444949A7D2FC6B48(
OrganizationId                  : NAMPR13A006.PROD.OUTLOOK.COM/Microsoft Exchange Hosted Organizations/Onlir
                                  NAMPR13A006.PROD.OUTLOOK.COM/ConfigurationUnits/OnlineExchangeBook.onmicro
AgeLimit                        :
RetainDeletedItemsFor           :
ProhibitPostQuota               : Unlimited
IssueWarningQuota               : Unlimited
MaxItemSize                     : Unlimited
LastMovedTime                   :
AdminFolderFlags                :
FolderSize                      : 0
HasSubfolders                   : False
FolderClass                     : IPF.Note
FolderPath                      : {Research, Calendar}
AssociatedDumpsterFolders       :
DefaultFolderType               : None
ExtendedFolderFlags             :
```

Important attributes here are 'MailEnabled', 'AgeLimit', 'RetainDeletedItemsFor', 'ProhibitPostQuota', 'IssueWarningQuota', 'MaxItemSize', 'HasSubFolders' and 'FolderPath'.   We can use these to make adjustments to the Public Folders. For example if we are working with a calendar folder, maybe we want the last 90 days to stay in the calendar only and make sure no one attaches large files (> 5 MB). In order configure this we'll need to take the Get-PublicFolder cmdlet and pipe the folder into the Set-PublicFolder cmdlet in order to configure it properly:

```
Get-PublicFolder '\Research\Calendar' | Set-PublicFolder -MaxItemSize 5MB -AgeLimit 90
```

For Max Item Size, valid values can be revealed in the Get-Help:

```
-MaxItemSize <Unlimited>
     The MaxItemSize paramet
     MaxItemSize parameter a
     value, qualify the valu

     When you enter a value,

     * B (bytes)
     * KB (kilobytes)
     * MB (megabytes)
     * GB (gigabytes)
     * TB (terabytes)
     Unqualified values are
```

To set an appropriate Age Limit on the items, this can also be found in the Get-Help:

```
-AgeLimit <EnhancedTimeSpan>
     The AgeLimit parameter specifies the overall age limit on the folder. Replicas of this public folder are
     automatically deleted when the age limit is exceeded.

     To specify a value, enter it as a time span: dd.hh:mm:ss where dd = days, hh = hours, mm = minutes, and ss
     seconds.
```

Validate these settings with:

```
Get-PublicFolder '\Research\Calendar' | FL
```

```
AgeLimit                          : 90.00:00:00
RetainDeletedItemsFor             :
ProhibitPostQuota                 : Unlimited
IssueWarningQuota                 : Unlimited
MaxItemSize                       : 5 MB (5,242,880 bytes)
```

Other parameters can also be set, make sure to review the Get-Help parameters for the Set-PublicFolder cmdlet before setting them.

Removing Public Folders

Now, imagine that an organization has created tons of folders for departments, tasks, projects, calendar needs, clients or whatever. The same folders have taken up a lot of space and you have been given a directive to clean these up. First, some specific folders need to be removed - Research. This department was recently sold off as a division to another company:

```
Get-PublicFolder '\Research\Calendar' | Remove-PublicFolder
```

```
[PS] C:\>Get-PublicFolder "\Research\Calendar" | Remove-PublicFolder

Confirm
Are you sure you want to perform this action?
Removing public folder "\Research\Calendar".
[Y] Yes  [A] Yes to All  [N] No  [L] No to All  [?] Help (default is "Y"): y
```

Get-PublicFolder '\Research' | Remove-PublicFolder

```
[PS] C:\>Get-PublicFolder "\Research" | Remove-PublicFolder

Confirm
Are you sure you want to perform this action?
Removing public folder "\Research".
[Y] Yes  [A] Yes to All  [N] No  [L] No to All  [?] Help (default is "Y"): y
```

Now, if you were to try and remove all Public Folders under one root folder, you would run into an issue, because the first folder found is the root folder, the root folder has subfolders and you cannot delete the root Public Folder with subfolders, but you can delete subfolders in the root folder:

```
PS C:\> Get-PublicFolder '\IT' -Recurse | Remove-PublicFolder
The folder '\IT' has subfolders, so it cannot be deleted.
    + CategoryInfo          : InvalidOperation: (\IT:PublicFolderIdParameter) [Remove-PublicFolder], InvalidOperationException
    + FullyQualifiedErrorId : [Server=CY4PR13MB1350,RequestId=ff390615-8446-492e-941e-309284710110,TimeStamp=12/15/2017 4:28:08 AM]
    [FailureCategory=Cmdlet-In validOperationException] D8F21234,Microsoft.Exchange.Management.MapiTasks.RemovePublicFolder
    + PSComputerName        : ps.outlook.com

Confirm
Are you sure you want to perform this action?
Removing public folder "\IT\Calendar".
[Y] Yes  [A] Yes to All  [N] No  [L] No to All  [?] Help (default is "Y"): y
```

Get-PublicFolder*

Same as we've done with other Exchange objects, we can get some basic feedback on how much is stored in the Public Folders in Exchange Online. The two cmdlets that can be used are:

Get-PublicFolderItemStatistics
Get-PublicFolderStatistics

These cmdlets can either be run by themselves as one-liners or when information about a Public Folder is piped (with the '|' symbol) to them. Let's take a look at the Get-Help -Examples for both of these cmdlets:

```
---------------------------- Example 1 ----------------------------
This example retrieves statistics about the public folder Marketing\2013\Pamphlets. The output of the
Get-PublicFolderStatistics command is piped to the Format-List command so that all the available information is
displayed in the result.
Get-PublicFolderStatistics -Identity "\Marketing\2013\Pamphlets" | Format-List
```

```
---------------------------- Example 1 ----------------------------
This example returns default statistics for all items in the Pamphlets public folder under the \Marketing\2013
path. Default information includes item identity, creation time, and subject.

Get-PublicFolderItemStatistics -Identity "\Marketing\2013\Pamphlets"

---------------------------- Example 2 ----------------------------
This example returns additional information about the items within the public folder, such as subject, last
modification time, creation time, attachments, message size, and the type of item by piping the results of the
Get-PublicFolderItemStatistics command to the Format-List command.

Get-PublicFolderItemStatistics -Identity "\Marketing\2013\Pamphlets" | Format-List
```

If you try to pipe the Get-PublicFolder cmdlets to the Get-PublicFolderStatistics cmdlet, you will need to specify some information in order to make the cmdlet more useful:

```
[PS] C:\>Get-PublicFolder | Get-PublicFolderStatistics

Name                                              ItemCount
----                                              ---------
IPM_SUBTREE                                       0
```

However, if you just run the Get-PublicFolderStatistics, you will get some base information:

```
Name                                              ItemCount
----                                              ---------
IPM_SUBTREE                                        0
Executive                                          0
Calendar                                           0
HR                                                 0
Calendar                                           0
IT                                                 0
```

If we explore a bit deeper with Format-List we can see that there are more properties revealed by this cmdlet:

```
RunspaceId               : d5e2291a-5389-4eb5-ade2-cefd5e5016d3
AssociatedItemCount      : 0
ContactCount             : 0
CreationTime             : 12/15/2017 3:40:29 AM
DeletedItemCount         : 0
EntryId                  : 000000001A447390AA6611CD9BC800AA002FC45A0300900AEA
FolderPath               : {Marketing, Calendar}
ItemCount                : 0
LastModificationTime     : 12/15/2017 3:40:29 AM
Name                     : Calendar
OwnerCount               : 0
TotalAssociatedItemSize  : 0 B (0 bytes)
TotalDeletedItemSize     : 0 B (0 bytes)
TotalItemSize            : 0 B (0 bytes)
MailboxOwnerId           : PFMailbox01
Identity                 : PFMailbox01
IsValid                  : True
ObjectState              : New
```

While the above folder is empty, we see that there are several measurements of the items in the Public Folder:

- AssociatedItemCount
- ContactCount
- ItemCount
- TotalAssociatedItemSize
- TotalDeletedItemSize
- TotalItemSize

Now if there are some items in the folders, we'll be able to explore them with the Get-PublicFolderItemStatistics:

Get-PublicFolderItemStatistics -Identity '\Marketing' | ft PublicFolderName,Subject,Identity

```
PublicFolderName  Subject                 Identity
----------------  -------                 --------
\Marketing        Second Test to Marketing PFMailbox01\RgAAAAAaRHOQqmYRzZvIAKoAL8RaCQCQCurayyGkRJSafS
\Marketing        Test Attachment          PFMailbox01\RgAAAAAaRHOQqmYRzZvIAKoAL8RaCQCQCurayyGkRJSafS
```

If we need more details, we can simply just use Format List:

Get-PublicFolderItemStatistics -Identity '\Marketing' |fl

```
RunspaceId            : d5e2291a-5389-4eb5-ade2-cefd5e5016d3
Subject               : Second Test to Marketing
PublicFolderName      : \Marketing
LastModificationTime  : 12/15/2017 4:49:34 AM
CreationTime          : 12/15/2017 4:49:34 AM
HasAttachments        : False
ItemType              : IPM.Post
MessageSize           : 3.428 KB (3,510 bytes)
Identity              : PFMailbox01\RgAAAAAaRHOQqmYRzZvIAKoAL8RaCQ
MailboxOwnerId        : PFMailbox01
IsValid               : True
ObjectState           : New

RunspaceId            : d5e2291a-5389-4eb5-ade2-cefd5e5016d3
Subject               : Test Attachment
PublicFolderName      : \Marketing
LastModificationTime  : 12/15/2017 4:49:12 AM
CreationTime          : 12/15/2017 4:48:59 AM
HasAttachments        : True
ItemType              : IPM.Post
MessageSize           : 207.4 KB (212,350 bytes)
Identity              : PFMailbox01\RgAAAAAaRHOQqmYRzZvIAKoAL8RaCQ
MailboxOwnerId        : PFMailbox01
IsValid               : True
ObjectState           : New
```

We can run this against each Public Folder individually, or we can create a short script to run it against each folder. Why do we need to do this? Because we cannot pipe the cmdlet 'Get-PublicFolder' into Get-PublicFolderItem-Statistics. So, in order to get the Public Folder Item Statistics for each folder we will first need to get a list of the Public Folder names and store it in a variable. Remember that when we run *Get-PublicFolder -Recurse '\'* we get a list of Public Folders with two columns - Name and Parent Path. However, these will not work for Get-Public-FolderItemStatistics. We need the Identity value for the folder. We will utilize the 'Name' column for this example:

```
$PFNames = (Get-PublicFolder -Recurse '\').Identity
Foreach ($PFName in $PFNames) {Get-PublicFolderItemStatistics $PFName | Ft PublicFolderName
,Subject, Identity}
```

```
PublicFolderName  Subject                     Identity
\IT               Agenda for Weekly IT MEeting PFMailbox01\RgAAAAAaRHOQqmYRzZvIAKoAL8RaCQCQCurayy...


PublicFolderName  Subject                     Identity
\Marketing        Second Test to Marketing    PFMailbox01\RgAAAAAaRHOQqmYRzZvIAKoAL8RaCQCQCurayyGkRJ...
\Marketing        Test Attachment             PFMailbox01\RgAAAAAaRHOQqmYRzZvIAKoAL8RaCQCQCurayyGkRJ...
```

Using this you could check for large items, or ones of a certain subject for discovery purposes.

Mail Enabled Public Folders

In previous versions of Exchange, the addition of mail enabled Public Folders was a feature used by SMTP application messages, workflows, for those who wished to deliver emails directly to a Public Folder, and more. There had been plans, multiple times, to remove Public Folders from Exchange, but based on customer feedback they remain today. As the use of Public Folders has diminished, so has the need for email delivery to them. Let's see what PowerShell cmdlets are available for Mail Enabling:

```
Get-Command *MailPublicFolder

Disable-MailPublicFolder
Enable-MailPublicFolder
Get-MailPublicFolder
New-SyncMailPublicFolder
Remove-SyncMailPublicFolder
Set-MailPublicFolder
```

By default, no Public Folders are mail enabled. As such, running Get-MailPublicFolder would display an empty result. How can we Mail Enable the Public Folders? Reviewing the cmdlets, we see that there is an 'Enable-Mail-PublicFolder':

```
Get-Help Enable-MailPublicFolder -Examples
```

```
------------------------------ Example 1 ------------------------------
This example mail-enables the top-level public folder My Public Folder.
Enable-MailPublicFolder "\My Public Folder"

------------------------------ Example 2 ------------------------------
This example mail-enables the public folder Reports that's in the parent folder Marketing.
Enable-MailPublicFolder "\Marketing\Reports"
```

Those default examples are a bit too basic. There are no options to choose SMTP address and other options you may want to use. To get a better idea what is available, make sure to run 'Get-Help Enable-MailPublicFolder'. You should concentrate on these options - 'HiddenFromAddressListsEnabled' and 'OverrideRecipientQuotas'. If we wish to set the email address we need to use the Set-MailPublicFolder.

Example – Enable

```
Enable-MailPublicFolder -Identity '\HR\Calendar'
Get-MailPublicFolder -Identity '\HR\Calendar' | Fl
```

```
RunspaceId                              : d5e2291a-5389-4eb5-ade2-cefd5e5016d3
Contacts                                : {}
ContentMailbox                          : PFMailbox01
DeliverToMailboxAndForward              : False
ExternalEmailAddress                    :
EntryId                                 : 000000001A447390AA6611CD9BC800AA002FC45A0300900AEADACB21A4
                                          44949A7D2FC6B486F90000000000280000
OnPremisesObjectId                      :
IgnoreMissingFolderLink                 : False
ForwardingAddress                       :
PhoneticDisplayName                     :
AcceptMessagesOnlyFrom                  : {}
AcceptMessagesOnlyFromDLMembers         : {}
AcceptMessagesOnlyFromSendersOrMembers  : {}
AddressListMembership                   : {\MailPublicFolders(VLV), \All Recipients(VLV), \Default
                                          Global Address List, \Offline Global Address List...}
AdministrativeUnits                     : {}
Alias                                   : Calendar
ArbitrationMailbox                      :
BypassModerationFromSendersOrMembers    : {}
OrganizationalUnit                      : nampr13a006.prod.outlook.com/Microsoft Exchange Hosted
                                          Organizations/OnlineExchangeBook.onmicrosoft.com
CustomAttribute1                        :
```

Example – Set-MailPublicFolder

First, check the assigned email address for the folder to be modified:

```
Get-MailPublicFolder 'HR\Calendar' | Ft EmailAddresses
```

```
EmailAddresses
--------------
{SMTP:Calendar@OnlineExchangeBook.onmicrosoft.com}
```

Now we can make the change:

```
Set-MailPublicFolder '\HR\Calendar' -EmailAddressPolicyEnabled $False -PrimarySmtpAddress 'HR-
Calendar@OnlineExchangeBook.onmicrosoft.com'
```

Public Folder Permissions

Client permissions on Public Folders are an important configuration step that is often overlooked when a folder is created. Permissions can determine who has access to Public Folders as well as the information contained in these folders. Restricting or granting access can be important depending on the information in the folders. If it's a company-wide folder, default permissions will probably be okay. However, if you need custom access and processes or security restrictions, then PowerShell is your tool for assigning these permissions.

PowerShell

What cmdlets are available when configuring the correct security on Public Folders? Well, let's check with Get-Command:

```
Get-Command *PublicFolderClientPermission
Add-PublicFolderClientPermission
Get-PublicFolderClientPermission
```

Remove-PublicFolderClientPermission

The default permissions on a newly created Public Folder would look something like this:

Get-PublicFolder '\Marketing' | Get-PublicFolderClientPermission

```
FolderName                User                      AccessRights
----------                ----                      ------------
Marketing                 Default                   {Author}
Marketing                 Anonymous                 {None}
```

Why would we want to change the default permissions? Some sample scenarios would be:

- **Departments Folders** - Lock the Public Folder down to a particular group.
- **Sensitive client or company data** - Limit access to those who need access and not the entire company.
- **Subsidiary consolidation** - Imagine two companies wanting to merge and they both have Public Folders. Access could potentially be restricted to folders by company membership.

Scenario 1 - Lock down to a Department

In this scenario we'll take each departmental Public Folder and lock it down to their respective group. First, let's see how we can assign permissions by checking for examples of the Add-PublicFolderClientPermission cmdlet:

Get-Help Add-PublicFolderClientPermission -Examples

```
-------------------------- Example 1 --------------------------

This example adds permission for the user Chris to create items in the public folder My Public Folder.
Add-PublicFolderClientPermission -Identity "\My Public Folder" -User Chris -AccessRights CreateItems
```

Reviewing the syntax above it seems that client permissions for Public Folders must be assigned by user as the cmdlet will not recognize the user of a group. Trying to add a group results in lots of red:

```
PS C:\> Get-PublicFolder '\Marketing' | Add-PublicFolderClientPermission -User Marketing@OnlineExcha
ngeBook.onmicrosoft.com -AccessRights Owner
The user "Marketing@OnlineExchangeBook.onmicrosoft.com" is either not valid SMTP address, or there
is no matching information.
    + CategoryInfo          : NotSpecified: (:) [Add-PublicFolderClientPermission], InvalidExterna
   lUserIdException
    + FullyQualifiedErrorId : [Server=CY4PR13MB1350,RequestId=c5696008-7680-4e3b-bda4-0bcb593b153c
   ,TimeStamp=12/15/2017 5:21:18 AM] [FailureCategory=Cmdlet-InvalidExternalUserIdException] B698
   2CFF,Microsoft.Exchange.Management.StoreTasks.AddPublicFolderClientPermission
    + PSComputerName        : ps.outlook.com
```

So how can we add all users for a department to a set of Public Folders? First, we will work with one department - Marketing - that we want to assign all users in Marketing to have access to Marketing. We also need to decide what level of access to grant these users. Exploring Get-Help for client permissions cmdlets reveals these levels:

ReadItems The user has the right to read items within the specified Public Folder.

CreateItems The user has the right to create items within the specified Public Folder.

EditOwnedItems The user has the right to edit the items that the user owns in the specified Public Folder.

DeleteOwnedItems The user has the right to delete items that the user owns in the specified Public Folder.

EditAllItems The user has the right to edit all items in the specified Public Folder.

DeleteAllItems The user has the right to delete all items in the specified Public Folder.

CreateSubfolders The user has the right to create subfolders in the specified Public Folder.

FolderOwner The user is the owner of the specified Public Folder. The user has the right to view and move the Public Folder and create subfolders. The user can't read items, edit items, delete items, or create items.

FolderContact The user is the contact for the specified Public Folder.

FolderVisible The user can view the specified Public Folder, but can't read or edit items within the specified Public Folder.

-- Combined Roles --

None FolderVisible
Owner CreateItems, ReadItems, CreateSubfolders, FolderOwner, FolderContact, FolderVisible, EditOwnedItems, EditAllItems, DeleteOwnedItems, DeleteAllItems
PublishingEditor CreateItems, ReadItems, CreateSubfolders, FolderVisible, EditOwnedItems, EditAllItems, DeleteOwnedItems, DeleteAllItems
Editor CreateItems, ReadItems, FolderVisible, EditOwnedItems, EditAllItems, DeleteOwnedItems, DeleteAllItems
PublishingAuthor CreateItems, ReadItems, CreateSubfolders, FolderVisible, EditOwnedItems, DeleteOwnedItems
Author CreateItems, ReadItems, FolderVisible, EditOwnedItems, DeleteOwnedItems, NonEditingAuthor, CreateItems, ReadItems, FolderVisible
Reviewer ReadItems, FolderVisible
Contributor CreateItems, FolderVisible

For a departmental Public Folder where all users would have equal access, something equivalent to 'PublishingAuthor' might be appropriate. For our Marketing example, we would first need a list of users to assign the rights to. We can use group membership in order to do this. We can do this first by getting the distribution group Marketing and then pipe this to a cmdlet that can get the membership of the group, like so:

Get-DistributionGroupMember -Identity Marketing

Now if we store this in a variable like $DepartmentMembers, we can use a Foreach loop to process each line of the variable (each line would represent one user in the group) and apply the client permissions to the Public Folder as we envisioned:

```
$DepartmentMembers = Get-DistributionGroupMember -Identity Marketing
Foreach ($DepartmentMember in $DepartmentMembers) {
   $User = $DepartmentMember.Alias
   Get-PublicFolder '\Marketing' | Add-PublicFolderClientPermission -User $User -AccessRight
   PublishingAuthor
}
```

Sample from the script running:

FolderName	User	AccessRights
Marketing	Damian Scoles	{PublishingAuthor}
Marketing	John Doe	{PublishingAuthor}
Marketing	Pete Blanket	{PublishingAuthor}

We can also verify the success or failure of the additions with the Get-PublicFolderClientPermissions cmdlet:

Get-PublicFolder '\Marketing' | Get-PublicFolderClientPermission

FolderName	User	AccessRights
Marketing	Default	{Author}
Marketing	Anonymous	{None}
Marketing	Pete Blanket	{PublishingAuthor}
Marketing	John Doe	{PublishingAuthor}
Marketing	Damian Scoles	{PublishingAuthor}

Now if we need to repeat this for a group of departments, we simply need a variable to hold these departmental names and then loop through each of those with the above permission assignment loop inside of that:

```
$Departments = 'Marketing','I','HR','Executives'
Foreach ($Department in $Departments) {
   $DepartmentMembers = Get-DistributionGroup $Department | Get-DistributionGroupMember
   Foreach ($DepartmentMember in $DepartmentMembers) {
     $User = $DepartmentMember.Alias
     Get-PublicFolder "\$Department" | Add-PublicFolderClientPermission -User $User -AccessRight
     PublishingAuthor
   }
}
```

Now we've assigned all the permissions, we can verify that they are correct with a script similar to the one that assigned the permissions:

```
$Departments = 'Marketing','IT','HR','Executives'
Foreach ($Department in $Departments) {
   Get-PublicFolder '\$Department' | Get-PublicFolderClientPermission
}
```

Scenario 2 - Lock down for Security

In this scenario not only will folders be locked down to a set of users, but the folder will also be hidden from enumeration by other users in the company who are in a different department. This will be done because the information is propriety to the company and the security team for the company would like to limit access as much as possible to the folders. The folder in question is called Sensitive and it is a root folder as well.

Requirements:

1. Make the folder visible to the department and invisible to all others.
2. Grant Access to departmental users only.
3. Grant Access to IT for all departments - to allow for management / support.

If you remember, the default permissions looked like this on any new Public Folder:

```
FolderName              User                    AccessRights
----------              ----                    ------------
Marketing               Default                 {Author}
Marketing               Anonymous               {None}
```

In order to remove access for other departments, we need to adjust the Default access rights. Currently the default is 'Author' for any account connecting to the folder. In order to make this adjustment we need to use the Remove-PublicFolderClientPermissions cmdlet. Let's check out some examples of the cmdlet:

```
Get-Help Remove-PublicFolderClientPermission -Examples
```

```
------------------------------ Example 1 ------------------------------
This example removes permission for the user Chris to the public folder My Public Folder.
Remove-PublicFolderClientPermission -Identity "\My Public Folder" -User Contoso\Chris
```

Get-PublicFolder '\Marketing' | Remove-PublicFolderClientPermission -User Default

```
[PS] C:\>Get-PublicFolder "\Marketing" | Remove-PublicFolderClientPermission -user Default
Confirm
Are you sure you want to perform this action?
Removing mailbox folder permission on "\Marketing" for user "Default".
[Y] Yes  [A] Yes to All  [N] No  [L] No to All  [?] Help (default is "Y"): y
```

Then we can verify this with the same Get-PublicFolder cmdlet used earlier:

```
[PS] C:\>Get-PublicFolder "\Marketing" | Get-PublicFolderClientPermission

FolderName           User                 AccessRights
----------           ----                 ------------
Marketing            Default              {None}
Marketing            Anonymous            {None}
```

Now we can remove access to a Public Folder. If we combine that and the script above, we can remove default access to anyone not in the right department and give the department users access to their folder. In addition to this we need to grant IT Owner access to all folders. Code combined below:

```
$Departments = 'Security','ITM'
$ITDepartmentMembers = Get-DistributionGroupMember 'IT'
Foreach ($Department in $Departments) {
   # Get a list of department users
   $DepartmentMembers = Get-DistributionGroupMember -Identity $Department
   # Remove the default permissions from this folder
   Get-PublicFolder $Department | Remove-PublicFolderClientPermission -User Default
   # Assign Department users to the folder
   Foreach ($DepartmentMember in $DepartmentMembers) {
      $User = $DepartmentMember.Alias
      Get-PublicFolder '\$Department' | Add-PublicFolderClientPermission -User $User -AccessRight
      PublishingAuthor
   }
   # Assign IT users to the folder
   Foreach ($IRDepartmentMember in $ITDepartmentMembers) {
      $User = $ITDepartmentMember.Alias
      Get-PublicFolder '\$Department' | Add-PublicFolderClientPermission -User $User -AccessRight
      Owner
   }
}
```

Because Public Folder client permissions do not support groups, a script like the above would need to be ran regularly to grant new users access to the folder. In addition, users who have left such a group would need to be removed. Permissions can also be managed using Outlook, for occasional additions and removes.

Troubleshooting

This cmdlet provides event level information for your Public Folders and can help assist you in troubleshooting issues with them. If we were to run the cmdlet against one of our mailboxes like so:

```
Get-PublicFolderMailboxDiagnostics -Identity pfmailbox01
```

We can see there is detailed information on the Sync status of the Public Folders:

```
RunspaceId      : d5e2291a-5389-4eb5-ade2-cefd5e5016d3
SyncInfo        : SyncedSourceMailbox: cc233ce3-f55f-4f16-bd0e-59caa06594df
                  IsFullSyncCompleted: True
                  NextPushSyncMessage: 1
                  NumberOfFoldersSynced: 18
                  NumberOfFoldersToBeSynced: 18
                  NumberOfBatchesExecuted: 1
                  BatchSize: 500
                  LastAttemptedSyncTime: 12/15/2017 3:35:32 AM
                  LastSuccessfulSyncTime: 12/15/2017 3:35:32 AM
                  FirstFailedSyncTimeAfterLastSuccess: 1/1/1601 12:00:00 AM
                  NumberofAttemptsAfterLastSuccess: 0
                  LastSyncCycleLog:
                      2017-12-15T03:35:32.097Z,,Entry,NAMPR13A006.PROD.OUTLOOK.COM/Microsoft Exchange Hosted
                  Organizations/OnlineExchangeBook.onmicrosoft.com - NAMPR13A006.PROD.OUTLOOK.COM/ConfigurationUnits/Onli
                  neExchangeBook.onmicrosoft.com/Configuration,cc233ce3-f55f-4f16-bd0e-59caa06594df,Sync
                  started,,21fd7511-4ad6-4c16-a10e-fe5c0cf0ae5e,29368d28-0dc7-46c2-80f4-0ccb8ae2c65f
                      2017-12-15T03:35:32.097Z,,Verbose,NAMPR13A006.PROD.OUTLOOK.COM/Microsoft Exchange Hosted
                  Organizations/OnlineExchangeBook.onmicrosoft.com - NAMPR13A006.PROD.OUTLOOK.COM/ConfigurationUnits/Onli
                  neExchangeBook.onmicrosoft.com/Configuration,cc233ce3-f55f-4f16-bd0e-59caa06594df,FLT:XRF=True,,21fd751
                  1-4ad6-4c16-a10e-fe5c0cf0ae5e,29368d28-0dc7-46c2-80f4-0ccb8ae2c65f
                      2017-12-15T03:35:32.144Z,,Verbose,NAMPR13A006.PROD.OUTLOOK.COM/Microsoft Exchange Hosted
                  Organizations/OnlineExchangeBook.onmicrosoft.com - NAMPR13A006.PROD.OUTLOOK.COM/ConfigurationUnits/Onli
                  neExchangeBook.onmicrosoft.com/Configuration,cc233ce3-f55f-4f16-bd0e-59caa06594df,PrimaryMailboxHierarc
                  hySyncFactory.CreateSourceMailbox. Initializing a
                  StorageSourceMailbox,,21fd7511-4ad6-4c16-a10e-fe5c0cf0ae5e,29368d28-0dc7-46c2-80f4-0ccb8ae2c65f
                      2017-12-15T03:35:32.144Z,,Verbose,NAMPR13A006.PROD.OUTLOOK.COM/Microsoft Exchange Hosted
                  Organizations/OnlineExchangeBook.onmicrosoft.com - NAMPR13A006.PROD.OUTLOOK.COM/ConfigurationUnits/Onli
                  neExchangeBook.onmicrosoft.com/Configuration,cc233ce3-f55f-4f16-bd0e-59caa06594df,Connecting to
                  Primary Hierarchy as source. [Mailbox:cc233ce3-f55f-4f16-bd0e-59caa06594df;
                  Server:MWHPR1301MB2029.namprd13.prod.outlook.com; Database:2ec50169-3689-4a69-88ec-4f8526e05e62; Partit
                  ionHint:<null>:NAMPR13A006.PROD.OUTLOOK.COM:OnlineExchangeBook.onmicrosoft.com:<null>],,21fd7511-4ad6-4
                  c16-a10e-fe5c0cf0ae5e,29368d28-0dc7-46c2-80f4-0ccb8ae2c65f
                      2017-12-15T03:35:32.300Z,,Verbose,NAMPR13A006.PROD.OUTLOOK.COM/Microsoft Exchange Hosted
                  Organizations/OnlineExchangeBook.onmicrosoft.com - NAMPR13A006.PROD.OUTLOOK.COM/ConfigurationUnits/Onli
                  neExchangeBook.onmicrosoft.com/Configuration,cc233ce3-f55f-4f16-bd0e-59caa06594df,PrimaryMailboxHierarc
                  hySyncFactory.CreateExecutor. Initializing PrimaryMailboxSyncInitializeExecutor,,21fd7511-4ad6-4c16-a10
                  e-fe5c0cf0ae5e,29368d28-0dc7-46c2-80f4-0ccb8ae2c65f
                      2017-12-15T03:35:32.316Z,,Verbose,NAMPR13A006.PROD.OUTLOOK.COM/Microsoft Exchange Hosted
                  Organizations/OnlineExchangeBook.onmicrosoft.com - NAMPR13A006.PROD.OUTLOOK.COM/ConfigurationUnits/Onli
```

As well as some Assistant status information:

```
AssistantInfo : LastAttemptedSyncTime: 12/15/2017 3:39:03 AM
                LastSuccessfulSyncTime: 12/15/2017 3:39:03 AM
                FirstFailedSyncTimeAfterLastSuccess: 1/1/1601 12:00:00 AM
                NumberofAttemptsAfterLastSuccess: 0
                LastSyncCycleLog:
                    2017-12-15T03:39:03.151Z,,Entry,NAMPR13A006.PROD.OUTLOOK.COM/Microsoft Exchange Hosted
                Organizations/OnlineExchangeBook.onmicrosoft.com - NAMPR13A006.PROD.OUTLOOK.COM/ConfigurationUnits/Onli
                neExchangeBook.onmicrosoft.com/Configuration,cc233ce3-f55f-4f16-bd0e-59caa06594df,Start,,897f3b2c-cf08-
                42fe-9e42-97a8fbad4d01,29368d28-0dc7-46c2-80f4-0ccb8ae2c65f
                    2017-12-15T03:39:03.245Z,,Verbose,NAMPR13A006.PROD.OUTLOOK.COM/Microsoft Exchange Hosted
                Organizations/OnlineExchangeBook.onmicrosoft.com - NAMPR13A006.PROD.OUTLOOK.COM/ConfigurationUnits/Onli
                neExchangeBook.onmicrosoft.com/Configuration,cc233ce3-f55f-4f16-bd0e-59caa06594df,Processing all
                public folders in two passes -dumpsters in the first pass and all other folders in next
                pass.,,897f3b2c-cf08-42fe-9e42-97a8fbad4d01,29368d28-0dc7-46c2-80f4-0ccb8ae2c65f
                    2017-12-15T03:39:03.245Z,,Verbose,NAMPR13A006.PROD.OUTLOOK.COM/Microsoft Exchange Hosted
                Organizations/OnlineExchangeBook.onmicrosoft.com - NAMPR13A006.PROD.OUTLOOK.COM/ConfigurationUnits/Onli
                neExchangeBook.onmicrosoft.com/Configuration,cc233ce3-f55f-4f16-bd0e-59caa06594df,DOUMDFIRE=False,,897f
                3b2c-cf08-42fe-9e42-97a8fbad4d01,29368d28-0dc7-46c2-80f4-0ccb8ae2c65f
                    2017-12-15T03:39:03.245Z,,Verbose,NAMPR13A006.PROD.OUTLOOK.COM/Microsoft Exchange Hosted
                Organizations/OnlineExchangeBook.onmicrosoft.com - NAMPR13A006.PROD.OUTLOOK.COM/ConfigurationUnits/Onli
                neExchangeBook.onmicrosoft.com/Configuration,cc233ce3-f55f-4f16-bd0e-59caa06594df,Trying to get all
                Public Folder move requests through GetPublicFolderMoveRequest. Current Mailbox under processing: ffa05
                940-c489-4dba-adce-c7e79ebaa914,,897f3b2c-cf08-42fe-9e42-97a8fbad4d01,29368d28-0dc7-46c2-80f4-0ccb8ae2
                65f
```

These three values provide a quick insight into the last sync attempt, last successful sync and first failure after a good sync. Lower in the results from the cmdlet we see this:

```
DumpsterInfo    :
HierarchyInfo   :
AutoSplitInfo   :
Identity        : PFMailbox01
IsValid         : True
ObjectState     : New
```

Notice that the 'Info' properties have no values. Are these typically populated? No. In order to populate these values we need to add two different switches.

-IncludeHierarchyInfo
-IncludeDumpsterInfo

We can add both of these switches to the previous cmdlet:

```
DumpsterInfo    : DumpsterHolderEntryId:
                  000000001A447390AA6611CD9BC800AA002FC45A0300900AEADACB21A444949A7D2FC
                  CountTotalFolders: 31
                  HasDumpsterExtended: True
                  CountLegacyDumpsters: 0
                  CountContainerLevel1: 1
                  CountContainerLevel2: 1
                  CountDumpsters: 25
                  CountDeletedFolders: 3
```

These two provide some background information for what is under the hood in your Public Folders.

In This Chapter

- Overview
- UM Basics
- Basic Configuration
- Skype Integration
- User Management
- Reporting

Overview

Unified Messaging for Exchange Online allows the end user to get a fuller experience out of Exchange. Not only can they get emails to their Inbox, but now they can work with faxes and receive voicemail to their mailbox as well. The integration of UM allows for the end user to play voicemails from OWA, Outlook and their phone. Enabling them to be more productive and not concerned which client they are on. Adding Skype and UM completes the circle of Unified Communications with voice, email and fax on one platform.

As with all parts of Exchange, there are many PowerShell cmdlets that we can use to configure, modify, report and troubleshoot the UM infrastructure. Using these cmdlets we will walk through the various parts of the UM service for Exchange as well as providing insight into the configuration and managing PowerShell without a GUI.

Exchange Online's integration with Skype is also an important aspect of Unified Messaging. Skype provides many additional features that enhances the end user experience. From presence to voicemail, end users will get more than email in their Outlook client. Integration goes a bit deeper in the enhancements that are also brought to the OWA web client with presence also available as well as the ability to schedule.

As with any other portion of Exchange Online, we can also generate reports with PowerShell. We can report on server settings, end user access to UM and how Dial Plans and UM Policies are configured. PowerShell also comes with some built-in cmdlets for troubleshooting Unified Messaging issues. These cmdlets can be used in conjunction with other detection methods to narrow down issues within Exchange's Unified Messaging.

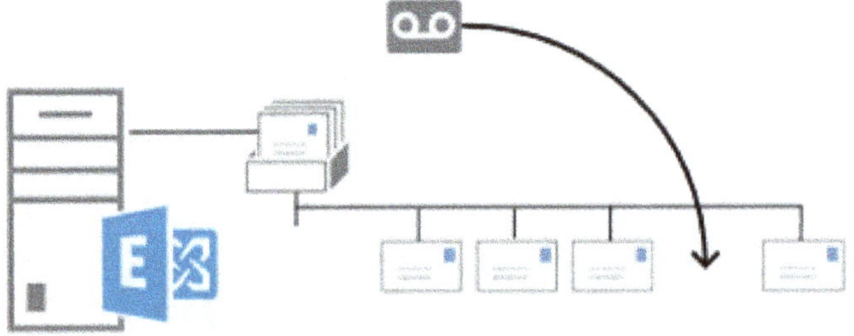

UM Basics

In previous on-premises versions of Exchange, Unified Messaging was included as a separate role. With the advent of Exchange 2013 and 2016, the roles have been collapsed into a single server role. With Exchange Online we don't have to worry about the physical architecture behind the feature, but just the features of Unified Messaging.

Features of UM in Exchange Online:

Access to Exchange information

Play on Phone

Voicemail Form

User Configuration

Call Answering

Call Answering Rules

Voicemail Preview

Message Waiting Indicator

Missed Call and Voicemail Notifications Using SMS

Protected Voicemail

Outlook Voice Access (OVA)

Group addressing with OVA

Unified Messaging in Exchange consists of a few components. These components can be configured in the EAC or with PowerShell. Combined together, these components will allow Exchange to provide end users voicemail. The voicemail feature is accessible with Outlook, phone, and web. Here are the components that make up Unified Messaging:

UM Dial Plan – Establishes a link between a user's extension and their mailbox in Exchange

UM Policy – Is a set of common parameters that are applied to a user mailbox

UM Service – Plays the users voicemail, greeting message and processes call answering rules

UM Call Router Service – Used to route calls to the Exchange server

Auto Attendant – Creates a menu system for users and callers to use

Outlook Voice Access – Gives users access to their voicemails using a phone call

Basic Configuration

In order to configure Unified Messaging in Exchange, we need to walk through the various components that make-up the Unified Messaging service in Exchange.

UM Dial Plan

First item that needs to be configured in order to enable Unified Messaging is a Dial Plan:

Get-Command *DialPlan

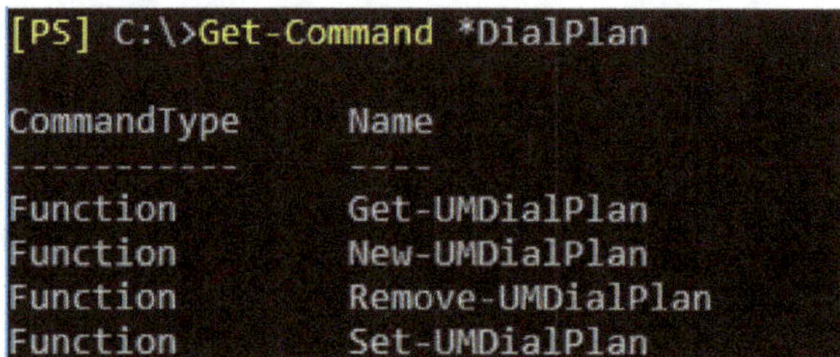

```
[PS] C:\>Get-Command *DialPlan


CommandType      Name
-----------      ----
Function         Get-UMDialPlan
Function         New-UMDialPlan
Function         Remove-UMDialPlan
Function         Set-UMDialPlan
```

The first cmdlet we need to run is Get-UMDialPlan to check for any Dial Plans that may have been created. On a Greenfield tenant for Exchange Online:

```
[PS] C:\>Get-UMDialPlan
Creating a new session for implicit remoting of "Get-UMDialPlan" command...
[PS] C:\>_
```

With no plans pre-created, we'll need to create a new Dial Plan. What options are there for configuring a new Dial Plan:

Get-Help New-UMDialPlan -Examples

```
-------------------------- Example 1 --------------------------
This example creates the UM dial plan MyUMDialPlan that uses four-digit extension numbers.
New-UMDialplan -Name MyUMDialPlan -NumberOfDigitsInExtension 4

-------------------------- Example 2 --------------------------
This example creates the UM dial plan MyUMDialPlan that uses five-digit extension numbers that support
SIP URIs.
New-UMDialplan -Name MyUMDialPlan -URIType SipName -NumberOfDigitsInExtension 5

-------------------------- Example 3 --------------------------
This example creates the unsecured UM dial plan MyUMDialPlan that supports E.164 numbers and that uses
five-digit extension numbers.
New-UMDialplan -Name MyUMDialPlan -URIType E164 -NumberOfDigitsInExtension 5 -VoIPSecurity Unsecured
```

For our sample configuration we'll configure a few of Dial Plans. Each of these Dial Plans will correspond to a different country in an Organization. These regions all require different default languages to be available in Exchange. The countries involved will be United States, France and Japan. The Dial Plans need country codes as well as language definitions. How can we find the country code for these plans?

Search Terms: Country Codes

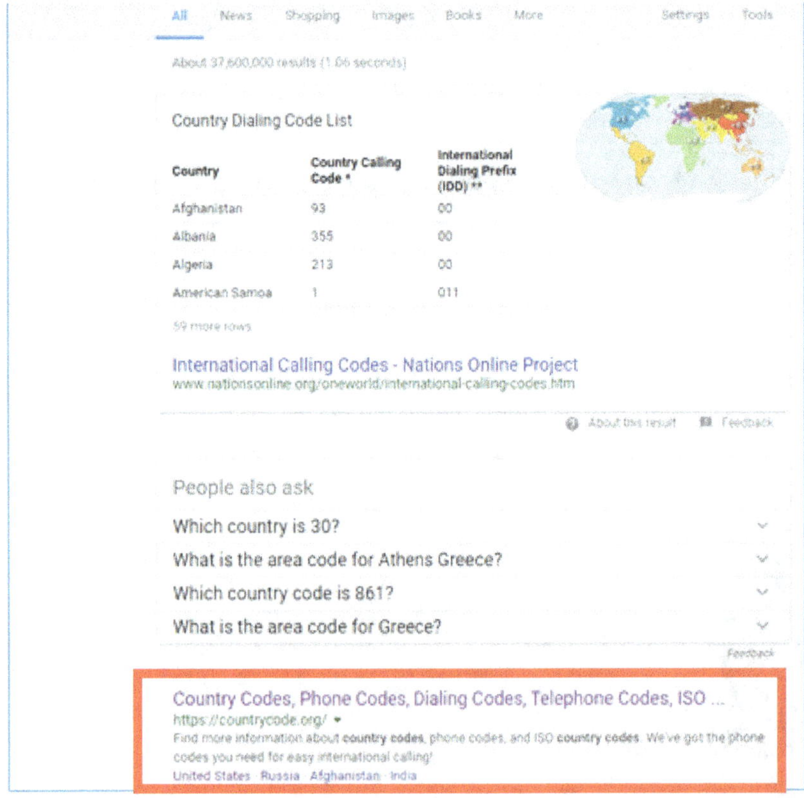

From that page we see that the country codes are as follows:

United States	1
France	33
Japan	81

After we have the country code we can also configure regionalized languages. In our case we have locations in non-English speaking countries and can change the language to what is used by the end user it will provide for a better end user experience. Exchange Server contains localized languages in something called Language Packs.

Search Terms: Exchange Server 2016 UM Language Packs

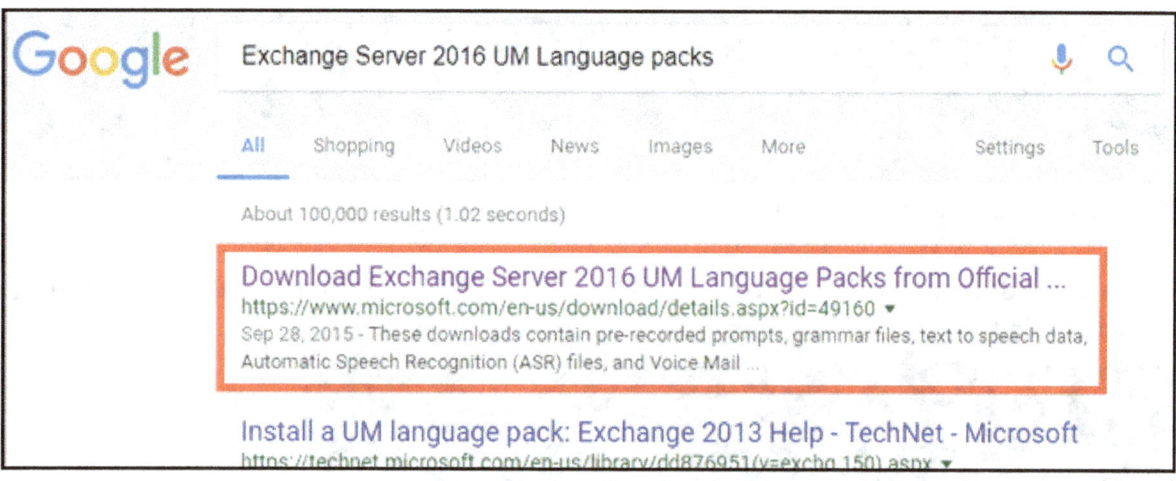

From that page we see there are a few languages that are supported by the Exchange UM:

Language	Country/Region	Code
Catalan	Spain	ca-ES
Danish	Denmark	da-DK
German	Germany	de-DE
English	Australia	en-AU
English	Canada	en-CA
English	United Kingdom	en-GB
English	India	en-IN
English	United States	en-US
Spanish	Spain	es-ES
Spanish	Mexico	es-MX
Finnish	Finland	fi-FI
French	Canada	fr-CA
French	France	fr-FR

Language	Country/Region	Code
Italian	Italy	it-IT
Japanese	Japan	ja-JP
Korean	Korea	ko-KR
Norwegian (Bokmal)	Norway	nb-NO
Dutch	Netherlands	nl-NL
Polish	Poland	pl-PL
Portuguese	Brazil	pt-BR
Portuguese	Portugal	pt-PT
Russian	Russia	ru-RU
Swedish	Sweden	sv-SE
Chinese (Simplified)	China	zh-CN
Chinese (Hong Kong)	China	zh-HK
Chinese (Traditional)	Taiwan	zh-TW

In our sample scenario, we will need to create three Dial Plans for the three different physical locations. Some of the options we will also need are DefaultLanguage, Number of digits for the extension and URIType.

With these parameters and the previous language and country codes, we can create the Dial Plans for the different geographic locations:

```
New-UMDialPlan -Name "USDialPlan" -NumberOfDigitsInExtension 4 -URIType "SipName"
-CountryOrRegionCode 1 –DefaultLanguage "en-US"
New-UMDialPlan -Name "FranceDialPlan" -NumberOfDigitsInExtension 4 -URIType "SipName" –
CountryOrRegionCode 33 –DefaultLanguage "fr-FR"
New-UMDialPlan -Name "JapanDialPlan" -NumberOfDigitsInExtension 4 -URIType "SipName"
-CountryOrRegionCode 81 –DefaultLanguage "ja-JP"
```

A successful creation of a UM Dial Plan should look like this:

```
PS C:\> New-UMDialPlan -Name "FranceDialPlan" -NumberOfDigitsInExtension 4 -URIType "SipName" -CountryOrRegionCode 3
3 -DefaultLanguage "fr-FR"

Name                    UMServers               UMIPGateway             Digits
----                    ---------               -----------             ------
FranceDialPlan          {}                      {}                      4
```

Luckily, since we are working with Exchange Online, we do not have to worry about installing Language Packs or having dial plans fail because they are missing.

Once the plans are created, we can also modify these plans with a PowerShell cmdlet called 'Set-UMDialPlan'. First, let's review what is in the new UM Dial Plans we just created:

```
[PS] C:\>Get-UMDialPlan

Name                    UMServers               UMIPGateway             Digits
----                    ---------               -----------             ------
USDialPlan              {}                      {}                      4
FranceDialPlan          {}                      {}                      4
JapanDialPlan           {}                      {}                      4
```

The base Get-UMDialPlan provides a good list of Dial Plans, but not a lot of useful information. If we run Get-UM-DialPlan | FL we can see a lot more information and a lot of values we can customize:

```
RunspaceId                            : f8fca2e7-7004-40ca-8594-06eae572a6d9
NumberOfDigitsInExtension             : 4
LogonFailuresBeforeDisconnect         : 3
AccessTelephoneNumbers                : {}
FaxEnabled                            : True
InputFailuresBeforeDisconnect         : 3
OutsideLineAccessCode                 :
DialByNamePrimary                     : LastFirst
DialByNameSecondary                   : SMTPAddress
AudioCodec                            : Mp3
DefaultLanguage                       : en-US
VoIPSecurity                          : Secured
MaxCallDuration                       : 30
MaxRecordingDuration                  : 20
RecordingIdleTimeout                  : 5
PilotIdentifierList                   : {}
UMServers                             : {}
UMMailboxPolicies                     : {USDialPlan Default Policy}
UMAutoAttendants                      : {}
WelcomeGreetingEnabled                : False
AutomaticSpeechRecognitionEnabled     : True
PhoneContext                          : USDialPlan.16-08.local
WelcomeGreetingFilename               :
InfoAnnouncementFilename              :
OperatorExtension                     :
DefaultOutboundCallingLineId          :
```

Some items that can be configured to further customize the UM Dial Plans. A sample of these values are:

- WelcomeGreetingFilename
- InfoAnnouncementFilename
- LogonFailuresBeforeDisconnect
- UMAutoAttendants
- DialByNameSecondary

** **Note** ** When a new UM Dial Plan is created, a new UM Mailbox Policy is also created:

Get-UMMailboxPolicy | FT –Auto

```
Name                           UMDialPlan      AllowCommonPatterns PINLifetime PINHistoryCount MinPINLength
----                           ----------      ------------------- ----------- --------------- ------------
USDialPlan Default Policy      USDialPlan      False               60.00:00:00 5               6
FranceDialPlan Default Policy  FranceDialPlan  False               60.00:00:00 5               6
JapanDialPlan Default Policy   JapanDialPlan   False               60.00:00:00 5               6
```

Assigning UM Mailbox Policy

Now that we've defined our UM Dial Plans we need to assign them to users. In order to do so, we'll need to find the right PowerShell cmdlet.

PowerShell

What cmdlets are available for assigning UM Mailbox Policies to mailboxes in Exchange Online? Similar to the CASMailbox cmdlets, there is a similar set with 'UMMailbox' in the cmdlet.

Get-Command *UMMailbox

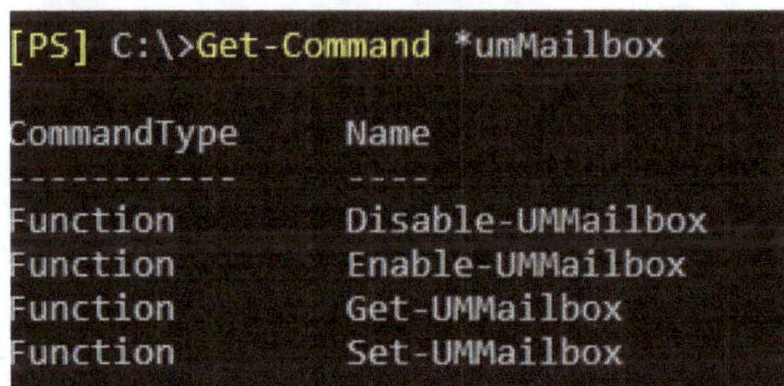

```
[PS] C:\>Get-Command *umMailbox

CommandType     Name
-----------     ----
Function        Disable-UMMailbox
Function        Enable-UMMailbox
Function        Get-UMMailbox
Function        Set-UMMailbox
```

From the list above, it looks like the obvious choice is 'Enable-UMMailbox'. Let's review the cmdlet's examples to see what we can do with the cmdlet:

Get-Help Enable-UMMailbox -Examples

```
------------------------ Example 1 ------------------------
Enable-UMMailbox -Identity tonysmith@contoso.com -UMMailboxPolicy MyUMMailboxPolicy
-Extensions 51234 -PIN 5643892 -NotifyEmail administrator@contoso.com -PINExpired $true

------------------------ Example 2 ------------------------
Enable-UMMailbox -Identity tonysmith@contoso.com -UMMailboxPolicy MyUMMailboxPolicy
-Extensions 51234 -PIN 5643892 -SIPResourceIdentifier "tonysmith@contoso.com"
-PINExpired $true
```

Sample Scenario

A company just migrated to Exchange Online and added Skype for Business for their voice solution. The company wants to enable the UM feature of Exchange for all of their users. In this scenario, a large number of users are being enabled and thus a CSV file was created to contain the user data. The CSV file has the following fields:

SMTP,Extension,PIN

A sample of the data file would looks something like this:

```
File  Edit  Format  View  Help
SMTP,Extenstion,PIN
damian@OnlineExchangeBook.onmicrosoft.com,4455,551155
john.doe@OnlineExchangeBook.onmicrosoft.com,3456,551155
dave.stork@OnlineExchangeBook.onmicrosoft.com,4679,551155
ljones@OnlineExchangeBook.onmicrosoft.com,2967,551155
```

To assign the correct plan to the user, we'll look up the properties of the mailbox and use the 'UsageLocation' property as a determining factor as to what UM plan is assigned. Let's create a script to accomplish this task.

Script

First, we need to import the UM configuration settings stored in a CSV in a variable called $CSV:

```
$CSV = Import-CSV 'C:\Source\UMSettings.csv'
```

Variables

We need to define a variable for the admin email address:

```
# Global variables
$Admin = 'administrator@OnlineExchangeBook.onmicrosoft.com'
```

At this point we can use a Foreach loop to read each line of the CSV file to configure each user for UM:

```
Foreach ($Line in $CSV) {
```

Next, we'll configure some variables we need within the loop:

```
# Local Variables
$Mailbox = $Line.SMTP
$Pin = [int32]$Line.Pin
$Extension = $Line.Extension
$Plan = $Null
```

Then we'll need to figure out which 'UsageLocation' is configured for a mailbox since that is our criteria for assigning the UM Mailbox Policy:

```
$Location = (Get-Mailbox $Mailbox).UsageLocation
```

Next, we can compare the user's OU versus the three sites and set the $Plan variable for the correct plan:

```
If ($Location -Eq 'France') {
    $Plan = 'FranceDialPlan Default Policy'
```

```
    }
    If ($Location -Eq 'Japan') {
        $Plan = 'JapanDialPlan Default Policy'
    }
    If ($Location -Eq 'United States') {
        $Plan = 'USDialPlan Default Policy'
    }
}
```

Finally, we can take all of the above and use it to configure the UM Mailbox using the Enable-UMMailbox cmdlet:

```
Enable-UMMailbox -Identity $Mailbox -UMMailboxPolicy $Plan -Extensions $Extension -PIN $Pin
-NotifyEmail $Admin -SipResourceIdentifier $Mailbox -Whatif
```

Combining all of those lines we now have a complete script that will configure all of the mailboxes for UM with the data populated in a CSV file:

Complete Script

```
# Global variables
$CSV = Import-CSV 'C:\reports\UMSettings.csv'
$Admin = 'administrator@OnlineExchangeBook.onmicrosoft.com'
Foreach ($Line in $CSV) {
    # Local Variables
    $Mailbox = $Line.SMTP
    $Pin = [int32]$Line.Pin
    $Extension = $Line.Extension
    $Plan = $Null
    $Location = (Get-Mailbox $Mailbox).UsageLocation
    $Location
    $Mailbox
    If ($Location -Eq 'France') {
        $Plan = 'FranceDialPlan Default Policy'
    }
    If ($Location -Eq 'Japan') {
        $Plan = 'JapanDialPlan Default Policy'
    }
    If ($Location -Eq 'United States') {
        $Plan = 'USDialPlan Default Policy'
    }
    Write-Host "The plan is $Plan"
    Write-Host "The extention is $Extension"
    Enable-UMMailbox -Identity $Mailbox -UMMailboxPolicy $Plan -Extensions $Extension -PIN $Pin
    -NotifyEmail $Admin -SipResourceIdentifier $Mailbox -Whatif
}
```

Secondary Dial Plans

An interesting feature available in Exchange UM is the concept of a secondary Dial Plan. These Dial Plans allow for a roaming user to use a different dial plan if they happen to be in a different location. If we were to continue to use our scenario above with the three different UM Dial Plans, we can configure a mailbox with a primary and a secondary UM Dial Plan.

**** Note **** A user can be assigned more than one secondary extension.

In order to do so, we need an extension to assign the user and a Dial Plan to assign to the mailbox. We can use an extension of '3245' since we configure the plans for four digit dialing before. This user travels between the US and France. That means that we will use the FranceDialPlan. While in the second location, the user will also need a second extension for dialing.

The caveat is that the plan cannot be configured with the Set-UMMailbox cmdlet and needs to be assigned with the Set-Mailbox cmdlet. We will use the SecondaryAddress and SecondaryDialPlan parameters to do so:

Set-Mailbox Damian.Scoles –SecondaryAddress 3245 –SecondaryDialPlan "FranceDialPlan"

Skype for Business Integration

In order for Exchange to work with Skype for voicemail, presence and other functionality, we need to configure Skype and Exchange as 'partnering apps'. Microsoft provides good documentation for this integration at this link - https://support.microsoft.com/en-us/help/2614614/how-to-integrate-exchange-online-with-skype-for-business-online--lync. To find links and helpful documentation like this, use your favorite engine. I found this link like so:

Search Terms: Skype for Business Exchange Online integration

Which delivers these search results:

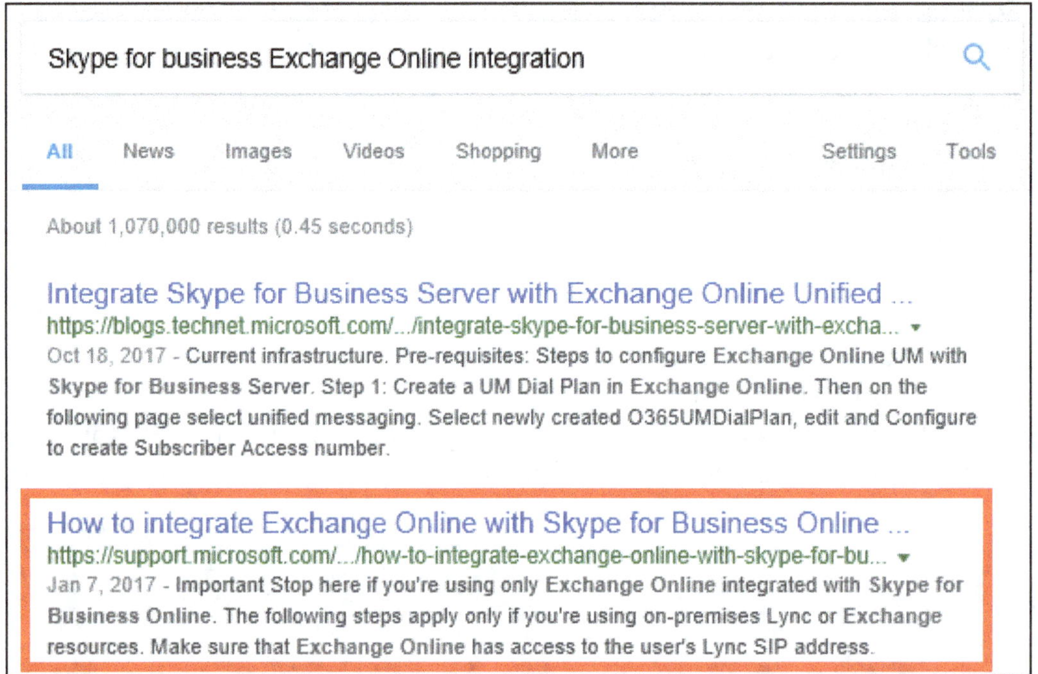

The link above brings us to the official Microsoft document for configuring Skype and Exchange for integration with each other:

https://technet.microsoft.com/en-us/library/jj688151.aspx

** **Note** ** Configuring Skype is out of scope of this book.

User Management

Once Unified Messaging is configured on the server, we now need to worry about the end user and any configuration / reconfiguration would need to be completed. On a day to day basis, UM configuration should be rather low and hopefully a set it and forget it setting. If there are any changes to made, Microsoft has provided a set of cmdlets to allow for this configuration. Let's review these cmdlets:

PowerShell

Get-Command *UMMailbox

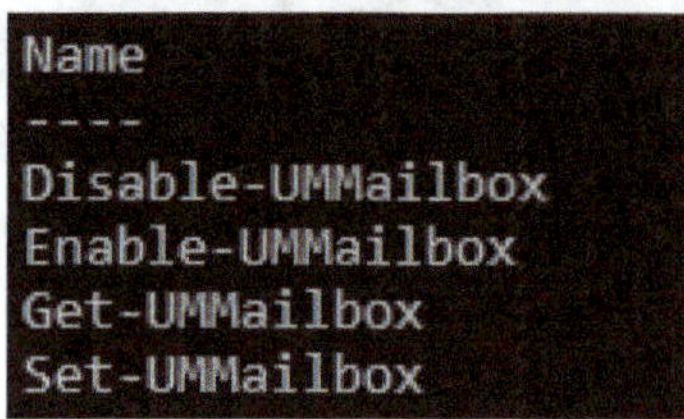

Modifying UM Mailbox

We can modify existing UM Mailboxes with the 'Set-UMMailbox'. What parameters exist?

PhoneNumber	ErrorVariable	PinlessAccessToVoiceMailEnabled
AirSyncNumbers	WarningVariable	AnonymousCallersCanLeaveMessages
VerifyGlobalRoutingEntry	InformationVariable	AutomaticSpeechRecognitionEnabled
UMMailboxPolicy	OutVariable	VoiceMailAnalysisEnabled
IgnoreDefaultScope	OutBuffer	PlayOnPhoneEnabled
DomainController	PipelineVariable	CallAnsweringRulesEnabled
Identity	WhatIf	AllowUMCallsFromNonUsers
ProxyToMailbox	Confirm	OperatorNumber
ProxyToServer	TUIAccessToCalendarEnabled	PhoneProviderId
Verbose	FaxEnabled	CallAnsweringAudioCodec
Debug	TUIAccessToEmailEnabled	ImListMigrationCompleted
ErrorAction	SubscriberAccessEnabled	Name
WarningAction	MissedCallNotificationEnabled	
InformationAction	UMSMSNotificationOption	

For example, when a UM Mailbox is enabled, the users mail messages and calendar are available over the phone. If this service needs to be removed for all UM Mailboxes or particular mailboxes, the TUIAccessToCalendarEnabled and TUIAccessToEmailEnabled values will need to be configured as false like so:

Set-UMMailbox Damian -TUIAccessToEmailEnabled $False –TUIAccessToCalendarEnabled $False

We can also remove the PIN requirement for users accessing their voicemail using this one-liner:

```
Set-UMMailbox Damian –PinlessAccessToVoiceMailEnabled $True
```

Lastly, we can change the format of the voicemail from MP3 to a different format:

```
Set-UMMailbox Damian -CallAnsweringAudioCodec WMA
```

We can also further integrate Skype with Exchange by saving the Skype contact list in the Exchange mailbox:

```
Set-UMMailbox Damian -ImListMigrationCompleted $True
```

Removing UM Mailbox

Removing the UM Mailbox from a user can be done after they are terminated or possibly during a change of Unified Messaging Systems. To remove the UM Mailbox features from an Exchange mailbox, we can use 'Disable-UM-Mailbox'. Let's review examples for using the cmdlet:

```
-------------------------- Example 1 --------------------------
This example disables Unified Messaging on the mailbox for tonysmith@contoso.com.
Disable-UMMailbox -Identity tonysmith@contoso.com
```

Looks like we only need the SMPT address of the mailbox to disable:

```
Disable-UMMailbox –Identity Dave@WorldCorp.Com
```

Now this user has no UM Mailbox and cannot receive voicemails.

```
[PS] C:\>Disable-UMMailbox -Identity Dave@WorldCorp.Com

Confirm
Are you sure you want to perform this action?
The UM mailbox "Dave@WorldCorp.Com" is being disabled.
[Y] Yes  [A] Yes to All  [N] No  [L] No to All  [?] Help (default is "Y"): y

Name                     UMEnabled Extensions UMMailboxPolicy PrimarySMTPAddress
----                     --------- ---------- --------------- ------------------
Dave Stork               False        {}                      Dave@WorldCorp.Com
```

Reporting

Like any other IT system, having a way to report settings or configuration information in it is a necessary function. With Unified Messaging in Exchange, PowerShell can provide an insight into how things are configured. It can also be used for verification of data. For Unified Messaging, reporting could involve the configuration of user mailbox, UM Mailbox Policies, UM Service configurations and more.

Sample User Report

One task that IT could take on is validating phone lists against what is configured in Unified Messaging. A validating of data to confirm that users with UM mailboxes are configured with the right extensions, or even a secondary extension. An audit may also reveal mailboxes that should not have one, or have the wrong extension assigned.

The easiest way to reveal information on Unified Messaging is the 'Get-UMMailbox' cmdlet. The default results are OK, but we don't need the Primary SMTP Address. Instead we'll simplify the results like so:

```
Get-Mailbox | Get-UMMailbox | FT DisplayName,UMDialPlan,UMMailboxPolicy,Extensions
```

```
DisplayName     UMDialPlan     UMMailboxPolicy             Extensions
-----------     ----------     ---------------             ----------
Damian Scoles   USDialPlan     USDialPlan Default Policy   {3245 (FranceDialPlan.16-08.local), 4455 (USDialPlan.16-08.loc
Dave Stork      FranceDialPlan FranceDialPlan Default Policy {3456, dave@WorldCorp.Com}
John Smith      USDialPlan     USDialPlan Default Policy   {4679, jsmith@WorldCorp.Com}
Larry Jones     JapanDialPlan  JapanDialPlan Default Policy {2967, LJones@WorldCorp.Com}
Sarah Wright    FranceDialPlan FranceDialPlan Default Policy {3756, swright@WorldCorp.Com}
Yamada Shinji   JapanDialPlan  JapanDialPlan Default Policy {2798, yshinji@WorldCorp.Com}
```

Another column that could be added would be the Phone Number field if the full phone number is populated and needs to be verified.

What if there are a lot of user moves and the IT department has noted a lot of users now have extensions for the wrong office, how would we go about validating the plans are correct? First, we would have to be sure that when a user moves, that either the user is put in the correct office site OU (if AD is configured that way) or maybe the user's office attribute is set to their new office. For this script we can use a check like the script that was used to configure the UM Mailboxes earlier in the chapter.

In this case we'll start with the usual variable definitions – locations and a variable to store all UM Mailboxes. Then we'll use a Foreach loop to examine the assigned plan ($ConfiguredPlan) for the mailbox and compare it against the plan that should be assigned ($ExpectedPlan) according to the OU the user is present in. Then, once the comparison is made, report a good configuration in cyan and the wrong configuration with red text.

Complete Check Script

```
# Global Variables
$UMMailbox = Get-UMMailbox

Foreach ($line in $UMMailbox) {
    $SMTP = ($line.PrimarySMTPAddress)
    $Mailbox = Get-Mailbox $SMTP
    $Org = $Mailbox.OrganizationalUnit
    $ConfiguredPlan = $Line.UMDialPlan
    $DisplayName = (Get-Mailbox $SMTP).DisplayName
    If ($Location -Eq 'France') {
        $ExpectedPlan = 'FranceDialPlan Default Policy'
    }
    If ($Location -Eq 'Japan') {
        $ExpectedPlan = 'JapanDialPlan Default Policy'
```

```
    }
    If ($Location -Eq 'United States') {
        $ExpectedPlan = 'USDialPlan Default Policy'
    }
    If ($ConfiguredPlan -eq $ExpectedPlan) {
        Write-Host "User $DisplayName has the correct UM Dial Plan configured." -ForegroundColor Cyan
    } Else {
        Write-Host "User $DisplayName has the wrong UM Dial Plan configured." -ForegroundColor Red
    }
}
```

If all of the plans are correctly assigned all of the results should show in cyan:

```
[PS] C:\source>.\UMPlanCheck.ps1
User Damian Scoles has the correct UM Dial Plan configured.
User Dave Stork has the correct UM Dial Plan configured.
User John Smith has the correct UM Dial Plan configured.
User Larry Jones has the correct UM Dial Plan configured.
User Sarah Wright has the correct UM Dial Plan configured.
User Yamada Shinji has the correct UM Dial Plan configured.
```

If things are not configured properly, we would expect to see some red from users with a Dial Plan that does not correspond to the office their account is in:

```
[PS] C:\source>.\UMPlanCheck.ps1
User Damian Scoles has the correct UM Dial Plan configured.
User Dave Stork has the correct UM Dial Plan configured.
User John Smith has the correct UM Dial Plan configured.
User Larry Jones has the wrong UM Dial Plan configured.
User Sarah Wright has the wrong UM Dial Plan configured.
User Yamada Shinji has the correct UM Dial Plan configured.
```

Thus, this script can be used as an audit mechanism for the Unified Messaging configuration for users.

## 18

Reporting

In This Chapter

- Screenshots
- TXT Files
- CSV Files
- HTML Files
- Delivery Methodologies
- File Copy

When managing environments like Exchange Online, often the concentration of work to manage these is reviewing the configuration with Get cmdlets or making configuration changes with Set cmdlets. Of course there are other cmdlets starting with New, Remove, and so on. Either way the daily tasks such as adding mailboxes, changing settings in Exchange Online, looking for issues and scouring through Message Trace or Admin Audit logs will take up the majority of time and little time is given to documenting an environment or being proactive and producing daily reports. While documenting a Exchange Online certainly requires less effort due to there not being any servers to manage, reporting on Exchange Online's configuration is still important for the administrator.

PowerShell makes creating reports easy and while there are third party products that can produce canned results, they are not usually as flexible as PowerShell. With PowerShell, an administrator can choose the parameters to be reported on, the formatting and delivering method. Scripts can also be scheduled and contain error correction as needed depending on the intended results.

In this chapter, we will explore various reporting formats like TXT, CSV, HTML, and more. Delivery methods will also be explored and ways to schedule the reports. Real world scenarios will be used to help illustrate the usefulness of each method as well as the possibilities that each of these formats will provide.

Screenshots

The simplest method for using PowerShell to document an Exchange Online environment is to use screenshots to capture script results. The advantages to this method are that it is quick, simple and somewhat flexible. The disadvantages are that the results are harder to manipulate post screenshot and not as flexible for generating good documentation.

Using programs like the Windows Snipping Tool, OneNote, SnagIt and others can make quick snapshots of your PowerShell Script results. However, since this is a PowerShell book, I would only recommend using these tools as enhancements for documentation or reports that were created in PowerShell.

> ** **Note** ** It is important to note, that while screenshots can be helpful for referring to a proper configuration for something in Exchange Online, the screens and sections of the Exchange Online administration pages will change over time.

Let's explore other options for creating documentation via PowerShell.

TXT Files

PowerShell provides a variety of ways to export results from cmdlets or scripts thus making results accessible for later review. One of these methods includes exporting any and all results to a text file.

Exporting the output can be done with a couple different methods. One is to use the '>' symbol and specifying a TXT file name for output. The second method for exporting the results via the Out-File cmdlet. The below examples will explore both of these options for real world scenarios.

First, reporting the statistics for mailboxes in an Exchange Online environment requires a couple of cmdlets to gather the data. Get-Mailbox, which is piped to Get-MailboxStatistics to derive the numbers needed for an accurate report of all mailbox sizes. In addition to these cmdlets, some formatting has been inserted for attributes that are reported on. Note that Select-Object is being used to facilitate this:

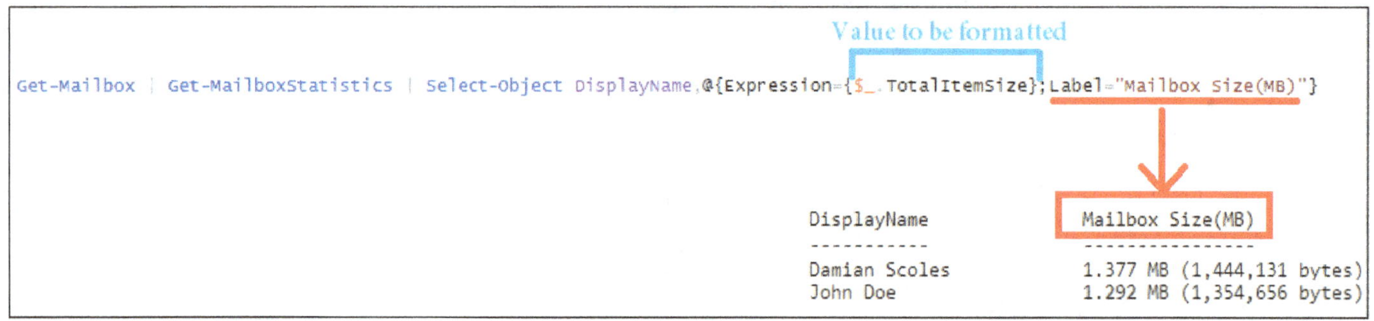

Example – '>'

```
Get-Mailbox | Get-MailboxStatistics | Select-Object DisplayName,@{Expression={$_.TotalItemSize};
Label="Mailbox Size(MB)"} | ft -Auto > C:\Downloads\MailboxStats.txt
```

> ** **Note** ** The '>' symbol can be used to create or overwrite an existing file, while using '>>' will append to an existing file.

This cmdlet drops the results of this cmdlet to a local text file:

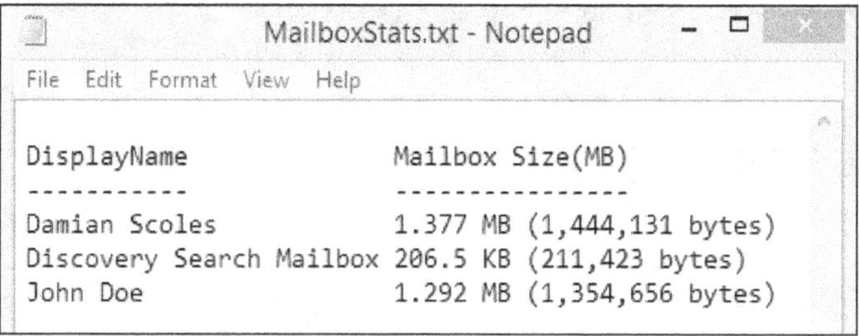

Example – Out-File #1

Similar to the '>' output symbol, the Out-File provides a method for exporting results of the cmdlet to a TXT file. However, Out-File provides more options for formatting the actual output; including Encoding, NoClobber, as well as width of the output.

```
Get-Mailbox | Get-MailboxStatistics | Select-Object DisplayName,@{Expression={$_.TotalItemSize};
Label="Mailbox Size(MB)"} | ft -Auto | Out-File -FilePath C:\Downloads\MailboxStats-OF.txt -NoClobber
```

This PowerShell cmdlet drops the results to a local text file:

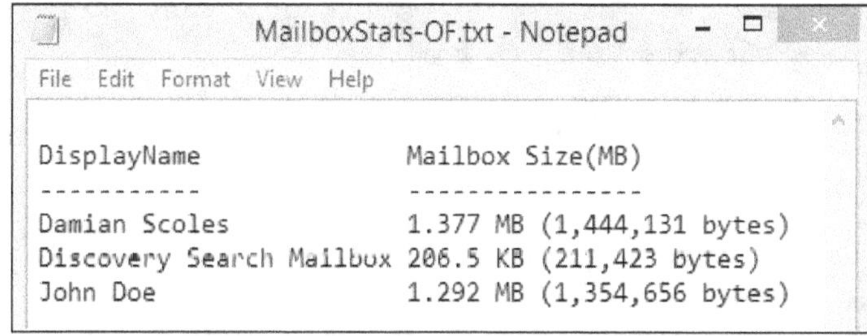

Notice that in terms of actual output or formatting, the text file is exactly the same for either '>' or 'Out-File'. The true differentiator will be the usage of NoClobber and Encoding. While Encoding was not used for this example, it is an available option. The NoClobber option is useful as it will prevent the overwriting a file by the output of this cmdlet. This is useful for running reports that may need to be reviewed later and having a script overwrite a file would make data analysis later impossible.

Example – Out-File # 2

The first example was a bit simple, based off a single cmdlet. In this example a script will be written to produce a report of licenses assigned to each user in Azure AD, then exported to a TXT file for reporting:

```
$Mailboxes = Get-MsolUser -All | Select-Object UserPrincipalName,Licenses
$Header1 = "Licensing for each mailbox:" | Out-File c:\Reports\Licenses.txt -NoClobber
$Header2 = "-------------------------" | Out-File c:\Reports\Licenses.txt -Append
Foreach ($Mailbox in $Mailboxes) {
    $LicenseAll = $Null
    $UPN = $Mailbox.UserPrincipalName
    $ServicePlans = $Mailbox.Licenses.ServiceStatus
    $Licenses = $Mailbox.Licenses
    $SKUs = $Licenses.AccountSKUID
```

```powershell
$LicenseCurrent = New-Object System.Object
$LicenseCurrent | Add-Member -Type NoteProperty -Name Mailbox -Value $UPN
Write-Host "$UPN" -ForegroundColor Cyan
Foreach ($Sku in $SKUs) {
    If ($SKU -eq "OnlineExchangeBook:ENTERPRISEPACK") {
        Foreach ($Line in $ServicePlans) {
            $ServicePlan = $Line.ServicePlan.ServiceName
            $ProvisioningStatus = $Line.ProvisioningStatus
            $ServicePlan
            $LicenseCurrent | Add-Member -Type NoteProperty -Name $ServicePlan -Value $ProvisioningStatus
        }
        $LicenseAll += $LicenseCurrent
    }
    $LicenseAll | Out-File c:\Reports\Licenses.txt -Append
    }
}
```

Contents of the resulting TXT file are:

```
Licensing for each mailbox:
---------------------------

Mailbox                    : john.doe@OnlineExchangeBook.onmicrosoft.com
BPOS_S_TODO_2              : Success
FORMS_PLAN_E3             : Success
STREAM_O365_E3            : Success
Deskless                  : Success
FLOW_O365_P2              : Success
POWERAPPS_O365_P2         : Success
TEAMS1                    : Success
PROJECTWORKMANAGEMENT     : Success
SWAY                      : Success
INTUNE_O365               : PendingActivation
YAMMER_ENTERPRISE         : Success
RMS_S_ENTERPRISE          : Success
OFFICESUBSCRIPTION        : Success
MCOSTANDARD               : Success
SHAREPOINTWAC             : Success
SHAREPOINTENTERPRISE      : Success
EXCHANGE_S_ENTERPRISE     : Success


Mailbox                    : damian@OnlineExchangeBook.onmicrosoft.com
BPOS_S_TODO_2              : Success
FORMS_PLAN_E3             : Success
STREAM_O365_E3            : Success
Deskless                  : Success
FLOW_O365_P2              : Success
POWERAPPS_O365_P2         : Success
TEAMS1                    : Success
PROJECTWORKMANAGEMENT     : Success
SWAY                      : Success
INTUNE_O365               : PendingActivation
YAMMER_ENTERPRISE         : Success
RMS_S_ENTERPRISE          : Success
OFFICESUBSCRIPTION        : Success
MCOSTANDARD               : Success
SHAREPOINTWAC             : Success
SHAREPOINTENTERPRISE      : Success
EXCHANGE_S_ENTERPRISE     : Success
```

Explanation of the Script

In the first part of the script, a header and underline are added for identification and documentation purposes. Note that the switch –append is not used on the first line. This is because the file needs to start fresh, with no content for the header, otherwise the 'header' would go to the bottom of the file and is then not a header.

```
$Header1 = "Licensing for each mailbox:"    Out-File c:\Reports\Licenses.txt -Append
$Header2 = "--------------------------"    Out-File c:\Reports\Licenses.txt -Append
```

```
Licensing for each mailbox:
--------------------------
```

The next section (inside the Foreach loop), a series of variables are set for the script user license query. The most complicate variable, $LicenseCurrent, is a system object because other information will be added to it a little later:

```
$LicenseAll = $Null
$UPN = $Mailbox.UserPrincipalName
$ServicePlans = $mailbox.Licenses.ServiceStatus
$Licenses = $mailbox.Licenses
$SKUS = $Licenses.AccountSKUID
$LicenseCurrent = New-Object System.Object
$LicenseCurrent | Add-Member -type NoteProperty -name Mailbox -value $UPN
```

Next, we validate that the SKU is the correct one, which is TenantName:LicenseLevel. In this case that value would be 'OnelineExchangeBook:ENTERPRISEPACK':

```
foreach ($Sku in $SKUs) {
    if ($SKU -eq "OnlineExchangeBook:ENTERPRISEPACK") {
```

This part of the script populates the $LicenseCurrent variable which is used to populate the results file like so:

```
$LicenseCurrent | Add-Member -type NoteProperty -name $ServicePlan -value $ProvisioningStatus
```

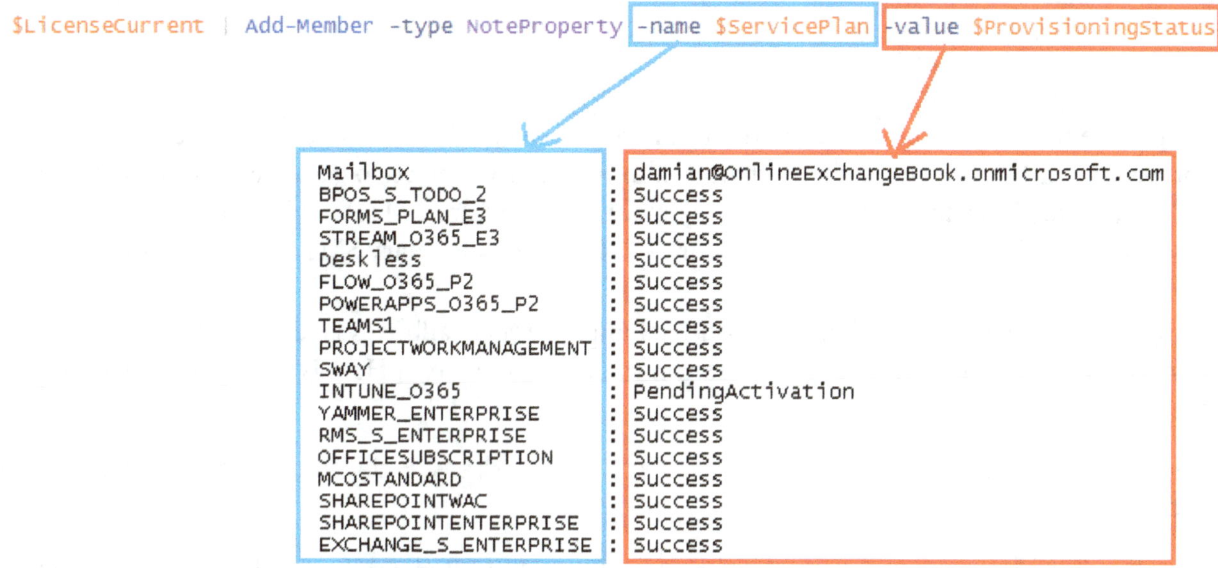

From the script above and the previous Out-File and '>' methodology, exporting the results of PowerShell can be used for reporting and can be formatted to your liking. The Out-File cmdlet is not a complex cmdlet and provides an easy way to create documentation or create a starting point for further reporting on an Exchange Server environment. The caveat is that it cannot be easily utilized for producing additional reports and these TXT reports are essentially just screen scrapes. The next section of this chapter, on CSV files, provides that next step of exporting data to a file that can be used for future reports and even as input to other systems or spreadsheets easily.

CSV Files

A CSV file can be constructed by using Export-CSV cmdlet in PowerShell. CSV files are a good data format for tables since their format can be used for future scripts. CSV file data is also similar in format to the format of an array of arrays used in PowerShell. They're typically used as either a temporary data storage for a script for further processing, used by a different script or just to document values found in Exchange. In terms of documenting an Exchange messaging environment CSV files are useful for creating large data tables to be analyzed/reported on. They can also easily be imported into Excel and other tools for further data analysis and usage.

In terms of real world examples, CSV files can be used to document things such as:

- **Mailbox Statistics** – name, number of items, database, server, mailbox size, quotas and more
- **Exchange Server Information** – name, site, role, version, mailboxes on a server, etc.
- **Transport Settings** – tracking logs, protocol logs and more
- **Mailbox Information** – name, database, UPN, primary SMTP address, SIP Address and more
- **SMTP Connectors** – server, connector name, connector type, Remote IPs, authentication and scoping

All of the examples above are good examples of what can be contained in these CSV files. How do we use Power-Shell to create a CSV file? Let's go through some practical examples of how to create files and use the data that is contained in the CSV file.

** **Note** ** The CSV delimiter value could be different depending on your region. Another sample delimiters is ';' which is used in German and Dutch language regions. Keep in mind that you can also specify a delimiter character if you wish.

Example 1

For this example, we have a project where IT Management has decided to upgrade Exchange 2016 to Exchange Online. In preparing for this project, as the Exchange administrator you need to gather a list of all mailboxes with the following data – Display Name, SAM Account Name, UPN, Primary SMTP Address and other values. This information will be stored as a CSV file for future work – UPN and/or Primary SMTP address corrections.

First, the main cmdlet for gathering information on Exchange Server mailboxes is 'Get-Mailbox'. However, does this cmdlet provide all the criteria we are looking for on the mailboxes? Yes. Here is the cmdlet we need to cover all mailboxes:

```
Get-Mailbox | ft Name, UserPrincipalName, PrimarySMTPAddress, HiddenFromAddressListsEnabled,
RetentionPolicy
```

** **Note** ** In most environments, the use of the -ResultSize Unlimited parameter should be used so that the number of results returned will not be capped at 1,000.

In a typical environment, this cmdlet will gather all user mailboxes in Exchange. At least one extraneous mailbox will show up in the report and it is the Discovery Mailbox. In order to eliminate this from the report we need to make an exception. The easiest way to make that exception is to use the filtering techniques used in Chapter 2.

Here is the filter to be used:

| Where {$_.Name -NotMatch "Discovery"}

This will exclude the Discovery Mailbox. The full one-liner is:

Get-Mailbox | Where {$_.Name -NotMatch "Discovery"} | ft Name, UserPrincipalName, PrimarySMTPAddress, HiddenFromAddressListsEnabled, RetentionPolicy

Before

```
Name                                           UserPrincipalName

damian                                         damian@OnlineExchangeBook.onmicrosoft.com
DiscoverySearchMailbox{D919BA05-46A6-415f-80AD-7E09334BB852}  DiscoverySearchMailbox{D919BA05-46A6-415f-80AD-7E09334B...
john.doe                                       john.doe@OnlineExchangeBook.onmicrosoft.com
```

After

```
Name       UserPrincipalName                           PrimarySmtpAddress                          HiddenFromAddressLists
                                                                                                                  Enabled

damian     damian@OnlineExchangeBook.onmicrosoft.com    damian@OnlineExchangeBook.onmicrosoft.com              False
john.doe   john.doe@OnlineExchangeBook.onmicrosoft.com  john.doe@OnlineExchangeBook.onmicrosoft.com            False
```

Now that we have all the mailbox properties lined up, the data needs to be exported to a CSV file. What cmdlets are available for CSV export? What cmdlets have 'CSV' in them:

Get-Command *csv*

```
Function        Stop-PcsvDevice
Cmdlet          ConvertFrom-Csv
Cmdlet          ConvertTo-Csv
Cmdlet          Export-Csv
Cmdlet          Import-Csv
Application     csvde.exe
Application     Microsoft.Exchange.Edge
```

Export-Csv has several useful parameters for exporting the data from the above one-liner and export it to a usable CSV file:

Append	InputObject	UseCulture
Delimiter	NoClobber	LiteralPath
Encoding	NoTypeInformation	
Force	Path	

Example 2

In this example there is a need to monitor mailbox growth over time. In order to do so, the Get-MailboxStatistics cmdlet will be used in conjunction with the Export-CSV cmdlet to create CSV files every day which when combined together will then provide historical data. Each file will be tagged with a date (no time stamp) and the files created must not be overwritten. Using a similar process to Example 1 where the results of a cmdlet are exported to a CSV file. The additional criteria is that a different file be generated and placed in a shared folder:

```
$Date = Get-Date -Format "yyyy-MM-dd"
Get-Mailbox | Get-MailboxStatistics | Select-Object  DisplayName,@{Expression={$_.TotalItemSize};
Label="Mailbox Size(MB)"}, ItemCount | Export-Csv $Date-MailboxStat.csv -NoClobber -NoType
```

This code is saved as a script and then scheduled to run once per day. The 'NoClobber' switch makes sure that none of the files are overwritten when the new daily file is generated. The 'NoType' switch makes sure that the format is clean for the CSV file.

Exporting the CSV file without using –NoType, results in the CSV file containing bad data (in the red rectangle):

	A	B	C
1	#TYPE Selected.System.Management.Automation.PSCustomObject		
2	DisplayName	Mailbox Size(MB)	ItemCount
3	Damian Scoles	1.377 MB (1,444,131 bytes)	409
4	Discovery Search Mail	206.5 KB (211,423 bytes)	51
5	John Doe	1.292 MB (1,354,656 bytes)	380
6			

Exporting the CSV file with the –NoType parameter removes this unneeded data:

	A	B	C
1	DisplayName	Mailbox Size(MB)	ItemCount
2	Damian Scoles	1.377 MB (1,444,131 bytes)	409
3	Discovery Search Maill	206.5 KB (211,423 bytes)	51
4	John Doe	1.292 MB (1,354,656 bytes)	380
5			

Then the Get-Date cmdlet is stored in the $Date variable which is used to tag the file name. Key to that cmdlet is the formatting of the date to year-month-day (i.e. 2016-08-16).

To schedule PowerShell scripts, store the scripts in a secure location – isolated by NTFS permissions and placed on a share that is also locked down by permissions. Then the scheduled task will also need stored credentials to run.

The data is stored into a CSV file as such:

```
"DisplayName","Mailbox Size(MB)","ItemCount"
"Damian Scoles","1.377 MB (1,444,131 bytes)","409"
"John Doe","1.292 MB (1,354,656 bytes)","380"
"Dave Stork","4.584 MB (2,709,212 bytes)","980"
```

This data could now be used to create charts for trending data, in Excel for example. Imported one day of data into Excel, a data set would look like this:

DisplayName	Mailbox Size(MB)	ItemCount
Damian Scoles	1.377 MB (1,444,131 bytes)	409
John Doe	1.292 MB (1,354,656 bytes)	380
Dave Stork	4.584 MB (2,709,212 bytes)	980

HTML Files

When it comes to creating reports, HTML provides the most flexible platform for customization, creativity and informational overload. Visually speaking, HTML is excellent with the customization allowing for reports that are more visually presentable to the consumer of the report. This is important because the reports should be usable and read by the recipient of the report. Reports should be meaningful, containing real data that the recipient can readily understand and not ignore because it's just a table of numbers.

The most useful and information oriented HTML reports contain good coloring, column sizing, spacing and more. In this section on HTML reporting three types of reports will be covered:

* Quick HTML Report
* Some Formatting Present
* Advanced Formatting

The first involves using just the Set-Content and ConvertTo-Html, basic, quick and easy. While the second involves some basic options for formatting using CSS and the ConvertTo-Html cmdlet. The last option is to use headers, table formatting and multiple sections of information put into an HTML file, using variables to assemble the content.

Quick HTML Reports

```
Get-Mailbox | Get-MailboxStatistics | Sort-Object TotalItemSize -Descending | ConvertTo-Html
DisplayName,@{Expression={$_.TotalItemSize}; Label="Mailbox Size(MB)"}| Set-Content c:\test.html
```

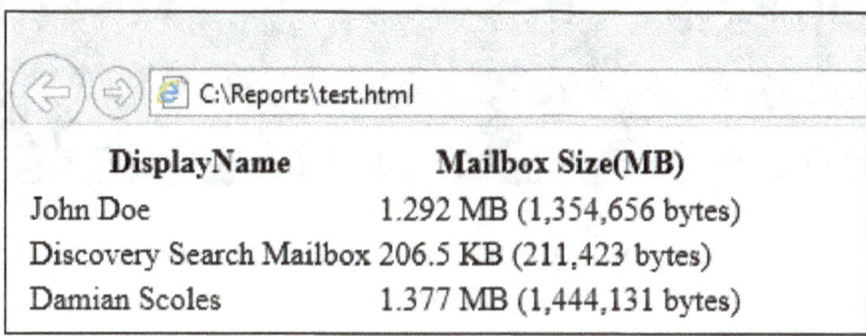


```
ConvertTo-Html  DisplayName,@{Expression={$_.TotalItemSize}; Label="Mailbox Size(MB)"}
```

The previous one-liner does the following:

Code Section	What it does
Get-Mailbox	Finds all mailboxes in Exchange
| Get-MailboxStatistics	Pipes the mailboxes into the Get-MailboxStatistics cmdlet
| Sort-Object TotalItemSize -Descending	Sorts the Size (descending order)
ConvertTo-Html DisplayName, @{Label="TotalItemSize(MB)";Expression={$_.TotalItemSize.Value.ToMB()}}	Formats the table columns and values
| Set-Content c:\Reports\Test.html	Exports content to an HTML file

As can be seen by the resulting HTML table, the results are really basic. For quick reports that need low effort, this report fits that need. HTML table can have as many fields as needed. Take for an example where a list of Retention Policy Tags in Exchange Online as part of documentation for the Exchange Online environment. A typical one-liner report allows for a formatted table of the results to be created:

```
Get-RetentionPolicyTag | ft Name,MessageClassDisplayName,RetentionEnabled,AgeLimitForRetention
```

```
Name                                         MessageClassDisplayName RetentionEnabled AgeLimitForRetention
----                                         ----------------------- ---------------- --------------------
Never Delete                                 All Mailbox Content      False
Recoverable Items 14 days move to archive    All Mailbox Content      True 14.00:00:00
Junk Email                                   All Mailbox Content      True 30.00:00:00
Deleted Items                                All Mailbox Content      True 30.00:00:00
Default 2 year move to archive               All Mailbox Content      True 730.00:00:00
Personal 1 year move to archive              All Mailbox Content      True 365.00:00:00
Personal never move to archive               All Mailbox Content      False
1 Week Delete                                All Mailbox Content      True 7.00:00:00
1 Month Delete                               All Mailbox Content      True 30.00:00:00
Personal 5 year move to archive              All Mailbox Content      True 1825.00:00:00
6 Month Delete                               All Mailbox Content      True 180.00:00:00
1 Year Delete                                All Mailbox Content      True 365.00:00:00
5 Year Delete                                All Mailbox Content      True 1825.00:00:00
```

Taking this same PowerShell one-liner and adding ConvertTo-Html, a portable document can be created and stored as part of an overall documentation of the Exchange Online Retention Policies:

```
Get-RetentionPolicyTag | ConvertTo-HTML Name, MessageClassDisplayName, RetentionEnabled,
AgeLimitForRetention | Set-Content c:\Reports\RetentionPolicyTags.html
```

Resulting HTML file:

Name	MessageClassDisplayName	RetentionEnabled	AgeLimitForRetention
Never Delete	All Mailbox Content	False	
Recoverable Items 14 days move to archive	All Mailbox Content	True	14.00:00:00
Junk Email	All Mailbox Content	True	30.00:00:00
Deleted Items	All Mailbox Content	True	30.00:00:00
Default 2 year move to archive	All Mailbox Content	True	730.00:00:00
Personal 1 year move to archive	All Mailbox Content	True	365.00:00:00
Personal never move to archive	All Mailbox Content	False	
1 Week Delete	All Mailbox Content	True	7.00:00:00
1 Month Delete	All Mailbox Content	True	30.00:00:00
Personal 5 year move to archive	All Mailbox Content	True	1825.00:00:00
6 Month Delete	All Mailbox Content	True	180.00:00:00
1 Year Delete	All Mailbox Content	True	365.00:00:00
5 Year Delete	All Mailbox Content	True	1825.00:00:00

Similar to the first HTML example, a portable HTML file is now available for IT to keep as a reference in case there are any issues. However, the formatting lacks quite a bit of finish – no header, no grid marking columns and rows.

Next, let's add some polish to these HTML reports.

Adding Polish – Refining HTML Reports

Creating better HTML reports start with formatting and refining the look of the HTML output itself. This requires several features of HTML - CSS Styling, headers and possibly a footer as well. Each of these will provide value to the final file when it is delivered or printed out for documentation.

In this first example, the report generated will have a Header, Title and more added to it. At the very top of the HTML report will be this block of text. The colorful 'rectangles' refer back to the sections of code that made them possible:

```
$InitialUserInfo = $InitialUserCSV | ConvertTo-Html -Fragment -As Table -PreContent "<h2>Current User Attributes Before Import</h2>" Out-String
$InitialReport = ConvertTo-Html -Title "Current State - User Data" -Head "<h1>PowerShell Reporting</h1><br>This report was run: $(Get-Date)" -Body
```

Starting with the first line and 'ConvertTo-Html' portion of this one-liner, notice the following parameters that are being used:

- **Fragment** - Defined because this section of code refers to only part of the HTML header being constructed
- **As Table** - Formatting the output as a table
- **PreContent** - Wording of this section of the HTML header

On the second line, starting with 'ConvertTo-Html' again, there are these parameters populated:

- **Title** - The title as seen in a browser window
- **Head** - Words to appear at the top of the spreadsheet

When coding the next part of the script, displayed in the next section, needs to include a CSS code section, for formatting the overall colors of the chart and other options. The value of the $CSS variable are stored between a pair of ' ' (single quotes). This example uses a black and white coloring scheme. <TD> sections are Black with White text and <TD> sections are White with Black text:

```
$Css='<style>table{margin:auto; width:98%};Body{background-color:Cyan; Text-
align:Center;};th{background-color:black; color:white;};td{background-color:white; color:Black; Text-
align:Center;};</style>'
```

The last line of the full code, which exists outside the configuration of the HTML file, is to actually export the HTML code to a text file:

```
$Report | Out-File $Filepath
```

Complete Coded Section

```
$FilePath = "c:\Reports\report.html"
$Css='<style>table{margin:auto; width:98%};Body{background-color:Cyan; Text-align:Center;};th{background-color:black; color:white;};td{background-color:white; color:Black; Text-align:Center;};</style>'
$RetentionTags = Get-RetentionPolicyTag | Select-Object Name, MessageClassDisplayName, RetentionEnabled, AgeLimitForRetention
$RetentionTags| Export-CSV c:\Downloads\InitialUserState-$date.csv -NoType
$RetentionTagsInfo= $RetentionTags| ConvertTo-Html -Fragment -As Table -PreContent "<h2>Current Retention Policy Documentation</h2>" | Out-String
$Report = ConvertTo-Html -Title "Current Retention Policy Tags" -Head "<h1>PowerShell Reporting</h1><br>This report was run on: $(Get-Date)" -Body "$RetentionTagsInfo $Css"
$Report | Out-File $FilePath
```

Sample results from this:

PowerShell Reporting

This report was run on: 12/19/2017 16:24:36

Current Retention Policy Documentation

Name	MessageClassDisplayName	RetentionEnabled	AgeLimitForRetention
Never Delete	All Mailbox Content	False	
Recoverable Items 14 days move to archive	All Mailbox Content	True	14.00:00:00
Junk Email	All Mailbox Content	True	30.00:00:00
Deleted Items	All Mailbox Content	True	30.00:00:00
Default 2 year move to archive	All Mailbox Content	True	730.00:00:00
Personal 1 year move to archive	All Mailbox Content	True	365.00:00:00
Personal never move to archive	All Mailbox Content	False	
1 Week Delete	All Mailbox Content	True	7.00:00:00
1 Month Delete	All Mailbox Content	True	30.00:00:00
Personal 5 year move to archive	All Mailbox Content	True	1825.00:00:00
6 Month Delete	All Mailbox Content	True	180.00:00:00
1 Year Delete	All Mailbox Content	True	365.00:00:00
5 Year Delete	All Mailbox Content	True	1825.00:00:00

Detailed, Complex HTML Reporting

For the last section on HTML reporting, the creation of complex, detailed and visually appealing HTML files are what would have a wow factor or just considered more 'accessible' with color coding. This section will concentrate on creating a full HTML report with coloring, multiple charts, legends and more. For this scenario we'll use a report of certain values for Exchange Server that should be configured a certain way. The report will contain the role, version, Operating System and more.

Caveats to this approach are that you must know HTML. Whole books have been written about HTML. Consider the next few pages a primer on how to combine HTML and PowerShell into one. Feel free to use snippets of code for your own scripts. This will make the script building process go quicker and allow one to explore the code to create more personalized reports.

First, a destination HTML file needs to be declared for holding the information to be gathered with PowerShell. To provide information on this code line, a comment will be included just above the file declaration line:

```
$HTMLReport = "c:\Reports\Book-Retention-Policy-Tags.html"
```

Next we'll need to begin building HTML files. This section starts with the variable which will store all information that will be exported to a HTML file:

```
$Output="<html><body>
```

Next, define the font for the header to be applied to the Header and the Subheader (if needed) – the two headers are defined with <h1> and <h3>:

```
<Font Size=""1"" face=""Calibri,Sans-Serif"">
<H1 Align=""Center"">Retention Policy Tags</H1>
<H3 Align=""Center"">Generated $((Get-Date).ToString())</H3>
</Font>
```

After the header has been created, a table is defined for the display of the data that will be gathered with PowerShell cmdlets – border is applied ("1") and some room around each cell ("3") is added. Also notice that there are double quotes around values, this is because it is being stored within a variable. This section is then closed off with a quote to end stop populating the $Output variable for now:

```
<Table Border=""1"" CellPadding=""3"" Style=""Font-Size:8pt;Font-Family:Arial,Sans-Serif"">
<tr bgcolor=""#3498db "">"
```

The HTML file now has a defined header with labels. After that, table headers need to be defined. Make sure there is one <th> per column (closed with '</th>') and value that will be displayed. For this block four columns are defined for the four values. Two lines are used for readability, four lines could be used or even one long line could be used:

```
# Build Server Table Headers
$Output += "<th Colspan=""10000""><Font Color=""#ffffff"">Policy Tag</Font></th>"
$Output += "<th colspan=""10000""><Font Color=""#ffffff"">Message Class</Font></th>"
```

** **Note** ** this section is ended with '</tr>' which will start a new section and a new line.

For the next section of the script, each Retention Policy Tag needs to have these values queries: Name, Message-

ClassDisplayName, RetentionEnabled and AgeLimitForRetention. First, it gathers the Tags information (stored in a variable called $RetentionPolicyTag) to process each tag in the Foreach loop:

```
$RetentionPolicyTag= Get-RetentionPolicyTag

# Build the Data Table
Foreach ($Tag in $RetentionPolicyTag) {
```

Here we set up all of the variables from the information provided by the current line ($Tag) in the $RetentionPolicyTag variable:

```
$Name = $Tag.Name
$MessageClassDisplayName = $Tag.MessageClassDisplayName
$RetentionEnabled = $Tag.RetentionEnabled
$AgeLimitForRetention = $Tag.AgeLimitForRetention
$Type = $Tag.Type
```

We use these values so that they can be placed into a column for the table. The column is started with '<td>' and ended with '</td>'. In between this will be the variable value for each of the values defined above. Also defined are the width of the column (10000), the alignment of the text (center) and the font color (#000000). The variable also is defined as '$Output +=' as this will append these lines to the $Output variable:

```
$Output += "<tr><td Colspan=""10000"" Align=""Center""><Font Color=""#000000"">$Name</Font></td>"
$Output += "<td Colspan=""10000"" Align=""Center""><Font Color=""#000000"">$MessageClassDisplayName</font></td>"
$Output += "<td Colspan=""10000"" Align=""Center""><Font Color=""#000000"">$RetentionEnabled </font></td>"
$Output += "<td Colspan=""10000"" Align=""Center""><Font Color=""#000000"">$AgeLimitForRetention</font></td>"
$Output += "<td Colspan=""10000"" Align=""Center""><Font Color=""#000000""> $Type</font></td></tr>"
```

At the end of the script, the $Output variable is closed up with "</body></html>" which closes off these sections in HTML.

```
# Ending the HTML FILE
$Output+="</body></html>"
```

Then the variable is exported to an HTML file:

```
# Export the Outlook variable to the HTML Report
$Output | Out-File $HTMLReport
```

The end result of the HTML script, looks like this:

Retention Policy Tags

Generated 12/19/2017 4:51:12 PM

Policy Tag	Message Class	Enabled	Age Limit	Type
Never Delete	All Mailbox Content	False		Personal
Recoverable Items 14 days move to archive	All Mailbox Content	True	14.00:00:00	RecoverableItems
Junk Email	All Mailbox Content	True	30.00:00:00	JunkEmail
Deleted Items	All Mailbox Content	True	30.00:00:00	DeletedItems
Default 2 year move to archive	All Mailbox Content	True	730.00:00:00	All
Personal 1 year move to archive	All Mailbox Content	True	365.00:00:00	Personal
Personal never move to archive	All Mailbox Content	False		Personal
1 Week Delete	All Mailbox Content	True	7.00:00:00	Personal
1 Month Delete	All Mailbox Content	True	30.00:00:00	Personal
Personal 5 year move to archive	All Mailbox Content	True	1825.00:00:00	Personal
6 Month Delete	All Mailbox Content	True	180.00:00:00	Personal
1 Year Delete	All Mailbox Content	True	365.00:00:00	Personal
5 Year Delete	All Mailbox Content	True	1825.00:00:00	Personal

Notice that some cells have a color assigned to them and that the table has defined columns. These column borders can be removed by changing its definition here - <table border=""0"">:

Retention Policy Tags

Generated 12/19/2017 4:54:32 PM

Policy Tag	Message Class	Enabled	Age Limit	Type
Never Delete	All Mailbox Content	False		Personal
Recoverable Items 14 days move to archive	All Mailbox Content	True	14.00:00:00	RecoverableItems
Junk Email	All Mailbox Content	True	30.00:00:00	JunkEmail
Deleted Items	All Mailbox Content	True	30.00:00:00	DeletedItems
Default 2 year move to archive	All Mailbox Content	True	730.00:00:00	All

If for instance, an additional table needs to be added to this HTML file, simply add some lines like this:

```
$Output += "<BR><BR>"
```

Then add a new table the same way as the previous section.

```
Complete Script:
# HTML File name
$HTMLReport = "c:\Reports\Book-Retention-Policy-Tags.html"

# Create the HTML Header for the report
$Output="<Html>
<Body>
<Font Size=""1"" face=""Calibri,Sans-Serif"">
<H1 Align=""Center"">Retention Policy Tags</H1>
<H3 Align=""Center"">Generated $((Get-Date).ToString())</h3>
```

```
</Font>
<Table Border=""1"" CellPadding=""3"" Style=""Font-Size:8pt;Font-Family:Arial,Sans-Serif"">
<tr Bgcolor=""#3498db "">"

# Build Server Table Headers
$Output += "<th Colspan=""10000""><Font Color=""#ffffff"">Policy Tag</Font></th>"
$Output += "<th colspan=""10000""><Font Color=""#ffffff"">Message Class</Font></th>"
$Output += "<th Colspan=""10000""><Font Color=""#ffffff"">Enabled</Font></th>"
$Output += "<th Colspan=""10000""><Font Color=""#ffffff"">Age Limit</Font></th>"
$Output += "<th Colspan=""10000""><Font Color=""#ffffff"">Type</Font></th></tr>"

# Build the Data Table
$RetentionPolicyTag= Get-RetentionPolicyTag
Foreach ($Tag in $RetentionPolicyTag) {
    # Variables for table
    $Name = $Tag.Name
    $MessageClassDisplayName = $Tag.MessageClassDisplayName
    $RetentionEnabled = $Tag.RetentionEnabled
    $AgeLimitForRetention = $Tag.AgeLimitForRetention
    $Type = $Tag.Type

    # Lines for HTML table
    $Output += "<tr><td Colspan=""10000"" Align=""Center""><Font Color=""#000000"">$Name</Font></td>"
    $Output += "<td Colspan=""10000"" Align=""Center""><Font Color=""#000000"">$MessageClassDisplayName</font></td>"
    $Output+="<tdColspan=""10000""Align=""Center""><FontColor=""#000000"">$RetentionEnabled</font></td>"
    $Output += "<td Colspan=""10000"" Align=""Center""><Font Color=""#000000"">$AgeLimitForRetention</font></td>"
    $Output += "<td Colspan=""10000"" Align=""Center""><Font Color=""#000000""> $Type</font></td></tr>"
}

# Ending the HTML FILE
$Output+="</table></body></html>"

# Export the Outlook variable to the HTML Report
$Output | Out-File $HTMLReport
```

Delivery Methodologies

Once a report has been created and validated, a delivery method might need to be chosen. One of the most common delivery mechanism is email, but a file copy could also be employed. For this section on delivery we will go through both options to see how this can be done via PowerShell to deliver the report to their destination.

SMTP Delivery

Sending a report created in PowerShell via Exchange Online is probably the most common delivery method for PowerShell reporting. Email delivery requires a few things:

- IP Address or FQDN of the Exchange Server to relay email through
- The location of the source document to be sent
- Determine if the file is to be attached or inserted into the body of an email
- The destination email address
- The sender email address
- Subject line of the email messages

Each of these parameters will fit into a variable to be defined and then placed into the section of code that handles the email sending. First, how do we send an email in PowerShell? Well, let's search for the cmdlet:

```
Get-Command *Message
Cmdlet          Protect-CmsMessage
Cmdlet          Send-MailMessage
Cmdlet          Unprotect-CmsMessage
```

There is a cmdlet called Send-MailMessage, which looks appropriate for our task at hand. Reviewing the parameters of the cmdlet using 'Get-Help Send-MailMessage –full' and we find these parameters are needed:

-Attachments	The location of the source document to be sent
-Body	Determine if the file is to be attached or inserted into the body of an email
-BodyAsHtml	Would be used if sending the report in the body of the email
-From	The sender email address
-SmtpServer	IP Address or FQDN of the Exchange EXO to relay email through
-Subject	Subject line of the email messages.
-To	The destination email address

Now that the parameters are known, variables can be defined and placed into the cmdlet to send the email:

```
$Body = "Forgot about today's meeting."
$From = "damian@OnlineExchangeBook.onmicrosoft.com"
$To = "ItDistributionGroup@OnlineExchangeBook.onmicrosoft.com"
$SMTPServer = "smtp.office365.com"
$Subject = "Test"
$Attachment = "C:\Reports\Test.Html"
```

** **Note** ** The server smtp.office365.com is Microsoft's defined connection point for SMTP traffic.

Incorporating all the variables above and using them for the Send-MailMessage cmdlet, the cmdlet looks like this:

```
$Credential = Get-Credential
Send-MailMessage -From $From -to $To -subject $Subject -body $Body -priority High -SmtpServer $SMTPServer -Credential $Credential -UseSsl -Port "587"
```

Make sure to include the 'Credential' parameter as the message will fail to send:

```
Send-MailMessage : The SMTP server requires a secure connection or the client was not authenticated. The server
response was: 5.7.57 SMTP; Client was not authenticated to send anonymous mail during MAIL FROM
[CY4PR1001CA0030.namprd10.prod.outlook.com]
At line:1 char:1
+ send-mailmessage -from "damian@OnlineExchangeBook.onmicrosoft.com" -t ...
+ ~~~~~~~~~~~~~~~~~~~~~~~~~~~~~~~~~~~~~~~~~~~~~~~~~~~~~~~~~~~~~~~~~~~~~~~~~~~~
    + CategoryInfo          : InvalidOperation: (System.Net.Mail.SmtpClient:SmtpClient) [Send-MailMessage], SmtpException
    + FullyQualifiedErrorId : SmtpException,Microsoft.PowerShell.Commands.SendMailMessage
```

We can also add an attachment using the '-Attachment' parameter and specifying a file to send to the recipient who can then open it up from their mail client:

```
$Credential = Get-Credential
Send-MailMessage -From $From -to $To -subject $Subject -body $Body -priority High -SmtpServer $SMTPServer -Credential $Credential -UseSsl -Port "587" -Attachment $Attachment
```

If, however, the report needed to be in the body of the message, the script would be changed as follows:

```
$Body = Get-Content "\\laptop.domain.com\c$\downloads\test.html" –Raw
Send-MailMessage -To $To -From $From -Subject $Subject -Attachment $Attachment -Body $Body -BodyAsHTML -SmtpServer $SMTPServer -Credential $Credential -UseSsl -Port "587"
```

We included the -Attachment also, in addition to replacing the body with the same HTML code. The $body variable stores the HTML file since it the message body will be the HTML file and the -RAW switch will help facilitate that. The email arrives in the destination mailbox as so, with the HTML document pasted into the body of the message.

File Copy

Copying reports to a central location can be a solid alternative to sending all reports through email. By doing so, these files are accessible and possibly kept indefinitely for historical reporting. What cmdlets can be used for moving files to file servers? The BITS Transfer service would be ideal for moving files. What cmdlets are available for this service?

```
Get-Help *BITS*
```

Name	Category	Module
Add-BitsFile	Cmdlet	BitsTransfer
Complete-BitsTransfer	Cmdlet	BitsTransfer
Get-BitsTransfer	Cmdlet	BitsTransfer
Remove-BitsTransfer	Cmdlet	BitsTransfer
Resume-BitsTransfer	Cmdlet	BitsTransfer
Set-BitsTransfer	Cmdlet	BitsTransfer
Start-BitsTransfer	Cmdlet	BitsTransfer
Suspend-BitsTransfer	Cmdlet	BitsTransfer

Reviewing the list above, what cmdlets from this list are needed for transferring files from place to place? Start-BitsTransfer will copy a file from a source to a destination. This cmdlet is similar to a file copy daemon on steroids. Start-BitsTransfer has quite a few options to choose for running the cmdlet:

-Asynchronous
-Authentication - Basic, Digest, NTLM or Negotiate
-Credential
-Description
-Destination
-DisplayName
-Priority - High, Normal and Low
-ProxyAuthentication:
    Basic, Digest, NTLM, Negotiate or Password
-ProxyBypass
-ProxyCredential
-ProxyList
-ProxyUsage:
    System Default, NoProxy, AutoDetect or OverRide
-RetryInterval - default is 600 seconds
-RetryTimeout - default is 1209600 seconds (14 Days)
-Source
-Suspended
-TransferPolicy
-TransferType
-UseStoredCredential

Depending on the destination and how a file needs to be transferred, BITS could be the ideal solution. It is useful if a large number of large files need to be transferred as BITS will dynamically associate bandwidth with a file transfer, run in the background and handle transfers even with network interruptions. In Chapter 3, this cmdlet is used in the script built to download files for use on servers. In the case of documentation, the cmdlets can now be used to move these documentation files to a central location.

In order to copy files to a central location, there is a need to define the source files that need to be moved, where the files will be moved to and if any sort of logging, authentication or priority needs to be assigned to these jobs. Retry intervals can be configured if the files are pulled from a source over a slow or notoriously high latency connection and to adjust for these connections 'RetryInterval' and/or 'RetryTimeout'.

Example

For this example the requirement for the script is to pull locally run results files like CSV, HTML and or text files from five different global locations. These results will deposited on one server and stored for analysis by the global IT team located in the US global headquarters. Locations and destinations are known, for three of the five links are to overseas locations are low latency. Two other links are high latency and need to be accounted for. Let's begin by focusing on the low latency links and work our way out to the high latency link. The jobs should log and if possible the transfer jobs should be described accurately. No special authentication is needed.

Low Latency

For the low latency links, the source and destination options are a given and are filled with the source and destination files. The priority is defined in case this needs adjustments later. To help identify the BITS Transfer, a description and name are given to the processes transferring files. Here are the three BITS Transfer PowerShell one-liners for this process:

```
Start-BITSTransfer –Displayname "Exchange HTML From GB" –Description "Exchange Information
– British Servers" -Priority Normal -Source \\GB-FILE01\Reporting\*.html –Destination \\US-SRV-FS01\
Reporting\Exchange
```

```
Start-BITSTransfer –Displayname "Exchange HTML From Poland" –Description "Exchange Information
– Polish Servers" -Priority Normal -Source \\POL-FILE01\Reporting\*.html –Destination \\US-SRV-FS01\
Reporting\Exchange
```

```
Start-BITSTransfer –Displayname "Exchange HTML From Canada" –Description "Exchange Information
– Canadian Servers" -Priority Normal -Source \\CAN-FILE01\Reporting\*.html –Destination \\US-SRV-
FS01\Reporting\Exchange
```

With the above cmdlets, all files are being copied to the same root folder and not a specific folder for each server. It is assumed that all files are unique and identifiable from the location that they come from. For example each set of files could be prefaced with a location and then the current date. This helps identity where and when these files are generated.

High Latency

For higher latency links, the same criteria above is used, with the addition of higher Retry Internal and Timeout. This is done because of the higher latency of the links. These values would be tweaked over time to adjust for any issues on these links.

```
Start-BITSTransfer –Displayname "Exchange HTML From China" –Description "Exchange Information
    – Chinese Servers" -Priority High -RetryInterval 900 -RetryTimeout 2419200 -Source \\CH-FILE01\
    Reporting\*.html –Destination \\US-SRV-FS01\Reporting\Exchange

Start-BITSTransfer –Displayname "Exchange HTML From SA" –Description "Exchange Information –
    South African Servers" -Priority High -RetryInterval 900 -RetryTimeout 2419200 -Source \\SA-FILE01\
    Reporting\*.html –Destination \\US-SRV-FS01\Reporting\Exchange
```

In summary, the BITS Transfer process can be used to move files between destinations with some advantages over a regular file copy. BITS transfer jobs that error or timeout can be examined with the Get-BITSTransfer cmdlet. There are policies that could be applied if necessary to manipulate the file transfer as well. For large file transfers the BITS Transfer can be monitored and manipulated while in flight (Set-BITSTransfer) and Get-BITSTransfer.

## 19

Troubleshooting

In This Chapter

- Breaking up the Script
  - Pause and Sleep
- Write-Host
- Comments
- PowerShell ISE
- Debugging
- Try and Catch
- ErrorAction
- Transcript
- Deciphering Error Messages
- Access Denied
- Variables
- Arrays
- Conclusion

An Intro to Troubleshooting

We're now at the point in the book where you, the reader, should be more comfortable with writing scripts for Exchange Online. You should be able to write scripts that manage, manipulate, and report on your Exchange Online tenant. Hopefully you've begun writing scripts for your Exchange Online tenant by now and are familiar with the various cmdlets at your disposal. As you've begun doing this, no doubt you have had issues with your scripts. From infamous red text of cmdlets failing to getting results that were not quite what you expect. This is where troubleshooting comes into play.

Troubleshooting PowerShell can be complicated by many factors. These factors include troubleshooting code you did not write, different variable data types, null variables when expecting a result and more. In order to tackle an issue, it is helpful to understand the end goal of the script that is being written. If the goal is simply to run a few PowerShell cmdlets and expect results, then there might not be a lot to troubleshoot and when there is a more complex goal, it might require a method to do so.

Let's explore some of the many options for troubleshooting scripts.

Breaking up the Script

PowerShell scripts can vary greatly in length. A very complex script can go well over a thousand lines and can go much higher. Troubleshooting something this complex may require different techniques depending what errors or problems are noted. One technique of many, is to break the script apart to find the problem. This could be a simple as commenting out whole sections of code or copying a whole section of code and copying that to a new script to run for testing.

Take for example a script that will modify Azure Active Directory (AAD) User Attributes to keep the GAL accurate and in the same script generates a before and after report in HTML with a copy of the results in a CSV file as well. The script has five distinct parts – the header (script description), the before report, the section that makes the changes, the part that reports on the change that was made, and the body of the script which defines variables and runs each function.

Pause and Sleep

Pause in PowerShell allows you to stop the scripts actions for a period of time while you examine what is either displayed in the PowerShell window or maybe the objects that were modified (Azure AD, Exchange, etc.). Once results have been confirmed or an error noted, then PowerShell can be stopped with a Break key or let it complete depending on the script. I have used the Pause key for scripts that run too quickly for results or error messages to be seen. The key with Pause is that it requires user interaction to allow the script to continue processing.

Sleep in PowerShell temporarily pauses the PowerShell script. Essentially allowing for the same functionality as Pause, with the notable exception that the Sleep command is time based and after the time parameter has expired, the PowerShell script will continue:

```
#Pause and Sleep

$N = 1
Write-Host "Number counts."
Pause

Do {

    Write-Host "This is the number $."
    If ($N -eq 5) {Sleep 5;Write-Host "Sleep for 5 successful." -ForegroundColor Cyan}
    If ($N -eq 10) {Sleep 2;Write-Host "Sleep for 2 successful." -ForegroundColor Cyan}
    If ($N -eq 15) {Sleep 7;Write-Host "Sleep for 7 successful." -ForegroundColor Cyan}
    $N++

} While ($N -lt 20)

Write-Host "Twenty numbers."
```

```
[PS] C:\>.\NumberCounts.ps1
Number counts.
Press Enter to continue...:
This is the number 0.
This is the number 1.
This is the number 2.
This is the number 3.
This is the number 4.
Sleep for 5 successful.
This is the number 5.
This is the number 6.
This is the number 7.
This is the number 8.
This is the number 9.
Sleep for 2 successful.
This is the number 10.
This is the number 11.
This is the number 12.
This is the number 13.
This is the number 14.
Sleep for 7 successful.
This is the number 15.
This is the number 16.
This is the number 17.
This is the number 18.
This is the number 19.
Twenty numbers.
[PS] C:\>_
```

Explanation of the script:

```powershell
$N = 1
write-host "Number counts."
Pause
Do {
    Write-Host "This is the number $N."
    If ($N -eq 5) {Sleep 5;Write-Host "Sleep for 5 successful." -ForegroundColor Cyan}
    If ($N -eq 10) {Sleep 2;Write-Host "Sleep for 2 successful." -ForegroundColor Cyan}
    If ($N -eq 15) {Sleep 7;Write-Host "Sleep for 7 successful." -ForegroundColor Cyan}
    $N++
} while ($N -lt 20)

write-host "Twenty numbers."
```

Pause

Sleep 3 times during the script.

The pauses in a script can help isolate sections of the script for troubleshooting. This method could be used inside of a function that does not seem to be working, to pausing between each function or pausing after a certain block of code runs. It would be best to use multiple pauses as it will help to isolate the cause of errors to a smaller section of code.

Write-Host

Write-Host tells PowerShell to each contents of variables, display strings of text and more. The cmdlet can be an excellent troubleshooting tool for PowerShell and it can be used to display information for troubleshooting.

Take for example working on a large script that may have generated an error some effort may be needed to figure out where the error was generated in the script. Using write-host, lines of code can be inserted into the script to display a number. A series of these the script can be broken up numerically so when the script breaks a numerical indicator will help determine the code causing the issue. With a more complex script, it may take several iterations.

Script Text

```
Write-Host "Start of the script"
$Mailboxes = Get-Mailbox
$N = 2
$RetentionPolicies = @()
Write-Host "STEP 1 Complete"
Foreach ($Mailbox in $Mailboxes) {
   $Name = $Server.RetentionPolicy
   Write-Host "The server $Mailbox has the $Name retention policy assigned!"
   Write-Host "STEP $N Complete"
   $Sites += $Name
   $N++
}
Write-Host "End of the script on STEP #$N"
```

Explanation of the Script

Showing progress

```
Write-Host "Start of the script"
$Mailboxes = Get-Mailbox
$N = 2
$RetentionPolicies = @()
Write-Host "STEP 1 Complete"
Foreach ($Mailbox in $Mailboxes) {
    $Name = $Server.RetentionPolicy
    Write-Host "The server $Mailbox has the $Name retention policy assigned!"
    Write-Host "STEP $N Complete"
    $Sites += $Name
    $N++
}
Write-Host "End of the script on STEP #$N"
```

Variable Contents

Output from the script

```
Start of the script
STEP 1 Complete
The server Damian Scoles has the Default MRM Policy retention policy assigned!
STEP 2 Complete
The server Discovery Search Mailbox has the Default MRM Policy retention policy assigned!
STEP 3 Complete
The server John Doe has the Default MRM Policy retention policy assigned!
STEP 4 Complete
End of the script on STEP #5
```

Comments

In previous chapters, comments were added to scripts for various reasons – a script description header and code line documentation and for blocking out lines of code. For this chapter, the latter options will mostly be used for troubleshooting. Comments in this text are simply blockers for preventing certain sections of code from executing.

Line Changes

For the first example the comment ('#') symbol can be used to save the contents of an old line in case the replacement line fails to work properly or to remove a line no longer needed or to remove a line from execution in case it is causing an issue. The code below examines message traces in Exchange Online and specifically is looking for SPAM messages filtered by EOP during a certain date range (defined by $Start and $End):

Example Code

```
# Script variables
$Page = 1
$PageSize = 5000
$TotalCount = 0
$Start = '11/29/17 12:01AM'
$End = '12/03/17 11:59PM'
Do {
   $N = 1
   $Results = Get-MessageTrace -StartDate $Start -EndDate $End -Page $Page -PageSize $PageSize |
   Where {$_.Status -eq 'FilteredAsSpam'}
   $Results2 = Get-MessageTrace -StartDate $Start -EndDate $End -Page $Page -PageSize $PageSize
   # Get-MessageTrace -StartDate $Start -EndDate $End -Page $Page -PageSize $PageSize | Where {$_.
   Status -eq 'FilteredAsSpam'} | ft Received, Recipientaddress, Renderaddress

   If ($Results2 -eq $Null) {
      # Set maximum number of pages to examine
      $Page = 201
   } Else {
      $Results2[0].Received
      $Count = $Results.Count
      Write-Host "Found $Count SPAM messages." -ForegroundColor Cyan
      Write-Host "Page Number - $Page" -ForegroundColor Yellow
      $Page++
   }
} While ($Page -lt 200)
```

A successful run would look like this:

```
Sunday, December 3, 2017 11:58:31 PM
Found 819 SPAM messages.
Page Number - 1
Sunday, December 3, 2017 9:18:48 PM
Found 858 SPAM messages.
```

Now imagine if the code were written close to the above, but maybe we had some misspelled words or maybe we want to get rid of certain steps, commenting out a line could help simply the script or block out bad code or allow one to copy a line to rewrite a different way, while retaining the original code for backup.

An example of this would be the line 'Get-Mailbox damian | ft RetentionPolicy'. Maybe the name for the PowerShell cmdlet was mistyped and an error occurred or a section of code needs to be removed because we don't want the service to be started, but only have the script notify because it's being run during the day.

Scripts like the above are built in blocks based on function. Then the script is assembled using these code blocks. Perhaps after the blocks are assembled an error occurs. One way to troubleshoot the script would be to comment ('#') out a script block to see if that alleviates the issue.

The script run with the misspelled cmdlet:

```
Get-Malbox : The term 'Get-Malbox' is not recognized as the name of a cmdlet, function, script file, or operable
program. Check the spelling of the name, or if a path was included, verify that the path is correct and try again.
At line:1 char:1
+ Get-Malbox damian | ft RetentionPolicy
+ ~~~~~~~~~~~~~~~~~~
    + CategoryInfo          : ObjectNotFound: (Get-Malbox:String) [], CommandNotFoundException
    + FullyQualifiedErrorId : CommandNotFoundException
```

Commenting out the first line:

    # Get-Malbox damian | ft RetentionPolicy

Then rewrite the line:

    Get-Mailbox damian | ft RetentionPolicy

Now the code block runs successfully. The old line was kept as a backup in case a recoded line fails again with a bad switch or invalid variable.

Comments would also come in handy when converting a script that is designed for a single mailbox, single user account or whatever to a script that can handle all mailboxes, user accounts or whatever in an environment. This requires some variable changes, a loop and a few other code changes. If this conversion process fails, comments could be used to remove the Foreach loop, variable changes and more and enabling troubleshooting of the new code.

Example

In the code sample below we have two ways in which to run the Import-Module cmdlet. One will just try and import the module and if it fails we get lots of red and some sort of error message. If it succeeds, there is no message relayed. The second code disabled the ErrorAction by stopping PowerShell from executing any further, avoiding the red error message text.

Code sample

```
# Import-Module MSOnline
Import-Module MSOnline -ErrorAction STOP
```

We can further enhance the second line by using Try {} Catch {} which will allow code to run in the event of an error.

Note See page 374 for an example of Try {} and Catch {}

PowerShell ISE

While not the obvious choice for troubleshooting, one of the advantages of using the Windows PowerShell Integrated Scripting Environment (ISE) is that in a longer script ISE can visually assist in finding misconfigured parts of the script. For example, bad brackets have red squiggly lines under them. What makes the ISE program even more powerful for troubleshooting PowerShell scripts, plug-ins can be installed that provide hints on misconfiguration, information on quotes that may be incorrect, and more.

When writing scripts and prior to executing them, make sure to load the script into PowerShell ISE along with a plug-in called ISE Steroids. Taken together, a script can be analyzed better, tweaks could be made or errors could be corrected before the script makes it into production. Here are some examples of this:

Example 1

If you were coding in Notepad or similar ASCII editor, then PowerShell syntax issues would not be obvious:

```
Foreac ($Line in $Test) {
Write-Host 'This is a test.'
}
```

However, the same text, in PowerShell ISE with the ISE Steroids plugin loaded would look this:

```
2 foreac ($line in $test) {
3     write-host 'This is a test.'
4 }
```

Here is what the ISE is pointing out:


```
2 foreac ($line in $test) {
3     write-host 'This is a test.'
4 }
```

Example 2

Quotes. As was discussed in Chapter 2 there are two types of quotes in PowerShell. A single quote (') and a double quote ("). In PowerShell, what quote that is used can determine what can be placed in those quotes:

```
$alias = 'DScoles'

write-host 'The mailbox alias is $alias.'
write-host "The mailbox alias is $alias."
```

Using the ISE and ISE Steroids, we are able to see where the blocks of quotes start and end (the type of quotes does not matter, as long as they match).

```
write-host 'The mailbox alias is $alias.'     write-host 'The mailbox alias is $alias.'
write-host "The mailbox alias is $alias."     write-host "The mailbox alias is $alias."
```

A mistake in the quotes will be pretty obvious using the plugin and ISE:

```
write-host 'The mailbox alias is $alias."
write-host "The mailbox alias is $alias.'
```

However, if you were using Notepad the mistake may or may not be as obvious:

```
write-host 'The mailbox alias is $alias."
write-host "The mailbox alias is $alias.'
```

Debugging

The ISE can also be used to set up various Breakpoints for in the script at certain lines, when variable values change, and when commands are run. Each of these have their value when it comes to PowerShell's debugging.

A Line Break allows for a pause at a certain point in the script. Could be good for running parts of the script at a time. Making troubleshooting easier by partitioning out the code looking for the weak points.

The Variable Breakpoint allows for a script to pause whenever a variable's value has changed. This could be potentially good if a value should not be changing or if the script should be paused to examine what has happened already before the variable changes.

Command Breakpoint is triggered when a certain command or function is about to run. Before that command or function is run, PowerShell will pause.

For each of these scenarios, the script is paused and while the script is paused, other commands can be run to examine the current state of the script. This includes checking variable values to running any command that provides output. In effect, this feature is even more useful than using Pause, Sleep or some of the other techniques listed in this chapter.

Breakpoints can also be enabled and disabled at will. This can be done via the menu. Below is an example of setting a Line Breakpoint from the menu and what it looks like in the ISE window:

Edit View Tools **Debug** Add-ons	
Step Over	F10
Step Into	F11
Step Out	Shift+F11
Run/Continue	F5
Stop Debugger	Shift+F5
Toggle Breakpoint	F9
Remove All Breakpoints	Ctrl+Shift+F9
Enable All Breakpoints	
Disable All Breakpoints	

```
# variables
$Filepath = (Get-Item -Path ".\" -Verbose).FullName
$Server = $env:computername

foreach ($line in $bpa) {
    $Name = $Line.Replace("Microsoft/Windows/","")
    $Model = $Line
    $CSV = "BPA-Results-$Name-$Server.csv"
    Invoke-BPAModel $Model -ErrorAction SilentlyContinue
    Get-BPAResult -BestPracticesModelId $Model -ErrorAction SilentlyContin
    $CSVFile = Import-CSV $CSV
    GenerateHTMLReport $Name $CSVFile $Filepath
}
```

Try and Catch

Basic PowerShell scripting involves very little error correction or data validation. Using the Try and Catch coding pair is not exactly troubleshooting as it is more like error correction or error handling. Take for example a scenario where with some data or results, PowerShell works perfect. With other data, the same PowerShell cmdlet may fail or generate an error which causes the rest of the script to fail. In the below examples, the use of Try and Catch will be demonstrated as a key part of building an effective PowerShell script.

Example 1 - Simple Module Import

For this scenario you are importing modules into your PowerShell session so you can perform certain actions or have access to specific PowerShell cmdlets. However, it is true that not all servers are built the same. Which means that if you have a script written for your particular server and expect it to run anywhere without error, then we need to build in Try and Catch coding to at least perform basic corrections. In the case of PowerShell modules specifically, you will find that not all servers with PowerShell have all modules. I think that should go without saying.

In the below code, we are simply trying to load the MS Online module so we can login to our tenant via PowerShell to perform administrative tasks with a script. The load process for the module is pretty simple

```
Import-Module MSOnline
```

The one-liner is pretty basic and gets the job done. However, if the module is not present, it will fail and so will the script. There are two ways to handle this, one would be with a '#Requires' statement and the other is with a Try and Catch code bracket. The first will simply stop the script entirely from running whereas the second option will allow us to make adjustments (register an error) or install the requisite module. Let's examine the second option.

Recoded module import (Register an error):

```
Try {
    Import-Module MSOnline -ErrorAction STOP
} Catch {
    Write-Host 'MSOnline module not found.'
}
```

The second option would be to have the script run a code block (maybe download and install the missing module):

```
$NotPresent = $False
Try {
    Import-Module MSOnline -ErrorAction STOP
} Catch {
    $NotPresent = $True
}
If ($NotPresent -eq $True) {
    <CODE BLOCK>
}
```

Example 2

This time we will use some code to add people to certain Distribution Groups in Exchange Online. This requires that the correct user or correct group or both are used in the script. We're all human and bound to make mistakes in typing and creating the scripts. This typo could occur in the name of the member to add or the group to be added to. Either way we should build in some sort of error checking in case there is an issue and we can be made aware. The below samples tackle this issue and incorporate error checking.

Example Run 1

```
$Group = 'Exchange Online Admins'
$Member = 'Damian'
Try {
    Add-DistributionGroupMember -Identity $Group -Member $Member -ErrorAction STOP
    Write-Host "Successfully added $Member to the group $Group." -ForegroundColor Cyan
} Catch {
    Write-Host "Could not add $Member to the group $Group." -ForegroundColor Yellow
}
```

** **Note** ** The above would work for non-synced or cloud only groups in Exchange Online as only that type of group would allow modification.

The above code does not seem to work as we generate lots of errors:

```
The operation couldn't be performed because object 'Exchange Online Admins' couldn't be found on
'DM5PR13A006DC03.NAMPR13A006.PROD.OUTLOOK.COM'.
    + CategoryInfo          : NotSpecified: (:) [Add-DistributionGroupMember], ManagementObjectNotFoundException
    + FullyQualifiedErrorId : [Server=CY4PR13MB1350,RequestId=8fcba7ac-32bb-4165-8e22-4ab81ff7432f,TimeStamp=12/19/201
7 5:25:51 AM] [FailureCategory=Cmdlet-ManagementObjectNotFoundException] FA6BEF20,Microsoft.Exchange.Management.Re
cipientTasks.AddDistributionGroupMember
    + PSComputerName        : ps.outlook.com

Successfully added Damian to the group Exchange Online Admins.
```

The 'successful' message at the end is actually a false positive as the group doesn't event exist. In order to get the Try and Catch feature to work, we sometimes need to capture the cmdlet results in a variable instead. Example Run 2 below is that attempt:

Example Run 2

```
$Group = 'Exchange Online Admins'
$Member = 'Damian'
Try {
    $ Add = Add-DistributionGroupMember -Identity $Group -Member $Member -ErrorAction STOP
    Write-Host "Successfully added $Member to the group $Group." -ForegroundColor Cyan
} Catch {
    Write-Host "Could not add $Member to the group $Group." -ForegroundColor Yellow
}
```

This time when the script is run, then it fails as expected and produces this result:

```
Could not add Damian to the group Exchange Online Admins.
```

Now we have a successful run and can expand this to more groups or mailboxes.

ErrorAction

ErrorAction is useful in numerous scenarios. In the previous section of this chapter, ErrorAction was used within the Try and Catch framework in order to make it work properly. By using '-ErrorAction STOP' when a cmdlet fails in the 'TRY { }' section of the code errors or fails, the cmdlet is stopped and fails to the 'Catch { }' section of PowerShell code. If no –ErrorAction were not specified, the Catch { } part of the code would never be executed.

ErrorAction can also be used to allow a command to continue silently without displaying an error message:

Without

```
C:\> Get-retentionpolicy '12 Months'
e operation couldn't be performed because object '12 Months' couldn't be found on
M5PR13A006DC03.NAMPR13A006.PROD.OUTLOOK.COM'.
    + CategoryInfo          : NotSpecified: (:) [Get-RetentionPolicy], ManagementObjectNotFoundException
    + FullyQualifiedErrorId : [Server=CY4PR13MB1350,RequestId=7ac5b9ed-bf36-4ac8-8e1a-666cde234195,TimeStamp=12/19/
7 5:43:34 AM] [FailureCategory=Cmdlet-ManagementObjectNotFoundException] 6A5F21DE,Microsoft.Exchange.Management.
sks.GetRetentionPolicy
    + PSComputerName        : ps.outlook.com
```

With

```
PS C:\> Get-retentionpolicy '12 Months' -ErrorAction SilentlyContinue
```

Using the –ErrorAction SilentlyContinue may be what is needed for a script to keep moving or prevent the script from failing and causing further issues. However, in a troubleshooting scenario, removing these switches may be what is needed as its removal could generate error messages that could potentially point to the issue.

Transcript

While not an active troubleshooting method, using the transcription feature in PowerShell provides value by recording what is entered into a PowerShell window and the resulting output from a script. Transcription will copy these entered cmdlets, their output and error messages to a .txt file for an examination of what happened.

Example

```
# Start Transcript Process
Start-Transcript -Path "C:\reports\ScriptLogging.txt" -NoClobber
# Starting the script part to be logged
$Groups = (Get-DistributionGroup).Name
Foreach ($Group in $Groups) {
    Write-Host "Group Membership for $Group is:"
    Write-Host "--------------------------------"
    Get-DistributionGroupMember -Identity $Group
    Write-Host ' '
}
# Ending the transcript process
Stop-Transcript
```

Transcript File Content

```
************************
Windows PowerShell transcript start
Start time: 20171218235653
Username: Domain\DScoles
RunAs User: Domain\DScoles
Machine: MyLaptop (Microsoft Windows NT 6.3.9600.0)
Host Application: C:\Windows\System32\WindowsPowerShell\v1.0\powershell.exe
Process ID: 7288
PSVersion: 5.1.14409.1012
PSEdition: Desktop
PSCompatibleVersions: 1.0, 2.0, 3.0, 4.0, 5.0, 5.1.14409.1012
BuildVersion: 10.0.14409.1012
CLRVersion: 4.0.30319.42000
WSManStackVersion: 3.0
PSRemotingProtocolVersion: 2.3
SerializationVersion: 1.1.0.1
************************
Transcript started, output file is C:\reports\ScriptLogging.txt
Group Membership for Marketing is:
--------------------------------------


Group Membership for Test Group is:
--------------------------------------

Name            RecipientType
----            -------------
damian          UserMailbox
john.doe        UserMailbox
Pete Blanket    MailUser
damian          UserMailbox
john.doe        UserMailbox
Pete Blanket    MailUser


************************
Windows PowerShell transcript end
End time: 20171218235655
************************
```


Notice that the PowerShell cmdlets that were contained in the script do not get recorded in the transcript file. The only items that are recorded is the output from each PowerShell cmdlet that was run. The exception is the header and the footer of the transcript file that are recorded. The header provides some information about the computer and user running the script, while the footer provides just the ending time.

Notice that the Start-Transcript cmdlet is using the '-NoClobber' switch. This switch simply prevents any other log files from being overwritten. If the script is being run multiple times and you want to overwrite the files, just remove the '-NoClobber' switch.

For troubleshooting, the Transcript is more useful on scripts that run unattended and only the output needs to be logged. Make sure to use date/timestamps for the file name. This will make troubleshooting much faster in case the file is copied or moved and the date/timestamp is not retained.

Deciphering Error Messages

PowerShell error messages; yes, this is a bit of a nebulous concept. There are literally thousands of error messages that could occur in PowerShell. This section will not address them all. No book could truly address them all. This section of this chapter is simply here to help guide the troubleshooting process for these error messages. Let's start with the basics.

Basic Steps

There are a lot of things that can go wrong in building and running a PowerShell script. As with any troubleshooting technique, start with the basics if the error message is not clear enough.

- Open the script in PowerShell IDE and look for syntax and formatting misuse clues.
- Check the spellings of all cmdlets, variables, arrays, switches, etc.
- Check the value of each variable using write-host, a line with the variable name in it or via a ISE breakpoint.
- If the error message contains a line number, see if that line can be isolated or run by itself so that it can be picked apart.
- Break out the section that is causing the error into a similar script or run the code one line at a time from the prompt.
- Check permissions, does the script need to be run as an administrator?

Sample Error Troubleshooting

Let's say you tried to start a service using the following cmdlet and received the error below:

Start-Service -Name "ADSync"

```
Start-Service : Service 'Microsoft Azure AD Sync (ADSync)' cannot be started due to the following error:
Cannot start service ADSync on computer '.'.
At line:1 char:1
+ Start-Service ADSync
+ ~~~~~~~~~~~~~~~~~~~~~
    + CategoryInfo          : OpenError: (System.ServiceProcess.ServiceController:ServiceController) [Start-
   Service], ServiceCommandException
    + FullyQualifiedErrorId : CouldNotStartService,Microsoft.PowerShell.Commands.StartServiceCommand
```

So, let's check the StartType of the Remote Registry service with this cmdlet:

Get-WMIObject WIN32_Service -Filter "Name = 'ADSync'" | Fl Name,StartMode,State

From the StartType returned, we can see the service is Disabled and therefore can't be started until the StartType is changed.

```
Name      : ADSync
StartMode : Disabled
State     : Stopped
```

Access Denied

Got an Access Denied error? The PowerShell windows or script may need to run as an Administrator. This can be done by right-clicking on the shortcut for Windows PowerShell and selecting "Run as Administrator".

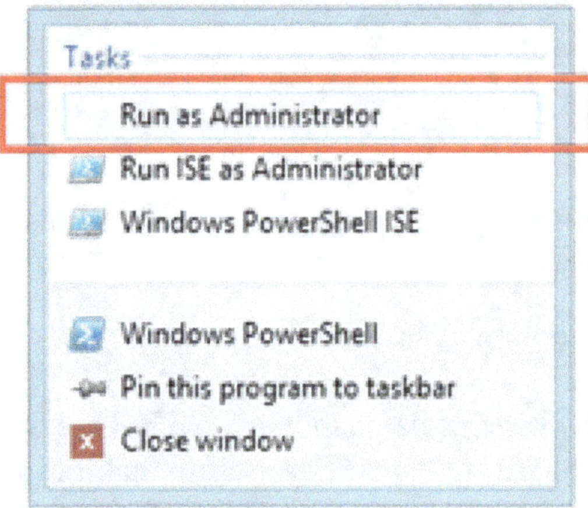

Opening PowerShell, using Run as Administrator allowed the Set-Service cmdlet to change the setting without error. It isn't uncommon to run into this issue as some PowerShell cmdlets require an elevated set of permissions in order to run. The use of 'Run as Administrator' should be limited to only when needed, versus doing it all the time. Elevated permissions should be restricted to an as needed basis. This will limit any possible exposure to malicious code running on a production server.

To fix the issue, a PowerShell cmdlet would be needed to change the startup mode from Disabled to something like Automatic. The cmdlet below will do this, but requires an elevated, Administrator, PowerShell sessions:

```
Set-Service -Name "Remote Registry"-StartupType Automatic
```

Attempting to run this cmdlet, brings up an error "Access is denied" error, if not run as an Administrator:

```
Set-Service : Service 'Remote Registry (remoteregistry)' cannot be configured due to the following error: Access is
denied
At line:1 char:1
+ Set-Service -name remoteregistry -StartupType automatic
+ ~~~~~~~~~~~~~~~~~~~~~~~~~~~~~~~~~~~~~~~~~~~~~~~~~~~~~~~~~
    + CategoryInfo          : PermissionDenied: (System.ServiceProcess.ServiceController:ServiceController) [Set-Servi
   ce], ServiceCommandException
    + FullyQualifiedErrorId : CouldNotSetService,Microsoft.PowerShell.Commands.SetServiceCommand
```

Back to the problem with starting the service, once the service Start Mode was set from Disabled to Automatic, the script now runs without error:

```
PS C:\> .\RemoteRegistryScript.ps1
PASSED - the Remote Registry Service is running.
PS C:\>
```

Because of this issue, a code block was put in place to check for the startup mode of the Remote Registry service:

Added Code Block

```
$StartUpMode = (Get-WmiObject Win32_Service | Where-Object {$_.Name -eq "RemoteRegistry"}).
StartMode
If ($StartUpMode -eq "Disabled") {
```

```
    Set-Service -Name RemoteRegistry -StartupType Automatic
    Start-Service -Name "Remote Registry"
    $StatusReg = (Get-Service -Name "Remote Registry").Status
}
```

Variables

Variable content can be quite crucial in a PowerShell script. Script troubleshooting may include validating the content of variables. A variable used to store values may not be storing the value the way one might think it's storing. Let's examine one scenario where the content of a variable does not match the expected results:

```
    Get-Mailbox "Damian" | fl PrimarySmtpAddress
```

This commend provides these results:

Now, say we want to store this for later use? A temporary variable might be the appropriate approach. The problem becomes when the value that is stored turns out to be the wrong value because the property that is stored is not a single value property but actually a multi-valued property. Take the above command where the Primary SMTP Address for a mailbox is stored in a variable. At first glance it appears to be a single value property – a string that makes up an email address. However, let's see what it really is. First, store the SMTP address as a variable (below):

```
    $PrimarySmtpAddress = (Get-Mailbox "Damian"). PrimarySmtpAddress
```

Now, using this Primary SMTP Address, let's attempt to query for the mailbox (yes, it is a circular reference, but it will make sense later):

```
    Get-Mailbox $PrimarySmtpAddress
```

This provides some surprising results:

```
Cannot process argument transformation on parameter 'Identity'. Cannot convert the "Damian@domain.com" value of type
"Microsoft.Exchange.Data.SmtpAddress" to type "Microsoft.Exchange.Configuration.Tasks.MailboxIdParameter".
    + CategoryInfo          : InvalidData: (:) [Get-Mailbox], ParameterBindin...mationException
    + FullyQualifiedErrorId : ParameterArgumentTransformationError,Get-Mailbox
    + PSComputerName        : ex01.domain.com
```

Not exactly the results that were expected. What's happening here? The property in question, PrimarySMTPAddress, is actually a multi-value property. To see the values stored, expand the contents of the variable with this command:

```
    $PrimarySmtpAddress | fl
```

And these results:

```
    Length          : 17
    Local           : Damian
    Domain          : domain.com
    IsUTF8          : False
    IsValidAddress  : True
```

Notice that the five values stored together, are all stored in the $PrimarySMTPAddress property. One solution to this problem is to store the address as a string instead, which will group these properties as we had originally expected:

```
[String]$PrimarySmtpAddress = (Get-Mailbox "Damian").PrimarySmtpAddress
Get-Mailbox $PrimarySmtpAddress
```

Then we get the desired results:

```
Name                    Alias           ServerName          ProhibitSendQuota
----                    -----           ----------          -----------------
DamianScoles            Damian          by2pr0801mb1494     99 GB (106,300,440,576 bytes)
```

Adding '| fl' after a variable name at the prompt, can be used to reveal if that variable is a multi-valued variable and therefore might need special handling to use it correctly.

Variables can also store empty values. Which may or may not be a desired result. The empty value could be because a PowerShell query (i.e. any mailbox alias is misspelled) did not work or an invalid value was provided for the query providing bad results (garbage in / garbage out). The $null value may not even provide any errors or cause the script to throw an error. The script may end up with invalid data as a result. Depending on the script, a check for the $null (or empty) variable may need to be put in place OR the cause of the empty (or null) variable may need to be investigated.

Example

In this example, there are say 20 databases on four Exchange 2016 servers in a Hybrid environment. We need to query all the mailboxes for an upcoming migration with a PowerShell script that has been written to find all mailboxes on a certain database. At the tail end of the script is a nice section of code that handles the formatting to create an HTML report. The script is also run on a scheduled basis. Yet, for a database with 150 mailboxes on it, the HTML is completely empty.

Sample Script Code

```
# HTML Formatting
$Css2='<Style>Table{Margin:Auto; Width:98%}
   Body{Background-Color: Black; Color:White; Text-Align:Center;}
   th{Background-Color:Black; Color:White;}
   td{Background-Color:White; Color:Black; Text-Align:Center;}
</Style>'
# Gather information
Try {
   $Groups = Get-DistributionGroup -ErrorAction STOP
} Catch {
   Write-Host 'No distribution groups were found.'
}
[String]$FilePath = "C:\downloads\report\GroupInfoReport.html"
Write-Verbose "HTML report will be saved $FilePath"
# Format the HTML Report
$GroupInfo = $Groups |ConvertTo-Html -Fragment -As Table -PreContent "<h2>Current Group
Attributes</h2>" | Out-String
```

```
$GroupReport = ConvertTo-Html -Title "Group Report" -Head "<h1>Exchange Group Reporting</
H1><br>" -Body "$GroupInfo $Css2"
# Generate Report
$GroupReport | Out-File $Filepath
```

Troubleshooting the failed report generation will require multiple steps – check the variable values, check the code for the HTML report and check to see if any mailboxes exist in the database. Because this book is a practical guide to PowerShell, let's examine the script to see where the problem lies.

As with any troubleshooting method starting with the absolute basics is key. Starting with the source of the mailbox data used to generate the HTML report:

```
Try {
    $Groups = Get-DistributionGroup -ErrorAction STOP
} Catch {
    Write-Host 'No distribution groups were found.'
}
```

No error is generated with the above code block (save in 'TestCommand.ps1'):

```
[PS] C:\>.\TestCommand.ps1
[PS] C:\>_
```

So, the code block above still does not provide the answer. The fact is, we know that there are mailboxes in every database on the server. So, we did not get an error and the HTML report is blank. Since the HTML report is generated from the $Groups variable its contents need to be validated. So, after the second attempt, with no error generated, we can do that by adding a line at the end of the script like this:

```
Try {
    $Groups = Get-DistributionGroup -ErrorAction STOP
} Catch {
    Write-Host 'No distribution groups were found.'
}
$Groups
```

The results are exactly the same:

```
[PS] C:\>.\TestCommand.ps1
[PS] C:\>_
```

This now proves that the $Groups variable is blank. However, no clues are provided by PowerShell. Let's isolate the code even further by just running the command without any extra switches or filters or variables. Just the base 'Get-DistributionGroup' to see if the data is good from the start:

```
$Groups = Get-DistributionGroup
```

After this is run…. The problem becomes self-evident:

```
Get-distributiongroup : The term 'Get-distributiongroup' is not recognized as the name of a cmdlet, function, script file, or oper
the name, or if a path was included, verify that the path is correct and try again.
At line:1 char:11
+ $Groups = Get-distributiongroup
+           ~~~~~~~~~~~~~~~~~~~~~~
    + CategoryInfo          : ObjectNotFound: (Get-distributiongroup:String) [], CommandNotFoundException
    + FullyQualifiedErrorId : CommandNotFoundException
```

In the above scenario we aren't connected to Exchange Online and thus are unable to run the cmdlets. Once we connect to Exchange Online, this script will run properly. Then once the script is fixed (just changing the source database name), an HTML report is generated.

Exchange Group Reporting										
					Current Group Attributes					
PSComputerName	**RunspaceId**	**PSShowComputerName**	**GroupType**	**SamAccountName**	**BypassNestedModerationEnabled**	**IsDirSynced**	**ManagedBy**	**MemberJoinRestriction**
ps.outlook.com	d92669ea-f574-4442-9760-d031e83596a5	False	Universal	Marketing5650511631816	False	False	damian	Open
ps.outlook.com	d92669ea-f574-4442-9760-d031e83596a5	False	Universal	Test Group56505670955889	False	False	damian	Open

The report generated is a bit awful looking, but it did work as planned. As you can see, checking data sources and the corresponding variables, can prove useful in determining the root of bad results.

** **Note** ** Reviewing the above information, you will note that the PSComputerName is returning ps.outlook.com which is in Exchange Online.

Arrays

Arrays can contain either a single line of values or an array of lines with data in them. To troubleshoot the contents of an array with PowerShell, there are two methods that could be used. If the data is stable, then the data only needs to validate it once. However, if the data source is more fluid or variable, it may need to be checked on a more constant basis.

Method One
```
$Array | ft
```

Method Two
```
Foreach ($Line in $Array) {
   $Array | ft
}
```

Each line that is stored in the array can now be evaluated and verified as good or bad data. From there it can be determined if the data source is bad, or if the PowerShell command that gathered the data is bad, or if the script that is using the data in the array is not handling the data types correctly.

Conclusion

Writing scripts isn't always a cut and dry process. Details may need to be worked out, variable names vetted and uses need to be worked out. Functions built, reporting code created and feedback to the user may need to be included.

This chapter covered several troubleshooting methods. The methods are by no means exhaustive on troubleshooting PowerShell. When troubleshooting script errors remember that there is no limit to the number of techniques described that can be used. It isn't unusual to use more than three methods (variables, transcript, commenting and write-host) on a single script to troubleshoot issues with it.

Before there is a real need for troubleshooting, practice with some of this chapter's PowerShell cmdlets and syntax to get familiar with how these tools will work. Make sure to also take advantage of the usual tools for PowerShell:

- ISE and ISE Steroids plug-in
- Get-Help
- Search Engine

Putting all of it together will make building a successful script that much easier.

Best Practices

In This Chapter

- What is a Best Practice?
- Summary of Best Practices
- PowerShell Best Practices
- Conclusion and Further Help

What is a Best Practice?

The use of PowerShell, like any other code in the IT world, requires guidance and best practices to make sure the experience of the coder and end-user are conducive to its use in the real world. As such, a series of best practices has been identified. Now, some of the best practices have already been covered, and will be noted as such, others have been developed over the years that PowerShell has been in use and lastly, some are matters of opinion. For this chapter, the bulk of our time will be spent on the middle topic of the developed best practices. At the end of the chapter we'll also explore some third party options that will help us code better with code analysis.

Summary of Best Practices

- Comment block at the top of the script
- Comments in script for documenting operation
- Useful comments
- Variable naming
- Variable block
- Matching variables to parameters
- Preference variables
- Verb-Noun-Functions and scripts
- Single task function
- Signing your code
- Filter vs. Where
- Error handling
- Write-Output / Write-Verbose
- # Requires
- Set-StrictMode
- Capitalization
- Using full command names
- Cmdlet binding
- Script structure
- Quotes
- Running applications

PowerShell Best Practices

Commenting

When it comes to PowerShell scripting, comments can be extremely useful when documenting a script, but also for troubleshooting a script's performance. Commenting is especially important for scripts that are meant for public disbursement. If someone else using your script runs into a problem, it would be ideal to either have copious commenting or to have some sort of documentation for them to reference. Below are samples we have used in the real world.

Example 1

Notice that the comment below lets us know that we are loading more modules:

```
# Load PowerShell Modules
Import-Module MSOnline
Import-Module ActiveDirectory
```

Example 2

Get users with retention policies assigned:

```
# Gets all servers that have a mounted database
$Mailboxes = (Get-Mailbox ).RetentionPolicy | Where {$_ -ne $Null}
```

Example 3

```
################################
#       Global   Definitions        #
################################
$DistributionGroup = "IT Department"
$RetentionPolicy = "AllItems"
$IssueWarning = "20GB"
```

** **Note** ** A more detailed description of PowerShell commenting is available on page 372 of this book.

Useful Comments

Another Best Practice for comments is simply to make sure to put useful information into the comment sections. Use comments to denote breaks. Use them to describe what a section does. Use them to describe variables purposes or maybe helpful troubleshooting information.

Variable Naming

Most of us are guilty of this one. Have you ever needed to create a quick script and in that script, for example, you needed a numerical counter so you could keep track of something for later? Well, I can almost guess that you used '$A++' or '$N++' to make your counters. This is a best practice that most of us need to break. The best way to handle such variables is to provide a meaningful name. If for example you need a list of all mailboxes, make the variable name '$Mailboxes'. If you need all users, make the variable $Users and so on.

Examples – Following the best practice

```
$GivenNames = (Get-User -Filter *).FirstName
$Counter++
$Mailboxes = Get-Mailbox
```

Examples – Not following best practice

```
$N = (Get-User  -Filter *).FirstName
$I++
$MBX= Get-Mailbox
```

Variable Block

In the spirit of previous best practices, another best practice concerning variables is creating a variable block. A variable block is an area of the script (at the top) that defines all the variables. It's usually started with a comment like so:

```
# Variable definition
```

Or

```
############### VARIABLES ###############
```

Then the variables to be used in the script are defined below that.

Example – from a working script

```
###############################
#      Global Variable Definitions      #
###############################
$NewProxy = $Null
$Domain = 'domain.com'
$TestUserUPN = 'licensing@domain*'

# Proxy Addresses
$Proxy = (Get-User -Filter * -Property * | Where-Object {$_.UserPrincipalName -Like $UserUPN}).
ProxyAddresses
```

Matching Variables to Parameters

Another naming convention that should be followed, is to name variables that match a parameter or value from a query. An example of this would be:

    $DisplayName = (Get-Mailbox).DisplayName

The reason for this is less confusion. This isn't necessarily a hard and fast rule. A variation of this is to name the variable after the content you intend to store. Using the above cmdlet as an example:

    $RetentionPolicy = (Get-Mailbox).RetentionPolicy

OR

    $Users = Get-MSOLUser

The intent is to keep the name of the variable as close as possible to the name of the parameter or value. This gives PowerShell variable names a purpose.

> ** **Note** ** One caveat to variable names, there are a set of predefined or 'Automatic Variables' that PowerShell has and you need to be aware of. These variables names are documented by Microsoft here:

https://docs.microsoft.com/en-us/powershell/module/microsoft.powershell.core/about/about_automatic_variables?view=powershell-6

Preference Variables

What is a Preference Variable in PowerShell? Preference Variables determine certain behaviors in PowerShell for how cmdlets should process certain conditions. These conditions include Errors, Debugging, WhatIf, Warnings, etc. To see which of these variables are available in PowerShell we can run this:

    Get-Variable *preference

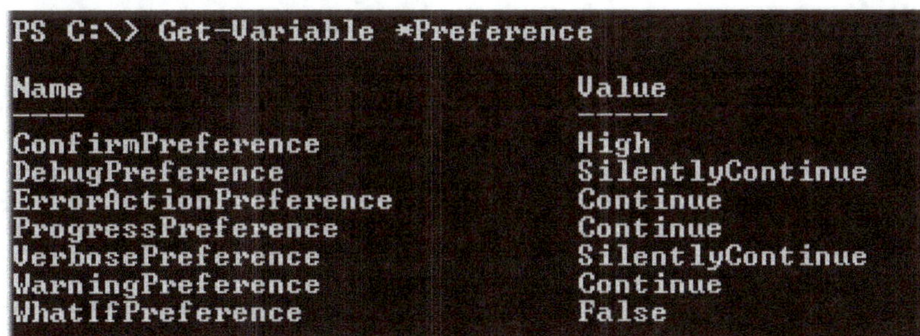

These are your default values for each Preference Variable in PowerShell. The best practice is not to change these settings globally because this configuration is what would be called expected behavior. If settings need to be changed, these should be changed on a case by case basis:

    Get-Mailbox Damian –ErrorAction STOP

Not

    $ErrorActionPreference = "STOP"

If we were to run this line we would change how all cmdlets would respond to errors when run. This makes troubleshooting more difficult and changes the expected behavior in PowerShell.

Naming Conventions, this time for Functions and Scripts

This is one thing we did not cover in the book in-depth or even at all. Earlier in the book we talked about naming conventions for variables in terms of capitalization and in this chapter we talked about using normal language instead of abbreviations for variables. This same concept can be extended to include functions and scripts. For these the best practice is to follow a similar naming convention as cmdlets in PowerShell. This would mean that function and script names should follow a 'Verb-Noun' naming format. Some examples are listed below:

Functions
```
Function Add-Licenses {}
Function Change-Quotas {}
Function Send-EmailMessages {}
```

Script Names
```
Set-RetentionPolicies.ps1
Test-ActivesyncOffice365.ps1
Set-MailboxSettings.ps1
```

As you can see from the above examples, we tried to be descriptive of what the function or script does. The same was done with scripts.

Singular Task Functions

This is an easy one. Functions can run all sorts of PowerShell cmdlets inside of them. However, the simpler more focused they are the better. As a best practice, functions should perform a single task like looking up a hotfix or installing a particular program or maybe making a registry change. The reason for this is to keep things simple and repeatable. That is the very definition of a function. Functions should be stackable in the sense that they can be called and used to build tasks (like LEGOs to build a house). We want to make sure the functions we construct are not overly complex or perform too many actions. This could complicate troubleshooting.

An example of this would be:

Example
This function will check for a certain module to be present which could affect a portion of the script:

```
Function Mail-ManagerDisabled ($GroupSmtpAddress) {
    $Manager = ((Get-DistributionGroup $GroupSmtpAddress).ManagedBy)
    $Manager | Foreach-Object {
      $EmailAddresses = (Get-Mailbox $_).EmailAddresses
        $EmailAddresses | Foreach-Object {
      If ($_ -CMatch "SMTP*") {
        $SMTPAddress = $_.Substring(5)
        $SMTP += @($SMTPAddress)
```

```
        }
      }
    }
  $DLName = (Set-DistributionGroup $GroupSmtpAddress).DisplayName
  [String] $Body = "<strong>NOTIFICATION</strong><BR><BR>As a part of regular maintenance, IT
  has decided to monitor the usage of Distribution # Lists.<BR><BR>This email is a notification that
  an Email Distribution Group that you manage has been inactive for over 12 months. This Distribution
  group has been deleted.<BR><BR>Please send an email to $AdminAddress if you have any questions.
  Thanks for your assistance with this matter."
  Foreach ($Line in $Smtp) {
    $MessageParameters = @{
      Subject = "Distribution Group Manager Alert - Removed Distribution Group - $DLName"
      Body = $Body
      From = $From
      To = $Line
      SmtpServer = $SmtpServer
    }
    Send-MailMessage @MessageParameters –BodyAsHtml
  }
} # End Function Mail-ManagerDisabled
```

Signing Your Code

Signing your code will help with two things. If downloaded by someone else, it ensures that the code has not been modified by anyone after it was signed, and if there is a strict PowerShell policy in place (which there is by default) the script can be run without changing this security feature.

As this is already covered, you can find more information on Code Signing on page 42 of this book.

Filter vs. Where

When it comes to manipulating data results, the Filter parameter and the Where operation are two different approaches to narrowing data to search from. With Filter the results are pre-filtered by a Domain Control or other system outside of PowerShell. With Where the results are all returned to PowerShell and then filtered. Because of this, the speed performance of the two results can vary greatly.

This is covered on page 33 of this book.

Error Handling

When first starting out to script, it isn't uncommon for there to be a reliance on '-ErrorAction SilentlyContinue' for pseudo error handling in a script. This allows for a one-liner or cmdlet to continue even if errors crop up that would otherwise end its operation. The problem with using this technique is that it can hide all errors. Errors that could be different from the original one that broke a script from running will now be hidden. A better way to handle this is to use Try and Catch. These two together can perform effective error handling where a cmdlet succeeds in the 'Try' part of the code block.

Try and Catch was covered earlier in the book and you can read more about this on page 376 of this book.

Write-Output / Write-Verbose

There are a few ways to output information while a script is running – Write-Host, Write-Verbose and Write-Output. Write-Host will immediately display the information to the PowerShell window as the script or line is run. For example, if we were to get a list of all Mail Contacts in Exchange and then display them in a certain way, we can use Write-Host to visually represent data:

```
$Contacts = Get-MailContact
Foreach ($Contact in $Contacts) {
    $Name = $Contact.Name
    Write-Host "$Name is a mail contact."
}
```

Using Write-Host is not recommended because a lot of scripts are run for automation and thus any output to a PowerShell window may be useless. A better option is to use Write-Verbose or Write-Output. Both of these provide a completely different option for your PowerShell script.

** **Note** ** Good reading on Write-Host can be found here -https://blogs.technet.microsoft.com/heyscriptingguy/2014/03/30/understanding-streams-redirection-and-write-host-in-powershell/.

Write-Verbose

Write-Verbose is an additional tool for troubleshooting the operation of a script. This cmdlet can be placed throughout the script at key points to help document.

Example
In this example, we use Write-Verbose to display information being gathered by a script:

```
Write-Verbose "The $DisplayName mailbox has had the $Policy retention policy applied."
Write-Verbose "A connection to Exchange Online could not be made."
Write-Verbose "No mailboxes were found."
```

If the script is run without the –Verbose switch, no output is displayed. However, if it experiences issues, we can use the –Verbose switch to trigger the Write-Verbose:

```
Damian Scoles mailbox has had the BigCorp 30 Day Retention retention policy applied.
A connection to Exchange Online could not be made.
No mailboxes were found.
```

Write-Output

This cmdlet can be used in two instances, it can be used to display the contents found from the running of a cmdlet/one-liner like so:

```
Get-UnifiedGroup | Write-Output
```

This is a bit redundant as the same output can be produced with:

    Get-UnifiedGroup

It can also be used to produce the output in a variable:

    $Mailboxes = Get-Mailbox
    Write-Output $Mailboxes

However, the same process can be done without the Get-Output cmdlet:

    $Mailboxes = Get-Mailbox
    $Mailboxes

Stick with Write-Verbose for most scripts and only use Write-Host if a visual answer / question or menu is needed.

'# Requires'

PowerShell scripts can be written to be standalone or they can be written to utilize other modules or components. If the latter is the case, then the use of '# Requires' should be in the script. Adding this to a script will prevent a script from running if the requirement is missing. This is important because without this a script that references to a module or particular component that is not available will fail. The PowerShell window will be covered with red text as the script fails to run. The most common usage that we've seen is when a certain level of PowerShell is needed. PowerShell's version level could determine important items like what cmdlets are available or what switch / parameters would be available to be run by the script.

What can we require? How do we figure that out? The easiest way is to fire up your favorite browser / search engine and look for the following:

    PowerShell #Requires

These search terms provide us with these results on the next page:

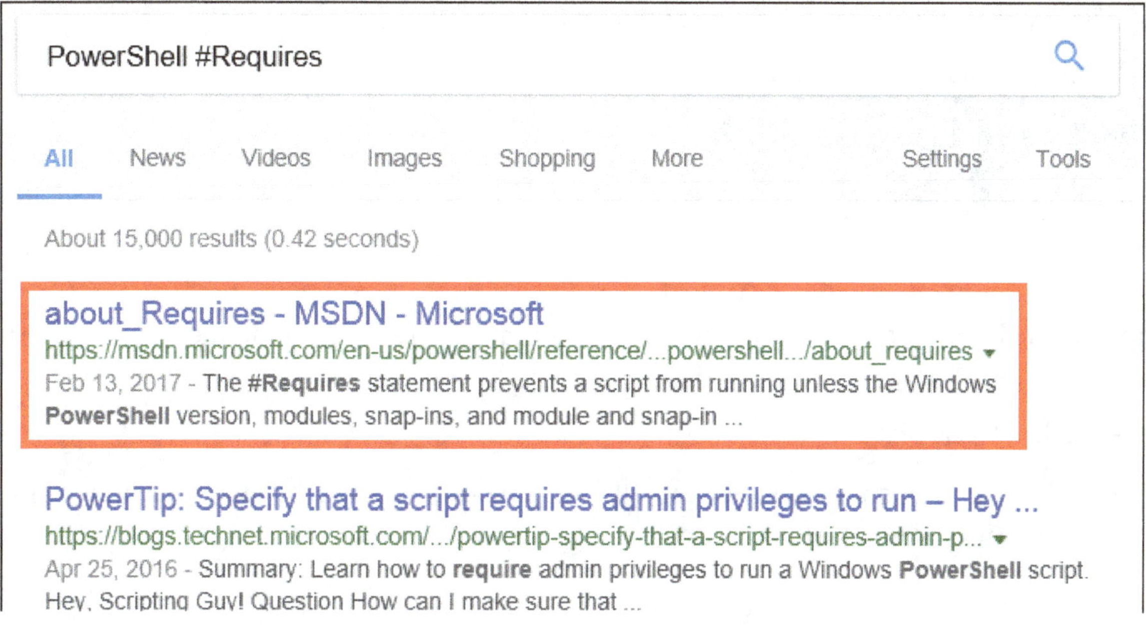

If we explore the resultant page, we find some more information on how to use the '#Requires' feature:

<table>
<tr><td>

SYNTAX

```
#Requires -Version <N>[.<n>]
#Requires -PSSnapin <PSSnapin-Name> [-Version <N>[.<n>]]
#Requires -Modules { <Module-Name> | <Hashtable> }
#Requires -ShellId <ShellId>
#Requires -RunAsAdministrator
```

</td><td>

RULES FOR USE

- The #Requires statement must be the first item on a line in a script.
- A script can include more than one #Requires statement.
- The #Requires statements can appear on any line in a script.

</td></tr>
</table>

Example 1

For our first example, we'll test requiring a certain version of PowerShell. The test will be run on a Windows 2008 R2 server. What version of PowerShell runs on Windows 2008 R2 by default?

$PSVersionTable reveals the following:

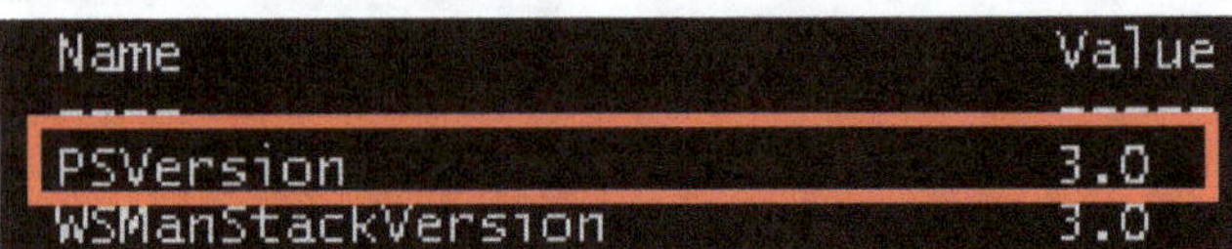

The PowerShell version is 3.0. As such, if we set the Requires for version for 4.0 like this:

    #Requires –Version 4.0

Then when the script is run, it will fail:

```
[PS] C:\downloads>.\Test-Requires.ps1
.\Test-Requires.ps1 : The script 'Test-Requires.ps1' cannot be run because it contained a "#requires" statement for Wind
version required by the script does not match the currently running version of Windows PowerShell version 3.0.
At line:1 char:1
+ .\Test-Requires.ps1
+ ~~~~~~~~~~~~~~~~~~~
    + CategoryInfo          : ResourceUnavailable: (Test-Requires.ps1:String) [], ScriptRequiresException
    + FullyQualifiedErrorId : ScriptRequiresUnmatchedPSVersion
```

The same script run on a Windows 2012 R2 server would not have any issue at all. It runs because if we check the $PSVersionTable, we see that Windows 2012 R2 is at version 4.0:

```
PS C:\Downloads> $PSVersionTable

Name                  Value
----                  -----
PSVersion             4.0
WSManStackVersion     3.0
```

Example 2

From the Syntax provided from the MSDN page, we see that we can also require certain modules before running like this:

    #Requires –Modules MSOnline

If the MS Online module is not loaded, the 'Requires' will force a module load. If the module cannot be loaded, a terminating error occurs and the script will exit.

PowerShell also provides a Get-Help for the #Requires feature. 'Get-Help Requires' will provide more detail on how to use '#Requires'.

```
[PS] C:\downloads>Get-Help Requires
TOPIC
    about_Requires

SHORT DESCRIPTION
    Prevents a script from running without the required elements.

LONG DESCRIPTION
    The #Requires statement prevents a script from running unless the Windows
    PowerShell version, modules, snap-ins, and module and snap-in version
    prerequisites are met. If the prerequisites are not met, Windows PowerShell
    does not run the script.

    You can use #Requires statements in any script. You cannot use them in
    functions, cmdlets, or snap-ins.

    SYNTAX
            #Requires -Version <N>[.<n>]
            #Requires -PSSnapin <PSSnapin-Name> [-Version <N>[.<n>]]
            #Requires -Modules { <Module-Name> | <Hashtable> }
            #Requires -ShellId <ShellId>

    RULES FOR USE

        - The #Requires statement must be the first item on a line in a script.
        - A script can include more than one #Requires statement.
        - The #Requires statements can appear on any line in a script.

    PARAMETERS
    -Version <N>[.<n>]
        Specifies the minimum version of Windows PowerShell that the script
        requires. Enter a major version number and optional minor version number.

        For example:
        #Requires -Version 3.0
```

Set-StrictMode -Version Latest

This is one that we've started adding to our scripts now. What this does is it enforces certain best practices in your PowerShell coding and forces the code to be 'Correct'. Think of this as a code check prior to execution of the script. One item that is checked is variable definition. Variables that are used in a script will need to be defined at the top of the script.

How can we configure this PowerShell cmdlet, let's review the Get-Help for the cmdlet to see:

Get-Help Set-StrictMode –Full

The valid values are "1.0", "2.0", and "Latest". The following list shows the effect of each value.

1.0
-- Prohibits references to uninitialized variables, except for uninitialized variables in strings.

2.0
-- Prohibits references to uninitialized variables (including uninitialized variables in strings).
-- Prohibits references to non-existent properties of an object.
-- Prohibits function calls that use the syntax for calling methods.
-- Prohibits a variable without a name ($\{\}).

Latest:

--Selects the latest (most strict) version available. Use this value to assure that scripts use the strictest available version, even when new versions are added to Windows PowerShell.

Version 1 - Example:

In this example we'll use an undefined variable (one without a value):

```
Set-StrictMode -Version 1.0
If($A > 2) {
   Write-Host "Large Number"
}
```

```
The variable '$a' cannot be retrieved because it has not been set.
At C:\Downloads\TestStrict.ps1:2 char:4
+ if($a > 2) {
+     ~~~
    + CategoryInfo          : InvalidOperation: (a:String) [], RuntimeException
    + FullyQualifiedErrorId : VariableIsUndefined
```

Now if we define a variable correctly and still use the strict mode, no error will occur:

```
Set-StrictMode -Version 1.0
$Count = (Get-command *Mailbox*).Count
If($Count > 2) {
   Write-Host "Large Number"
}
```

```
[PS] C:\>.\TestStrict.ps1
[PS] C:\>
```

Version 2 - Example

In this example we review one of the Version 2 best practices. Let's try out the restriction on calling nonexistent properties.

No sub-properties to call and no version defined:

```
$Mailboxes = "Dave"
$Mailboxes.DisplayName
```

No results or errors will show with that code.

Now we try the same code with StrictMode Version 2:

```
Set-StrictMode -Version 2.0
$Mailboxes = "Dave"
$Mailboxes.DisplayName
```

```
The property 'DisplayName' cannot be found on this object. Verify that the property exists.
At line:1 char:1
+ $Mailboxes.DisplayName
+ ~~~~~~~~~~~~~~~~~~~~~~~
    + CategoryInfo          : NotSpecified: (:) [], PropertyNotFoundException
    + FullyQualifiedErrorId : PropertyNotFoundStrict
```

Best practice Followed:

```
Set-StrictMode -Version 2.0
$Mailboxes = Get-Mailbox
$Mailboxes.DisplayName
```

This last example worked because the variable $Mailboxes has a sub-property called DisplayName and when called it displays its value.

The last value for –Version is a bit deceptive. 'Latest' is the same as '2.0' for now. As such the best practice is to use 'Latest' so that if something is added later on, you are not stuck with old code looking for '2.0' restrictions and not something newer that was added.

Capitalization

Capitalization is just another best practice that has more to do with readability and formatting than a strictly PowerShell best practice.

** **Note** ** This is already covered in the book on page 26. See that section for more detail on this best practice.

Using full command names

PowerShell contains quite a few aliases (or shortcuts) that are basically shortcuts to common cmdlets like 'Foreach-Object', 'Where-Object' and 'Write-Output'.   Aliases are typically used for a couple reasons:

- It's quicker to type the shortened version:

Example

 '%' rather than typing the equivalent 'Foreach-Object'

- Simplifies the coding, can point aliases towards commands and functions.

Why not use aliases? Aliases should not be used when coding a script for the public consumption or trying to explain PowerShell coding to another person. Make sure to put full commands in so that there will be no confusion as to why something was used. For learning purposes, using the Verb-Noun format of PowerShell is more conducive then trying to get someone to learn the multitude of aliases that are present in PowerShell. For example, Exchange Online has 158 aliases.

How do we find that out?

(Get-Alias).Count

```
PS C:\> (Get-Alias ).count
158
```

In addition to this, when building a new script, it would be better to have the correct syntax / commands so that if you need help troubleshooting something there won't be any head-scratching on trying to decipher aliases. Thus having the full commands is better for you and someone helping you.

Details of PowerShell aliases are covered on page 410 of this book.

Cmdlet Binding

Cmdlet binding is used to add additional functionality to functions within a PowerShell script. Using cmdlet binding also allows for the use of Write-Verbose. Write-Verbose can be useful for troubleshooting a script or providing more information on a particular section of a script.

How do we use this? In this example we'll see if we can get the Write-Verbose cmdlet to work:

```
Function Test-AdvancedFeatures {
  [CmdletBinding()]Param()
  Try {
     Import-Module MSOnline -ErrorAction STOP
  } Catch {
     $Failed = $True
     Write-Verbose "Cannot load the MSOnline module."
  }
}

Test-AdvancedFeatures -Verbose
```

Without the verbose switch, no feedback is given:

```
PS C:\> .\TestVerbose.ps1
PS C:\>
```

However, with the verbose switch:

```
PS C:\> .\TestVerbose.ps1
VERBOSE: Cannot load the MSOnline module.
PS C:\>
```

In addition to this, Cmdlet Binding can also add functionality like –WhatIf or –Confirm, or even ErrorVariable and ErrorAction to a script or function. The use of this option expands options that are available for use with PowerShell functions to the point of them operating like cmdlets specifically with the switch options.

Further reading on Cmdlet Binding - https://msdn.microsoft.com/en-us/powershell/reference/5.1/microsoft.powershell.core/about/about_functions_cmdletbindingattribute

Script Structure

For ease of use, readability, and general flow, a good script structure is generally recommended. In general a script should follow something like this:

Comment block – script description, parameter definitions, versioning and more

Global variable definitions – define arrays and other variables that may need to be pre-populated like dates

Functions – there should be a section of the script near the top that defines the functions that will be used in the script (not required)

Script body – where the script starts to run and use the variables and functions that were predefined in order to accomplish some task

Example Script - Structure

Comment Block	<pre>###
	# SCRIPT DETAILS
	# Created a charet of licensing options configured on each user
	#
	# SCRIPT VERSION HISTORY
	# Current Version : 1.1
	# Change Log : 1.1 - Added comments and fixed some bugs (export)
	# : 1.0 - First iteration
	#
	# OTHER SCRIPT INFORMATION
	# Wish list : Better comment based help
	# Rights Required : MSOL PowerShell Module
	# Author : Damian Scoles
	# My Blog : http://justaucguy.wordpress.com
	# Disclaimer : You are on your own. This was not written by, supported by, or endorsed by Microsoft.
	#
	# EXECUTION
	# .\Office365Licenses.ps1
	#
	###</pre>

Global Variables	<pre># Variables
	$AllSKUIDs = (Get-MsolAccountSku).AccountSKUID
	$Mailboxes = Get-MsolUser -All
		Select-Object UserPrincipalName,Licenses</pre>

Script Body	<pre># Variables
	$AllSKUIDs = (Get-MsolAccountSku).AccountSKUID
	$Mailboxes = Get-MsolUser -All
		Select-Object UserPrincipalName,Licenses
		
		#Script Body
		ForEach ($SKUID in $ALLSKUIDs) {
		    $LicenseAll = $Null
		    $LicenseCurrent = $Null
		    $LicenseAll = @()
		    $FileName = "c:\Downloads\ExchangeBook-Licenses.csv"
		
		    foreach ($mailbox in $mailboxes) {
		        $UPN = $Mailbox.UserPrincipalName
		        $ServicePlans = $mailbox.Licenses.ServiceStatus
		        $Licenses = $mailbox.Licenses
		        $SKUs = $Licenses.AccountSKUID
		
		        foreach ($sku in $SKUS) {
		            if ($SKU -eq $SKUID) {
		                $LicenseCurrent = New-Object System.Object
		                $LicenseCurrent
			Add-Member -type NoteProperty -name Mailbox -value $UPN
			                Foreach ($Line in $ServicePlans) {
			                    $ServicePlan = $Line.ServicePlan.ServiceName
			                    $ProvisioningStatus = $Line.ProvisioningStatus
			                    $LicenseCurrent
				Add-Member -type NoteProperty -name $ServicePlan -value $ProvisioningStatus
				                }
				                $LicenseAll += $LicenseCurrent
				            }
				        }
				    }
				    $LicenseAll
					Export-CSV $FileName -NoType
					}</pre>

Quotes

Quoting in a PowerShell script may not seem important, but it can determine if a script runs correctly. The use of single quotes (') versus double quotes (") makes a vast difference in scenarios with variables that may need to be called from inside the quotes. This topic was covered earlier on page 40 of this book.

Running Applications

This is the easiest of the best practices in PowerShell. When calling an executable from PowerShell, make sure to use the '.exe' file extension. If you were to call an application without the extension and the application name happens to match a PowerShell alias, then the alias is called and not the executable. One example of this would be 'sc'.

```
Get-Alias sc
```

Whereas the sc.exe executable file would need to be called directly with 'sc.exe' instead.

Conclusion and Further Help

When it comes to PowerShell, best practices are defined in order to guide us into producing better code for ourselves and others that we are coding for. Whether it means more consistent capitalization, easy to remember variables or signing the script code, the purpose is the same. The list in this chapter is in no way a comprehensive list of all best practices for PowerShell. Make sure to follow the rules suggested, but also use external information to validate. In addition to the list provided, there are vendors besides Microsoft that produces PowerShell tools to help keep your script quality. One of these products is called 'PsScriptAnalyzer'. This tool is available on Github:

https://github.com/PowerShell/PSScriptAnalyzer

The ISE from Microsoft, the one newest versions, come with the Script Analyzer built in.

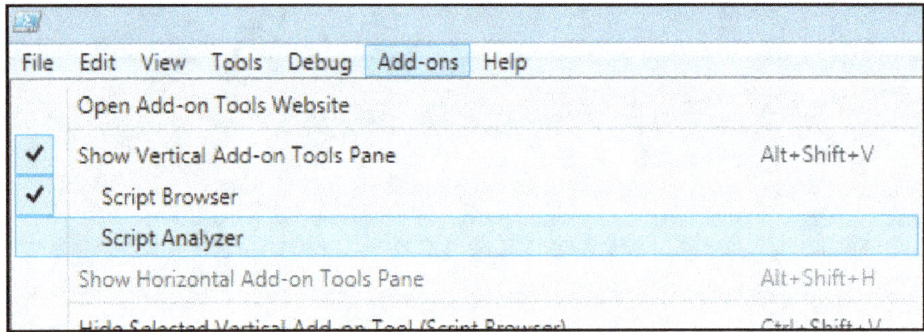

Once you have a script opened, you can run the tool with this:

On the right will be a list of suggested fixes:

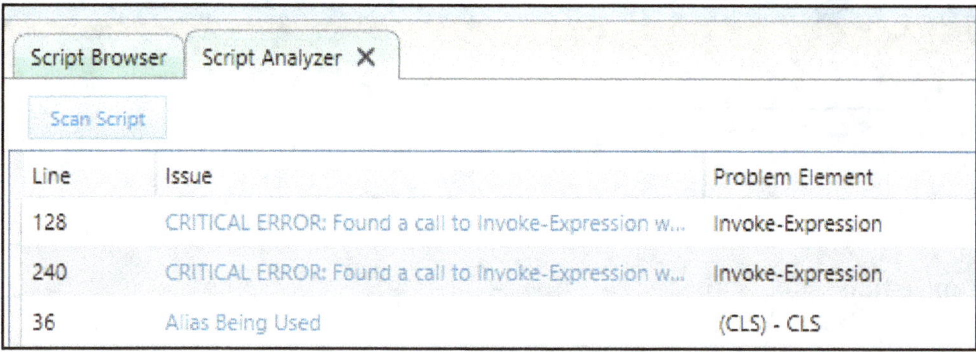

You might find the analysis to be a bit over picky, but if you would like your script to be more stream-lined and accurate, then this is the way to go.

B   Miscellaneous

In This Chapter
- Menus
- Aliases
- Foreach-Object (%)
- PowerShell Interface Customization
- Command Logging

In this book, we've covered numerous topics from how to start out scripting, to customizing Exchange Online topics in PowerShell. The topics picked are, as with the rest of the book, based on practical experience and are ones that should prove useful in a production environment.

For this chapter, we'll cover menus, aliases, Foreach-Object filtering, and special permission cmdlets. Each of these provide some added benefit to managing Exchange Online with PowerShell. Aliases provide a way to customize PowerShell for easier coding. These shortcuts simply make coding easier. In addition to this, the shell can also be customized in terms of path, colors and window sizing.

An additional filtering option will also be covered in this chapter. This cmdlet helps sort through or manipulate results of cmdlets and can be used to provide an 'in-flight' cleanup for results for readability. Foreach-Object is indeed a useful cmdlet for your PowerShell scripts or one-liners.

Menus

Building menus is not a task that is necessary for one off scripts. Menus should be used on scripts that will be run on multiple occasions, for example supporting a large number of mailboxes in Office 365 or for occasions where occasional input may be necessary. Another reason to use it is for a reusable script, which is especially useful for consultants who run their scripts in dozens of environments a year. The menu simply makes running the script quicker and more flexible.

In a PowerShell script, the menu can consist of two parts. The first part is the text for the menu which is the visual part of the script. The menu can be simple and singular in color or very colorful like the example given in Chapter 2. The second part is the infrastructure or back-end of the menu itself. This is where the executable code is stored and where coding needs to be performed in the form of functions that will complete the tasks the menu has called.

Sample Menu Code

```
$Menu = {
    Write-Host "******************************************************************"
    Write-Host "Office 365 Mailbox Management"
    Write-Host "******************************************************************"
    Write-Host "1) UPN Check "
    Write-Host "2) Configure Retention Policy"
    Write-Host "3) Configure Client Access"
    Write-Host "4) Set Legal Hold"
    Write-Host ""
    Write-Host "99) Exit"
    Write-Host ""
    Write-Host "Select an option.. [1-99]?"
}
```

The above menu has been snipped from a script that is used to manage mailboxes and their settings in Office 365. By itself this menu is just a variable that holds a bunch of text that looks like a menu. Next, we need to build the backbone on the infrastructure part of the menu. This is where PowerShell will make calls to functions in the rest of the script to perform the functions you code for.

To start this section, construct a 'Do { } While' code block. The reason for this is that script will keep running options and displaying the menu until an exit code is chosen. So the 'Do { } While' block would look something like this:

```
Do {
    Invoke-Command -ScriptBlock $Menu
    $Choice = Read-Host
} While ($Choice -ne 99)
```

Notice that with this code, the loop will keep displaying the menu after each option is chosen until the value of 99 is selected. At that point the script will stop and exit to a PowerShell prompt. The Read-Host will store the value type in $opt to be used for selecting which code block to run. Next, there needs to be a way to decide which option will run. What PowerShell cmdlet will allow for this?

```
Switch ($Choice)
```

However, a review of the help on 'Switch' does not reveal a lot of clues for its usefulness/functionality. However with a little bit of help from your favorite search engine, one can find this MSDN link for PowerShell functionality:

https://technet.microsoft.com/en-us/library/hh847750.aspx

We find that Switch will act like a condition tester, if a condition is fed to it, it will select that option within the Switch code section. For example:

```
$Choice = 3
   Switch ($Choice) {
   1 {Write-Host "1"}
   2 {Write-Host "2"}
   3 {Write-Host "3"}
}
```

The result of this will display the number 3:

Let's incorporate this into our menu infrastructure. Using the above as an example, we'll need to build code blocks for each function we'll need to call from our example on the previous page. To make this process simpler (in terms of the scope of the menu) functions are pre-created:

Correct mailbox UPN: Modifies a users UPN for Exchange Online
Configure Retention Policy: Applies a retention policy to a mailbox
Configure Client Access: Configures mailbox access to client protocols like ActiveSync
Set Legal Hold: Configures a hold on a mailbox in Exchange Online

With these functions created they can be referred to in each option code block. Note that it is assumed that a connection to the MSOL Service has already been made prior to running any of the options. Refer to Chapter 5 on how to connect to Exchange Online with PowerShell.

Option 1

This option calls the Mailbox UPN check function:

```
Function UPN Check {
   $BaseDomain = '@OnlineExchangeBook.onmicrosoft.com'
   $Users = Get-MSOLUsers -All
   Foreach ($User in $Users) {
      $DisplayName = $User.DisplayName
      $UPN = (Get-MSOLUser $User).UserPrincipalName
      If ($UPN -like $BaseDomain) {
         Write-Host 'The UPN for $DisplayName has the correct domain base' -ForegroundColor Cyan
      } Else {
         Write-Host 'The UPN for $DisplayName has an incorrect domain base' -ForegroundColor Yellow
      }
   }
}
```

Option 2

This option calls the Retention Policy Configuration function:

```
Function RetentionPolicy {
    $Mailbox = Get-Mailbox
    $Policy = '18 Month Email Delete and Purge'
    Foreach ($Line in $Mailbox) {
        $Name = $Line.DisplayName
        $Retention = $Line.RetentionPolicy
        If ($Retention -eq $Policy) {
        Write-Host "The mailbox for $Name " -ForegroundColor White -NoNewLine
        Write-Host "has the right Retention Policy." -ForegroundColor Green
    } Else {
        Write-Host "The mailbox for $Name " -ForegroundColor White -NoNewLine
        Write-Host "has the wrong retention policy!" -ForegroundColor Red
        Set-Mailbox $Mailbox -RetentionPolicy $Policy
    }
} # End Retention Policy Function
```

```
The mailbox for user01 has the wrong retention policy!
The mailbox for user02 has the wrong retention policy!
The mailbox for user03 has the wrong retention policy!
The mailbox for user04 has the wrong retention policy!
The mailbox for user05 has the wrong retention policy!
The mailbox for user06 has the wrong retention policy!
The mailbox for user07 has the wrong retention policy!
The mailbox for user08 has the wrong retention policy!
The mailbox for user09 has the wrong retention policy!
The mailbox for user10 has the wrong retention policy!
The mailbox for User11 has the wrong retention policy!
The mailbox for User12 has the wrong retention policy!
```

Option 3

This option calls the Configure Client Access function. The reason I want this function is to 'normalize' all access to mailboxes in Exchange Online. Let's say for example the tenant has multiple Global Admins and maybe some mistakes have been made or experimenting with settings. This could potentially lead to problems for end user access. For example, the users below are different, but they should match:

```
PS C:\> Get-Mailbox | Get-CASMailbox | where {$_.name -notlike 'disco*'}

Name      ActiveSyncEnabled OWAEnabled PopEnabled ImapEnabled MapiEnabled
----      ----------------- ---------- ---------- ----------- -----------
damian    False             True       False      False       True
john.doe  True              True       True       True        True
```

This function needs to make sure all services are enabled for the user and not disabled like we see above. We will need to get a list of all mailboxes and then use the Set-CASMailbox cmdlet to change the ActiveSync, OWA, POP, IMAP and MAPI settings to be 'Enabled' or set to True ($True in PowerShell). We can add a little feedback if we want to let the admin know what has changed or who was misconfigured if we want to.

```
Function CASChanges {
    $Mailboxes = Get-CASMailbox | where {$_.Name -NotLike 'disco*'}
    Foreach ($Mailbox in $Mailboxes) {
        $Access = Get-CASMailbox | where {$_.Name -NotLike 'Discovery*'}
```

```powershell
    Foreach ($Line in $Access) {
      $Name = $Line.Name
      If ($Line.ActiveSyncEnabled -ne $True) {
          Write-Host "ActiveSync is misconfigured for $Name!" -ForegroundColor Yellow
          Set-CASMailbox $Name -ActiveSyncEnabled $True
      }
      If ($Line.OWAEnabled -ne $True) {
          Write-Host "OWA is misconfigured for $Name!" -ForegroundColor Yellow
          Set-CASMailbox $Name -OWAEnabled $True
      }
      If ($Line.POPEnabled -ne $True) {
          Write-Host "POP is misconfigured for $Name!" -ForegroundColor Yellow
          Set-CASMailbox $Name -POPEnabled $True
      }
      If ($Line.IMAPEnable -ne $True) {
          Write-Host "IMAP is misconfigured for $Name!" -ForegroundColor Yellow
          Set-CASMailbox $Name -IMAPEnabled $True
      }
      If ($Line.MAPIEnabled -ne $True) {
          Write-Host "MAPI is misconfigured for $Name!" -ForegroundColor Yellow
          Set-CASMailbox $Name -MAPIEnabled $True
      }
    }
  }
} # End of CAS Changes function
```

Sample run of this function:

```
PS C:\> .\CAS-Fix.ps1
ActiveSync is misconfigured for damian!
POP is misconfigured for damian!
IMAP is misconfigured for damian!
```

Option 4

The option calls the Legal Hold function:

```powershell
Function LegalHold {
    Write-Host 'Enter the email address for the user to be put on Legal Hold. ' -NoNewLine
    $Email = Read-Host
    Write-Host 'How many days for Legal Hold? [0 for no end] ' -NoNewLine
    $Days = Read-Host
    # Set $Days variable to 'Unlimited if a '0' was entered.
    If ($Days -eq '0') {
      $Days = 'Unlimited'
    }
    Set-Mailbox $Email -LitigationHoldEnabled $True -LitigationHoldDuration $Days
} # End of Legal Hold function
```

```
Enter the email address for the user to be put on Legal Hold. damian@OnlineExchangeBook.onmicrosoft.com
How many days for Legal Hold? [0 for no end] 0
WARNING: The hold setting may take up to 60 minutes to take effect.
```

Notice that a comment is included in each option block for documentation purposes. For the last option the script provides a way to exit the script cleanly:

Option 99

```
99 {# Exit
   Write-Host "Exiting..."
}
```

When option 99 is selected, the script exits because of the Do {} While code block.

Pulling all of the previous code together into one script:

```
$Menu = {
   Write-Host "*********************************************************************"
   Write-Host "Office 365 Mailbox Management"
   Write-Host "*********************************************************************"
   Write-Host "1) UPN Check "
   Write-Host "2) Configure Retention Policy"
   Write-Host "3) Configure Client Access"
   Write-Host "4) Set Legal Hold"
   Write-Host ""
   Write-Host "99) Exit"
   Write-Host ""
   Write-Host "Select an option.. [1-99] " -NoNewLine
}
Do {
   Invoke-Command $Menu
   $Choice = Read-Host $Menu
   Switch ($Choice)  {
      1 { # UPN Check
        UPNCheck
      }
      2 { # Configure Retention Policy
        RetentionPolicy
      }
      3 { # Configure Client Access
        CASChanges
      }
      4 { # Set Legal Hold
        LegalHold
      }
      99 {# Exit
        Write-Host "Exiting..."
      }
      Default {
         Write-Host "You haven't selected any of the available options. "
      }
   }
```

} While ($Choice -ne 99)

Running the script provides a menu as displayed below:

```
*************************************************
Office 365 Mailbox Management
*************************************************
1) UPN Check
2) Configure Retention Policy
3) Configure Client Access
4) Set Legal Hold

99)
```

Option 99 allows for the script to exit:

```
Select an option.. [1-99]  99
Exiting...
```

If an option is typed in wrong, say 77, an error message is provided:

```
Select an option.. [1-99]  77
You haven't selected any of the available options.
```

Aliases

PowerShell aliases are shortened versions of PowerShell cmdlets. Consider aliases to be a convenience in reducing the amount of text in a script. Aliases are not necessary for writing a script but they do provide shortcuts to coding. Without aliases, each command in PowerShell just takes longer to type. The downside of aliases is that normally PowerShell is a very readable scripting language and using aliases can obscure the ability to read PowerShell in plain English. Another downside is that there is no guarantee that the alias will exist in a different environment. If the script is meant to be portable, it would be advisable to not use them or at least limit their usage. If a script will be read by someone other than you, using aliases might make the script unreadable to others.

```
Get-Alias -Definition Foreach-Object

CommandType     Name
-----------     ----
Alias           % -> ForEach-Object
Alias           foreach -> ForEach-Object
```

However, what if you don't know the command that the alias is for? The above can be reverse engineered to show all aliases. To look up all aliases, simply type in 'Get-Alias':

```
CommandType     Name
-----------     ----
Alias           % -> ForEach-Object
Alias           ? -> Where-Object
Alias           ac -> Add-Content
Alias           asnp -> Add-PSSnapin
Alias           cat -> Get-Content
Alias           cd -> Set-Location
Alias           chdir -> Set-Location
Alias           clc -> Clear-Content
Alias           clear -> Clear-Host
```

Without listing them all here, all told, there are 148 aliases defined. What may be more interesting is that aliases can be created and modified. This certainly provides for some flexibility or customization of PowerShell.

New-Alias

If there is a desire to make custom aliases for PowerShell, New-Alias is the cmdlet to use.

** **Note** ** The aliases are only good for the current session. If you close the current session, the alias is lost and when you reconnect to Exchange Online PowerShell the alias will not be there.

Get-Help New-Alias -Examples

```
------------------------- EXAMPLE 1 -------------------------

PS C:\>new-alias list get-childitem
This command creates an alias named "list" to represent the Get-ChildItem cmdlet.
```

```
------------------------- EXAMPLE 2 -------------------------

PS C:\>new-alias -name w -value get-wmiobject -description "quick wmi alias" -option ReadOnly
PS C:\>get-alias -name w | format-list *
This command creates an alias named "w" to represent the Get-WMIObject cmdlet. It creates a description, "quick wmi
pipes it to Format-List to display all of the information about it.
```

Sample Usage

We can create an alias for just about anything in PowerShell that we want. For this example we can create aliases for any of the *-Mailbox cmdlets if we wanted to.

To create these aliases, we'll use a series of New-Alias one-liners:

```
New-Alias dmbx Disable-Mailbox -Description 'Disable Mailbox cmdlet'
New-Alias embx Enable-Mailbox -Description 'Enable Mailbox cmdlet'
New-Alias gmbx Get-Mailbox -Description 'Get Mailbox cmdlet'
New-Alias nmbx New-Mailbox -Description 'New Mailbox cmdlet'
New-Alias rmbx Remove-Mailbox -Description 'Remove Mailbox cmdlet'
New-Alias smbx Set-Mailbox -Description 'Set Mailbox cmdlet'
```

Example result of a new alias creation:

```
PS C:\temp> New-Alias dmbx Disable-Mailbox -Description 'Disable Mailbox cmdlet'
PS C:\temp> Get-Alias dmbx

CommandType     Name                                               Version    Source
-----------     ----                                               -------    ------
Alias           dmbx -> Disable-Mailbox
```

There are a few parameters that can be used to customize this new alias during creation. One of the parameters is 'Option' which provides for a way to limit when the alias can be used – Global, Local, Script or Private. An alias could be enabled for only when a script runs or only while in a local session. The purpose of this option is to possibly isolate the usage of a cmdlet as to prevent unwarranted changes using the aliases. A description should be added so that the purpose of the alias is known by others.

Set-Alias

This cmdlet is used to modify any of the existing aliases to the specifics that you may want to configure for a particular alias. One of the exceptions is if the alias is set to ReadOnly. To modify one of those aliases, a '-Force' switch must be used. Here are some sample uses of the cmdlet:

Get-Help New-Alias -Examples

```
------------------------------ EXAMPLE 1 ------------------------------

PS C:\>set-alias -name list -value get-childitem
This command creates the alias "list" for the Get-ChildItem cmdlet. After you create the alias, you can use "list"
in place of "Get-ChildItem" at the command line and in scripts.
------------------------------ EXAMPLE 2 ------------------------------

PS C:\>set-alias list get-location


This command associates the alias "list" with the Get-Location cmdlet. If "list" is an alias for another cmdlet,
this command changes its association so that it now is the alias only for Get-Location.
```

Sample Usage

In practical terms, this cmdlet would likely only be used to modify existing aliases that you've created yourself.
Taking some of the aliases created in the previous section, let's make sure that the aliases are ReadOnly:

Set-Alias dmbx Disable-Mailbox -Option ReadOnly
Set-Alias embx Enable-Mailbox -Option ReadOnly
Set-Alias gmbx Get-Mailbox -Option ReadOnly
Set-Alias nmbx New-Mailbox -Option ReadOnly
Set-Alias rmbx Remove-Mailbox -Option ReadOnly
Set-Alias smbx Set-Mailbox -Option ReadOnly

What's interesting is that this same cmdlet ('Set-Alias') can be used to create a new alias as well. For example, if a
new alias were needed for creating a new mailbox on-premises. The Set-Alias could be used to create this alias as
well:

```
PS C:\> Set-Alias gmt Get-MessageTrace -Description 'Get Message Trace cmdlet'
PS C:\>
```

Removing an Alias

Reviewing the PowerShell cmdlets with the word 'Alias' there are no cmdlet with the word 'remove' in it. How
then can an alias be removed? If the solution cannot be found in PowerShell, then searching for a solution via your
favorite search engine is the next step:

Search string: remove powershell alias

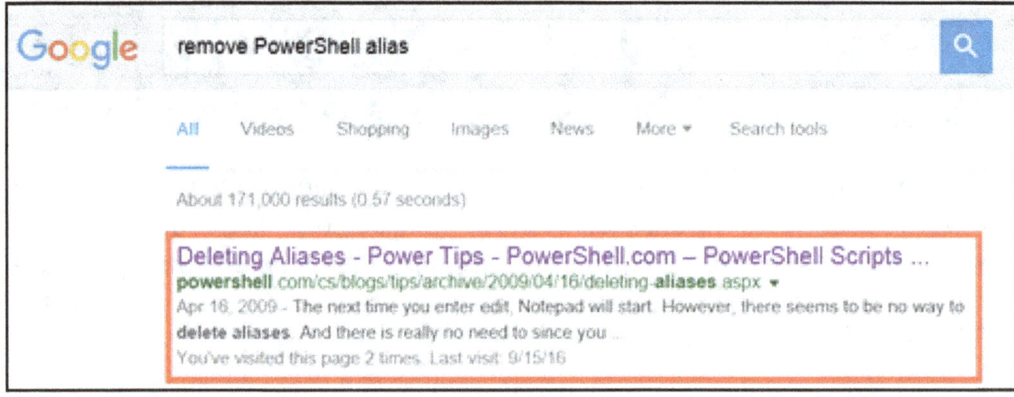

Reviewing the first link from the search, the solution to removing the alias is:

Remove-Item Alias:<alias to remove>

To remove one of the previous aliases that were created use this cmdlet:

    Remove-Item Alias:dmbx

However, there is an error:

```
C:\> Remove-Item Alias:dmbx
Remove-Item : Alias was not removed because alias dmbx is constant or read-only.
line:1 char:1
Remove-Item Alias:dmbx
~~~~~~~~~~~~~~~~~~~~~~~
    + CategoryInfo          : WriteError: (dmbx:String) [Remove-Item], SessionStateUnauthorizedAccessExcepti
    + FullyQualifiedErrorId : AliasNotRemovable,Microsoft.PowerShell.Commands.RemoveItemCommand
```

That means the 'ReadOnly' setting that was applied worked as expected. To remove the ReadOnly option, run this:

    Set-Alias nrm New-RemoteMailbox –Force –Option None
    Remove-Item Alias:nrm

```
PS C:> Set-Alias dmbx Disable-Mailbox -force -option none
PS C:> Remove-Item Alias:dmbx
PS C:>
```

Now if the alias is tried once more, PowerShell fails as the references have been removed:

```
PS C:> dmbx
dmbx : The term 'dmbx' is not recognized as the name of a cmdlet, function, script file, or operable program. Check
the spelling of the name, or if a path was included, verify that the path is correct and try again.
At line:1 char:1
+ dmbx
+ ~~~~
    + CategoryInfo          : ObjectNotFound: (dmbx:String) [], CommandNotFoundException
    + FullyQualifiedErrorId : CommandNotFoundException
```

In the end, creating your own aliases is not required, nor are they necessary, but creating custom aliases may be a more efficient way to write code in PowerShell.

Foreach-Object (%)

While on the topic of PowerShell aliases, there are indeed some useful aliases that point to some rather useful cmdlets that we have not covered. One useful alias is '%'. What does the '%' symbol stand for or abbreviate in PowerShell. We can still use the Get-Alias cmdlet, but we need some criteria for finding just the '%' character in the results. If you recall from the Filtering section earlier in the book, the 'where' filter can help find the '%' symbol. From the screenshot, we also know that the field called 'Name' will contain the value:

    Get-Alias | Where {$_.Name -eq "%"}

```
CommandType     Name
-----------     ----
Alias           % -> ForEach-Object
```

By using that cmdlet we now know that the alias % refers to Foreach-Object. Some other examples of other aliases:

    Get-Alias | Where {$_.Name -eq "ft"}

```
CommandType     Name
-----------     ----
Alias           ft -> Format-Table
```

    Get-Alias | Where {$_.Name -eq "fl"}

```
CommandType     Name
-----------     ----
Alias           fl -> Format-List
```

Circling back to the '%' symbol or Foreach-Object. This particular alias provides for some interesting processing of data. Take for example a scenario where we need to get the SIP address for a user's account in Exchange Online. The address exists in the EmailAddresses property for a mailbox. It is one of a number of addresses that exist there. We can write a one-liner that can pull the entire EmailAddresses property and pull out just the SIP address. In the end, a report that shows this criteria needs to be created and the PowerShell one-liner looks like this:

```
Get-Mailbox | Select-Object DisplayName, @{Expression ={$_.EmailAddresses};Label='SIPAddress'}
| % {$Mail = $_.SIPAddress ; $Email =$Null; Foreach ($Line in $Mail) {$Address = $Line -split ':'; $Prefix
= $Address[0]; if ($Prefix -cmatch 'SIP') {$Email = $Address[1]}};if ($Email -eq $Null) {$Email = 'No SIP
Address'};$_.SIPAddress = $Email;Return $_} | FT -Auto
```

OK. Maybe that was a bit too much at once. Think of the above as what IT Management is looking for. To learn how the Foreach-Object or '%' alias fit into this, start with the results of just the 'Get-Mailbox' that we need for the replication information.

```
Get-Mailbox
```

```
Name                          Alias                 ServerName        ProhibitSendQuota
----                          -----                 ----------        -----------------
damian                        damian                mwhpr1301mb2078   11 GB (11,811,160,064 bytes)
DiscoverySearchMailbox...     DiscoverySearchMa...  mwhpr1301mb2205   50 GB (53,687,091,200 bytes)
john.doe                      john.doe              by2pr13mb0391     99 GB (106,300,440,576 bytes)
```

Notice that we get Name, Alias, ServerName and ProhibitSendQuota. This isn't what we need for our report. Yes, we can use Name and if we want an alias, but we really need to SIP address. So let's user the Get-Mailbox cmdlet to reveal these mailbox properties in table format:

```
Get-Mailbox | where {$_.name -notlike 'Disc*'} | ft Name,Alias,EmailAddresses
```

```
Name      Alias     EmailAddresses
----      -----     --------------
damian    damian    {SPO:SPO_de374a39-6500-4a91-b3e7-dc0b95f8a6b5@SPO_29368d28-0dc7-46c2-80f4-0ccb8ae2c65f, SIP:
john.doe  john.doe  {SIP:john.doe@OnlineExchangeBook.onmicrosoft.com, SMTP:john.doe@OnlineExchangeBook.onmicroso
```

** **Note** ** I also filtered out the Discovery Mailbox as this is not a user mailbox.

The table looks alright, however the EmailAddresses field is a mess. We also see the SIP address in the field, but we also see every other email address as well. We need to parse that field for that address. For readability sake we will also rename the field to 'SIPAddress'.

From the field data, we can determine that there are several address types stored in the EmailAddresses field - SMTP, smtp, SIP and SPO. SPO is for SharePoint Online, SMTP and smtp are our email addresses and SIP is used for Skype Online.

Let's start with the renaming of the column for the EmailAddresses property. This can be done instead of using 'Format-Table' we can use 'Select-Object' in conjunction with 'Expression' and 'Label' formatting method, like so:

```
Get-Mailbox | Where {$_.Name -NotLike 'Disc*'} | Select-Object DisplayName, @{Expression ={$_.
EmailAddresses};Label='SIP Address'
```

This will then change the column heading to show as 'SIP Address' instead of 'Email Addresses':

```
DisplayName     SIP Address
-----------     -----------
Damian Scoles   {SPO:SPO_de374a39-6500-4a91-b3e7-dc0b95f8a6b5@SPO_29368d28-0d
John Doe        {SIP:john.doe@OnlineExchangeBook.onmicrosoft.com, SMTP:john.d
```

Now that this is in place, we can now work with the data in the field and pull out just the SIP Address. How do we go about doing this? Well, we already have the data with we will use the 'Select-Object' cmdlet. We can now manipulate this data with a Foreach-Object, or it's alias of '%'. With this we can manipulate the data using what amounts to a PowerShell code block. In this code block we need to pull out the SIP value from the series of values in the EmailAddresses field. One of the best ways is a Foreach loop to examine each one. We only store the one value that has the key letters 'SIP' in front of it. We can also register a 'No SIP value' phrase if we do not match these letters. First is the 'Foreach-Object' to kick it off:

```
| %
```

We store all of the Email Addresses in a new variable called $Mail. Notice the EmailAddresses value can be turned in a variable by putting '$_.' in front of it. We can do this with any property if we wish to do so:

```
{$Mail = $_.EmailAddresses
```

Next we configure the $SIP variable as $Null. This variable will be used to store a SIP value if found or be left empty and used to trigger the phrase about no SIP address ($Null):

```
$SIP =$Null
```

The next code section is a Foreach loop that will process each entry stored in $Email in a loop:

```
Foreach ($Line in $Mail) {
```

Each entry in the field has a Prefix (SIP, SMTP, etc) that precedes the data we need. We can split that up the values in the $Line variable using a parameter called '-Split'. With this parameter we can then decide which character to separate out with. See these sample values we need to split:

```
Prefix
      Separator Value

  SPO: SPO_de374a39-6500-4a91-b3e7-dc0b95f8a6b5@SPO_29368d28-0dc7-46c2-xxx-0ccb8ae2c65f
  SIP: damian@OnlineExchangeBook.onmicrosoft.com
  SMTP: damian@OnlineExchangeBook.onmicrosoft.com
```

We can store this separated value with the $Address like so:

```
$Address = $Line -split ':'
```

Now the $Address variable stores each part of the original field as a separate column and is numbered starting with the number '0':

```
$Prefix = $Address[0]
```

Once we store the Prefix value in the $Prefix variable we can check it to see if it contains our three special characters of 'SIP' and we also make sure that these letters are capitalized as well:

```
If ($Prefix -cmatch 'SIP') {
```

If there is a match, we can then process it by storing the address value ($Address - field 1) in a variable called SIP, like so:

```
$SIP= $Address[1]}}
```

Once this is done and all the addresses are processed, we can then check to see if the $SIP variable is empty. If it is empty, then the $SIP value is populated with 'No SIP Address' to indicate that no SIP address was found.

```
If ($SIP -eq $Null) {$SIP = 'No SIP Address'}
```

At the very end of the line, we need to then return this information back to be displayed, This requires we first use the original variable from the beginning ($EmailAddresses) as well as a 'Return' cmdlet:

```
$_.EmailAddresses = $SIP
Return $_}
```

Once all of these pieces are in place we now have a one-liner that will give us a mailbox's DisplayName and SIP address in a nicely formatted and labeled table:

```
Get-Mailbox | Select-Object DisplayName, @{Expression ={$_.EmailAddresses};Label='SIP Address'} | % {$Mail = $_.EmailAddresses ; $SIP =$Null; Foreach ($Line in $Mail) {$Address = $Line -split ':'; $Prefix = $Address[0]; If ($Prefix -cmatch 'SIP') {$SIP = $Address[1]}};If ($SIP -eq $Null) {$SIP = 'No SIP Address'};$_.EmailAddresses = $SIP ; Return $_} | FT -Auto
```

However, when we run this code, we get LOTS of red. What went wrong?

```
% : Exception setting "EmailAddresses": "The property 'EmailAddresses' cannot be found on this object. Verify that the
property exists and can be set."
At line:1 char:99
+ ... Address'} | % {$Mail = $_.EmailAddresses ; $Email =$Null; Foreach ($L ...
+
    + CategoryInfo          : NotSpecified: (:) [ForEach-Object], SetValueInvocationException
    + FullyQualifiedErrorId : ExceptionWhenSetting,Microsoft.PowerShell.Commands.ForEachObjectCommand
```

Well, the error message doesn't make sense, does it? The error states that the property 'EmailAddress'cannot be found on the object. It appears that the error message is related to the Mailbox object and its EmailAddresses object. However, this is not the case. The error relates to the label of the column, which is 'SIP Address' and the variable used in the Foreach-Object which is '$EmailAddresses'. These values are different, which causes the error message to occur. Instead, these values need to match like so:

```
PS C:\> Get-Mailbox | Select-Object DisplayName, @{Expression =($_.EmailAddresses);Label='SIPAddress'} | % {$Mail =
$_.SIPAddress ; $Email =$Null; Foreach ($Line in $Mail) ($Address = $Line -split ':'; $Prefix = $Address[0]; if ($Prefi
-cmatch 'SIP') ($Email = $Address[1]};if ($Email -eq $Null) ($Email = 'No SIP Address');$_.SIPAddress = $Email;Return
$_} | FT -Auto

DisplayName                      SIPAddress
-----------                      ----------
Damian Scoles            damian@OnlineExchangeBook.onmicrosoft.com
Discovery Search Mailbox No SIP Address
John Doe                 john.doe@OnlineExchangeBook.onmicrosoft.com
```

Code Summary

Taking all of the above information and synthesizing it, we get this long one-liner to handle the heavy lifting for us. What is nice is that we can substitute the 'SIP' phrase for 'SMTP' or even 'smtp' if we want to customize it for a different search.

```
Get-Mailbox | Select-Object DisplayName, @{Expression ={$_.EmailAddresses};Label='SIPAddress'} | % {$Mail = $_.SIPAddress ; $Email =$Null; Foreach ($Line in $Mail) {$Address = $Line -split ':'; $Prefix = $Address[0]; If ($Prefix -cmatch 'SIP') {$Email = $Address[1]}};If ($Email -eq $Null) {$Email = 'No SIP Address'};$_.SIPAddress = $Email;Return $_} | FT -Auto
```

```
DisplayName                      SIPAddress
-----------                      ----------
Damian Scoles            damian@OnlineExchangeBook.onmicrosoft.com
Discovery Search Mailbox No SIP Address
John Doe                 john.doe@OnlineExchangeBook.onmicrosoft.com
```

PowerShell Interface Customization

Working space is important in PowerShell and this means screen buffering. Why is this important?   The default line buffer limit is 300 which can be too small depending on what script output of cmdlet output is being run. For example, just running 'Get-Help New-ReceiveConnector' can overrun that buffer. This makes it hard to use PowerShell to its fullest. So, just changing the buffer size will make PowerShell that much easier to work with.

** **Note** ** These changes are local to the machine where the changes are made.

Before - 300 Character Buffer

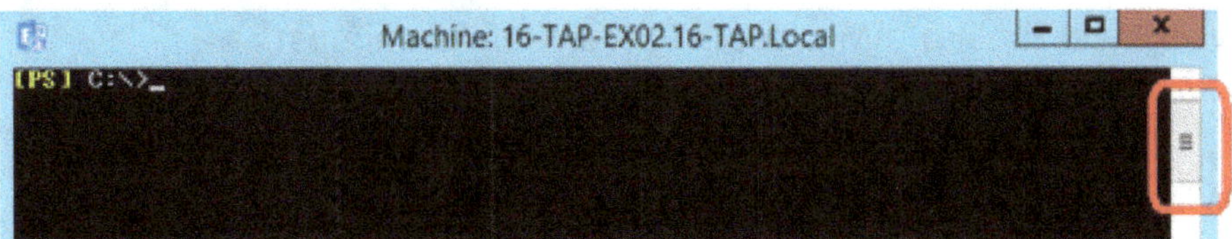

To make the change, click on the icon in the upper left and select Properties (see below):

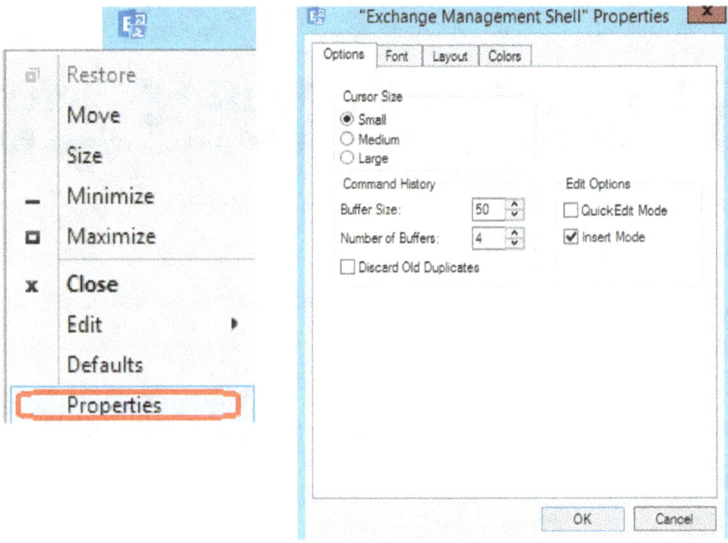

Adjust the 300 to 9999:

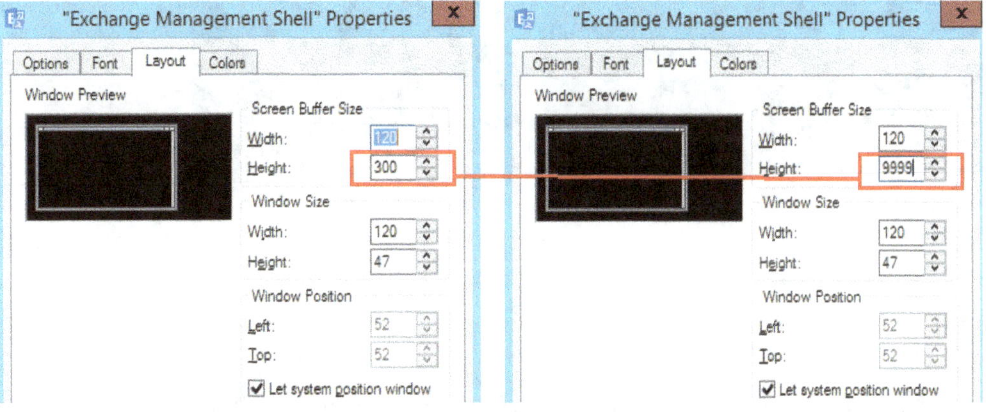

After - 9999 Character Buffer

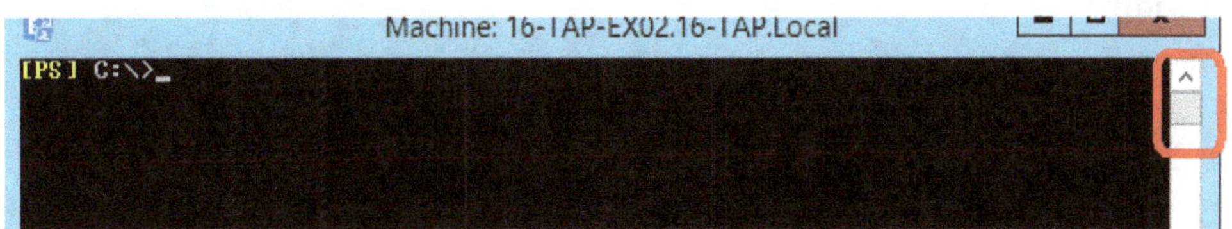

Notice the smaller size of the slider on the right. Now output from most, if not all cmdlets, will not exceed the window buffer size. If the output is in excess of 9999 lines, it may be better to export the results to a TXT, CSV or some other sort of file. Make sure to save these settings so we won't have to keep making this change.

In addition to the above, startup options can be created for the PowerShell window to customize it more. There are several locations for customization files for PowerShell and they vary in their functionality. The two we will work with for this chapter are:

For all users - PowerShell

%windir%\system32\Windows¬PowerShell\v1.0\Microsoft.Powershell_profile.ps1

Current user - PowerShell

%UserProfile%\Documents\WindowsPowerShell\Microsoft.Powershell_profile.ps1

Before creating a new one, verify that one has not yet been created. Backup the old profile if needed for later. First verify the current PowerShell profile:

$Profile

```
PS C:\> $Profile
C:\Users\administrator.16-TAP\Documents\WindowsPowerShell\Microsoft.PowerShell_profile.ps1
PS C:\>
```

To see if the file was already created and in use (if $True, then the file exists, otherwise it does not):

Test-Path $Profile

```
PS C:\> Test-Path $Profile
False
PS C:\>
```

In the above case, the profile has not been created and if we wish to add customizations we'll need to create our own file.

New-Item -Path $Profile –ItemType File –Force

```
PS C:\> New-Item -Path $Profile -ItemType File -Force


    Directory: C:\Users\administrator.16-TAP\Documents\WindowsPowerShell


Mode                LastWriteTime         Length Name
----                -------------         ------ ----
-a---          2/26/2017    6:49 PM              0 Microsoft.PowerShell_profile.ps1
```

Once the file has been created you can open this in your favorite editor.

What Can Be Added to This File

The following is a list of some of the customizations that can be performed with the profile file:

- Window sizing (height and width)
- Load custom scripts
- Windows colors

Window Sizing and Coloring

The size of the console is stored in this variable $Host which is a known variable in PowerShell.

$Host

```
PS C:\> $Host


Name               : ConsoleHost
Version            : 4.0
InstanceId         : 6d3a530c-8f0f-48cd-b4c1-0f5d73a3eb78
UI                 : System.Management.Automation.Internal.Host.InternalHostUserInterface
CurrentCulture     : en-US
CurrentUICulture   : en-US
PrivateData        : Microsoft.PowerShell.ConsoleHost+ConsoleColorProxy
IsRunspacePushed   : False
Runspace           : System.Management.Automation.Runspaces.LocalRunspace
```

Notice the UI parameter is for the User Interface. To find out what is stored in it, run this:

$Host.UI

```
PS C:\> $Host.UI

RawUI
-----
System.Management.Automation.Internal.Host.InternalHostRawUserInterface
```

That was rather unhelpful, how do we see the values stored for the UI so that changes can be made?

$Host.UI.RawUI

```
PS C:\> $Host.UI.RawUI

ForegroundColor        : DarkYellow
BackgroundColor        : DarkMagenta
CursorPosition         : 0,43
WindowPosition         : 0,0
CursorSize             : 25
BufferSize             : 120,3000
WindowSize             : 120,50
MaxWindowSize          : 120,72
MaxPhysicalWindowSize  : 242,72
KeyAvailable           : False
WindowTitle            : Administrator: Windows PowerShell
```

We now see the buffer size and Window Size as well as colors for the window. For this sample, the window will have a background of gray and a foreground of black. The buffer will be widened to 160 and shortened to 6000. Next the Window Size will increase to 160 and then length to 85.

```
$Shell = $Host.UI.RawUI
$Shell.ForegroundColor = "Black"
$Shell.BackgroundColor = "Gray"
$Buffer = $Shell.BufferSize
$Buffer.Width = 160
$Buffer.Height = 6000
$Shell.BufferSize = $Buffer
$Window=$Shell.WindowSize
$Window.Width = 160
$Window.Height = 50
```

```
$Shell.WindowSize = $Window
```

The custom colors change the PowerShell window like this:

```
PS] C:\Windows\system32>cd \
PS] C:\>
PS] C:\>_
```

In the end, when the new customized PowerShell window is opened, there may be an error message displayed. The reason is that in order to load a script with the PowerShell window, the permissions for Script Execution need to be something above Restricted, which is the default permission. For example, the 'RemoteSigned' permission will allow the script to be loaded.

```
Set-ExecutionPolicy RemoteSigned
```

That will ensure the customizations will work. Loading scripts when opening a PowerShell window requires a couple of items. First changing the location of the PowerShell window to a directory where the scripts are stored:

```
Set-Location C:\Psscripts
```

As a final step of configuring the profile script, we could run another script (below) stored the above folder:

```
.\CheckMailboxConfig.PS1
```

The example script above, would return various settings for our mailboxes - retention policies, quotas, OWA Mailbox Policy Mobile Device policies and more. Combining all of these steps together would results in this profile script:

```
# Load all shell parameters
$Shell = $host.UI.RawUI
$Shell.ForegroundColor = "Black"
$Shell.BackgroundColor = "Gray"
$Buffer = $Shell.BufferSize
$Buffer.Width = 160
$Buffer.Height = 6000
$Shell.BufferSize = $buffer
$Window=$Shell.WindowSize
$Window.Width = 160
$Window.Height = 50
$Shell.WindowSize = $Window
# Run Exchange Services check script
Set-Location C:\Psscripts
.\ExchangeServices.PS1
```

There are plenty of other options and additions that can be made to your PowerShell profile, but they will not all be listed here.

Command Logging

PowerShell is very important to Exchange Online and even the Exchange Administration Console leverages PowerShell. The question is, can this be made visible? The answer is yes, it can. What benefits does this give to those who want to use PowerShell to maintain their Exchange Online environment? For starters, when the PowerShell commands are revealed, insight may be gained into how to use the various switches and parameters when config-uring an item in PowerShell. That's great, but how do we turn it on? By logging into the Exchange Administration console, click on the Administrator drop down button and selecting the 'Show Command Logging' option.

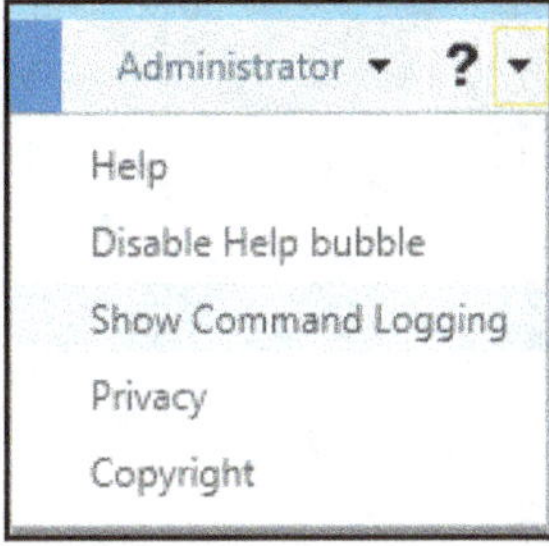

Once this is done, another window will pop-up so have your pop-up blocker turned off. The window looks some-thing like this:

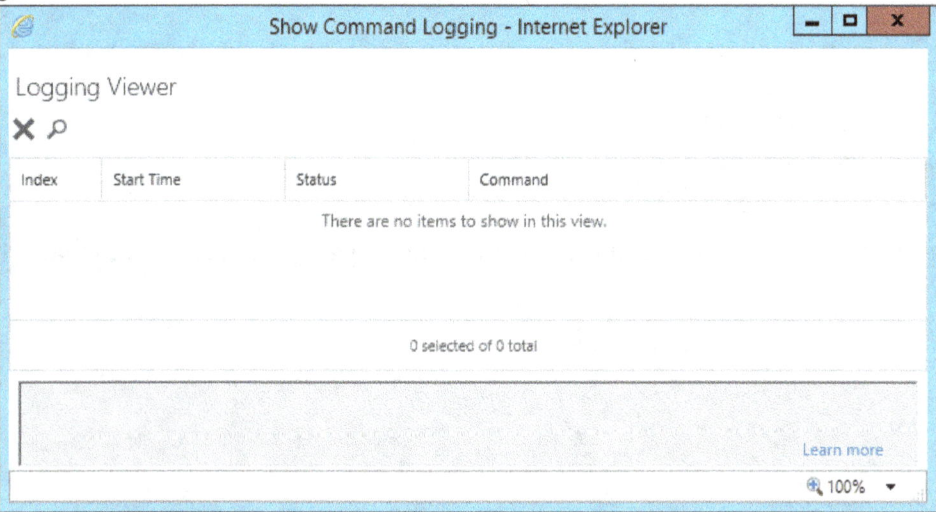

Notice that all boxes in the window are completely empty. To get commands to show here, we now need to manage our Exchange Server. Let's take for an example that I want to perform a Message Trace for all messages coming into the environment. First click on 'Mail Flow' and then click on 'Message Trace':

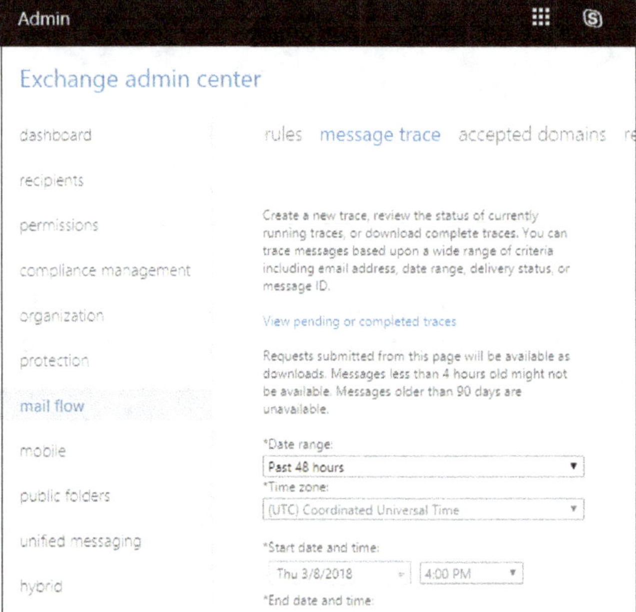

Now we can enter some parameters for a Message Trace - Date Range, Delivery Status and Recipient:

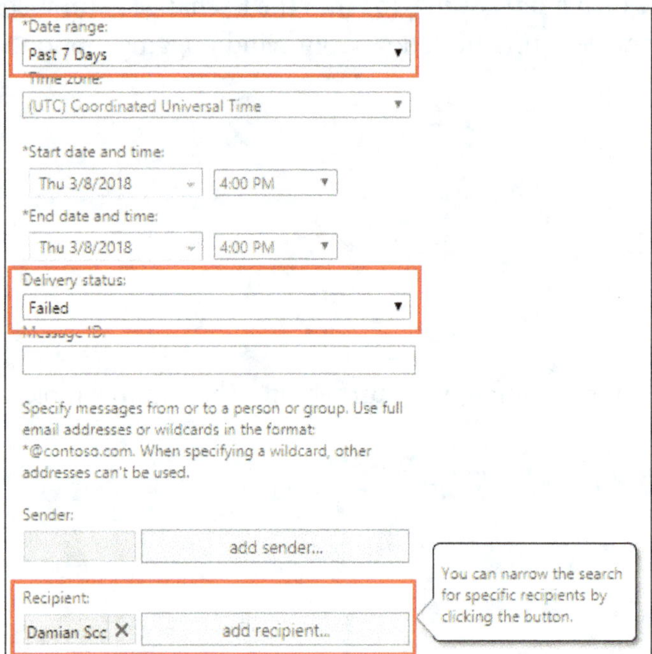

Then we can click 'Search' to get our results and then we review the Command Logging window to see what actions were taken in PowerShell:

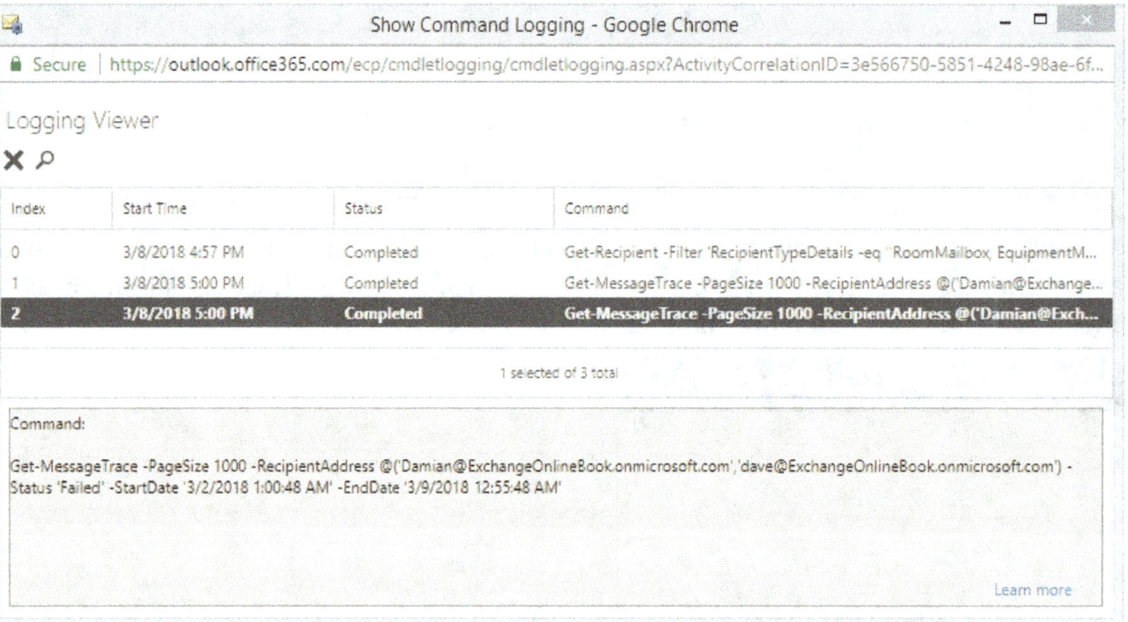

What can be gleaned from this information and how can an administrator use it to improve knowledge of Power-Shell? First, take a look at the cmdlets that are listed. Notice that there are two cmdlets listed, Get-Recipient:

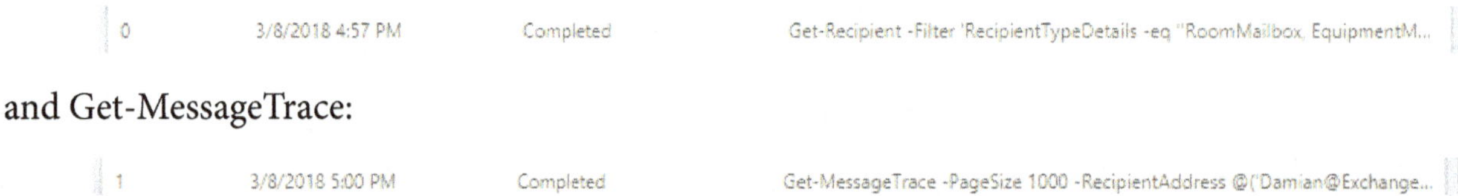

and Get-MessageTrace:

The two Get-MessageTrace cmdlets have a -PageSize of 1000 which is the default size for a Message Trace query and as we learned earlier in the book, we can manipulate how many results or records are queried. The other nice part of this Command Logging window is that we can copy and paste the cmdlets and the three that ran in our example copy and paste here as (second and third are duplicates):

```
Get-Recipient -Filter 'RecipientTypeDetails -eq "RoomMailbox, EquipmentMailbox, LegacyMailbox,
LinkedMailbox, UserMailbox, MailContact, DynamicDistributionGroup, MailForestContact, MailNon-
UniversalGroup, MailUniversalDistributionGroup, MailUniversalSecurityGroup, MailUser, PublicFolder,
TeamMailbox, SharedMailbox, RemoteUserMailbox"' -Properties 'PrimarySmtpAddress,Display-
Name,ArchiveGuid,AuthenticationType,RecipientType,RecipientTypeDetails,ResourceType,Window-
sLiveID,Identity,ExchangeVersion,OrganizationId,City,Company,CountryOrRegion,Department,Of-
fice,Title' -ResultSize 500


Get-MessageTrace -PageSize 1000 -RecipientAddress @('Damian@ExchangeOnlineBook.onmicrosoft.
com','dave@ExchangeOnlineBook.onmicrosoft.com') -Status 'Failed' -StartDate '3/2/2018 1:00:48 AM'
-EndDate '3/9/2018 12:55:48 AM'
```

Now we can use the above Get-MessageTrace cmdlet and try it in PowerShell to see what we get as a result. In this case the 'Failed' status provides us with zero results and is helpful in determining that these two users did not have any messages that failed to deliver. If we were to remove that condition, so that it were to look for all messages, the cmdlet would look like this:

```
Get-MessageTrace -PageSize 1000 -RecipientAddress @('Damian@ExchangeOnlineBook.onmicrosoft.
com','dave@ExchangeOnlineBook.onmicrosoft.com')  -StartDate  '3/2/2018  1:00:48  AM'  -EndDate
'3/9/2018 12:55:48 AM'
```

Which does provide results:

Received	Sender Address	Recipient Address	Subject	Status
3/6/2018 7:11:52 AM	damian@practicalpowershell.com	dave@exchangeonlinebook.onmicrosoft.com	test journaling	Delivere
3/6/2018 7:04:13 AM	damian@practicalpowershell.com	damian@exchangeonlinebook.onmicrosoft.com	Test	Delivere

Index

A

abbreviation 159, 178, 221, 391, 421
AcceptedDomains 210-211
AcceptLargeDataLoss 297
AcceptMessagesOnlyFrom 195-196
AccessLevel 310, 312
AccessRights 158, 168, 176-178, 330-332
account 10-11, 36, 68-69, 72, 76, 79, 81-82, 84, 90, 94, 100, 102, 109-112, 148-152, 160, 211, 216, 225, 262, 279, 281, 305, 313-314, 331, 347, 353, 373, 413
AccountDisabled 150
AccountPassword 100
accounts viii, xiii, 10-11, 80-81, 84-85, 90, 100, 108, 153-154, 178, 217, 280, 317, 373, 423
AccountSkuId 109, 111, 116, 350
Acknowledgments vii
ActiveDirectory 50-51, 85, 87, 99, 388
ActiveGroups 49, 53-54
ActiveSync xiii, 9-11, 119-122, 156-157, 239, 242, 304-305, 311, 313-315, 317, 405-407
ActiveSyncAllowedDeviceIDs124, 313
ActiveSyncBlockedDeviceIDs 124
ActiveSyncDebugLogging 122
ActiveSyncEnabled 120, 156, 317, 407
ActiveSyncMailboxPolicy 150, 157, 306-307
AddAdditionalResponse 156
Add-ADGroupMember 114
Add-ADPermission 177
Add-Content 63-64
AddDays 48, 52
Add-DistributionGroupMember 377
AdditionalResponse 156
AddLicenses 111, 116, 391
Add-MailboxFolderPermission 158
Add-MailboxPermission 157-158, 176-177
Add-ManagementRoleEntry 263
Add-Member 351
ADDomain 105
AddOrganizerToSubject 156
Add-RecipientPermission 158, 177-178
address ix, x, 2, 10, 16, 28, 48-49, 52-56, 58, 74, 80-81, 85, 88-92, 100-101, 119, 122, 129-136, 147-151, 153-154, 158, 160, 162, 170, 174, 203, 208-211, 216-217, 221, 232-236, 241, 263, 292-294, 296, 304, 314, 327-328, 341, 345-346, 353, 364, 380, 382-383, 407, 413-415

AddressBookPolicy 136, 150
addressing 336
AddressList 2, 131, 132, 135-136
AddressSpaces 203
Add-RoleGroupMember 254, 272
Add-WindowsFeature 51
AddXHeader 221
AdfsAuthentication 142-143
AdminAddress 49, 56-57, 392
AdminAudit 281
AdminAuditLogCmdlets 282
AdminAuditLogExcludedCmdlets 282
AdminAuditLogParameters 282
administrator vii, 48, 66-67, 76, 113, 156, 168, 172, 177, 233, 262, 271, 273, 281, 284, 286, 293, 316, 319, 341-342, 348, 353, 380-381, 420-421
administrators 66-67, 121, 188, 213, 216, 222, 262, 286
AdminMailRecipients 311
ADSIEdit 10-11
ADSync 103, 106, 380
AgeLimit 324
-AgeLimit 324
AgeLimitForRetention 357, 359, 361, 363
AirSyncNumbers 344
AirWatch 314
alerting 54
alerts 69, 188
aliases xv, 35, 82, 100, 211, 398-399, 403, 409-412
alleviates 373
AllGroups 49, 53
AllItems 388
AllMailboxCount 199
AllMailboxes 13
AllowAccess 143, 145
AllowCamera 309
AllowIncrementalSyncs 294, 295
AllowLargeItems 297
AllowNonProvisionableDevices 242, 307
AllowRedirection 51, 62, 76, 115, 203, 224, 250
AllowUMCallsFromNonUsers 344
AllowUnknownColumnsInCsv 294
AllSigned 44
alphabetically 52
alphanumeric 307
AlphanumericPasswordRequired 308
AlwaysShowFrom 155
Android 68, 70, 72-73, 122, 157, 304, 307, 310

anonymous   167
anti-hammering   309
Anti-Malware 214, 249
Anti-Spam   170, 249
anti-virus   214
AnyOfAuthenticationTypes   142
AnyOfClientIPAddressesOrRanges   142
AnyOfProtocols   142-145
anyone 9, 43, 148, 193, 201, 224, 228, 308, 332, 392
anything   10, 20, 39, 272, 291, 296, 319, 410
Anywhere   120, 296, 376
append   208, 349, 350-352, 354, 361
Appendix   219, 388, 390, 392, 394, 396, 398, 400, 402, 404, 406, 408, 410, 412, 414, 416, 418, 420, 422
ApplicationImpersonation   263, 279-280
ApplyHtmlDisclaimerLocation   208
ApplyHtmlDisclaimerText   19, 208
ApplyOME   245
ApplyRightsProtectionTemplate   241-242
ApprovalRequired   188
Archive   xi, 5, 10, 23, 39, 77, 79, 147-148, 151, 157, 294, 297
ArchiveApplication   264
ArchiveGuid   422
ArchiveName 151
ArchiveOnly   294, 297
ArchiveQuota 13
archives   23
ArchiveState   80
ArchiveStatus   39
archiving   79, 234, 249
Argumentlist 50, 61, 115
arrays viii, xv, 12-14, 16, 47, 49, 353, 368, 380, 385, 400
AsPlainText   149
AsSecureString   50, 149
assign 116, 128-129, 131-132, 136, 157, 160, 175-176, 217, 249, 254, 256, 272-273, 279-281, 306-307, 329-330, 332, 340-341, 343
assigned   44, 54-55, 58-59, 62, 81, 109, 113, 115, 123, 126, 129, 131, 149, 152, 157-158, 172, 176-178, 189, 209, 211, 251-253, 262-263, 266-268, 270-277, 279-280, 305-306, 328-329, 331, 341, 343, 346-347, 350, 362, 366, 371, 388
AssignedRoles 252, 276
assigning   xiii, 58, 112-113, 116, 129, 157, 176-177, 272, 306, 328, 340-341

assignment   113, 156-157, 251, 272-273, 275, 277-279, 281, 331
Assignments   153, 157, 251, 276
Assigns   188
AssociatedItemCount 326
asterisk   32
Asynchronous 365
Attach 72
AttachmentNameMatchesPatterns   208-209
attachments   69, 72, 126, 208, 209, 227, 228, 230, 249, 84, 302, 314, 364-365
AttachOriginalMail   209
Attendant   336
attribute   53-54, 58, 89-91, 96-97, 101-102, 136, 144, 167, 199, 250, 296, 298, 346
attributes   10-11, 32-33, 74, 76, 88, 97-101, 105, 144, 147-148, 150, 152, 161-162, 294, 300, 324, 349, 369, 383
auditable   282
AuditAdmin   286
AuditAndNotify   226-227
AuditDelegate 286
audited   281-282, 286-287
AuditEnabled 286
auditing   xiii, 154, 162, 172, 262, 281, 286-287
AuditLog   286
AuditLogAgeLimit   286
AuditOwner   286
Audits   282, 286
authenticate   62, 95, 292, 309
authenticated 148
authentication 50, 51, 62, 6, 77, 86, 95, 115, 142-143, 146, 202, 203, 213, 224, 250, 304, 307, 353, 365, 366
AuthenticationType   145, 422
Authority   10, 99, 178
AutoAccept   156, 179-180
AutoAddSignature   155
AutoBooking   178-179
AutoCleanDeletedItems   157
AutoComplete   293-294
Auto-Completion   23
AutoDetect   365
AutoDiscover   158
AutoExpanding   151
AutoExpandingArchive   151
Automapping   158
AutomateProcessing   156, 179-180

Automation   1, 50, 61, 115, 393
AutoReplyState   159
AutoStart   293, 294
AutoSuspended   301
availability   69, 72, 94, 158, 179, 313, 319
AvailabilityOnly   168
AzureAD   6-7
azure-ad-connect-staging   108

B

background   xiii, 212, 261, 304, 318, 334, 366, 418
BackgroundColor   358-359, 383 418-419
backup   373, 417
BadItemLimit   293-296, 297
BadSMTP   91-92
bandwidth   366
BaseDomain   405
BasicAuthentication   142-143
Batches   292, 294-298, 300-301
BatchMove   293-294
batchname   293, 297-298, 301
BccMessage   221
Behalf   72, 157-158
Bgcolor   360, 363
bifurcation   52
BigEndianUnicode   228
binary   228
binding   xv, 387, 399
bleeding   70
blocked   xiii, 44, 126-127, 170, 180, 194, 209, 218, 277, 308, 310-311, 313, 316
BlockedFileTypes   126-1288
Bluetooth   309
BodyAsHtml   56-58, 64, 364-365, 392
BookInPolicy   180
Book-Retention-Policy-Tags   360, 362
Border 360, 362-363
borders   362
BoxAttachmentsEnabled   126
bracket   21, 30-31, 199, 376
bracketing   22, 26
brackets   ix, 14, 17, 19-23, 26, 30, 62, 374
branded   247
branding   246
breaches   160

Breaking   xiv, 28, 287, 368-369
breakpoint   375, 380
breaks   108, 201, 371, 388
browser   120, 358, 394
buffer   416-419
BufferSize   418-419
built-in   20, 119, 213, 225, 251, 256-257, 268, 335
button   iii, 184, 231, 245, 420
bypass   44

C

Calendar   xi, 70, 72-73, 148, 155-159, 166-168, 174-175, 178, 180, 198, 302, 304, 322-324, 328, 344
calendars   148, 178
CallAnsweringAudioCodec   344, 345
CallAnsweringRulesEnabled   344
camera   305, 309
CAN-FILE   366
Capacity   181-182, 308
Capitalization ix, xv, 26-27, 55, 387, 391, 398, 401, 414
CASChanges   406, 408
case-insensitive   27, 64
CASMailbox x, 120, 138, 340
CASMailboxPlan   x, 123
CellPadding   360, 363
Centralized   xi, 201, 206-207, 249
certificate   45-46, 203, 304
CertificateBasedAuthentication   142-143
ChangeOwner 176
ChangePermission   176
Change-Quotas   391
characteristic 174, 310-311
CheckBeforeSend   155
CheckMailboxConfig 419
Check-OldDisclaimers   19
ChronologicalNewestOnTop 155
circular   382
claims 86
classes 311
classification   72, 228-230, 232, 248-249, 254
Clear-ActiveSyncDevice   314
Clear-MobileDevice 314
ClientAccessServerEnabled   239, 242
Cloud-Only   viii, 9-10, 149

CloudServicesMailEnabled 202, 203
cmatch 55, 57, 391, 413-415
CmdletBinding 399
cmdletbindingattribute 399
CmdletCheck 61, 63-65
code-signing 46
CodeSigningCert 46
coexistence 66, 74, 88, 97, 291
Colspan 360-361, 363
commas 295
comma-separated 180
comment 27-29, 46-47 , 57, 59, 71, 360, 372-373, 387-389, 400, 408
comments xiv, xv, 21-23, 26-29, 65, 208, 241, 245, 259, 368, 372-373, 387-388
Compare-Object 53, 127-128
CompleteAfter 298-299
CompletedRequestAgeLimit 299
CompletedWithWarning 301
Complete-MigrationBatch 295
CompletionInProgress 301
Compliance xii, 69, 72-73, 75, 160, 212, 214, 216, 218, 220, 222-226, 228, 230, 232, 234-236, 238, 240, 242, 244, 246, 248-250, 252, 254-256, 258-260, 262-264, 266, 268, 270-272, 274, 276, 278, 280-282, 284, 286, 288, 290, 424
conditional 17, 87, 142, 304, 307
conditions 72, 138, 241, 262, 291, 390
confidential 228-230, 241, 251, 256-257, 423
ConfidentialInformation 225, 258
configurable 69, 72, 105, 122, 139, 153, 214, 282
configuration x, xiv, 2-3, 10-11, 44, 74, 79, 82, 86-88, 96, 106-107, 119, 124, 130, 141, 147, 153, 156, 159, 161, 165-166, 170-173, 194, 201-202, 206-207, 212-215, 219, 221-222, 234, 239-240, 244-247, 262-264, 279, 281-282, 295, 306, 308, 312, 328, 335-337, 341, 344-349, 359, 390, 406
-ConfigurationName 51, 62, 76, 115, 203, 224, 250
ConfiguredPlan 346-347
configure-policy-templates 240
Confirm 58, 59, 152, 179, 239, 260, 344, 346, 399
confirmation 69, 314
Connect-AzureAD 7
connected 62, 148, 157, 160, 210, 225, 250, 258, 305, 315, 384
Connect-EXOPSSession 152
ConnectionFilter 218

ConnectionUri 51, 62, 75, 76, 115, 203, 224, 250
Connect-MSOLService 77, 115, 117, 152
connector iv, xi, 105-106, 201-207, 353
connectors x, xi, 105-106, 201-202, 204-206, 353
ConnectorSource 202-203
ConnectorType 202-203
console iii, 10-11, 37, 84-85, 108, 112, 240, 248-250, 254, 418-420
consumer 72, 319, 356
contact 49, 72, 147-148, 151, 153, 216, 312, 329, 345, 393
ContactCount 326
Contacts xi, 48, 148, 151, 159, 304, 393
contain 13-14, 56, 63, 107, 135, 193, 208, 254, 294, 309, 318, 341, 348, 356, 360, 385, 412
containing 13, 212, 313, 355-356
contains 13-14, 16, 34, 52, 58, 89, 100, 108, 126, 151, 188, 216, 227-229, 243, 262, 294, 321, 338, 380, 398, 414
ContentIndexStatus 5
context 189, 208, 251
ControlPanel 241, 259
ConversationSortOrder 155
conversion 373
convert 49, 83, 160-161, 198-199
converted 81, 84, 160, 185, 229
ConvertFrom-SecureString 49-50, 115
Converting xi, 147, 160, 198, 373
ConvertTo-Html 356-359, 383-384
ConvertTo-SecureString 49-50, 61, 100, 115, 149
corrupt 293-294, 302
corrupted 297
counter 16-18, 189, 389
countries 234, 337-338
country 111, 150, 234-235, 337-339
CountryOrRegion 143, 422
CountryOrRegionCode 339
counts 199, 369
CreateItems 329-330
creates 33, 233, 280, 292, 297, 336
CreateSubfolders 329-330
CreationAgeInDays 256
creations 226
Credential 550, 1, 62, 76, 115, 203, 224, 250, 364-365
credentials 49-50, 61-62, 76-77, 111, 292, 293, 314, 355

criteria 34, 89, 117, 131, 133, 142, 145, 177, 182, 187-188, 209, 212, 225-227, 240, 259, 284, 341, 353-354, 367, 412-413
crossover 224
cross-premises 203
CSVData 293-294
CSVFileData 15-17
cumulative 44, 112, 305
CurrentChanges 64-65
CurrentChart 61, 63
CurrentFileTypes 127-128
CustomAttribute 53-54, 58, 131, 136, 143, 145, 234-235
CustomExternalBody 216
CustomExternalSubject 216
CustomFromAddress 216
CustomFromName 216
CustomInternalBody 216
CustomInternalSubject 216
customizable 256
customization 71, 155, 223, 267, 356, 403, 409, 416-417, 419
CustomizedSyncCycleInterval 104
customizing 240, 403
CustomNotifications 216
CustomRecipientWriteScope 281
Cutting 109

D

daemon 365
dashboard 66-68, 72
database 4, 29, 33-34, 94, 148, 154, 172, 185, 232, 297, 300, 303, 318-319, 353, 383-385, 388
databases 4-5, 16, 33, 148, 174, 185, 291, 297, 303, 318-319, 383
datacenters 281
dataClass 230
DateFormat 159
Date-MailboxStat 354
dd-MM-yy 159
Debugging xiv, 368, 375, 390
decrypting 49, 245
DefaultAccessLevel 311, 312
DefaultLanguage 338-339
defaults 31, 97, 154, 221, 314

dehydrated 267
delegate 156, 270, 277, 286-287
DeleteAllItems 329-330
DeleteItem 176
DeleteMessage 209
DeleteOwnedItems 329-330
Delete-QuarantineMessage 70
delimited 295
delimiter 353-354
delineated 9
DeliverToMailboxAndForward 153
DenyAccess 144-145
Department 100, 143, 177, 179-180, 187, 195, 197, 208, 216-217, 233-234, 260, 273, 322-324, 329, 331-332, 346, 388, 422
departmental 174, 322-323, 329-331
DepartmentMember 330-332
Departments 174, 212, 322, 324, 329, 331-332
deprecated 60, 259, 306-307, 311, 314-315
Descending 356
describe 2, 29, 388
described 27, 303, 366, 386
description 7-8, 26, 28, 47, 51, 72, 181-182, 194, 220, 229, 253, 260, 297, 366-367, 369, 372, 388, 400, 410
Determinationx, 110, 138
determine 39, 54, 88, 138, 170, 189, 217, 264, 272, 274, 280, 294, 307, 320, 328, 364, 371, 374, 390, 394, 401, 413
determined 108, 233, 385
determines 188, 227
device xiii, 97, 120, 156-157, 242, 304-316, 419
DeviceAccessState 316
DeviceEncryptionEnabled 306
DeviceFriendlyName 316
DeviceID 313, 316
DeviceModel 310-312
DeviceOS 310-311, 314-315
DevicePasswordEnabled 242
devices xiii, 9, 97, 157, 242, 304-316
DeviceType 310-311, 315
Devicetypes 315
DeviceUserAgent 310-311
DeviceWipeSucceeded 316
diagnose 122
diagnostics 122
DialByNameSecondary 340

DialPlan 336
dictionary 68-69
DictionaryLanguage 155
DifferenceObject 128
differences 9, 14, 53, 191
Digest 365
Digits 155, 308, 338
Directory ix, x, 1-2, 5-6, 10-11, 23, 35, 48-51, 61, 65, 72, 74, 76-77, 79-84, 86-88, 90, 93-99, 101-106, 113, 115-116, 138, 148-150, 162, 171, 175, 187, 225, 237, 279, 296, 369, 419
DirectReports 196
DirSync 87
dirteam vi, 87
disable 58-59, 110, 140, 150, 156, 160, 236, 239, 307, 309, 345, 410
disabled xiii, 48-49, 54, 57-59, 110, 113-115, 120, 122, 126, 130, 141, 148, 154, 156-157, 226, 236, 240, 317, 373, 375, 380-381, 406
Disable-DistributionGroup 59
DisabledOptions 110-111, 116
DisabledOptionsIW 115
DisabledOptionsMKT 115
DisabledOptionsWH 114
DisabledPlans 111, 116
Disable-Journal 236
Disable-JournalRule 236
Disable-Mailbox 152, 266, 410-411
Disable-MailPublicFolder 327
Disable-SweepRule 70
Disable-UMMailbox 266, 345
Disclaimer 19-20, 208, 247
DisclaimerText 246
discoverable 198
Discovery viii, 5, 140, 212, 240, 273-274, 327, 353-354, 406, 413
DiscoveryHolds 170
DisplayName 17, 29, 36, 39, 56-57, 82-84, 100, 126, 128, 133, 140, 149, 150, 175, 184, 189-190, 276, 303, 323, 346-347, 349-350, 354-356, 365-367, 390, 392-393, 397-398, 405-406, 413, 415, 422
DistinguishedName 89-91, 132-134, 196
distributed 2, 319
DistributionGroup 388
Distribution-Group-Cleanup-59
DistributionGroupCount 199-200
DistributionGroups 189-190

DLIdentities 198
DLName 56-58, 392
dlpcustomtypes 258
DlpKeywordDictionary 69
DlpSensitiveInformation 257
DlpSensitiveInformationType 225
documentation 8, 80, 99, 139, 142, 202, 204-205, 343, 349, 352, 357-359, 366, 372, 388, 408
documented 27, 69, 204-206, 390
documenting 205, 323, 348, 353, 387-388
documents 228, 231-232, 417
domain xii, 2, 49, 79, 81, 85, 87, 96, 105, 109-111, 136-137, 149, 154, 203, 209-211, 213-214, 260, 281, 296, 365, 389, 392, 405
DomainController 239, 344
DomainName 210-211
DomainValidation 203
Dropbox 126
DropboxAttachmentsEnabled 126
DynamicDistribution 190
DynamicDistributionGroup 422
DynDistributionGroupCount 199-200
earlier 58-59, 103, 219, 249-250, 260, 292, 321, 332, 346, 391, 393, 401, 412, 422

E

eDiscovery 72-73, 240, 248-249, 253, 259, 272-274
eDiscoveryManager 252-254
eDiscoverySuperUserEnabled 239-240
EditAllItems 329-330
EditOwnedItems 329-330
EditSubsetGroups 157
EmailAddress 55, 57, 85, 160, 293-294, 328, 413-415
EmailAddressPolicy 92
EmailAddressPolicyEnabled 91, 149, 328
Emailtext 246
EmployeePII-Form 228
EmployeeRemoval 102
EnabledCmdlets 266
Enable-JournalRule 236
Enable-Mailbox 79, 150-151, 266, 410-411
Enable-MailPublicFolder 327-328
Enable-MailUser 83-84
Enable-RemoteMailbox 84
Enable-SweepRule 70

Enable-UMMailbox   266, 340, 342

Encoding   225, 228, 246, 258, 302-303, 350, 354

encrypt   49, 50, 237, 243, 245-247 , 308, 314

Encryption   xii, 50, 72, 212, 237, 243-247, 306-308

EndDate   51-53, 191-192, 235, 285, 289, 372, 422

Endpoint   292-293

ENTERPRISEPACK   109, 111, 116, 351-352

Entourage   156

Equipment   xi, 148, 155-156, 161-162, 165, 174, 178-180, 199

EquipmentMailbox   180, 199, 422

EquipmentMailboxCount   199

errata   vii

ErrorAction   82-83, 90-91, 102, 114, 205, 211, 344, 368, 373, 376-378, 383-384, 390, 392, 399

ErrorActionPreference   390

ErrorFileName   89-92

errors   iii, vii, 1, 22, 88-92, 227, 292, 299, 369-370, 374, 377-378, 383, 386, 390, 392, 397

ErrorVariable   344, 399

EventAgeInDays   256

events   vi, 59, 70, 72, 175

EventsFromEmailEnabled   166

EwsAllowEntourage   156

ExceptAnyOfAuthenticationTypes   143

ExceptAnyOfProtocols   143

ExchangeActiveSync   142-143, 315

ExchangeActiveSyncDevices   314-315

ExchangeAdminCenter   142-143

ExchangeLocations   256

ExchangeNum   61, 64

ExchangeOnline   61, 63-64

ExchangeRemoteMove   293

ExchangeServices   419

ExchangeVersion   422

ExchangeWebServices 143

ExecutionPolicy   44

ExpectedPlan   346-347

Export-Clixml 285, 289

Export-CSV   viii, 14, 18, 302-303, 353-354, 359

Expression   53, 349-350, 354, 356, 413, 415

ExternalAccount   176

ExternalEmailAddress 84, 151

ExternalLicensingEnabled   239, 240

ExternalRelay 210

ExternalSenderAdminAddress   216

F

fabrikam   154

FaceBook   208

Facility   159

fasttracktips   213

FaxEnabled   344

feature 3, 10, 51, 67, 69-71, 87, 119, 129, 142, 156-158, 183, 196, 198, 212-213, 219, 221-222, 228, 232, 237, 239, 243, 279, 291, 307, 309, 314, 327, 336, 341-342, 375, 377-378, 392, 395-396

features   ix, xii, 2, 20, 23, 60, 66-71, 74, 85, 87, 93, 97, 113, 119, 123, 125, 148, 153, 157, 161, 166, 196, 198, 201, 212, 222-224, 232, 237, 246, 248-249, 262, 268, 304-305, 309, 335-336, 345, 358, 424

federated   79, 95, 155, 157, 263

FederatedEmail   79

Federation   86, 95

FederationTrust   2

FileData   225, 229, 258

FilePath   89-92, 350, 359, 383-384

Filter   x, xv, 28, 33-34, 62, 77, 91, 101, 119, 129-130, 133, 136, 150, 178, 180, 184, 190, 193, 196, 199, 215, 217-221, 250, 280, 316, 354, 380, 387, 389, 392, 412, 422

filtered 77, 90, 96, 192, 372, 392, 413

FilteredAsSpam   192, 372

filtering   ix, 26, 31, 33-34, 87, 97, 154, 172, 192, 214, 220, 281, 353, 403, 412

filters   34, 143, 178, 213-214, 218-219, 303, 384

fingerprint   228-230, 232, 307

fingerprinted   228

fingerprinting xii, 223, 228, 232

Fingerprints   229-230

FocusedMailbox   2

Folder xi, xiii, xiv, 72, 147-148, 154, 157-159, 167-170, 172, 174, 185-187, 199, 271, 291, 303, 318-332, 354, 366, 419

FolderContact 329-330

FolderOwner   329-330

FolderPath   324

Folders   xiii, xiv, 6, 48, 69, 97, 148, 157-159, 167-172, 174, 176, 185-187, 263, 303, 318-334, 423

FolderScope   169

FolderType   159

FolderVisible   330

Font-Family 360, 363
Font-Size 360, 363
footer 358, 379
footsteps 235
ForceOffline 291, 299
forces 396
forcibly 211
Foreach viii, 4, 16-17, 19-20, 38-39, 47, 53-54, 56-58, 61, 63, 82-85, 89, 91, 100, 102, 111, 114-116, 133, 141, 182, 189-190, 196, 203, 205-206, 210-211, 253, 260, 265, 270, 303, 327, 330-332, 341-342, 346, 350-352, 361, 363, 371, 373, 378, 385, 392-393, 405-407, 413-415
Foreach-Object xv, 55, 57, 391, 398, 403, 409, 412-415
foreground 418
ForegroundColor 19, 37-40, 83, 102, 114-115, 127-128, 189-191, 193, 199-200, 205, 211, 253, 265, 347, 351, 369, 372, 377, 405-407, 418-419
format 14, 28, 31-32, 61, 81, 89-90, 99, 109, 155, 159, 172, 208, 234-235, 293, 298, 303, 323, 326, 345, 353, 355, 383, 391, 398, 413
Format-List 42, 125, 137, 161, 213, 265, 302, 310, 326
Format-Table 213, 265, 270, 315, 413
formatted 56, 265, 308, 352, 357, 415
formatting ix, 21, 26, 28, 31, 33, 38-39, 56, 161, 199-200, 313, 323, 348-350, 355-356, 358, 380, 383, 398, 413
Forums v, 108
forward iii, 148, 153, 225, 258
forwarded 151, 175, 237
forwarding 15, 148, 151, 153
ForwardingSmtpAddress 153
Fragment 358, 359, 383
FromMemberOf 208
FromScope 245
FullAccess 158, 176
FullChart 63-64
FullDirectory 258
function 2-3, 9, 14, 19-20, 26-27, 30, 49, 54, 56-59, 113, 201, 224, 345, 369-370, 373, 375, 387, 391-392, 396, 399, 405-407
functions xv, 12, 19, 25, 29, 47, 54, 57, 59, 66, 196, 248, 259, 386, 391, 398-400, 404-405

G

GenerateIncidentReport 209
Get-AcceptedDomain 3, 137, 210-211
Get-ActiveSyncDevice 311
Get-ActiveSyncDeviceAccessRule 311
Get-ActiveSyncDeviceStatistics 314
Get-ActiveSyncMailboxPolicy 306
Get-ADDomain 23
Get-AddressBookPolicy 3
Get-AddressList 132
Get-ADGroup 115
Get-AdGroupMember 115
Get-AdminAuditLogConfig 282
Get-ADSyncConnector 106-107
Get-ADSyncRule 107-108
Get-ADSyncScheduler 103-104
Get-ADSyncServerConfiguration 107
Get-ADUser 23, 28, 82, 85, 91-92, 101-102
Get-Alias 399, 401, 409, 412
Get-BITSTransfer 367
Get-CalendarProcessing 165-166, 180
Get-CaseHoldPolicy 71
Get-CaseHoldRule 71
Get-CASMailbox x, 3, 120-121, 124, 126, 128, 138, 173, 266, 317, 406
Get-CASMailboxPlan 123
Get-ClientAccessRule 142, 144
Get-Clutter 3
Get-cmdlets 3
Get-Command 5-7, 9, 62-63, 77-78, 103, 106, 109, 120, 124, 132, 134-136, 139, 153, 176, 183, 186-187, 197, 201, 208-210, 213, 215, 218-219, 221, 223, 225, 227, 230, 232, 239, 241, 246, 250-251, 255, 257, 263, 266, 271, 275, 280-281, 286, 292, 320-321, 327-328, 336, 340, 344, 354, 364, 397
Get-ComplianceSearch 260-261
Get-ComplianceTag 70
Get-ComplianceTagStorage 70
Get-Content 64, 225, 228-229, 246, 258, 365
Get-Credential 76, 203, 224, 250, 293, 364-365
Get-DataClassification 230
Get-DataEncryptionPolicy 70
Get-DataRetentionReport 70-71
Get-Date 48, 52, 89-90, 354-355, 359-360, 362
Get-DistributionGroup 53-55, 57-58, 189-190, 196, 199, 331, 378, 383-384, 391

Get-DistributionGroupMember 184, 189-190, 196, 330-332, 378
Get-DkimSigningConfig 213
Get-DlpDetailReport 232
Get-DlpDetectionsReport 232
Get-DlpIncidentDetailReport 70, 232
Get-DlpKeywordDictionary 69
Get-DlpPolicy 3, 223, 226
Get-DlpPolicyTemplate 224
Get-DynamicDistributionGroup 132-134, 190, 199, 234-235
Get-Group 307
Get-GroupMailbox 266
Get-Help 2, 7-9, 12, 49, 51, 55, 61, 65, 81, 83-84, 100-101, 104, 121-122, 130, 134-135, 137, 139, 142, 180, 183, 186, 188, 191, 193-195, 197, 202, 204, 215-218, 222, 225-228, 239, 241, 257, 260, 272, 278, 280, 283, 286, 322, 324-325, 327, 329, 331, 337, 340, 364-365, 386, 396, 410-411, 416
Get-HoldCompliancePolicy 71
Get-HoldComplianceRule 71
Get-HostedContentFilterPolicy 220
Get-ImapSubscription 139
Get-InboundConnector 202, 205
Get-IntraOrganizationConnector 202
Get-IRMConfiguration 239, 245
Get-JournalRule 233, 236
Get-Mailbox 2-5, 7, 13, 15, 29-30, 33-34, 39, 55, 57, 62, 79, 85, 90-91, 122, 126, 128, 136, 141, 159, 162-163, 177-178, 180, 184, 187, 199, 210-211, 266, 269, 276, 286-287, 317, 341-342, 346, 349-350, 353-354, 356, 371, 373, 382-383, 388-391, 394, 398, 406, 410-411, 413, 415
Get-MailboxCalendarFolder 167
Get-MailboxFolder 167
Get-MailboxFolderPermission 168
Get-MailboxFolderStatistics 159, 168-169
Get-MailboxPermission 171-172, 177-178
Get-MailboxStatistics 3-4, 170, 172-173, 199, 349-350, 354, 356
Get-MailContact 393
Get-MailDetailATPReport 70
Get-MailPublicFolder 327-328
Get-MailTrafficATPReport 70
Get-Malbox 373
Get-MalwareFilterPolicy 215
Get-MalwareFilterRule 215

Get-ManagementRole 131, 251, 253, 263-265, 270
Get-ManagementRoleAssignment 263, 270, 279-280
Get-ManagementRoleEntry 263, 269-270
Get-MessageTrace xi, 51-53, 191-192, 235, 372, 421-422
Get-MessageTrackingLog 51, 191, 282
Get-MigrationBatch 42-43, 293, 301
Get-MigrationConfig 295
Get-MobileDevice 3, 310-311, 313, 315-316
Get-MobileDeviceMailboxPolicy 242, 305-306
Get-MobileDeviceStatistics 314, 316
Get-Module 62, 103, 250
Get-MoveRequest 298, 300-301, 303
Get-MoveRequestStatistics 42-43, 298, 301-303
Get-MsolAccountSku 109
Get-MSOLGroup 140
Get-MSOLGroupMember 140
Get-MsolUser 36, 109-112, 115-118, 153, 162, 350, 390, 405
Get-MsolUserRole 153
Get-MSOLUsers 405
Get-OMEConfiguration 246
Get-OutboundConnector 202, 205
Get-OutlookProtectionRule 241
Get-Output 394
Get-OwaMailboxPolicy 124-125, 127-128
Get-PolicyTipConfig 227
Get-PSSession 53, 63, 65
Get-PublicFolder xiv, 4, 318, 321-327, 329-332
Get-PublicFolderItemStatistics 325-327
Get-PublicFolders 322-323
Get-PublicFolderStatistics 4, 325
Get-QuarantineMessage 3
Get-Recipient 190, 421-422
Get-RecipientPermission 178
Get-RecycleBin 116
Get-RemoteMailbox 54, 79-80
Get-ReportExecutionInstance 70
Get-RetentionCompliancePolicy 71
Get-RetentionComplianceRule 71
Get-RetentionPolicy 7-8
Get-RetentionPolicyTag 357, 359, 361, 363
Get-RoleAssignmentPolicy 275-276, 278
Get-RoleGroup 252-253, 271, 275
Get-RoleGroupMember 253, 272

Get-SendConnector 203
Get-Service 382
Get-SiteMailbox 266
Get-SupervisoryReviewPolicyV 70
Get-SupervisoryReviewReport 70
Get-SupervisoryReviewRule 70
Get-SweepRule 70
Get-SyncRequest 3
Get-TransportConfig 130
Get-TransportRule 19, 230
Get-UMDialPlan 337, 339
Get-UMMailbox 3, 266, 346
Get-UMMailboxPolicy 340
Get-UnifiedGroup 3, 32, 197, 393-394
Get-Unique 315
Get-User 196, 389
Get-Variable 390
Get-WmiObject 380-381
github 65, 401
GivenName 83, 100, 389
GlobalAddressList 134-136
GlobalAdmin 50, 61
GoogleDriveAttachmentsEnabled 126
Governance 249
granting 119, 174, 271, 328
GrantSendOnBehalfTo 158
Greenfield 337
GroupDetails 190
GroupInfo 383-384
GroupInfoReport 383
Group-Object 52-53
GroupObjectId 140
groups ix, xi, xiii, 3, 47-49, 52-59, 65, 68, 70, 72-73, 87, 97, 99, 108, 113-114, 130-131, 133, 135, 138, 140, 154, 174, 176, 178, 181, 183, 185, 187-191, 193-194, 196-200, 217, 234, 251-252, 259, 262-263, 271-272, 275, 277, 307, 318, 332, 377-378, 383-384
GroupSmtpAddress 54-57, 391-392
GroupsToUsers 114

H

HasSubFolders324
HeaderRow 63
headers 356, 358, 360, 363
HiddenFromAddressListsEnabled 58, 80, 328, 353-354

hierarchy 185, 318-319, 321
HighSecurity 157
HostedContentFilter 219
HostedOutbound 221
hotfix 391
HTMLReport 360-363
Hybrid 10-11, 74, 77-80, 85-86, 88, 97, 99, 201-202, 206-207, 383
Hygiene xii, 212-213, 263

I

identifier 23, 62, 97, 108, 293, 296, 310
identities 4, 86, 98-99
Identity x, 28, 86, 88, 90-92, 94, 96, 98, 100, 102, 104, 106, 108, 110, 112, 114, 116, 118, 150, 158, 161, 176, 178, 204, 294, 296, 303, 313-314, 323, 326-327, 344-345, 366, 422, 424
-Identity 54, 58-59, 82, 84, 90, 92, 102, 114, 127-128, 150, 152-159, 161-163, 165-173, 177, 184, 189-190, 205, 210, 214, 246, 254, 269-270, 281, 289, 293, 295, 298-299, 302-303, 306-309, 312-315, 321, 326, 328, 330, 332-333, 342, 377-378
IgnoreDefaultScope 344
IgnoreMixedDigits 155
IgnoreUpperCase 155
-Image 246
IMAPAccess 140
IMAPAcess 140
IMAPEnable 407
IMAPEnabled 120, 139-140
-IMAPEnabled 122, 124, 141, 156, 407
ImapGroup 140
ImapSuppressReadReceipt 139
ImapUseProtocolDefaults 139
ImListMigrationCompleted 344, 345
impersonate 262, 279, 280
Import 72, 85, 89, 91, 224-225, 228, 244, 258, 263, 272-273, 341, 373, 376
Import-CSV 15, 17, 61, 82, 84-85, 89, 91, 100, 102, 110, 114, 182, 341-342
Import-Module 50, 85, 103, 373, 376, 388, 399
Import-PSSession 51, 62, 76-77, 115, 203, 224, 250
InactiveGroups 49, 53, 58
inactivity 48, 53, 56, 58, 309

Inbound   202, 204-206
InboundConnector   202, 205
IncidentReportContent   209
IncludeDumpsterInfo   334
IncludeOldestAndNewestItems   169
IncludeReport   42-43, 302-303
IncrementalSyncInterval   298-299
indentation   20-22
indenting   21
indexing   14
InfoAnnouncementFilename 340
InformationAction   344
information-protection   240, 243
InformationVariable   344
InheritanceType   158, 176
InPlaceHolds   80
in-policy   180
InputObject   53, 128, 354
Install-Module   6, 51
InternalLicensingEnabled   239-240, 244
InternalMessage   159
InternalOnly   143
InternalRelay   210
InternalSenderAdminAddress   216
international   214
Intune   110-111, 304, 314
Invoke-Command   38-39, 404, 408
InvokeSynchronizer   321
-IPAllowList   218-219
-IPBlockList   218-219
IRMEnabled   242
isesteroids   23
IsInherited   171-172
IsLicensed   111, 115
IsRecordLabel   256
-IsReplyAllTheDefaultResponse   155
IssueWarning   388
IssueWarningQuota   16, 39, 154, 324
ItemCount   326, 354-355
ItemType   417

J

JITUsers   178
Journal   232-236, 240
journaled   202, 212, 232-235, 240

JournalEmailAddress 233-236
Journaling   xii, 201-202, 206, 212, 232-236, 240, 249, 263
JournalingReportNdrTo   233
JournalReportDecryptionEnabled   239-240

K

keepanddelete   256
keyword   2, 23, 78, 176, 259, 271, 274-275, 286
KeywordSearch-CI   259

L

Labels   xii, 248-249, 254-256, 360
language   23, 56, 155, 159, 172, 227, 259, 337-339, 353, 391, 409
LargeItemLimit   294, 297
LastName   81-83, 100, 149-150
LastSuccessSync   316
LastSyncAttemptTime316
latency   366-367
LegacyMailbox   422
LegalHold   407-408
LegalHoldApplication 264
length   287, 307, 369, 418
letter-spacing   208
license   10-11, 108-113, 116, 123-124, 149, 152, 160, 223, 243, 309, 352
LicenseAll   350-351
LicenseCurrent   351-352
licensed   110-111, 115-116, 149
LicenseLevel   352
LicenseOptions   111-112, 116
licenses   108-110, 112-113, 115-116, 123, 148, 151-152, 243, 249, 350-351
licensing   x, 86, 108-109, 112-113, 115-116, 123, 196, 212, 237, 239-240, 243-244, 350, 389
LicensingLocation   239
LimitedDetails   168
line-height   208
linked   148, 160, 162, 196
LinkedMailbox   422
LinkID   94

LiteralPath   354
litigation   80, 154, 274
LitigationHoldDuration   80, 407
LiveCred   50-51, 61-62, 203, 224, 250, 296-300
locale   227
LocalizeDefaultFolderName   159
location   10, 44, 89, 94, 111, 115-116, 166, 168, 175, 181-183, 209, 228, 232, 244, 279, 285, 294-295, 341-343, 346-347, 355, 364-366, 419
logged   172, 209, 286, 378-379
logging11, 85, 90, 92, 122, 219, 262, 281, 286, 288, 290, 366, 403, 419-422
Login-AzureRmAccount   111
LogLevel   282
LogonFailuresBeforeDisconnect   340
looped 14, 182
looping   13, 17

M

mailbox   xi, xiii, xiv, 2-6, 10-11, 13-17, 29-30, 34, 37-40, 43, 55, 65, 70, 72, 77, 79-81, 83-84, 90-92, 110, 120, 122-126, 128-129, 132, 138-141, 147-162, 165, 167-180, 182, 185-186, 199, 210-211, 213, 234-235, 248-249, 260, 262-263, 266, 268, 272-277, 279-280, 284, 286-288, 291-307, 310, 313-314, 318-321, 335-336, 340-346, 349-351, 353-356, 365, 371, 373, 382-384, 393, 397, 404-406, 408, 410-411, 413, 415, 419
MailboxAudit   286
MailboxData   15
mailboxid   298-299
MailboxManagement 281
MailboxNames   27
MailboxSearch   274
MailboxSearchApplication   264
MailboxStats   349
MailboxType   294
MailContact   422
MailEnabled   152, 324
MailForestContact   422
Mail-ManagerDisabled   57, 59, 391-392
Mail-ManagerHidden 54, 57-58
MailNonUniversalGroup   422
MailPublicFolder   327
MailRequired   64
MailTips   226

MailUniversalDistributionGroup   422
MailUniversalSecurityGroup 422
MailUser   13, 83, 422
MakeDefault   210
Malware   213-219
MalwareFilter   215
MalwareFilterPolicy   217
ManagedBy   54-55, 57, 188, 391
ManagedCustomFolder   170
ManagementRole   263, 265
ManagementScope   280
manager   iii, iv, 48, 54-59, 70, 77, 121, 175, 196, 234, 253, 259-260, 294-295, 321, 391-392
mandatory   150-151, 157, 202, 240, 308
MAPIEnabled   120, 122, 124, 407
MAPIHTTPEnabled 122
margin   358-359, 383
MarkAsSpamEmbedTagsInHtml   221
MarkAsSpamFormTagsInHtml   221
MarkAsSpamFramesInHtml 221
MaxInactivityTimeLock   309
MaxItemSize   324
MaxNumberOfBatches   295
MaxPasswordFailedAttempts 309
MaxReceiveSize   294
MaxSendSize   294
MCOSTANDARD   110-111, 114
Member   114, 138, 143, 187, 196, 254, 262-263, 377
MemberDepartRestriction   188
MemberJoinRestriction   188
MemberOf   140
MemberOfGroup   133-134
Members   184
message   xii, 5-6, 48, 51, 54, 56-57, 60, 67, 72, 82-83, 92, 153-154, 159, 165, 193-195, 201, 203-204, 207-209, 212-213, 216-217, 221-222, 225-229, 231-235, 237, 240-247, 263, 267, 284, 297, 301, 311, 336, 348, 360, 363-365, 372-373, 377-378, 380, 409, 415, 419-422
MessageClassDisplayName   357, 359-361, 363
MessageParameters   56-58, 392
messages   xv, 16, 48, 51-52, 79, 138, 155, 170, 174, 191-193, 202, 206-207, 212-214, 216, 225-227, 232-233, 235-237, 239-241, 243, 245-246, 318-319, 327, 344, 364, 368-369, 372, 378, 380, 420, 422
MessageTrace 191
Messaging   xiv, 2, 12, 83, 120, 188, 201, 212, 218,

237, 247, 263, 335-338, 340, 342, 344-347, 353
migrate 159, 291, 299, 303
migrated 81, 188, 293-296, 341
migrating 34
Migration xiii, 42, 48, 81, 263, 279, 291-298, 300-301, 303, 383
MigrationBatch 294, 301
MigrationEndpoint 292
Migrations xiii, 34, 43, 104, 262, 279, 291-292, 294-296, 298, 300, 302-303
MigrationService 279, 298, 301
mincount 259
MinPasswordComplexCharacters 308
MinPasswordLength 307
MissedCallNotificationEnabled 344
misspelled 373, 383
Mobile xii, xiii, 9, 71, 73, 122, 124, 156-157, 242, 304-310, 312-316, 419
MobileDevice 304, 306
MobileIron 314
mobiles 308
moderated 174, 193
ModerateMessageByUser 259
Moderation xi, 174, 188, 193-194, 198
moderators 194
Modern xiii, 9, 23, 28, 72, 148, 198, 303, 308, 318
ModificationAgeInDays 256
ModifiedObjectResolvedName 282
ModifiedProperties 282
module 2, 6-7, 20, 23, 51, 62-63, 75, 85, 103, 108, 209, 248, 250-251, 264, 373, 376, 390-391, 394-395, 399
ModuleName 62-63, 77-78, 103, 106, 250-251
modules viii, 2, 6, 23, 50-51, 62, 75, 250, 376, 388, 394-395
MoveRequest 301, 303
Move-Request 296, 297, 301, 303
MoveStatus 301
MoveToJmf 220-221
MReceiveQuota 17
MRSEndpoint 293-294
MsolUser 153
MSOnline 50-51, 209, 373, 376, 388, 395, 399
Multi-dimensional 13
MultiFactor 77, 152
Multi-Factor 77
multi-line 32

MultiValuedProperty 126, 239
MyAddressInformation 263
MyBaseOptions 168, 263, 278
MyContactInformation 263, 278
MyDisplayName 263
MyDistributionGroupMembership 263, 278
MyDistributionGroups 263
MyDomain 293
MyMailboxDelegation 263, 278
MyMailSubscriptions 263
MyMobileInformation 263
MyName 263
MyPersonalInformation 263
MyProfileInformation 263
MyRetentionPolicies 263, 278
MyScript 46
MyTeamMailboxes 263, 278
MyTenant 50, 61
MyTextMessaging 263, 278
MyVoiceMail 263, 278

N

nested 13
network 72, 95, 147, 366
Networking 321
networks 319
New-ActiveSyncDeviceAccessRule 310
New-ActiveSyncMailboxPolicy 307
New-AddressBookPolicy 135-136
New-AddressList 132-133
New-AdminAuditLogSearch 283-284
New-ADUser 83, 100
New-Alias xv, 410-411
New-ClientAccessRule 142-145
New-ComplianceCase 260
New-ComplianceSearch 259-260
New-ComplianceTag 255-256
New-DataClassification 229
New-DistributionGroup 183-184, 188
New-DlpKeywordDictionary 69
New-DlpPolicy 225-226
New-DynamicDistributionGroup 130-131, 183, 234-235
NewEmployees 100
NewExchangeNum 63-64

NewFileTypes   128
New-Fingerprint   228-229
New-GlobalAddressList   134
New-ImapSubscription   139
New-InboundConnector   202
New-Item   417
New-JournalRule   233-235
New-Mailbox   10, 151, 175, 179, 182, 186, 266, 269-271, 320-321, 410-411
New-MailboxAuditLogSearch 287-289
New-MailboxImportRequest   270
New-MailboxRelocationRequest   71
New-MailboxRepairRequest   302
New-MailContact   151
New-MailUser   83-84
New-MalwareFileRule   217
New-MalwareFilterRule   217
New-ManagementRole   263, 266
New-ManagementRoleAssignment   263, 272-273, 279, 281
New-ManagementScope   280-281
New-MigrationBatch   293-295, 297, 301
New-MigrationEndpoint   292-293
New-MobileDeviceMailboxPolicy   306-307
New-MoveRequest   291-292, 296-299, 301
New-MsolDomain   209-210
New-MsolLicenseOptions   111, 116
New-MsolUser   149, 153
New-Object   50, 61, 115, 351
New-OfflineAddressBook   135
New-OutboundConnector   203
New-OutlookProtectionRule 241-242
New-PolicyTipConfig   227-228
New-ProtectionServicePolicy 70
NewProxy   389
New-PSSession   51, 61-62, 76, 115, 203, 224, 250
New-PublicFolder   187, 321-322
New-ReceiveConnector   416
New-RemoteMailbox   11, 80-81, 412
New-RetentionCompliancePolicy   256
New-RetentionComplianceRule   256
New-RoleAssignmentPolicy   275, 278
NewRow   63-64
New-SafeLinksPolicy   70
New-SchedulingMailbox   266
New-SiteMailbox   266

New-SweepRule   70
New-SyncMailPublicFolder   327
New-TransportRule   10-11, 208, 230, 241, 245, 259
New-UMDialPlan   337, 339
New-UnifiedGroup   197
NewUserPrincipalName   152
NoAlias   82
NoChange   64
NoClobber   350, 354-355, 378-379
non-ASCII   303
NonBasicAuthentication   142-143
non-capitalized   27
Non-Delivery   233
non-destructive   3, 105
NonEditingAuthor   330
NoNewLine   37-38, 127-128, 253, 265, 406-408
non-Exchange   74, 81, 159
Non-Provisionable   307
Non-User   xi, 157, 174, 176, 178, 180, 182, 184, 186, 188, 190, 192, 194, 196, 198, 200
NoOfflineOWA   157
NoProxy   365
NoteProperty   351
NotificationEmailAddresses   314-315
NotificationEmails   295
-NotificationEmails   293-295
notifications   48-49, 58-59, 67, 69, 72, 214, 216-217, 222, 336
NotifyEmail   342
NotifyOnly   227
NotifyOutboundSpam   222
NotifyOutboundSpamRecipients   222
NotifySender   230
-NotLike   178, 406, 413
-NotMatch   354
NotPresent   376
NoType   18-19, 254, 355, 359
NoTypeInformation   354
NumberOfDigitsInExtension 339

O

OAuthAuthentication 142-143
Obfuscated   ix, 26, 42
object   10-11, 13, 32-33, 53, 67, 76, 79, 81, 83-85, 92,

99-102, 117, 148-149, 152-153, 160, 162, 176, 187, 197, 199, 276, 293, 302, 313, 351-352, 396, 415
OBJECTCLASS   89, 91
ObjectClass-eq   90
ObjectId   117-118, 140
objects   iii, x, xi, 1, 10-11, 13, 15, 31-33, 47, 76-78, 81, 83, 86-89, 91, 96-102, 105, 116-118, 135, 147, 149, 157, 160-162, 174, 176, 178-180, 182, 184, 186, 188, 190, 192, 194, 196, 198, 200, 248, 293, 296-297, 323, 325, 369, 423
Office v, vi, ix, xi, xii, 7, 10-11, 35, 47-48, 50-54, 60-62, 64, 66-77, 79-81, 84-88, 95, 97-102, 104-106, 108, 110-112, 115-117, 119-123, 126, 129, 136-137, 139, 142-143, 150, 154, 159-161, 165, 170, 174-175, 177-178, 196-199, 201-203, 206-207, 212, 218, 224, 226, 232, 237, 243-244, 246, 248-249, 251, 254-256, 259, 282, 291, 293-294, 303-304, 314, 318, 346-347, 364, 404, 408, 422-424
OfficeExtensionApplication   264
OfficePhone   100
OFFICESUBSCRIPTION   110-111, 114
Offline x, 119, 126, 129, 133, 135, 148, 157, 291, 299
OfflineAddress   135
OfflineAddressBook   135-136, 143
OMECon   246
OneDrive   69-70, 72, 126, 248-249, 254, 256-257
one-liner   3, 23, 29, 42, 50-52, 54, 103, 108, 117, 128, 159, 178, 180, 186, 204, 210, 216, 222, 233, 244, 246, 345, 354, 357-358, 376, 392-393, 413, 415
OneNote   40, 198, 349
one-off225, 258
onmicrosoft   5, 50, 61, 80, 105, 136, 162-163, 198, 208-209, 233, 244, 281, 293-294, 296-300, 328, 341-342, 364, 405, 422
on-screen   308
operators   viii, 12, 15-16, 34, 72
option x, 14, 18-19, 38, 41-42, 46, 49, 62, 73, 77, 87, 93-95, 112-113, 129, 138, 150, 152, 157-158, 176, 179, 188, 195, 201, 203, 209, 211, 217, 224, 231, 239, 241, 291, 308, 310-311, 314, 316, 350, 356, 376, 393, 399, 403-410, 412, 420
options   1-2, 7-8, 28-29, 44, 47, 61, 71-72, 74, 87, 93-94, 97, 105, 109-116, 124-126, 138-139, 142, 147, 149, 152-153, 156, 159-160, 176, 181, 188, 191, 198, 201-202, 206-209, 213-214, 216, 220, 226, 229, 233, 245, 249, 264, 278, 280, 286, 291, 299, 301, 305, 309-310, 317, 327-328, 337-338, 349-350, 356, 358, 363,

365-366, 368, 372, 387, 399, 404-405, 408, 417, 419
organization   74, 102, 120, 128, 154-156, 159-160, 165, 174-175, 178, 181-182, 188, 193, 198, 201, 206, 210, 218, 222, 228, 233, 259, 262-263, 271-274, 294, 305, 307, 310, 312-313, 324, 337
Organizational   113, 161, 178, 272
OrganizationalUnit   346
OrganizationId   422
OrgUnit   100
OtaNotificationMailInsert   311
Outbound   201-202, 204-207, 214, 221-222
OutboundConnector 205
OutBuffer   344
Out-File   50, 89-92, 115, 349-352, 359, 361, 363, 384
Outlook   x, xii, 51, 62, 68-73, 75-76, 115, 119-120, 124, 138, 148, 151, 154-159, 166, 170, 172, 194, 196, 203, 223-224, 226, 228, 241-242, 245, 250, 256, 296, 302, 304, 308, 332, 335-336, 361, 363, 385
OutlookAnywhere   143
OutlookWebApp   143-144
output iii, ix, 3-4, 14, 16-18, 26, 29, 31-33, 37-38, 42, 92, 103, 170, 206, 210, 235, 264-265, 278, 280, 285, 298, 305, 311-312, 315, 349-350, 358, 360-363, 375, 378-379, 393-394, 416-417
Outputs   8
outsidevi, 14, 32, 46, 63, 151, 154, 156, 165, 195, 207, 212, 227-228, 230, 233, 240, 259, 272, 359, 392, 401
Out-String   359, 383
OutVariable   344
override   154, 227, 309, 313, 365
OverrideRecipientQuotas   328
overrule   294, 313
overruled   160
OWAEnabled 120, 407
OWAMailboxPolicy   122,126, 128, 129, 157
OwaMailboxPolicy-Default   125-128
OWAPolicyName   127-128

P

Pagefile   29
PageSize   191-192, 372, 422
parameter   2, 29, 39, 44, 92, 101, 109, 122, 130, 143, 149, 151, 159-161, 169, 172, 175-176, 179-180, 183-184, 186, 188, 191, 195-196, 199, 203, 208, 221,

226-227, 229, 258-259, 269, 272, 282-283, 286, 288, 293-295, 297-298, 301, 310, 313, 315, 322, 353, 355, 364-365, 369, 390, 392, 400, 414, 418

parameters   xv, 2-3, 8, 12, 16, 48, 51-52, 76, 91, 110, 122, 124, 137, 140, 142-144, 149-151, 180, 186, 191-192, 194-195, 203, 216, 218, 220-222, 228-230, 239, 241, 256, 260, 262, 282, 284, 286, 293-295, 297, 299-300, 306, 309-310, 323-324, 336, 339, 343-344, 348, 354, 358, 364, 387, 390, 394, 410, 419-421

parentheses   199

parsed   36

Parsing   34, 271

partnership   304-305, 310, 314

partnerships   315-316

Pass-Through 95

password   49-50, 61, 86-87, 95, 97, 99-100, 115, 149, 263, 304-305, 307-309, 365

PasswordEnabled   242, 307

PasswordExpiration   308

PasswordHistory   308

passwords   49, 86, 97, 100, 149, 307-308

pattern   143, 307

patterns   214

paused   104, 375

pauses   369-370

pausing   370

payloads   214

PeopleIdentity 241, 259

per-group   176

PermanentlyDisable   152

permission   2, 44, 131, 148, 158, 171, 176-178, 270-271, 273-274, 279, 331, 403, 419

permissions   xi, xii, xiii, xiv, 2, 50, 63, 72, 131-132, 148, 152-153, 157-159, 168, 171-172, 176-178, 248-249, 251-252, 262-264, 266, 268-272, 274, 276, 278, 280, 282, 284, 286, 288, 290, 318, 328-332, 355, 380-381, 419

per-user   176

phishing   72

Phone   182

PhoneNumber 344

PhoneProviderId   344

pipeline   3-4, 241

PipelineVariable   344

pipelining   3

piping   viii, 3-4, 302

PlainPassword 149

Planner   110, 113, 174, 196

PlayOnPhoneEnabled 344

plugin   374-375

plug-in   viii, 23-25, 245, 374, 386

policies   xi, xii, xiii, 44, 68-69, 119, 124, 126, 129, 135-136, 150, 153, 156-157, 160, 212, 215, 217, 219-220, 223, 225-226, 248, 254, 256, 263, 277, 304-307, 309, 314, 335, 340, 345, 357, 367, 388, 419

policy   x, xii, 10-11, 33, 37-38, 44, 69, 72, 90-91, 105, 119, 122, 124-126, 128-130, 135-136, 138, 143, 149-151, 157, 160, 213, 215, 217-218, 220, 222-223, 225-228, 231, 242, 248, 256-257, 275, 277-278, 305-307, 309, 336, 340-342, 346-347, 357, 359-360, 362-363, 371, 392-393, 404-406, 408, 419

PolicyApplied   91

PolicyTip   227

PolicyType   105

POPAccess   140-141

POPEnabled   120, 122, 124, 139-141, 156, 407

PopGroup   140

PortalText   246, 247

PostalCode   143

Postmaster   xii, 209-211

PowerMTA   213

PowerShell-aware   20

powershell-liveid   75, 224, 250

powershellmagazine   25

PowerShellWebServices   143, 145

powertheshell 23

PreContent   358

Prefix   413-415

PrepareAD   79

pre-stage   292

pre-staging   298, 300-301

prevent   40, 44, 46-47, 174, 193, 228, 237, 262, 297, 299, 308-309, 313-315, 350, 378, 394, 410

PreventCompletion   299

preventing   292, 372

Prevention   xii, 206, 212, 222, 248-249, 263

pricing   243

PrimaryAndArchive   294

PrimaryOnly   294, 297

PrimarySmtpAddress 28, 53, 81-82, 84, 90, 149, 234-235, 281, 346, 353-354, 382-383, 422

PrimarySmtpAddress 85, 328

profile 23, 277, 296, 417, 419

ProhibitPostQuota   324

Prohibits 396
ProhibitSendQuota 33-34, 154, 413
ProhibitSendReceiveQuota 154
PROJECTWORKMANAGEMENT 110-111, 114-115
properties 32-33, 53, 79, 88, 90, 101, 106, 109, 121, 124-126, 138, 143, 154, 160, 197-198, 204, 209, 228, 252, 282, 323, 326, 333, 341, 354, 383, 396-397, 413, 416
ProPlus 72, 110, 148
Protection xii, 11, 44, 68, 72, 75, 170, 202, 212-214, 218, 221-222, 224, 237-242, 244-245, 250, 254
protocol 9, 120-122, 138-139, 145, 212, 296, 317, 353
protocols 9, 119-122, 124, 138, 142-144, 146, 156, 173, 317, 405
ProtocolSettings 317
ProvisioningStatus 351
ProxyAddress 90
ProxyAddresses 90-92, 389
ProxyAuthentication 365
ProxyBypass 365
ProxyCredential 365
ProxyList 365
ProxyToMailbox 344
ProxyToServer 344
ProxyUsage 365
PSComputerName 385
PSCredential 50, 61, 115
PSharp viii, 25
PSScriptAnalyzer 401
Psscripts 419
PSSession 65
PSTManagement 273
PSVersionTable 395
PublicFolder 6, 186-187, 199, 320-321, 422
PublicFolderClientPermission 328
PublicFolderMailboxCount 199
PublicFolderName 326-327
publish 156, 256
-PublishComplianceTag 256

Q

Quarantine 310-313, 316
-QueryString 310
quotas 16, 32, 154, 162, 353, 419

quotations 2, 149
quotes ix, xv, 24, 26, 40-42, 298, 358, 360, 374-375, 387, 400-401

R

ranging iii, 308
readability 21, 27, 360, 398, 400, 403, 413
readable 26-27, 33, 308, 409
ReadAllBytes 293-294
ReadCount 225, 258
Read-Host 50, 115, 127-128, 149, 404, 407-408
ReadItems 329-330
ReadOnly 10, 410-412
ReadPermission 176
ReadWriteMailbox 263, 278
reboot 308
rebuild 204
Receipts 69
receive 5-6, 17, 44, 148, 169, 195, 201, 204, 206, 234, 266, 297, 335, 345
Receive-ApplicationRelay 205
recipient x, 39, 52, 119, 129-130, 132-133, 143, 158, 191, 208, 213, 222, 230-234, 236, 243, 246-247, 263, 266, 271, 356, 365, 421
RecipientAddress 52-53, 199, 372, 572
RecipientDomains 203
RecipientFilter 131, 133-134, 150, 190 , 234-235
RecipientPreviewFilter 190
RecipientRestrictionFilter 281
recipients 11, 79, 175, 190, 221, 233, 237, 239-240, 243, 263-264, 267-268
RecipientType 13, 133, 422
RecipientTypeDetail 162
RecipientTypeDetails 180, 184, 199, 422
reconnect 132, 410
Recoverable 170
RecoverableItems 170
Recurse 323, 326-327
Recycle x, 86, 102, 116-118
Redirect 62, 221
redirection 62
redundant 394
ReferenceObject 128
RefreshServerCertificates 240
region 150, 159, 178, 181-182, 262, 299, 353

regionalized   338
regions   119, 234, 337, 353
Registry   380-382, 391
rehydrate   267
rejected   154
RejectMessageReasonText   230
RejectMessagesFrom   195
RejectMessagesFromDLMembers   195
RejectOverride   227-228
RelatedRecipientAddress   52
RemoteAddress   145
RemoteCredential   296-300
RemoteHostName   296-299
RemoteMailbox   79
RemotePort   145
RemotePowerShell   143, 145
RemoteRegistry   381-382
RemoteRoutingAddress   80
RemoteServer   293
RemoteSigned   44, 419
RemoteUserMailbox   422
Remove-ActiveSyncDevice   315
Remove-ActiveSyncMailboxPolicy   307
Remove-ADUser   102
Remove-CalendarEvents   70
Remove-ClientAccessRule   142, 146
Remove-DlpKeywordDictionary   69
RemoveFromRecycleBin   117-118
Remove-InboundConnector   204
Remove-Item   65, 411-412
Remove-JournalRule   236
Remove-Mailbox   5, 152, 266, 410-411
Remove-MailContact   151
Remove-ManagementRole   263, 268
Remove-ManagementRoleEntry   263
Remove-MigrationBatch   295
Remove-MobileDevice   311, 315
Remove-MoveRequest   300
Remove-MRSRequest 71
Remove-MsolDomain 211
Remove-MsolUser   117-118, 153
Remove-MSOLUsers 117
RemoveOME   245
Remove-OutboundConnector   204
Remove-OWAMailboxPolicy 129
Remove-PSSession   53, 63, 65
Remove-PublicFolder 321, 324-325

Remove-ReceiveConnector   204
Remove-RoleAssignmentPolicy   276
Remove-RoleGroupMember 254
Remove-SweepRule   70
Remove-SyncMailPublicFolder   327
Renderaddress372
replication   xiv, 83, 185, 292, 303, 318-319, 413
replies 154, 158, 165, 245
ReplyAll   155, 193
report vii, 5, 16, 33-34, 37, 39-40, 42-43, 83, 90, 172, 177, 180, 189-190, 199-201, 204, 209, 279-280, 283-284, 289, 302-303, 314, 335, 345-346, 349-350, 353, 356-365, 368-369, 383-385, 413
Reporting   xi, xii, xiii, xiv, 1, 19, 32, 37, 39, 68, 83, 99, 147, 152, 161, 168-169, 199, 204, 213, 236, 250, 279, 302-304, 315, 335, 345, 348-350, 352, 354, 356, 358-360, 362, 364-367, 384, 386
reports xiii, xiv, 3, 33, 39, 42-43, 72, 83, 195-196, 209, 233, 249, 262, 282, 284, 291, 300, 303, 335, 342, 348-353, 356-360, 362, 364-365, 369, 378
require 1, 4, 10-11, 23, 119, 131, 138, 148, 152, 154, 159-160, 168, 170, 172, 179, 186, 189-190, 201-202, 212-213, 237, 294-295, 299, 303, 306-309, 311, 315, 337, 368-369, 381, 384, 394-395
required   20-22, 27, 37, 40, 60, 62, 93, 108, 112-113, 149-150, 152, 155, 157-158, 160-161, 165, 208, 228, 245, 268-269, 283, 288, 293-295, 298, 303-304, 306-307, 311, 313, 316, 400, 412
RequireDeviceEncryption   242, 308
requires   xv, 44, 47, 75, 112, 118, 150, 156, 160, 170, 177, 186, 188, 207, 212-213, 219, 223, 225, 240, 279, 291, 318, 320, 348-349, 358, 364, 369, 373, 376-377, 381, 387, 394-396, 415, 419
RequireStorageCardEncryption   308
RequireTls   202
ResourceCapacity   182
ResourceType   422
Restore-MsolUser   153
RestrictDomainsToCertificate202
RestrictDomainsToIPAddresses   202
ResultSize   3, 53, 161, 189-191, 285, 301, 303, 315, 353, 422
Resume   59, 300
Resume-MoveRequest300
Resume-MRSRequest 71
retain   154, 299
RetainDeletedItemsFor   154, 324

RetainDeletedItemsFor   154

retained   91, 154, 219, 256, 274, 379

retaining   373

Retention   10-11, 33, 37-38, 68, 80, 151, 154, 156-157, 233, 248-249, 254, 256, 263, 277-278, 357, 359-360, 362, 371, 388, 393, 404-406, 408, 419

RetentionAction   256

RetentionDuration   256

RetentionEnabled   357, 359, 361, 363

RetentionHoldEnabled   13, 80

RetentionPolicies   371

RetentionPolicy   37-39, 150, 353-354, 371, 373, 388, 390, 406, 408

RetentionPolicyTag   361, 363

RetentionPolicyTags   357

RetentionTags   359

RetentionTagsInfo   359

RetentionType   256

RetryInterval   365-267

RetryTimeout   366

ReturnDeletedUsers   116-118

Reviewer   vi, 249, 330

Reviewing   vi, 51, 70, 122, 137, 176, 179-180, 183, 194-195, 230, 249, 254, 259, 274, 282-283, 288, 327, 329, 348, 364-365, 385, 411

rights   2, 72, 76, 110, 115, 143, 175-178, 212, 237-239, 244, 251, 254, 262-263, 268, 271, 279-281, 286, 330-331

RMSOnline   244

RMSOnlineKeySharingLocation   240, 244

Roadmap   ix, 66-67, 70

road-warriors   124

roaming   343

robust   292

RoleAssigneeName   270, 280

RoleAssigneeType   270

RoleAssignmentPolicy   150, 156, 275-276

RoleAssignments   252, 276

RoleEntries   264-265

RoleGroup   271

RoleName   253, 265

Rolling   ix, 66, 70, 85

RoomList   135-136, 182-184

RoomMailbox   184, 199, 422

RoomMailboxCount   199

RoomName   182

RoomTest   13

RouteAllMessagesViaOnPremises   206

RouteAllMessagesViaOnPremises   206-207

routes   206

Routing   x, 80, 119, 129-130, 207, 209, 257

RSAT-AD-AdminCenter   51

RSAT-AD-PowerShell 51

RuleCheck   19

RuleErrorAction   208, 241, 245, 259

S

SamAccountName   28, 80, 100, 114

SamAccountNameGroup   113

scenario   ix, 10-11, 26, 34-36, 47-48, 60, 79, 81, 85, 113, 121, 130, 132, 138, 143, 153, 177, 181, 188-189, 192-193, 195, 202, 208, 210, 222, 226, 228, 232, 234, 237, 240, 278, 281, 291, 321-322, 329, 331, 338, 341, 343, 360, 376, 378, 382, 384, 413

scenarios   10-11, 14, 34, 37, 54, 74, 86, 122, 143, 178, 202, 208, 222, 232, 237, 258-259, 282, 291, 329, 348-349, 375, 378, 401, 424

schedule   98, 103-104, 179, 249, 298, 335, 348, 355

scheduled   49, 60, 63, 65, 348, 355, 383

scheduler   103-104, 141

schedules   175

scheduling   1, 72, 87, 154, 165, 175, 178-179

Schema   107

Scope   233-235

scoped   69, 279

Scopes   xiii, 143, 262, 280

scoping   353

screen   18, 21, 33, 113, 211, 281, 285, 309, 352, 416

screenshot   111, 126, 137, 209, 220, 349, 412

screenshots   xiv, 93, 161, 348-349

script   iii, iv, ix, xiv, xv, 10, 12-15, 17-20, 22-23, 26-31, 34, 40-41, 43-51, 53-54, 56, 58-61, 63, 65, 81-85, 89-92, 99-100, 110, 112-114, 127, 138, 140-141, 161, 182, 187, 189-190, 192-193, 195, 199-200, 206, 210-211, 225, 234, 250, 253, 258, 262, 265, 268, 326, 330-332, 341-342, 346-347, 349-350, 352-353, 355, 358, 360-362, 365-366, 368-389, 391-396, 398-402, 404, 408-410, 416, 419, 424

ScriptBlock   39, 404

scripter   43

ScriptErrors   89-92

scripting   iii, ix, 4, 12, 20, 26-27, 37, 46, 85, 110, 114-115, 182, 293-294, 374, 376, 388, 403, 409, 424
ScriptLogging 378
scripts v, ix, xv, 1, 9-10, 12, 15, 20-21, 23, 26-29, 44-48, 50, 52, 54, 56, 58, 60, 62, 64-65, 74-75, 86, 92, 110, 159, 291, 348-349, 353, 355, 360, 368-369, 372-374, 377, 379, 386-388, 391, 393-394, 396-397, 403-404, 417, 419, 423-424
scrolling   iii
search xii, 2, 8, 34, 51, 65, 72, 111, 183, 192, 228, 235, 240, 248-249, 255, 258-260, 263, 269, 274, 287, 337-338, 343, 364, 386, 392, 394, 405, 411, 415, 421
Search-AdminAuditLog   283, 285
SearchEnabled 240
searches   xii, 248-249, 259-261, 274, 282-283, 286-287
searching   2, 6, 208, 259, 283, 287, 411
Search-MailboxAuditLog   287-289
SecondaryAddress   343
SecondaryDialPlan   343
section   ix, 8, 15-18, 21, 26-31, 40, 54, 56, 58-59, 64, 70, 82, 89-92, 103, 111, 152, 161, 182, 194, 199, 208, 222, 226, 244, 258, 275, 286, 297, 352, 356, 358-360, 362-364, 369-370, 373, 378, 380, 383, 388, 398-400, 404-405, 411-412, 414
sections   8, 28-30, 37, 59, 349, 356, 358, 361, 369-370, 372, 388
secure 49-50, 100, 120-121, 179, 204, 243, 246, 308, 314, 355
SecurePassword   149
SecureString 50, 100, 115
SecureString-MyTenant   50, 61
Security   xii, 50, 63, 68-69, 75, 77, 126, 148-150, 156-157, 176, 202, 204, 223-225, 237, 240, 248-250, 252, 254-258, 260, 262-263, 268, 271, 275, 279, 281, 286, 304-305, 307-309, 314, 328, 331-332, 392, 423-424
seemingly   27, 62
Segmentation x, 119, 129-130, 135
Segregation   119
Select-Object 53, 62, 140, 178, 349-350, 354, 359, 413-415
Select-ObjectName   63
--Selects   397
self-destruct   309
self-evident   384
self-explanatory   67, 281, 321
self-managed 10

self-management   10
Self-Service   198
self-signed   46
SendAs   177
Send-As   158, 175-178
Send-Connector   203
Send-EmailMessages 391
sender 154, 158, 213, 216, 226, 240, 244-245, 364
SenderAddress   51, 191, 235
SenderAddressLocation   208, 241, 245-246, 259
SenderDomains   202
senders   188, 194, 208, 233, 245
sending   155, 174, 192, 194, 201, 206, 218, 243, 364-365
SendMailApplication 264
Send-MailMessage   56-58, 64-65, 364-365, 392
Send-Message 56
Sensitive   xii, 26, 68-69, 212, 222-223, 226, 245, 249, 251, 254, 256-257, 259, 308, 329, 331
SentTo   242
SentToMemberOf   217
SentToScope 208, 230, 241-242, 245, 259
server iii, iv, v, vi, 1-2, 4, 10-11, 13, 20, 29, 33-34, 39, 48-51, 54, 56, 63, 69, 74, 77-81, 83, 85, 88, 94, 99, 103, 106-107, 119, 148, 150, 156, 202-204, 210, 212, 218, 222, 228, 230, 232-233, 236, 239, 264, 267, 279, 291-292, 294, 296, 298, 304, 310, 318, 335-336, 338, 344, 352-353, 360, 363-364, 366, 371, 376, 381, 384, 395, 420, 423-424
ServerName   29, 34, 413
servers iii, v, vi, 1, 13, 20, 33-34, 39-40, 47-48, 66, 79, 81, 120, 149, 204, 206, 213-214, 218, 237, 272, 281-282, 291-292, 321, 348, 365-367, 376, 383, 388
service iii, 5, 34, 63, 67, 71-72, 74-75, 77, 79, 94, 103, 108, 110, 113, 115, 140, 143, 151-152, 156, 175, 201, 204, 211, 213-214, 218, 232-233, 235, 237, 262, 279-280, 292, 303, 335-336, 344-345, 365, 373, 380-381, 405
ServiceName 351
ServicePartner 244
ServicePlan   351
ServicePlans   350-351
services   v, vi, vii, 10, 66-67, 75, 86-88, 95, 113, 156, 179, 212, 232, 237, 241, 251, 406, 419, 423
ServiceStatus 109-110, 112, 350
Set-AcceptedDomain   137, 210
Set-ActiveSyncDeviceAccessRule   312
Set-ActiveSyncMailboxPolicy   307

Set-ADSyncScheduler 104
Set-ADUser   28, 85, 90, 92, 100-101
Set-Alias   xv, 410-412
SetAuditSeverity   209
Set-AuthenticodeSignature   45-46
Set-BITSTransfer   367
Set-CalendarProcessing   156, 179-180
Set-CalenderProcessing   156
Set-CASMailbox   120-122, 129, 138-141, 156-157,
266, 306-307, 313, 406-407
Set-CASMailboxPlan 70, 124
Set-ClientAccessRule 142
set-command   138
Set-Content   356-357
Set-DataClassif   ication 229
Set-DataEncryptionPolicy   70
Set-DistributionGroup   54, 56-58, 193-196, 392
Set-DkimSigningConfig   214
Set-DlpKeywordDictionary   69
Set-ExecutionPolicy   44, 419
Set-Group   58-59
Set-GroupMailbox   266
Set-HostedContentFilterPolicy   219, 221
Set-ImapSubscription 139
Set-IRMConfiguration   239-240, 242, 244
Set-Location   419
Set-Mailbox   15-16, 28, 85, 91, 136, 141, 149,
153-154, 157-158, 160-161, 266, 269, 286-287, 343,
406-407, 410-411
Set-MailboxCalendarFolder   155-156
Set-MailboxFolderPermission158
Set-MailboxRelocationRequest   71
Set-MailboxSettings   391
Set-MailPublicFolder 327-328
Set-MalwareFilterPolicy   215-216
Set-ManagementRoleAssignment   263, 281
Set-ManagementRoleEntry   263
Set-MigrationBatch   295
Set-MigrationConfig 70, 295
Set-MobileDeviceMailboxPolicy   242, 306-309
Set-MoveRequest   296, 299-300
Set-MsolUser 111, 116, 149, 153
Set-MsolUserLicense 111-112, 116, 153
Set-MsolUserPassword   153
Set-MsolUserPrincipalName 152-153
Set-OMEConfiguration   246
Set-Organization   70

Set-OutboundConnector   206-207
Set-OwaMailboxPolicy   126-128
Set-ProtectionServicePolicy 70
Set-PublicFolder   321, 324
Set-RemoteMailbox   80
Set-RetentionPolicies   391
Set-RoleAssignmentPolicy   276, 278
Set-SafeLinksPolicy   70-71
Set-Service   381-382
Set-SiteMailbox   266
Set-StrictMode   xv, 387, 396-398
Set-SweepRule   70
Set-TenantAnalyticsConfig   70
Set-TransportConfig   130, 233, 294
Set-TransportRule   226
Set-UMDialPlan   339
Set-UMMailbox   266, 343-345
Set-UnifiedGroup   3
Set-UserAnalyticsConfig   70
Shared xi, 10, 86, 147-148, 150-152, 160-162, 165, 167,
174-177, 179, 196, 198-199, 227-228, 290, 354
SharedMailbox   199, 422
SharedMailboxCount 199
SharePoint   66, 69, 71, 75, 110, 174, 196, 248-249,
254, 256-257, 259, 413, 423
SHAREPOINTENTERPRISE 110-111, 114
SHAREPOINTWAC 110-111
SharingPolicy 150, 156, 157
signature   46, 155, 208, 213
signed 43-44, 46, 392
sign-in 94-95
Signing   ix, xv, 26, 43-45, 213, 387, 392, 401
Sign-On   95
SilentlyContinue   54, 211, 378, 392
SingleItemRecoveryEnabled 80
Singular   xv, 99, 102, 391, 404
SIPAddress   413, 415
SipName   339
SipResourceIdentifier 342
SkuPartNumber   109
SmartHost   203
SMTPAddress 56-57, 233, 391
SmtpServer   49, 56-58, 64, 364-365, 392
SnagIt 349
Sort-Object   52-53, 315, 356
source 10, 19, 36, 86, 88-89, 95-96, 99, 113, 171, 203,
218, 228, 259, 292, 294, 296, 302, 341, 364-366, 384-

385
SourceEndpoint   293-294
specialized   249, 262
Splitting   ix, 26, 34, 52, 265, 413-415
Start-ADSyncSyncCycle   104-105
StartAfter   298-299
Start-BITSTransfer   365-367
Start-ComplianceSearch   261
StartDate   52-53, 191-192, 235, 285, 289, 372, 422
started v, vi, 82, 87, 91, 156, 241, 260-261, 298-299, 361, 373, 380, 389, 396
Start-MailboxSearch 70
Start-MigrationBatch 293, 295
StartMode   380-381
Start-Service 380, 382
Start-Transcript   378-379
StartType   380
StartUpMode 381
StartupType   381-382
StateOrProvince   143
statistics   170, 172, 235, 301, 303, 316, 326, 349, 353
status xiii, 4-5, 52, 72, 112, 159, 192, 235, 283, 289, 291, 293, 295, 299-301, 304, 316, 333, 372, 382, 421-422
StatusMailRecipients   283, 288
StatusReg   382
Stop-MailboxSearch 70
Stop-MigrationBatch 295
StopRuleProcessing   208, 241, 245, 259
Stop-Transcript   378
StrictMode   397
Structure   viii, xv, 2, 61, 322, 387, 400
Subdomains   137
subfolders   170, 322-323, 325, 329
Subheader   360
Subject 54, 56-58, 64, 152, 156, 165, 168, 216, 222, 227, 235, 247, 326-327, 364-365, 392
SubjectContainsWords   245
SubjectMatchesPatterns   241
SubjectMatchPatterns 241
SubscriberAccessEnabled   344
subscription   243
-SuppressStatus   321
Suspending   292, 300
Suspend-MoveRequest   300

Suspend-MRSRequest   71
SuspendWhenReadyToComplete   296, 299-301
switch 2, 5, 8, 32-33, 38, 42-43, 47, 50, 56, 99, 116, 150-151, 168, 183, 211, 227, 291, 296-297, 299-300, 314, 320, 352, 355, 365, 373, 379, 393-394, 399, 404-405, 408, 410
switches   7-8, 42, 264, 267, 297, 299, 334, 378, 380, 384, 420
SwitchParameter   239-240
symbol 3, 21, 29, 325, 349-350, 372, 412-413
synced viii, 9-11, 35, 48, 76, 86-87, 95, 97-98, 100-101, 149, 176, 291-292
synchronization   x, 10, 74, 86-88, 93-95, 97-98, 100, 103-104, 106, 294-295, 299, 314, 316
synchronizations   104, 298

T

TaggedAgeInDays   256
TargetDeliveryDomain   293-294, 296-300
TeamMailbox 422
TeamMembers 195-196
template   223-226, 228, 240-241, 258
templates   xii, 44, 69, 207, 222-226, 237, 240, 257
tenant 1, 5, 7, 10, 48, 51, 53-54, 61, 63, 66-67, 70, 76-77, 79-80, 88, 95, 99, 101, 104-106, 108-109, 111, 115-117, 126, 128, 136, 144, 146, 154, 192, 197, 201-202, 206, 210, 214-215, 218, 220-221, 223, 237, 239, 243, 248-251, 254, 267, 291, 293, 318, 320, 337, 368, 376, 406, 423-424
TenantAdmins   254
TenantID   109
TenantManagement   244
tenantname   111, 116, 352
TestActiveSyncConnectivity 313
Test-ActivesyncOffice   391
Test-AdvancedFeatures   399
Test-ClientAccessRule   142, 145
TestCommand   384
Test-IRMConfiguration   240, 244
TestModeAction   221
TestModeBccToRecipients   221
Test-Path   417
Test-SiteMailbox   266
Throttling   191, 315
TLSDomain   203

TlsSenderCertificateName   202
TLSSettings   203
ToString   360, 362
TotalAssociatedItemSize   326
TotalCount   192, 372
TotalDeletedItemSize   326
TotalItemSize   326, 349-350, 354, 356
TouchID   307
Tracing   xii, 201, 207
Transcript   xv, 368, 378-379, 386
Transport   xi, xii, 10-11, 19, 69, 79, 142, 179, 201-202, 206-209, 212-213, 222-223, 225-226, 228-230, 232-233, 240-241, 245, 254, 257-259, 263, 272, 353
TransportDecryptionSetting   240
TransportRule   208
troubleshoot   iii, 22, 39, 201, 236, 292, 335, 368, 373, 385-386
troubleshooting   xiv, xv, 27-29, 65, 168-170, 213, 232, 318, 333, 335, 368-376, 378-380, 382, 384, 386, 388, 390-391, 393, 399
TrustedSendersAndDomains   154
Trustee   158, 177
TUIAccessToCalendarEnabled   344
TUIAccessToEmailEnabled   344

U

UMAutoAttendants   340
UMDialPlan   346
UMMailbox   268, 340, 344, 346
UMMailboxPolicy   342, 344, 346
UMSettings   341-342
UMSMSNotificationOption   344
Undo-SoftDeletedMailbox   266-267
unicodelookup   35
UnifiedAuditLog   282
UnifiedGroup   197
UnifiedGroupCreation   27
Unique   62, 196, 315
UniversalOutlook   311, 313
unlicensed   110
Update-PublicFolderMailbox 266-267, 321
Update-Recipient   70
Update-SiteMailbox   266-267
Upgrade-DistributionGroup   198

UPNCheck   408
URIType   338, 39
UsageLocation   111, 115, 116, 149, 341-342
UseCulture   354
UseDatabaseRetentionDefaults   154
UseMxRecord   203
UserAgent   310
UserApplication   264
UserCanOverride   242
UserDisplayName   316
UserID 28, 100
UserMailInsert   311, 312
UsernameMatchesAnyOfPatterns   143
UserPrincipalName   80, 89-90, 115, 117-118, 149, 152, 350, 353-354, 389, 405
UserRecipientFilter   143, 145
UserUPN   389
UseSsl   364-365
UseStoredCredential   365

V

variable   xv, 4, 12-13, 15-20, 23, 27, 34-36, 38-39, 41-42, 46, 49-56, 58-59, 61-62, 64, 76-77, 82-83, 90-91, 109, 111, 126-128, 133, 138, 140, 182, 184, 189, 192, 195-196, 203, 210-211, 228-229, 260, 265, 303, 326, 330-331, 341, 346, 352, 355, 358, 360-361, 363-365, 368, 373, 375, 377, 380, 382-387, 389-390, 394, 396-398, 400, 404, 407, 414-415, 418
variables   viii, xv, 12-14, 16, 20-21, 23, 25, 31, 39, 41, 48-49, 53, 59, 76, 82, 91, 100, 114-115, 145, 189, 192, 341-342, 346, 352, 356, 361, 363-364, 368-369, 371-372, 380, 382-391, 396, 400-401
Verb-Noun   1, 391, 398
Verb-Noun-Functions 387
Verbose   42-43, 282, 344, 393, 399
VerifyGlobalRoutingEntry   344
View-Only   264
voicemail   335-336, 343, 345
VoiceMailAnalysisEnabled   344
voicemails   335-336, 345

W

warning   32, 39, 144, 151, 161, 211, 304
WarningAction   54, 344
Warnings   37, 44, 390
WarningVariable   344
webmail   314
webpi-azps   75
Well-Known   159, 168, 172
WhatIf   2, 5, 47, 59, 260, 344, 390, 399
Where-Object   15, 140, 381, 389, 398
WindowsAzureAD   108
WindowSize   418-419
WindowsLiveID   422
WindowsPowerShell   417
WorkDays   155
WorkingHours   155
Write-AdminAuditLog   70, 264
writeback   97
write-back   86
Write-Host   xiv, 16-19, 30, 37-42, 83-84, 102,
114-115, 127-128, 189-191, 193, 199-200, 205, 211,
253, 265, 342, 347, 351, 368-369, 371-372, 374, 376-
378, 380, 383-384, 386, 393-394, 397, 404-408
Write-Output   xv, 387, 393-394, 398
Write-Verbose   xv, 383, 387, 393-394, 399

X

X-Header   221
xmlscript   225, 258
XMWSLHeader   310

Y

Yammer   68, 110, 114, 196

Books by the Authors

Exchange Server 2016 - Second Edition

This book is in its second edition of our first book! It has been updated to reflect changes in Exchange 2016 over the past six months as well as an additional 100+ pages of new material covering Public Folders, security and more. Dave and I literally spent hundred of hours researching, testing and writing the material that is in this book. With the additional topics we have covered the breadth and width of Exchange 2016. With this book you will be able to confidentially manage your Exchange server with PowerShell.

Already for sale here - www.PracticalPowerShell.com

COMING SOON!

Microsoft Azure

Managing Virtual Machines and Users is important no matter if they are on-premises or in the cloud. With the growing popularity of Azure and PowerShell, this book takes the same premise as the previous book, that is a practical approach to using PowerShell. Azure is one of the most exciting products from Microsoft. The range and breadth of what is available is amazing. In this book we will tackle how to use PowerShell to manage your user accounts in AD as well as your objects in your Azure Tenant. We will take you from the basics of PowerShell to how to use powerful PowerShell scripts to manage your tenant. This is THE PowerShell book to get for Azure PowerShell management.

Look for the book here - www.PracticalPowerShell.com

COMING SOON!!

Office 365 - SharePoint, Teams and More

The authors of this book are looking to cover a wide variety of services in Office 365 that have not been covered by any other book in the series. As such, topics like SharePoint and Teams are fair game along with many other topics. The book itself is still under development. Any updates on this title will be placed on the publishers website here:

www.PracticalPowerShell.com